~15th Edition~

Radio Control
Buyers Guide

MW01248847

©1991 RADIO CONTROL BUYERS GUIDE
Published by Model Retailer
A Division of Kalmbach Publishing Co.
14121 Parke-Long Court, Suite 112
Chantilly, Virginia 22021

ISBN 0-89024-123-6

TABLE OF CONTENTS

OFFICIAL AMA SAFETY CODE—January 1, 1991

Model Flying Must Be In Accordance With This Code In Order For AMA Liability Protection To Apply

GENERAL

1. I will not fly my model aircraft in competition or in the presence of spectators until it has been proven to be airworthy by having been previously, successfully flight tested.

2. I will not fly my model higher than approximately 400 feet within 3 miles of an airport without notifying the airport operator. I will give right-of-way to, and avoid flying in the proximity of full-scale aircraft. Where necessary, an observer shall be utilized to supervise flying to avoid having models fly in the proximity of full-scale aircraft.

3. Where established, I will abide by the safety rules for the flying site I use, and I will not willfully and deliberately fly my models in a careless, reckless, and/or dangerous manner.

4. If my model weighs over 20 pounds, I will only fly it in accordance with paragraph 5 of this section of the AMA Safety Code.

5. At air shows or model flying demonstrations a single straight line must be established, one side of which is for flying, with the other side for spectators. Only those persons essential to the flight operations are to be permitted on the flying side of the line; all others must be on the spectator side. Flying over the spectator side of the line is prohibited, unless beyond the control of the pilot(s). The only exceptions which may be permitted to the single straight line requirement, under special circumstances involving consideration of site conditions and model size, weight, speed and power, must be jointly approved by the AMA President and the Executive Director. The maximum permissible takeoff weight of models is 55 lbs.

6. I will not fly my model unless it is identified with my name and address or AMA number, on or in the model. Note: This does not apply to models flown indoors.

7. I will not operate models with metal-bladed propellers or with gaseous boosts, in which gases other than air at normal atmospheric pressure enter their internal combustion engine(s); nor will I operate models with extremely hazardous fuels such as those containing tetranitromethane or hydrazine.

8. I will not operate models with pyrotechnics (any device that explodes, burns or propels a projectile of any kind) including, but not limited to, rockets, explosive bombs dropped from models, smoke bombs, all explosive gases (such as hydrogen-filled balloons), ground mounted devices launching a projectile. The only exceptions permitted are rockets flown in accordance with the Safety Code of the National Association of Rocketry or those permanently attached (as per JATO use); also those items authorized for Air Show Team use as defined by AST Advisory Committee (document available from AMA HQ). Note: A model aircraft is defined as an aircraft with or without engine, not able to carry a human being.

9. I will not fly any model using turbojet power (axial or centrifugal flow) unless I have obtained a special waiver for such specific flights from the AMA President and Executive Director and I will abide by any restrictions imposed on such flights by them. (Note: This does not apply to ducted fan models using piston engines or electric motors.)

RADIO CONTROL

1. I will have completed a successful radio equipment ground range check before the first flight of a new or repaired model.

2. I will not fly my model aircraft in the presence of spectators until I become a qualified flier, unless assisted by an experienced helper.

3. I will perform my initial turn after takeoff away from the pit or spectator areas, and I will not thereafter fly over pit or spectator areas, unless beyond my control.

4. I will operate my model using only radio control frequencies currently allowed by the Federal Communications Commission. (Only properly licensed Amateurs are authorized to operate equipment on Amateur Band frequencies.) Further, any transmitters that I use at a sanctioned event must have a certified R/CMA-AMA gold sticker affixed indicating that it was manufactured or modified for operation at a 20kHz frequency separation (except 27MHz and 53MHz).

FREE FLIGHT

1. I will not launch my model aircraft unless at least 100 feet downwind of spectators and automobile parking.

2. I will not fly my model unless the launch area is clear of all persons except my mechanic and officials.

3. I will employ the use of an adequate device in flight to extinguish any fuses on the model after it has completed its function.

CONTROL LINE

1. I will subject my complete control system (including safety thong, where applicable) to an inspection and pull test prior to flying.

2. I will assure that my flying area is safely clear of all utility wires or poles.

3. I will assure that my flying area is safely clear of all non-essential participants and spectators before permitting my engine to be started.

APPLICATION—1991 A.M.A. MEMBERSHIP

Academy of Model Aeronautics
1810 Samuel Morse Drive, Reston, VA 22090
Insurance Coverage Effective on Date of Dues Receipt at AMA HQ
(1991 Membership Expires December 31, 1991)

For Everyone: Fill in Date of Birth: MONTH DAY YEAR

Main Interest (check only one): ☐ CL ☐ FF ☐ RC ☐ Indoor ☐ Scale ☐ All   ☐ New ☐ Renewal   (number if known _____)

For Those 19 or Over by July 1, 1991—Check One Only!

☐ **OPEN FULL MEMBERSHIP** $40.00
All membership and competition privileges, liability and accident/medical insurance, and subscription to *Model Aviation* magazine**.

☐ **OPEN LIMITED MEMBERSHIP** $36.00
Same as above, except no magazine.

☐ **EXTRA FAMILY MEMBERSHIP** $20.00
For 2nd adult (immed. family) at same address—no publication.

_____
Name and AMA No. of Other Family Member

☐ **SPECIAL SENIOR CITIZEN RATE** $21.00
For those age 65 or over—must submit proof first time. Same privileges as Open Full Member.

For Those Not 19 by July 1, 1991—Check One Only!

☐ **YOUTH FULL MEMBERSHIP** $16.00
Same privileges as Open Full Member.

☐ **YOUTH NO-PUB MEMBERSHIP** $7.00
Same as at left, but no magazine.

INSTRUCTIONS: PRINT CLEARLY IN CAPITAL LETTERS.

FIRST NAME _____ INIT _____ LAST NAME _____

MAILING ADDRESS (TYPICALLY NUMBER AND STREET) _____

MAILING ADDRESS CONTINUATION (USE ONLY IF REQUIRED FOR YOUR ADDRESS) _____

CITY _____ STATE _____ ZIP CODE _____

☐ VISA ACCOUNT NO. ☐ MASTER CHARGE ACCOUNT NO. *Only Visa or Master Charge

Total: $ _____
☐ Enclosed
☐ Charged*

EXPIRATION DATE OF CREDIT CARD

AMA membership ends each year on December 31, regardless of the date a membership application is received. If a subscription is included with membership, it begins with the first issue available for the year of application after the application and payment are received; it expires with the issue printed in December (which is dated February of the following year). Those whose applications are received between October 1 and December 31 with next year's dues rate receive membership for the following year plus whatever days of membership remain in the year of application; however, the application and payment must be received by December 15 to assure being sent the publication that is mailed in January (which is dated March).

**Of the dues, $10 is for the *Model Aviation* magazine subscription.

Applications Without Signature(s) Will Be Returned!

I hereby agree to comply with the current AMA Safety Code for all model aircraft operations and the NAR Safety Code for all model rocket operations (as printed on the reverse side). I understand that my failure to comply with the applicable Code will result in failure of liability coverage for any damages or claim so caused. I further understand that written notice must be provided within 60 days of the occurrence of any incident of bodily injury and/or property damage.

_____
Signature of Applicant

_____
Parent or Guardian of Applicant Under Age 18 Must Also Sign

PUBLISHER
George Zombakis

MANAGING EDITOR
Karen Boothe

EDITORIAL ASSISTANTS
Carol Collier
Peter Exton
Anne Hoke
John McCaw

CONTRIBUTING EDITORS
Tyree Phillips
Doug Pratt
Michael Shaw
Jim Zombakis

PHOTOGRAPY
Karen Boothe
Jennifer Hanscome

HALFTONE PRODUCTION
Jennifer Hanscome
John McCaw

ADVERTISING SALES
Barbara Freson
George Zombakis

PRODUCTION MANAGER
Leslie Orr

PRODUCTION COORDINATOR
Christine Hilbert

PRODUCTION STAFF
Mitzi Beneck
Irene Day
Claire Escobar

COVER ART
GeoGrafik Design Group, Inc.

**R/C SHOWCASE
PRODUCTION/DESIGN**
Claire Escobar

OFFICE MANAGER
Karen Proefrock

EXECUTIVE PUBLISHER
Geoffrey Wheeler

WALTER J. MUNDSCHAU
President
Kalmbach Publishing Co.

ROBERT A. MAAS
Vice President
Sales/Marketing

ABOUT THE COVER

The cover of the 15th Edition of the *Radio Control Buyers Guide* was created by GeoGrafik Design Group Inc. of Alexandria, Virginia. It depicts all the major product groups covered in detail in this *Guide*. The computer-illustrated design was generated entirely on state-of-the-art desktop publishing equipment.

INTRODUCTION

The 15th edition of the *Radio Control Buyers Guide* has no equal and was written with you in mind. Its purpose is to be the most complete source possible for the entire radio control hobby—planes, cars, boats, trucks, helicopters, and accessories. One volume covers it all!

Every year, we pool all of our resources and expertise to give you the best reference *Guide* possible at a reasonable cost. The 15th edition reflects our best improvements yet.

First, we have increased the size of each product listing by 25%. By doing so, we can now show you a larger photograph and a more detailed description of each product.

Second, we have increased the number of color pages significantly, again to show you more finished models of all types.

Third, we have carefully selected "how-to" topics, written by people who know the hobby, to help you better understand each segment of the hobby. We'll make you better prepared in not only selecting the best model but selecting the one that will give you the most enjoyment at a price you can afford.

The *Radio Control Buyers Guide* is easy to use. In looking for a particular product, refer to the Product Index in the back of the *Guide*. This index tells you the page for each product description.

The Manufacturers Index, also in the back of the *Guide*, gives you information on each company that has products advertised or listed. This index also identifies companies whose products are only available through hobby shops and those that accept orders direct from consumers. The manufacturers index also identifies the page each product can be found.

A new addition to this year's *Guide* is the introduction of Rebate Coupons and Special Offer Coupons. These valuable coupons, located in the back of the *Guide*, represent significant savings to you and are designed to help you communicate directly with advertisers.

We also list a group of hobby shops that specialize in radio control products. These shops have qualified sales people to help you make the correct purchasing decision, give you tips, and answer your questions as you're building your model. We strongly recommend you work with your local hobby shop when starting a new project.

It has been our experience that you will enjoy your hobby to the fullest if you join a club in your town and participate in its activities. Not only will you benefit from their expertise but friendly competition is the key to keeping you active and will maximize your enjoyment for many years to come. You will be amazed how helpful club members can be as they eagerly share advice and their experiences with you.

We want you to become a part of the *Guide*. As you saw in the color sections of the *Guide*, many of the photos came from modelers like you. If you have a model that you are particularly proud of, send us a color slide. You may see your model in the next edition!

We are always open to suggestions and encourage you to send us your comments about this edition and how we can improve future editions.

Finally, we want to thank the members of the Westchester Radio Aeromodelers (WRAM) club of White Plains, N.Y. and the Vintage Radio Control Society of Fairfax, Va. for sharing their unique models with us.

Happy modeling!

**George Zombakis
Publisher**

Published by Model Retailer, a division of Kalmbach Publishing Co., 14121 Parke-Long Ct., Ste. 112, Chantilly, VA 22021, phone (703) 263-0900. Circulation: Available at better hobby shops. If not available at a hobby shop in your area, send $9.95 (plus postage and handling: $1.00 U.S.; $1.50 foreign; Wisconsin residents add 5% sales tax) to Kalmbach Publishing Co., 21027 Crossroads Circle, PO Box 1612, Waukesha, WI 53187. Standard trade discounts are allowed on multiple copy orders. Copyright © 1991 by Kalmbach Publishing Co. All rights reserved. Printed in USA.

How to Shop for Airplanes

By Douglas R. Pratt

When you first walk into a hobby shop, you're likely to be bewildered by what you have to choose from. There are a lot of airplanes out there! Of course, this is one of the things that makes model aviation a lifelong hobby; there are always new challenges and new things to spark your interest.

If you're a beginner, the thing you need most is information. You made your first smart move by buying this *Guide;* it'll save you a lot of time and money! Your hobby dealer will have other books you should buy—ones written for beginners, not experts who know all the jargon. Some good ones are *"The Beginner's Guide to RC Sport Flying," "The Sportflier's Guide to RC Soaring,"* and *"The Beginner's Guide to Flying Electric Powered Airplanes."* There are also some very good model magazines that you should buy to give you an idea of products that are currently available. *Radio Control Modeler, Model Airplane News, Model Aviation, Model Builder, Flying Models, RC Report, RC Car Action, RC Modeler, Competition Plus, Heli Scene, Boat and Ship Modeler,* and *RC Boat Modeler* are all excellent publications. Most have regular columns for beginners.

Your hobby dealer is your most important source of information. He can guide you in selecting the best equipment to buy. Since he wants you as a steady customer, he'll steer you to what you really need. Ask your dealer about the best places to fly in your area. If there's a local flying club, join it. It's the best way to get instruction and have a good place to fly.

Why A Trainer Plane?

Unless you've flown an R/C model before, you need a trainer plane. If you have a full-scale pilot's license, it doesn't mean you can fly an R/C model...it's a whole different experience. Prepare to learn! And, pick a plane that will help you do it without surprises or challenges.

First, the best trainer planes are the ones that practically fly themselves. There are plenty of planes around that will do just that. A student pilot usually tends to fight the airplane, over-controlling it. During a recent training session, I told one student pilot, "Remember, the plane knows how to fly better than you do! Let it!"

The best planes to train with are high-wing designs; that is, the wing is mounted on top of the fuselage. These planes tend to be more stable in turns, and will roll back to a level altitude when the controls are returned to neutral. More importantly, they are easy to see, and it's easy to recognize what attitude they're in. Flying R/C is largely a matter of hand-eye coordination.

Second, look for a kit that has a good set of instructions. Carl Goldberg Models set the standard for instruction books years ago with its "Eaglet" and "Gentle Lady" kits. Every step is spelled out in simple language and has a photo or drawing to illustrate it.

Your first kit should have instructions that will tell you clearly and simply what you need to do. Here's an advantage of buying your kit from a hobby shop—you can open it up and look at it before you buy.

If a plane meets these tests, then your choice should be based on what looks the best to you. If you like the looks of the kit, you'll be more willing to spend the time necessary to get it built right.

Almost Ready to Fly

Should you buy an Almost-Ready-to-Fly (ARF) airplane? Maybe. The old adage that "time is money" applies here. If you buy a plane that you don't have to spend time building, it'll cost you more than a kit. On the other hand, if you don't have spare time to build or don't trust your ability to build it straight, an ARF is a good choice. Ask your hobby shop which ARF kits they like. They'll have one or two that they can recommend based on their customers' experiences.

Three or four channels?

A three-channel airplane will give you control of the rudder, elevator, and throttle. These planes are designed to fly without ailerons (control surfaces on the wings). Three-channel planes tend to roll back out of a turn by themselves, and many people consider them easier to fly. They are also simpler to build, since no control linkage is needed in the wing.

A four-channel plane will have controls for throttle, elevator, rudder and ailerons. They are more maneuverable than three-channel planes. If one of your early goals is to fly aerobatics, you need a four-channel plane.

Pilots sometimes talk about making the transition from three to four channels, as if the two kinds of plane flew so differently that it was difficult to fly one if you learned on the other. Well, it ain't necessarily so. If you learn to fly on a three-channel plane, you'll be doing your turning with the right transmitter stick, which controls rudder (with side-to-side movement) and elevator (up-and-down).

You'll use the same stick for turning a four-channel plane, only the side-to-side movement will control the ailerons instead of the rudder. The only transition will be in learning to use the rudder, which is now on the left stick. Rudder is rarely used in the air on a four-channel trainer plane. You'll use it most on the ground, where its linkage to the nose wheel will steer the plane.

How big?

Another factor to consider when you're selecting your trainer is size. As a rule, the bigger the plane is the slower it will fly. If it flies slowly, you'll be able to think ahead of it, anticipate your control inputs, and enjoy flying it more. If it's fast, you'll be struggling to keep up with it, reacting to what it does instead of leading it the way you want to go. Who's the pilot here, after all?

Most trainer planes are designed around .40 size engines. This is certainly the most popular engine available, and there are several brands to choose from. One of the largest .40 sized trainers is the Sig Kadet Senior, which is one of the best-flying trainers you can find, but can be a challenge to build.

You should seriously consider getting a trainer that is designed for a .60 engine. The engine is more expensive than a .40, but the bigger plane is easier to see and has better flying characteristics. You may want to consider Hobby Lobby's big Telemaster which comes in a kit or a ready-to-cover version.

Gas or electric power?

You'll see several electric-powered trainers on your dealer's shelves. Are they better than gas models?

Well, they're certainly simpler. There's no fuel tank to hook up, you don't have to tweak a needle valve to get the engine running right, you don't even have to flip the engine to start it. Electric planes are generally built light, to fly slowly and glide for a long time. This makes them a good choice for modelers who don't want to take the time to turn an airplane.

On the other hand, you can only expect flights of four to six minutes from an electric plane, then you have to land and charge the battery. Your flight plan will typically involve taking off and flying up to a good altitude, then shutting off the motor and gliding back down. This is a good way for a beginner to practice, and it's one of the resons that many electric trainers resemble sailplanes, with long, curved wings.

Refer to the Aircraft: Electric Kit section in this *Guide* for information on some of the more popular kits available.

Whatever plane you choose, ask the advice of your hobby dealer. He's helped a lot of people get started in this sport, and he can make it a lot easier for you.

We strongly suggest you visit your local R/C flying field on weekends and talk to club members. There's nothing like seeing an R/C airplane performing stunts like the full-size airplanes. If your local club is like most others, you'll get more suggestions and offers for help than you could possibly handle.

Happy flying!

Aircraft

Ready to Fly

COX HOBBIES, INC.

The *Cox Space Probe* (No. 4600 Flying Saucer; Retail: See your dealer) is a flying disk! The saucer accelerates from your hand and climbs hundreds of feet, sometimes hovering before coming to soft landing.

COX HOBBIES, INC.

The *E-Z Bee II* (No. 90474 or No. 90475 with 2-channel Cobra radio and Video-Copilot™, and No. 90475G with 2-channel Gold radio and Video-Copilot™; Retail: See your dealer) enables novice flyers to advance to exciting loops, wingovers, and dives, yet they can rely on E-Z Bee stability to restore level flight. A Cox .049 engine and a second servo for separate elevator and rudder control produce flight characteristics that have brought success to 125,000 beginners. The plane, made of polystyrene foam, is 32 in. long and has a wingspan of 55 in. It requires a 2-channel radio and uses a Cox .049 Babe Bee engine with Snap Starter®.

COX HOBBIES, INC.

The *Electric Sundance* (No. 90464, No. 90465 with 2-channel Cobra radio and Video-Copilot™, and No. 90465G with 2-channel Gold radio and Video-Copilot™; Retail: See your dealer) can be flown by anyone, anywhere. The electric motor and durable, crash-resistant construction insure long-lasting fun. The plane is made of polystyrene foam, is 32 in. long and has a 55-in. wingspan. It uses a Mabuchi RK-370 motor and requires a 2-channel radio.

COX HOBBIES, INC.

The *Cessna Skylane* (No. 90420, or No. 90421 with Cobra radio and Video-Copilot™, and No. 90421G with 2-channel Gold radio and Video-Copilot™; Retail: See your dealer) is a new "turn on a dime" R/C airplane with formed blow-molded fuselage. It is 31 in. long with a 36-in. wingspan, the plane is stable, yet can do loops and split S's. Requires 2-channel radio and uses Cox .049 Ranger engine with Snap Starter®.

COX HOBBIES, INC.

The *Fairchild 24* (No. 90424, Fairchild 24, or No. 90425, Fairchild 24 with 2-channel Cobra and Video-Copilot™, and No. 90425G with 2-channel Gold radio and Video-Copilot™; Retail: See your dealer) is a replica of the award-winning Fairchild that is in the EAA Antique Classics Hall of Fame. Easy to assemble, the Cox Fairchild has a high wing for beginners' stability, and a large rudder and elevator control for aerobatics. The plane, with OPS laminate wing and blow-molded fuselage, is 28 in. long, has a 38-in. wingspan, requires a 2-channel radio and uses a .049 Ranger engine.

COX HOBBIES, INC.

The *Airwolf™ Free Flight* (No. 4700; Retail: See your dealer) is the most famous helicopter ever flown! It's featured in the ever-popular Airwolf™ television series—and the Cox model is a miniature replica of the real Airwolf™. It's super-detailed right down to the realistic guns and cannons. Authentically colored, it's free flying with a Cox .049 engine. Newly designed rotor head with extra-wide rotor blades enhances climb and descent characteristics. Rotor diameter is 20 in.

COX HOBBIES, INC.

The *Super Chipmunk* (No. 9300; Retail: See your dealer) is an extraordinary stunt plane that can execute any aerobatic maneuver with flawless precision, owing to full symmetrical airfoil and dual ported .049 Cox engine. Made of low density polystyrene foam and high impact styrene, the plane is 20 in. long and has a 31-in. wingspan.

COX HOBBIES, INC.

The *.020 powered Turbo Centurion* (No. 90430; Retail: See your dealer), equipped with the Cox Failsafe rudder-only radio system is a natural for the first time flyer, yet relaxing fun for the experienced R/Cer. ''Failsafe'' neutralizes the rudder automatic-ally, preventing overcontrol, yet pulsing the left or right turn button will increase the turn rate.

LANIER R/C

The *P-51 Sport* (No. 74112, $124.95 retail) is a Sport scale model which features symmetrical airfoil, plywood spar, and a beautiful high-gloss finish. It's rugged and durable, fuel proof, painting's not necessary, and parts are easily available. Made of a plastic and ply fuselage and a foam wing with plastic covering, the P-51 has a 63-in. wingspan that gives a 630-sq.-in. area. It requires a 4-channel radio and a .45/.60 or 4-stroke .80/.90 engine. Flying weight is 6-7 lbs.

ROYAL PRODUCTS CORP.

The *Royal-Air 40T* ($134.95 retail) is an ideal, inexpensive ready-to-fly trainer. It comes complete with wheels, tank, motor mount, push rods, and spinner. It is pre-constructed of a balsa wing and plywood fuselage just like a balsa kit and covered with a pre-painted polyester film. The wingspan is 64 in., the length is 49 in., and a .40-.45 engine and a 4-channel radio are required.

ROYAL PRODUCTS CORP.

The *Royal-Air .20* ($99.95 retail) comes factory assembled. It features a balsa and ply fuselage and a balsa wing and comes pre-covered with a multi-colored mylar film. The wingspan is 50 in. and the area is 437-1/2 sq. in. Wheels, tank, spinner, and pushrods are included. High-, mid-, or low-wing options are available. A .20-.25 engine and a 4-channel radio are required.

ROYAL PRODUCTS CORP.

The *Royal Air .40* ($129.95 retail) comes fully assembled. It features balsa construction and comes pre-covered with a multi-colored Mylar film. Wheels, tank, spinner, and pushrods are included. High-, mid-, or low-wing options available. The wingspan is 57-1/4 in. and the area is 572-1/2 sq. in. A .40-.45 engine and a 4-channel radio are required.

Aircraft

Almost Ready to Fly

COX HOBBIES, INC.

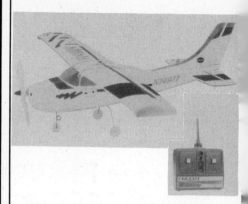

The *Electric Flyboy* (No. 90440) is an easy-to-fly radio-control airplane. The Flyboy is almost fully assembled and requires taping the elevator, strapping the wing down with rubber bands, and snapping on the landing gear.

ALTECH MARKETING

Altech Marketing is pleased to introduce a new 4-channel R/C trainer that will outfly and outlast all others; it's the *Sage 25*. This durable almost-ready-to-cover kit of wood construction is almost completely factory assembled, so you can spend more time making it pretty and learning to fly. The Sage 25's fuselage is constructed of lightweight wood in a laminated form that is extremely tough to resist shock and vibration. The main wing uses a foam core with wood sheeting. With a length of 38 inches and a wingspan of 56 inches, it's easily transportable.

ALTECH MARKETING

Altech Marketing has always catered to the discriminating modeler; the one who wants only the best engine in his prize airplane. We chose an almost-ready-to-cover, wood airplane kit as the latest item preferred by knowledgeable modelers. We selected a biplane for its outstanding appeal. The end result is Altech Marketing's *Super Stearman Kit IE300;* it's everything you wanted in an almost-ready-to-cover airplane kit and more!

The Super Stearman was a modified version of the aircraft used to train hundreds of pilots. The Super Stearman version featured a "hot" radial motor for exciting aerobatics. Our kit version will give you the same thrills but in much quicker time because we've built all the hard parts for you.

ALTECH MARKETING

The *Zlin Akrobat* airplane is well known by real pilots and modelers alike. Made in Czechoslovakia, this low wing monoplane was an important factor in world aerobatic championships. Altech Marketing has recreated this plane in a 4-channel .40 size almost-ready-to-cover kit that will outperform "plastic" airplane kits of the same size and type.

We designed a wood kit that features low building time. We've built the fuselage and foam core wings to save your time for building and flying. Try our Enya SS40 or SS40BB for screaming performance; the Enya 53-4C will give the Zlin the vertical performance of a scared cat climbing a tree! Try flying inverted in a circle; the Zlin won't roll out of position like other so-called aerobatic planes.

FUTABA

The newest in Futaba's line of pre-constructed aircraft is the *Acrostar 60*, a semi scale replica of the European Aerobatic Champion. Faithfully reproduced using our advanced ARF design, Futaba's Acrostar looks great just taxiing down the runway. All graphics and markings of the original are already applied and fuelproofed. No painting or covering is necessary, the Acrostar is factory-finished and over 90% pre-constructed. And the detailing is accurate right down to the wheel pants. This aircraft uses a .60 2-cycle or .90 4-cycle engine. The plane has a 57.09" wingspan and a 600 sq. in. wing area. Requires a 4-channel radio.

HOBBICO

Hobbico's *P-40 Warhawk* (No. HCAA-2650, $299.95 retail) is a highly detailed, realistic ARF model of the full-size P-40 Warhawk, as flown by Rudy Frasca. The ASAP (as-soon-as-possible) P-40 is 80% pre-built, as it only requires 16-20 hours to complete. The aircraft offers extremely stable, pattern-like performance combined with incredible detail. It can be equipped with 90° rotating retracts available from Hobbico (HCAA-4050). It has a wingspan of 61-in., weighs 6.25-7 lbs., and runs on a .46-.61 2-cycle engine.

HITEC R/C USA, INC.

Hitec's *Wind Cruiser II* (No. HAP0010) is an ARF electric-powered glider for 2 or 3 channel flying. With its special blow-molded fuse, ready built, and covered balsa core wing and tail surfaces, the Wind Cruiser II goes together very rapidly and weighs a mere 38.86 oz. Ready-to-fly. Included is a Mabuchi 540 motor with direct drive folding prop assembly, pre-attached servo trays, and all hardware to get you in the air.

HOBBY DYNAMICS DISTRIBUTORS

The *Yoshioka Liberty 25/45* ($139.99/$359.99 retail) is an excellent choice for the intermediate or advanced flyer. It is constructed of plastic foam, with a 50-in. or 57-in. wingspan, depending on your choice. It comes with all necessary hardware including fuel tank, and is 90% preassembled. A .20/.45 engine and 4-channel radio are required.

HOBBY DYNAMICS DISTRIBUTORS

The *Long Tai Shin Das Ugly Stick 40/60* ($159.99/$189.99 retail) is almost ready-to-fly, pre-covered in brilliant red, white, and black graphics. This all-balsa-and-plywood airplane is 44 in. or 46 in. long with a 52-in. or 60-in. wingspan, depending on your selection. It includes motor mount, spinner, landing gear, wheels, fuel tank, control rods, horns, hinges, and simple step-by-step plans. A .40-.60 engine and 4-channel radio are required.

HOBBY DYNAMICS DISTRIBUTORS

The *Ultra 40 ARF* (No. HDDULTARP, $159.95 retail) utilizes flat bottom wings and plenty of dihedral. For convenience this fuselage has plenty of space for the radio gear. Proper drag coefficients make for easy landings.

HOBBY DYNAMICS DISTRIBUTORS

The *Sportee 40 ARF* (HDDSPTARF, $159.95 retail) has a stable air platform capable of any maneuver. It utilizes a hardwood leading dowel wing that makes building a snap and adds durability no other style can offer.

KYOSHO

Kyosho's *Soarus* (No. KYOA1083, $209.95 retail) is the first electric powered ARF sailplane that is competition ready out-of-the-box. Utilizes a Seleg 3021 airfoil for excellent power-off thermaling capabilities. Included are the LeMans AP36L electric motor and spinner-equipped folding propeller. Made of tough, blow-molded polypropylene fuselage, balsa ribs and pre-covered flying surfaces. This plane, painted for you in high-visibility yellow, has a wingspan of 77 in. A 2- or 3-channel radio is required.

LANIER R/C

The new *Invader* (No. 87207, $199.95 retail) is 80% complete and, based on its jet-looking appearance, it will get a lot of attention. It is 40 in. long with a 55-in. wingspan and requires a 4-channel radio and a .40-.60/2-C engine. A high performance plane and a flying weight of 5-6 lbs.

LANIER R/C

New! The *Sea Bird* (No. 87206, $229.95 retail) is the only 90% pre-built amphibious seaplane on the market today. Good looks and a great performer, it is 46 in. long with a 60-in. wingspan and requires a 4-channel radio and a .45-.60/2-C or .60-.80/4-C engine. It has a semi-symmetrical airfoil and a flying weight of 5-1/2 - 6-1/2 lbs.

LANIER R/C

The new *Lanier Laser* (No. 87205, $189.95 retail) is a high-performance fully aerobatic, 90%-built aircraft that will attract a lot of attention at any flying field. It is 43 in. long with a 59-1/2-in. wingspan and requires a 4-channel radio and a .45-.60/2-C or .60-1.20/4-C engine. It has a flying weight of 6-7-1/4 lbs.

LANIER R/C

The *Vulcan* (No. 84200, $159.95 retail) is high performance, 90% finished, retract ready, has symmetrcial airfoil, plywood spar. It has a plastic and ply fuselage and a foam wing with plastic covering. The wingspan is 63 in. with a 630-sq.-in. area. Vulcan requires a 5-channel radio and a .45/.60 or 4-stroke .80/.90 engine. No covering or painting necessary. The plane has a high-gloss finish, is fuel proof and durable, parts are easily available. Flying weight is 7 lbs.

LANIER R/C

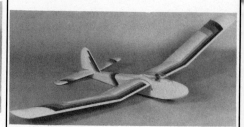

The *Hawk* (No. 74109, $115.95 retail) is a trainer glider that comes 95% finished for high start launch or slope flying. It has flat bottom airfoil, plywood spar, high-gloss finish. No painting or covering needed. It has a plastic and ply fuselage and a foam and plastic wing. The wingspan is 75 in., giving an area of 750 sq. in. It requires a 2-channel radio. It's durable, rugged, and parts are available. Flying weight is 2-1/2 - 3-1/4 lbs.

LANIER R/C

The *Dart* (No. 74104, $124.95 retail) is a Sport pattern model which is 90% finished. It has symmetrical airfoil, plywood spar, high-gloss finish and is rugged, durable and fuel proof. No covering or painting necessary. Dart has a 63-in. wingspan and 630-sq.-in. area. The fuselage is plastic and ply and the wing is foam with plastic covering. A 4-channel radio is required, along with a .40/.60 or 4-stroke .80/.90 engine. Flying weight is 6 lbs.

LANIER R/C

The *Rebel* (No. 78129, $249.95 retail) is a high-performance Sport biplane, 80% finished, with symmetrical airfoil, plywood spars, and high-gloss finish. The fuselage is plastic and ply, the wings are foam with plastic covering. Wingspan is 50 in. and total wing area is 700 sq. in. It requires a 4-channel radio and a .45/.60 or 4-stroke .80 engine. It's rugged and durable, parts are easily available, and no painting or covering is necessary. Flying weight is 7 lbs.

LANIER R/C

The *Jester* (No. 74116, $124.95 retail) features high performance, is 90% finished, has symmetrical airfoil, plywood spar. Constructed of a plastic and ply fuselage and foam wing with plastic covering, it has a 63-in. wingspan that offers a 630-sq.-in. area. No covering or painting is necessary. The plane comes with a high gloss finish, is fuel proof, durable, rugged, and parts are easily available. Jester requires a 4-channel radio and a .45/.60 or 4-stroke .80/.90 engine. Flying weight is 6 lbs.

LANIER R/C

The *Caprice* (No. 74116, $124.95 retail) is a high-performance aircraft. It is 90% finished and has a symmetrical airfoil and a plywood spar. The wingspan is 63 in., giving an area of 630 sq. in. The fuselage is plastic and ply and the wing is foam with plastic covering. It has a high-gloss finish; no covering or painting is necessary. Fuel proof, durable and rugged, Caprice requires a 4-channel radio and a .45/.60 or 4-stroke .80/.90 engine. Parts are easily available. Flying weight is 6 lbs.

LANIER R/C

The *TR-260* (No. 91210, $189.95 retail) is an excellent aerobatic performer! Foam wings covered in ABS plastic are symmetrical with a 60 in. span and an area of 620 sq. in. Engine sizes range from .45-.60 or .60-.91 4-cycle. Firewall engine mount with cowling. Materials consist of ABS plactic, foam, plywood, and balsa wood.

LANIER R/C

The *Fun-Fly 40* (No. 91209, $99.95 retail) is for fun or sport flying. Semi-symmetrical airfoil spans 48 in. with an area of 516 sq. in. The fuselage length is 35-1/2 in. with a finished weight of 3-3/4 to 5 lbs. Foam wings are covered in ABS plastic; tail surfaces require covering or painting. The recommended engine sizes are .19-.46.

LANIER R/C

The *Stinger* (No. 90208, $299.95 retail) has a vacuum-formed plastic turtledeck, wing cover, and fuel tank cover. Foam wings have balsa spars that require partial balsa sheeting and cap stripping. Canopy, cowling, and wheel pants included. Wing span is 84 in. with an area of 1596 sq. in. Recommended engine sizes are 1.2-4.2 cubic in. Flying weight is 14 lbs. and up.

O.S. ENGINES

For the *O.S. Engines Ryan ARF* (No. OSMA0010, $399.95 retail), advanced construction means no covering, no painting and no lengthy assembly. All major hardware is included along with the O.S. .40 FP already installed. Made of a balsa frame with multi-layered film, the plane is 41 1/2-in. long and has a 58-in. wingspan. It requires a 4-channel radio and uses an O. S. MAX .40 FE engine (incl.).

ROYAL PRODUCTS CORP.

The *Royal-Air Powersoar* ($109.95 retail) is a new gas-powered ARF that features factory assembled and covered sections that assemble quickly. It's a good beginner aircraft and comes with a complete hardware package. The wing is balsa and the fuselage is ply. It has a 66-1/2-in. wingspan and is 40-1/2-in. long. A .049-.10 engine and a 2- or 3-channel radio are required.

ROYAL PRODUCTS CORP.

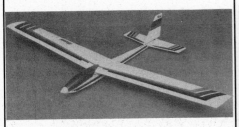

The *Royal-Air Easysoar* ($109.95 retail) is a new ARF that features pre-built and covered modular sections for quick building. It is designed for light duty high start and comes complete with hardware package. It's a good beginner, fun fly aircraft. With a balsa wing and ply fuselage, it has a 66-1/2-in. wingspan and a length of 40-1/2 in. An electric 540 motor and a 2-channel radio are required.

ROYAL PRODUCTS CORP.

The *Royal-Air 20T* ($102.95) boasts more prefabrication and less assembly time than any other balsa ARF. It comes 95% factory assembled with pre-covered paint design on both sides of the wing and stab.

ROYAL PRODUCTS CORP.

The *Royal-Air Electrosoar III* ($139.95 retail) balsa/ply ARF comes 90% complete from the factory with an electric 550 engine, folding prop, switch harness, and paint scheme on both sides of wing and stab. Its wingspan is 78-1/4 in. and length is 42 in.

U.S. AIRCORE

The *AirCore™ Family Trainer* (No. AC2030, $119.95 retail) is completely pre-decorated in vivid red, white, and blue. This quick-built, super tough aircraft is made of AirCore™ material, resulting in an airplane that is three to four times tougher than balsa. The AirCore 40's large high lift, 64" wing allows excellent flight characteristics. Included is the Power Cartridge™, which slides into the nose of the plane, containing your engine, radio, tank, and servos. The PC can be removed for service or easily inserted into other PC compatible airplanes. Engine .40-.46 2-stroke, .50 4-stroke. Radio 4-channels. Complete easy-to-follow instruction manual included. 100% Made in U.S.A.

U.S. AIRCORE

The *CoroStar 40™ Warbird Extraordinair* (No. AC2010, $89.95 retail) is a quick-built, super tough taildragger. Shown here with optional Explorer™ Floats, it is made of AirCore™ material. The CoroStar™ is three to four times tougher than balsa planes. Pre-finished in white, it can be decorated with paint or trim tape to resemble the warbird of your choice. Included is the Power Cartridge™ or 'PC,' a tray which slides into the nose of the plane, containing your engine, radio, tank, and servos. The PC can be removed for service or easily inserted into other PC compatible airplanes. Engine .40-.46 2-stroke, .50 4-stroke. Radio 4-channels. Complete easy-to-follow instruction manual included. 100% Made in U.S.A.

U.S. AIRCORE

The *Classic 40™, the Ultimate Bush Plane* (No. AC2040, $129.95 retail) is a quick-built, super tough taildragger. Made of AirCore™ material, the Classic™ is three to four times tougher than balsa planes. Pre-finished in cub-yellow, it can be decorated as a cub (shown) or the classic of your choice with simple trim tape and decals. Included is the Power Cartridge™ or 'PC,' a tray which slides into the nose of the plane, containing your engine, radio, tank, and servos. The PC can be removed for service or easily inserted into other PC compatible airplane. Engine .40-.46 2-stroke, .50 4-stroke. Radio 4-channels. Complete easy-to-follow instruction manual included. 100% Made in U.S.A.

UNITED MODEL DISTRIBUTORS

The *Union Tsunami* ($239.99 retail) is a stand-off scale, electric ARF plane for the experienced flier. The Tsunami is easy to assemble and includes a 7.2 volt, 600 mah flight pack and charger. The Tsunami can fly with two to four channels which enable it to do many aerobatics.

UNITED MODEL DISTRIBUTORS

The *Union EP Challenger* ($169.95 retail) is a geared, electric-powered trainer designed specifically for the newcomer to R/C flying. It is 26.5 in. long, has a 33.4-in. wingspan, is powered by an electric 380-size engine, and requires a 2-3 channel radio. Construction is fast and easy. Made from expanded polystyrene foam, the EP Challenger is both light and durable. Mini radio equipment is not needed. Both battery and charger are included with this highly prefabricated ARF kit.

UNITED MODEL DISTRIBUTORS

The *Union Cessna Centurion* ($189.99 retail) is a stand-off scale electric ARF model of the popular light plane. The Centurion is easy to assemble and fly. Construction time is 2-4 hours due to the high degree of prefabrication. The Cessna Centurion is great looking and requires 2 channels of control.

UNITED MODEL DISTRIBUTORS

UNITED MODEL DISTRIBUTORS

This electric-powered model, the *Union EP Champion* ($199.99 retail), is a step up in flying characteristics and performance from the Union EP Challenger. It is 27.1 in. long, has a 33.4-in. wingspan, is powered by an electric 380-size engine, and requires a 2-3 channel radio. The geared motor unit is powerful and flies the Champion for 3-1/2-4-1/2 minutes. All foam/expanded polystyrene construction makes for quick assembly and lightweight durability. Battery and charger included. Mini radio not necessary.

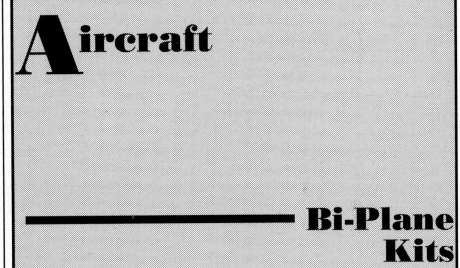

Aircraft

Bi-Plane Kits

The *Union EP Rocky* is a European motor-glider-styled electric plane intended for the experienced flier. It is 25.9 in. long, has a 42.1-in. wingspan, is powered by an electric 380-size engine, and requires a 2-3 channel radio. 3-1/2 to 4-1/2 minute motor run times and exciting performance will please the R/C enthusiast. All foam/expanded polystyrene construction combines quick assembly, durability, and good looks in one great package. Battery and charger included. Mini radio system not required.

ACE R/C, INC.

The *4-120 Bipe* (No. 50K228, $169.95 retail) is the ideal plane for those that believe that it isn't a plane unless it's got two wings. The plane, made of lite ply and spruce, has wingspans of 60 in. and 62.5 in. and a length of 60 in. It requires a 1.20/4-C engine and a 4-channel radio. This biplane is truly majestic in the air. Its long moments make smooth maneuvers easy and predictable. COMPLETE hardware is provided, including fiber-filled landing gear and heavy duty linkage.

ALTECH MARKETING

Altech Marketing has always catered to the discriminating modeler; the one who wants only the best engine in his prize airplane. We chose an almost-ready-to-cover, wood airplane kit as the latest item preferred by knowledgeable modelers. We selected a biplane for its outstanding appeal. The end result is Altech Marketing's *Super Stearman Kit IE300;* it's everything you wanted in an almost-ready-to-cover airplane kit and more!

The Super Stearman was a modified version of the aircraft used to train hundreds of pilots. The Super Stearman version featured a "hot" radial motor for exciting aerobatics. Our kit version will give you the same thrills but in much quicker time because we've built all the hard parts for you.

CARL GOLDBERG MODELS, INC.

The *Ultimate Byplane* ($199.99 retail) kit is designed around the proven "slot-tab" method of construction, so you will find this the "Ultimately-easiest" biplane to build. Simple built-in fixtures assure warp-free wing assembly. All screws, hardware (including glass-filled engine mounts) etc., are included to finish the airframe. Formed bolt-together aluminum cabanes deliver precise "hassle-free" wing alignment. Full-size plans and clearly photographed instructions guide you through every step. Also furnished are rugged molded cowl, canopy and wheel pants, and two large sheets of full-color decals for the finishing touches of your "Ultimate" model.

GREAT PLANES MODEL MFG.

The *Sportster Bipe 40* (No. GPMA0510, $105.95 retail) can't be beat when it comes to downright barnstorming. You can count on our precision-cut and sanded parts to help speed the building of two wings. Wings are held on with bolts and screws to save assembly time at the field—no cumbersome interplane struts are used. Uses .35-.45/2C or .40-.60/4C engine; ideal aircraft for .45-.61 4-cycle. Made of balsa fuselage and wings, the plane has a 45-in. wingspan and a 716 cu. in. area. It requires a 4-channel radio.

MODEL ENGINEERING OF NORWALK

Big John (Retail: See your dealer) has a 76-3/4-in. wingspan that yields a 1500-sq.-in. wing area, yet it can be built in 25 to 45 hours. M.E.N.'s kit engineering was specifically planned for fast, easy building. Our "Thru-Cut" die cutting combined with "Tri-Square-Loc" construction of lite plywood and balsa makes construction fast and simple. The inherent strength of lite plywood construction provides durability and lasting performance. The kit features Thru-Cut die cutting, quality materials, rolled plans, building instructions, wing jig building fixtures, complete hardware package, pre-bent landing gear, cabane strut wires. It requires a .60-.90 engine and a 4-channel radio.

ROYAL PRODUCTS CORP.

Royal brings the classic *Curtiss Hawk P-6E* ($284.95 retail) alive in this beautiful balsa/ply kit. It comes complete with super-detail decal set and loads of extra scale information. The wingspan is 63 in. and the length is 1010 sq. in. A 4-channel radio and a .60/2C or .90/4C engine are required.

ROYAL PRODUCTS CORP.

The *Stearman PT-17* ($364.95 retail) is an exciting military flight trainer that comes to life in Royal's new balsa kit. Designed exclusively for 4-cycle engines, this model comes complete with dummy radial engine. The wingspan is 68 3/8 in. A .60-.90/2C or .90-1.20/4C is required.

ROYAL PRODUCTS CORP.

The *Pitts S-2A* ($109.95 retail) is a new member of Royal's semi-scale family and provides a small alternative to the larger S-2 and S-1 Pitts. The wingspan of this balsa kit is 31 1/2 in. and the area is 335 sq. in. A .09-.21 engine and a 4-channel radio are required.

ROYAL PRODUCTS CORP.

The *Pitts S2* ($214.95 retail) is the big brother of Royal's Little Stinker. The wingspan of this balsa kit is 52 in. and the wing area is 830 sq. in. The extra fuselage length of this two-seat version really smooths out its flying capabilities. A .60-.80 engine and a 4-channel radio are required.

SIG MANUFACTURING CO.

The *Liberty Sport* (No. RC-33, $114.95 retail) is a full-scale model that flies like a sport design and isn't difficult to build. This balsa kit includes three views and photos of the prototype airplane. The wingspan is 57 in. A .45-.60 engine and a 4-channel radio are required.

SIG MANUFACTURING CO.

The *Skybolt* (No. RC-34, $116.95 retail) features a molded plastic cowl, wheel pants, and turtle deck. It comes in a double or single aileron configuration. It's very aerobatic! The wingspan of this balsa plane is 51-1/2 in. and the area is 798 sq. in. A .60 engine and a 4-channel radio are required.

SIG MANUFACTURING CO.

The *Smith Miniplane* (No. RC-38, $94.95 retail) is a sport-scale model of a colorful home-built design. It features semi-symmetrical wings, and is very aerobatic. It's a fun airplane to build and fly. It's made of built-up balsa, with a 44-in. wingspan and a 650-sq. in. wing area. It requires a .40-.45 engine and a 4-channel radio.

Aircraft ——— Control Line Kits

CARL GOLDBERG MODELS, INC.

The *Little Toot* (No. 22, kit G-4, $19.99 retail) is our sporty biplane with a 16-in. wingspan. It is designed for an .049 engine and it is easy to build and fly. All parts are die-cut balsa.

CARL GOLDBERG MODELS, INC.

The *Lil' Wizard* (No. 23, kit G-5, $19.99 retail) is the ideal "first" kit for line control modelers. It has a shaped balsa wing, die-cut balsa fuselage, and tail surfaces with a 21-in. wingspan. It was designed for an .049 engine and can be flown on a 40- to 50-ft.-long line.

CARL GOLDBERG MODELS, INC.

The *Shoe String Stunter* (No. 30, kit G-9, $39.99 retail) is our best stunt flyer. It has all die-cut balsa parts and a 42-in. wingspan designed to be flown with a .19 to .35 engine. All die-cut balsa parts. It's an ideal starter model for larger line control models.

CARL GOLDBERG MODELS, INC.

The *Stuntman 23* (No. 24, kit G-6, $19.99 retail) is our simplest stunt model with a 23-in. wingspan. It has all die-cut balsa parts and has been designed to fly with a .049 to .09 size engine.

CARL GOLDBERG MODELS, INC.

The *Swordsman 18* (No. 21, kit G-3, $19.99 retail) is our large control line model designed to fly with a .049 engine. It has an 18-in. wingspan and all die-cut balsa parts. It's easy to build and easy to fly.

SIG MANUFACTURING CO.

The *Banshee* (No. CL-11, $39.95 retail) is an attractive profile stunter that sports flaps, good-looks, and super flight performance. The full-size plans make it easy to build even for the novice. Made of built-up balsa and plywood, it has a 49-in. wingspan and requires a .29-.40 engine.

SIG MANUFACTURING CO.

The *Magnum* (CL-24, $92.95 retail) evolved over several years of competition and represents state-of-the-art design for precision aerobatics. This deluxe kit features a cored foam wing and a balsa fuselage. The wingspan is 60 in. and the length is 46 in. A .40-.60 engine is required.

SIG MANUFACTURING CO.

The *Mustang Stunter* (No. CL-21, $61.95 retail) features the classic lines of the P-51 blended into an ideal C/L stunter layout. It also has pre-cut foam wing core, balsa fuselage construction, plastic cowl, and top deck. Wingspan is 50 in., area is 480 sq. in. A .29-.40/2-cycle engine is required.

SIG MANUFACTURING CO.

The *Skyray* (No. CL-23, $11.95 retail) uses a one-piece balsa wing for quick assembly. Designed for beginners, this super-strong model is easy to fly. Decals are included! The wingspan is 23-3/4 in. and a .049 engine is required.

SIG MANUFACTURING CO.

The *Skyray 35* (No. CL-25, $39.95 retail) is an easy-to-build profile model for stunt, combat, racing, or general sport flying. Strong built-up balsa wing with spruce spars and Lite-Ply plywood ribs. The wingspan is 44 in. and the area is 396 sq. in. A .19-.35 cu. in. engine is required.

SIG MANUFACTURING CO.

The *Super Chipmunk* (No. CL-19, $62.95 retail) features outstanding flight performance that has resulted in several Nats victories. The molded cowling and bubble canopy set this model apart from the average stunter. Constructed of built-up balsa and plywood, it has a 53-1/2-in. wingspan and requires a .29-.40 engine.

SIG MANUFACTURING CO.

The *Twister* (No. CL-22, $39.95 retail) profile stunter is excellent for aerobatic training—it performs like a competition model! With flaps, pre-bent pushrods, and complete hardware. Constructed of built-up balsa and plywood, and has a 48-in. wingspan and requires a .29-.40 engine.

Aircraft

Electric Kits

ALTECH MARKETING

The *Clipped-Wing Piper Cub* (No. IQ002; Retail: See your dealer) features a gear reduction system for longer flights. The plane has a balsa/styrofoam fuselage and balsa wing. Included is pre-colored paper, two propellers, and detailed full-size plans and instructions.

CARL GOLDBERG MODELS, INC.

The *Electra* (No. 40/EL1 for deluxe, $79.99 retail; No. 41/EL2 for basic, $49.99 retail; Wing Kit K-80, $24.99 retail) is based on Goldberg Models' popular Gentle Lady sport sailplane. This model can give you up to 12 minutes of flight. It's the perfect "first" electric plane. The all-balsa Electra is 41 in. long and has a 78-1/4-in. wingspan. It is designed for a .05 electric engine and 2 or 3 channel radio.

CARL GOLDBERG MODELS, INC.

The *Mirage 550* (No. 42, $79.99 retail; Wing Kit K-91, $24.99 retail) is a new breed of electric sport-trainer. It climbs easily using less power so you spend more time flying. The 54-in. wingspan and generous wing area—464 sq. in.—gives Mirage gentle trainer-like handling. Expect flight times of over 10 minutes from standard 6 or 7 cell car packs. This all-balsa kit includes Turbo 550 motor and complete electric harness, special Dave Brown ''lite-wheels,'' hinges, pushrods and more. It requires a 2 or 3 channel radio. Beautiful cowl, windshield, wheel pants add a final touch of class!

GREAT PLANES MODEL MFG.

The *Electrostreak* (GPMA0385, $79.95 retail) offers aerobatic performance never thought possible in an electric powered plane. This kit features step-by-step illustrated instructions and pre-cut parts with motor and prop included. Made of balsa and ply, the Electrostreak is 39.5 in. long and has a 44-in. wingspan. A Great Planes Goldfire 550 engine is included. A 4-channel radio is required.

KYOSHO

The *Valencia* (No. KYOA1140, $249.95 retail) is an easy-building, stylish, great-flying electric motor glider ARF. It features an Eppler 178 airfoil and unique T-tail. A super-tough fuselage contributes to this glider's stability. Made of blow-molded plastic and balsa, the Valencia has a 70-in. wingspan and requires a 2- or 3-channel radio. A LeMans 240E electric motor is included.

THE MIDWAY MODEL COMPANY

The *Electra Glide II* ($47.95 retail). This 73 in. span 4500 sq. in. area design is a modern, high performance, 3-channel electric sailplane. It features the popular Eppler 205 airfoil. While the Electra Glide II is primarily for direct drive 035 to 05 motors, it can also be easily modified to accommodate a gear drive unit and a large (12 in.) folding propellor. It is a good beginning flyer's plane. The kit has all machine cut and sanded balsa, ply, and spruce parts, rolled plans, detailed instructions, and basic R/C hardware.

THE MIDWAY MODEL COMPANY

The *Lightning Aerobatic kit* ($39.95 retail). This 39 in. span, 280 sq. in. area plane is designed for 035 and 05 direct drive electric motors and six or seven-cell packs. It is very fast and highly aerobatic using aileron and elevator controls. Intended originally for club racer rules, it has become the plane of choice for electric pattern type aerobatics. An on-off switch or motor control is recommended to manage the power. Although the kit is extremely simple to build, the flying is best left to the intermediate to advanced flyer. The kit features parts of machined cut and sanded balsa, ply, and spruce pieces, rolled plans, detailed instructions, and basic hardware. It is available at the best hobby shops nationwide. Another high quality kit made in the USA.

THE MIDWAY MODEL COMPANY

The *Air Trails Sportster* ($47.95 retail) was designed in 1939. It has a 50 in. wingspan, 380 sq. in. area, and weighs approximately 32-38 oz. ready to fly. For 3-channel radios, and .09 to .15 gas engines for power. This model will also accept electric power. The kit includes top quality machined and sanded balsa, ply, and spruce parts of prime grade woods. The kit also features detailed full size plans, complete assembly instructions, basic R/C hardware, and special electric propulsion conversion installation instructions. Available at leading hobby shops everywhere. Made in the USA.

THE MIDWAY MODEL COMPANY

The *Thermic Traveler Electric Powered Sailplane* ($47.95 retail) is a high-performance electroflight glider. Its classic looks are from the pre-WWII model aircraft designs that were based on Wolf Hirth's full size sailplane, The Wolf. As an R/C model, it incorporates an Eppler 205 airfoil giving it an excellent soaring glide along with the ability to penetrate high winds. While the kit is designed with an Astro Geared Cobalt 05 system in mind, the plans also show a direct drive version as well as a pure glider version.

THE MIDWAY MODEL COMPANY

The *Ultra Mk IV* ($59.95 retail) is a multi-use electric sailplane that has the unique option of being constructed two ways: one is an 86 in. span with 750 sq. in. wing area for 035 or 05 gear drive units, or a 75 in. wing span with 615 sq. in.wing area for 05 direct or gear drive drive units. The kit comes with top quality hand-machined ply and balsa parts, rolled plans, hinges, horns, clevises, and the wing joiner parts.

THE MIDWAY MODEL COMPANY

The *Fast Eddie Sport/Pylon Racer* ($39.95 retail) is small, light, and the fastest electric model available today! It holds the FAI unofficial world speed record (92.85 MPH) in level flight over a two way measured course. The plans and instructions show three different wing spans; a 29 in. for maximum speed, and a 33 in. or 38 in. for pylon racing or acrobatics. The battery compartment will accommodate either a six or seven cell 1200 MAH battery and three servos, or two servos and a speed control/motor control unit. Intended for the experienced flyer.

THE MIDWAY MODEL COMPANY

The *Skyknight for Direct 05 electric* ($39.95 retail). Span: 44 in. area: 330 sq. in. 3-channel radio required (For rudder, elevator and throttle.) There has been a need for a simple basic trainer ever since R/C electric models became popular. In a very lightweight and compact package our Skyknight is a real looking airplane with ''Citabria'' like eye appeal. It features a flat-bottom Clark ''Y'' type airfoil for slower, more predictable flying speeds. This kit has complete step by step instructions, full size plans, and fully machined parts of prime grade balsa and ply, along with pre-bent landing gear and basic hardware.

PECK-POLYMERS

The *1300 Blimp Kit* (No. PP035, $349.95 retail) incorporates all the best features we have learned. It gives you the most maneuverable and efficient blimp ever flown. The blimp bag is vinyl and fills to a volume of 150 cu. ft. The gondola is plastic and the fins are balsa. Overall length is 12 and 13 ft., and wingspan is 55 in. The new 1300 also features propeller guards for safety. The Blimp comes complete with plans, die-cut balsa, ply, formed plastic gondola, propeller guards, all hardware, and finished vinyl bag. The Power Kit ($300.00 retail) completes the Blimp with three Peck 035 electric motors, battery, charger, helium filler, adaptors, switch harness, and electric speed control. A 4-channel radio is required.

ROYAL PRODUCTS CORP.

The *Royal-Air Electrosoar III* ($139.95 retail) balsa/ply ARF comes 90% complete from the factory with an electric 550 engine, folding prop, switch harness, and paint scheme on both sides of wing and stab. Its wingspan is 78-1/4 in. and length is 42 in.

Aircraft

Free-Flight & Rubber Power Kits

ALTECH MARKETING

The *Skylark* (No. IS022; Retail: See your dealer), shown above, is a new addition to Altech's growing family of rubber-powered airplanes. Also available is the Joy-Star (IS020). These rubber-powered stick airplanes feature foam wings and tail surfaces, and snap-together parts.

ALTECH MARKETING

These *Rubber Powered Aircraft* (See your dealer for details) are for the free-flight enthusiast in all of us. Eight different aircraft, all made of polystyrene foam, are available in three different style groups to match your price/performance wishes. The Piper, assembles with tape and self-sticking decals for flights within 15 minutes of opening the box. The Zero and Spitfire have prepainted airframes plus water-soluble decals for tops in scale looks. You get instructions on how to add extra details to make your model a masterpiece, plus you get a display stand to show it off. The Rya STA model is excellent for you to paint and detail to your heart's content. Each kit contains at least one spare rubber band. The custom kits have spare propellers, too.

PECK-POLYMERS

Each of these *11 Peanut Scale* ($8.95 retail) models is a proven good flier. Made of balsa and powered by rubber, they have 13-in. wingspans and areas of 30 to 40 sq. in. Included are full-size plans, photo instruc-tions, quality balsa, complete with propeller wheels, rubber, and tissue.

PECK-POLYMERS

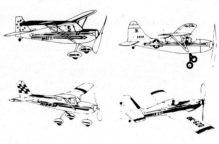

All *Busy People Kits* (No. PP-25 for Citabria, No. PP-26 for Stinson, No. PP-27 for Cessna, No. PP-28 for Zlin 50L; $8.95 retail) are die-cut balsa Profile rubber-powered. Wingspan is 16 in.

PECK-POLYMERS

The *Peck R.O.G.* (No. PP-10, $2.95 retail) is great to teach the basics of building models, and it's fun to fly. Made of balsa and powered by rubber, it has a 10-in. wingspan and an area of 30 sq. in. All materials, except glue, are included. It's used by many schools and groups.

PECK-POLYMERS

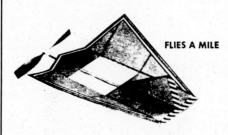

FLIES A MILE

The *Stringless Wonder* (No. PP-4, $5.95 retail) is easy and quick to build. It flies a mile. It's ideal for classes, because very little adjustment is needed. The kit is complete except for glue. Made of balsa and rubber powered, it has a 10 x 12 (measurement) flying wing with an area of 58 sq. in.

SIG MANUFACTURING CO.

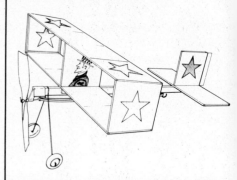

The *Uncle Sam* (No. FF-28, $3.50 retail) was designed by small-model expert Bill Hannan. This unique rubber-powered biplane flies with great stability. Made of balsa, it is 10-in. long with a 10-1/4-in. wingspan. The plan is the covering material and is recommended for beginners.

SIG MANUFACTURING CO.

The *Sig Classic Series* includes six rubber-power designs. All feature proven flight characteristics and complete building and flying instructions. All are constructed of balsa, and wingspans range from 20 to 24 in. All kits include propeller, rubber motor, wheels, and covering material. Choose between the Sig Tiger (No. FF-22, $8.95 retail), Cabinaire (FF-20, $9.95 retail), the '29er (FF-21, $8.95 retail), Mr. Mulligan (FF-23, $11.95 retail), Monocoupe (FF-25, $11.95 retail), and Customaire (FF-26, $11.95 retail).

SIG MANUFACTURING CO.

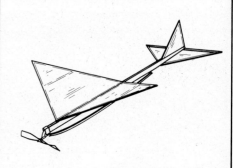

The *AMA Cub* (No. FF-5, $1.65 retail) was designed especially as a beginner's first model. Over 1.5 million have been built and flown. Made of balsa, this rubber-powered model has a 12-1/2-in. wingspan, and is available in quantity with your message printed on the wing covering material.

SIG MANUFACTURING CO.

The *Parasol* (No. FF-15, $3.95 retail) is a super-fun rubber-powered ''profile'' model for indoor or outdoor flying. Made of balsa, it has an 18-in. wingspan. The plan is the covering material. Wheels are included.

SIG MANUFACTURING CO.

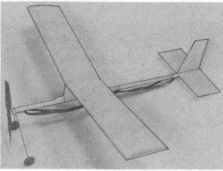

The *Sig Cub* (No. FF-1, $5.25 retail) is an ideal kit for learning how to build and fly rubber-powered models. Simple to build, yet turns in flights up to a surprisingly long 1000 feet! Made of balsa, it is 22-3/4-in. long with a 23-1/2-in. wingspan.

SIG MANUFACTURING CO.

THERMAL DART

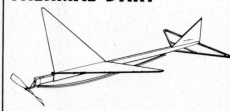

The *Thermal Dart* (No. FF-12, $4.50 retail) is an enlarged AMA Cub. Made of balsa and rubber-powered, its big 24-in. wingspan provides long, majestic flights. It's built right on the covering material. Great for kids of all ages!

WILLIAMS BROS.

Corben Super-Ace (Model 525). This 1935 aircraft was designed for amateur construction, and was powered by a modified Ford Model A engine. The Super-Ace had a top speed of about 100 miles per hour. Injection molded in 1/48-scale and highly detailed. NOW AVAILABLE IN H.O. SCALE FOR YOUR RAILROAD.

WILLIAMS BROS.

Curtiss C-46 (Model 72-346). The Curtiss Commando transport carried supplies over the Himalayan Hump during World War II, and served with the Chinese Air Force. War surplus C-46s flew with air lines, including the famous Flying Tigers. It features injection molded parts, three and four blade propellers, and decals for three different subjects. Giant 18 inch span, 1/72-scale.

WILLIAMS BROS.

Wedell-Williams (Model 32-121). These popular racers were flown during the golden age of aviation by such well known pilots as Roscoe Turner, Jimmy Wedell, Jim Haizlip and Mary Haizlip, winning many trophies. Beautifully recreated in 1/32 scale, this kit features two types of landing gear and comes complete with all decals to build any one of three different aircraft.

WILLIAMS BROS.

Northrop Gamma (Model 72-214). Jack Northrop's 1933 design featured such advanced concepts as multi-cellular wing construction, full span flaps, and momocoque fuselage. Flown by Frank Hawks, it set many records. Highly detailed and molded in 1/72 scale, this Williams Bros. kit includes two different engines, two different cowlings and canopies, and a complete decal sheet.

WILLIAMS BROS.

Pitcairn Autogiro (Model 48-161). The Pitcairn Autogiro was the forerunner of today's helicopter, the 1931 PCA-2 Autogiro was operated regularly by commercial firms and experimentally by the U.S. Navy and Marines. The recently restored Miss Champion is owned by Stephen Pitcairn, son of the original builder. The kit features injection molded parts, comprehensive instructions and drawings, as well as decals for both civil and military versions. 1/48 scale.

WILLIAMS BROS.

Seversky P-35/S2 (Model 32-135). Designed during the 1930s, the U.S. Army P-35 was an ancestor of the World War II P-47 Thunderbolt. The S/2 Seversky competed in the Bendix and Thompson Trophy races. This kit is injection molded in 1/32 scale, includes two types of decals, two types of canopies, and all other parts required to complete either the military or racer version.

R/C Flying is fun for the whole family!

WILLIAMS BROS.

Gee Bee R-1 Racer (Model 32-711). The Gee Bee R-1 is perhaps the most famous racing aircraft of all time. The Granville Brothers R-1, flown by Jimmy Doolittle, won the 1932 Thompson Trophy race and broke the world's speed record. This 1/32-scale kit is detailed to the traditionally high standards of William Bros. The kit includes injection molded parts, hard or flexible tires, and includes all parts to complete either the R-1 or the R-2.

WILLIAMS BROS.

Gee Bee "Z" Model Kit (Model 32-426). The Gee Bee "Z" was the first of the Granville Brothers barrel shaped racers, the Gee Bee "Z" won the 1931 Thompson trophy race and was the direct forerunner of the famous Gee Bee R-1 racer. This 1/32-scale model kit features injection molding, high quality decals, monofilament rigging, and two types of cowlings.

Aircraft

Giant Scale Kits

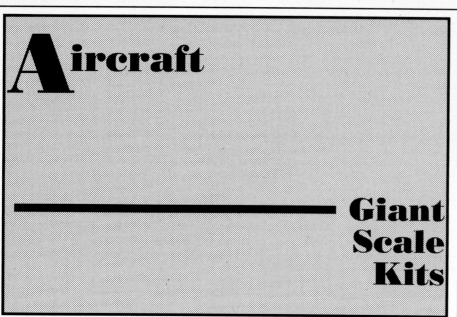

ACE R/C, INC.

The *Extra 230* (No. 50G5033, Retail: see your dealer) features a fiberglass cowl, formed landing gear, detailed rolled plans and asssembly manuals. It is made of balsa and foam and has a wingspan of 96 in. It requires an engine 2.6 cubic inches or larger. Top notch quality and impressive performance. Great for the aerobatic enthusiast.

ROYAL PRODUCTS CORP.

The *F4U-1A Corsair* ($629.95 retail) is a new 1/5-scale offering from Royal sure to delight the big bird enthusiast. The wingspan is 98-5/16 in. and the wing area is 1814 sq. in. This balsa kit comes complete with spun aluminum cowl and super-detail decal set. A 35-50cc engine and a 4-channel radio are required.

SIG MANUFACTURING CO.

This *1/4-Scale Clipped Wing Cub* (No. RC-47, $199.95 retail) is a deluxe giant-scale version of Hazel Sig's world-famous Clipped Wing Cub. It offers the same smooth, stable flight characteristics you expect from a Cub coupled with improved aerobatic capability. The kit features a molded cowling with scale engine details, scale tailwheel assembly, pushrods, decals, hardware, plans, and illustrated instructions. Constructed of balsa, ply, and spruce, it is 67-in. long and has an 86-in. wingspan. It requires a 4-channel radio and a .60-.90/2C or .90-1.6/4C engine.

ROYAL PRODUCTS CORP.

The *Super Cub PA18* ($419.95 retail) is a classic design kit that comes alive again in 1/4 scale. It features all balsa/ply construction and fiberglass cowl. The wingspan is 105-1/2 in. and the wing area is 1733 in. A .90-1.20/2C or 1.20-1.60/4C engine and a 4-channel radio are required.

SIG MANUFACTURING CO.

The *1/3-Scale Spacewalker* (No. RC-61, $349.95 retail) is a popular new home-built inspired by Aviation's Golden Era. The deluxe, highly accurate scale kit includes fiberglass cowling, wheel pants, and wingtips, plastic dummy cylinders, tailwheel assembly, three-piece wing with aluminum wing joiners, four plan sheets, and complete hardware. Constructed of balsa, plywood, and spruce, it is 72 in. long with a 104-in. wingspan. It requires a 1.5-2.4/2C or 1.8-3.0/4C engine and a 4-channel radio. This plane flies as good as it looks!

SIG MANUFACTURING CO.

1/4-Scale Piper J-3 Cub (No. RC-48, $209.95 retail) This plane is constructed of balsa/ply/spruce. It has a wingspan of 105 in. and a length of 67 in. It uses a .60-.90/2-c or .90-1.6/4-c engine and requires a 4-channel radio. The kit features a molded cosling with scale engine details, scale tailwheel assembly, fiberglass pushrods, decals, complete hardware, plans and illustrated instructions.

SIG MANUFACTURING CO.

The *Morrisey Bravo* (No. RC-57, $309.95 retail) is constructed of balsa/ply/spruce and has a wingspan of 86 in. with an area of 1,375 ft. It requires a 1.6-3.0 cu. in. engine and a 4-channel radio. The kit features a fiberglass cowl and wheel pants, scale tailwheel, pushrods, decals, hardware, plans, and illustrated instructions.

Aircraft

Glider Kits

ACE R/C, INC.

The *Easy Eagle* (No. 50K233, Retail: see your dealer) is a glider with a wingspan of 78-1/2 in. Whether on your first plane, experienced sport pilot, or a seasoned competition-oriented veteran, this plane has the simplicity and the latest technology to fit the need. Computer-generated and wind-tunnel tested. Quick assembly, gapless hinge lines, bolt-on wing, and complete hardware are included.

AG INDUSTRIES, INC.

The *WhiteWings Original Series* (No. AG-1500, $16.00 retail) model kit contains 15 classic airplane models printed on specially created fiber paper. The planes have an average wingspan of 7 in. and an average length of 9 in. An in-depth 60-page manual gives step-by-step instructions for building and tuning each plane. Models are designed by international champion of model airplane design, Dr. Yasuaki Ninomiya.

CARL GOLDBERG MODELS, INC.

The *Sophisticated Lady* (No. 59, $49.99 retail; Wing Kit K-80, $24.99 retail) is made of balsa-ply, has a wingspan of 78 in., and a length of 41 in. Features include: scale rendition of a high performance glider; T-tail for higher efficiency and safer landings; formed detailed cockpit interior; easy access radio compartment; removable canopy; fly with hi-start launch, slope soar, or optional electric Power Pod; easily responds to lift due to low sink-rate; designed from Goldberg Models' Gentle Lady; detailed illustrated construction booklet and plans.

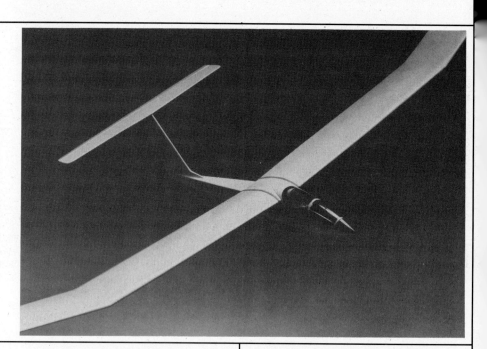

CARL GOLDBERG MODELS, INC.

The *Gentle Lady* (No. 60/SP-1, $34.99 retail; Wing Kit K-80, $24.99 retail) is a natural beginner's choice, yet efficient enough for 2-meter competition. Gentle, responsive, and just plain fun to fly. Made of balsa-bass-ply and balsa-ply, it has a 78-1/4-in. wingspan and 663 sq. in. area. It's excellent for Tow, Slope, or Power flying. It has pre-shaped leading and trailing edges, and fast, simple, and lightweight construction. All linkage hardware, including the tow hook, is included. Also, a complete step-by-step photo instruction booklet, geared for beginners, and full-size plans are included. A 2 or 3 channel radio is required.

CARL GOLDBERG MODELS, INC.

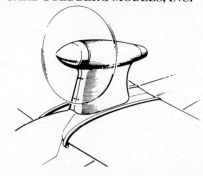

Although the *Power Pod* (No. 678, $44.99 retail) is designed to fit both Sophisticated Lady and Gentle Lady, this model adapts well to all other sailplanes. Features include: Turbo 550 motor with Tamiya connector and fuse; 8 x 4 prop and Goldberg spinner; operates from standard 6 or 7 cell car battery pack; complete instructions included.

GREAT PLANES MODEL MFG.

The *Spectra* (No. GPMA0540, $79.95 retail) has an unmatched climbing ability in an entry-level electric sailplane. The Great Planes Goldfire 550 motor allows the Spectra to soar from ground-zero to 500-ft. in just 60 seconds. The triple-taper wing with a modified Selig 3010 Airfoil provides longer soaring time. It is constructed out of balsa and ply, has a wingspan of 78.5-in., weighs 48-oz. RTF, and comes with a detailed, photo-illustrated instruction manual, full-sized plans that explain every step of the assembly, canopy, and all required hardware.

GREAT PLANES MODEL MFG.

The *Sprit* (No. GPMA0530, $49.95 retail) is the perfect entry-level sailplane. The Sprit is a sailplane that can fly slowly, giving new pilots time to learn, or fast, for contest flying in the hands of an experienced pilot. Featuring a modified Selig 3010 airfoil, state-of-the-art triple taper planform, polyhedral shape, and low wing loading, making the Sprit and excellent thermal chaser. Made of balsa with basswood spars, the Sprit has a 78.5-in. wingspan and requires a 2- or 3-channel radio.

HOBBY DYNAMICS DISTRIBUTORS

The *Yoshioka On Air E* ($199.99 retail) was awarded 1989 Model of the Year, Glider Division, at the International Toy and Model Show in Nuernberg, Germany. This is a high-quality glider that performs incredibly. It is 40.9 in. long with a 67.3-in. wingspan.

KYOSHO

The *Kyosho Stratus 2000 Sailplane* (No. KYOA1082; Retail: See your dealer) is designed for beginners and experienced sailplane pilots. It features an LSS one-piece molded fuselage and pre-built balsa ribbed wing and tail sections; the wing and tail sections are pre-finished in Excelcote covering material. A 3-channel radio with 6- or 7-cell battery pack and 550 size engine are required. The Stratus 2000 is 34.8 in. long and has a 76.4-in. wingspan.

HOBBY DYNAMICS DISTRIBUTORS

The *Yoshioka On Air S Sailplane* (No. YMFA2004, $175.99 retail) is an ARF that features a pre-molded wing with the popular E-205 airfoil. The fuselage requires minor assembly and radio installation. The specifications of this sailplane make it ideal for slope soaring or thermal duration flying.

THE MIDWAY MODEL COMPANY

The *Gnome 2-M* ($59.95 retail) is a 2-Meter sailplane with a 78 in. wingspan, 628 sq. in. wing area, and a flying weight of 32-38 oz. A 2- (or more) channel radio control unit is required. It is a strong, highly maneuverable model that is designed for power "zoo" launches from 12 volt electric winches or for heavy duty Hi-starts. Top notch hand-machined balsa and ply parts and all hardware necessary are included. Also included are step by step instructions and details for installing the optional spoilers.

THE MIDWAY MODEL COMPANY

The *Gnome HLG* ($41.95 retail) is truly "the high performance compact glider." With a 12-15 oz. flying weight, the glider measures 60 in. long and has a 375-sq. in. wing area. The Gnome is designed for a two-channel radio with medium to small servos. A standard size receiver will fit under the canopy/hatch. At its normal weight the wing loading range is 4.6 to 5.8 oz/sq. ft. The kit features the highest quality contest grade balsa, all machined ply and balsa parts, full size plans and detailed instructions. Basic hardware is included.

MODEL ENGINEERING OF NORWALK

The *Gobbler* (Retail: See your dealer) will allow faster and higher launches with its engineered 30-G bolt-on wing joiner system. Its stiffened stabilator gives a smoother flight profile. The wingspan is 114 in., the area 938 sq. in., and the wing loading range is 8-1/2 - 20 oz./sq. ft. The fully-sheeted Eppler 205 wings incorporate spoilers and wing ballast tubes. Optional configurations are shown for flaperons or aileron with separate flaps. A minimum of three to a maximum of seven servos are required for radio installation. A complete hardware package is included. Optional carbon fiber stiffening package is available also.

PECK-POLYMERS

The *Genesis R/C Flying Wing* (No. PP040, $39.95 retail) is for hand launch, cliff soaring, and Hi-Start. Made of die-cut balsa and plywood and covering plastic film, it is 22-1/2 in. long with a 59-in. wingspan yielding a 346-sq.-in. wing area. A 2- or 3-channel radio with small servos is required. No engine is required. Complete instructions with three elevon systems shown, die-cut balsa and ply, all hardware except mixer.

SIG MANUFACTURING CO.

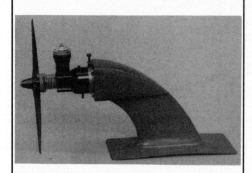

The *Sailplane Power Pod* (No. SH-660, $5.25 retail) is an easy way to launch your 2-meter sailplane without the hassle of a high-start. Made of balsa and plywood, it is designed for a .049-.051 engine and is easy to build.

SIG MANUFACTURING CO.

The *Ninja* (No. RC-63, $59.95 retail) is an aerobatic R/C glider that will satisfy both rookie and experienced slope soaring enthusiasts. It's smooth, responsive, and easy to fly. Deluxe foam, Lite-Ply, and balsa kit features precision-cut foam wing cores, 1/16-in. balsa wing sheeting, pre-cut balsa tail surfaces, and a quick-building Lite-Ply fuselage. Pushrods, Easy Hinges, and a complete hardware pack are included. The length is 39 in. and the wingspan is 58 in. A 2-channel radio is required while the engine is not.

SIG MANUFACTURING CO.

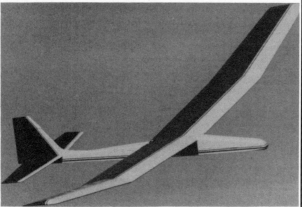

The *Riser 100* (No. RC-62, $67.95 retail) is a standard-class sailplane with a 100-in. wingspan and 1,000 sq. in. of wing area and a modified Eppler-205 airfoil for excellent performance in all types of conditions. It has great thermal capability! Fast construction of ply, spruce, and balsa, it features a die-cut Lite-Ply fuselage, rugged two-piece wing, spoiler option, pushrods, complete hardware, plans, and illustrated instructions. The Riser 100 is 51-1/2-in. long and it requires a 2- or 3-channel radio. No engine is required.

SIG MANUFACTURING CO.

The *Riser* (No. RC-52, $38.95 retail) is a 2-meter sailplane with typical balsa, ply, and spruce construction. Full-size plans and photo-illustrated instructions show optional spoilers. Power pod (.049) is available. The wingspan is 78 in. and the area is 620 sq. in. A 2-channel radio is required.

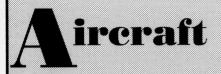

Aircraft

Helicopter Kits

COX HOBBIES, INC.

Sky Jumper (No. 4800; Retail: See your dealer) is great for beginning Heli fans! Wow! Think of it! This free-flight Huey UH-1D climbs to 200 ft., the engine shuts off, and then—the door opens and the Sky Jumper ejects, parachute opening. The Huey's main rotor blades then automatically phase into autorotate and it descends slowly to a soft landing. What a trip!

ALTECH MARKETING

The *Hirobo Shuttle Series* (Retail: See your dealer) is distributed in the U.S. exclusively by Altech Marketing. The *Shuttle,* which requires a .30-.35 size engine and a 4- or 5-channel radio, is the original .30-.35 size heli that trained thousands of pilots, while the *Shuttle XX* features full ball bearings in the control system and tail boom reinforcement struts. Both are excellent choices for novices and can be upgraded with optional parts available through Altech Marketing.

The *Shuttle Z* and *Shuttle ZX* are designed to please intermediate modelers, yet the novice can enjoy their enhanced capabilities. The Z version features longer, weighted main rotor blades and a longer tail boom, while the ZX carries full ball bearings, a metal clutch, and tail boom reinforcement struts. Both the Z and ZX feature the new FZ rotor head for increased performance. In all Hirobo Shuttle Series, the Enya SS35 Heli TN engine is included in specific assembled versions. The photo shows the optional Jet Ranger Fuselage on a standard series Shuttle. Order No. 0402977 for Shuttle Standard Assembled with Engine, No. 0402982 for Shuttle Standard Assembled without Engine, No. 0402978 for Shuttle XX Assembled with Engine, No. 0402983 for Shuttle XX Assembled without Engine, No. 0402979 for Shuttle Z Assembled with Engine, No. 0402984 for Shuttle Z Assembled without Engine, No. 0402980 for Shuttle ZX Assembled with Engine, No. 0402985 for Shuttle ZX Assembled without Engine, No. 0402981 for Shuttle ZX Unassembled Kit.

R/C FLYING IS FUN FOR THE WHOLE FAMILY!

ALTECH MARKETING

The *MH-10 helicopter* (No. 0408901, MH-10 without Engine; No. 0408902, MH-10 with BK-117 Body without Engine; Retail: See your dealer) is the latest innovation by Hirobo engineers, introduced and distributed proudly by Altech Marketing. This amazing little machine is powered by .10-.15 size engines (not included), yet carries a collective pitch mechanism similar to its bigger brothers. It comes factory assembled, requiring only minor assembly and 5-channel radio installation (a gyro can be fitted). The new clutch system and swashplate type and location defies description; you have to see it to understand it, yet it works wonderfully. Available in a pod/boom style or with a Bolkow BK117 ABS plastic body, the Hirobo MH-10 will become the experienced pilots' ''Sunday flier'' machine. The photo shows both styles of bodies available.

ALTECH MARKETING

The *Hirobo SST Eagle* (No. 0404937, SST Eagle with SSR-II Assy. without Engine; Retail: See your dealer) is a fantastic .60 size machine that offers championship level performance. With available optional parts from Altech Marketing, you can recreate the 1989 F3C World Championship machine. However, its out-of-the-box performance will leave the experienced flyer breathless with excitement. The SSR rotor head delivers sharp response, with a coning angle of 1 degree for better stability. The photo shows the optional Ecureuil 2 body installed. Requires .60 size engine (not included) and radio with 5 or more channels.

ALTECH MARKETING

The *Hirobo SST Condor EX* (No. 0404943, SST Condor EX w/FFZ R/H Assy. without Engine; Retail: See your dealer), sold exclusively by Altech Marketing, is an excellent sport .60 size helicopter. It utilizes an FFZ rotor head, comprised of high strength resin plastic that delivers both low weight and high performance. Other features include a belt drive tail rotor system, a C.G. balanced stabilizer paddle set, weighted main rotor blades, and a cone starter system. We are sure you will be pleased by its ability to attract a crowd's attention as you perform aerobatics. Requires .60 engine (not included) and radio with 5 or more channels.

ALTECH MARKETING

The Hirobo model of the *Vertol KV-107 II Tandem Rotor Helicopter* (No. 0406902, Vertol KV-107 II FFZ R/H Assy. without Engine; Retail: See your dealer) is sure to attract a crowd while at rest. In flight, the 3-bladed flybarless rotor heads keep the scale appearance while delivering a smooth realistic flight using a toothed belt transmission system. The Hirobo Vertol (of the CH-46 variety) uses a .32 to .35 size engine (not included), has a fiberglass reinforced plastic fuselage, and comes with decals for the U.S. Marines or Japanese Self Defense Force prototypes. The experienced flyer will enjoy this scale machine as sold and serviced by Altech Marketing. Requires 5-channel radio.

FUTABA

The *G153BB/G133BB* ($149.95 retail) is a ball bearing, single axis gyro. Power required: 4.8V shared with receiver or 6V external. Current drain: 20 ma (amplifier @ 4.8V), 100 ma (motor). Gyro body: 1.57-in. x 1.65-in. x 1.34-in./2.86 oz. Control amplifier: 1.73-in. x 2.28-in. x 0.63-in./1.61 oz. Control box: 0.94-in. x 1.34-in. x 0.59-in./0.54 oz.

FUTABA

The *G154/G134* ($89.95 retail) is a single axis, two-piece gyro. Power required: 4.8V. Current drain: 20 ma (amplifier), 100 ma (motor). Gyro body: 1.57-in. x 1.65-in. x 1.60-in. Amplifier: 1.06-in. x 1.89-in. x 0.63-in. System weight: 3.6 oz.

HELI IMAGES LTD.

HELISCENE ($6.00 per copy, $36.00 annual subscription) is quite simply the finest radio controlled model helicopter publication with full-size coverage. Complete information on this fascinating hobby/sport for the beginner, novice, intermediate and expert flyer/modeller. 84 full-color pages every issue with unbiased facts, reviews, information, and stunning photography.

HOBBY DYNAMICS DISTRIBUTORS

The *Kalt Whisper* (No. K40000, $299.99 retail; No. K40001, $349.99 retail) is an epoch-making electric-powered R/C helicopter. It's a breakthrough in helicopter technology incorporating exceptional performance and reliability in a 2-ft. 11-in. machine weighing in at just over two pounds. It is made of durable lightweight materials, is capable of longer flight times, and has superior hovering ability. It's great as a trainer for the first-time pilot, and also for experts who are searching for a combination of fun and performance flying. Watch for this electric helicopter to be at the top of everyone's wish list.

HOBBY DYNAMICS DISTRIBUTORS

The *Kalt Enforcer 30 Size Helicopter* ($429.99 retail) is a high quality modular design heli that is fully aerobatic. It has a planetary gear system. There is very low power loss and it's well sealed to protect the gears from dust and dirt. It is 41-in. long and requires a Heli .28-.35 engine and a 4-channel radio. Available in kit or ready-to-fly.

HOBBY DYNAMICS DISTRIBUTORS

The new *Kalt Baron Alpha II* (No. K66002500, $99.99 retail) is a top-of-the-line competition heli, designed with the FAI pilot in mind. It features a 800mm tail boom, 9.78:1:5.4 gear ratio and top cone start for convenience. The SII competition rotor head and competition tail gear are designed for great performance. The heavy-duty aluminum side frames are lightweight but durable.

HOBBY DYNAMICS DISTRIBUTORS

The *Excalibur* ($999.99 retail) features a K-5 rotor head, ABS plastic body, tinted windshield, autorotation system, K-series weighted rotor blades, a new shaft start system which eliminates starting belts, all necessary control linkages and hardware, including fuel tank. It requires a .60 engine and a 5-channel radio. A gyro is recommended. Gear ratio (engine:main:tail) is 8.7:1:4.5.

HOBBY DYNAMICS DISTRIBUTORS

The *Cyclone II Helicopter* (No. K81002500, $539.99 retail; No. K82002500, $829.99 retail) is available in kit or ready-to-fly. It comes equipped with a K-5 rotor head and a high-performance, single-axle head, and it's made of light, fiber-filled plastic. It has a one-piece blade axle that features an all-ball-bearing flybar assembly and mixing levers.

KYOSHO

The Kyosho *EP Concept Helicopter* (No. KYOE0230, $399.95 retail) is an electric-powered helicopter. It is 32.7 in. long and weighs only 42 oz. The main rotor diameter is 35.1 in. This helicopter is designed for the experienced flyer who is looking for high performance with the ease and quiet of electric power.

KYOSHO

Kyosho's *Concept 30 SX* (No. KYOE0280, $519.95 retail) is the newest version of the Concept 30 series. The SX evolved from the needs of top-level flyers. The newest features include greater collective pitch range, thrust bearings in the rotor head, metal pivot balls used throughout entire rotor head as well as on the swash plate, and a new canopy with improved decals.

KYOSHO

The *Concept 60's* main structure is an improvement over the Concept 30. It has modular construction, an inclosed drive system, an inverted engine inclined at 9° below horizontal, a piano wire tail drive, a stronger drive gear, optional stainless steel tube drive and constantly driven tail for autorations. It features stainless steel pivot balls through for precision steering, a see-saw with stablizer bar in same plane as main blade, automatic flapping compensation—dependent on rotor head rpm. It is easy to assemble, the links are easy to adjust, has a +20° to -10° pitch range, the gear ratio is 9.79:1:5.38, and weighs 8.8 lbs. (4000g).

MORLEY HELICOPTERS R/C MODELS, U.S.A.

The *Bell UH-I "Huey"* (Retail: See your dealer) is the most widely produced aircraft in the world and as a robust workhorse of the air has reached classic status. The 1/10 near scale model from this kit captures the character that has made the full-size aircraft so famous. It is 17 in. high, 4-1/2 in. wide, and 57 in. long. Blade span is 50 in. The model specification includes a 48" (1.2m) diameter rotor with cyclic and collective pitch control and the weight is 8 1/2 lbs. (3.9 kg). A .40 cubic-inch engine and 4 to 5 function radio, with 5 servos, is required. The comprehensive kit includes a quality G.R.P. body shell 454" long, ballraced main and tail gearboxes with steel gears, and an aluminum chassis with all links and fasteners.

THE MIDWAY MODEL COMPANY

The *R/C Table Trainer* ($18.95 retail) has been featured in R/C Modeler Magazine. Here is a chance for new life in that old pre-1991 radio system or just to "burn in" that new one! This handy gadget will sharpen your flying skills for planes or helicopters and can be used in the den, living room, or the shop. For the beginner, learn how to handle the reversal of directional controls that occur when an R/C aircraft is flying toward you. All kit parts are completely prefab-ricated of sturdy materials for simple, fast assembly.

MORLEY HELICOPTERS R/C MODELS, U.S.A.

The *Tow Cobra Fuselage* is designed for MXA Mechanics. It is 17 in. high, 4-1/2 in. wide, and 57 in. long. Blade span is 50 in.

Safety is no accident

MORLEY HELICOPTERS R/C MODELS, U.S.A.

HUGHES 300   BELL 47 G   AGUSTA 109

Morley Helicopters (Retail: See your dealer) require .40-.46cc engines and 4- or 5-channel radios. Blade span and length vary with model. Hughes 300—comes with optional 3-bladed head for the experienced scale enthusiast. Bell 47G—great for all levels of experience. Includes retractable under carriage very much like the real thing.

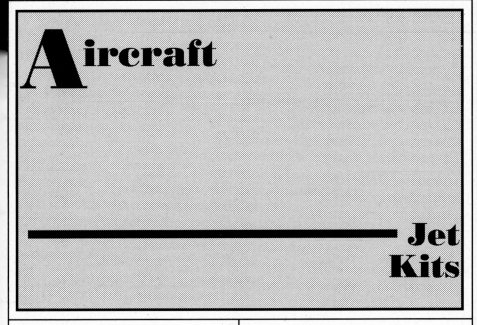

Aircraft
Jet Kits

ROYAL PRODUCTS CORP.

The *Cessna Citation-1* ($314.95 retail) is a beautiful balsa kit designed around .20 size ducted fan units and comes complete with epoxy glass fan inlet and exit cowls. The wingspan is 67 in. and the area is 653 sq. in. A .20-.25 twin-ducted fan engine and a 4-channel radio are required.

ROYAL PRODUCTS CORP.

The *Phantom F4J* ($184.95 retail) is a hot-flying, all-scale ship which is capable of doing pattern maneuvers. The kit features hand-cut balsa pre-fabrication. The wingspan is 45 in. and the area is 477 sq. in. A .49-.80 engine is required. Aircraft is prop driven.

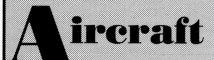

Aircraft

Pattern Kits

GREAT PLANES MODEL MFG.

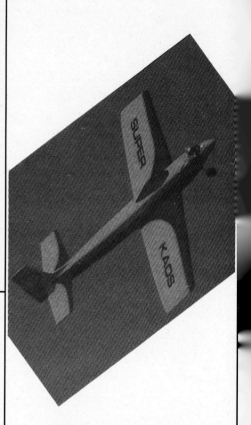

GREAT PLANES MODEL MFG.

The *Super Kaos 60* (No. GPMA0180, $106.95 retail) has been purchased by thousands of modelers who say model airplanes don't come any more handsome or fly any better than this. With a clean front end, generous wing fillets and healthy Schneurle ported .60, this streamlined plane will approach 100 mph for smooth graceful flight. Like all Great Planes kits, the Super Kaos kit is complete with engine mount, fixed gear, canopy, plans (showing both fixed and retract installation), and hardware pack. If you like 'em fast 'n smooth, then the Super Kaos is for you! Made of a balsa fuselage and wing, the plane has a 58-in. wingspan and 644-sq. in. area. It requires a .60 engine and 4- to 5-channel radio.

The *Super Kaos 40* (No. GPMA0390, $85.95 retail) was designed with simplicity in mind. Its fixed tricycle landing gear is both rugged and functional and the kit is a breeze to build with the basic box fuselage. The streamlined front end adds to looks and performance. A double tapered, symmetrical airfoil wing is great in both rolling and looping maneuvers, and builds in a minimum of time. Made of a balsa fuselage and wing, the plane has a 52-in. wingspan and 507-sq. in. area. It requires a size 40 engine and a 4-channel radio.

Aircraft

Scale Kits

ROYAL PRODUCTS CORP.

The *Staggerwing Beech* ($204.95 retail) is an excellent scale project for the biplane enthusiast, scale builder, or sport modeler. The wingspan is 56 in. and the area is 907 sq. in. This balsa kit requires a .60-.80 engine and a 4-channel radio.

ALTECH MARKETING

The *Zlin Akrobat* airplane is well known by real pilots and modelers alike. Made in Czechoslovakia, this low wing monoplane was an important factor in world aerobatic championships. Altech Marketing has recreated this plane in a 4-channel .40 size almost-ready-to-cover kit that will outperform ''plastic'' airplane kits of the same size and type.

We designed a wood kit that features low building time. We've built the fuselage and foam core wings to save your time for building and flying. Try our Enya SS40 or SS40BB for screaming performance; the Enya 53-4C will give the Zlin the vertical performance of a scared cat climbing a tree! Try flying inverted in a circle; the Zlin won't roll out of position like other so-called aerobatic planes.

ROYAL PRODUCTS CORP.

The *P-51D Mustang* ($64.95 retail) is a semi-scale model and Royal's newest addition to the P-51 scale series. The cockpit is included. The wingspan is 35-1/4 in. and the area is 217 sq. in. This balsa kit requires a .045-.051 engine and a 2-channel radio.

ROYAL PRODUCTS CORP.

The *Cessna 310Q* ($259.95 retail) is an all-scale twin that flies as good as it looks. The kit features all-balsa construction and cockpit. The wingspan is 72-7/8 in. and the area is 725 sq. in. Twin .35-.60 engines are required.

ROYAL PRODUCTS CORP.

The *Cessna Skymaster* ($259.95 retail) is a unique twin that delivers the performance of two engines, yet offers the handling of a single-engine aircraft. It flies as well on one engine as it does on two. The scale kit features balsa construction and includes cockpit. The wingspan is 76-1/8 in. and the area is 754 sq. in. A .40-.61 engine and a 4-channel radio are required.

ROYAL PRODUCTS CORP.

The *Spitfire Sr.* ($184.95 retail; Spitfire Jr., $144.95 retail) is a true handcrafted balsa kit. Its workmanship and construction are further complemented by its flyability. The wingspan is 64-1/2 in. and the area is 736 sq. in. A .60-.80 engine is required. The cockpit is included in Sr. size.

ROYAL PRODUCTS CORP.

The *BF 109E Messerschmitt* ($64.95 retail) is a new addition to Royal's Mini Series. It is semi-scale and utilizes balsa construction. The wingspan is 35-1/2 in. and the area is 220 sq. in. A .051-.09 engine and a 4-channel radio are required.

ROYAL PRODUCTS CORP.

The *Victor P-68* ($174.95 retail) is an ideal scale project for the twin enthusiast featuring select building materials combined with stable flight characteristics. This balsa kit has a wingspan of 62-3/4 in. and an area of 502 sq. in. It requires twin .19-.25 engines and a 4-channel radio.

ROYAL PRODUCTS CORP.

The *Zero Sr.* ($204.95 retail; Zero Jr., 475 sq. in. and cockpit included, $159.95 retail) is a true scale kit handcrafted to exacting standards in both authenticity and flyability. The wingspan of this balsa kit is 62-5/8 in. and the area is 706 sq. in. A .60-.80 engine is required.

ROYAL PRODUCTS CORP.

The *JU 87D-5 Stuka* ($204.95 retail) is a scale balsa version of the famous WWII fighter with wheel pants included. It has planked covering. The wingspan is 71 in. and the area is 670 sq. in. A .60-.80 engine and a 4-channel radio are required.

ROYAL PRODUCTS CORP.

The *F8F Bearcat* ($209.95 retail) is one of the newer additions to Royal's line of scale balsa kits and flies as well as it looks. The cockpit is included. The wingspan is 62-3/16 in. and the area is 652 sq. in. A .60-.80 engine is required.

ROYAL PRODUCTS CORP.

The *Hayabusa (Oscar)* ($199.95 retail) is a balsa, scale kit whose hand-cut pieces fit together well enough to win the Japanese Scale Championships. The wingspan is 59 in. and the area is 613 sq. in. A .45-.80 engine is required.

ROYAL PRODUCTS CORP.

The *P-51D Mustang* ($219.95 retail; P-51 Junior, 576 sq. in., $164.95 retail) is one of the military classics! The cockpit is included. The wingspan is 64-3/4 in. and the area is 777 sq. in. A .60-.80 engine and a 4-channel radio are required.

ROYAL PRODUCTS CORP.

In this *P38* ($314.95 retail) kit, hand-cut balsa pre-fabrication builds up to capture, in true scale, one of the all-time WWII favorites. The cockpit is included. The wingspan is 74-1/4 in. and the area is 695 sq. in. Twin .35-.60 engines are required.

ROYAL PRODUCTS CORP.

The *Beechcraft Baron 58P* ($239.95 retail) is a newer member of Royal's line and features all-balsa construction. Detailed plans are included (feature retract layout). The wingspan is 70-1/2 in. and the area is 682 sq. in. Twin .35-.40 engines and a 4-channel radio are required.

ROYAL PRODUCTS CORP.

The *Hein Senior (Tony)* ($214.95 retail; Junior Series, 168 sq. in., $169.95 retail) all-balsa and all-scale kit has found its way into many a winner's circle over the years. The wingspan is 68-1/4 in. and the area is 676 sq. in. A .45-.80 engine is required.

ROYAL PRODUCTS CORP.

The *P-26A Peashooter* ($364.95 retail) is a scale beauty designed around the 1.20 4-cycle engine (not included), but will fly well on .60-.90 2-cycle. This 1/5-scale balsa model is sure to receive attention at the flying field. The wingspan is 68 in. and the length is 57-1/2 in. A 4- to 5-channel radio is required.

ROYAL PRODUCTS CORP.

This *B-25* ($234.95 retail) is a true scale project which uncompromisingly combines flyability and scale beauty. This balsa kit includes spun aluminum cowls and cockpit. The wingspan is 70-7/8 in. with an area of 750 sq. in. Twin .40-.61 engines are required.

ROYAL PRODUCTS CORP.

The *Piper Colt* ($229.95 retail) is an all-scale kit which features balsa construction and flies as well as it looks. The wingspan is 74-13/16 in. and the area is 946 sq. in. A .60-.80 engine and a 4-channel radio are required. It's available in a Jr. Series (56-1/2-in. span), cockpit included.

ROYAL PRODUCTS CORP.

The *ME109 Messerschmitt* ($209.95 retail) has select balsa building materials combined with stable flight characteristics to make this offering from Royal quite attractive. The wingspan is 61-5/8 in. and the area is 602 sq. in. A .60-.80 engine and a 4-channel radio are required.

ROYAL PRODUCTS CORP.

This *P-51D Mustang* ($114.95 retail) is a scaled-down version of Royal's .60 size and displays the same quality and flyability at a smaller size (1.25 in. per foot) and price. The cockpit is included. Made of balsa with planking covering, it has a wingspan of 46-1/4 in. and an area of 372 sq. in. A .19-.40 engine and a 4-channel radio are required.

ROYAL PRODUCTS CORP.

The *Corsair* ($209.95 retail) is an all-balsa/all-scale kit version of the famous WWII fighter. Its wingspan is 61-1/2 in., and a .60-.90 engine is required. The kit includes spun aluminum cowl, cockpit, four decal sheets, and dummy radial engine.

ROYAL PRODUCTS CORP.

The *Cessna 182 Senior* ($209.95 retail; Junior, 405 sq. in., $159.95 retail) is an excellent scale project for combining balsa pre-fabrication with flyability. The wingspan is 72-1/2 in. and the area is 700 4/5 sq. in. The cockpit is included. and a .45-.60 engine is required.

ROYAL PRODUCTS CORP.

The *Douglas C-47* ($274.95 retail) is an excellent scale project for the twin-engine enthusiast. Select balsa materials and handcrafted pre-fabrication make this twin-engine plane a pleasure to scale and fly. The wingspan is 83-1/8 in. and the area is 767 sq. in. Twin .40-.60 engines and a 4-channel radio are required.

ROYAL PRODUCTS CORP.

The *A6M3 Zero* ($64.95 retail) is a semi-scale model and its the newest addition to Royal's Zero Scale Series. Cockpit included. The wingspan of this balsa kit is 34-7/8 in. and the area is 232 sq. in. A .049-.051 engine and a 2-channel radio are required.

ROYAL PRODUCTS CORP.

The *Bleriot* ($64.95 retail) is a semi-scale version that quite aptly captures the features of this memorable aircraft. Constructed of hardwood and balsa, the wingspan is 46 in. and the area 356 sq. in. A .09-.15 engine and a 3-channel radio are required.

ROYAL PRODUCTS CORP.

The *Stinson Reliant SR-8* ($364.95 retail) has graceful lines and superior aerial handling that characterize both the real Stinson Gull wing and this new balsa model kit from Royal. This aircraft was designed to fly best on 4-cycle 1.20 engines. The wingspan is 84-1/3 in. and the area is 1348 sq. in. It requires a .60-.90/2C or .90-1.20/4C engine.

ROYAL PRODUCTS CORP.

The *F4-U-1D Corsair* ($144.95 retail) is an ideal size! It's a scaled-down version (1.25 in. to the foot) of Royal's .60 size Corsair. Made of balsa with planked covering, its wingspan is 54-1/4 in. and the area is 480 sq. in. A .35-.51 engine and a 4-channel radio are required. The cockpit is included.

ROYAL PRODUCTS CORP.

The *F4U Corsair* ($64.95 retail) is a scale model that is the newest addition to Royal's line of Corsair kits. Made of balsa, it has a 35-1/2-in. wingspan and a 229-sq. in. area. The cockpit is included. A .049-.051 engine and a 2-channel radio are required.

ROYAL PRODUCTS CORP.

The *Little Stinker (Pitts Special)* ($209.95 retail) is an all-scale bipe which offers all the thrills and realism of the full-size aircraft. The kit features hand-cut, balsa pre-fabrication. The wingspan is 51-13/16 in. and the area is 856 sq. in. A .49-.80 engine is required.

ROYAL PRODUCTS CORP.

This *Spitfire MK I* ($64.95 retail) is a welcome addition to Royal's Mini Series of kits. It features all-balsa construction, with a 35-1/4-in. wingspan and a wing area of 217 sq. in. It requires a .049-.09 engine and a 4-channel radio.

ROYAL PRODUCTS CORP.

This balsa *Corsair* ($119.95 retail) kit contains spun aluminum cowl and a special 17 x 22 in. full-color data sheet. The wingspan is 44-3/4 in. and the area is 372 sq. in. A .19-.40 engine and a 4-channel radio are required.

ROYAL PRODUCTS CORP.

This *Cessna 172 Skyhawk* ($134.95 retail) model displays, at 1.5-in. to the foot, impressive scale accuracy and is a fairly docile flyer. Made of balsa with planking covering, it has a 53-7/8-in. wingspan and an area of 388 sq. in. A .19-.35 engine and a 4-channel radio are required. The cockpit is included.

ROYAL PRODUCTS CORP.

The *B-17 Flying Fortress* ($294.95 retail) is an exciting scale project to build and fly; a sure attention-getter. Made of balsa with planked covering, it has a 77-3/4-in. wing–span and an 806 sq. in. area. Four .20 engines and a 4-channel radio are required and the cockpit is included.

ROYAL PRODUCTS CORP.

This *Bleriot* ($104.95 retail) is a true scale version that quite aptly captures the features of this memorable aircraft. The kit has a scale ratio of 1-7/8-in. to one foot, and features all-balsa construction. The wing cover has open-rib structure. The wingspan is 51-3/4 in. and the area is 564 sq. in. A .35-.40/2C or .40-.60/4C engine and a 3-channel radio is required.

ROYAL PRODUCTS CORP.

This *A6M3 Zero* ($114.95 retail), at 1.2-in. to the foot, is a scaled-down version of our .60 size that flies well on a .19-.35 size engine (not included). Made of balsa, it has a wing-span of 46.2 in. and an area of 356.5 sq. in., with cockpit included.

ROYAL PRODUCTS CORP.

The *Focke Wulf 190* ($204.95 retail) is the newest addition to our line of scale balsa WWII kits. It flies as good as it looks and includes cockpit. The wingspan is 60-3/4 in. and the area is 642 sq. in. A .45-.80 engine is required.

ROYAL PRODUCTS CORP.

The *P-61 Black Widow Kit* ($364.95 retail) is the only American WWII night fighter. It is fabricated from balsa/ply/ABS, has a wing span of 71-15/16-in. and length of 54-1/16-in., runs on twin .40-.60 engines. The scale is 1 3/32-in:1 ft. The Black Widow is sure to attract attention wherever it is flown.

SIG MANUFACTURING CO.

The *Citabria* (No. RC-30, $108.95 retail) features a new instruction booklet, revised plans, plastic cowling and wheelpants, and complete hardware. With a balsa wing and balsa-ply fuselage, it has a length of 47 in. and a wingspan of 69 in. A 4-channel radio and a .35-.50/2C or .45-.61/4C engine are required. Ideal for Sunday flying or sport-scale competition.

SIG MANUFACTURING CO.

The *Zlin Akrobat* (No. RC-23, $108.95 retail) is an exact-scale model with Pattern-style flight characteristics and it's a National Scale winner. It features formed plastic cowl, complete decals, and special scale spinner. The fuselage is balsa and the wing is balsa-covered foam. It has a 70-in. wingspan and an area of 680 sq. in. A .60 engine and a 4- or 5-channel radio are required.

SIG MANUFACTURING CO.

The *Ryan STA Special* (No. RC-27, $152.95 retail) is the most outstanding exact-scale kit ever offered. It includes 43 formed plastic parts. The fuselage and wing are constructed of balsa. It has a 72-in. wingspan and an area of 770 sq. in. It requires a .60/2C engine, and a 4-channel radio with no flaps or a 5-channel radio with flaps.

SIG MANUFACTURING CO.

The *Piper J-3 Cub* (No. RC-3, $71.95 retail) is a 1/6-scale replica of America's favorite lightplane. It features traditional built-up balsa and ply construction and is easy to fly. The wingspan is 71 in. A .25-.40/2C or .40-.45/4C engine is required.

SIG MANUFACTURING CO.

This *Clipped Wing Cub* (No. RC-26, $71.95 retail) is a 1/6-scale model of Hazel Sig's Clipped Wing Cub. Constructed of balsa, it has a 56-in. wingspan and requires either a .25-.40/2C or .40-.45/4C engine. It's fun to fly.

SIG MANUFACTURING CO.

The *Beechcraft Bonanza's* (No. RC-41, $122.95 retail) balsa box fuselage with molded plastic top and molded clear cabin windows make it easy to build. A photo instruction book is included. The wing is foam-balsa, and has a span of 64 in. with an area of 652 sq. in. A .60 engine and a 4- or 5-channel radio is required.

SIG MANUFACTURING CO.

The *P-51 Mustang* (No. KBRC-6, $129.95 retail) model is designed for sport scale flying. It has a balsa fuselage and a foam wing with 64-in. span and 648-sq. in. area. Photo-illustrated instructions show optional flap and retract installation. A .60-engine and a 4- to 6-channel radio are required.

SURE FLITE ENTERPRISES

The *ARF Spitfire* ($68.95 retail) is a super fast, responsive elliptical winged fighter. A great-looking, fine performing warbird that turns on a dime and dogfights with the best of them. Its strong, unreinforced wing will take retracts. For the experienced flyer. This plane is all molded foam with a 35.5-in. fuselage. Wingspan is 50 in. and has an area of 450 sq. in. Engines are .45-.50 4 stroke or .35-.45 2 stroke, and requires a 4-5 channel radio.

SURE FLITE ENTERPRISES

The *ARF P-40 Warhawk* ($72.95 retail) is a wide stance taildragger, fast and fully aerobatic. This warbird is a top performer. Fast building, the P-40 features include a vacuum-formed cowl, canopy, land gear, decals, push rods, and most hardware. A popular, exciting fighter. Constructed of molded foam with a wingspan of 51 in., an area is 450 sq. in., and a fuselage length of 39.5 in. Engines needed are .40-.45 2 stroke or .40-.60 4 stroke and requires a 3-5 channel radio.

SURE FLITE ENTERPRISES

The *ARF P-39 Airacobra* ($68.95 retail) is a tricycle gear warbird that is easy handling, looks great, and is a superior aerobatic fighter. Can be flown with three channels but excels with ailerons. Comes complete with landing gear, canopy, decals, exhausts, and most hardware. Constructed of molded foam, has a wingspan of 51 in., an area is 450 sq. in., and a fuselage length of 37.5 in. Engines are .40-.45 2 stroke or .45-.60 4 stroke and uses a 3-5 channel radio.

TOP FLITE MODELS, INC.

The *F4U-1A Corsair* (No. TOPA0100, $199.95 retail) is an exciting stand-off scale model that recreates the legendary Black Sheep Squadron model. It is an all-balsa kit and features injection-molded cowl, pre-formed fuselage shells, authentic markings and heavy-duty 3/16-in. diameter landing gear. Its wingspan is 61 in., has a 50 cu. in. engine and flies with grace and agility.

R/C Flying is fun for the entire family!

Aircraft

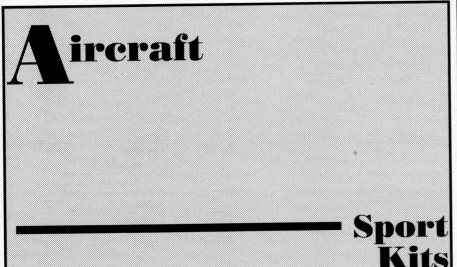

Sport Kits

ACE R/C, INC.

The *Bingo* (No. 50K232, $89.95 retail) is great for the beginner through the advanced pilot. The plane is made of balsa and hardwood, with a wingspan of 70 in. and a length of 54 in. The ease and speed of construction, great looks, versatility, and performance envelope make this the best sport plane you could ask for. It requires a .40-.60 2-cycle engine or a .48-.90 4-cycle engine and a 4-channel radio.

ALTECH MARKETING

The *Zlin Akrobat* airplane is well known by real pilots and modelers alike. Made in Czechoslovakia, this low wing monoplane was an important factor in world aerobatic championships. Altech Marketing has recreated this plane in a 4-channel .40 size almost-ready-to-cover kit that will out-perform "plastic" airplane kits of the same size and type.

We designed a wood kit that features low building time. We've built the fuselage and foam core wings to save your time for building and flying. Try our Enya SS40 or SS40BB for screaming performance; the Enya 53-4C will give the Zlin the vertical performance of a scared cat climbing a tree! Try flying inverted in a circle; the Zlin won't roll out of position like other so-called aerobatic planes.

ALTECH MARKETING

Altech Marketing has always catered to the discriminating modeler; the one who wants only the best engine in his prize airplane. We chose an almost-ready-to-cover, wood airplane kit as the latest item preferred by knowledgeable modelers. We selected a biplane for its outstanding appeal. The end result is Altech Marketing's *Super Stearman Kit IE300;* it's everything you wanted in an almost-ready-to-cover airplane kit and more!

The Super Stearman was a modified version of the aircraft used to train hundreds of pilots. The Super Stearman version featured a "hot" radial motor for exciting aerobatics. Our kit version will give you the same thrills but in much quicker time because we've built all the hard parts for you.

FUTABA

Our *Acrostar* is also a complete kit, including everything you need except glue, radio, engine, and engine accessories. A thoroughly illustrated, step-by-step instruction manual guides you through assembly and installation of the radio and engine. The *Acrostar 60* is even more impressive on the flight field. Like the full-scale classic, the Futaba Acrostar climbs, knife-edges, snap rolls and maneuvers with precision and surprising ease. Using a built-up wing with a true airfoil section our Acrostar is an athletic and exciting performer. Futaba's advanced preconstruction techniques, materials, and extensive flight-testing of prototypes all contribute to the exceptional and startling performance of the Acrostar 60. What would not be a surprise would be for the Futaba Acrostar 60 to start turning up in pattern competition...and winning. This aircraft uses a .60 2-cycle or .90 4-cycle engine. The plane has a 57.09" wingspan and a 600 sq. in. wing area. Requires a 4-channel radio.

AIRCRAFT: SPORT KITS

CARL GOLDBERG MODELS, INC.

The *Sky Tiger* (No. 64, kit G31, $99.99 retail; No. 84, Wing Kit G31W, $29.99 retail) is one of the best flying low-wing Sport models ever. It features fast and easy ply/ balsa construction, a 63-in. wingspan, and 715-sq.-in. area. A 32-page booklet describing each phase of building, covering, radio installation, and flying (including a full-size plan) is included. It comes complete with 4-channel hardware, steerable nosegear, large decals, vac-formed canopy, wing tips, and pilot. A .40-.61 engine and 4-channel radio are required.

CARL GOLDBERG MODELS, INC.

CARL GOLDBERG MODELS, INC.

The *Piper Cub J3* (No. K63/G30, $99.99 retail; No. 86/G33W for Wing Kit, $29.99 retail) is a scale-like floater with a 4-cycle .45, and with a clipped wing and a .60 (or a 4-stroke .90). It's aerobatic! It comes with recessed firewall and mounting options, highest quality materials and die-cutting, plus a complete hardware package, formed cowling, windows, dummy engine, snap-in struts, decals, and advice on how to add even more details for Sport/Scale competition. The plane has a 76-1/2-in. wingspan and 744-sq.-in. area. It requires a .40-.61/2 engine and 4-channel radio.

The *Super Chipmunk* (No. 52, $139.99 retail; Wing Kit K-87, $39.99 retail) is an easy-to-handle Sunday flyer that will put on an airshow with all the flash and flair of its full-size cousin. Just turn it loose! Its beautiful formed molded parts, full-color peel-off decals and complete hardware package are the kind of deluxe accessories you'd only expect to find in kits costing a lot more. Plus you'll find the same kind of high quality materials, precision cutting, straightforward construction planning and superbly illustrated instructions that have made all of our kits so popular. The Super Chipmunk's well-designed flap and retract options offer an added dimension of realism. The plane, all balsa-ply, is 53-in. long and has a 64-in. wingspan. A .45-.60/2-C or .60-.90/4-C engine and 4- to 6-channel radio are required.

GREAT PLANES MODEL MFG.

The *Ultra Sport 40* (No. GPMA0410, $109.95 retail) from Great Planes is designed as the next-step purchase for experienced flyers. It has been designed with computer-enhanced airfoil and correct wing and power loadings. It is made from top-quality balsa parts and all hardware items are included. It has a wingspan of 55 in., and a wing area of 566 sq. in. The fuselage is 49-1/2-in. long and requires 4- or 5-channel radio, and either a .40-.45 2-cycle or a .60-.70 4-stroke engine.

Your local hobby shop is there to help you select the best equipment and to answer your questions

GREAT PLANES MODEL MFG.

Our *CAP 21 40* (No. GPMA0230, $99.95 retail) will give you a scale plane that flies the full turnaround pattern...all with an economical .40 engine! Easy-building balsa kit gets you in the air fast. Photo-illustrated instructions, dural gear, and decals are included. The CAP 21 40 has a 60-in. wingspan and wing area of 550 sq. in. It requires a .40-.45 engine and a 4-channel radio.

GREAT PLANES MODEL MFG.

The *P-51D Mustang* (No. GPMA0175, $109.95 retail) is a fully aerobatic, semi-scale, mid-sized authentic WWII fighter plane. Authentic details include wing guns and exhaust stacks. It has a wingspan of 57-in., weighs 6 lbs., uses a .40-.46 2-cycle or .60-.70 4-cycle engine, is constructed of balsa and ply and comes easy to build with interlocking construction and complete instructions. The retractable landing gear is optional.

GREAT PLANES MODEL MFG.

The *CAP 21 60* (No. GPMA0240, $176.95 retail) means excitement, whether you're a scale enthusiast, Turnaround Pattern flyer, or general Sport modeler. Construction techniques are what you'd expect for a high-performance machine. Built-up tail surfaces help keep the tail light. A foam core, sheeted with balsa, makes quick work of the turtleneck. The wing is straightforward, with quality dural gear for strength and durability. Decals are included. Made of a balsa/ foam fuselage and balsa wings, the CAP 21 60 has a wingspan of 72 in. and a wing area of 756 sq. in. It requires a .60-1.2/2C or .90/4C engine and a 4-channel radio.

GREAT PLANES MODEL MFG.

The *Ultra Sport 60* (No. GPMA0420, $124.95 retail) is a .60-size sport model that enables fliers to perform expert maneuvers with only moderate low wing experience. The Ultra Sport 60 offers stable performance in a wide speed range, form easy high-speed aerobatics to gentle low-speed landings. It is made of balsa/ply, has a wingspan of 61.5-in., and wieghs 71 lbs. It comes complete with hardware, and step-by-step photo-illustrated instructions and interlocking design.

Radio Control Flying is fun for the entire family!

GREAT PLANES MODEL MFG.

The *Super Sportster 40* (No. GPMA0200, $85.95 retail) is ideal for .45-.61 4-cycle engine. It has a balsa fuselage and wings. The high quality of these precision-machined balsa parts and photo-illustrated instructions help you breeze through fast and effortless construction. Parts are included to build it as a taildragger (with wheel pants included) or with tricycle gear, in addition to the motor mount, hardware pack, canopy, and rolled plans. The wingspan is 56 in. and the wing area 550 sq. in. It requires a .35-.45/2C or .40-.60/4C and a 4-channel radio. Also available are the Super Sportster 60 and the Super Sportster 90/120.

GREAT PLANES MODEL MFG.

The *Super Sportster 20* (No. GPMA0190, $69.95 retail) is a low-wing plane with a larger-than-average wing that makes it an ideal first flyer. Construction of the balsa fuselage and wing is virtually effortless, due to machine-cut parts, razor-cut ribs, and sheet balsa used in tail. The engine mount is glass-filled nylon. The instructions are easy to read with photos and rolled plans. The kit also provides hardware for either 2- or 3-gear set-ups. The wingspan is 48 in. and the area 400 sq. in. A .19-.25/2C or .30/4C engine and a 4-channel radio are required.

HOBBICO

Hobbico's *ASAP "As Soon As Possible"* ($159.95 - $229.95 retail) ARF sport planes require no sanding, covering, painting, hinging, or other time-consuming tasks. The ASAP series of planes is available in .25 to .40-size sport planes and are 90% factory assembled. Kits available now are Diablo .40, Chipmunk .40, Telstar .40, Cessna .40, Super Chipmunk .25, and Cherokee .25 size. The Chipmunk .40 and Telstar .40 offer a retract option.

HOBBICO

Hobbico's *Extra 300* (No. HCAA2600, $259.95 retail) is a carefully detailed version of the full-scale German Extra 300 recreated right down to the simulated rivets. Included are the chrome spinner, plastic canopy, and scale landing gear. The Extra 300 offers aerobatic performance for the intermediate to experienced flyer. A balsa and ply structure with foam covering, the Extra 300 has a 53.75-in. wingspan. It requires a .40-.46 2-stroke or .70-.91 4-stroke engine and a 4-channel radio.

HOBBY DYNAMICS DISTRIBUTORS

The *Sportee 40* ($72.99 retail) is aerobatic and can instantly recover from spins and snaps. It comes with all hardware and a photo-illustrated instruction book. It is 41 in. long with a 58-in. wingspan and requires a .25-.40 engine and 4-channel radio. This outstanding sport plane is made in the U.S.A.

HOBBY DYNAMICS DISTRIBUTORS

The *P-51 Mustang Sport Scale* (No. HDDP51, $79.99 retail) airplane is easy to build so you can be in the air in record time. This plane has a stable air platform which allows for better control. It is 41 in. long with a 58-in. wingspan. Make this P-51 Mustang part of your inventory.

HOBBY DYNAMICS DISTRIBUTORS

The simplistic design and stable flight characteristics of the *P-39 Airacobra Sport Scale* (No. HDDP39, $79.99 retail) make this one of the hottest Hobby Dynamics planes. This WWII model is a classic in sport scale design. It is 41 in. long, has a 20.5-in. wingspan, and offers a tri-gear with superior performance.

HOBBY DYNAMICS DISTRIBUTORS

The *ME-109 Messerschmitt Sport Scale* (No. HDDME109, $79.99 retail) WWII fighter has impressive performance capabilities. Best of all, it is quick and easy to build. It is 41 in. long with a 58-in. wingspan. High altitudes are no problem because the ME-109 Messerschmitt has a large wing area.

HOBBY DYNAMICS DISTRIBUTORS

Acrobatic maneuvers are at your fingertips with the Hobby Dynamics *MK-14 XIV Spitfire Sport Scale* (No. HDDMK14, $79.99 retail). It is 41 in. long with a 58-in. wingspan. Although designed as a .40 size kit, it will fly great with a .25 size engine. It is lightweight and easy to build.

HOBBY DYNAMICS DISTRIBUTORS

The *RFB Fan Trainer 600 Sport Scale* (No. HDDFANT, $139.99 retail) is a pusher style jet with all the thrills of a ducted fan without the high price. This striking jet is a replica of the Fan Trainer 600 which was designed in West Germany in the 1970s. It is 64 in. long and has a 58-in. wingspan. A .45-.50 size ABC engine is recommended for best performance.

LANIER R/C

The *Sky Scooter* (No. 84203, $99.95 retail) is a trainer aircraft with pre-covered wings. The vertical stabilizer, horizontal stabilizer, elevators, and ailerons require Monokote covering. The fuselage is plastic and ply and the wing is foam with ABS covering. The wingspan is 50 in. and the area 350 sq. in. A 4-channel radio and .19-.45 engine are required. Flying weight is 3-3/4 - 4-1/2 lbs.

LANIER R/C

The *Javelin* (No. 84204, $99.95 retail) is an intermediate sport airplane. The wings are pre-covered and have a 50-in. span and 350-sq.-in. area. The fuselage is plastic and ply and the wing is foam with ABS covering. The vertical stabilizer, horizontal stabilizer, and elevators require Monokote covering. A 4-channel radio and .19-.45 engine are required. Flying weight is 3-3/4 - 4-1/2 lbs.

THE MIDWAY MODEL COMPANY

The *1938 POWERHOUSE* ($47.95 retail) was designed by the great Sal Taibi in 1938, and our 50 in. span, 380 sq. in. area and 32-38 oz. weight version faithfully reproduces that ''Classy gassie'' look. For 3-channel radios and .09 to .15 gas engines. It can also can be powered by 05-15 electric direct drive motors. The kit includes top quality, prime grade balsa, ply and spruce parts. Other features are: rolled full size plans, basic R/C hardware, and special electric propulsion conversion installation instructions. Available at quality hobby shops throughout the USA.

THE MIDWAY MODEL COMPANY

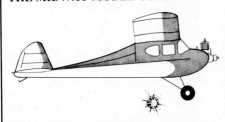

The *70% BOMBSHELL* ($47.95 retail) is an original Old Timer Design from 1940. It is a smaller version of the classic 6 Ft. Bombshell, for the .09 to .15 class engines. It has a 50.4 inch wingspan, 423 sq. in. area and normally weighs between 32 and 38 ounce. It is for 3-channel radios operating rudder, elevator, and throttle or it can be flown as a free flight in class A Old Timer events. It can also be powered by 035 to 05 electric direct drive motors. The kit includes top quality, prime grade balsa, ply, and spruce parts with all parts machine cut and sanded. Made in the USA.

MIDWEST PRODUCTS CO.

Midwest Mustang (No. 170, $109.95 retail), is a quick-building warbird model that flies like a sport plane so you'll enjoy learning to fly a taildragger. The wingspan is 54 in., and uses 35-40 2-stroke or 40-50 4-stroke engines. This all-wood kit includes Micro-Cut Quality wood parts, vacuum-formed canopy and exhaust stacks, authentic self-adhesive military markings, Success Series Construction Manual, and full-size plan sheet with 4-cycle conversion drawings. A Success Series kit available only from your local hobby shop.

MIDWEST PRODUCTS CO.

Midwest Messerschmitt (No. 171, $109.95 retail), is a low-wing taildragger that's easy to fly. This quick-building warbird model includes Micro-Cut Quality Wood parts, vacuum-formed canopy and exhaust stacks, authentic self-adhesive military markings, Success Series Construction Manual, and full-size plan sheet with 4-cycle conversion drawings. A Success Series kit available only from your local hobby shop.

MIDWEST PRODUCTS CO.

Midwest Zero (No. 172, $119.95 retail). Fly a dawn patrol with this low-wing taildragger that flies like a sport plane. This all-wood kit includes Micro-Cut Quality Wood parts, a crystal clear molded canopy, beautifully formed plastic cowling, authentic self-adhesive military markings, Success Series Construction Manual, and full-size plan sheet with 4-cycle conversion drawings. A Success Series kit available only from your local hobby shop.

MIDWEST PRODUCTS CO.

Midwest Mustang .60 (No 174, $179.95 retail) is a BIG, quick-building warbird model that flies like a sport plane, so you'll enjoy flying this low-wing taildragger. This all-wood kit includes Micro-Cut Quality Wood parts, a side-mounted .60-.90 2-stroke engine for a more scale appearance, a large wing that easily accepts retracts, a cockpit insert that makes a great looking area to mount a pilot, authentic military markings, Success Series Construction Manual, and full-size plan sheet. A Success Series kit available only from your local hobby shop.

PECK-POLYMERS

The *Mini Bell* (No. PP-16, $18.95 retail!) is a peanut-size R/C plane that sports a 25-in. wingspan (100-sq.-in. wing area), has .020 power for 2- or 3-channel mini-radios and R/O pulse, and comes with die-cut balsa and plywood, formed landing gear, a canopy, building photos, and easy-to-understand plans.

SIG MANUFACTURING CO.

The *Kobra* (No. RC-53, $59.95 retail) is a compact sport plane that flies like its big brother, the Kougar. It features a foam wing, balsa fuselage, and formed plastic fuselage top. The required .19-.35 engine makes it easy on fuel. The wingspan is 45 in.

SIG MANUFACTURING CO.

The *Mustang 450* (No. RC-28, $84.95 retail) is a very fast, competitive Formula I Pylon Racer. It's stable at low speeds for easy handling and ground handling. Easy to build, it's constructed of balsa and has a 49 1/2-in. wingspan. A .40 engine is required.

SIG MANUFACTURING CO.

The *Four-Star 40* (No. RC-44, $72.95 retail) is an outstanding low-wing sport model featuring an ultra-simple Lite-Ply fuselage and easy-to-build balsa and spruce wing. Pre-cut tail surfaces, aluminum landing gear, and a stylish molded canopy make this one of the fastest-building kits around. It comes complete with pushrods, Easy Hinges, full-size plans, and photo-illustrated instruction book. The wingspan is 59-3/4 in. and the length is 47 in. A .30-.40/2-stroke, or .40-.50 4-stroke engine and a 4-channel radio are required.

SIG MANUFACTURING CO.

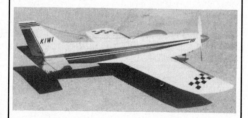

The *Kiwi* (No. RC-42, $72.95 retail) is an R/C sport pattern model that's ideal for Sunday flying and fun-fly events. It's made of strong, simple balsa-ply construction and comes with a built-up wing, sheet balsa tail surfaces, full-size plans, etc. The wingspan is 54 in. A .35-.45 engine and a 4-channel radio are required.

Learn to fly safely. Join your local flying club.

SIG MANUFACTURING CO.

The *Colt Kit* (No. RC-43, $42.95 retail) scale-like sportster combines the convenience of a ready-to-use foam wing with the strength and durability of a balsa fuselage and tail. The wingspan is 45 in. A .09-.15 engine and a 2- or 3-channel radio are required.

SIG MANUFACTURING CO.

The *Kavalier* (No. RC-39, $82.95 retail) is an intermediate-level model that features a special wing design with built-in washout and a semi-symmetrical airfoil for smooth control response without sacrificing aerobatic potential. It's a great all-round model for the active sport flier. The 46-in. fuselage is ply and the wing is balsa, with a 55-1/2-in. wingspan. Full-size plans and illustrated instructions are included in this complete deluxe kit. A .29-.40/2C engine and a 4-channel radio are required.

SIG MANUFACTURING CO.

The *Kougar Mark II* (No. RC-35, $79.95 retail) is a sleek jet-styled model that is easy to build and exciting to fly. Incorporating balsa, ply, and foam in construction, it has pre-cut foam wing cores that have "washout" to eliminate tip stalling and a fully symmetrical airfoil for smooth pattern-like maneuvers. The wingspan is 50 in. and the length is 45-1/2 in. A molded plastic fuselage top makes building this deluxe kit quick and easy. It's an ideal advanced aerobic trainer! A .40-.50/2C engine and a 4-channel radio are required.

SIG MANUFACTURING CO.

The *Super Sport* (No. RC-37, $41.95 retail) combines the convenience of a ready-to-use molded foam wing with the strength of a balsa fuselage. The kit includes molded plastic cowling, aluminum landing gear, and tailwheel. The wingspan is 45 in. and the area is 290 sq. in. A .09-.15 engine and a 2- or 3-channel radio are required.

SIG MANUFACTURING CO.

The *Hummer* (No. RC-50, $29.95 retail) kit contains complete hardware, formed aluminum landing gear, wheels, canopy, nylon pushrods, full-size plans, and a photo-illustrated instruction book. It has a balsa fuselage and wing, with a 34-in. wingspan and a 212.5-sq. in area. A .049-.051 engine and a 2- or 3-channel radio are required.

SIG MANUFACTURING CO.

The *Astro Hog* (No. RC-55, $102.95 retail) is one of R/C modeling's classic designs. It offers perfect stability plus great maneuverability provided by a thick semi-symmetrical airfoil, large wing area, and light wing loading. It is constructed of built-up balsa and has a 71-in. wingspan giving an area of 824 sq. in. A .45-.60/2C or .60-.80/4C engine and a 4-channel radio are required.

SIG MANUFACTURING CO.

The *King Kobra* (No. RC-54, $102.95 retail) is a sport and pattern model for use with .60s. When equipped with a standard .60 engine, it's docile and easy to fly. When it's equipped with optional retracts and a hot .60 and pipe…WOW! It has a foam wing and balsa fuselage. The wingspan is 58 in. and the area is 700 sq. in. A .60 engine and a 4-channel radio are required.

SIG MANUFACTURING CO.

The *Scamp* (No. RC-45, $41.95 retail) is a fast-building molded foam wing fun-flier with the classic look of the light planes of the 1930s. The photo-illustrated step-by-step instruction book makes construction easy for beginners. The fuselage is balsa. The wingspan is 45 in. and the area is 290 sq. in. A .09-.15 engine and a 2- or 3-channel radio are required.

SIG MANUFACTURING CO.

The *Komander* (No. RC-32, $86.95 retail) is an aileron trainer with unusually good lines. Wing-mounted gear provide good ground handling and the balsa and foam construction is strong and simple. An easy-to-access hatch to the tank is included. The wingspan is 62 in. and the area is 640 sq. in. A .40-.50 engine and a 4-channel radio are required.

SIG MANUFACTURING CO.

The *Klipper* (No. RC-36, $42.95 retail) kit includes a ready-to-use foam wing for a compact performer. The balsa fuselage and tail build quickly. A coil-sprung nose gear (with nylon bearing and steering arm) is included. The wingspan is 45 in. and the area is 290 sq. in. A .09-.15 engine and a 2- or 3-channel radio are required.

SIG MANUFACTURING CO.

The *Doubler II* (No. RC-40, $49.95 retail) is a 1/4-scale Midget Racer and sport model. Made of balsa, it has simple design, built-up wing, and is fast-building. Full-size plans, illustrated instruction book, and complete hardware pack are included. Wingspan is 36 in. A .15 engine and a 4-channel radio are required.

GLEN SPICKLER RADIO MODELS

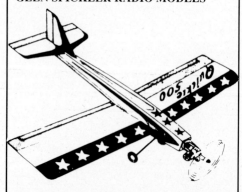

The *Quickie 500* ($58.00 retail) is an Original 500 Club Racer that's fast, easy to assemble, and stable to fly. All wood parts are machine-cut for precise fit. This is a proven, classic aircraft design. Made of wood, it has a 50-in. wingspan and an area of 500 sq. in. A .19-.55 engine is required.

GLEN SPICKLER RADIO MODELS

The *Quickie 200* ($28.00 retail) is a fast 1/2A design that was published in R.C.M. It uses an easy-to-finish wood fuselage, foam wing, and can be totally ready-to-fly in less than a day. It requires a .049-.051 engine and a 2-channel radio.

GLEN SPICKLER RADIO MODELS

The *Quickie Sport* ($63.00 retail) has strong and simple construction, machine-cut parts, full-size plans, canopy, hardware, etc. It has a balsa and ply fuselage and a balsa wing. The wingspan is 50 in. and the area is 500 sq. in. A 25-40-50 engine and a 3- or 4-channel radio are required.

GLEN SPICKLER RADIO MODELS

The *Tally Whacker* ($63.00 retail) has simple construction, machine-cut parts, full size plans, canopy, hardware, etc. Docile and stable with a .25, fast and quick with a .40. It has a balsa wing and ply fuselage. The wingspan is 50 in. and the length is 45 in. A 25-40 engine and a 4-channel radio are required.

SURE FLITE ENTERPRISES

The *ARF Cessna 180* ($47.95 retail) is a smaller plane that does not require an engine with a throttle, but can use a throttle by using mini-servos for control. A flat bottom, high wing fun flying plane for small places. This plane has an injection molded fuselage, length 25.75 in., and balsa tail. Wingspan is 41.75 in. and has an area of 250 sq. in. Uses a .049-.10 engine and requires a "SPORT" 2-4 channel radio.

SURE FLITE ENTERPRISES

This *ARF Piper J-3 Cub* ($47.95 retail) is a fun flying, stable, high winged sport plane which can easily be hand-launched for small spaces. Add a throttle and some ailerons for real excitement and action. Can go electric also. This plane has an injection-molded foam fuselage, length 25 in., and balsa wings. Wingspan is 41.25 in. and area is 250 sq. in. Uses a .049-.10 engine and requires a 2-4 channel radio.

SURE FLITE ENTERPRISES

Sure Flite's *ARF Benny Howards DGA-3 "Pete"* ($44.95) is a hot little classic 1930 racer for the challenged and knowledgeable. Use small servos and put in ailerons and you will have a hot flying, responsive model. Comes with aluminum gears, vacuum-formed cowl, decals, and more. This plane is all injected-molded foam with a fuselage length of 31.5 in. Wingspan is 36 in. and has an area of 250 sq. in. Uses a .10 engine and requires a 2-4 channel radio.

Aircraft

Trainer Kits

ALTECH MARKETING

Altech Marketing is pleased to introduce a new 4-channel R/C trainer that will outfly and outlast all others; it's the *Sage 25*. This durable almost-ready-to-cover kit of wood construction is almost completely factory assembled, so you can spend more time making it pretty and learning to fly.

The Sage 25's fuselage is constructed of lightweight wood in a laminated form that is extremely tough to resist shock and vibration. The main wing uses a foam core with wood sheeting. With a length of 38 inches and a wingspan of 56 inches, it's easily transportable.

DURACRAFT INC.

DuraPlane II—wingspan of 45 inches. For .20- to .25-size engines and 3-channel radio control. Radio system controls elevator, rudder, and engine speed. Instructions include optional aileron installation for more advanced pilots. The DuraPlane II is available in either the standard version with unfinished foam wing or in a deluxe version featuring the Durahide® coated foam wing.

DURACRAFT INC.

DuraBat—wingspan of 45 inches (400 sq. in.). For .40- to .46-size 2-cycle engines and 4-channel radio control. Designed for the intermediate flier who can already pilot a basic radio controlled model airplane. The DuraBat is available in either the standard version with unfinished foam wing or in a deluxe version featuring the Durahide® coated foam wing.

FUN-LINE MODELS

The *Ole Reliable "Deluxe"* ($79.95 retail) is a machine-cut, hand-fitted, top-quality kit. It features spruce and plywood fuselage construction and a balsa and spruce wing for high strength and low weight. The plane has a 70-in. wingspan with a 660-sq.-in. area. It requires a .19-.35 engine. The kit includes rolled plans, an illustrated building guide, top-quality wheels, and hardware. Dealer inquiries invited. Send $1.00 for catalog.

FUTABA

The *Professor 40/ARF Trainer* ($189.95 retail) is designed for quick construction and durability, using a combination of advanced ARF techniques. Over 90% pre-constructed, the Professor 40 is a complete kit. Futaba provides a thoroughly illustrated, step-by-step instruction manual. Futaba uses only the finest grade hardwoods, selected balsas, and lightweight materials to construct the Professor 40.

FUTABA

With the new *Professor Almost-Ready-to-Fly (ARF) Electric Powered R/C Trainer* ($209.05 retail), Futaba has made electric-powered R/C flying easier than ever. Extremely stable design and quiet operation make the Professor the ideal first plane for beginners. Special, lightweight materials are used for exceptional strength and rigidity, and built-up, pre-covered wing, stab and tail make assembly simple and easy. Pushrods and 540SH motor are factory installed.

CARL GOLDBERG MODELS, INC.

The *Eaglet 50* (No. 61/G28, $59.99 retail; No. 82G28W for Wing Kit, $19.99 retail) kit is easy to build and fly (Novice or Sport). It features quality fittings, formed main and steerable nosegear, etc. Made with a birch-ply wing and balsa-ply fuselage, this plane has a 50-in. wingspan and 450-sq.-in. area. It requires a .09-.20 engine and 2- to 4-channel radio. Plans, etc. included.

CARL GOLDBERG MODELS, INC.

The *Freedom 20* ($59.99, Wing Kit: $19.99 retail) instruction booklet makes building easy—even if you've never built a model before. Clear illustrations guide you through every step of construction and equipment installation. Covering materials and techniques are described, plus there's a section on adjusting and flying your plane. The Freedom 20 is 43 in. long with a 55-1/2-in. wingspan. A .20-.30 engine and 4-channel radio are required.

CARL GOLDBERG MODELS, INC.

The new *Eagle 2* (No. 56, $89.99 retail; No. 90 for Wing Kit, $29.99 retail) replaces the very popular Eagle 63 sport-trainer. It has the same easy-to-build, sturdy Eagle 63 construction and forgiving flight characteristics, plus much more. Realigned engine placement, redesigned tail, improved climb-to-glide transition, and repositioned landing gear make the Eagle 2 even more forgiving in flight and allows smoother takeoffs and landings. It includes molded hinges, servo tray, and ready-to-use aileron linkage and more. With a ply fuselage and balsa wings, the Eagle 2 has a 63-in. wingspan and 715-sq.-in. area, and requires a 4-channel radio. Expanded instruction manual includes more photos and details on 4-cycle engine, electric motor, and float options.

GREAT PLANES MODEL MFG.

The *Great Planes PT-E* (No. GPMA0110, $79.95 retail) is the perfect electric trainer, featuring excellent wood quality, precision parts, and easy-to-understand illustrated instructions. The stability and quality that went into the PT-20 and PT-40 is now an electric. Made of balsa and ply, the PT-E is 39 in. long with a 56-in. wingspan. It requires a 3-channel radio and uses a Great Planes Thrustmaster 550 engine.

CARL GOLDBERG MODELS, INC.

SR. FALCON, KIT G16

The *Senior Falcon* (No. 51/G16, $119.99 retail; No. 76/G16W for Wing Kit, $39.99 retail; and No. 145/G16N for Nose Gear, $3.49 retail) is the standard big trainer for 4-channel proportional. Top quality fittings, Symmet-TRU wings construction, etc. Made of balsa, the plane has a 69-in. wingspan and 810-sq.-in. area. It requires a .35-.40 engine and a 4-channel radio.

GREAT PLANES MODEL MFG.

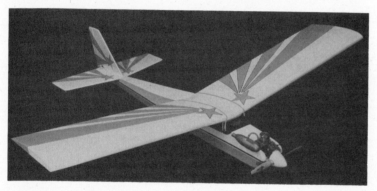

The *PT-40* (No. GPMA0117, $69.95 retail) is the perfect trainer for you if you're looking for the easiest-building, best-flying first airplane. Made of a ply/balsa fuselage and balsa wing, it has a wing area of 675 in. and requires a size .40 engine and 3- or 4-channel radio. It features interlocking balsa and plywood parts, complete hardware, and an illustrated instruction manual. This airplane practically flies itself, making learning much easier. Lay the foundation for your R/C hobby.

GREAT PLANES MODEL MFG.

The *Great Planes Super Decathlon 40* (No. GPMA0185, $109.95 retail) was computer-designed for great performance and easy assembly. The kit features pre-shaped and notched wing leading and trailing edges, aluminum main gear. Constructed of balsa and ply, it is 45-in. long with a 64-in. wingspan. A molded ABS cowl and wheel pants, plus molded clear plastic windshield and side windows, add sharp detailed looks to this outstanding performer. A 4-channel radio and .40-.46 2-stroke or .48-.70 4-stroke engine are required.

GREAT PLANES MODEL MFG.

The *Trainer Sixty* (No. GPMA0120, $109.95 retail) is for those modelers who prefer a large plane and engine. It's the "daddy" of our line. The larger size is appealing to many because of the increased radio installation area, greater flight stability in winds, plus it's easier to see in the air! Trike gear provides the best ground handling. This model can be a docile beginner's ship (with a 40, and control throws reduced), but bolt on a 60, increase the throws, and you'll find performance not really fitting the Trainer name. With balsa fuselage and wing, the Trainer Sixty has a 65-in. wingspan and 764-sq. in. wing area. It requires a .40-.60 or .60-.90/4C engine. Instructions for 4-cycle conversion are included.

GREAT PLANES MODEL MFG.

The *Big Stiks* (No. GPMA0145, 20-size, $49.95 retail; No. GPMA0146, 40-size, $57.95 retail; No. GPMA0147, 60-size, $68.95 retail) feature a classic design, advanced construction methods, and the highest quality materials. The interlocking balsa/ply structure makes it easy to build a Big Stik, and these kits are designed to handle fast, aerobatic flight and hand launchings. With a high wing area to size ratio, Big Stiks fly more like real airplanes. Roomy fuselages make it easy to install engine, radio gear, etc. Parts and hardware are included for both tricycle or taildragger landing gear configurations. Size 20 Big Stik is 44 in. long with a 53-1/4-in. wingspan and requires a .19-.28/2-C or .25-.40/4-C engine. Size 40 Big Stik is 48-1/2-in. long with a 59-in. wingspan and requires a .35-.46/2-C or .46-.61/4-C engine. Size 60 Big Stik is 55-1/2-in. long with a 67-1/2-in. wingspan and requires a .50-.61/2-C or .80-1.20/4-C engine.

HOBBICO

Hobbico's *Flightstar 40* (No. HCAA2050, $149.95 retail) is an all-wood, almost-ready-to-fly trainer that can be assembled in about 10 hours. The flatbottom airfoil provides stability to beginning pilots. The Flightstar 40 is built to survive mishaps with minimal damage. It has a 64-in. wingspan and requires a .40-.46 2-cycle engine and a 4-channel radio.

HOBBICO

Hobbico's *Avistar* (No. HCAA2010, $144.95 retail) is an outstanding ARF trainer, and will appeal to beginners for its hand-crafted quality, durability, and ease of assembly. The illustrated instructions will take you quickly from the box to the air. Made of balsa and polyester film, the Avistar is 45 in. long with a 60-in. wingspan. It requires a 2-stroke .40 size engine and a 4-channel radio.

The Academy of Model Aeronautics promotes safety. JOIN TODAY!

HOBBICO

Hobbico's *Sturdy Birdy* (No. HCAA1000, $64.95 retail) is a trainer that is capable of surviving even the roughest landings and wingtip-to-wingtip cartwheels. An excellent first R/C airplane that assembles in a short time. It includes ABS fuselage, molded foam wing and aluminum main channel and tail boom, and has a 53-in. wingspan. A 2-stroke .25 engine and 3-channel radio are required. Also available is the Sturdy Birdy II version. This includes ailerons.

HOBBICO

Hobbico's *Hobbistar 60* (No. HCAA2100, $199.95 retail) is an easy-to-assemble kit that offers smooth flight. The high-wing design with a semi-symmetrical airfoil, huge wing area, and a trainer-like wing loading, makes the Hobbistar 60 a pleasure to fly. It has all wood, almost ready to fly construction, and a 71-in. wingspan. It requires a .60 2-cycle engine and a 4-channel radio.

HOBBY DYNAMICS DISTRIBUTORS

The *Ultra* (No. HDDULT 20, $68.99 retail; No. HDDULT 40, not yet available) is an attractively designed trainer that can be assembled easily with the photo illustrated instruction book. Its performance is outstanding with its flat bottom wing for high lift slow speed, steerable nose gear, and strong 3/8" dowel leading edge.

HOBBY DYNAMICS DISTRIBUTORS

The *Gobee 20/40* (20 size, $59.99 retail: 40 size, $77.99 retail) is made in the USA. This trainer requires a .25-.40 engine. It is easy to assemble, includes all hardware, motor mounts, and hardwood leading edge. In 40 size, the Gobee is 45 in. long with a 62-in. wingspan. In 20 size, it is 40 in. long with a 54-in. wingspan. A 4-channel radio is required.

LANIER R/C

The *Comet* (No. 74105, $115.95 retail) is an intermediate trainer, 90% finished. Features include symmetrical airfoil, ply spar, beautiful high gloss finish. The wingspan is 63 in., giving an area of 630 sq. in. The fuselage is plastic and ply and the wing is foam with plastic covering. No painting necessary. Rugged, durable, fuel proof parts are easily available. A 4-channel radio and .40-.60 or 4-stroke .49-.90 engine are required. Flying weight is 5-1/2 - 6-1/2 lbs.

LANIER R/C

The *Cessna* (No. 72119, $109.95 retail) is a basic trainer, 95% finished. The fuselage is plastic and ply and the wings are foam with plastic covering. Wingspan is 49 in. giving a 490-sq.-in. area. A .25-.40 or 4-stroke .40-.45 engine and a 3-channel radio are required. Features include flat bottom airfoil, ply spar, high-gloss finish. No painting or covering required. Parts available. Rugged, durable, fuel proof. Flying weight is 4 lbs.

LANIER R/C

The *Pinto* (No. 73, $109.95 retail) is a basic trainer, 95% finished. The fuselage is plastic and ply and the wings are foam with plastic covering. Wingspan is 49 in. giving a 490-sq.-in. area. A .25-.40 or 4-stroke .40-.45 engine and a 3-channel radio are required. Features include flat bottom airfoil, ply spar, high-gloss finish. No painting or covering required. Parts available. Rugged, durable, fuel proof. Flying weight is 4 lbs.

LANIER R/C

The *Slo Comet* (No. 74111, $115.95 retail) is a basic trainer, 90% finished. The fuselage is plastic and ply and the wing is foam with plastic covering. Wingspan is 75 in., area is 750 sq. in. A 3-channel radio and .40-.60 or 4-stroke .49-.90 are required. Rugged, durable, fuel proof. Features include flat bottom airfoil and high-gloss finish. No painting or covering necessary. Parts available. Flying weight is 6 lbs.

LANIER R/C

The *Transit* (No. 73108, $109.95 retail) is a basic trainer with symmetrical airfoil, ply spar and beautiful high-gloss finish. It's 95% finished—needs no painting or covering. Parts available. Rugged, durable, fuel proof. Wingspan is 63 in., area is 520 in. The fuselage is plastic and ply and the wings are foam with plastic covering. A 3-channel radio and .29-.60 or 4-stroke .49.60 engine are required. Flying weight is 5 -6 lbs.

MIDWEST PRODUCTS CO.

Aero-Star .40® (No.159, $99.95 retail), is the perfect trainer aircraft. This all wood kit features Micro-Cut Quality® wood parts for ease of construction, 3 or 4 channel R/C wing, full-size plans and large decal sheet. A Success Series kit available only from your local hobby shop. Its wingspan is 62 in., the engine is .30-.40 2/C, .40-.45 4/C.

MODEL ENGINEERING OF NORWALK

The *Buzzard Bombshell* (Retail: See your dealer) is a recreation of a classic Old-Timer FF that meets the SAM requirements for R/C Old-Time competition. With a wood fuselage and balsa wing, it has a 72-in. wingspan that yields 850 sq. in. of wing area. It requires a .25-.40 engine and a 3-channel radio.

MODEL ENGINEERING OF NORWALK

The *M.E.N. Trainer* (Retail: See your dealer) is a stable basic trainer for the novice, and a Sport plane for the intermediate pilot. The fuselage is made of balsa, lite ply, and spruce for durability. The balsa wing has a 58-in. span. This Trainer requires a .15-.20 engine and a 3-channel radio.

MRC

The *Trainer Hawk II* (No. IF101; Retail: See your dealer) is an all-foam ARF kit which requires very little assembly. It even comes with an Enya .15 TV already installed. Made of foam, it has a 48-in. wingspan. The fuselage has molded cavities for your R/C gear. A 3-channel radio is required. Fuel tank, landing gear, pushrods, and wheel pants are included.

R/C Flying is fun for the whole family!

MODEL ENGINEERING OF NORWALK

The *M.E.N. Trainer 40* (Retail: See your dealer) is for the ''second plane'' in your R/C flying program. It has a 52-in. wingspan and a 518-sq.-in. area, and features tri-square-loc construction, thru-cut die cutting, quality material, rolled plans, building instructions, pre-shaped spruce leading edge, die-cut light ply spars, and a complete hardware package. It requires a .35-.45 engine and a 4-channel radio.

PECK-POLYMERS

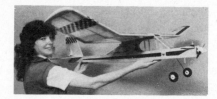

The *Prairie Bird 50* (No. PP-29, $49.95 retail) is an easy-to-fly trainer. It's slow flying, very stable, and is made of die-cut balsa and ply. Large full-size plans and instructions with photos are included. Electric (.5) or gas (.10-.15) power may be used. The wingspan is 49 in., yielding a wing area of 423 sq. in. A 2- or 3-channel radio is required.

ROYAL PRODUCTS CORP.

The *Cessna 206* ($219.95 retail) is an excellent-flying scale project which combines balsa pre-fabrication with flyability. It flies as good as it looks. The cockpit is included. The wingspan is 73-1/4 in. and the area is 654 sq. in. A .49-.60 engine is required.

ROYAL PRODUCTS CORP.

The *Royal-Air 20T* ($102.95) boasts more prefabrication and less assembly time than any other balsa ARF. It comes 95% factory assembled with pre-covered paint design on both sides of the wing and stab.

SIG MANUFACTURING CO.

The *Kadet Seniorita* (No. RC-60, $56.95 retail) is a compact version of the famous "Hands Off Trainer." It has the same super-light wing loading and slow, forgiving flight characteristics in a smaller size that gives the student pilot time to think and react, so learning to fly will be fun, not nerve racking. The big instruction book makes building a breeze. Constructed of balsa, ply, and spruce, it has a 63-in. wingspan and a length of 50 in. A 3-channel radio and a .15-.25/2C or .21-.35/4C engine are required.

SIG MANUFACTURING CO.

The *Kadet Junior* (No. RC-46, $51.95 retail) is a reduced-size version of the inherently stable, high-wing model that's perfect for the student pilot. Easy to build (with a full set of instructions and drawings—that have been called "a beginner's course in model building") it's rugged enough to withstand the hard knocks of learning. A .15-.25/2C engine and a 3-channel radio are required— the 3-channel radio system tightly controls the economical lower displacement engine. The ply fuselage is 39 in. long and the balsa wing has a 48-in. span.

SIG MANUFACTURING CO.

The *Kadet Senior* (No. RC-58, $76.95 retail) is the original "Hands Off Trainer!" It flies along so slowly and gently that almost anyone can handle it on their very first try. If the student pilot gets confused, let go of the sticks and the Senior will return to level flight. Includes full-size plans and complete step-by-step photo-illustrated instructions. Made of balsa, spruce, and ply, the Senior is 62 in. long with a 78-in. wingspan. A .29-.40/2C engine and a 3-channel radio are required.

SURE FLITE ENTERPRISES

The *ARF Sure Flite Tri-Pacer* ($68.95 retail) is a high-winged, flat-bottomed trainer that has excellent ground handling and superior flight characteristics. Though a tough trainer, repairs are quick and easy and inexpensive replacement parts are available. The Tri-Pacer is excellent with floats and can go electric. Constructed of injected-molded foam with a wingspan of 49.5 in., an area of 420 sq. in., and a 37.5 in. long fuselage. Uses any of the following engines: .19-.25 2 stroke, .20-.26 4 stroke, or .05 electric and requires a 3-4 channel radio.

SIG MANUFACTURING CO.

The *Kadet MK II* (No. RC-49, $72.95 retail) is a rugged, snap-to-build trainer with printed fuselage sides, injection-molded cowling, formed-aluminum landing gear. Features include a high-wing configuration for stability, flat-bottom airfoil for precisely controlled flight speed, tri-cycle gear for smooth take-offs and landings, ply fuselage and strong sheet balsa construction for durability. The wingspan is 57-1/4 in. and the length is 44 in. Includes full-size plan, 40-page instruction book, and installation/flying checklists and drawings. A .25-.40/2C engine and a 4-channel radio are required.

SURE FLITE ENTERPRISES

Sure Flite's *ARF Piper J-3 ''Old Yeller'' Cub* ($62.95 retail) has been the trainer for thousands of new modelers. With a wide stance aluminum landing gear and a high lift flat bottom wing, this fast assembling, easy-to-repair trainer is a long time favorite. Constructed of injection-molded foam, has a wingspan of 49.5 in., an area of 420 sq. in., and a fuselage length of 37.5 in. Engines are .20-.26 4 stroke, .15-.25 2 stroke, or .05 electric and uses a 3-4 channel radio.

SURE FLITE ENTERPRISES

The *ARF Cessna Skylane 182* ($62.95 retail) has excellent ground handling for take offs and landings. A smooth, stable flyer, with a high semi-symmetrical wing, the Cessna is a fine trainer for three channels or with four channels. A great aerobatic plane. Made of injection molded foam, has a 53-in. wingspan, an area of 420 sq. in., and fuselage length of 36.5 in. Engine size is .19-.25 and requires a 3-4 channel radio.

PRICES AND SPECS ARE SUBJECT TO CHANGE

R/C Boating—An Introduction

By Michael Shaw, Hobbico Inc.

Looking through today's R/C boating magazines, one cannot help but become mesmerized by all the different types of boats. engines, drive systems, and hull designs available today. To begin understanding radio control boating, we must first go over the basic formats in which boats can be propelled and then describe the various types of boats available.

Radio-control boats can be propelled with wind, gas, steam, and the most popular form, electric power. Each of these methods has its own special features.

Powering Your Boat

Gas engines can be the glow fuel type and range in size from .10 cubic in. all the way up to .90 cubic in. for the larger boats. They offer very high power-to-weight ratio and operate at higher RPM ranges. The key factor with glow engines is that they have a water-cooled jacket around them to keep the engine cool while running. In some cases, an airplane or buggy engine can be used if they have a "cool clamp" around the cylinder head. There are several ways of accomplishing this. See your hobby shop for assistance.

A typical glow fuel engine drive system has the engine attached to a pair of rails on an engine mount attached to the hull. A heavy flywheel at the rear of the engine facilitates the use of a starting belt, for starting the engine and it also helps to maintain engine RPM. The drive shaft can be of the flexible or straight type which is encased in a "stuffing box" and the shaft then exists the full. Grease is applied into the stuffing box to both lubricate the driveshaft and also to keep water from entering the hull. The propeller—or in the case of dual shafts, the props—is then attached to the shaft and the engine drive system is complete.

Outboard glow fuel engines are simpler in comparison to the inboard engines. They require no running hardware. Simply bolt the engine to the stern, hook up the full lines and steering rods, and you're off and running. Outboard engines are much more nimble than inboards and require more attention. By angling the outboard system you determine the "planing" speed of the boat. But remember, if you over-compensate the angle of the outboard, it can cause the boat to "blow-over" or flip and the boat could possibly sink.

Steam Power

Boats powered by steam engines are normally those that are the most expensive, such as riverboats, tugs, and other boats of yesteryear. Be prepared to spend a considerable amount of money if this is your area of interest.

Electric Power

Electric-powered boats are the most popular because they are quiet and easy to start. Just hook up the batteries, turn on the transmitter and the receiver and you're off. Electric-powered boats come in single and dual motor power plants, with single or dual battery packs for higher speeds. Speaking of speeds, electric-powered boats can travel as fast as some of the gas-powered models. The only negative of electric powered boats is the duration they run on a single charge. Don't expect more than 15 minutes running time and always plan to be near shore when you are approaching that time limit.

Wind Power

Sailboats rely on the wind for power and require more skill than gas- or electric-powered boats.

Here's a quick description of the various types of boats available:

Hydroplanes

Hydroplanes are most popular with modelers looking for speed and size. A racing hydroplane, when running at flank speed, rests upon the rear of the two outside hulls, called sponsons, and the stern of the boat. Typical examples of hydroplanes are the Dumas Miller Unlimited and the Miss Circus Circus. Another name for this class is the unlimited hydroplanes, which are highly detailed, fast and not recommended for the novice boat modeler.

Another variation of the hydroplane is the outrigger hydro which has sponsons connected to the mail hull by a few supports to reduce weight and wind/water friction. This design is perhaps the fastest radio control boat available.

Tunnel Hulls

Tunnel hull boats are a refinement of the three-point design boats described above. The sponsons are extended aft until they meet the end of the transom. The boat now rides on two long sections similar to a catamaran. The effect is that the boat is supported partially by a cushion of air trapped beneath the hull. Tunnel boats are powered mostly by outboard motors. Typical examples of this type of boat are the Dumas Hotshots and Sprint, the G. P. Marine Wildcat, and the Kyosho Hurricane.

V-Hulls

V-hulls are the famous "Cigarette" class off-shore racing boats you have seen many times on television engaged in endurance high-speed competition. The V-hulls are shaped exactly like a V and the hulls are called "monohull" or "one-hull" boats. Noted for their ability to knife through rough water, they are powered by inboard power plants. V-hull boats are the most popular with all types of modelers because they are the easiest type boats to handle and learn with. Examples are the Dumas Scarabs and Deep Vees, the Kyosho Jet Stream and Viper, and the G. P. Stinger.

Sailboats

Sailboats offer quiet and relaxation and are ideal for the neighborhood pond or lake. These boats can be operated rudder only, or you can add a sail-winch to take in or let out the main sail. As with all hobbies, you will enjoy it more if you understand the principles of sailboating before you put out to sea. For example, do you know what the terms "tack", "reach", or "run" mean? A. G. Industries, Polk's, and Robbe are just a few of the companies manufacturing radio-control sailboats in all sizes and price ranges.

Scale Boats

Finally there are scale boats. Scale boats, like scale airplanes, are replicas of actual full-size boats. Considerable skill is required to successfully build a scale model. Many of these scale models find their way into studies and offices as "static" models once completed. You will find a wide assortment of scale models ranging from military-type boats, tugs, fishing boats, and even ocean liners.

Boating is widely regarded as a truly family hobby. Visit your nearest pond and you'll see whole families enjoying model boating. Remember, radio-control boating is not a toy. These boats are fast and heavy and it's easy to get hurt or hurt someone else if you don't practice safety first. Remember: take your time building your model and practice caution and courtesy.

Why not introduce a friend to radio-control boating? It will help you enjoy the hobby even more.

Happy boating!

Boats

Ready to Run

R/C Boating is a Family Sport!

Join in some family fun!

DUMAS PRODUCTS INC.

The *Scarab S Type with Line Trimmer Engine* (No. 1438, $695.00 retail) will now be available built-up with a McCulloch 22cc engine installed. This combination of the Dumas Scarab and the McCulloch engine fires a one-two punch that is sure to please. Each boat is handmade by one of Dumas' very own in-house builders. Just install your radio and make some minor adjustments, fill up the tank, and you're in business. It is 45 in. long, has a 14-1/2-in. beam, is made of fiberglass, and is powered by a McCulloch 22cc water-cooled gas engine.

TRAXXAS

The *Traxxas Villain IV* (No. 1508) is the ultimate fully assembled 'deep V' offshore racer. The Villain IV is 31-in. long and has a 8-1/4-in. beam. It comes equipped with twin RS-540S motors, adjustable 2:1 gear reduction, and adjustable trim angle on the outdrives. The props are counter rotating and utilize the latest in surface piercing technology. The fully assembled Villain IV comes with the two-channel radio system and a FWD/REV electronic speed control. The Villain IV is also available as a kit with mechanical speed control (No. 1501).

Boats

Almost Ready to Run

HOBBY DYNAMICS DISTRIBUTORS

The *CESA 1882* ($204.95 retail) is a deep-vee, off-shore racer with twin high performance motors which provide awesome speed. Made of orange molded ABS plastic, the hull is 36-1/4 in. long. The model is easy to assemble, weighs only four pounds, and comes with dynamite decals for great looks.

HITEC R/C USA, INC.

The *Sea Nymph* (No. HAP0020) is hitec's newest entry into the exciting world of radio controlled boats. An ARF electric, the Sea Nymph's molded ABS hull design offers an exciting blend of speed and stability for extraordinary performance. The Sea Nymph comes with its hull and deck pre-joined along with the motor and most hardware already installed for speedy assembly. Powered by a strong 540 motor and stretching 27" long and 9-3/4" wide, it's sure to be a winner.

KYOSHO

The affordable *Kyosho Viper* (No. KYOB1400, $149.95 retail) high-performance semi-vee comes 70% prebuilt. It is compact and lightweight (measuring 25.2-in. long x 8.7-in. high, weighing 2.7-lbs.) so it can be raced in tighter areas than larger R/C boats, yet offers stable handling unique to small boats. Its efficient direct drive system comes with a LeMans 360ST motor, prop, and speed control. The Viper comes with pilot figures, smoked windshield, exhaust stacks, trim, decals, and stand.

HOBBY DYNAMICS DISTRIBUTORS

The *Hustler Boat* (No. HDD3000, $499.95 retail) is new and exclusively available from Hobby Dynamics Distributors! This boat has a modified deep vee design and rigid construction for durability. The heavy-duty strut drive assembly and McCulloch 22cc gasoline engine make it a powerful machine. Even with such high-performance this boat still has a 40-minute run time on a single tank of fuel. Impressive performance and unyielding power make this ready-to-run boat one you won't want to miss!

LINDBERG/CRAFT HOUSE CORP.

The *PT-109—Motorized Torpedo Boat* (1/32 scale, No. 87012, $65.00 retail) has a one-piece hull that's 30 in. long with an 8-in. beam. Made of injection-molded plastic, it includes R/C conversion instructions, movable gun mounts, crew, twin props, rudders, metal shafts/tubing, electric motor, battery box, flags, and decals.

R/C BOATING IS A FAMILY SPORT.

MRC

The *Nordic Deep Vee Turbo* (No. IF240; Retail: See your dealer). Made of ABS plastic, it is 29-in. long with an 8-in. beam. It has a modified 540-type electric motor. Superior out-of-the-box speed is provided by factory motor break-in. An extruded finned heat sink lets this deep vee run longer and cooler. The gear box was designed to handle two 550 motors, and the stainless steel prop shaft resists bending and corrosion.

MRC

MRC introduces the new *Thunder Streak* R/C hydroplane boat kit with super steering, amazing speed, and easy assembly. It is more than 25 inches long with a 9-inch beam and twin 540 electric motors. 1.5:1 gear ratio which powers a steerable outdrive. Highly efficient outdrive unit which couples the propeller and rudder for maximum power output and super responsive steering. Strong ABS hull assembles in a snap. Stainless steel propeller shaft for strength and corrosion resistance. Premolded tray for efficient radio installation. Four spring loaded clips make the canopy easy to remove for maintenance. Two 7.2 volt NiCad batteries give the Thunder Streak blazing performance!

Boats

Electric Kits

G.P.M.

The *G.P. Marine Wildcat* (No. GPMB1000, $149.95 retail) has pre-joined ABS deck and hull with motors and drive system mounted. Twin turn tabs and rudders make for 180 degree turns at full throttle. Marine Wildcat is 27 in. long and takes two Thrustmaster 550 engines.

G.P.M.

The *G.P. Marine Stinger* (No. GPMB1005, $169.95 retail) has a revolutionary twinline drive system that uses two in-line 550 size motors to provide 5-7 minute run times. Features pre-joined ABS hull (24-in. long) and deck for quick assembly time and comes with speed control. If you don't want to paint it, just apply the decals provided on the white hull.

J & M PRODUCTS CO.

The *Super Sport Fisherman* (No. ESF-320, 32 in., $134.95 retail; No. SSF-480, 48 in.. $199.95 retail) was designed by Gerald A. WoBrock for full-scale appearance and performance. Hand-shaped hull ready for planking, planking and parts precision-cut for 6-hour assembly. Construction cradle included. Unsinkable and no hollow sound. Length is 32 in. and 48 in., beam is 9 in. and 13 in. Constructed of aircraft plywood, balsa, and foam. Takes single or twin electric engine.

J & M PRODUCTS CO.

The *Panther* (No. PM-340, gas, $118.95 retail; No. PM-340-E, electric, $112.95 retail) is a high-performance beauty with only 16 parts. Constructed of aircraft plywood and foam, it is 34 in. long with a 11-1/4-in. beam and takes a 3.5/single or twin electric engine. Features include four-hour assembly, precision-cut planking and parts, and construction cradle. It's strong with no hollow sound and it's unsinkable.

KYOSHO

The *Kyosho Hurricane* (No. KYOB1500, $229.95 retail) is an electric catamaran hull boat that utilizes the proven jet stream's outdrive system combined with twin LeMans 360ST motors (2 included). Made of ABS plastic, it is 31-in. long and has a 10.6-in. beam. The Hurricane comes complete with twin adjustable trim tabs which improves stability and high-speed handling. The Kyosho Hurricane can even withstand a full speed 180 degree turn. It comes complete with colorful decals or it can be painted.

R/C BOATING IS FAMILY FUN!

KYOSHO

The *Kyosho Jet Stream 800* (No. KYOB1600, $194.95 retail) is a deep-vee offshore electric racing boat. It comes complete with speed control and drive system. The ABS hull and deck are pre-joined for fast assembly time. An efficient drive system pivots the rudder and propeller to minimize rudder distortion. The Jet Stream 800 is 34.6-in. long with a 8.1-in. beam and takes a LeMans 360ST engine.

LINDBERG/CRAFT HOUSE CORP.

The *Chris Craft Constellation* (1/20 scale, No. 70814, $130.00 retail) is a true classic. This boat kit is 30 in. long with a 9-1/2-in. beam plus one-piece injection-molded red plastic hull, removable rear deck section—all decks molded in color, complete cabin (removable) with clear windows, chrome-plated fittings, curtains, Venetian blinds, etc. The drive-train consists of two brass tube stuffing boxes, solid brass prop shafts, complete brass universal joints, and left- and right-hand nylon props. Included are die-cast rail posts, music wire railings, anchor, davits, rudders with brass brushings, etc. Other features include plywood platform to mount motors and R/C equipment, dingy with oars, two folding chairs, two control rods with connectors, rudder retainers, trim tape, flags, and decals. All that's needed to complete this model for R/C operation is a 2-channel R/C system and one Lindberg No. 8000 drive system.

LINDBERG/CRAFT HOUSE CORP.

Unique is the best description of this first all-in-one *Radio Control Disel Tug Boat* model kit (No. 70817, $58.00 retail). Everything needed to produce a complete R/C model of an HO scale (1/87) diesel tug boat, except the two channel radio, is included. It is 14 in. long and has a 3-3/4-in. beam. Any standard two channel radio will work.

LINDBERG/CRAFT HOUSE CORP.

The *Sport Fisherman* (1/16 scale, No. 70811, $155.00 retail) has a one-piece hull. It is 30 in. long with a 10-in. beam. and is made of vacuum-formed and injection-molded plastic. It includes R/C conversion instructions, chrome-plated parts, Delrin gears, clear plastic windshield windows, and twin propellers.

MIDWEST PRODUCTS CO.

Boothbay Lobsterboat (No. 964, $169.95 retail) is a large version of the typical Maine launch, specifically designed for radio control. A large interior and several access hatches make it easy to install and maintain R/C equipment. The kit contains Micro-Cut Quality Wood parts, Success Series Construction Manual and full-size rolled plan sheet. A Success Series kit available only from your local hobby shop.

MRC

When the *Wellcraft Portofino Cruiser* (No. IF230; Retail: See your dealer) hits the pond, a hush falls over the crowd. From the chrome-like handrails to the meticulously crafted cockpit fittings, its striking ornamentation is reminiscent of a finely detailed yacht. But a sluggish cruiser she's not—just fire up that RS-540 racing motor with 3:1 gear reduction and you'll feel the fury within. Made of an ABS plastic hull with chrome plastic fittings, Portofino is 28.8 in. long with a 9.7 in. beam. Use a 2-channel radio and leave lesser boats in your wake as the Portofino's deep vee racing hull slips and slices through the pack. You'll be amazed at the silky smooth handling, lightning speed, and fast assembly of this awesome ready-to-float racer.

MRC

MRC introduces the new *Thunder Streak* R/C hydroplane boat kit with super steering, amazing speed, and easy assembly. It is more than 25 inches long with a 9-inch beam and twin 540 electric motors. 1.5:1 gear ratio which powers a steerable outdrive. Highly efficient outdrive unit which couples the propeller and rudder for maximum power output and super responsive steering. Strong ABS hull assembles in a snap. Stainless steel propeller shaft for strength and corrosion resistance. Premolded tray for efficient radio installation. Four spring loaded clips make the canopy easy to remove for maintenance. Two 7.2 volt NiCad batteries give the Thunder Streak blazing performance!

MRP

MRP's new *Outboard Motor* (No. 10-3500, $99.95 retail) has a "HIGH SPEED" surfacing propeller and strong, corrosion resistant, stainless, brass, and aluminum components. This record-holding outboard motor comes with "EVINRUDE," "JOHNSON," and "MERCURY" decals to suit the racer's desire. Now sold separately, this is the same motor that powered MRP's "BUD LIGHT" Tunnel Boat to the A.P.B.A. Championship!

MRC

The *Nordic Deep Vee Turbo* (No. IF240; Retail: See your dealer) features superior out-of-the-box speed provided by factory motor break-in. Other features include wet magnets with a balanced and skewed armature. Made of ABS plastic, the Turbo is 29-in. long with an 8-in. beam. An extruded finned heat sink lets this deep vee run longer and cooler. The gear box was designed to handle two 550 motors or a modified 540-type electric motor, and the stainless steel prop shaft resists bending and corrosion.

MRP

Continuing the MRP tradition of fast electric boats, we proudly present the *Bud Light Team* (No. 10-1941, $209.50 retail). This O.P.C. tunnel hull gives you all the thrill and excitement of the real boat. The outboard motor, powered by twin 6 cell battery packs, gives you all the action you can handle and more. Your skill as a driver translates to your racing performance.

MRP

With twin motors, twin battery packs, and surface drive for unbelievable speed and action, the *MRP Miss Budweiser Unlimited Hydroplane* (No. 10-2011, $264.95 retail) streaks across the water leaving a long rooster tail behind. Dancing through the corners, hanging on the turn fin, this is one fast electric that will give you the feel and excitement of the full-sized Miss Budweiser. The turbine-like sound of the twin .05 electric motors and gear whine are guaranteed to speed up the heart of any boat racing fan.

MRP

The *41" Fountain Superboat* (No. 10-5001, $189.95 retail), the latest addition to MRP's "Rough Water Series," is powered by the A.P.B.A. record breaking MRP electric motor. Realistic down to the last detail, this boat is modeled after Reggie Fountain's 47' record holding superboat. The deep vee design slices through white-caps just like the real thing. Real speed, real sound, and real affordable. It's all yours with the Fountain 41" Superboat.

MRP

WET 'N WILD WATERHEATER—That's the way to describe *MRP's Skater* (No. 10-3001, $299.95 retail). This is the largest off-shore, electric outboard Catamaran available. It is also the fastest. Powered by two MRP race-proven 550 Wizzard Outboard Motors, you'll find the same bone-crunching, wave jumping action in this boat as in the real Skater Off-Shore Cats.

PORTA-POWER INDUSTRIES

"X12 TURBO"
23" LENGTH

The *PPI Fast Electric Series Boats* were designed to give advanced hobbyist speed, with novice experience in kit building. Each kit is available with optional upgrade motors and matched prop combinations, which can substantially increase speed and performance without any modifications to the boat. This change can be made in 10-15 minutes. Assembly is made easy due to modular design and fully illustrated and simplified computer-generated instructions. This line of high speed boats is designed primarily for blistering out-of-the-box speed and handling; but for the racing enthusiast, the "X-12 Turbo" with optional twin racing motors and gear drive with high strength alloy prop, powered by twin battery packs, will surely leave all other boats in its wake!!!

MRP

Fun is what you'll have when you drive *MRP's 28" Outrageous* (No. 10-2018, $209.95 retail) Flat Bottom Racing boat. This "K" racing class unlimited flat bottom rockets over the water. Speed comes from a special wind .05 electric motor and twin 5 volt NiCad battery packs. A heat-sink motor mount offers longer engine life.

MRP

At a length of over 43 inches, with three 550 electric motor driven props, MRP proudly introduces the *Gentry Eagle* (No. 10-2101, $249.95). Modeled after the real 110 foot racing yacht which holds the record for crossing the Atlantic Ocean, this sleek cruiser is capable of speeds in excess of 20 miles per hour. Utilizing MRP's new heavy-duty microswitch speed control, this racing yacht runs straight and true in the roughest water.

Boats
Gas Kits

DUMAS PRODUCTS INC.

The *Skater .67* (No. 1436 for kit, $235.00 retail; No. 2352 for running hardware, $87.00 retail) is simply one of the fastest models we have come across in a long time. With a .67 size gas engine, this boat provides you with unlimited speed and magnetic maneuverability. This all hand laid fiberglass kit comes with deck and hull joined. It is 40 in. long and has a 13-1/4-in. beam. The engine rails are mounted and drilled for a Dumas/Steve Muck 5" motor mount. Use Dumas Running Hardware kit No. 2352.

DUMAS PRODUCTS INC.

The *Hot Shot Sprint 3.5* (No. 1326, $85.00 retail) features precision die cut birch and mahogany plywood construction and a pre-formed ABS cowl. The boat is 24 in. long with a 11-1/4-in. beam; it requires a 3.5 Outboard Marine engine. Step-by-step instructions with lots of photos and a complete plan set makes building a snap. We have even included the building jig in the kit. No running hardware required.

DUMAS PRODUCTS INC.

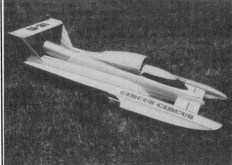

DUMAS PRODUCTS INC.

This big *Wellcraft Scarab 38KV* (No. 1435 for kit, $275.00 retail; No. 2354 for Running Hardware, $87.00 retail) is for big boating enthusiasts and, with its sleek lines, it means all-out power. The boat is 55 in. long with a 14-1/2-in. beam; it requires a .60-.90 engine. This fiberglass kit comes with deck and hull joined and is finished in white gel coat.

Building the *Miss Circus Circus Unlimited Hydroplane* (No. 1325 for kit, $235.00 retail; No. 2346 for Running Hardware, $80.00 retail) will be as much fun as driving it. With a preformed ABS cowling/center section and premium die cut birch and mahogany plywood construction, your Circus Circus will seem to materialize on your workbench. The boat is 43 in. long with a 21-in. beam; it requires an 11cc Inboard Marine engine. A complete set of decals will add the finishing touch to your model.

DUMAS PRODUCTS INC.

The all-new *Hot Shot Sprint* (No. 1323, kit, $110.00) can be built for either a 7.5cc engine or 11cc engine. The 7.5cc version is 31 in. long, the 11cc version is 36 in. long. Both have a 13-1/2-in. beam. This boat has all the latest design features including a shallow tunnel to reduce blow-overs and auxiliary sponsons for faster acceleration out of the turns. This is an all mahogany and birch plywood kit for easy and lightweight construction.

DUMAS PRODUCTS INC.

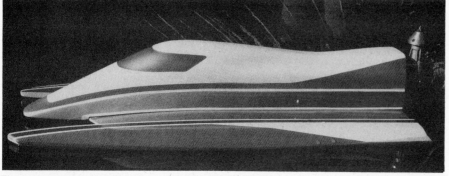

The unsurpassable *Hot Shot Sprint 3.5* (No. 1327, $140.00 retail) is now available in preformed ABS plastic. Whether you are looking for your first gas-powered boat, or are an experienced model boat racer knowing what this boat can do, the ABS Hot Shot Sprint 3.5 is for you. The Sprint is pulled out of .060-thick ABS plastic, with the deck and hull assembled at the factory. The kit will include: fuel tank, control linkage, throttle linkage, push rods, push rod seals, and adjustable motor mount. It is 24 in. long; has an 11-1/4-in. beam, is made of ABS plastic, and is powered by a 3.5 Outboard Marine Engine.

J & M PRODUCTS CO.

The *Fury* (No. OBT-350, gas, $159.95 retail; No. OBT-290, gas, $148.95 retail; No. OBT-290, 3.5 electric, $138.95 retail) features aerodynamic design for outstanding performance and jig-assembled hand-shaped foam hull ready for planking. All parts are precision-cut aircraft plywood. No fins required for turning. The Fury is 35 in. long with a 15-in. beam. It takes a 7.5 or .67 outboard engine. It has sealed radio compartment and six-hour assembly time.

KYOSHO

The *Kyosho Jet Stream GP-10* (No. KYOB1605, $319.95 retail) is a gas-powered deep-vee off-shore racing boat. It is 35-in. long with a 8.2-in. beam; an O.S. 10FP-M engine is already installed. The ABS hull and deck are pre-joined. It uses stainless steel gear drive system. Stern drive unit and gear-drive shaft steering system pivot the propeller to minimize rudder distortion.

PRATHER PRODUCTS

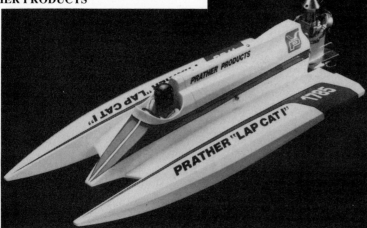

The *Lap Cat I, II, and III* all incorporate the latest design features for speed and turning ability. All three Lap Cat Tunnels have set World Speed Records and are consistant winners in competition. Fast construction time and easy-to-follow photo instructions make the Lap Cats a great choice for competition and sport boaters alike.

PRATHER PRODUCTS

PRATHER PRODUCTS INC.

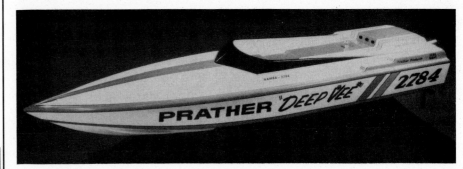

These *Prather Deep Vees* (31-in., $124.95 retail; 40-in., $149.95 retail; 46-in., $179.95 retail) are fast-building and consistent winners in competition. They hold more national records than any other deep vee boats. They feature a factory-joined deck and hull with optional running hardware, radio boxes, and hatch covers. These complete packages make building a real pleasure. Made of epoxy glass, they use 3.5, 7.5, and 11cc engines.

Boats

Military Kits

The *Spitfire I and II* (30" length, $219.95 retail; 36" length, $249.95 retail) are a tremendous step forward in boating technology. The Spitfires' unique one-piece design insures quick, accurate construction while their record breaking speed brings model boating performance to a new level. The prototypes quickly set new national Straight-A-Way records and oval course records. Now even a novice can achieve record-breaking performance using the new Spitfire Hydros and popular K&B 3.5cc and 7.5cc outboard engines.

LINDBERG/CRAFT HOUSE CORP.

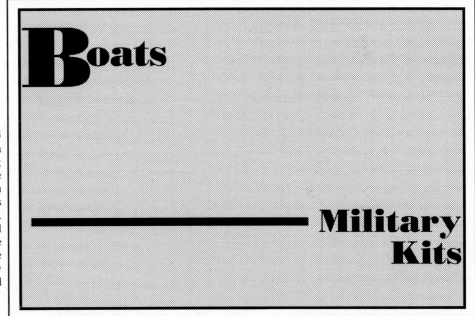

The *Blue Devil Destroyer—Motorized* (1/125 scale, No. 70815, $45.00 retail) is a "Fletcher Class" destroyer. It has a one-piece hull that's 36 in. long with a 3-in. beam. Included are R/C conversion instructions, gun turrets, radar screens, torpedo tubes, twin propellers, flags, and decals.

DUMAS PRODUCTS INC.

This *PT-109* (No. 1227 for boat kit, $275.00 retail; No. 2358 for Running Hardware, $36.00 retail) is a larger model—48-in. length, 12-3/4-in. beam—with a fiberglass hull, mahogany and birch plywood deck and super structure, and detail, detail, detail. The PT-109 can be either gas or electric power.

R/C Boating is a Family Sport.

Boats

Sailboat Kits

AG INDUSTRIES, INC.

The *Cup Racer 12* (No. AG-124RC, $239.00 retail) is the official model of the The America's Cup Challenge '87 which was best in its class. The hull is constructed of ABS plastic and has a length of 19-5/8 in. and a beam of 4-1/4 in. The sails are mylar and have a surface area of 211 sq. in. It comes complete with a 2-channel R/C system that allows full control of both sails and rudder and is constructed of high-quality components for easy assembly.

AG INDUSTRIES, INC.

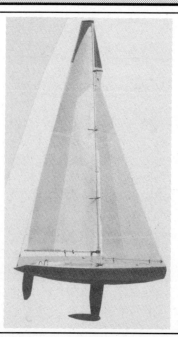

The *Cup Racer 610* ($249.00 retail with R/C, $119.00 retail w/o R/C) is another new official America's Cup-style racer. Easy to operate and assemble, the boat has a length of 24 in., a height of 44 in., and a sail area of 2.1 sq. ft. The hull is constructed of precision-engineered ABS. Perfect for interior display as well as exciting action racing. It comes complete with 2-channel R/C system for full control of both sails and rudder.

DUMAS PRODUCTS INC.

This *Huson 36* (No. 1115 for built, $500.00 retail; No. 1119 for kit, $325.00 retail; No. 3702 for Sail Control) is a sharp looking 36-in.-long fiberglass sailboat that comes completely built and painted with a 48-in. finished wood mast with Dacron sails.It has a 600-sq.-in. sail area and a 10-in. beam. It has a silver bottom, white deck, and a choice of maroon or blue topsides. Rigging and stand included. A 2-channel radio and Dumas sail control are required for sailing. Also available in kit form.

KYOSHO

The *Kyosho Rivera Sailboat* (No. KY-OB1010, $124.95 retail) is more than three feet tall and can be operated with one channel, or add a sail winch and sail with two channels. The laminated polystyrene foam/hull, metal mast, and nylon sail come with all required hardware, wooden stand, and decals. The mast removes for easy transportation. The boat is 38 in. high and 19.75 in. long.

KYOSHO

The *Kyosho Fairwind Sailboat* (No. KY-OB1005, $249.95 retail) features a molded ABS hull, aluminum mast, nylon sail with battens and scale fittings. It is 61.5-in. high and 36-in. long, and can be sailed with one channel or add a sail winch and use two channels.

Boats
Miscellaneous Kits

DYNAMIC MODEL PRODUCTS

One of Dynamic Models' new 'Master Series' semi-kits is the *ATF Tug* (No. 145M, $259.00 retail) which includes fiberglass hull, deck, cabin, super structure, funnel, and more. The ATF Tug is 51-1/4-in. in length, has a 9-5/8-in. beam, and requires a Hecto-perm w/Maxi-Pile engine (sold separately). Deck fittings and running hardware are sold separately.

DUMAS PRODUCTS INC.

The *Prime Time* (No. 1229 for kit, $275.00 retail; No. 2360 for Running Hardware, $60.00 retail) kit features hand laid-up fiberglass hull and premium die cut plywood deck and super structure parts. 48 in. long with a 9-3/4-in. beam, the Prime Time is setup for twin electric power and can use either our 6-volt or 12-volt system. Step-by-step instructions, complete plans, and photo hints are included.

DUMAS PRODUCTS INC.

A beauty from yesteryear! Create a legendary masterpiece from our all-wood kit of the *1930 24' Chris-Craft Mahogany Runabout* (No. 1230, $225.00 retail). The construction of this kit features a double planked hull with birch plywood on the inside with mahogany strip planking on the outside. A complete set of deck fittings and running hardware, including the shaft, stuffing box, rudder, strut, and a bronze three bladed propeller will also be in the kit. It is 36 in. long, has a 10-in. beam, is made of birch and mahogany plywood, and is powered either by gas or electric.

DUMAS PRODUCTS INC.

The *Creole Queen* (No. 1222 for kit, $275.00 retail; No. 2349 for Running Hardware, $60.00 retail) is a 48-in. scale model of the stern-wheeler built by Halter Marine for the New Orleans tourist and business trade on the Mississippi. It's a wood kit with lots of opportunity for innovative R/C controls and details. The boat has a 10-in. beam and is designed to run on either electric or steam power.

DUMAS PRODUCTS INC.

The *Jolly Joy* (No. 1231, $100.00 retail) is great for the modeler who is looking for smaller models and who enjoys strip-plank construction. The Jolly Jay has many things going for it, such as mahogany plywood frames, balsa wood planking, preformed ABS plastic cabin parts, and complete drive line running hardware, including a 4.8 volt electric motor. Jolly Jay can be radio controlled with a two-channel radio or build for display only. It is 24 in. long; has a 8-1/2-in. beam; is made of mahogany plywood, balsa wood, and ABS plastic; and is powered by a 4.8 volt electric motor (included in the kit).

DUMAS PRODUCTS INC.

We have done a make-over of our legendary *33" PT-109* (No. 1201, $90.00 retail). Updated plans and instructions, improved running hardware installation instructions, and added detailing galore are all part of the new improved 33" version of the PT-109. Construction of this all-wood kit will be out of mahogany plywood and mahogany veneer planking. Powering methods include scale electric power, high-speed electric power, and gas power with a .10 size engine. It is 33 in. long, has a 9-in. beam, is made of mahogany plywood and mahogany veneer, and is powered by either gas or electric.

NOVAK ELECTRONICS, INC.

Finally a waterproof casing that provides direct-injection cooling for your Novak speed control. The *Novak Hydro Cooling System* ($30.00 retail) includes a waterproof Lexan case (with screws), a rubber ''O'' ring, water-cooled heat-sink, thermal insulator for brake transistor(s), and pick up and exhaust tubing. It is 1.85" x 2.15" x 1.25" and weighs 1.80 oz. No. 6420 fits T4, T1, T1X, 828-Hv, M1c, MXc, and M5. No. 6410 fits the 610-RV reversible speed control.

Making The Right Choice:
Which R/C Car Or Truck To Buy?

By the Staff of Model Retailer

Perplexed. That's a one-word description for the first-time R/C buyer. And it doesn't get much easier with the purchase of a second vehicle. Although the hobby has matured to the point where almost any decision you make will yield acceptable results, is acceptable all you expect? How do you make the *best* choice?

Start with the pocketbook

We suggest that you look to your piggy bank first. How much can you truly afford? Don't make the mistake of having to buy the best in any product line. You'll find that even some of the economy models in a manufacturer's selection are durable and enjoyable.

You *will* have to set a budget for the model and other major items such as rechargeable batteries, a battery charger or quick charger, a surface frequency radio control system, necessary tools and paints, and perhaps some spare parts to keep your model going.

Pinpoint your preference

Next, choose a model best suited to your personal preferences. Choose the class of car or truck that will please you the most, but do consider the area of operation you have.

Do you like off-road cars? If so, do you have a place to run such a car? Off-road cars are at home on dirt tracks. Grassy lawns should be shunned for most R/C vehicles anyway.

Are Indy CART or Formula I cars your "cup of tea"? You can select between various models made by Kyosho, MRC-Tamiya, and other companies.

The class of stock cars is also booming with entries by BoLink, Team Associated, and MRP. The question here is: do you have a clean, flat surface to run these cars on? A dirt surface may not do so well here.

As for trucks, they are relatively independent of the type of surface they can operate on. Trucks have diversified though. You'll have to decide which type of truck to choose. As examples, the MRC-Tamiya Blackfoot is a two-wheel-drive monster truck, as is the new Associated RC10T truck. There's also the Kyosho USA-1; a four-wheel-drive/ four-wheel steering monster truck; the Team Losi Junior T, a "stadium-class" racing truck; and the Parma California Sport Truck, typical of the new breed of low-slung street cruiser truck without the ground clearance of the other truck classes.

Kit or RTR?

A relatively new choice in R/C is whether to buy a kit or a ready-to-run (RTR). Kits have strong merits—their costs are relatively low, building a kit helps you understand their construction for later tune-ups and repairs; and they are supported in hobby shops with spare parts and accessories.

The RTR cars and trucks recently introduced have broken the "toy" image that was applied to their predecessors. The Traxxas Sledgehammer RTR truck with radio system and the MRC-Tamiya Thunder Shot Q.D. RTR off-road car with radio system are prime examples of prebuilt vehicles with pre-installed electronics made of hobby-quality materials. These vehicles have the road speed to match many of the kit types. You should check out RTRs if your time or personal ability to build a kit is lacking.

Other considerations

Another whole subcategory is the fuel-powered model car. The Kyosho Turbo Burns DX and the Team Associated RC500 models are proven winners. The sound alone of one of these racers is impressive enough to make many modelers go out and get one. The initial higher cost and greater need for maintenance may be considerations, but any gas modeler will tell you that the higher level of enjoyment and speed is worth it.

Are you in the market for a "fun" vehicle or one for racing? Some vehicles are meant solely for the sheer enjoyment of operation. A Parma Hemi Coupe goes fast but may not have a class to race in at a local track. Certainly, the always-popular Team Associated RC-10 or the Team Losi Junior Two were designed for racing but that doesn't mean you *have* to race them to enjoy them.

Spending more money on racing accessories doesn't make you a better driver. The experienced racer will tell you that talent wins over technical support most of the time. By the way, where will you race, and what classes of racing are open? Answers to these questions alone will be strong factors as to what vehicle you buy.

After the purchase

There is one other consideration: the level of support for a product. Can you get spare parts for your vehicle? Where do you get your parts? From the hobby dealer? From the manufacturer/importer? Or can you obtain parts from both sources?

Having the parts at the shop is helpful, but if you live miles away from the nearest shop, recourse to direct sales for parts is necessary. We recommend shopping at your local hobby shop whenever possible because they can help you with any problems.

Do other companies make spare parts and accessories for the model you are considering? Such support usually is a good indication of the popularity of a model. But, be sure to inquire if support is available for your model if none is shown in magazines or advertisements. You may find that products for your chosen model are under development or new.

Who can you turn to for help with your model? A hobby shop with a knowledgeable staff will probably be your best bet, although you will also find that many of the top manufacturers have a service or technical staff available. Although toll free 800 numbers are available, they're not an indication of a manufacturer's commitment to help the customer. You pay for such a call in the price of the model. It's the *ability* of the service staff to help you that should guide your decision.

Question various manufacturers about the compatibility of radio systems, spare parts, and other accessories with their products. They may steer you to products you haven't considered but may be closer to your preferences. Your questions may reveal factors you haven't considered in making a choice. Soon, you'll be able to judge which vehicle is best suited for you. And, the cost of making a phone call will be offset by *knowing* you have made the right choice.

Radio-control cars, trucks, and other surface vehicles have diversified over the past few years. But, don't let that frighten you! It merely means that this segment of the hobby industry has matured to the point where alternatives to the most popular classes of cars or trucks are available to suit your personal taste. If you take the time to make a check list based upon our suggestions, we're sure you'll make the right choice. Then, instead of being perplexed you'll be having fun. And, that's what *any* hobby is all about!

Cars

Off-Road Ready to Run

MRC-TAMIYA

The *Super Sabre QD* (No. RK002; Retail: See your dealer) is part of the MRC-Tamiya QD (Quick Drive) series. This 1/14-scale ready-to-run car just needs batteries and it's on the track! Powered by an electric motor, it has an injection-molded plastic body and an ABS resin plastic chassis. It incorporates features found in the best R/C cars: an electronic speed controller with a two-step forward and a fixed speed reverse; a sealed gear box with precision differential; a turbo speed option; a functional suspension for smooth-going in rough spots; and spiked tires. Sold with wheel-type 2-channel transmitter, the Super Sabre has all it takes to get the checkered flag. Here's the really hot look in today's R/C car world.

MRC-TAMIYA

When it comes to ready-to-run R/C off-road car fun, the new leader is MRC-Tamiya with the Q.D. (Quick Drive) series of vehicles. A case in point is the *Monster Beetle Q.D.*; it's a fabulous Volkswagen Beetle body on a monster truck chassis that's begging to be driven!

The Monster Beetle Q.D. injection-molded body comes in your choice of patriotic colors; red, white, or blue. Chrome-like exhaust pipes and engine detail. This 2-wheel drive Beetle carries a powerful electric motor driving a differential gear that can be switched by its owner for high speed or for high torque obstacle climbing.

Fine touches such as coil springs, a steering servo saver, plus optional hop-up parts make the Monster Beetle Q.D. in 1/14-scale a step above the rest.

MRC-TAMIYA

The *Thunder Shot QD* (RK001; Retail: See your dealer) is ideal for taking to the sport for the first time. QD stands for Quick Drive and this is a 1/14-scale, ready-to-run Special (a ready-to-run product with none of the ready-to-run problems). Powered by an electric motor, it has an injection-molded plastic body and an ABS resin plastic chassis. Includes wheel and trigger type 2-channel proportional transmitter, switch selected turbocharging, proportional right and left steering plus forward and reverse, electronic speed control with two-step forward and reverse, coil spring damped front and rear suspension, sealed gear box with differential, and much more! Enjoy the excitement of car racing fast with a Tamiya Quick Drive buggy.

NIKKO AMERICA INC.

The *1/10-scale Dandy Dash* (No. 10060; Retail: See your dealer) is new! Features include full-time frictionless 4WD with power tooth timing belt, pinion front and rear differential gears, independent 4-wheel suspension. Includes front and rear stabilizer set, racing end ball set, torque limiter metal parts set, with low profile block pattern tires for excellent track contact under all conditions!

TRAXXAS

Radicator is the only car in its class which can be purchased factory-assembled with the pistol grip radio system and a forward/reverse speed control already installed (Model No. 1706). In addition, it has great features like high-volume oil-filled shocks, and fully independent suspension with upper and lower control links. The fiber-reinforced tub chassis is a compact design which securely holds the battery and radio equipment. The sleek streamlined body comes with precut painting masks for the windows and colorful neon decals. Kit without electrics is Model No. 1701.

Cars

Off-Road 1/10 Scale Kits

ASSOCIATED ELECTRICS

The *Yokomo YZ-10* ($399.00 retail) won the world championships. It's easy to build and maintain and is the most popular 4WD car raced. This 1/10-scale car has a Lexan body and is powered by an 05 electric motor (not included). No speed control.

ASSOCIATED ELECTRICS

Associated's all new *RC10T Stadium Truck* is a totally new competition stadium racing truck. At its first race ever, the 1991 Florida Winter Champs with 450 entries, we entered three trucks and finished 1st and 2nd. This is currently the hottest truck out.

ASSOCIATED ELECTRICS

This *RC-10 Off-Road Car* (Cat. No. RC10; $150.00 retail) is the best engineered and most rugged off-road car in the world. It was U.S.A. ROAR National Champion and IFMAR World Champion. If you want the best, this is it! This 1/10-scale car has a Lexan body and an aluminum chassis. It is powered by an .05 motor.

FUTABA

The *FX 10/All Terrain* ($129.95 retail) 1/10-scale off-road car is a product of Futaba's international team of R/C experts. It incorporates many of the features of serious competition models. Four-wheel drive/independent suspension with 4-link rear/monocoque racing chassis/sealed gearbox and differential/lightweight polycarbonate body shell/ and a whole lot more! Powered by a 540/05 motor, it offers 3-stage speed control, high-speed capability, and all the excitement of fast tracking with ease of assembly.

KYOSHO

The *Kyosho Slingshot* (No. KYOC0110, $339.95 retail) is a 1/10-scale 4WD designed specifically for dirt oval racing, that uses a two-belt drive system. Included are one way differential in the front, special oval-type low shock towers, graphite chassis (slotted for batteries to be placed on one side), Kyosho Gold Shocks, and ball bearings. Electric motor, speed control, and body are not included.

KYOSHO

The *Kyosho Ultima II* (No. KYOC0176, $199.95 retail) is the next generation of Ultima performance. It accepts most of the original Ultima hop-up parts, and features oil-filled shocks, duraluminum shock towers, a new adjustable rear wing mount, a lightweight and strong Kellron chasssis with a Lexan body. It is 14.2-in. long and weighs 52.6-oz.

KYOSHO

The *Kyosho Turbo Raider Pro 2WD* (No. KYOC0183, $149.95 retail) is an entry-level 2WD off-road car. An improved version of the Raider, it comes with oil-filled shocks and ball bearings. New high-traction rear tires, orange racing wheels, and decal sheet are included. This 1/10-scale car has a Lexan body with ABS chassis, speed control, and is powered by an Outlaw Stock Mega Motor.

KYOSHO

The *Kyosho Raider Pro ARR* (No. KYOC0182, $139.95 retail) is a two-wheel-drive off-road that's almost ready to race right out of the box. This 1/10-scale model has an ABS chassis with Lexan body, and comes with speed control and a LeMans Stock 05 motor installed. The Raider ARR makes an excellent entry-level car that is capable of accepting many hop-up parts.

R/C RACING IS A FAMILY SPORT

KYOSHO

The *Kyosho Turbo Ultima II Off-Road Racer* (No. KYOC0184, $279.95 retail) has many of the standard features found on the Ultima II plus gold shocks, FRP shock towers, 14 ball bearings, ball-type differential, a Kyosho Mega Outlaw stock motor, and a mechanical speed control.

MRC-TAMIYA

The *Avante 2001* (No. 58085) off-road racer represents the latest technology from MRC/Tamiya. The chassis features a double deck that places the motor battery between the decks to provide the lowest center of gravity. Many other upgrades are available for the Avante 2001.

KYOSHO

The *Kyosho Ultima Pro XL* (No. KYOC0176, $269.95 retail) has a lightweight graphite chassis with a longer wheel base that improves stability. Wider suspension and longer arms, 30 degree "kick-up," adjustable rear toe-in linkage, and adjustable upper suspension arm turnbuckles allow for adjustable front and rear suspension geometry. This 1/10-scale car includes Lexan body, full ball bearings, Kyosho gold shocks, and low-profile front and rear pin-spike tires. Electric motor and speed control are not included.

Safety is Contagious..

MRC-TAMIYA

The *Manta Ray 1/10-scale 4WD Off-Road Racer* (No. 58087) features a 540-type electric motor and a three-speed forward and reverse speed control. Optional ball bearings and motors such as the Dynatech 02H are available for increased performance.

MRC-TAMIYA

The *Fire Dragon* (No. RB878; Retail: See your dealer) is a 1/10-scale high-performance off-road racer from MRC-Tamiya. It has features galore—a four-wheel, front/ rear, independent double wishbone suspension, an adjustable coil over oil-filled dampers for road hugging performance. An anti-roll, front end stabilizer, and a differential gearing for superb cornering. It includes a three-step forward and reverse speed controller, a 540 type motor, lightweight, one-piece wheels, and is made of polycarbonate, resin, and plastic.

MRC-TAMIYA

The *Egress* (No. RB879; Retail: See your dealer) is a race-designed 1/10-scale kit that sports a 2-plate carbon graphite chassis, polycarbonate body, titanium screws, and aluminum nuts. Front and rear axle ball differentials and a center torque splitter allow optimum power transfer ratio. Eight ball bearings provide minimum-friction, tight-control steering. Three-speed forward and reverse speed control is included. It is powered by an electric 540-type motor.

MRC-TAMIYA

The *Astute* (No. RB880; Retail: See your dealer) has a unique toe-in adjustment that increases stability, and optional ball bearings in the steering system that provide near frictionless motion. This 1/10-scale model has a polycarbonate body and RFP chassis. Three-speed forward and reverse speed control is included. The adjustable front suspension and steering permit camber changes with minimum play. It's powered by an electric 540-type motor. Higher-performance upgrades are available, including scaled bearings, Hi-Cap Mini and Short Shocks, and the Dynatech 01R motor.

MRC-TAMIYA

The *Vanquish* (No. RB876; Retail: See your dealer) boasts robust 4WD off-road performance and a ton of potential. Both front and rear suspension arms are tough and adjustable to accommodate different road conditions. With a polycarbonate body and a monocoque resin plastic chassis that holds it all together, this 1/10-scale kit includes a slick midship-mounted 540 motor. The three-step forward and reverse speed control is mounted on top of the chassis for quick adjustment. Coil-over, oil-filled shock dampers and lightweight, one-piece wheels and pin spike tires keep it on an even keel, even on tight corners! It's in the forefront of 1/10-scale technology!

MRC-TAMIYA

This *Nissan King Cab* (No. RB881; Retail: See your dealer) 1/10-scale monster truck has sleek looks and flashy lines that pair with guts and power. Adjustable C.V.A. oil-filled coilover shocks at all four suspension points smooth out the ride, and the adjustable double wishbone suspension in the front and rear enables racers to match track conditions. The body is polycarbonate and the chassis is ABS resin plastic. Three-speed forward and reverse speed control is included. The Nissan King Cab is powered by an electric 540-type motor.

MRC-TAMIYA

The *Super Sabre* (No. RB866; Retail: See your dealer) 4WD off-road from MRC-Tamiya uses high power, efficient shaft-drive mechanics, plus a four-wheel independent double wishbone suspension system to achieve track hugging performance! Wow! Look at that wedge-shaped aerodynamic body with the enclosed cockpit and the integral rear wing! Watch this buggy slice through the air effortlessly! This 1/10-scale dandy has a sturdy ABS resin plastic bathtub-type frame, polycarbonate body, a three-step forward/reverse speed control, and a 540 type competition motor. And the oval block front and rear tires are ready for action. Here's excellent performance at an economical price.

MRC-TAMIYA

The *Terra Scorcher* (No. RB875; Retail: See your dealer) is a 1/10-scale, off-road racer to satisfy R/C enthusiasts from novice to expert alike. This racer is made of a polycarbonate body and a resin plastic chassis and powered by a 540 electric motor (included). It features race-oriented 4WD mechanics. The bathtub chassis combines strength and futuristic styling. The front and rear double wishbone suspension is damped by four large-capacity, coil-over, oil-filled shock absorbers. And the upper wishbone arms are adjustable for fine tuning to road conditions. Anti-roll stabilizers are used on both front and rear suspensions for rock-solid handling. Speed control is included and, best of all, the power is transmitted by a race-proven, shaft-driven system. It's tough, yet its sleek appearance is a pleasure to watch! It's got it all!

MRC-TAMIYA

The *Thunder Dragon* (No. RB873; Retail: See your dealer) combines an ultra-sleek wedge-shaped polycarbonate body styling with state-of-the-art, shaft-driven, 4-wheel drive mechanics for 1/10-scale off-road excitement from MRC-Tamiya. Economically priced, a snap to assemble—yet this buggy has all the sophistication found in quality models! It's great for first-time dragging. Yet, for the serious competitor, the Thunder Dragon is a natural for upgrading for more power, more control, sleeker looks! It features double wishbone suspension system with three oil-filled dampers, sealed gear boxes with differentials, and a steel drive shaft. The chassis is resin plastic. Speed control and a 540 electric motor are included. Turn it loose and watch it go!

MRC-TAMIYA

The *Thunder Shot* (No. RB867; Retail: See your dealer) is economically priced and easily assembled, but offers high performance. The 1/10-scale off-road Thunder Shot 4WD from MRC-Tamiya has a sturdy resin plastic bathtub chassis, double wishbone suspension system, futuristic polycarbonate body. A three-step forward/reverse speed control with BEC connector permits a low racing weight. New style one-piece wheels with pneumatic spike tires are ideal for off-road use. It comes with competition-type 540 motor. Offers sophisticated mechanics, yet it's ideal for the modeler just getting started.

MRC-TAMIYA

The *Grasshopper II* (No. RB874; Retail: See your dealer) is the ideal beginning buggy for those just getting started in R/C cars. It offers rugged construction, yet ease of assembly and a budget price! This 1/10-scale model from MRC-Tamiya has an impact resistant, injection-molded styrene plastic body with a resin plastic bathtub-type chassis, a front independent swing axle suspension, rear rolling rigid axle with four large, shock-absorbing coil springs, and a sealed gearbox with differential. The speed control is heavy duty, three-step forward and reverse type. And a 380-type motor is included. Yes, indeed, here's the machine for experiencing quick first-time track success!

MRC-TAMIYA

MRC-Tamiya has brought new life into the R/C off-road car sport with the introduction of the *Bear Hawk* (No. 58093).

The Bear Hawk has an engineering plastic bathtub chassis that provides extreme toughness. The double wishbone front and rear suspension uses friction dampers. Pin spike tires provide plenty of traction in the dirt. The 2WD planetary differential gear is held in a sealed gearbox to prevent damage from dirt. A 540-type motor and a 3-speed forward and reverse speed control perform the power chores.

There's no other R/C off-road car for beginners quite like the Bear Hawk, created by the leader in off-road technology, MRC-Tamiya.

MRC-TAMIYA

The *Avante* (No. RB872, w/o motor; No. RB872M, w/ Technigold motor; Retail: See your dealer) is the future of 4WD off-road racing! This 1/10-scale car is the very last word in engineering! With a polycarbonate body and a fiberglass reinforced plastic chassis, it's designed to be the fastest racing machine around! Featuring shaft-drive, full-time four-wheel mechanics, with the motor mounted amidships, it has double wishbone independent suspension on all wheels, with long-stroke oil shock absorbers for smoother all-out handling on corners! Includes full ball-bearing set to transmit motor (RX-540VZ Technigold) power to all wheels with minimal friction. The Avante is a mature product of Tamiya success in off-road innovation.

SCHUMACHER

COUGAR (No. U-415-T). Designed using advanced tech-nology to give you European Championship winning performance for competition or street racing. Simple rugged lightweight design with High Torque kevlar drive belt will give experts and beginners alike superb handling and performance straight out of the box.

SCHUMACHER

U-770-R *Slipper Clutch* for 2WD or 4WD. This Slipper Clutch gives greatly improved car control on loose and slippery surfaces, increased stability over rough terrain and reduces wear and tear to the transmission. As used by the Team.

SCHUMACHER

U-745-S *Hex Super Diff All 2WD U-769-Q Hex Super Drum Diff All 4WD.* The Hex Super Diffs are fully supported by ball bearings and uses aluminum parts to give a really smooth action capable of transmitting enormous power to the drive wheels.

SCHUMACHER

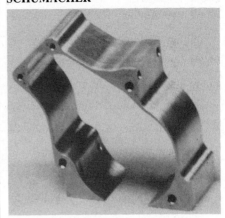

U-771-S *Aluminum Inner Trans. Housing-4WD U-781-C Aluminum Transmission Housing-2WD.* Precision alignment of all transmission parts and excellent dissipation of motor heat.

SCHUMACHER

U-366-W *Aluminum Eccentric Bearing Housings.* Achieve total accuracy of belt tension with 24-step adjustment and precision mounting of rear diff. 2WD or 4WD.

SCHUMACHER

U-200-L *Rear Wishbones "Long Wheel Base" 2 & 4 WD;* U-268-C *Rear Wishbones "Medium Wheel Base" 2 & 4 WD;* U-294-C *Rear Wishbones "Short Wheel Base" 4 WD* only. The shorter wishbones will improve the traction to the rear wheels.

SCHUMACHER

U-623-T *Transmission Side Plates "BLACK"-4WD;* U-781-C *Transmission Side Plates "BLACK"-2WD.* These Aluminum Side Plates are anodized black for improved heat dissipation and strength.

SCHUMACHER

U-289-X *Front Overdrive Pully "48T" 4-WD.* Overdriving the front wheels adds power-on stability in slippery conditions.

SCHUMACHER

U-743-Q *Q.C. Saddle Pack Trays and Straps; 2WD.* These quick change tray and straps are used in our 2WD cars and truck. Can be used with most any flat chassis. U-744-R *Q.C. Saddle Pack Strap "pair" 4WD.* These are used in our 4WD, replacements for the U-743-Q or can be fitted to most saddle pack chassis.

SCHUMACHER

The *Procat* (No. U-409-N) is fully specified for competition use and is race proven by British and European Championship victories. The sophisticated design features fully ballraced four wheel drive, two ball differentials, one way drive shafts, kevlar drive belts and precision machined alloy shock absorbers.

CARS: OFF-ROAD, 1/10 SCALE KITS

SCHUMACHER

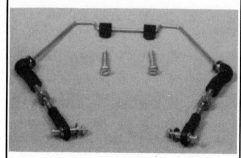

U-739-M *Rear Anti Roll Bar 2WD*; U-766-N *Rear Anti Roll Bar 4WD*; U-765-M *Front Anti Roll Bar 4WD*; U-814 *Rear Anti Roll Bar 2WD Nitro-10.*

SCHUMACHER

911 Turbo SE (No. U-417-V). Stunning rear motor 2WD racer. Four wheel independent suspension, tough alloy chassis, smooth handling, fantastic speed and incredibly tough. Racing in the street, over dirt, or just burning rubber. DO IT WITH STYLE.

TEAM LOSI INC.

The new *Junior Two 1/10 Racing Buggy Kit* (No. A-0030) represents a giant step forward in R/C car technology as well as offering the entrance level racer a truly race-proven and competitive car at an incredibly reasonable price. All suspension components, tough transmission, wheels, and tires are race-proven pieces as used on Team Losi's eight time National Champion JRX series of cars and trucks.

SCHUMACHER

RS COSWORTH 4X4 (No. U-416-U). Aggressive, no compromise, mean machine. Fully ballraced, four wheel drive, kevlar drive belts, alloy shocks, serious specification, serious performance. Competition bred for circuit racing, rallycross or JUST RAISIN' DUST.

SCHUMACHER

The *SHOTGUN* (No. U-419-X) was created to master the most demanding off road conditions, this truck can handle anything you can throw at it. The huge tires and massive ground clearance will eat up any terrain. The SHOTGUN is one tough truck. BLAST AWAY THE OPPOSITION!

TEAM PIT STOP

The *TPS NOVA* (#1000 Series) is available in five different models. They are national, regional, and state champions and include all the finest R/C car components made, i.e,. advanced aerospace designs using graphite, titanium, and aluminum components. Combine the NOVA basic kit with either the Off-road, Oval, or Monster truck kits to make the car of your choice, or own all three. The On-road Transmission and Sprint Cars are also available.

TEAM LOSI INC.

The *JRX-PRO 1/10 Racing Buggy Kit* (No. A-0020, $309.95 retail) offers the latest in race-proven technology for the serious racer. Having won many major national events in its development, the JRX-PRO features a longer graphite/carbon fiber chassis, longer travel shocks, H-arm rear suspension, revised steering mechanism, battery cup, shock mounts, wheels, tires, body, and numerous competition developed pieces.

R/C RACING IS A FAMILY SPORT

Cars

Off-Road 1/8 Scale Kits

KYOSHO

KYOSHO

The *Kyosho Burns DX* (No. KYOC0532, $379.95 retail) is a 1/8-scale gas 4-wheel-drive racing car with a heavy-duty shaft drive system with three gear-type differential units. It has a Lexan body and flat-pan aluminum chassis with nylon double wishbones for maximum wheel travel. Features include oil-filled shocks, bronze bushings, disk brake, tuned pipe, and manifold. Requires a .21 size buggy engine and 2-channel radio. Speed control is not included.

The *Kyosho Turbo Burns* (No. KYOC0535, $649.95 retail) is the 1/8-scale gas performance version of the Burns DX. It has a 3mm-thick aluminum main chassis with Lexan body, and includes complete ball bearings, large volume shocks, and rear anti-roll bar. It features adjustable rear wing mount, quick-fill fuel tank, tuned pipe, and header. It requires a .21 size gas buggy engine and 2-channel radio for on- or off-road high speed excitement. Speed control is not included.

OFNA RACING DIVISION

OFNA Racing is the exclusive distributor in North America for the *Pirate M1* 1/8-scale 4WD gas off-road racer (No. HB-M1-1 standard kit; No. HB-M1-1ENG standard kit with RF-B type .21 engine; No. HB-M1-1G standard kit with graphite kit). Standard kit includes full bearings, 3 differentials, universal joints, large knob tires, adjustable engine mounts, large oil shocks, 3 shoe racing clutch, tuned exhaust, disc brake, quick fill fuel tank, rear wing, sealed gear boxes, and many more quality features. Also, OFNA Racing has a large stock of upgrade racing components for competition.

Cars

On-Road 1/12 Scale Kits

ASSOCIATED ELECTRICS

The *RC12L Car* (No. 4302; Retail: See your dealer) is the best 1/12-scale car in the world. Won the ROAR Nationals and the IFMAR World Championships. The chassis is graphite (no body). No speed control.

C&M MFG.

Cobra LTOOR 12 ($215.95 retail)—the best in 1/10 just got smaller! ROAR Region 3 on-road oval champion! LTOOR—Left Turn Only Or Road—5/3 battery cut out is designed for loading batteries on one side for oval or balanced for road. The chassis is made of the highest quality graphite. Has a wide read pod for easy motor access, heat sink motor mount with ride height spacers, velvet drive titanium pro dif with bearings and varilok adjustment, axle cone washers for precision rear end adjustment, titanium axle and turnbuckles, pivot balls with tweak adjustments, super shock for maximum dampening, Delron hubs, and much more!

COX HOBBIES, INC.

The brand new *Cox .049 GTP Nissan* (No. 9060, or No. 9065 with radio) is an on-road dandy that captures all the sights, sounds, and smells of fuel-powered on-road racing! A snap to assemble and customize. It features an efficient fiberglass chassis design, molded suspension components, nylon wheels and foam tires, and a fully proportional throttle control and brake—all for highly responsive control and top performance! Includes a ratchet pull starter, a 1.5 oz. fuel tank giving 15 minutes of running time and all hardware for assembly. Now with Maples E.G.R. Throttle System.

COX HOBBIES, INC.

Featuring design and engineering technology utilized in the Cox .049 GTP Nissan and .049 Stocker, the *.049 Indy Car* (No. 9600, No. 9665 with 2-channel Sidewinder radio; Retail: See your dealer), with the 'Maples EGR' throttle system is ready for Mini-Indy 500s, Detroit, and Long Beach Grand Prix racing. With 15-minute runs per tank full (no recharging here!), experience true long distance racing!

COX HOBBIES, INC.

With chassis and running gear taken from the Cox GTP Nissan, the *.049 Stocker* (No. 9160, No. 9165 with 2-channel Sidewinder radio; Retail: See your dealer) provides the excitement of American Super Speedway racing. Equipped with the new 'Maples EGR' (exhaust gas recirculation) throttle system, a lower, more reliable idle and a smoother transition to racing RPM will provide faster pit stops!

MRC-TAMIYA

The *Toyota Celica Gr. B. Rally Special* (No. RB864; Retail: See your dealer) is a 4WD, dual-purpose 1/12-scale rally racer crackling with the ultimate in automotive technology! With shaft driven mechanics, and precision differentials at each end of the shaft, and a center differential to equalize the differences in speeds between the front and rear ends. Other features include semi-pneumatic rally tires, coil and oil damped, 4-wheel independent suspension system for the roughest trail, ABS plastic resin chassis, and a light but sturdy polycarbonate body, the product of state-of-the-art blow molding technology. Even operable headlights add to the realism! Powered by a 540 Technigold electric motor, with speed control included.

MRC-TAMIYA

The *Porsche 959* (No. RB859; Retail: See your dealer) is two dominating racers in one, made with equal portions of off-road and on-road technology. It's a thrilling track speedster and an off-road warrior. This 1/12-scale racer has a polycarbonate body, resin chassis, and three-step forward/reverse speed control. It features full-time four-wheel shaft drive—for firm footing, brisk cornering, and brutal no-slip acceleration; a sophisticated coil and oil damped, four-wheel independent double wishbone suspension that's fully adjustable for making the most of any surface; a choice of two gear ratios—one for top speed racetrack blasts, the other for responsive low-end bursts on- or off-road; and the torque of MRC-Tamiya's monstrous RX-540VZ Technigold motor (included).

MRC-TAMIYA

The *Lunch Box* (No. RB863; Retail: See your dealer) is a custom Dodge van that sits atop massive pneumatic tires a full 4.5 in. in diameter and 2.7 in. wide! It's unique! It's hot! It's wild! Paint it (its injection-molded plastic body is perfect for sharp paint schemes and detailing). Modify it by adding windows or radical spoilers or whatever you like. It's got a resin plastic chassis. This 2WD, 1/12-scale Lunch Box from MRC-Tamiya has chrome-like, metal-plated front and rear bumpers and exhaust mufflers. And once you've created the look you want, check out its beefy 540 motor (incl.), sealed gearbox, three-step forward and reverse speed control, 5-in. high coil spring shocks at each end, and much more! You've got to experience it going over bumps, bogs, and boulevards. This is power fun!

MRC-TAMIYA

(58070)

The *Midnight Pumpkin* (No. RB870; Retail: See your dealer) is the latest in the high-rolling pickup line from MRC-Tamiya. It's a classic '53 Ford F-100 customized pickup body on a rugged ABS resin plastic chassis with humongous tires nearly 5 in. high! It's a classic beast! The carefully sculptured 1/12-scale injection molded plastic body recalls the 1953 Ford F-100 down to its smallest details. (In the '50s, the name "Pumpkin" was used to describe the vehicle's bulging hood and fenders and its round-contoured body styline). The gloss black body paint scheme and blue flame decals give the Midnight Pumpkin a rarin' to go appearance that matches its well-proven engineering marvels! Speed control is included and it's powered by a 540-type electric motor.

Cars

On-Road 1/10 Scale Kits

ASSOCIATED ELECTRICS

The *RC10L* (Fiberglass Basic Kit, $170.00 retail; Graphite Basic Kit, $235 retail) car has proved to be one of the best 1/10-scale on-road cars available anywhere. This electric powered car comes in two versions: Fiberglass Basic Kit or Graphite Basic Kit.

C&M MFG.

Cobra SS ($254.95 retail) the fastest, best handling super speedway 1/10-scale car on the market! Lake Whippoorwill Race of Champs winner a main stock! ROAR Region 3 on-road oval champ stock! This new narrowed high-tech chassis is made of the highest quality graphite. It has velvet drive titanium pro differential with full bearings and varilok adjustment, hardened chromally steel threaded front axles, heat sink motor mount with ride height spacers, titanium turnbuckles, tweak plate with pivot balls, 4-way rear pod adjustment, axle cone washers for precision rear end adjustment, and much more!

C&M MFG.

Cobra LTOOR ($269.95 retail) Lake Whippoorwill Race of Champs TQ/Winner a main modified! Road Region 6 on-road oval stock and modified champion! TQ modified Thunderdome! LTOOR—Left Turn Only Or Road—the only car designed to run all six batteries on inside for oval racing, or balanced saddle packs for road racing. Made of the highest quality graphite, it has velvet drive titanium pro differential with full bearings and varilok adjustment, hardened chromally steel threaded front axles, heat sink motor mount with ride height spacers, titanium turnbuckles, tweak plate with pivot balls, 4-way rear pod adjustment, axle cone washers for precision rear end adjustment, and much more!

HYPERDRIVE RACING SYSTEMS

The *H10SE,* bred on the super speedways. From it's predecessor the legendary Hyper 10 (the first narrow super speedway car) designed and first raced in 1988 where it won 4 out of 8 of the super speedway races, including TQs and wins at both Whippoorwill and RC Thunderdrome. Has been refined to be the car to beat on the high banked tracks from the East to the West. HYPERDRIVE: Pioneering the way in a total free-floating rear pod with correct rear suspension geometry and dialabilty to any track. ''With out the box'' build it and race it with no expensive ''hop up parts'' needed. The H10SE is a winner and a pleasure to own, build, and drive. HYPERDRIVE: The Ultimate in Racing.

KYOSHO

In the *Kyosho Scale Series* ($199.95 retail) the 1/10-scale Penske PC19 and McLeren Honda F-1 chassis absorb rugged on-road punishment. Also available: Ferrari F1, Toyota, and Nissan body styles. Electric motor, speed control are included.

KYOSHO

Kyosho announces the *XJ-220 Prototype* (No. KYOC0122, $299.95 retail), a 4-wheel-drive 1/10-scale electric car. This car is one of the latest of the Kyosho super-scale car series. The super-scale XJ-220 Prototype is based on the full-size version XJ-220 Prototype. It measures 31.3-in. long x 5.2-in. high and weighs 4.7 lbs. and the interior comes complete with seats, dashboard, instrument panel, and more. Other features include a totally new glass-reinforced chassis that can be lengthened, and a double wishbone suspension that helps the XJ-220 handle curves.

KYOSHO

Kyosho's *Nissan 300 ZX* (No. KYOC0172, $199.95 retail) is a realistic 1/10-scale model of Nissan's high performance sports car. Its Kelron chassis is based on the proven Ultima 2WD chassis design. The Nissan 300 ZX features glass reinforced independent suspension with oil-filled shocks. Accurately molded Lexan body, radial pattern tires and scale wheels make this car one of the new series of realistic classic scale cars. It is powered by a LeMans Stock 05 motor and includes speed control. Overall length is 18.7 in., the wheelbase is 10.7 in., and the width is 9.6 in. It weighs 3.8 lbs.

KYOSHO

The *Kyosho Ferrari F-1* (No. KYOC0173; Retail: See your dealer) is an exciting 1/10-scale replica of a Ferrari Formula 1 racing car. It has an aerodynamic Lexan body with front and rear wings, and high strength resin chassis. Coil-over dampeners are mounted in a streamlined inboard position. The Kyosho Outlaw Stock Motor (included) is also mounted inboard for ideal balance. Speed control and scale all-independent suspension are included. This is one of Kyosho's scale car series. Overall length is 16.3 in., wheelbase is 9.7 in., width is 7.3 in., and weight is 2.9 lbs.

KYOSHO

The *Nissan-R89C* ($199.95 retail) is a 1/10-scale electric version of a group-c racing car. The Nissan-R89C 2-wheel-drive, on-road model includes a speed control with three forward and one reverse speeds. The authentically styled, all-independent suspension system with coil-over dampeners and the accessories add to the realism of group-c racing. All that's required for operation is a 2-channel radio system, 7.2 volt 1200/1700 mAH battery pack, and battery charger. The unit measures 17.7-in. long x 7.5-in. wide x 3.9-in. high, has a wheelbase of 9.7-in., and weighs 2.9 lbs.

KYOSHO

Kyosho's *Porsche 911 Turbo Flatnose* (No. KYOC0171, $199.95 retail) is a realistic scale model of Porsche's world-class sports car. Its Kelron chassis is based on the Ultima 2WD chassis design. This model accepts all hop-up parts for the Ultima. It is powered by a Stock LeMans 05 motor and has speed control and independent suspension with oil-filled shocks. Accurately molded Lexan body, radial tire pattern and scale wheels make this car part of the new series of realistically detailed scale cars by Kyosho. Length is 21.3 in., wheelbase is 10.7 in., width is 9.6 in., and weight is 3.9 lbs.

KYOSHO

Experience authentic F-1 racing in electric 1/10-scale with the *McLaren Honda MP4/5B* ($199.95 retail). An extremely detailed all-independent suspension with coil-over dampeners and high strength resin chassis is reproduced in a scale model that is very popular at the F-1 racing events held world wide. The McLaren Honda MP4/5B measures 17.7-in. long x 7.5-in. wide x 4.3-in. high, has a wheelbase of 9.7-in. and weighs 2.9 lbs., has a clear poly-carbonate Lexan body, and comes complete with electric motor, and the speed control has 3 forward and one reverse speed.

KYOSHO

The *Corvette ZR-1* (No. KYOC0515, $359.95 retail) is a 1/10-scale gas-powered buggy manufactured by Kyosho. It is 19.8 in. long, 9.4 in. wide, and 5.6 in. high. It features a four-wheel independent wishbone suspension with oil-filled shocks and a belt drive for maximum efficiency. Everything except fuel, a two-channel radio, and four D-cell batteries is included in the kit. The O.S. .12 CZR engine features a unique pull starting and priming system for easy starting.

KYOSHO

Kyosho's Lamborghini Diablo (No. KY-OC0164, $299.95 retail) is a super-scaled, 4-wheel-drive, electric, realistically detailed sports car. The Lamborghini Diablo is scaled from the full-size exotic, and features a display-quality interior complete with seats, steering wheel, gear shift, and dashboard. In action, the Lamborginin Diablo is equally impressive. It comes with a LeMans stock 05 motor, speed control, double wishbone suspension, and strong, glass-reinforced chassis.

KYOSHO

The *25th Anniversary Lamborghini Countach* ($199.95 retail) is a 1/10-scale electric 2-wheel-drive, on-road car for R/C modelers and full-size car enthusiasts. It includes a speed control with three forward and one reverse speeds, a stock LeMANS 05 electric motor, oil filled shocks, aluminum hock towers, Lexan body, and Kelron chassis. The authentic scale detail makes it an excellent showpiece. The Lamborghini Countach measures 19.9-in. long x 10.2-in. wide x 4.7-in. high, has a wheelbase of 10.7-in., weighs 3.9 lbs., is based on the Kyosho Ultima II Chassis, and accepts all of the Ultima hop-up parts.

KYOSHO

The *Toyota Group-C* ($199.95 retail) features a realistically styled all-independent suspension system with coil-over dampeners and a detailed Lexan body for fine on-road racing performance. A 2-channel radio system, 7.2 volt 1200/1700 mAH battery pack and battery charger are not included and are required for operation. The Toyota Group-C measures 17.7-in. long x 7.5-in. wide x 3.9-in. high, has a wheelbase of 9.7-in., weighs 2.9 lbs., and has a high-strength, resin chassis.

KYOSHO

Kyosho announces the 1/10-scale electric *Ferrari Testarossa* ($199.95 retail). The Ferrari Testarossa is a highly-detailed 2-wheel-drive model featuring a fully adjustable, 4-wheel independent suspension with double wishbones, oil filled shocks with coil-over springs, aluminum shock towers, a Kelron chassis, Lexan body and speed control with three forward and one reverse speeds. It measures 19.7-in. long x 9.6-in. wide x 5.3-in. high, has a wheelbase of 10.7-in., and weighs 3.9lbs.

MCALLISTER RACING

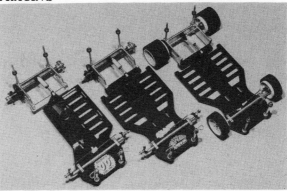

''0'' Oval Only Chassis Kit (No. MX-1003, $249.99 retail) is the ultimate for stock car oval set-up. Weight jacking adjustments, full bearing dif with graphite chassis and more.

MX-Pro Chassis Kit (No. MX-1002, $159.95 retail) is for the experienced racer. Accepts stick or saddle pack batteries. Has graphite rear axle and full bearing diff.

''Outlaw Stocker Kit'' (No. MX-1000 with axle bushings, $110.00 retail; No. MS-1001 with axle bearings, $149.00 retail) is maximum performance for a minimum budget. The Outlaw kit comes complete with wheels and tires, body, decals, and instructions.

MRC-TAMIYA

The *Williams FW-11B* (No. RB869; Retail: See your dealer) is the fierce running machine that swept away its Formula 1 competitors. This 1/10-scale model of the Williams FT-11B Honda from MRC-Tamiya incorporates a V-6 turbo-charged engine, a fiberglass reinforced plastic (FRP) double deck chassis, and a three-point suspension system with an enlarged oil damper in the rear. Provide your own speed control, but a 540 electric motor is included. Sponge tires on all four wheels grab the road as never before! Decorate its polycarbonate body with authentic Williams Team colors and markings for concourse-winning appearance. Enjoy track racing to its utmost!

MRC-TAMIYA

The *Mercedes Benz C-11 1/10-scale Racer* (No. 58088) is an exact replica of the real racing machine that is famous all over the world. It features a 3-point suspension, 540-size electric motor, and ball differential.

MRC-TAMIYA

The *Lotus Honda 99T* (No. RB868; Retail: See your dealer) is a Grand Prix winner from MRC-Tamiya! This 1/10-scale racer captures the look and feel of Formula 1 racing with many high-tech features. Incorporating Honda's awesome V6 cylinder, turbo-charged engine...a three-point, active computerized suspension system...a double deck, fiberglass reinforced plastic (FRP) chassis setup under a polycarbonate body. It comes with a 540 electric motor, along with differential gearing for increased cornering traction. Plus both Lotus and Camel decals for either British or continental style markings. No speed control.

MRC-TAMIYA

The *Toyota Celica Gr. B. Rally Special* (No. RB864; Retail: See your dealer) is a 4WD, dual-purpose 1/12-scale rally racer crackling with the ultimate in automotive technology! With shaft driven mechanics, and precision differentials at each end of the shaft, there is a center differential to equalize the differences in speeds between the front and rear ends. Other features include semi-pneumatic rally tires, coil and oil damped, 4-wheel independent suspension system for the roughest trail, ABS plastic resin chassis, and a light but sturdy polycarbonate body, the product of state-of-the-art blow molding technology. Even operable headlights add to the realism! Powered by a 540 Technigold electric motor with speed control included.

MRC-TAMIYA

Now you can own a Formula I R/C car that wears the Tamiya name for two reasons: the new *Lotus 102B Judd Formula I* (No. 58095) kit is typically easy to build and handles excellently; and the real car is sponsored by Tamiya!

The R/C car kit features the recently introduced 1/10-scale road chassis, with its one and a half fiberglass reinforced plastic (FRP) deck design for light weight with the proper amount of stiffness. The independent coil spring front suspension and single point coil-over oil-filled shock damper for the rear suspension ensure top notch handling when used with the sponge tires in the kit. With you own speed control and our 540-type electric motor, speedway thrills are within your grasp!

MRC-TAMIYA

Sports car racing is fast, furious, and fun. MRC-Tamiya has created a new 1/10-scale R/C car, the *Nissan 300ZX IMSA GTO Racer* (No. 58091) that will astound you with its innovative features.

The Nissan uses a new engineering plastic chassis combined with a FRP portion that is stiff where stiffness is needed yet flexes for optimum handling when necessary. A new Sport Tuned 540 electric motor is controlled through a 3-step forward and reverse speed control yet permits the use of optional electronic speed controls. The rear axle brace is mounted on an FRP T-bar plate that flexes with the track surface; the shock damper plate can be adjusted for track conditions.

PARMA INTERNATIONAL

This 1/10 scale *Days of Thunder™ Mello Yello® car* (No. 15070, $119.95 retail), is just like the one driven by Cole Trickle in the movie! Also available is Cole Trickle's *City Chevrolet* (No. 15071, $119.95 retail) or *Bad Guy Hardee's® Stock Car Kit* (No. 15072, $119.95 retail). Make some noise in your neighborhood. Pick up one of these complete rolling chassis kits.

MRC-TAMIYA

When it comes to R/C racing excitement, 1/10-scale electric track cars are a "hot item" on any modeler's list. MRC-Tamiya adds fuel to the fire with the release of the *Tyrrell 019 Ford Formula One* (No. 58090) race car kit.

The FRP deck-and-a-half chassis builds quickly. The rear suspension consists of a motor mount unit sitting on top of a T-bar that permits the rear sponge tires to grab uneven road surfaces. Lightweight one piece wheels and bushings on all axles are part of Tamiya's racing technology that puts this car ahead of its class.

To top the Tyrrell off, you'll find a dependable 540-type motor, driving a precision ball bearing differential for smooth handling. With optional parts such as a Dynatech motor and sealed ball bearings, the Tyrrell 019 Ford will be a top race contender.

MRC-TAMIYA

One of the hottest teams in Group C racing worldwide is Jaguar. Their fast and fabulous-looking XJR-12 is now the subject of a 1/10-scale R/C car kit by MRC-Tamiya that will continue its winning ways on R/C road courses.

The *Jaguar XJR-12* (No. 58092) features the new bathtub chassis developed by Tamiya engineers that is easy to adjust both for ride height and track conditions, using the coil spring front end and the adjustable coil-over oil-filled shock absorber rear suspension. The ball differential can be adjusted for varying amounts of slip. This kit will come with a 3 speed forward and reverse speed control, yet the chassis easily permits the use of electronic speed controls is preferred. The Sport Tuned motor adds extra power for road racing as well.

MRC-TAMIYA

The *Lancia LC2* (No. RG203; Retail: See your dealer) was Lancia's first C Group racer and it's a racer you've got to see, especially in this super-precise 1/24 scale. Sports car racing was never this formidable. The mammoth front air scoop will take your breath away. The mirrors mounted on the sweeping fenders will make you sit up and look. From the bottom of its track-hugging silhouette to the top of its convex cockpit cowling, this injection-molded body of impact-resistant styrene plastic has all the details of speed. The roar comes from a powerful Mabuchi FK-180SH Mini-Black motor, the roll is along sponge tires that just tack to the track. The coil-damped suspension soaks up the shocks—it's independent in the front, link-type, with stabilizer in the rear. And it's all nestled in an easy-to-assemble monocoque chassis engineered from lightweight, durable resin plastics. You can get the Lancia LC2 together in a Tamtech package that includes NiCad battery, charger, special R/C radio, and receiver variable speed control system.

PARMA INTERNATIONAL

The Parma *California Sport Truck Kit* (No. 15060, $99.95 retail) is a rolling chassis design with many extras. All packaged in this sporty box with convenient carrying handle. Also available separately is replacement *California Chevy Body with decal* (No. 10318, $24.00 retail) and an alternative choice, the *California Ford Body* (No. 10337, $24.00 retail) with it's own unique decal design.

Safety is no accident!

PARMA INTERNATIONAL

The Parma *Hemi Coupe* (No. 15080, $129.95 retail) will capture the attention of both R/C hobbyists and scale modelers. It features a highly-detailed 1/10 scale Hemi Motor kit and a crystal clear Lexan, 3 window coupe body. The concept of a rolling chassis design will stimulate sales of motors, batteries, radios, paints, decals, and more. To order, call your distributor today.

TWISTER MOTORS

Twister's new *"Cyclone"* car (Retail: See your dealer) is a 10th-scale on-road designed to be one of the hottest new cars of the nineties. Features like an ultra-low center of gravity, centrally mounted motor, carbon fiber construction, and easy tuning and assembly make the "Cyclone" the hottest car on the market.

MRC-TAMIYA

The *Porsche 962C* (No. RG201; Retail: See your dealer) says sleek from the dual headlamps recessed in the airfoil fenders to the outboard braced stabilizer wing. This car is the endurance race legend that embodies the essence of aerodynamics. Newly developed technology allows Tamiya to fashion the body of impact-resistant styrene plastic that's injection molded for precise detailing down to the wiper blade. The body is plastic, and the chassis is a monocoque design made of durable engineering resin plastics. The front suspension is a coil damped independent, while the rear is link type, also coil-damped, complete with stabilizer. The muscle of this 1/24-scale monster comes from the Mabuchi FK-180Sh Mini-Black electric motor (included). Electronic proportional forward/reverse speed control is included. Poise it all on wheels premounted with high-grip sponge racing tires and you're ready to rip.

Cars —On-Road 1/8 Scale Kits

KYOSHO

The 1/8-Scale *Kyosho BMT Blitz* (No. KYOC0540, $669.95 retail) is the Kyosho BMT 891 4WD on-road racer. It took five of the top ten spots, including first place, in the 1989 1/8-scale On-Road IFMAR World Championships in Italy. A two-speed gear box, clutch, and ball differential are factory installed. It also features a 4mm thick duraluminum flat pan chassis, four Kyosho oil-filled shocks, 20 total ball bearings, fuel tank, wing, and full set of sponge racing tires. A .21 size engine and a 2-channel radio are required.

MOODY AUTOMOTIVE, INC.

The *Moody "American" Sprint Car* (Deluxe Kit, $675.00 retail; Standard Kit, $595.00 retail) has all-metal structural components. Nickel-plated wire roll cage and nerf bars, steel rod ends, in-line drive, rear axle disc brake, heavy-duty clutch. With an aluminum chassis and an ABS body, this 1/8-scale car is powered by a .21 engine (not included). Dirt or asphalt oval racer. Plans and instructions easy to follow.

PARMA INTERNATIONAL

If you're looking for a "new look" for your 1/8 scale car, look no further. Parma International; pioneers in Lexan body manufacturing, now offers this beautifully detailed *1/8 scale Lumina NASCAR* (No. 1249, $19.95 retail). Now you can race in the fastest growing segment of R/C with a bold new look; a 1/8 scale Lumina NASCAR. Ask for Parma bodies at your local raceway or hobby shop.

Cars ———— Military Vehicles

MRC-TAMIYA

The *West German Flakpanzer Gepard R/C Tank* (No. RA230; Retail: See your dealer) is the most advanced R/C tank ever introduced by MRC-Tamiya. This 1/16-scale model is of the West German Flak Tank, based on the Leopard tank chassis. It has a plastic body, metal chassis, 540 electric motor, proportional speed control, 360-degree rotating turret, dual flak guns that raise and lower automatically, plus a rotating radar dish.

MRC-TAMIYA

The *King Tiger Tank* (No. RA240; Retail: See your dealer) is an exact 1/16-scale R/C model of the WWII German tank. Chassis and suspension are of heavy-duty aluminum and cast-metal, and the body is plastic. The large 540 electric motor works the gearbox through a dual clutch mechanism which permits proportional turns left or right. Proportional speed control is also provided for forward and reverse. A 2- to 4-channel radio is required; with a third R/C channel you can turn the turret; a fourth channel utilizes the strobe light mounted in the gun to simulate cannon fire.

MRC-TAMIYA

1/35th SCALE

This *West German Leopard A4 Tank* (No. RA201; Retail: See your dealer) consists of factory-assembled, gear-and-clutch system which allows quick building and tight turning. This 1/16-scale tank has a plastic body, metal chassis, and is powered by a 540 electric motor that enables it to climb 40-degree hills. A 2-channel radio is required.

R/C RACING IS A FAMILY SPORT

Cars

Motorcycles

ROYAL PRODUCTS CORP.

The *Honda RC30 Motorcycle* (No. 79-422, complete with radio, $149.95 retail) is a 16-1/2-in. long, 1/5-scale cycle that's ready-to-run, complete with radio. Made of ABS, it's powered by a Mabuchi 380 motor. It features electronic speed control and braking. This unit is beautifully painted and can be hopped up to double speed.

ROYAL PRODUCTS CORP.

SUPER KIT

The *Honda NC30 Supersport Kit* (No. 80-390, $99.95 retail) is the 16-1/2-in. long 1/5-scale kit version of the RC30 R.T.R. Royal Honda. Made of ABS, it comes with electronic speed control and steer servo. Parts are pre-painted in MC30 paint scheme and it's powered by a Mabuchi 380 motor.

ROYAL PRODUCTS CORP.

The *Kawasaki Motorcycle* ($234.95 retail) is ready-to-run and ready for thrills. It is 1/5 scale, powered by a 540 Mabuchi motor and measures 16-1/2-in. long. It comes complete with a radio and training extensions. It features electronic speed control and is beautifully painted in black, charcoal grey and red paint scheme.

ROYAL PRODUCTS CORP.

The *Yamaha Motorcycle* ($234.95 retail) comes ready-to-run. It is 1/5 scale, powered by a 540 Mabuchi motor and measures 16-1/2-in. long. It comes complete with a radio and training extensions. It features electronic speed control and is painted in red, white, and blue.

ROYAL PRODUCTS CORP.

The *Royal Kawasaki Motorcycle* ($149.95 retail) is beautifully detailed. It is 1/5 scale, powered by a 380 Mabuchi motor and it comes complete with a radio and training extensions, launch stand, and electronic speed control. Just add a standard 7.2V flat NiCad battery and you're ready-to-run.

Cars
Robotics

OWI INC.

Completed using only basic hand tools, the yellow and smoke-colored *MOVIT Manta* kit (No. MV-966, $41.95 retail) is designed for both the educational and adult-hobby markets. Its preassembled electronics, visible through a clear plastic housing, use a sound and pressure sensor for directional control. This enables the three-wheeled Manta to reverse direction when it contacts a surface or "hears" a sound. The Manta's front wheel automatically pivots when reversing, steering the robot in a new direction 45 degrees from its previous course.

OWI INC.

The red and smoke-colored *MOVIT Spider* kit (No. MV-962, $75.95 retail) is intended for both the educational and adult-hobby markets, and can be finished using only basic hand tools. A clear plastic housing displays the preassembled electronics that provide directional control. An infrared beam and sensor detect obstacles in the Spider's path, directing it to turn to a new course. Six legs driven by crank motion propel the robot.

Cars ———————— Trucks

KYOSHO

The *1/10-scale Kyosho Chevy Custom Sport Truck* (No. KYOC0159, $219.95 retail) has electric 2-wheel-drive excitement. It is 18.8-in. long, 6.4-in. high, weighs 3.8 lbs. and comes equipped with air dams, door mirrors, wipers, rear spoiler, and visor. More customizing options are included with the kit such as a bed wing, two sets of colorful decals, a durable Kelron chassis, double wishbone suspension, LeMans stock 05 motor, heavy-duty speed control, and a sealed gear box which provides superb on-road performance. The unit can also accept many Ultima hop-ups.

J.G. MANUFACTURING

The *Stadium Race Truck* is based on race-proven J.G. Mfg. components. Kit features ultra light direct bolt on nylon truck rims, Special Stadium truck tires, 11-1/2" long wheel base Graphite truck chassis, ultra tuff steering and servo saver linkage plus steering rack with ball bearings, complete stainless ball bearing kit, wide front end with in-line steering, extra-long Teflon-coated truck shocks, front and rear truck shock towers, front Stadium truck bumper, skid plate, body mount, 48 pitch final drive gears, Stealth transmission, new design long wheel base truck body, and rear spoiler. Does not include electronics, motor, radio, or batteries. Order Nos.: P/N 2201-01 S.R.T. with stick pack chassis and Chevy truck body; P/N 2201-02 S.R.T. with stick pack chassis and Ford truck body; P/N 2202-01 S.R.T. with saddle pack chassis and Chevy truck body; and P/N 2202-02 S.R.T. with saddle pack chassis and Ford truck body.

KYOSHO

Kyosho's USA-1 (No. KYOC0242, $319.95 retail) is the 1/10-scale official replica of the USA-1. The R/C version was designed in cooperation with the full-size USA-1 owner, Everett Jasmer, who clinched the 1988 Monster Truck World Championship. The model is powered by 2 Outlaw Stock Mega motors, and has an ABS chassis with Lexan body. It is 17.6-in. long, 12-in. high, and 16-in. wide. Chrome highlights have been added to match the full-sized USA-1 detail for detail. Featured is a new heavy-duty speed control. Upper control arms offer adjustable camber. Front steering blocks have 10 degrees of caster, metal bushings, and two coil-over shocks for each wheel. Suspension travel is an impressive 1-1/4-in.

KYOSHO

Kyosho announces the *Outlaw Ultima Racing Truck* (No. KYOC0210, $229.95 retail). It is based on the design of the Kyosho Ultima II, having a 4-wheel, independent, double wishbone suspension, a Kyosho Super Stock 34° engine, 4 long shocks with Kyosho's new adjustable collars, duraluminum shock towers, lightweight wheels, and pin-spiked tires with removable Lexan dirt shields. The Outlaw Ultima Racing Truck also features large dirt guards on the chassis sides, a new front bumper/body mount and full color decals. It accepts most of the Ultima hop-up parts.

KYOSHO

KYOSHO

The *Kyosho Outlaw Rampage Truck* (No. KYOC0518, $359.95 retail) combines 1/10-scale off-road stadium truck racing and gas powered action. It comes with a powerful O.S. .12CZ-R engine with recoil pull-start, fuel tank, and gearbox installed. It weighs 4.2-lbs., it's 16.7-in. long and 7.3-in. high. It features the power of nitro action, four-wheel independent suspension with adjustable oil-filled shocks, and a tough aluminum chassis for maximum strength.

KYOSHO

The *Kyosho USA-1 Nitro Crusher* (No. KYOC0525, $479.95 retail) is a combination of aggressive, high-speed excitement of gas racing with the styling of the most popular full-size truck. The USA-1 Nitro Crusher .21-size (scaled precisely after Everett Jasmer's ESPN superstar) R/C monster truck is based on the proven Burns DX 4-wheel-drive chassis, weighs 9.8-lbs., is 19.7-in. long, and 15.0-in. high. The muffler, air cleaner, manifold, decals, and lots of chrome accessories are included. The .21-size buggy engine is required.

MCALLISTER RACING

The *Kyosho Big Boss* (No. KYOC0225, $179.95 retail) is a 1/10-scale chrome accented Ford F-250 body with plenty of detail. It is powered by a LeMans Stock 05, and has speed control and a Lexan body. Fully enclosed gearbox and 4-wheel independent suspension with strong ABS chassis, and 5.8 in. x 2.9 in. tires make this an excellent off-road 4-wheel drive truck.

The *Fly'N "M" 18 Wheeler* (No. MX-2001, $159.95 retail) is a real eye-opener! Complete 7-part body for cab and trailer, with chassis, suspension, axles, and hubs. Also includes window mask, decals, and instructions.

KYOSHO

Kyosho's Heavy Metal (No. KYOC0280, $299.95 retail) 1/10-scale electric monster tank is more than big—it's unstoppable! The unique caterpillar tracks on bogey wheels take the Heavy Metal up, over, and through dirt, sand, rocks, snow—practically any terrain is open territory. Heavy Metal weighs 4.6-lbs., is 14.8-in. long, and 7.8-in. high. The kit includes a pre-assembled gear box with variable speed, 2 380-size electric motors, speed control, and decals. Optional ball bearings are also available.

MRC-TAMIYA

The *1/10-scale Toyota Hi-Lux Radio-Control Truck* (No. 58086) features the Tamiya bathtub chassis plus a separate sub-chassis for extra strength. This chassis technique allows for easy access to the radio components. The precision 2WD gearbox provides maximum performance and comes with a 540-type electric motor.

MAXTRAX

The *Maxtrax Elliminator Sled* (No. MTXC1200, $399.95 retail) is the official 1/10-scale pulling sled of the NR/CTPA (National Radio Control Truck Pulling Association). Its sturdy one-piece extruded anodized aluminum construction is rated for 400 lbs., and it features roller chain drive system with 1/4 hardened steel axles.

MRC-TAMIYA

The *Bullhead Monster Truck* (No. 58089) from MRC-Tamiya is the boldest and biggest monster truck on the market today. The tires measure 6.5 in. in diameter and 4.3 in. in width. The Bullhead kit features a semi-rig body and plenty of chrome detail. Four-wheel steering is featured, just like the real thing.

MRC-TAMIYA

The *Mud Blaster* (No. RB877; Retail: See your dealer) from MRC-Tamiya beats all in down-and-dirty big-wheel fun. Sitting high and mighty above the tough-looking realistic monster truck chassis is the ever popular Subaru Brat pickup body. It's tough, too! The tractor-pin spike tires are excellent dirt grabbers. The body is injection molded plastic and the ABS plastic resin space frame chassis holds the 2-channel R/C system. A 540-type electric motor powers the 2WD system through a proven durable gear exchange, and speed control is included. A double wishbone front suspension and rear trailing arms provide a fully independent suspension ride with coil springs all around. A sure pleaser among R/C monster movers, the 1/10-scale Mud Blaster will please the most discriminating modeler.

MRC-TAMIYA

The *4WD Clod Buster* (No. RB865; Retail: See your dealer) from MRC-Tamiya is the ultimate all-terrain car crusher. There's little that can stop this 1/10-scale giant. This monster is 480mm long and 340mm high, and its mammoth semi-pneumatic tires are nearly 165mm in diameter. Dual 540-type turf-tearing electric motors can be run in parallel for power climbing or in series for endurance driving. Speed control is included. The body is injection-molded plastic and the chassis is ABS plastic resin. Its 4-wheel steering lets you navigate around fallen obstacles, and maneuver on wet or dry surfaces. And there's much more—link-style single trailing arm suspension with rigid axles front and rear, eight heavy-duty, long-stroke coil spring shocks, steering tie-rods and engineering uprights a full 1-1/2 in. in diameter. Hey, now, this has got to be the BIG mover in R/C monster trucks!

MRC-TAMIYA

The *Monster Beetle* (No. RB860; Retail: See your dealer) has nearly a 2-in. ground clearance which means it can climb over and through obstacles that would stop lesser off-roads. Together with its 2.36-in. x 5.11-in. deep tread tires, there's little it can't overcome. It doesn't just move, but attacks with its 540S electric motor (incl.)...which is soup-up-able to Black or Technigold. The 1/10-scale Monster Beetle is your ticket to ride. It has a high-impact plastic body, resin chassis, and three-step forward/reverse speed control. Four-wheel independent suspension, wishbone in front, trailing arm in rear, and oil-filled dampers lick and stick to even the most uneven track. Differential gearing hugs the corners close, while a sealed gear box keeps out the gunk. In all, this crunchin' crusher is an all-terrain terror.

MRC-TAMIYA

(58070)

MRC-TAMIYA

The *Ford F-10 Ranger Blackfoot* (No. RB858; Retail: See your dealer) electric-powered pickup comes with large 125mm.-dia. tires. This 1/10-scale kit includes a sealed gear box, injection molded body, 3-step forward and reverse speed control, 540S electric motor, ABS space frame chassis and front double wishbone rear trailing arm, and 4-wheel independent suspension.

The *Midnight Pumpkin* (No. RB870; Retail: See your dealer) is the latest in the high-rolling pickup line from MRC-Tamiya. It's a classic '53 Ford F-100 customized Ford pickup body on a rugged ABS resin plastic chassis with humongous tires nearly 5-in. high! It's a classic beast! The carefully sculptured 1/12-scale injection molded plastic body recalls the 1953 Ford F-100 down to its smallest details. (In the '50s, the name ''Pumpkin'' was used to describe the vehicle's bulging hood and fenders and its round-contoured body styline). The gloss black body paint scheme and blue flame decals give the Midnight Pumpkin a rarin'-to-go appearance that matches its well-proven engineering marvels! Speed control is included. Powered by a 540-type electric motor.

MRC-TAMIYA

This *Nissan King Cab* (No. RB881; Retail: See your dealer) 1/10-scale monster truck has sleek looks and flashy lines that pair with guts and power. Adjustable C.V.A. oil-filled coil-over shocks at all four suspension points smooth out the ride, and the adjustable double wishbone suspension in the front and rear enables racers to match track conditions. The body is polycarbonate and the chassis is ABS resin plastic. Three-speed forward and reverse speed control is included. The Nissan King Cab is powered by an electric 540-type motor.

MRC-TAMIYA

Your local hobby shop is there to help you select the best equipment and to answer your questions

The *Lunch Box* (No. RB863; Retail: See your dealer) is a custom Dodge van that sits atop massive pneumatic tires a full 4.5 in. in diameter and 2.7 in. wide! It's unique! It's hot! It's wild! Paint it—its injection molded plastic body is perfect for sharp paint schemes and detailing. Modify it by adding windows or radical spoilers or whatever you like. It's got a resin plastic chassis. This 2WD, 1/12-scale Lunch Box from MRC-Tamiya has chrome-like, metal-plated front and rear bumpers and exhaust mufflers. And once you've created the look you want, check out its beefy 540 motor (included), sealed gearbox, three-step forward and reverse speed control, 5-in. high coil spring shocks at each end, and much more! You've got to experience it. Going over bumps, bogs, and boulevards. This is power fun!

MRC-TAMIYA

When it comes to ready-to-run R/C off-road car fun, the new leader is MRC-Tamiya with the Q.D. (Quick Drive) series of vehicles. A case in point is the *Monster Beetle Q.D.*; it's a fabulous Volkswagen Beetle body on a monster truck chassis that's begging to be driven!

The Monster Beetle Q.D. injection-molded body comes in your choice of patriotic colors; red, white, or blue. Chrome-like exhaust pipes and engine detail. This 2-wheel drive Beetle carries a powerful electric motor driving a differential gear that can be switched by its owner for high speed or for high torque obstacle climbing.

Fine touches such as coil springs, a steering servo saver, plus optional hop-up parts make the Monster Beetle Q.D. in 1/14-scale a step above the rest.

ROYAL PRODUCTS CORP.

The *Royal Crusher* ($109.95 retail) is a 1/10-scale off-road monster truck. Features include 4-wheel steering, chrome bumper, chrome rims and roll bar, twin wishbone suspension and big 5 1/4 in. tires. Powered by an electric 540 motor, this truck has speed control, a polycarbonate body, and a fiberglass-filled nylon chassis. 4-wheel drive conversion is available for under $30.00.

NOVAK ELECTRONICS, INC.

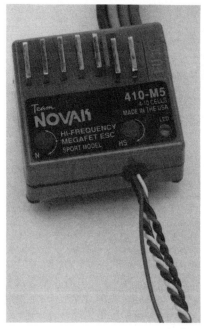

Team Novak continues to develop state-of-the-art high frequency technology with the introduction of the *410-M5 Sport Model MEGAFET Speed Control* (No. 1920, $119.00 retail). The M5 offers the entry-level driver an economical and easy way to experience the ultra-smooth driving and efficiency of Novak's top-of-the-line M1c and MXc speed controls. Features protection against reverse voltage with our exclusive, user-repairable Solder Pop Fuse™, MEGAFET transistors for lowest on resistance, 2500Hz high frequency pulse-width-modulation for more efficient recharging of the batteries, and perfect linearity for smooth acceleration. Includes heat sinks and motor capacitors, pot adjustment screwdriver, mounting tape, Novak Input Plug System™, pot hole plugs, complete instructions, a multi-color decal sheet, and the Novak 90-day warranty.

SKYWARD R&D LABORATORY

The *MEANer MUDDER* (No. 8902H, $325.00 retail) is an ARR 1/8-scale, gas-powered monster truck with PVC Chevrolet truck body. It has four-wheel-drive double wishbone independent suspension with oil-filled shocks and massive 3-5/8-in. x 7-in. pneumatic tires. It also includes a double disc braking system with aluminum chassis, chromed bumper and roll bar, and functional muffler. There's an optional 19:1 gear ratio, optional with Skyward 21Fsr motor installed, and optional built-in recoil starter.

SKYWARD R&D LABORATORY

The *MEANer MUDDER* (No. 8902HE, $499.00 retail) is an ARR 1/8-scale, gas-powered monster truck with PVC Chevrolet truck body. It has four-wheel-drive double wishbone independent suspension with oil-filled shocks, massive 3-5/8-in. x 7-in. pneumatic tires, double disc braking system with aluminum chassis, chromed bumper and roll bar, and functional muffler. There's an optional 19:1 gear ratio, optional with Skyward 21Fsr motor installed, and optional built-in recoil starter.

SKYWARD R&D LABORATORY

SKYWARD R&D LABORATORY

The *MEANer MUDDER* (No. 8903, $295.00 retail) is an ARR 1/8-scale, gas-powered monster truck with roll cage. It has four-wheel-drive double wishbone independent suspension with oil-filled shocks, massive 3-5/8-in. x 7-in. pneumatic tires, double disc braking system with aluminum chassis, and functional muffler. There's an optional 19:1 gear ratio, optional with

SKYWARD R&D LABORATORY

The *MEANer MUDDER* (No. 8903H, $325.00 retail) is an ARR 1/8-scale, gas-powered monster truck with roll cage. It has four-wheel-drive double wishbone independent suspension with oil-filled shocks, massive 3-5/8-in. x 7-in. pneumatic tires, double disc braking system with aluminum chassis and functional muffler. There's an optional 19:1 gear ratio, optional with Skyward 21Fsr motor installed, and optional built-in recoil starter.

The *MEANer MUDDER* (No. 8903HE, $499.00 retail) is an ARR 1/8-scale, gas-powered monster truck with roll cage. It has four-wheel-drive double wishbone independent suspension with oil-filled shocks, massive 3-5/8-in. x 7-in. pneumatic tires, double disc braking system with aluminum chassis, and functional muffler. There's an optional 19:1 gear ratio, optional with Skyward 21Fsr motor installed, optional built-in recoil starter.

SKYWARD R&D LABORATORY

The *MEANer MUDDER* (No. 8902, $295.00 retail) is an ARR 1/8-scale, gas-powered monster truck with PVC Chevrolet truck body. Four wheel drive double wishbone independent suspension with oil-filled shocks, massive 3-5/8-in. x 7-in. pneumatic tires, double disc braking system with aluminum chassis, chromed bumper and roll bar, and functional muffler. There's an optional 19:1 gear ratio, optional with Skyward 21Fsr motor installed, and optional built-in recoil starter.

PRICES AND SPECS ARE SUBJECT TO CHANGE

TEAM LOSI INC.

The *JRX-T Racing Monster Truck* (No. A-0050; Retail: See your dealer) has won every national championship for its class to date. Using the race proven JRX-2 technology and real rubber "naturals" tires, the 1/10 scale JRX-T is the ultimate racing monster truck. Kit includes carbon fiber graphite chassis, LRM transmission, 5 link suspension, Lexan body, lightweight hardware, and easy-to-follow instructions. Speed control and electric motor not included.

TEAM LOSI INC.

Utilizing many of the suspension components developed for the National Champion JRX-T and JRX-PRO, the *New Junior T Monster Truck Kit* (No. A-0060, $219.95 retail) represents the first competition-proven entrance level monster truck kit. The ultra tough ball bearing equipped LRM transmission, oil filled coil-over shocks, natural rubber racing tires, and revolutionary matrix fiber/resin molded chassis are identical to those used in the Junior Two and/or JRX-T.

TRAXXAS

The *Traxxas Blue Eagle Graphite Racing Truck* features an efficient new transmission specifically designed for truck racing with a slipper clutch and a ball differential. Other features include a graphite chassis, graphite shock towers, long suspension arms, shallow offset front wheels, T-6 aluminum long shocks, 48-pitch gears, and full ball bearings. The Blue Eagle is the current N.O.R.R.C.A. National Champion. A new bellcrank steering system is also used. Kits without motor and speed control are available as Model No. 1902.

TRAXXAS

TRAXXAS

The new *Traxxas Hawk* is the least expensive 1/10-scale truck on the market. Yet, it still has the features and performance you would expect to find on trucks costing much more. Features such as 4 oil-filled shocks, T-6 aluminum and nylon construction, fully independent suspension, and metal-finish nylon wheels. Hawk is great for beginners because it's inexpensive, durable, and with the detailed instructions, it's easy to build and maintain. Model 2810 is fully assembled with radio and mechanical speed control. Model 2806 is fully assembled with radio and electronic speed control. Model 2801 is an unassembled kit without the radio system.

The *Traxxas Sledgehammer* is the king of two-wheel drive monster trucks. It has 8 oil-filled shocks, T-6 aluminum and nylon construction, fully independent suspension, hardened steel axle shafts, and the highest usable ground clearance of any 1/10-scale truck. Metal-finish nylon wheels look like real aluminum. Handy turnbuckles are provided to tune the adjustable suspension. Sledgehammer is the only serious monster truck which can be purchased fully factory-assembled with the pistol grip radio system and electronic speed control installed (Model 1806). The unassembled kit without the electrics is Model No. 1801.

We have selected a wide variety of finished radio control models that have been completed by modelers just like you who have taken the time to carefully build these models to achieve the results you see here. Also shown are the equipment & accessories from various manufacturers.

Many of the finished models come from John Worth of the Vintage Radio Control Society and by members of the Westchester Radio Aeromodelers (WRAM) Club of White Plains, N.Y.

Clockwise from top left:
The Parma Int'l. *Hemi Engine* shown with spark-plug wires installed. *Building and Racing Electric RC Cars and Trucks* from Kalmbach Publishing Co.   *Baby Ace* in flight, built by Bob Burnstein, a member of the WRAM club. The Novak Electronics *Hydro Cooling Speed Controller* for R/C boats.

The following photographs were supplied by the Vintage Radio Control Society.
Clockwise from top left:
Bud Schenck's *Debolt Champion.* Ed Kazmirski's *Orion* and *Taurus,* built by Lynn Fondots. Nats winner, *Zue,* by Bob and Dolly Wicher. MGA's aces of WWII USAAF and Luftwaffe *pilot busts.* Carl Schmaedig's *Rudder Buf* from the Vintage RC Society. An assortment of *Black Baron* covering material from Coverite.

Clockwise from top right:
The *Max 6 FM System* from JR Radios. John Worth of the Vintage RC Society with Debolt's *Live Wire* trainer. Byron's *P-51 Mustang*, built by Dick De Beradinis, a member of the WRAM club. The old time *Commodore* from the files of Vintage RC Society. Midwest's *SuperHots*, built by Ron Fannes, WRAM.

Clockwise from top:
The Traxxas *TRX-T Eagle* monster truck.
A DC-powered *starter* from Royal
Products. The *Hustler* gas-powered boat
from Hobby Dynamics. The *Sledge
Hammer* monster truck from Traxxas.

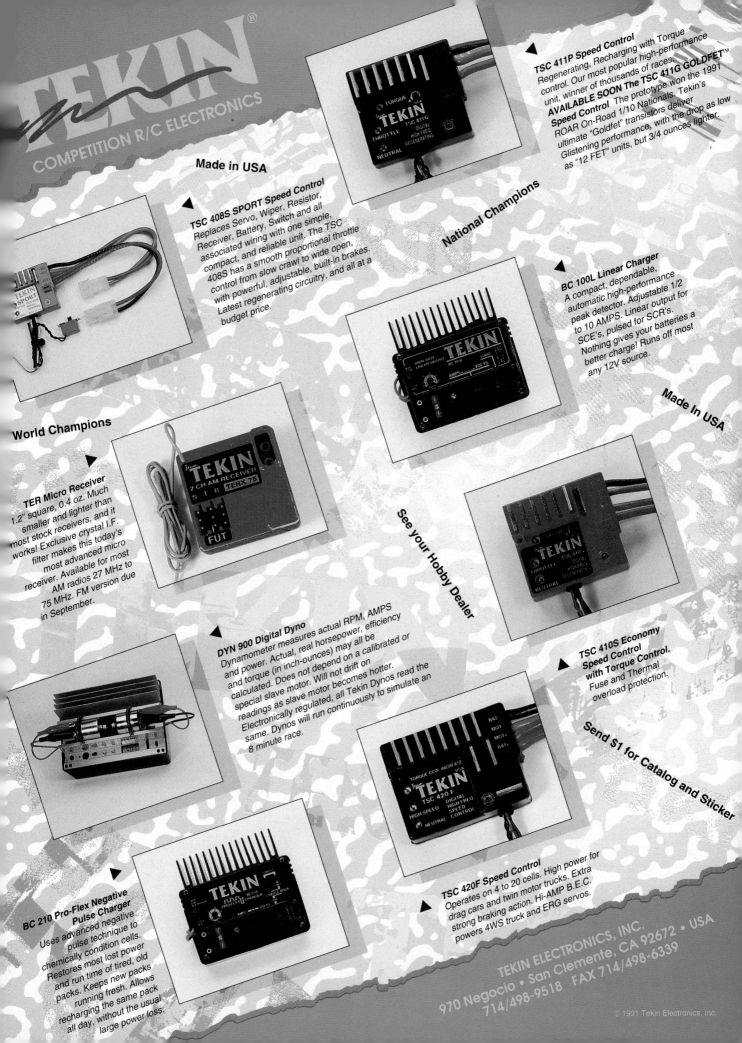

TEKIN®
COMPETITION R/C ELECTRONICS

Made in USA

TSC 411P Speed Control
Regenerating, Recharging with Torque control. Our most popular high-performance unit, winner of thousands of races.
AVAILABLE SOON The TSC 411G GOLDFET™ Speed Control The prototype won the 1991 ROAR On-Road 1/10 Nationals. Tekin's ultimate "Goldfet" transistors deliver Glistening performance, with the drop as low as "12 FET" units, but 3/4 ounces lighter.

TSC 408S SPORT Speed Control
Replaces Servo, Wiper, Resistor, Receiver, Battery, Switch and all associated wiring with one simple, compact, and reliable unit. The TSC 408S has a smooth proportional throttle control from slow crawl to wide open, with powerful, adjustable, built-in brakes. Latest regenerating circuitry, and all at a budget price.

National Champions

BC 100L Linear Charger
A compact, dependable, automatic high-performance peak detector. Adjustable 1/2 to 10 AMPS. Linear output for SCE's, pulsed for SCR's. Nothing gives your batteries a better charge! Runs off most any 12V source.

Made In USA

World Champions

TER Micro Receiver
1.2" square, 0.4 oz. Much smaller and lighter than most stock receivers, and it works! Exclusive crystal I.F. filter makes this today's most advanced micro receiver. Available for most AM radios 27 MHz to 75 MHz. FM version due in September.

See your Hobby Dealer

DYN 900 Digital Dyno
Dynamometer measures actual RPM, AMPS and power. Actual, real horsepower, efficiency and torque (in inch-ounces) may all be calculated. Does not depend on a calibrated or special slave motor. Will not drift on readings as slave motor becomes hotter. Electronically regulated, all Tekin Dynos read the same. Dynos will run continuously to simulate an 8 minute race.

TSC 410S Economy Speed Control with Torque Control.
Fuse and Thermal overload protection,

Send $1 for Catalog and Sticker

BC 210 Pro-Flex Negative Pulse Charger
Uses advanced negative pulse technique to chemically condition cells. Restores most lost power and run time of tired, old packs. Keeps new packs running fresh. Allows recharging the same pack all day, without the usual large power loss.

TSC 420F Speed Control
Operates on 4 to 20 cells. High power for drag cars and twin motor trucks. Extra strong braking action. Hi-AMP B.E.C. powers 4WS truck and ERG servos.

TEKIN ELECTRONICS, INC.
970 Negocio • San Clemente, CA 92672 • USA
714/498-9518 FAX 714/498-6339

Clockwise from top:
Beautifully detailed *monster-truck bodies* from Parma Int'l. The legendary *RC-10* off-road racer from Associated. The new *RC-10 Stadium Truck* from Associated. *Glow Plug igniter* from Royal Products.

Clockwise from top right:
The *Mini Mite* power tool from Dremel. *Mag wheels* for 1/4-scale cars from Rick's R/C; and a new release for the Associated *RC-10 stadium truck without the body*. The *Big Hammer* monster truck from Altech Marketing. The Parma 1/10-scale *Ford Sport* body. Tekin's *Mosfet ESC PX* speed controller.

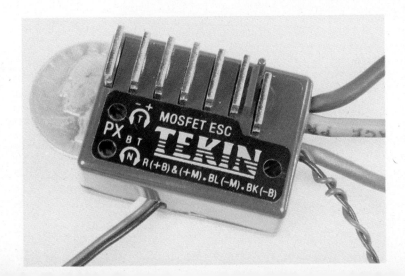

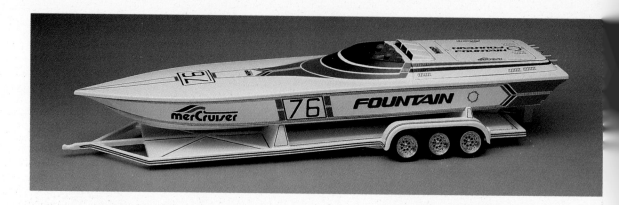

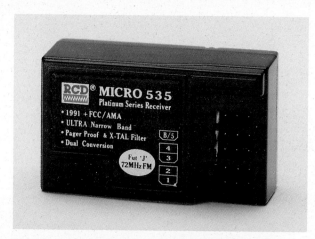

Clockwise from top:
The *MRP Fountain* boat on a trailer. RCD's *Shredder 2-Channel Receiver*. Hitec R/C *USA Sea Nymph* RTR boat. Novak's *NER 3 FM Receiver*. Parma's *Hemi Coupe*. RCD's *Micro 535 Platinum Receiver*.

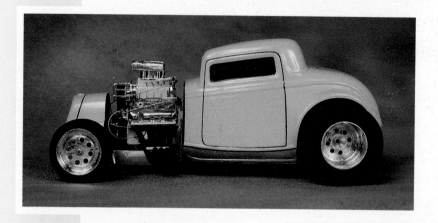

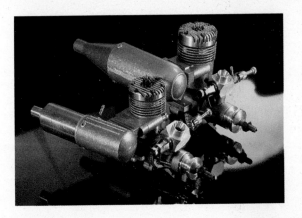

Clockwise from top right:
The *Nordic* from MRC and the
U90 Unlimited from Robbe. R/C
tank from CMI. The *Jeep
Cherokee* truck body from
McAllister. The *Jet Wave* 1/16-
scale car from Nikko. The *Kalt
Enforcer* helicopter from Hobby
Dynamics. Webra's *WE 1020*
size .61 and *WE 1022* RCS size
.40 engines

FAIRCHILD 24 38″ Wingspan
28″ Length
Cox .049 Engine Powered
A classic favorite among scale airplane buffs, the Cox .049 Fairchild provides an attractive, stable scale R/C airplane at a very affordable price.

CESSNA SKYLANE 36″ Wingspan
31″ Length
Cox .049 Engine Powered
Cox's fastest model, this "turn-on-a-dime" R/C airplane also provides the stability novices need to learn intermediate level aerobatics.

To The ARF Claim . . .

ELECTRIC SUNDANCE 55″ Wingspan
31″ Length
Electric Motor Powered
Large, glider-style wings and two-servo rudder/elevator control enable beginners to learn to fly and advance to basic aerobatic maneuvers.

TURBO CENTURION 27″ Wingspan
20″ Length
Cox .020 Engine Powered
The easiest to fly gas powered R/C airplane ever. The accompanying FailSafe radio system replaces transmitter sticks with buttons. To turn, just push the right and left buttons.

FLYBOY 27″ Wingspan
20″ Length
Electric Motor Powered
Everything possible . . . motor, radio system, rudder, push rods and even decals . . . is factory assembled. Incredibly easy to fly, the special FailSafe radio system enables anyone over 9 years old to fly.

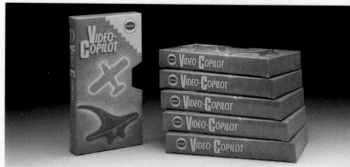

VIDEO-COPILOT™ E-Z Bee II, Electric Sundance, Fairchild 24, Cessna Skylane
Cox is the only company to include an instructional video with your airplane. Cox Video-Copilots enhance written assembly and flight instructions, helping you to correctly assemble your Cox ARF and fly successfully.

Avoid ARF Shock

COX Airplanes Live Up

Take the lid off the package of any Cox brand R/C airplane and it's immediately apparent that Cox has set the standard for the term "ARF" by providing the world's most complete, "user friendly" R/C airplanes.

Right at the factory, Cox takes care of all the difficult, time-consuming, error-prone steps that are common to the R/C airplane building process.

All the construction prevalent with other ARF brands has already been done by Cox. In fact, every Cox R/C airplane is designed with such extreme attention to ARF considerations that even the most common step in typical ARF kits, that of gluing, has been completely eliminated! All that remains is for you to assemble the finished component parts.

Purchasing a Cox R/C airplane requires no additional, costly accessories. When you purchase a Cox R/C airplane with radio, your only required separate purchases are Alkaline batteries for the radio system and, if your model is engine powered, a Cox 400 or 990 kit with fuel and starting battery. Cox electric airplanes always include Nickel Cadmium motor batteries.

Each Cox ARF is outstanding in flight. They all have different flight and performance characteristics. Read about each individual airplane and ask your local hobby store for the one that fits your needs best.

E-Z BEE II 55″ Wingspan
31″ Length
Cox .049 Engine Powered
The most stable, best flying engine powered beginner R/C airplane. Now, two servos provide independent rudder and elevator control.

Cox Hobbies, Inc.
350 West Rincon St.
Corona, CA 91720
©Cox Hobbies, Inc. 1991

Clockwise from top right: hitec's *Windcruiser* electric-power airplane kit. *Big John* biplane built by Fred Coleman of WRAM. Cox Hobbies' *Turbo Centurion.* *Rudder Buf* built by Jimmy Grier from the Vintage RC Society.

Clockwise:
U.S. AirCore's *Classic 40* with optional floats. *Live Wire Trainer,* a famous Hal DeBolt design, shown with Bob Langelius. This old-time control line design was converted to R/C by Leon Shulman. Photographs supplied by the Vintage RC Society.

TEAR OUT OF THE PACK-JOIN *Team* **SHREDDER**

RCD TEAM SHREDDER SPONSERS YOU!
With Price/ Performance That "TEARS UP" The Competition

RCD Team Shredder Packs— The only COMPLETE "Road Packs" out there! Every pack features RCD/Hitec's winning combination of Team Players:

■ **RCD SHREDDER RECEIVER** ■ **HITEC SPEED CONTROLS** ■ **RCD APOLLO 10 SERVO**

MONSTER PACK
■ SP-520 Speed Control
■ Shredder Receiver
■ Apollo 10 Servo

PRO- STOCK PACK
■ 1802N Speed Control
■ Shredder Receiver
■ Apollo 10 Servo

PRO- COMP PACK
■ 1802DL Speed Control
■ Shredder Receiver
■ Apollo 10 Servo

The smallest most reliable 2-Channel on the circuit.

SP 520
For Monsters

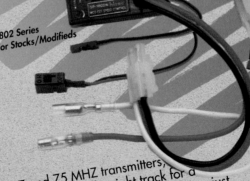

1802 Series
For Stocks/Modifieds

Apollo 10 Servo-
Powerful, Fast
5 pounds of thrust
under 1/5 of a sec.

To
"TEAR 'EM UP"
Call For More
Information:
1 800 "NOW GO RC"
(1-800-669-4672)

Runs with most 2-Channel AM 27 and 75 MHZ transmitters, RCD "Team Shredder" Race Packs get you on the right track for a winning price. So, whether you're out to "Shred the Competition" or just "Cruising for Fun", we have the performance pack for you!

© RCD 1991

Radio Control Development, Inc.
9419 Abraham Way • Santee, CA 92071
Ph: (619) 449-1112 • FAX: 449-1002
Distributed In Canada by Hobbycraft Canada
(416) 738-6557 FAX 738-6329

RCD™

What Radio Control System Should I Buy?

Before you make a decision on what type of radio you should buy, you should ask yourself these questions:

How far do I plan to get into the hobby?
What type of model will the radio be used in?
How much money am I willing to spend?
Can the same radio be used on more than one model?

Needs to consider

What type of modeler am I? Beginner, sport, advanced, or FAI/competition modeler? Knowing your needs is important because radio control systems are available in many levels and types.

Almost all manufacturers market two-channel and four-channel AM aircraft or surface model systems for the entry-level modeler where price is the primary factor. A four-channel and six-channel FM or PCM aircraft system is designed for entry or sport level flyers. The five- and seven-channel FM or PCM aircraft systems are for the advanced modeler and the nine-channel PCM aircraft radios are for the serious FAI/competition aircraft modeler.

Beginners' needs are generally very modest. The model should be very simple whether it is a boat, car, or aircraft. These basic systems are available from all manufacturers. Since everyone is different, an individual may benefit by selecting the next higher level radio, if he plans to move up to more complex models. This decision may save money in the long run.

We recommend that a beginner start with an entry/sport or a deluxe radio. Avoid top of the line FAI/competition radio control systems because experience is needed to use the features of the model itself and to program the various special advanced features of the transmitter. Sport or advanced modelers on the other hand, can take advantage of entry/sport radios, deluxe, or FAI/competition radio control systems depending on the application.

Your budget will help determine the type of model with which you decide to get started. The more complicated the model, the more expensive the hobby becomes in dollars and time spent.

What type of model?

Boats and cars: A minimum of two channels are required for basic function boats and cars. If your boat has special features, it will require an additional channel for each feature. A two-stick, two-channel or pistol grip AM system is used for this application. FM and PCM systems are available for the advanced modeler.

Gliders: Gliders generally use only two channels, elevator and rudder. However, high performance gliders can require more channels depending on the special features such as flaps and spoilers. In addition, advanced-level gliders now require special transmitter mixing functions to achieve higher levels of glider performance.

Generally, a transmitter that has a two-axis stick to allow elevator and rudder to be controlled from one stick is preferred. A four-channel AM, FM, or PCM system is your answer, however, a two-stick, two-channel system can be used if price is a major concern.

Power planes: Basic power planes with a high wing require four channels: aileron, elevator, throttle, and rudder control. Sport planes are mid- or low-wing planes that use four channels. Advanced planes can have retractable landing gears, flaps, and many more functions.

Some planes require special advanced transmitter mixing such as elevons or V-tail mixing. A four-channel AM, FM, or PCM system is all that is required. Features should be selected based upon budget and needs.

Helicopter: The line of helicopters currently available, with rare exception, are collective pitch type which means they require five channels and special collective pitch mixing in the transmitter. Advanced-level, high-performance helicopters still only need five channels but require transmitters with special mixing functions usually found in deluxe or competition-level radio control systems.

To effectively fly current helicopters, a transmitter that is specifically designed for helicopters is required. These systems are usually FM or PCM type radios to minimize the effect of metal to metal noise found in helicopters.

How much money to spend?

Radio control systems are now very reliable and of high quality. From today's entry-level systems to the most expensive competition systems reliability and quality are equal. The price difference between the least expensive and the most expensive system of a given manufacturer lies in the number of its features, not due to better reliability or higher quality. Select your radio based on your needs.

What features do I need?

The features you decide on for your radio will depend on the model you select and your budget. Radio manufacturers have made the selection easier with products tailored to specific groups of modeler needs — whether beginner or advanced competitor. Multi-task radios such as the Futaba FP-7UAP Super 7, are deluxe-level radios with special advanced features that enable a modeler to fly power planes, helicopters, or gliders from one transmitter rather than having multiple transmitters.

Frequency: Select a frequency that is suitable for your model. For surface models, a frequency on the 27 MHz band or channel on the 75 MHz band are FCC legal. Aircraft operate on the 72 MHz band. Surface and aircraft models operate on separate frequency bands to eliminate the possibility of crashes between the two groups when they are nearby. It's a good idea to check with local modelers for "good" frequencies to operate on.

Individuals who have a valid Amateur Radio Operators license can use systems on the 50 or 53 MHz bands.

Modulation and Data format—AM/FM, PPM/PCM: There are two methods of carrying information to the receiver. One is called AM (Amplitude Modulation) and the second is FM (Frequency Modulation). Both are effective in getting information to the receiver. However, FM is characteristically better in limiting electrical noise interference on data being transmitted and allowing transmitters to meet AMA transmitter narrow band specifications.

The data that is sent can be either PPM (Pulse Position Modulation) or PCM (Pulse Code Modulation). In a basic sense, PPM, sometimes called pulse width modulation, is analog information much like the signal that is used on phonograph records. Like records, the signal is affected by electrical noise and other RF interference which lengthens or shortens the control signal much like dust or dirt will affect the sound of a record.

PCM is a digital signal like that used in compact discs. Analog information is converted in the transmitter to digital code for transmission. Electrical noise and RF interference cannot alter the digital code just as dust and dirt will not alter the sound of a CD.

A microprocessor in the receiver processes the data received for errors. Should the information be damaged due to noise or RF interference, the microprocessor will go into a "hold" mode until good data is received.

Some PCM systems also have a failsafe feature in which servos will go to a preset position programmed by the user.

Servo Reversing: This transmitter feature allows the servo travel direction to be reversed by a switch in the transmitter or by software in computer-type transmitters. Servo reversing helps to make servo linkage hookup easy because it allows you to position servo and linkage for efficient movement without concern for servo travel direction.

Trainer function: Trainer capability allows the connection of two compatible transmitters. One is used as the master and the other as a trainer. This feature makes learning easier since the transmitter is not passed between instructor and student. A convenient switch is triggered to pass control of the model.

Advanced transmitter features:

Dual Rate electronically reduces servo throw with full control stick or wheel throw.

Exponential rate provides non-linear servo response and is used to reduce servo sensitivity close to neutral (sometimes referred to as end point adjustment).

ATV (Adjustable Travel Volume) lets you preset the maximum travel of a servo either side of neutral (sometimes referred to as end point adjustment).

ATL (Adjustable Throttle Limit) allows the throttle trim to function at low throttle settings. High throttle end point does not change.

Special advanced transmitter mixing—for planes: elevon mixing, V-tail mixing, Differential Ailerons, Flaperons; *for helicopters:* pitch mixing, invert mixing, throttle hold, idle up, revolution mixing.

The final choice

Whatever your needs, there is a radio control system that is tailored to your specific requirements. It is always wise to find someone you feel confident with and who is knowledgeable and experienced with radio control models to share experiences with.

Our thanks to Futaba Corporation of America for providing this information.

Radios

Aircraft Up to 4 Channels

ACE R/C, INC.

The *Olympic V Dual and Single Stick* (Retail: See your dealer) is an American-made alternative to the plastic imports. It was originally introduced with the standard dual stick configuration, but is now available in a single stick version also. The Olympic V comes standard with four channel servo reversing. A fifth channel and up to three dual rates are optional. The Olympic V has NiCads throughout and it comes less servos. System includes: Transmitter with NiCads, Receiver, Receiver NiCad pack with Switch Harness, System Charger, Deans Servo Connectors and Frequency Flag.

ARISTO CRAFT/POLK'S MODEL CRAFT HOBBIES INC.

The *2 Channel Radio*, which features a 1 oz. micro receiver that is the size of a quarter, is our very best servo. This radio is full featured with servo reversing, battery, charging jack, and LED metering of battery voltage. The servo is high quality with top and bottom bearings, and a high speed Mabuchi motor. This makes this servo the best offered in any two channel radio. The receiver is as small and light as specialty receivers that sell for far more than the price of our total radio. The connectors are industry compatible, and are of the highest grade as well.

COX HOBBIES, INC.

The *Cobra & Cobra III* are 2- and 3-channel, 72 Mhz radios that include advanced circuitry, servo reversing switches, and nickel cadmium Tx charging ports as outstanding features. Two servos. Order No. 918320A for Cobra Gold "AA" Battery Box, No. 918320D for Cobra Gold "AAA" Battery Box, No. 918330A for Cobra Three Gold "AA" Battery Box, and No. 918330D for Cobra Three Gold "AAA" Battery Box.

Now a new narrow band, dual conversion 1991 receiver with the latest in AM design concepts that exceeds AMA requirements and features SMT (surface mount technology) highly complements the Gold label approved Cobra 2 and 3 channel transmitters.

FUTABA

The *2NCS* ($89.95 retail) is a 2-channel dual stick system. R102JE BEC receiver, two S148 servos are included. 75 and 72 (aircraft) MHz.

FUTABA

The *4NBP Conquest* ($359.95 retail) is a four-channel PCM aircraft system. Included are R124DP receiver, three S148 servos, adjustable sticks, servo reverse, trainer system. All NiCad. 50 and 72 MHz.

FUTABA

The *4NBF Conquest* ($249.95 retail) is a four-channel FM aircraft system. It includes R127DF receiver, three S148 servos, adjustable sticks, servo reverse, trainer system. All NiCad. 50 and 72 MHz.

FUTABA

The *2NBR Attack R* ($114.95 retail) is a 2-channel dual stick system. It includes R102JE BEC receiver, two S148 servos, servo reverse. 27, 75, and 72 (aircraft) MHz.

FUTABA

The *4NBL Attack G* ($259.95 retail) is a 4-channel glider system. Includes R114H receiver, two S133 servos, servo reverse, 250mAh and transmitter NiCad. 72 MHz.

FUTABA

The *4NBL Attack E* ($299.95 retail) is a 4-channel electric system. Included are MCR-4A receiver/speed control, two S133 servos, servo reverse. Transmitter NiCad. 72 MHz.

Safety is no accident

FUTABA

The *4NBL Attack S* ($244.95 retail) is a 4-channel aircraft system. Includes R114H receiver, three S148 servos, servo reverse. Transmitter NiCad. 72 and 75 (surface) MHz.

HOBBY DYNAMICS DISTRIBUTORS

The *JR Max 4 AM* ($199.99 retail) has quality and dependability in a system that's great for beginners and experts alike. Besides ABC&W receiver, Tx and airborne NiCads, NiCad charger, complete servo accessories and hardware, the Max 4 has four channels, three servos, and has been 1991 approved for narrow band frequency (72 MHz).

HOBBY DYNAMICS DISTRIBUTORS

The *JR Max 2* ($79.99 retail) is an economical two channel style radio with two servos. 27-75 MHz. It comes with standard servo and Max series case.

HOBBY DYNAMICS DISTRIBUTORS

The *JRHD2C* ($69.99 retail) is a 2-channel, 2-servo radio that offers trims on both channels. It has ABC&W receiver and BEC-battery eliminator circuitry.

HOBBY DYNAMICS DISTRIBUTORS

The new *Max 4 FM* (No. JRP41, Mode 1 and No. JRP42, Mode 2; $249.99 retail) is the perfect training radio and has an ABC&W 7-channel receiver to provide added flexibility. The Max 4 FM also has servo-reverse and comes complete with three JR 507 servos. It's proven '91 Super Narrow Band Transmitter ensures performance for years to come! Frequency: 72 MHz.

Radios

Aircraft 5-6 Channels

FUTABA

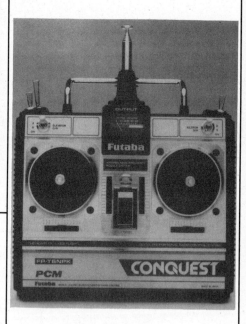

The *6NPK Conquest* ($459.95 retail) is a 6-channel PCM aircraft system. Included are R127DP receiver, four S148 servos, adjustable sticks, retract switch, dual rates (2), servo reverse, trainer system. All NiCad. 50 and 72 MHz.

FUTABA

The *5UAP* ($499.95 retail) is a 5-channel PCM 1024 aircraft system. Included are R129DP receiver, four S148 servos, control panel with ATV, dual rate and servo reverse, plug-in RF module, trainer system. All NiCad. 50 and 72 MHz.

FUTABA

The *6NHP* ($599.95 retail) is a 6-channel PCM helicopter system. Includes R128DP receiver, four S148 servos, invert switch, dual rate (2), mixing, servo reverse, plug-in RF module. All NiCad. 50 and 72 MHz.

FUTABA

The *6NFK Conquest* ($329.95 retail) is a 6-channel FM aircraft system. It includes R127DF receiver, four S148 servos, adjustable sticks, retract switch, dual rates (2), servo reverse, trainer system. All NiCad. 50 and 72 MHz.

FUTABA

The *5NLH* ($399.95 retail) is a 5-channel FM helicopter system. It includes R128DF receiver, four S148 servos, mixing (30), AST (2), hover memory (fixed), throttle hold, idle up, servo reverse. All NiCad. 50 and 72 MHz.

HITEC R/C USA, INC.

Hitec R/C USA announces the release of the exciting new Focus Series radio systems. Four systems are available for R/C aircraft. These include the *FOCUS-4* (No. HRS2200) a four-channel standard; the *FOCUS-4E* (No. HRS2400) a four-channel electric; the *FOCUS 6* (No. HRS3200) a 6-channel; and the *FOCUS HELI-5* (No. HRS2800) a 5-channel helicopter. The Focus systems include the latest SMT design and component technology to assure the modeler of a top quality, yet affordable, system. Exclusive features include the popular RCD Platinum receiver, high-quality precision gimbals with adjustable stick length and tension, Sanyo NiCad airborn pack, and an ergonomically-designed transmitter case for fatigue-error-free operation. All systems are AMA listed 1991 FM, dual conversion, and RCMA gold-stickered.

HOBBY DYNAMICS DISTRIBUTORS

The *Max 5 Radio Systems* ($299.99 - $399.99 retail) emerge as one of the highest quality systems available in today's market. Available in FM helicopter, FM aircraft and PCM aircraft, the Max 5 is fully engineered to operate in the narrow band radio signal environment of 1991 and beyond. These 5-channel radios have four servos in the aircraft systems, five in the heli version. Frequencies: 72, 50, 53 MHz.

HOBBY DYNAMICS DISTRIBUTORS

The *JR Max 6* ($479.99 - $579.99 retail) is a 6-channel radio system that combines computer technology and JR sophistication for first-class performance. Choose heli or aircraft, both are loaded with features and engineered to operate in the narrow band radio signal environment of 1991 and beyond. Frequencies: 72, 50, 53 MHz.

HOBBY DYNAMICS DISTRIBUTORS

JR's new system, the *Max 6 FM* (No. JRP61, Mode 1; No. JRP62, Mode 2; $319.99 retail), has an ABC&W 7-channel receiver for added flexibility and a trainer function for easy, safe learning. Other features include servo-reverse, dual rates, three-position flap switch, and retrace switch. Frequencies: 72, 50, 53 MHz.

KYOSHO

The *Kyosho Series 91 Advance Radios* (No. KYO30**, 7-channel FM, $319.95 retail; No. KYOJ30**, 5-channel PCM, $299.95 retail) are now available in a 7-channel FM and a 5-channel PCM configuration. The Advance 7-channel system is 1991 certified. It includes a dual conversion narrow band FM receiver, two auxiliary channels, select V-tail control or aileron/rudder mixing, and servo reversing. It comes with four KS100 servos. The same features are found on the Advance 5-channel PCM system.

Radios

Aircraft 7-8 Channels

FUTABA

The *7UHFS* ($649.95 retail) is a 7-channel FM helicopter system. Included are R128DF receiver, four S5101 servos, computer LCD screen, ATV, dual rate, exponential, programmable mixing, timer, invert switch, hover memory, pitch mixing, tail rotor mixing, servo reverse, memory, trainer system, plug-in RF module 1000mAH receiver NiCad. 50 and 72 MHz.

FUTABA

The *7UAPS* ($699.95 retail) is a 7-channel PCM 1024 aircraft system. Included are R129DP receiver, four S148 servos, computer LCD screen, ATV, dual rate, exponential, programmable mixing, timer, snap roll (4), servo reverse, memory, plug-in RF module, trainer system. All NiCad. 50 and 72 MHz.

FUTABA

The *8SSA* ($999.95 - $1,079.95 retail) is an 8-channel PCM single stick system. Included are R128DP receiver, four S5101 servos, dual rate, VTR (3), mixing (7), ATL, ATV, DSC, servo reverse, tachotimer, plug-in RF module. All NiCad. 50 and 72 MHz. (Also available with four S9201 servos.)

FUTABA

FUTABA

HITEC R/C USA, INC.

Hitec's Master-7 (No. HRS1400, $299.95 retail) is a top-of-the-line 7-channel FM system which features ATV for all 4 main channels, dual rates on elevator and aileron, vee tail and elevon mixers, 1-4 and flap mixing and hitec's innovative "Master-Student" trainer cable system. Included with the Master-7 is the RCD receiver, 4 HS-422 servos, all NiCad and plug-in RF module. AMA listed and RCMA gold stickered.

HOBBY DYNAMICS DISTRIBUTORS

The *8SSH* ($1,179.95 retail) is an 8-channel single stick PCM helicopter system. Includes R128DP receiver, five S9201 servos, invert switch, dual rate/VTR, mixing, ATL, ATV, DSC, servo reverse, tachotimer, plug-in RF module 1000mAH receiver NiCad. 50 and 72 MHz.

The *7UAFS* ($499.95 retail) is a 7-channel FM aircraft system. Included are R128DF receiver, four S148 servos, computer LCD screen, ATV, dual rate, exponential, programmable mixing, timer, snap roll (4), servo reverse, memory, plug-in RF module, trainer system. All NiCad. 50 and 72 MHz.

HITEC R/C USA, INC.

The *Master Heli-7* (No. HRS1500, $439.95 retail) is a full house 7-channel heli system featuring hovering throttle and pitch controls, tail rotor rev mixing, full pitch curve control, high idle and throttle hold and dual rates for aileron, elevon, and rudder. Standard equipment includes 5 servos, whip-style antenna, and 1000 mah battery pack. Exceeds all 1991 guidelines.

The *JR X-347* ($644.99 - $699.99 retail) is a revolutionary radio system from JR Remote Control that has gone beyond state-of-the-art technology. This three-in-one 7-channel system is the only one of its kind. With the X-347 radio you can fly a helicopter, airplane, or glider with the touch of a finger. The X-347 also has the world's first programmable trainer system. It comes complete with the system accessories necessary to fly one of three types of aircraft (helicopter, airplane, glider). Affordable flight packs are available that allow its owner to fly additional types of aircraft. Frequencies: 50, 53, 72 MHz. Of course, it's 1991 approved. Now available in FM with choice of servos.

KYOSHO

Radios

Aircraft Over 8 Channels

The *Kyosho Series 91 Advance Radios* (No. KYO30**, 7-channel FM, $319.95 retail; No. KYOJ30**, 5-channel PCM, $299.95 retail) are now available in a 7-channel FM and a 5-channel PCM configuration. The Advance 7-channel system is 1991 certified. It includes a dual conversion narrow band FM receiver, two auxiliary channels, select V-tail control or aileron/rudder mixing, and servo reversing. It comes with four KS100 servos. The same features are found on the Advance 5-channel PCM system.

ACE R/C, INC.

The *micropro8000* (Retail: See your dealer) is a micro-processor driven transmitter that offers computer power, features, and versatility never seen before in the R/C world. In addition to all the common features of the competition, it has auto-trim, eight aircraft memory, totally universal mixing, plus extremely easy, logical layout and set-up. This single, multi-task transmitter is for all applications including pattern, helicopters, hi-tech soaring, scale, racing, and sport. That makes this computer-age transmitter the perfect solution for any R/C modeler's needs from the most demanding competition pilot with sophisticated mixing requirements to the average Sunday flier that wants to enjoy flying and not be intimidated by an overly complicated transmitter. Programmed and built by Americans so that it is understandable, not overwhelming. Trust the micro-pro8000; so advanced, it's simple.

FUTABA

The *9VA* ($999.95 - $1,079.95 retail) is a 9-channel PCM 1024 aircraft system. It includes a R129DP receiver, four S5101 servos, computer LCD screen, ATV, AFR, ATR, programmable gang mixing, variable pitch propeller mixing, dual rate (3), exponential, adjustable VTR, timer, snap roll (3), servo reversing, mutual mixing, plug-in RF module, DSC. All NiCad. 50 and 72 MHz. (Also available with four 9101 servos.)

Safety is Contagious...

FUTABA

The *9VH* ($1,199.95 retail) is a 9-channel PCM 1024 helicopter system. Included are a R129DP receiver, five S9201 servos, computer LCD screen, ATV, AFR, ATR, programmable gang mixing, pitch mixing, CCPM mixing (5), dual rate (3), exponential, adjustable VTR, four-way timer, snap roll (3), servo reverse, mutual mixing, DSC, 1000mAh receiver NiCad, plug-in RF module. 50 and 72 MHz.

HOBBY DYNAMICS DISTRIBUTORS

The *PCM-10* ($1,199.99 - $1,299.99 retail) is the latest breakthrough in a new generation of computer radios. Available in helicopter and aircraft, this radio has an endless list of functions that you have to see to believe. The PCM-10 is engineered to operate in today's narrow band radio signal environment. Frequencies: 72, 50, 53 MHz. Now available with a choice of servos.

VANTEC

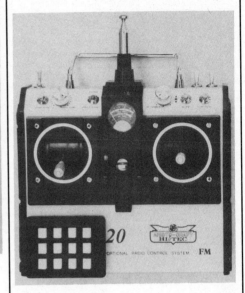

The *Keycoder* (No. KYU-18, $539.95 retail) is a modified Futaba FP-7UAF 720 radio with 18 channels consisting of six servo channels and 12 on-off channels that electrically switch up to 28V DC at 4 amps. It has air and surface frequencies.

Radios

Boat & Car

COX HOBBIES, INC.

The *Sidewinder* (No. 8250, with standard servos, No. 8251 with micro servos and "AAA" battery box; Retail: See your dealer) from Cox has been specially designed for the driver. It is perfectly angled and balanced for precise control and maximum comfort. This two-channel, two-servo radio features servo reversing switches, independent trim controls, quick changing crystals and NiCad battery charging jack. 27 Mhz only.

ALTECH MARKETING

Altech Marketing is proud to announce the latest, most stylish R/C system 2-channel pistol-grip wheel radio yet made. It's the *ACOMS Technisport AW-75 MK-III System* (No. HU168). This R/C system will set a new standard for performance and utility that will be hard to beat.

The new shape of the transmitter is designed for true hand comfort. The steering rate adjuster is conveniently located above your thumb. The trims for steering and throttle are recessed to prevent accidental bumping, as is the on-off switch and both servo reversing switches.

The BEC receiver is compact and light, yet still delivers a strong 42 ounce-inch punch of torque. With the BEC switch harness included in the set, the ACOMS Technisport R/C System is bound to be a favorite for most electric cars, trucks, and boats.

The ACOMS Technisport AW-75 MK-III 2 Channel Pistol Grip Wheel R/C System is available on 75 MHz only.

FUTABA

The *2PB Magnum Sport* ($119.95 retail) is a 2-channel pistol grip system. R102JE BEC receiver, two S148 servos, servo reverse included. 27 and 75 MHz.

FUTABA

The *2PB Magnum Sport ESC* ($169.95 retail) is a 2-channel pistol grip system with speed control. Features include R102JE BEC receiver, one S148 servo, MC112B MOS/FET electronic speed control, servo reverse. 27 and 75 MHz.

FUTABA

The *3PB Magnum* ($449.95 - $499.95 retail) is a 3-channel PCM 1024 pistol grip system. It features a R113IP receiver, two S9601 servos, electronic trim with sub trim, programmable mixing for four-wheel steering, boats, dual rate, exponential (2), servo reverse, plug-in RF module, adjustable steering lock-to-lock angle and throttle trigger position, DSC, transmitter NiCad. 75 and 27 MHz. (Also available with two S9301 or two S132H servos).

FUTABA

Futaba's *FP-3UCP Super System* for cars and boats. This PCM 1024 radio includes: R113IP/PCM 1024 receiver, two S9301 servos and transmitter NiCad power pack. Six Model Memory with car and boat software. LCD computer screen, ATV, ATL, Dual Rates, Exponential, Programmable Mix, Timer, One-Touch Key programming, servo reverse, plug-in RF module. 27 and 75 MHz. Also available with S132H servos.

FUTABA

The *2PD Magnum* ($249.95 - $299.95 retail) is a 2-channel pistol grip system. Features include a R102JE BEC receiver, two S9301 servos, dual rate, sub trim, servo reverse, ATV (2). 27 and 75 MHz. (Also available with two S9601 or two S132H servos).

FUTABA

The *2PBKA Magnum Junior ESC* ($199.95 - $214.95 retail) is a 2-channel pistol grip system with speed control. It includes a R102JE BEC receiver, one S148 servo, MC112B MOS/FET electronic speed control with reverse, steering dual rate, fine trim, throttle ATV, servo reverse. 27 and 75 MHz. (Also available with one S132H servo).

FUTABA

The *2PBKA Magnum Junior* ($159.95 - $189.95 retail) is a 2-channel pistol grip system. It features a R102JE BEC receiver, two S148 servos, steering dual rate, fine trim, throttle ATV, servo reverse. 27 and 75 MHz. Also available with two S132H servos).

HITEC R/C USA, INC.

The *hitec Challenger 260* (No. HRS0300, 75 mhz; No. HRS0310, 27 mhz) system features a reversible wheel assembly for right or left hand operation, an anti-break wheel that has a special clutch mechanism to prevent breakage. Included are 2 servos, B.E.C. receiver and dry battery holder with switch. Also available with the RCD Micro Shredder (No. HRS0500, 27 mhz).

HITEC R/C USA, INC.

The *Challenger 250* (No. HRS0100, 75 mhz; No. HRS0110, 27 mhz) is a 2-channel, two stick AM radio system for surface use. Included are two standard servos, B.E.C. receiver, dry battery holder with switch and features servo reversing for easy installation. Also available with the RCD Shredder Micro Receiver (No. HRS0400, 27 mhz).

HOBBY DYNAMICS DISTRIBUTORS

The *JR Alpina* ($118.99 retail) offers great control at a great price. The ABC&W receiver features BEC, two JR 507 servos, BEC switch harness, battery holder, interchangeable frequency crystal. Other features include servo reverse, variable rate steering, end point adjustments, throttle, and steering trims. Frequency: 27 MHz.

HOBBY DYNAMICS DISTRIBUTORS

The *JR Alpina PCM* ($139.99 retail) is our top of the line 2-channel ABC&W receiver featuring BEC, BEC switch harness, battery case, interchangeable frequency crystals, servo reverse, variable rate steering, throttle and steering trims, fail safe. Two servos. Frequencies: 27 and 75 MHz.

KYOSHO

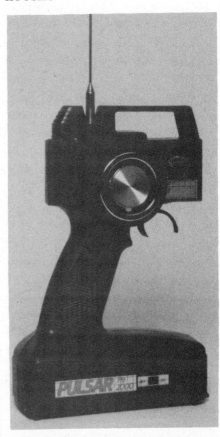

The *Kyosho Pulsar Pro-2000* (No. KYOP10**, $99.95 retail) and *EXP-2001* (No. KYOP15**, $129.95 retail) are pistol grip, 2-channel systems that capture the realism and thrills demanded by car racers. The transmitter features servo reversing, easy left/right hand conversion, and unique Precision Balanced™ design. Additionally, the EXP-2001 is equipped with variable (dual) rate steering, easy access and point adjustment, and exponential rates for steering and throttle.

KYOSHO

Kyosho's Pulsar EXP-2001 (No. KYOJ15**; Retail: See your dealer) is a 2-channel radio with 2 servos. It includes point adjustments, exponential-rate throttle and steering controls, variable steering rate control.

MRC

The *MRC 2-Channel System* (No. PK106, with BEC receiver; Retail: See your dealer) is a feature-packed part of the MRC High Performance Series ("Advanced engineering at a not-so-advanced price"). It comes with 2 channels, 2 servos, and 2 frequencies: 27 and 75 MHz, with click trims next to each stick for fine adjustments, an instant-glance battery meter, a recessed on-off switch and an easily accessible battery panel, plus a collapsible antenna, a charging jack, a carrying handle on a sure-grip case. Its sticks (with non-slip knurled knobs) are mounted on a self-centering, single-axis gimbal for smooth control. There's servo reversing and interchangeable crystals. We're really talking top performance here!

MRC

The *MRC Top Gun 2-Channel Wheel Radio* (No. PK108; No. PK109, with electronic speed control; Retail: See your dealer) is a 2-channel pistol grip radio that enables you to keep control of the action in the toughest terrain or around the tightest tracks. It's got it all—sure-grip handle; short travel trigger for speed control (from crawl to full throttle); oversized battery meter that's easy to read even in the heat of racing; servo reversing switches for both channels; 2 servos, 2 frequencies: 27 and 75 MHz. And it's a winner to use, with non-slip rubber surrounding the steering wheel and conveniently located throttle trim and end point adjustments for both sides of the throttle servo travel. There's even a recessed on-off switch to prevent accidental movements, and a charging jack in a recess in the grip!

MRC-TAMIYA

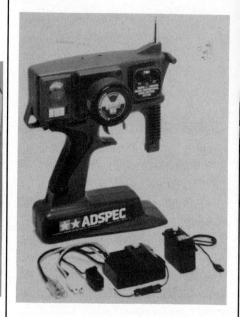

The *ADSPEC ("Advanced Specification") 2-Channel Pistol Grip Radio System* (No. RB309; Retail: See your dealer) from MRC-Tamiya has a highly sophisticated combined receiver and speed control in one package, the C.P.R. (Control Processing Receiver). It's got 2 channels and uses 2 frequencies: 27 and 75 MHz. Saving weight and space, this unit has 1 servo and 1 speed control, which eliminates the separate speed control in the model. And the ADSPEC is packed with power features: electronic trims for throttle and steering for finger adjustments, servo reversing switches, large battery meter, retractable antenna, dual rate on steering with thumb-wheel adjuster, and much more! The LCD (Liquid Crystal Display) lap timer, for instance, is built into the wheel for finger-tip control. So, write for more information and learn about how you can get utmost performance from the ADSPEC System!

VANTEC

The *Keycoder* (No. KYU-18, $539.95 retail) is a modified Futaba FP-7UAF 720 radio with 18 channels consisting of six servo channels and 12 on-off channels that electrically switch up to 28V DC at 4 amps. It has air and surface frequencies.

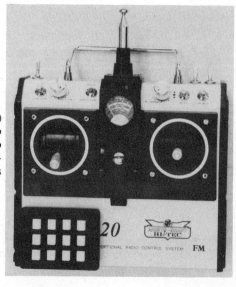

R/C RACING IS A FAMILY SPORT

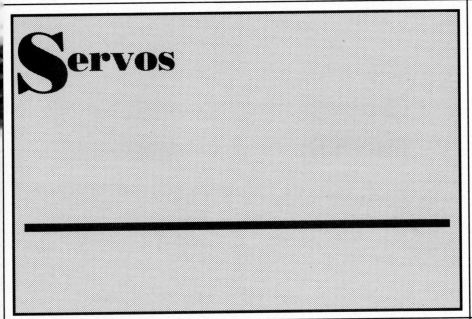

Servos

ARISTO CRAFT/POLK'S MODEL CRAFT HOBBIES INC.

The *Servo ARI 0341* (T-3360) has high speed and torque which provides high performance and reliability. One chip precision I.C. provides strong standing torque and narrow dead band and highly trackability is also stable working in low voltage. Double sided through the hole P.C. board improves durability against shock and vibration. Indirect drive for gear train protection. Precise and sturdy heavy duty gears improve high neutral position and minimal backlash. Double oilless bearing provides smooth working and especially top oilless bearing prevents wearing out of the top case plastic. Serviceable part and accessory available.

CONDOR R/C SPECIALTIES

The *MS-747WB Heavy Duty Servo* (No. 747WB, $38.95 retail) is a superior servo at a bargain price. Extensively used in costly UAVs (unmanned aerial vehicles). Features H.D. output shaft w/ball-bearing; extra strong gears, output arm and disk; O-ring sealed case and shaft. Specs: 167 oz./in torque, 0.26 sec./60° speed, 4 oz. weight, 2.15x2.05x1.05 in. size. Futaba J, Airtronics, or JR connector.

CONDOR R/C SPECIALTIES

The *SSPS-102 Heavy-Duty Watertight Servo* ($339.00 retail) for RPV/Robotics is ''reliable muscle for the big ones.'' Latest version has over 1,700 oz./in. torque, 0.7 sec./90° speed, 12 or 28V DC power. 3.60 in. high, 3.74 in. flange dia., 2.87 in. body dia., and 10 oz. weight. Compatible with all modern positive pulse R/C system.

CONDOR R/C SPECIALTIES

The *SSPS-105 H.D. Precision Servo* ($439.00 retail) ''super muscle'' gives over 5,000 oz./in. torque! 0.9 sec./90° speed, 12 or 28V DC power. Watertight die-cast aluminum case is 5.12 in. long, 2.17 in. wide, 4.37 in. O/A height, and 27.5 oz. weight. Compatible with all modern positive pulse R/C systems.

R/C Boating is a Family Sport.

COX HOBBIES, INC.

Servo/Micro Servo (No. 801020 for Standard Servo Clockwise, No. 80111 Micro Servo Clockwise; Retail: See your dealer) is preferred for small aircraft flying. Weighing less than one ounce, the Micro Servo provides powerful, exacting control.

FUTABA

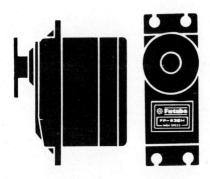

The *S132* (S32/S32L) ($54.95 retail) is a mini servo; 0.68" x 1.43" x 1.18", 1.1 oz./33.4 oz./in., 0.16 sec./60 degrees.

The *S132H* (S32H/S32HL) is a high speed mini servo; 0.68" x 1.43" x 1.18", 1.1 oz./25.0 oz./in., 0.13 sec./60 degrees.

FUTABA

The *S136G (S36G)* ($69.95 retail) is a compact landing gear retract; 0.87" x 1.75" x 1.00", 1.48 oz./76.4 oz./in., 0.50 sec./60 degrees.

FUTABA

The *S133 (S33/S33L)* ($59.95 retail) is a micro precision servo; 0.50" x 1.06" x 1.12", 0.6 oz./27.8oz./in., 0.22 sec./60 degrees.

FUTABA

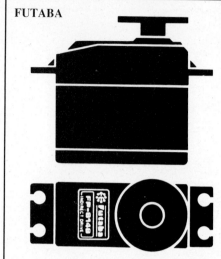

The *S148 (S48)* ($39.95 retail) is a precision servo; 0.77" x 1.59" x 1.58", 1.5 oz./42.0 oz./in., 0.22 sec./60 degrees.

FUTABA

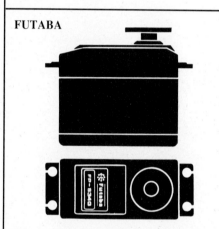

The *S134* ($64.95 retail) is a quarter-scale servo; 1.14" x 2.32" x 1.97", 2.7 oz./112.6 oz./in., 0.22 sec./60 degrees.

The *S134G (S34G)* ($74.95 retail) is a quarter scale retract; 1.14" x 2.32" x 1.97", 2.8 oz./173.8 oz./in., 0.33 sec./60 degrees.

FUTABA

The *S9201* (Air/Heli) & *S9301 (S131S)* ($79.95 retail); coreless, BB servo; 0.79" x 1.59" x 1.40", 1.7 oz./69.5 oz./in., 0.22 sec./ 60 degrees.

FUTABA

The *S9101* ($79.95 retail) is a coreless, ball bearing servo; 0.77" x 1.52" x 1.36", 1.5 oz./ 41.7 oz./in., 0.17 sec./60 degrees.

FUTABA

The *S9601 (S135)* ($79.95 retail) is a coreless, mini servo. Metal gear/ball bearing output, 0.62" x 1.21" x 1.118", 1.1 oz./36.1 oz./in., 0.17 sec./60 degrees.

HOBBY DYNAMICS DISTRIBUTORS

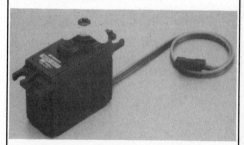

The *JR 517 Servo* (No. JRS517, $39.99 retail) is a high-torque dual ball-bearing servo. This mid-size servo has very precise centering capabilities. It also features indirect pot drive. Torque: 40.2 oz./inches. Weight: 1.70 oz.

HOBBY DYNAMICS DISTRIBUTORS

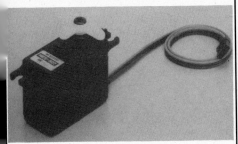

Get high speed and torque at an economical price with the *JR 507 High-Speed Servo* (No. JRS 507, $18.99 retail). Features include: high-speed, 5-pole motor; low gear ratio for power; silver-plated, triple-contact connector. The servo comes complete with a servo accessory package, servo horns, and mounting materials.

HOBBY DYNAMICS DISTRIBUTORS

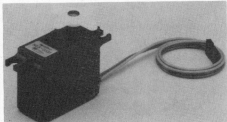

The *JR 2031 High-Torque, Coreless Servo* (No. JRS2031, $79.99 retail) has dual ball-bearing output and high-quality centerings. Its over-sized gear train provides smooth servo response under load. The JR 2031 also has gold-plated servo connectors. Torque: 61.1 oz./in.; Transit: 25 second/60 degrees; Weight: 1.6 oz.

NOVAK ELECTRONICS, INC.

The *NES-1H High Speed Servo* (No. 2120; $60.00 retail) is a high-speed precision servo with a transit time of 0.18 sec/60 degrees, 30 in-oz. of torque and will center within a half of a degree of its total throw. It features glass-filled nylon gears and a new long life feedback pot along with the Novak Input Plug System™ which allows the input harness to be compatible with the Airtronics, Futaba J, KO, Kyosho, or JR systems. Its size is 1.50" x 0.75" x 1.18" and weighs 0.98 oz.

RADIO CONTROL DEVELOPMENT, INC.

The *Apollo 20* (No. RCD920X) is a lightweight micro servo that is ideal for electrics, gliders, and many other applications with space limitations. Size: 1.25x0.55x1.2 inches; Weight: 0.95 ounces; Torque: 28 ounce/inches; 60 degree speed: 0.22 seconds; Position accuracy: 1/2 degree. Available with Futaba G, J, and Airtronics plugs.

RADIO CONTROL DEVELOPMENT, INC.

The *Apollo 05* (No. RCD905X) is an excellent sport servo featuring hard nylon output bearings. The RCD 905 is available with Futaba G, J, and Airtronics plug styles. Size: 1.43x0.79x1.6 inches; Weight: 1.55 ounces; Torque: 42 ounce/inches; Position accuracy: 3/4 degree; 60 degree speed: 0.24 seconds.

RADIO CONTROL DEVELOPMENT, INC.

The *Apollo 10* (No. RCD910X) is a pro-quality servo offering extremely tight position accuracy at 1/3 degree through its iron/oilite bearing system. Size: 1.48x0.79x 1.6 inches; Torque: 42 ounce/inches; 60 degree speed: 0.24 seconds; Weight: 1.55 ounces.

RADIO CONTROL DEVELOPMENT, INC.

The *RCD Apollo 15 Giant Scale Servo* (No. RCD915X) is ideal for large aircraft, cars, and boats. Producing 130 ounces of torque, this servo is a real powerhouse. Size: 1.97x1.14x2.3 inches; Weight: 3.5 ounces; Speed: 0.23 seconds; Accuracy: 1/2 degree; Bearing type: Ball bearing/oilite.

ROYAL PRODUCTS CORP.

The *Titan II Servo* ($16.95 retail) is a 1.87 x 1.62 x .75 in. servo and has 48.7 ounces-inch of torque. It weighs 1.8 oz. and has transit time of .24 sec./60 degrees. It will fit Futaba, Airtronics, or World and Aristo systems.

ROYAL PRODUCTS CORP.

The *Micro Titan II Servo* ($32.95 retail) is a 1.5 x 1.22 x .6 in. servo and has 27 ounces-inch of torque. It weighs .9 oz. and has transit time of .14 sec./60 degrees. It will fit Futaba, Airtronics, JR, World and Aristo systems.

ROYAL PRODUCTS CORP.

The *Shorty Titan II Servo* ($18.95 retail) is a 1.68 x 1.62 x .75 in. servo and has 44 ounces-inch of torque. It weighs 1.4 oz. and has transit time of .23 sec./60 degrees. It will fit Futaba, Airtronics, JR, World and Aristo systems.

ROYAL PRODUCTS CORP.

The *Mini Titan II Servo* ($24.95 retail) is a 1.43 x 1.43 x .69 in. servo and has 33.5 ounces-inch of torque. It weighs 1.1 oz. and has transit time of .16 sec./60 degrees. It will fit Futaba, Airtronics, JR, World and Aristo systems.

ROYAL PRODUCTS CORP.

The *Maxi Titan* ($32.95 retail) is a 2 1/4 in. x 1 3/32 in. x 2 5/16 in. servo and has 112 ounces/inch of torque. It weighs 3.7 oz. and has a transit time of .22 sec/60°, has top bearing support and fits Futaba, Airtronics, JR, World and Aristo systems.

Radios
Miscellaneous Accessories

ARISTO CRAFT/POLK'S MODEL CRAFT HOBBIES INC.

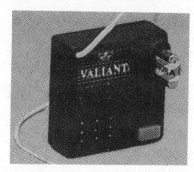

The *2 Channel Micro Receiver* is one chip I.C. design, one of the smallest and lightest in the world. Equipped with a ceramic filter to increase the selectivity while reducing interference, high-grade Crystal socket eliminates poor contact under heavy stock and vibration conditions.

CONDOR R/C SPECIALTIES

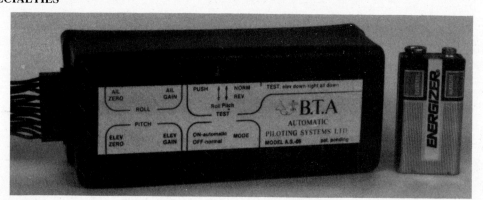

The *B.T.A. Automatic Pilot (Auto Level-izer) Model AS-05* ($330.00 retail) is aerospace technology on a R/C budget! This new "R/C autopilot" recovers your aircraft to "straight and level" flight whenever you get in trouble. Also lets you fly safely through the worst interference!

When "engaged," both pitch and roll are limited; making flying as easy as driving a car. Anybody can do it!

Use any radio with a free switching channel. Simple, plug-in installation. Only 7 ozs. and small enough, 2"x2"x5", for most .40 size models and a few .25 size.

Call, write, or fax today...the life of your model may depend on it!

CONDOR R/C SPECIALTIES

VTX-100 Video Transmitter (No. VTX-100, $300.00 retail)—miniature airborne video for R/C models! License-free, 100 mW transmission to ordinary TV on ground. Over 1/2 mile range. Just 3.5 oz. w/antenna. Only 3"x2"x3/4". Needs only videocam, switch, and 12V battery. A must for R/C aerial photography, mapping, inspection, surveillance, etc. Use any VCR to record data for post-flight thrills, analysis, history, etc. Lightweight miniature videocams also available.

DU-BRO PRODUCTS

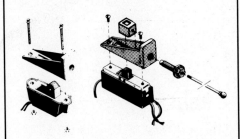

These *Aircraft/Surface Identification Flags* (No. 466, 72 MHz Red Aircraft Identification Flag, 1/pkg, $1.25 retail; No. 467, 75 MHz Yellow Surface Identification Flag, 1/pkg, $1.25 retail) are brightly colored, 1 in. wide x 8 in. long, and meet the new AMA frequency regulations. The flags come with Du-Bro Hook & Loop material that makes it easy to attach and remove from your antenna.

DU-BRO PRODUCTS

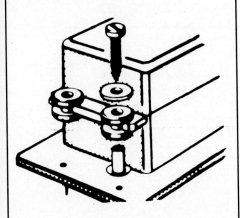

The *Kwik-Switch Mount* (No. 203, $2.50 retail) is a complete switch mounting set that enables you to install your battery switch in minutes, anywhere in the fuselage, by drilling one 1/16-in. hole! It's excellent for use in planes, helicopters, boats, and cars. The attractive, black nylon switch mount is adaptable to any wall thickness up to 3/8 in.

DU-BRO PRODUCTS

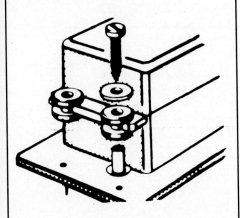

This small *Servo Mounting Hardware* (No. 114, 5 per set, $1.55 retail) contains 60 pieces (20 sheet-metal screws, 20 fibre washers, 20 spacers), enough for five servos.

DU-BRO PRODUCTS, INC.

Small servo natural rubber grommets (No. 115, $1.55 retail) come 20 per pack.

DU-BRO PRODUCTS, INC.

The *Frequency Identification Numbers* ($.60 retail, 2/pkg.) are vinyl numbers 1-1/2" high with a 1/4" stroke. The adhesive backing adheres permanently to Du-Bro No. 465 Frequency Identification Number Clip. Numbers are available in black only.
No. 455—Freq. Ident. Number 0 (2/pkg.);
No. 456—Freq. Ident. Number 1 (2/pkg.);
No. 457—Freq. Ident. Number 2 (2/pkg.);
No. 458—Freq. Ident. Number 3 (2/pkg.);
No. 459—Freq. Ident. Number 4 (2/pkg.);
No. 460—Freq. Ident. Number 5 (2/pkg.);
No. 461—Freq. Ident. Number 6 (2/pkg.);
No. 462—Freq. Ident. Number 7 (2/pkg.);
No. 463—Freq. Ident. Number 8 (2/pkg.);
No. 464—Freq. Ident. Number 9 (2/pkg.).

DU-BRO PRODUCTS, INC.

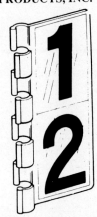

The design of the *Frequency Identification Number Clip* (No. 465, $2.20 retail, 1/pkg.) makes it easy to snap on and off your antenna. Guide lines on face of clip help to center numbers. Available in white only.

DU-BRO PRODUCTS, INC.

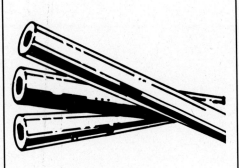

Our new *36" Antenna Housing* (No. 511, 24/tube, $.75 each retail) works great for airplanes, cars, boats, and helicopters.

DU-BRO PRODUCTS, INC.

We feel the *1/4" R/C Protective Foam Rubber* (No. 513, 1/pkg. 7x11" sheets, $2.00 retail) and the *1/2" R/C Protective Foam Rubber* (No. 514, 1/pkg., 7x11" sheets, $3.00 retail) are the highest quality on the market. It works great for protecting your receiver and fuel tank from vibration and also gives you protection during a crash.

FUTABA

The *M-TC-AM Trainer Cord* ($14.95 retail) fits 3 pin miniconnector systems (1.3 ms). The M-TC-FM Trainer Cord fits all J-connector systems (1.5 ms) and current systems.

FUTABA

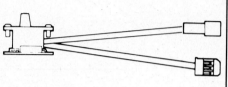

SWH-11 (Switch Harness) ($10.00 retail); J-Mini-Switch with BEC connectors.

FUTABA

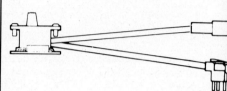

SWH-10 (Switch Harness) ($10.00 retail); Mini-Switch with BEC connectors.

FUTABA

The *NR-4M (NR-4J)* ($19.95 retail) is a flat pack NiCad. Specs are: 2.25" x 1.97" x 0.56"; 4.8V/500mAH; 3.3 oz. Parentheses indicate power packs with J connectors for 3PG/G Series—FM, J Series—PCM.

FUTABA

The *NR-5* ($29.95 retail) is a high-voltage NiCad. Specs are: 2.87" x 1.97" x 0.59"; 6V/500mAh; and 4.2 oz.

HAYES PRODUCTS

The *Hayes 12-in. Whip Antenna* (No. 186; Retail: See your dealer) is designed as a replacement antenna. For receivers with a 36-in. or longer antenna, use as is, combined with a pigtail provided. Follow directions for shorter antennas.

HITEC R/C USA, INC.

The *GY100* (No. HGY0020) bushing and the *GY100BB* (No. HGY0010) ball bearing gyro are three piece, single axis, dual rate systems designed with both the novice and expert in mind. Priced competitively with the low end single rate gyros, the GY100s offer the versatility of having two separate sensitivity rates to work with for outstanding control response.

HITEC R/C USA, INC.

Hitec's *Jam Check'R* (HMS0110) is the simplest most effective way to check for and help eliminate excessive current drain due to servo and linkage jam-ups. By plugging this unit between the receiver and battery pack when a servo is operated, a yellow or red LED will light if an excessive amount of current is drawn letting you know there is a jam.

HOBBICO

Hobbico's *Custom Radio Cases* (No. HCAP2000, $64.95 retail; No. HCAP2100, $79.95 retail) are made of high-quality aluminum to protect expensive radio equipment. Upper lid is foam-lined. Extra foam pads (included) allow for custom fitting any transmitter and they're available for single transmitter or in a double case design.

KDI

The *Stabilizor* ($49.95 retail) is the lightest, most comfortable transmitter tray ever. The brushed aluminum and oiled walnut base are not only handsome but functional. The wide non-slip neckstrap is comfortable and length adjustable. This is the tray being used by many top-notch pattern and heli flyers. It will accommodate any radio.

NOVAK ELECTRONICS, INC.

The *Stutter Stopper* (No. 5450; $12.00 retail), when plugged into the receiver's battery terminal, prevents the radio from stuttering during heavy acceleration. The Stutter Stopper acts as a memory capacitor which filters the signals to the radio system, allowing the model to run smooth. Harnessed with the two-pin JST plug, it includes the Novak Input Plug System™ making the plug compatible with the Airtronics, Futaba J, KO, Kyosho, or JR systems.

NOVAK ELECTRONICS, INC.

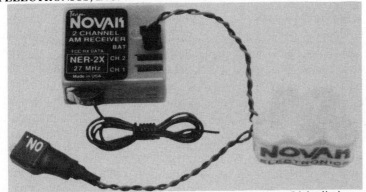

The *Micro Pack* (No. 5550; $32.50 retail) supplies constant power which eliminates common radio problems such as glitching and momentary loss of power to the receiver, and reduces motor noise in the receiver power supply line. This external battery pack consists of five 1.2 volt, 50 MAH nickel-cadmium batteries and is fully assembled with an on/off switch and a JST connector ready to plug into the battery terminal of the receiver. Recommended for use with Novak 828-HV ESC when using 14 or more cells. Includes the Novak Input Plug System™ to make the plug compatible with the Airtronics, Futaba J, KO, Kyosho, or JR system.

L.A.W. RACING PRODUCTS

The *Radio Transmitter Tray* has shoulder straps and frame assembly machined from polished, anodized aluminum. The straps are fully adjustable for a comfortable fit and are spring tensioned for easy on and off. The lightweight, ultra strong KOMATEX base plate will not conduct static electricity and is machined to fit all two stick transmitters. The transmitter is safely and securely mounted on the tray by means of a retention spring and a positive lock safety clip.

NOVAK ELECTRONICS, INC.

The *Novak Input Plug Kit* (No. 5300; $7.25 retail) will end the clutter and confusion of carrying six different input harnesses. It includes a three-wire harness and compatible plug plastics to easily make an Airtronics, Futaba J, KO, Kyosho, JR, or the two-pin JST input harness. The plug plastic simply clicks onto the wire pins.

RADIO CONTROL DEVELOPMENT, INC.

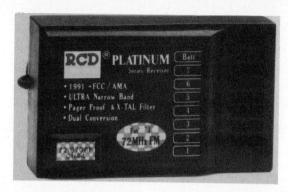

Touted as the premiere receiver in the industry, the *RCD Platinum Grade 7-Channel* offers the best in protection and reliability. These AMA 1991-listed AM and FM receivers block 2 IM, 3 IM, adjacent-channel, and pager-repeater interference. RCD Platinum Receivers are plug compatible to most 80s and 90s FM and AM Airtronics, Aristo, Cirrus, Expert, Futaba, and JR products. Compact and lightweight, the RCD Platinum Grade, bullet-proof receivers will fit nearly all your needs. No. RCD0100 for Futaba "G" AM, No. RCD0200 for Futaba "J" FM, No. RCD0400 for Airtronics FM, No. RCD1500 for Futaba "J" AM, No. RCD0300 for Airtronics AM, and No. RCD0600 for JR FM.

RADIO CONTROL DEVELOPMENT, INC.

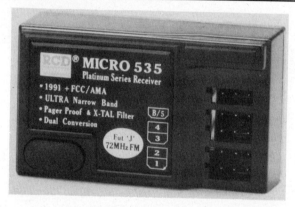

In response to the demands from racers, electric, and sailplane pilots for a small multi-channel receiver, RCD introduces the *Micro 535 FM 5-channel dual conversion receiver*. Smaller than most 2-channel receivers, the 535 weighs less than an ounce yet still offers the same outstanding "bulletproof" performance as the 7-channel RCD Platinum receivers. The Micro 535 surpasses all AMA 1991 guidelines and will be available with most popular connectors. No. RCD2200 for Futaba "J" FM, No. RCD2500 for Hitec FM, No. RCD2400 for Airtronics FM, and No. RCD2600 for JR FM.

TEKIN ELECTRONICS

The *Tekin TER 75 Professional Receiver* is designed specifically to reject electric motor noise. All receivers have new ceramic crystal filters which dramatically increases rejection of other transmitters operating on a frequency close to yours. These receivers are small and very light and use new Futaba J plugs and Airtronics plugs. KO plugs may also be used with minor modifications to the plug. FM version (world's smallest) due soon.

NOVAK ELECTRONICS, INC.

Introducing the Novak *NER-3FM*. A compact, 3-channel, narrow band FM receiver for use in all surface model applications. The NER-3FM is specifically designed for use with electronic speed controls and is compatible with all popular FM transmitters—including Futaba's 1024 PCM and Airtronics' CS2P and Caliber 3P transmitters. Features low voltage operation to prevent annoying glitches during heavy acceleration and to minimize adjacent channel interfere. This receiver works on 20 kHz channel spacing and is immune to pager frequencies. The 3FM is offered with the Futaba J type plug. Airtronics' servos and speed control harnesses are easily converted by use of the included Futaba J type plug plastics. Available on the 27 and 75 Mhz frequency bands with a user-friendly 18 inch antenna. The 3FM has the ability to use a Direct Servo Controller (DSC) harness. Made in the U.S.A. Size: 1.39" x 1.42" x 0.57". Weight: 0.58 oz.

Batteries

A & D RACING PRODUCTS

Having just won another national championship, *A & D Select Cells* (price varies with match time) are fast becoming the batteries of choice for serious racers. All of the cells are conditioned to enhance both voltage and run time, and matched on the third cycle to within three seconds before being shipped out. For stock class racing, A & D recommends the Sanyo SCR cells because of their high-voltage output. A & D Select Cells are available in 4-, 6-, and 7-cell packages of individual cells.

AEROTREND PRODUCTS

Monster Truck Battery Packs from Aerotrend are 2000 and 4000 mah battery packs to fit your truck or boat—including the very popular "CLODBUSTER" and a special 4000 mah pack for the "DOUBLE DARE."

AEROTREND PRODUCTS

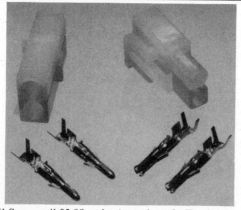

The *Gold Plug Set* (Special $2.25! Sug. retail $2.99 and up) consists of a Tamiya-type male and female plug and gold connectors. Each connector is stripped, then copper plated, then nickel plated, and finally finished in gold. This process produces a superior connector giving you exceptional performance. Gold Plug Set is stock no. 3901 (2 male connectors only—No. 3903). The Gold Plug Set is also available with "VERIFLEX" wire—No. 3913. "VERIFLEX" wire is high-quality, multi-strand 14-gauge silicone —No. 3915 (4 feet of red and black wire per package).

AEROTREND PRODUCTS

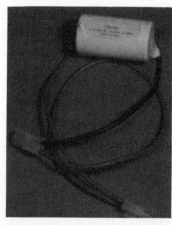

Add the *"X-Tra Cell Set-Up"*—On Sale! (Nos. 3020, 3021, and 3022, $12.99 - $24.99 retail) to increase your car's speed. It comes in 1200mah, 2000mah, and 4400mah.

BUD'S RACING PRODUCTS

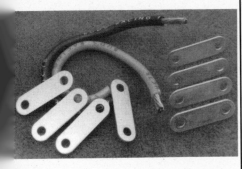

Battery assembly *Bud's Barz* (No. 6924, $5.95 retail) are 1% silver bearing, 1/2 hard copper, silver-plated for easy soldering, have better conductivity, and are corrosion resistance. Bud's 14 GA silicone wire included for assembly of saddle packs! Also bulk Barz available (No. 6923, $22.50 retail).

DURATRAX

Duratrax now offers an incredible price on *SCR and SCE Battery Packs* (No. DTXC2025, $39.95 retail; No. DTCS2030, $45.95 retail; No. DTCS2035, $57.95 retail). Available in 6- and 7-cell 1400 mAh packs, 6-cell 1700 mAh battery packs are also available. The SCRs are perfect for fast charge and discharge applications for both stock and modified racers. The 1700 mAh SCE packs are great for high-drain modified motors where the driver needs a slight advantage for run times.

DURATRAX

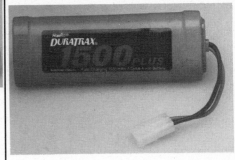

The new *1500mAH Plus Batteries* ($24.95 retail) are now available from Duratrax. They are offered in 6-cell and 7-cell packs as well as in flat or hump styles. Duratrax 1500mAH cells are available with Tamiya and Kyosho connectors.

DURATRAX

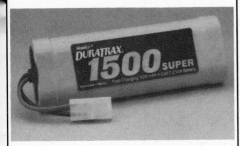

The *Duratrax/Sanyo 1500 Super Battery Packs* (Nos. DTXC2050, DTXC2055, DTXC2060, DTXC2065) are available in 6 or 7 factory matched cell packs. Sanyo 1500 mAH cells are incased in bright yellow shrink wrap with Kyosho or Tamiya connectors. Duratrax Super Packs are a step-up—"premium quality" from the "economy" battery pack at a low price.

GONZO PRODUCTS/AKS DISTRIBUTING

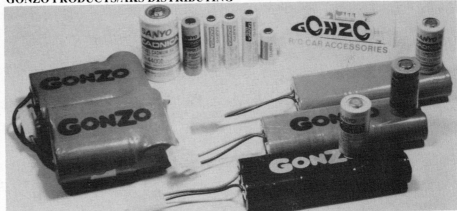

Gonzo Batteries (Retail: See your dealer) feature computer matched Sanyo NiCad SCR and SCE batteries in 4, 6, and 7-cell packs unassembled, and 6-cell assembled packs with Tamiya connectors. Also Sanyo "D" 4400 mah 6-cell packs for the Clodbuster, Sanyo "AA" transmitter batteries from 550 mah to 700 mah. Gonzo products are available through AKS Distributing.

HOLESHOT RACING PRODUCTS

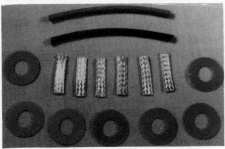

Our *24KT Gold Braided Wire Battery Kit* (No. 7000, $4.79 retail) will give your batteries more current flow due to less resistence and better conductivity, plus no corrosion. Each kit includes enough material to assemble up to a seven-cell pack. Kit includes six one-inch 24KT gold plated braided wire; six plastic insulators; two three-inch 13 gauge wire. Also available are 100/bag 24KT braided wire.

HORIZON HOBBY DISTRIBUTORS, INC.

The *Dynamite 6-Cell Stick Packs* (No. DYN1000, $32.95 retail; and No. DYN1100, $44.95 retail) and the Dynamite 7-Cell Stick Packs (No. DYN1050, $37.95 retail; and No. DYN1150, $52.50 retail) use top-quality Sanyo cells for maximum performance. The Nitro Sticks use Sanyo's KR cells (1300 mAh), which have slightly higher capacity. Both 7-cells and 6-cells are available. The Dynamite Nitro Stick XL uses Sanyo's SCE cell (1700mAh) which results in one third longer run time.

HORIZON HOBBY DISTRIBUTORS, INC.

The *Dynamite 1400 SCR Sport Pack* (No. DYN1010, $24.95 retail) is perfect for sport or fun drivers. This economical 6-cell stick pack features rugged 1400mAh Panasonic cells, welded tabs, and a special end cap that allows wire clearance in cars such as the RC10 and JR-X2.

BATTERIES

HORIZON HOBBY DISTRIBUTORS, INC.

The *Dynamite 7-Cell Hump Pack* (No. DYN1060, $37.95 retail and DYN1160, $52.50 retail) adds to the range of top-quality Sanyo-cell battery packs available from Dynamite. These Dynamite packs have a 7-cell hump configuration that's perfect for the RC10. The Nitro Stick pack uses economical, high-performance Sanyo KR cells; the Nitro Stick XL uses Sanyo's special SCE cells for an extended run time. Hump packs are available with an unprecedented end-cap design that allows the lead wires to be located either horizontally or vertically without chafing the wires. This makes the battery perfect for cars such as the RC10, where battery caps can put tremendous strain on ordinary batteries.

KYOSHO

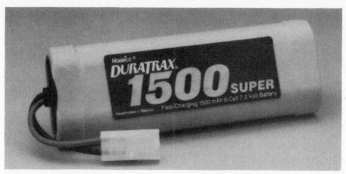

Kyosho Power Battery Packs (6-cell packs, $27.95 retail; 7-cell packs, $32.95 retail) are factory matched according to discharge rate to insure high capacity packs. Powerful, reliable, and affordable, Power Batteries are available in 6-cell and 7-cell flat and hump pack styles. Order No. KYOC0600 for 6-cell flat with Kyosho connector ($27.95), No. KYOC0602 for 7-cell flat with Kyosho connector ($32.95), No. KYOC0605 for 6-cell hump with Tamiya connector ($27.95), No. KYOC0610 for 7-cell hump with Tamiya connector ($32.95), No. KYOC0630 for 6-cell flat with Tamiya connector ($27.95), and No. KYOC0635 for 7-cell flat with Tamiya connector ($32.95).

HORIZON HOBBY DISTRIBUTORS, INC.

The *Dynamite Nitro Stick Battery* (No. DYN1200, $54.95 retail; and No. DYN1250, $99.95 retail) is made specifically for big trucks such as Tamiya's mammoth Clod Buster. Available in both 2000mAh (for trucks like Blackfoot) and 4400mAh (for the Clod Buster) capacities, these 7.2V, 6-cell batteries give a significantly extended run time. Only the best Sanyo cells are used in these Dynamite packs to ensure top performance and reliability.

KYOSHO

The *Kyosho 6-Cell 7.2V Racing Pack* (No. KYOC0700, $45.95 retail) and the Kyosho 7-Cell 8.4V Turbo Racing Pack (No. KYOC0707, $49.95 retail) are flat-style packs designed for high-level racing competition and feature only matched Sanyo cells for superior results. The 6-Cell Racing Pack is ideal whenever a standard 6-cell battery pack is needed. The 7-Cell Turbo Racing Pack was designed especially for the Kyosho Turbo Optima. Because of its awesome power and voltage, its use is cautioned in some 6-cell cars.

MRC

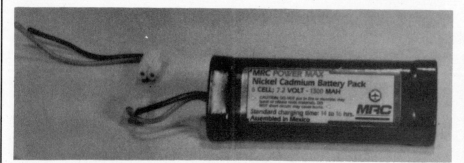

Here's the *Power Max Battery* (No. RB422; Retail: See your dealer)—the leading, longest lasting 7.2 volt flat pack battery, with the technology that gives your R/C vehicle the boost it needs to really perform! It delivers results! Actual capacity is 1400 mAH, for longer running time. It has heavy gauge wire with premium insulation and high-quality NiCad cells that are welded (not soldered) together. This means instantaneous current, for quicker torque, faster acceleration. Includes a matching 7.2 volt connector for applications with other surface vehicles, plus instructions on battery use.

MRC-TAMIYA

This *TamPack 7.2V/270 MAH Battery* (No. RG530; Retail: See your dealer) was made for the Tamtech 1/24 R/C cars by MRC-Tamiya and made only one way: excellently! Don't settle for less. Ask for the TamPack Battery for the Tamtech cars for best performance.

MRC

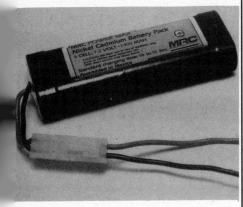

The *7.2V/1200 MAH Racing Pack* (No. RB441; Retail: See your dealer) from MRC is a long, snug battery pack for the new-wave R/C cars.

MRC-TAMIYA

Tamiya's *8.4V/1200 MAH Gold Power Battery* (No. RB439; Retail: See your dealer) has seven 1.2V cells for peak performance plus a special connector and internal circuit breaker.

STAGE III

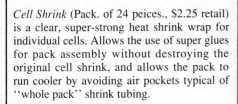

Cell Shrink (Pack of 24 peices., $2.25 retail) is a clear, super-strong heat shrink wrap for individual cells. Allows the use of super glues for pack assembly without destroying the original cell shrink, and allows the pack to run cooler by avoiding air pockets typical of "whole pack" shrink tubing.

PARMA INTERNATIONAL

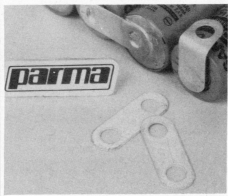

Big Mama Battery Bars (No. 11504, $3.95/6 retail) are silver-plated for maximum power flow. They are easier to solder on than braid, and look neater too. Remember power = voltage x current; increase your car's power, use Parma's "Big Mama" battery bars.

PROCELL

Procell Batteries—stocking 1200, 1400, and 1700 MA Sanyo batteries—now being matched at a 20 amp discharge with clearly marked labels. Neatly packaged in clear packages with bright color Procell header cards. Contact Procell at (1-800) 966-1616.

PARMA INTERNATIONAL

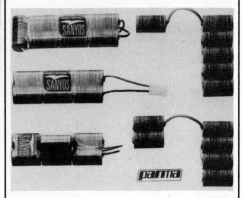

Parma/Sanyo Racing & Sport Packs. Parma batteries are available in unmatched, matched, or the new Final Match™ versions in dozens of configurations for every R/C application.

11210—24 bulk matched, Sanyo SCE $180.00

11211 "AA" Rechargeable batteries, Sanyo —$25.00/8

11212—24 bulk matched 1400 MAH, Sanyo SCR—$145.00

11217—6-cell matched 1400 MAH oval saddle pack/ 5-1 set-up, Sanyo SCR—$43.00

11218—7-cell matched 1400 MAH, Sanyo SCR—$43.50

11220—7-cell matched 1400 MAH hump pack w/Tamiya plug, Sanyo SCR—$46.50

11222—7-cell super-matched 1400 MAH, Sanyo SCR—$56.50

11224—2000 MAH matched saddle pack for Clod Buster, Sanyo C—$55.00

11225—C-size 6-cell mixed fun pack, Sanyo C—$50.00

11238—6-cell super matched, Sanyo SCE— $55.00

11239—7-cell super matched, Sanyo SCE— $65.00

11253—6-cell matched pack w/Tamiya plug, Sanyo SCE—$45.95

11258A—6-cell matched oval saddle pack/4-2 set-up, Sanyo SCE—$50.00

11259—6-cell matched saddle pack, pre-assembled, Sanyo SCE—$50.00

11265—7-cell matched flat pack, Sanyo SCE—$52.50

See our latest catalogue for complete listings.

STAGE III

Stage III is an independent cell testing lab that conditions and tests new and used Ni-Cad cells for the racer serious about winning. Using *Programmable Variable Load Discharge* as a load technique (for a more representative test and match), they condition and test cells for racers, retailers, and distributors throughout the world. Stage III cells have powered four national champions to victory and have enabled the non-sponsored racers to beat the team drivers. Infinitely programmable discharging and charging circuitry has been built in to enable Stage III to simulate different use conditions (Oval, Drags, Pulling, etc.) and to allow Pulse, Linear, Reflex, and any other charging method required to satisfy specific customer requests. Daily capacity for processing exceeds 1800 cells. For state-of-the-art precision and national championship power, contact Stage III.

STAGE III

Ultrabraid (2-ft. pkg., $4.50 retail; 50-ft. roll, $90.00 retail; 100-ft. roll, $160.00 retail) high-capacity, low resistance 12 ga. 99.9% pure copper braid for maximum current flow! Used as a shunt between cells in pack assembly. Ultrabraid has the lowest cost per connection, low resistance, and flexibility too!!

UNITED MODEL DISTRIBUTORS

The *Dymond Sport Pack* (No. DYM 7013, $29.99 retail) is a 6-cell, 7.2 volt battery pack for use in cars, boats, planes, and electric helicopters. The pack is constructed of the highest quality, 1300 mah matched cells and gives unmatched performance from a pack this size.

UNITED MODEL DISTRIBUTORS

The *Dymond Mega Pack* (No. DYM 7015, $24.99 retail) is a 6-cell, 7.2 volt 1500 mAh battery pack for electric planes, cars, and boats. The *Mega Pack* is constructed with matched SAFT cells for performance and durability. The *Dymond Mega Pack* is a great battery pack for competition or fun running.

UNITED MODEL DISTRIBUTORS

The *Dymond 1700 mAh Ultra Pack* is a 6-cell flat pack that can be charged at a voltage rate suitable for 1200 mAh SC or SCR cells. This eliminates the need for special battery chargers.

PARMA INTERNATIONAL

Parma's long trusted SCRs and SCEs just got better. Our new computer matching equipment not only lets our batteries be matched according to average run time and voltage, but also to internal resistance. The internal resistance factor allows us to more accurately match the cells. Packs matched only according to run time and amps without consideration of the internal resistance, may be far from identical. Insist on Parma *"Final Matched"* Sanyo 1400 and 1700 SCRs and SCEs.

Battery Chargers

ACE R/C, INC.

The *Digipace I - Assembled* (No. 34G16B, $104.95 retail) discharges and recharges receiver and transmitter batteries simultaneously and independently. There are three transmitter voltages and two receiver voltages. This unit is available in kit form also (experience advised).

AEROTREND PRODUCTS

The *Trickle Charger* (No. 3900, Special $7.00! Sug. retail $9.99) is designed to safely charge a 6- or 7-cell NiCad battery within 10 to 36 hours. Slow charge as often as possible for longer lasting NiCads.

ARISTO CRAFT/POLK'S MODEL CRAFT HOBBIES INC.

We are showing two D.C. only peak detection *Chargers,* which are both variable rate. The standard model does everything the deluxe does, but the deluxe has built-in volt/amp meter and coulomb meter for measuring incoming current. The compact size and performance will please you. Twin L.C.D. digital displays monitor the charging status of the battery capacity and charging volt/amps at the same time. Coulomb meter measures the power flowing into the batteries, and has a read out capacity of the batteries to help rate the cells and estimate running time. Volt/amp meter displays charging V/A, and features an auto peak volte memory hold, and also displays the input volts from the power supply (12v car battery), and it allows checking any other volt sources by connecting probes to the external jacks on the panel. Peak detection charging circuit for the most reliable full charge. Adjustable constant charge rates from 2-9 amps. High efficiency heat sink. Ultra bright LED indicator that can be seen even in bright daylight. Heat resistant and tough plastic case.

COMPETITION ELECTRONICS

Competition Electronics *Turbocharger* (No. CEI 2050, Standard, $299.95 retail; No. CEI 2060, Linear, $329.95 retail) offers more than an ultra reliable battery charger. It combines a peak detecting charger, an automatic turn-off discharger, a volt meter, an ammeter, and a discharger in a single unit! Winning drivers know the importance of having matched cells in their packs and race results show that more and more drivers are winning with the Turbocharger. Available as a pulse current (standard) or a constant current (linear) model.

CONDOR R/C SPECIALTIES

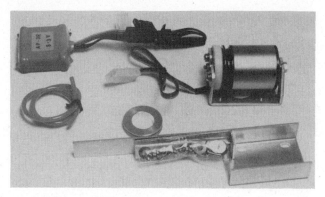

DYNA STAR AP-3 Brushless Alternator Set (No. AP-3, $139.00 retail) is a miniature, on-board alternator w/regulator for in-flight charging and powering of receiver and servos while the engine is running. Just 4.2 oz. total.

Features include no low-battery loss of control, allows use of a smaller battery pack, compensates for the heavy drain of many servos in large models, ideal for helos, fixed-wing, powerboats, enduros, and X-C, 5.3V output, 3W continuous, and 5W instantaneous.

HITEC R/C USA, INC.

The hitec *Kwick Chargers, CG-72* (No. HCG0070, 7.2 volt) and CG-84 (No. HCG0080, 8.4 volt) are for the racer on a budget. Simple and effective, these two DC to DC chargers use a mechanical 30-minute timer for charging 1200 to 1500 mAh battery packs.

CUSTOM CHROME PARTS

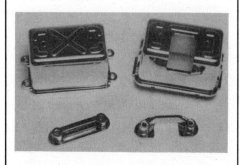

The *Clod/Bullhead Battery Covers* (No. CCP1012, $9.95 retail) comes 2 to a pack and will enhance the appearance of your monster truck, especially when used with CCP 1009 Clod/Bullhead Chrome Chassis. No better chrome plating available anywhere.

FUTABA

The *FBC-5B NiCad Charger* ($17.95 retail) is a special NiCad charger for use with Futaba's NR-41, 1000 mAh, 4.8V power supply, and has a LED charging indicator.

HITEC R/C USA, INC.

Hitec's lowest priced DC peak charger, *CG-315* (No. HCG0010), features a constant 3.4A rate and can handle 5 to 7 cell (6-8.4V) battery packs with a charge capacity of 1200-1800 mAh. One touch charging, auto trickle, and polarity protection circuitry are all standard.

HITEC R/C USA, INC.

Ideal for most field charging applications, the *CG-320* (No. HCG0015) will work with 4 to 10 cell packs from 270-1800 mAh capacity and has a variable charge current of 0.9 to 4.5A. Special features include a battery power checker which tells you the percent of charge, DC to DC power booster for batteries over 9.6V, and input power condition warning if input power drops below 12V.

HITEC R/C USA, INC.

The *CG-325* (No. HCG0020) is a top-of-the-line charger which has all the features of the CG-320 plus a discharge circuit for cycling and efficiency tester to determine the capacity of the battery being tested.

HITEC R/C USA, INC.

This hitec switching power supply, the *CG-300* (No. HCG0060), provides smooth ripple-free output for clean charging performance. Features include rush current prevention circuit, 75% power efficiency, built-in circuit breaker, and a 5A, 13.5 DC capacity.

HOBBY DYNAMICS DISTRIBUTORS

The *Hobby Dynamics AC 12V 600mAH Battery Adapter* (No. HDD103, $14.49 retail) provides the power to charge your HD 12V wet-cell or sealed battery.

KYOSHO

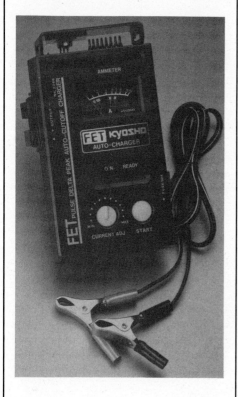

Kyosho's *FET Peak Charger* (No. KYOP1055, $139.95 retail) automatically switches to trickle charge when the battery is fully charged.

MODEL ENGINEERING OF NORWALK

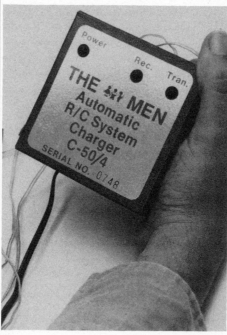

This *Automatic R/C System Charger* (No. C-50/4 (blue label 4-cell/8-cell standard model), $62.95 retail) is a state-of-the-art NiCad charger, simple to operate and super fast. It can be left connected to batteries until ready to fly (next day, next week, next year). Now the question of when to charge and how long is in the past. Batteries are charged by suitable control of pulse width and rate. Many simple tests can be performed with this charger to detect battery problems that can lead to disaster.

MRC

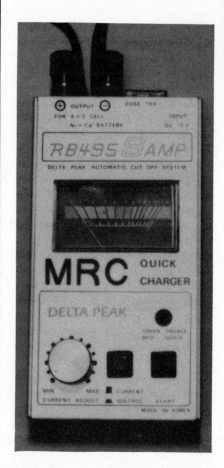

The *RB495 Delta Peak Quick Charger* (No. RB495; Retail: See your dealer), powered from 12 volts DC, uses race-car technology and can charge NiCads from 450-1800 mAH, in 4-7 cell configuration, with an adjustable current output from 1-9 amps. Standard features include a high-grade current/voltage meter, and a unique melody-maker to notify you of the completed quick-charge.

MRC

The *RB-460 Quick Charger* (No. RB-460; Retail: See your dealer) is the latest 12V DC quick-charger by MRC intended for 6V/1200 mAH batteries used in MRC-Tamiya cars. It features charge-rate of 15 minutes using auto cigarette lighter, mechanical timer, meter which gives current draw readout, and built-in discharge circuit which allows equalization and discharge of battery for peak performance.

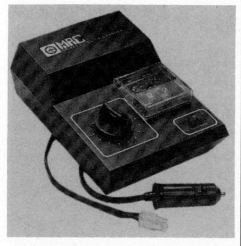

MRC

The *RB465 Quick Charger* (No. RB465; Retail: See your dealer) plugs into any wall outlet for convenient quick charging of 6V/1200 mAH NiCad packs. Features include a mechanical timer for 15-minute (or less) shut-off, and a meter which displays current input to NiCads. The meter, functional during discharge, allows judging of NiCad pack capacity and permits equalization of cells (or a safe discharge level) before pack recharge. Trickle charge circuit is now included.

MRC

The MRC *AC/DC Q.D. Quick Charger* (No. RK950; Retail: See your dealer) was engineered especially for 1/14-scale ready-to-run buggies, such as MRC-Tamiya's Q.D. series (including the Thundershot Q.D. and the Super Sabre Q.E.) that use eight 1.2 volt rechargeable NiCad batteries. It can operate from an AC wall outlet or from a 12-volt DC cigarette lighter socket. Its 15-minute mechanical timer and easy-to-read 6-0-6 amp current meter help you keep track of the condition of the battery. And a discharge mode is available to help cycle effectively and to extend the life of your batteries safely. It includes a fuse protection circuit, a trickle charge capability for topping off batteries, and a handy battery holder.

MRC

The *RB475 AC/DC Quick Charger* (No. RB475; Retail: See your dealer) can charge 7.2-volt or 8.4-volt 1200 mAH batteries quickly and safely. It comes with an AC wall outlet plug, and 12-volt DC cord with cigarette lighter or alligator clip adapter.

MRC-TAMIYA

The *TamPack Quick Charger* (No. RG532; Retail: See your dealer) is for use with 1/24-scale cars, enabling you to quick-charge your 7.2V Tampack battery in about 15 minutes using a car cigarette lighter. The charger is equipped with a timer and a pilot lamp to ensure safe trouble-free charging of your battery.

Safety is Contagious...

PORTA-POWER INDUSTRIES

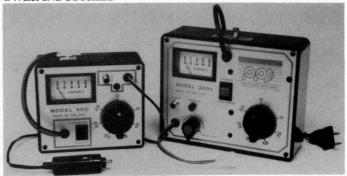

The *Model 3001 AC/DC Charger* ($75.00 retail) features: AC/DC w/adjustable current 0-6 amps for 4-8 cell packs; charges Sub "C" as well as AA, AAA, C, or D NiCads; discharge circuit; 30 minute timer; automatic switch over to trickle charge with indicator light; adjustable 75-150 ma trickle charge for slow charge or cell equalization; high tech components w/internal & external heat sinks for faster repeat cycles; voltmeter jack w/peak voltage capability (utilizing optional PPI-PVM meter); higher voltage output; fused and polarity protected. New dual charge/discharge meter. Optional "C" and "D" battery charging caddys are available with Tamiya plug. Made in U.S.A. Available with fan cooling option for heavy duty use.

PORTA-POWER INDUSTRIES

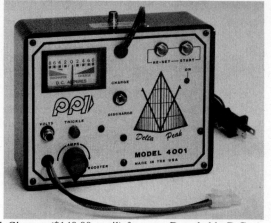

PORTA-POWER INDUSTRIES

The *Model 4001 AC/DC Super Peak Charger* ($140.00 retail) features: Detachable D.C. cord; charges 4-9 cell packs; charge/discharge meter; trickle charge w/light; voltmeter receptacle; adjustable 0-6 amps; charge/discharge mode; reset & start switch; charging indicator light; peak (Delta) voltage shut off; hi-tech circuitry eliminates false shut off from RF radio noise and AC line surges; also charges AA, C, or D, fast charges NiCads; lifetime warranty. Made in U.S.A. Available with fan cooling option for heavy duty use.

The *"Pro" Charger* ($299.00 retail) is a hi-tech electronic DC unit which can charge up to 30 cells in 15 minutes. Features include adjustable current, digital amp and volt meter, discharge circuit, mode indicators, fan cooled with vented case and carrying handle.

PRO-TECH MODEL CRAFT MFG.

The *706 and 707 AC/DC Pro-Tech Autopeak Dual Chargers* (Retail: See your dealer) from Model Craft automatically power your NiCads to peak performance. Both feature built-in peak detecting circuit with simple press button to start, four bright LED moving lights to indicate fast charge mode, automatic trickle charge circuits with green lights. The 706 has a hi-tech digital meter, the 707 a large analog meter. And both have two output lead wires (with a reverse polarity warning light) and two-way input sources —120V AC heavy duty transformer or two DC cords.

PRO-TECH MODEL CRAFT MFG.

The *701 AC/DC Charger* (No. 701, $68.50 retail) is designed to charge 4- to 8-cell battery packs. It features two DC cords, cigarette lighter plug and alligator clips. Automatic trickle charger with pilot light discharge circuit, clear DC ampere meter, volt meter jack and built-in universal output jack.

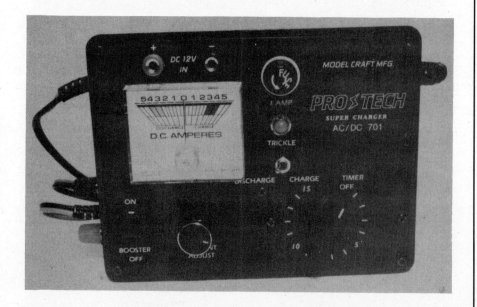

ROYAL PRODUCTS CORP.

These *Pre-Wired NiCad Packs for Off-Road Cars* ($19.95 - $28.95 retail) are for fast and slow charge. A 7.2V/1500 mah type is included with male/female connectors to fit most electric cars. It comes available in flat, camel-back, and twin-camel 8.4V hot racing packs. Its light weight and small size are features of this shrink-wrap style.

ROYAL PRODUCTS CORP.

The *Royal 12V/5.5A Wet Cell* ($17.95 retail) is top quality and has plenty of capacity to handle electric engine starters or other hobby accessories.

ROYAL PRODUCTS CORP.

This *Car Charger* ($6.95 retail) is an overnight style charger ideal for charging 6-, 7.2-, or 8.4-volt car packs. Unit comes with Tamiya-style connector and is excellent for "topping-off" a fast charge or battery maintenance charges.

ROYAL PRODUCTS CORP.

These *Battery Chargers* ($12.95 retail) are designed for wet-cell charging. They have indicator lights and the 12V model has a fuse. There are three models to choose from: 2V/1000 mah, 6V/500 mah, and 12V/600 mah.

ROYAL PRODUCTS CORP.

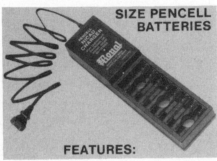

The *Pencell Charger* (No. 80-026; $17.95 retail) will charge 4 or 8 "AA" size Pencell type NiCads. Dual charging indicator lights provide charge info on multiple charging of 4 or 8 cells.

SERMOS R/C SNAP CONNECTORS, INC.

These *High-Amp Powerpole Snap Connectors* (Retail: Available from Sermos) are modular "silver-plated" connectors for your electric planes, cars, or boats. They're designed for a high-vibration environment. Cycled ten thousand times without electrical failure, they're designed for anything electrical requiring quick disconnects. Color coordinated and rated 30 amps at 600 DC, internal resistance is rated 250 micro ohms. Silver-plated contact accepts AWG sizes 12 to 16. For dealer information send to Sermos.

SCHUMACHER

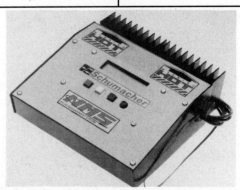

N.M.S. NiCad Management System (Part No. G-821). The N.M.S. is a charger, discharger, and cycler with data memory for 9 packs of 6- or 7-cell batteries. The charge made may be PEAK or THERMAL and features constant charge current between 2.5 and 8 amps. The discharge operates at a constant 10 amps and gives both a capacity reading in mA. Hours and a % figure compared to stored data. In this way, packs can be replaced or cycled to bring them back to life when performance falls to say 95% of new, or the gear ratio can be increased if there is over 10% capacity left at the end of the race. The N.M.S. will automatically cycle packs for reviving old packs. The memory will store information on 9 packs showing total number of charges and the best ever capacity reading. This can, of course, be reset when new packs are introduced.

TEAM CLASS RACING PRODUCTS

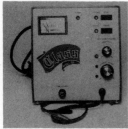

All your track-side charging needs are found in this small but powerful package. With over 8 amps of charging power, the *Class Charger* (Model 188, $239.95 retail) can really juice up your SCRs. With adjustable peak sensitivity, the Class Charger is very gentle to those delicate SCEs. The Class Charger will also break-in new motors and brushes. All this performance combined with the convenience of AC, with no need to carry bulky power supplies any more.

TEKIN ELECTRONICS

The *Tekin BC100L Linear Output Charger* (No. BC-100, $110.00 retail) is a 5 amp linear output charger that goes up to 10 amps pulsed and down to 1/2 amp to charge 50 mAh receiver packs. The BC100L is powered off 12V and can be pushed up to 10 amps for highest peak charging. It also has a trickle on/off switch. World champions, nothing gives your batteries a better charge.

TEKIN ELECTRONICS

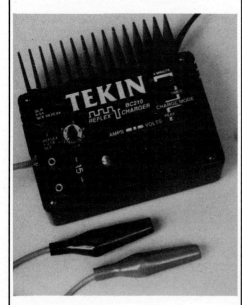

The *Tekin BC210 Peak Charger* (No. BC-210, $210.00 retail) with Pro•Flex circuit uses negative pulses to recondition worn cells, partially restoring power and run time. The BC210 Peak Charger allows recharging the same pack all day without damaging cells and with minimum loss of performance. Keeps new cells running fresh as only the Pro•Flex circuit can.

TRAXXAS

The *Max Peak II* (No. 3002) is the affordable peak-detecting charger. Now your batteries will always be perfectly charged to their maximum potential without overcharging. The Max Peak II's features include: current adjust for 4-8 cell packs, charge mode indicator lights, buzzer alert upon completion of the rapid charging cycle, and the Max Peak automatically powers down into pulsed trickle charge after the buzzer sounds. It is truly the foolproof way to charge batteries! The Max Peak II may also be used to charge your 'AA' transmitter packs.

VANTEC

This *Dual Forward/Reverse Speed Control* (No. DFRM-2 through 26 EB, $199.95 retail) has a series of dual controllers with built-in steering mixing for tanks, twin screw boats, and robots or any vehicle powered by a right motor and a left motor.

R/C RACING IS A FAMILY SPORT

VICTOR ENGINEERING

Release the ''beast'' from your racing batteries and motors with six types of Linear Chargers—cycling, grading/matching, motor conditioning/ analysis, and much more.

The *HI-IQ STANDARD* ($349.00 retail) has 9 standard functions, charges up to 15A, and discharge in excess of 15A (20A max.). Ideal for standard 10A Discharge method.

The *HI-IQ ''SENIOR''* ($449.00 retail) has 16 functions and carrying case. Designed for HI-RATE 20A Discharge method (25A max.).

The *SUPER-IQ* ($579.00 retail) is for 30A Discharge method with many new radical features. State-of-the-art.

The *IQ-POWER-1* ($139.00 retail) has a sub-compact switching power supply which delivers up to 12A, regulated 14VDC. Great for ANY CHARGER.

Many optional features are available. The most significant one is the *IQX8 8 CHANNEL MULTIPLEXER* ($399.00 retail) for up to 8 single cell—or up to 8 pack grading or conditioning. Direct printer hook-up for labels or PC hook-up for database.

FIRST, THE TURBOCHARGER.
NOW, THE TURBOMATCHER.

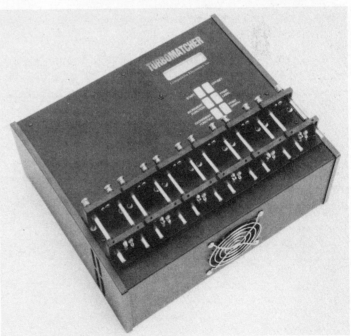

The Turbocharger offers more than a battery charger. It combines a peak detecting charger, an automatic turn-off discharger, a volt meter, an ammeter and a discharger in a single unit. Available as a pulse current (standard) and a constant current (linear) model. The linear model is specifically designed to get the optimum life out of SCE batteries.

Now, Competition Electronics introduces the Turbomatcher. The ultimate battery matcher. You can simultaneously test 6 cells in either 20-amp or 30-amp models.

Combine the Turbomatcher with a PC compatible printer using a Centronics parallel connector and get print-out labels for each cell. The second printer port will give discharge graphs.

Turbocharger and Turbomatcher obtain maximum performance from batteries to give you the winning edge.

Suggested Retail Prices:
Standard Turbocharger $299.95
Linear Turbocharger $329.95
20 amp Turbomatcher $1,395.00
30 amp Turbomatcher $1,995.00
Single-cell Battery Box $34.95

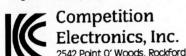

Competition Electronics, Inc.
2542 Point O' Woods, Rockford, IL 6111

(815)874-8001
FAX (815)874-8181

Testing & Cycling Equipment

C&M MFG.

COMPETITION ELECTRONICS

Competition Electronics Turbomatcher (No. CEI 2070, 20 amp, $1,395.00 retail; No. CEI 2080, 30 amp, $1,995.00 retail) is the ultimate battery matcher. You can simultaneously test 6 cells in either 20-amp or 30-amp models. Both feature automatic charge/repeak/discharge cycles. Charge setting from 2 to 10 amps. Discharge settings from 5 to 20 amps or 5 to 30 amps. Settable discharge end volts. Combine the Turbomatcher with a PC compatible printer and get print out labels and graphs for each cell.

Cobra VR3000 ($159.95 retail) for those who take the battery wars seriously! The only 30 amp variable rate battery discharger! It discharges, trains, matches, determines run time, determines best pack! This state-of-the-art discharger is microchip controlled for maximum accuracy, has Mosfets for power transfer, a variable cut-off voltage, and massive heat sink to assure optimum cooling. It has a variable discharge rate of 0-30 amps—this is a true discharge rate, not calculated! Discharge either single cells or entire packs. Use with stopwatch or optional Team Cobra Timer, the VR3000T ($99.95 retail) shown here.

COMPETITION ELECTRONICS

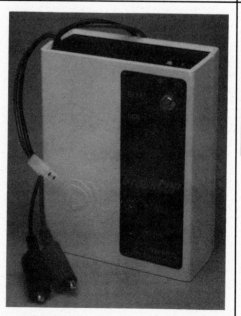

Competition Electronics StockCop (No. CEI 2100, $125.00 retail) is a cheaters nightmare. This unit checks the armature of a motor by measuring the resistance of the windings to determine if it is stock. Simply hook the StockCop up to a user provided volt meter and 6 cell SCR pack and your ready to eliminate illegal motors. Over 90% effective!

TEKIN ELECTRONICS

The *DYN 900 Digital Pro Dyno* ($350.00 retail) applies a fixed, known quantity of power into the motor. The power loss of the motor is then accurately measured. The power output of the motor is the power input minus power loss. The DYN 900 has a built-in fully regulated power supply and runs off 12V 25 amp power source. No other dyno on the market today is capable of giving readings as accurate and sensitive as the Tekin DYN 900.

Electric Motors

Aircraft

CARL GOLDBERG MODELS, INC.

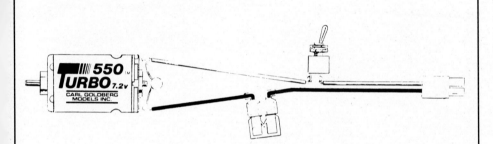

The *Motor Turbo 550* (No. 675/T-550, $24.99 retail) is a high-performance electric motor ideal for CG Electra, for best performance with 8-in. prop. This motor is READY-TO-RUN—no soldering required! Includes motor, 10-amp switch, and Tamiya connector. Lightweight fuse block for overload protection is included.

CARL GOLDBERG MODELS, INC.

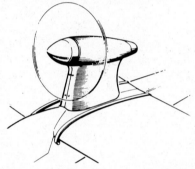

Although the *Power Pod* (No. 678, $49.99 retail) is designed to fit both Sophisticated Lady and Gentle Lady, this model adapts well to all other sailplanes. Features include: Turbo 550 motor with Tamiya connector and fuse; 8 x 4 prop and Goldberg spinner; operates from standard 6- or 7- cell car battery pack; complete instructions included.

Electric Motors

Boat

DYNAMIC MODEL PRODUCTS

The *Dynamic Hectoperm Engine W/Maxi-File* (No. 516 for 6 volt and No. 517 for 12 volt) is an electric, top-of-the-line motor to use with any large-scale model boat. They have stackable stage gears with possible ratios from 3 to 360:1. Size/Displ: 5 in. x 2-2/3 in. x 2-2/3 in.

ALTECH MARKETING

Electric Motors (Nos. R08522, R0821, RH26517, RH0918, RH25524, MT0824, MT0821, MT06527; Retail: See your dealer) are available from Altech in eight different models in two categories to fit your particular need. Wet magnets mean higher magnetic stretch and retention of strength. That translates into more enjoyment for modelers. The R series features dynamically balanced, skewed armatures. The RH versions have precision ball bearings and adjustable timing. The MT series motors include dynamically balanced, skewed armatures plus oilless metal bushings. All motors are NORCA and R.O.A.R. legal.

MRC

The *RB485 7.2V/8.4V Quick Charger* (No. RB485; Retail: See your dealer) represents the pinnacle of charger value and performance. All MRC chargers are in a class by themselves, but this feature-packed unit charges ahead of the pack. Features include a large easy-to-read meter; attractive, brushed aluminum face plate; choice of power options —including 120 volt AC, 12 volt cigarette lighter and 12 volt battery (all cords included); convenient compatibility with 6-cell 7.2 volt and 7-cell 8.4 volt batteries; trickle charge circuit with indicator lamp; fuse protection; banana post terminals for hook-up to other meters and connectors.

SERMOS R/C SNAP CONNECTORS, INC.

These *High-Amp Powerpole Snap Connectors* (Retail: Available from Sermos) are modular "silver-plated" connectors for your electric planes, cars, or boats. They're designed for a high-vibration environment. Cycled ten thousand times without electrical failure, they're designed for anything electrical requiring quick disconnects. Color coordinated and rated 30 amps at 600 DC, internal resistance is rated 250 micro ohms. Silver-plated contact accepts AWG sizes 12 to 16. For dealer information send to Sermos.

Electric Motors

Car

ASSOCIATED ELECTRICS

Associated-Reedy Motors ($20.00 - $70.00 retail) feature hand-wound armatures, diamond trued comms, balanced and epoxied, broken in, dyno-tuned.

ALTECH MARKETING

Electric Motors (Nos. R08522, R0821, RH26517, RH0918, RH25524, MT0824, MT0821, MT06527; Retail: See your dealer) are available from Altech in eight different models in two categories to fit your particular need. Wet magnets mean higher magnetic stretch and retention of strength. That translates into more enjoyment for modelers. The R series features dynamically balanced, skewed armatures. The RH versions have precision ball bearings and adjustable timing. The MT series motors include dynamically balanced, skewed armatures plus oilless metal bushings. All motors are NORCA and R.O.A.R. legal.

BUD'S RACING PRODUCTS

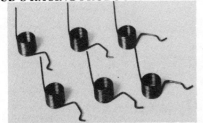

"DA" Spring ($2.50/pr., 6 pr. per bag, $15.00) is precision-formed music wire that is then heat-treated in its formed shape which gives you stable spring tensions as your motor gets hot. No need to change springs after several runs.

    No. 7185—Lite Tension, Blue
    No. 7186—Med. Tension, Green
    No. 7187—Heavy Tension, Red
    No. 7188—Super Heavy Tension, Purple
    No. 7190—3-Sprint Set (1 pr. Blue, 1 pr.
       Green, 1 pr. Red), $7.00.

C&M MFG.

Team Cobra Motors (Stock on-road/stock off-road $28.00 retail; modifieds, $80.00 retail) TQ Thunderdome! TQ/Winner Region 7 Dirt Oval! Winner Region 6 on-road ovals! At Team Cobra we don't simply repackage a can under our label. Using state-of-the-art dynos, brushes, springs and balancer, we go through an eight-step process to bring you the best motors available on the market! Our modifieds are all handwound with adjustable timing and bearings, cut and polished stacks, commutators trued to .0002 for minimal brush bounce. Also available in progressives and hybrids. Give our motors a try—you'll quickly see why at Team Cobra we're setting a new level for motor performance!!

PARMA INTERNATIONAL

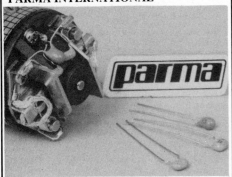

Today's competitive racer knows the value of those high-frequency speed controls. To make your motors compatible, count on Parma's *Hi-Frequency Capacitor Kit* (No. 4043, $2.00 retail). It includes two .01 microfarred capacitors and one 2.2 tantalum capacitor. Get the winning edge, use Parma electrics.

GREAT PLANES MODEL MFG.

The *Goldfire Motor* (No. SUPG0270, $479.95 retail) is a newly developed motor from Great Planes Mfg. It was designed to improve performance over stock "540" motors. The Goldfire is used in several GP kits presently and is said to offer up to 30% more running time than the LeMans 360PT. The motor will develop up to 19,800 rpms unloaded, and can run off 8.4V battery packs. The motor should fit most standard installations in cars, planes, and boats.

HOBBY PRODUCTS INT'L INC.

HPI offers series of *UNO Modified, Club Racer, Sports, Stock,* and *M.Truck Motors* ($28.00 to $65.00 retail) to R/C enthusiasts. (The labels shown are proto-type version.) The newly introduced UNO M.Truck motors are carefully engineered to provide smooth power band and high top-end speed for Monster/Stadium Trucks. The M.Truck motors are provided with already soldered-on capacitors and push-in type Tamiya compatible connectors.

KYOSHO

Kyosho announces the *ROAR-Legal 24° Stock Motor* (No. KYOG2024, $28.00 retail). It meets all the requirements set forth by ROAR for stock motors—24° timing, fixed endbell, and 27 turns of .65mm wire. Includes wet magnet for more torque and maximum allowable timing for high RPMs. Other features include heat sink endbell and necessary capacitors.

KYOSHO

Kyosho Mega Electric Motors ($24.95, $39.95 retail, depending on stock number) are available in 2WD, 4WD, on-road, dirt oval, paved oval, monster truck, and outlaw stock application. These inexpensive competition motors feature durable, high-torque, wet-processed magnets for extra power.

MRC-TAMIYA

The *Sport Tuned Motor* (No. U53068) is designed to handle 5- to 7-cell batteries (6 to 8.4 volts) and is factory set at 15-degree timing. At maximum efficiency, it produces 350 grams per centimeter of torque, uses 12.0 amps, and delivers 18,300 RPM. No-load RPM is rated at 21,500 at 2.2 amps. This motor is designed for use in all cars and trucks.

MRC-TAMIYA

The *Dynatech 02H* (No. U53044; Retail: See your dealer) is cool running, and to win a race, you and your motor must keep cool. A lightweight miniature fan ventilates this car and rotor, and the case has cooling fins. To adjust brush tension, you merely move the end of the brush springs to one of three settings. Hop-up options are available.

PROCELL

1000 Stock Motor use AYK can pink end bell with 30 degs timing complete with soft compound brushes and medium springs. ROAR and NORRCA approved. Average rpm between 26,000-27,000.

2000 Pro Stock use air supply cans with 34 degs timing complete with soft compound brushes and medium springs. ROAR and NORRCA approved. Average rpm between 24,000-26,000.

Modified motors use air supply cans, strong magnets, ball bearing, precision balancing, hand wound, adjustable timing. Available in custom winds for monster trucks, drag, boat, and cars. Single, double, triple, and quad winds obtainable.

PARMA INTERNATIONAL

These *48 Pitch Precision Machined Steel Pinions,* ($4.50 each, retail) now available from Parma, are all available at your local Parma dealer. Order No. 6019A–13 tooth, No. 6019B–14 tooth, No. 6019C–15 tooth, No. 6019D–16 tooth, No. 6019E–17 tooth, No. 6019F–18 tooth, No. 6019G–19 tooth, No. 6019H–20 tooth, No. 6019I–21 tooth, No. 6019J–22 tooth, No. 6019K–23 tooth, No. 6019L–24 tooth, No. 6019M–25 tooth, No. 6019N–26 tooth, No. 6019O–27 tooth, No. 6019P–28 tooth, No. 6019Q–29 tooth, No. 6019R–20 tooth.

PARMA INTERNATIONAL

The *World's Renowned Parma Cyclone II Motor.*
14100–Cyclone II Roar Stock motor, 27 T-single–$25;
14150–Cyclone II Super Stock motor, 25 T-single–$25.00;
14200–Cyclone II Ultra Stock motor, 17 T-single–$25.00;
14250–Cyclone II Pro Modified motor, adj. timing w/bushings, 18 T-double–$30.00;
14251–Cyclone II Pro Modified motor, adj. timing w/bushings, 16 T-double–$30.00;
14300–Cyclone II Super Modified motor, adj. timing w/bearings, 17 T-double– $45.00;
14301–Cyclone II Super Modified motor, adj. timing w/bearings, 15 T-double– $45.00;
14302–Cyclone II Super Modified motor, adj. timing w/bearings, 13 T-double– $45.00;
14353–Cyclone II T.Q. Series motor, handwound w/bearings, 17 T-triple–$65.00;
14354–Cyclone II T.Q. Series motor, handwound w/bearings, 16 T-single–$65.00;
14356–Cyclone II T.Q. Series motor, handwound w/bearings, 12 T-triple–$65.00;
14357–Cyclone II T.Q. Series motor, handwound w/bearings, 13 T-single–$65.00;
14361–Cyclone II T.Q. Series motor, handwound w/bearings, 15 T-quad–$65.00;
14362–Cyclone II T.Q. Series motor, handwound w/bearings, 16 T-double–$65.00;
14364–Cyclone II T.Q. Series motor, handwound w/bearings, 17 T-quad–$65.00;
14366–Cyclone II T.Q. Series motor, handwound w/bearings, 13 T-quad–$65.00.
See our latest catalogue for complete listings.

PARMA INTERNATIONAL

Cobalt Magnets and Handwound Armatures. 14800–Outlaw Cobalt Magnets for .05 motors, Not ROAR legal–$42.50 pr.; 14901–16 gauge fluorescent silicone wire, 2 ft.–$2.50; 14450–Cyclone II T.Q. Series armature, handwound, 21 T-double–$30.00; 14451–Cyclone II T.Q. Series armature, handwound, 20 T-triple–$30.00; 14452–Cyclone II T.Q. Series armature, handwound, 19 T-quad–$30.00; 14453–Cyclone II T.Q. Series armature, handwound, 17 T-triple–$30.00; 14454–Cyclone II T.Q. Series armature, handwound, 16 T-single –$30.00; 14455–Cyclone II T.Q. Series armature, handwound, 14 T-double–$30.00; 14456 –Cyclone II T.Q. Series armature, handwound, 12 T-triple–$30.00; 14457–Cyclone II T.Q. Series armature, handwound, 13 T-single– $30.00; 14458–Cyclone II T.Q. Series armature for drag, handwound, 8 T-single–$30.00; 14459–Cyclone II T.Q. Series armature for pullers, handwound, 30 T-single–$30.00; 14460–Cyclone II T.Q. Series armature, handwound, 11 T-double–$30.00; 14461– Cyclone II T.Q. Series armature, handwound, 15 T-quad–$30.00; 14462–Cyclone II T.Q. Series armature, handwound, 16 T-double– $30.00; 14463–Cyclone II T.Q. Series armature, handwound, 19 T-double–$30.00; 14464 –Cyclone II T.Q. Series armature, handwound, 17 T-quad–$30.00; 14465–Cyclone II T.Q. Series armature, handwound, 18 T-quad– $30.00; 14466–Cyclone II T.Q. Series armature, handwound, 13 T-quad–$30.00. See our latest catalogue for complete listings.

SERMOS R/C SNAP CONNECTORS, INC.

These *High-Amp Powerpole Snap Connectors* (Retail: Available from Sermos) are modular "silver-plated" connectors for your electric planes, cars, or boats. They're designed for a high-vibration environment. Cycled ten thousand times without electrical failure, they're designed for anything electrical requiring quick disconnects. Color coordinated and rated 30 amps at 600 DC, internal resistance is rated 250 micro ohms. Silver-plated contact accepts AWG sizes 12 to 16. For dealer information send to Sermos.

PARMA INTERNATIONAL

Cyclone II w/CommLock™.

14101–Cyclone II Roar '91 Stock motor w/CommLock™ 24°, dry magnets 27 T-single–$28.00;

14102–Cyclone II Roar '91 Stock motor w/CommLock™ 24°, wet magnets 27 T-single–$28.00.

More Motor Goodies. 3570–Motor bearing for Yokomo-type motor–$6.50;

3572A–Motor springs, light tension, silver–$2.00 pr.;

3572B–Motor springs, medium tension, black–$2.00 pr.;

3572C–Motor springs, heavy tension, gold–$2.00 pr.;

3573–Hard motor brushes–$3.50 pr.;

3574–Medium motor brushes–$3.50 pr.;

3577–Timed motor brushes–$4.50 pr.;

3578–Cut motor brushes–$4.50 pr.; 3579–Medium-soft motor brushes–$3.50 pr.;

3580–Medium-hard motor brushes–$3.50 pr.;

4011–1 ohm resistor with adjustable brake–$8.50;

4042–Motor Capacitor kit–$2.25/set; 4043–Motor Capacitor kit for High Frequency Speed Controllers–$2.00;

4050–16 gauge silicone hook-up wire, 2 ft.–$2.50.

See our latest catalogue for complete listings.

PARMA INTERNATIONAL

''Get It In Gear!'' Here's How!

6048–48 tooth spur gear for Parma-Associated differential–$3.25;

6310–1/8-in. precision differential balls–$2.50/20;

6312–1/4-in. precision thrust bearing–$4.00;

6313–Parma-Associated differential rebuild kit–$7.00;

17301–1/8-in. differential balls, 12/bag–$7.50/6 bags;

17310–98 tooth 64 pitch, spur gear–$4.00;

17311–102 tooth 64 pitch, spur gear–$4.00;

17312–106 tooth 64 pitch, spur gear–$4.00;

17313–110 tooth 64 pitch, spur gear–$4.00;

17314–115 tooth 64 pitch, spur gear–$4.00;

17315–120 tooth 64 pitch, spur gear–$4.00;

17317–79 tooth 48 pitch, spur gear–$4.00;

17318–84 tooth 48 pitch, spur gear–$4.00;

17319–88 tooth 48 pitch, spur gear–$4.00;

17320–92 tooth 48 pitch, spur gear–$4.00.

See our latest catalogue for complete listings.

TEAM CLASS RACING PRODUCTS

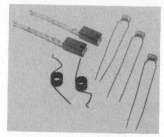

The *Class Stock Motor Performance Kit* (No. 7501, $6.99 retail) is great for races with handout motors or when setting up new stock motors. The kit includes everything needed to get top performance out of stock motors—3 high frequency capacitors, a pair of our legendary Venturi soft brushes and super heavy brush springs for low-end punch. This kit is being used by the fastest stock drivers around the country.

TEAM CLASS RACING PRODUCTS

The *Class Motor Maintenance Center* (No. 6000, $16.95 retail) is a convenient motor workshop that makes motor tuning much easier. The clip that holds the motor is superior to similar products currently on the market. Also, the stand has slots for custom brush cutting. You will also find a handy magnetic strip for organizing motor screw, springs, etc. The small fan, ''Turbo Prop,'' is placed on the motor during break-in, this keeps the motor very cool.

STAGE III

Dragin' Wire (Packaged with 2 ft. of black and 2 ft. of orange silicone-coated 12 gauge wire, $7.50 retail) is extra-capacity, high-performance wire, designed for high current flow and high voltages typical in R/C powerboating, drag racing, and truck pulling. With 1,666 strands; this new 12 gauge wire has 33% more capacity than its state-of-the-art Super 13 wire which has all the same quality and features: 99.9% pure copper stranding, tinned for fast soldering and corrosion resistance, super flexibility, and burn-proof silicone insulation. Dragin' Wire was recently top-rated by R/C Car Action Magazine. When only the best will do, Stage III is the only way to go!

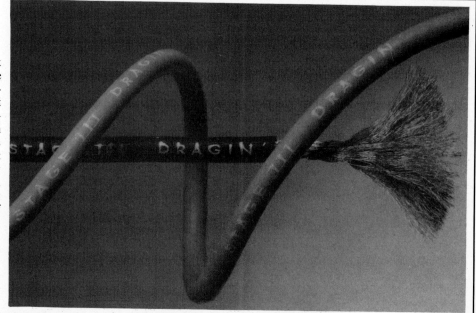

STAGE III

Super 13 Wire (2 ft. each of black and orange, $5.25 retail; Rolls available: 25 ft., $33.00 retail; 50 ft., $60.00 retail.) and *Super 13 B* (2 ft. each of black and orange, $3.00 retail; Rolls available: 25 ft., $33.00 retail; 50 ft., $60.00 retail.) were recently top-rated by R/C Car Action Magazine. They are high performance wires for all types of R/C. The wire is composed of 805 strands of 99.9% pure copper, tinned for easy soldering and corrosion resistance, and coated with super flexible silicone. Super 13 and 13 B are rated at a whopping 55 amps, and have 20% less resistance than typical 14 gauge wire.

TEAM LOSI INC.

The *Super Insane Stock Racing Motor* (No. TL 6024, $28.00 retail) was designed from the ground up, using the latest, strongest 4.9 wet magnets, precision-formed can, and of course, the unique slotted armature. Timing has been precisely locked at 24 degrees. This exceptional combination of engineering and production gives you a motor that produces the power and RPM of higher timed old technology motors while running cooler and more reliably. Let Team Losi give your stock racer ''Super Insane'' horsepower.

TEAM LOSI INC.

''*Revolution*'' *Modified Motors* ($75.00 retail) won every 2WD modified off-road national championship in 1989! This unequaled performance reflects the top quality components in these electric motors, as well as constant testing, development and, above all, unequaled workmanship. Motors for 1/10 scale on-road, off-road, 2WD, 4WD, and trucks available.

TEAM PIT STOP

From our ROAR legal ''Radical Duke'' Stock Motors ($24.99 retail) through our hand wound Modifieds, Team Pit Stop has the widest range of motors available. Our *Winner* ($27.99 retail) and *T.Q.* ($44.99 retail) series are budget modifieds with super speed available in 14, 15, and 18 winds. Our *Super Series* ($59.99 retail) are Yokomo-based, argon welded, hand-wound, precision-balanced, and double-trued available in 16 custom winds from 28 single to 11 double.

TWISTER MOTORS

Twister Motors (Retail: See your dealer) are available in many different price ranges, winds, and styles and are well known for their performance and reliability. Whether you're an experienced champion or just having fun in your back yard, there's an ultra hot ''Twister'' or ''Pocket Rocket'' motor for you.

WIMPY MOTORS/AKS DISTRIBUTING

Wimpy Modified Motors (Retail: See your dealer) are high performance, hand wound, welded, natural diamond trued comm, precision balanced, and computer timed for optimum performance. Specific winds for 1/12 and 1/10, SCR or SCE, oval, on and off road awesome performance. Available exclusively through AKS Distributing. 27T 22 gauge NORRCA/ROAR legal motor. Featuring the ''Gonzo'' Slick Brush.

Engines

Aircraft .010 to .40

ALTECH MARKETING

The *Enya SS-30 BB TV* (No. JB30B; Retail: See your dealer) is the next step for those fliers that demand more power and rpms for critical aerobatics. A larger Enya G5.5 carburetor increases the breathing ability of the engine while still permitting a smooth transition from idle to top speed. This .83 HP, glow type engine has an rpm range of 2500 to 16,000 (.83 HP @ 16,000 rpm), which means you can fly your craft to your heart's content knowing you are in command of a real "tiger" of an engine. The engine weighs 8.04 oz. w/o muffler and has a displacement of .30 cu. in. Two ball bearings on the crankshaft take the strain with ease. The M251 muffler is standard.

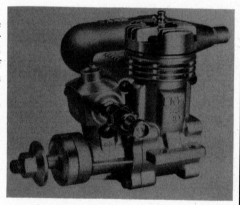

ALTECH MARKETING

The *Enya SS25 BB TV* (No. JB25Z, Retail: See your dealer) is a Schnuerle-ported .25 cu. in. displacement glow type engine. It features two ball bearings to support the crankshaft for low-friction running and higher rpms up to 16,000. The SS stands for "Super Sport" but it's not just a fancy name. It really can produce .73 HP with all the quality and reliability you've come to expect from Enya engines. The Enya secret is the cast iron piston riding in a nitrogen gas hardened steel cylinder for outstandingly easy starting, break-in and long-term use. An Enya G5.5 carburetor does the mixing chores for great throttle control from low to high speed. A specially matched muffler also keeps the noise down while permitting terrific engine performance. Without muffler, the engine weighs 8.04 oz.

ALTECH MARKETING

The *Enya SS30 Ring Marine* (No. JB30M, Retail: See your dealer) packs some of the basic components of the famous SS30 helicopter engine into a marine product. Here's a Schnuerle-ported power plant with a low expansion aluminum alloy piston running in a steel cylinder. A G5.5 carburetor eases fuel adjustment, and two water-line taps keep it cool. This .30 size glow type, 2-cycle engine cranks 0.8 HP @ 16,000 rpm, weighs 235 grams, and has a .30 cu. in. displacement.

ALTECH MARKETING

ALTECH MARKETING

ALTECH MARKETING

The *Enya SS30 TV* (No. JB30A, Retail: See your dealer) is the first engine in the lineup of Enya SS .30 cu. in. displacement engines. It features a Schnuerle-ported steel cylinder which has been gas hardened for longevity. A cast-iron piston, bronze bushing around the crankshaft, and an easy-to-adjust Enya carburetor makes this model a great investment for the beginning sport modeler. With about .73 HP on tap at 15,000 rpm, there's needed power during those first solo flights with a reverse for stunts when he's brave enough. This glow type engine weighs 7.5 oz. without muffler. The muffler is included and easy to attach.

The *Enya SS40 TV* (No. JB38A, Retail: See your dealer) is a glow type 2-cycle engine designed for Schnuerle-ported power at a price the sport flyer can afford. It has a .40 cu. in. displacement, 10.7 oz. net weight, and cranks 1.1 HP @ 15,000 rpm. The bronze-bushed crankshaft delivers the reliability you need for flight. Each SS40 TV engine comes with a bolt-on muffler plus Enya reliability and easier break-in.

The *Enya SS40 BB TV* (No. JB38B, Retail: See your dealer) is a 2-cycle, glow-type engine for the sport flier who doesn't mind paying a little extra. The SS40 BB TV provides the thrill in R/C flying he didn't think possible at this price. Two ball bearings on the crankshaft, a larger carburetor, plus muffler pump out this Enya's steady beat. The engine weighs a net 11.8 oz., has a .40 cu. in. displacement, and cranks 1.2 HP @ 16,000 rpm.

ALTECH MARKETING

ALTECH MARKETING

Safety is no accident

The *Enya 11 CX* (No. JB11M for aircraft, No. JB11W for cars; Retail: See your dealer) is an ideal engine for use in miniature aircraft and in small versions of off-road gas cars. This glow type engine puts out 0.4 HP @ 27,000 rpm, weighs 5.4 oz. w/o muffler, and has a .11 cu. in. displacement.

The *Enya .15 IV TV* (No. JA15W for aircraft, No. JD15M for marine; Retail: See your dealer) has a bronze main bearing. This glow type engine weighs 5.7 oz. w/o muffler, has a displacement of .15 cu. in., and puts out 0.23 HP @ 14,000 rpm. Muffler is included. Available in marine version.

ALTECH MARKETING

The *Enya SS25 TV* (No. JB25Y, Retail: See your dealer) is a welcomed Altech product for many reasons. First, this glow-type engine is Schnuerle-ported for the power the sport modeler has come to expect from more expensive engines. A bronze bushing supports the crankshaft, allowing trouble-free operation. An Enya carburetor is standard for steady throttle control from idle to top speed. Advanced metallurgy allows Enya to make piston/cylinder match-ups work better and longer. A cast iron piston is fitted to a nitrogen gas hardened steel cylinder. This combo results in a high quality unit producing .63 HP and revs up to 15,000 rpm. Yet, the SS25 is easy to start and easy to break in. The engine weighs 7.5 oz. w/o muffler and has a .25 cu. in. displacement.

ALTECH MARKETING

The *Enya SS35 Heli TN* (Retail: See your dealer) shows how Enya continues to pioneer new designs and develop new engines that can further advance the hobby of model helicopter flying. The 2-cycle glow-type SS35 Heli TN will deliver plenty of ''hover power'' for all .30 size helicopters and then some. Its heat-sink head and ringed aluminum piston take the heat...while the ''new'' twin needle 5.6mm carb allows for smooth mixture control at all rpms. The engine has a net weight of 8.46 oz., displaces .35 cu. in., and puts out 0.9 HP @ 16,000 rpm.

ALTECH MARKETING

The *Enya .09 TV* (No. JA9W, Retail: See your dealer) is a lightweight engine for R/C sport fliers. This glow-type engine puts out 0.16 HP @ 14,000 rpm, weighs 4.1 oz. w/o muffler, and has a displacement of .099 cu. in. The exhaust has been rotated 180 degrees to allow normal installation. Also, a washer between the drive-washer and front housing is included to reduce front-end wear. The muffler is included.

COX HOBBIES, INC.

The *.010 Tee Dee* (No. 130; Retail: See your dealer) is the world's smallest production engine. This 2-cycle, glow type engine is perfect for feather weight, free flight, and R/C planes. Tolerances are held within a few millionths of an inch! Displacement is .010 cu. in. and it attains 25,000 RPM with 3-in. x 1 1/4-in. pitch prop.

COX HOBBIES, INC.

The new *Cox Medallion .049 and .09 engines* (No. 2501, .049 cu. in. displ.; No. 2901, .09 cu. in. displ.; Retail: See your dealer) now include throttle control and muffler to fly quietly and experience higher Medallion performance. These are 2-cycle, crankshaft induction type engines.

COX HOBBIES, INC.

The *Cox Pee Wee w/Throttle* (No. 1001 with throttle, No. 100 without; Retail: See your dealer) is a low cost R/C reed valve induction type engine for smaller aircraft and gliders. It comes complete with an integral R/C tank. The engine weighs .86 oz. without muffler and cranks .035 BHP @ 18,500 RPM.

COX HOBBIES, INC.

The *Texaco .049* (No. 4506; Retail: See your dealer) is a unique, extended-duration production engine. Achieves both fuel economy and power. This 2-cycle, .049 cu. in. displacement engine features a high velocity .062 in. diameter intake venturi, a new free flowing reed holder, and a lightweight polymer tankback. Weighs 1.86 oz. net and attains 9,100-9,600 rpm with 7D3.5P prop.

COX HOBBIES, INC.

The *.074 Queen Bee* (No. 3701 for engine, No. 3785 for mount; Retail: See your dealer) comes standard with conventional replaceable glow plug. This is a reed valve induction type, two-cycle engine that cranks .080 BHP @ 16,000 RPM. It weighs 3.9 oz. net. Special mount available.

COX HOBBIES, INC.

The *Cox Dragonfly .049* (No. 4505; Retail: See your dealer) has an oversized fuel tank, throttle control, and muffler to provide long, quiet, and controlled flights. This two-cycle, reed valve induction type engine has a .049 cu. in. displacement. It is easy to start and smooth running. The Dragonfly is perfect for beginners and experts alike.

COX HOBBIES, INC.

The *Cox Black Widow .049* (No. 150: See your dealer) has always been considered one of the best .049s available. This reed valve induction type engine comes with Snap Starter® and integral gas tank, and works well even in the inverted position. It weighs 2.22 oz. without muffler, has a .049 cu. in. displacement, and delivers .078 BHP @ 15,500 RPM.

COX HOBBIES, INC.

The *Cox .049 QRC* (No. 4501: Retail: See your dealer) is an ideal small R/C engine designed with an integral fuel tank and muffler. This reed valve induction type engine includes patented Snap Starter for ease of starting and operation. It has a .049 cu. in. displacement, weighs 2.44 oz. with muffler, and delivers .070 BHP @ 14,000 RPM.

COX HOBBIES, INC.

The *Cox Tee Dee Designs* (No. 160, .020; No. 170, .049; No. 200, .051, No. 210, .09; Retail: See your dealer) are high-performance competition engines. They're ideal for use where maximum power and speed are required. These are crankshaft induction type engines. Size/displacements are .020, .049, .051, and .09 cu. in; weight: 1.5 oz. (049/051).

HOBBY DYNAMICS DISTRIBUTORS

The *Quickee 500 Pylon Speed .40* (with Muffler) (No. WE1034PABC, $249.99 retail) is a hot new .40-size Webra engine that offers high-speed performance in the lightest castings available. The all-new pipe-style muffler provides optimum back-pressure yet considerably quiets the engine. Compared with the standard Webra .40, the Quickee 500 has an all-new cylinder head and combustion chamber with much higher compression.

HOBBY DYNAMICS DISTRIBUTORS

The *Webra .32 Airplane Engine* (No. WE 1028RCABCD, $190.99 retail) offers the finest in German engineering at a great price. It will power your airplane to levels of performance you have only thought about. This features an aluminum piston, chrome plated brass sleeve, and a Dykes ring for easy starting.

O.S. ENGINES

O.S. FSR Classic Engines ($159.95 - $379.95 retail) are easy to start and exceptionally reliable. With standard features such as Schnuerle porting, ball-bearing supported crankshafts, specially-designed carburetors for maximum efficiency, mufflers, and parts that fit to precision tolerances, FSR Classics have been favored by flyers for years. Available are the .32 F ABC and the large 1.08 FSR. These engines weigh from 8.3 oz. to 26.5 oz.; have outputs ranging from 1.02 to 3.0 BHP @ 16,000 RPM; all are glow type.

O.S. ENGINES

The *O.S. SF Series Engines* ($134.95 - $349.95 retail) offer R/C pilots features and performance available nowhere else. Available in .25, .40, .46, and .61 sizes; both in ringed and ABC versions. The .61 long strokes offer more power in the 12,000 RPM range. The .46 and the .61 are available in pumped versions. All SF engines offer Schnuerle porting, double ball bearings, competition-type 4D carburetors, expansion mufflers and one-piece crankshafts, and are available with rings or ABC pistons. These engines weigh from 7.59 oz. to 20.44 oz. and all are 2-cycle glow type.

O.S. ENGINES

O.S. designed its *FP Series Engines* ($74.95 - $104.95 retail) with the sport flier in mind. These engines offer reliable performance and the most popular sizes at a reasonable price. FP Series Engines feature expansion mufflers and each are built to exact standards to ensure quick starting and smooth operation. These engines range in size from .10 to .60; weigh from 4.2 oz. to 8.6 oz.; have outputs of .29 to 1 BHP @ 17,000 RPM; and all are 2-cycle glow type.

ROYAL PRODUCTS CORP.

The *Royal .28 R/C Engine* ($104.95 retail) is Schnuerle-ported ABC and features full fuel-metered carburetion, twin ball bearings, and has massive one-piece shaft. This is a glow type, 2-cycle engine with .28 cu. in. displacement. The muffler is included.

ROYAL PRODUCTS CORP.

The *Royal .40 R/C Engine* ($117.95 retail) is Schnuerle-ported and ABC to provide power when needed. It is designed to operate on low-nitro fuels, is machined for quick break-in, and is priced less than most sport engines. It is designed for sport flying, but has the power if ever needed. The muffler is included and the engine has twin ball bearings.

ROYAL PRODUCTS CORP.

The *Royal .25 R/C Engine* ($99.95 retail) is a Schnuerle-ported and ABC to provide power when needed. It operates on low-nitro fuels, is machined for quick break-in, and priced less. It has twin ball bearings and comes with muffler.

SKYWARD R&D LABORATORY

The *Skyward 21* (No. 21 BC; Retail: See your dealer) is a 21 size, glow type, 2-cycle engine that is hand casted and machined for superior performance. It cranks 1.1 HP @ 25,000 RPM, is black anodized, ball bearing, and Schnuerle ported, with ABC construction. Net weight is 310 gr. and displacement is 3.44 cc.

SKYWARD R&D LABORATORY

The *Skyward 40FSR-H Engine* (No. 40RSRH) has an adjustable exhaust that can be side or rear, super quiet tune pipe supplied, special ABC construction allows engine to run hotter than normal, and is smaller in size than a regular 40. The engine features RPM of 15,500, weighs 375g, has a 6.47cc cylinder, and puts out 1.15 HP.

SKYWARD R&D LABORATORY

The *Skyward 40* (No. 40F SR; Retail: See your dealer) is a 40 size, glow type, 2-cycle engine that is hand casted and machined for superior performance. It cranks .97 HP @ 15,000 RPM, is black anodized, ball bearing, and Schnuerle ported with ABC construction. Muffler included. Net weight is 420 gr. and displacement is 6.40 cc.

Engines

Aircraft .45 to .60

ALTECH MARKETING

The *Enya SS45 Ring* (No. JB38R, Retail: See your dealer) is a 2-cycle, glow-type engine that puts out 1.25 HP @ 16,000 rpm. Just as the name describes, this Super Sport series Enya utilizes a ringed piston for easy break-in, a feature sport fliers can appreciate. Each SS45 Ring engine comes with an Enya G carburetor and bolt-on muffler for easy installation. It has a .45 cu. in. displacement.

ALTECH MARKETING

ALTECH MARKETING

The *GP 60XF-4* (No. JB60A for side exhaust version, No. JB60C for rear exhaust version, No. JB60B for side exhaust helicopter version; Retail: See your dealer) with gear pump is an excellent choice for severe aerobatic conditions. The GM-10GP carburetor delivers excellent throttle response at any rpm setting. The gear pump is preset at the factory. This 2-cycle, glow-type engine delivers 1.8 HP @ 17,000 rpm, weighs 19.36 oz. net, and has a size/displacement of .60 cu. in. No. JB60A is shown.

The *Enya SS50 Ring Marine* (No. JB50M, Retail: See your dealer) is a 2-cycle, glow-type engine that delivers 1.3 HP @ 16,000 rpm. Not-so-friendly water environments can make model boaters appreciate easy starts. The aluminum alloy ringed-piston Schnuerle porting, and a hardened steel cylinder on this solidly built marine engine deliver power. And the G-7 carburetor makes mixture adjustments a snap while the standard M402X muffler keeps the sound down. This .50 size engine weighs 325 grams net and has a .50 cu. in. displacement.

ALTECH MARKETING

The *Enya .60 XF IV TV w/Ring* (No. JB60F, without muffler; No. JB60Y, with muffler; Retail: See your dealer) is a new version of the 60 XF IV. It has a ringed piston for even easier break-in and starting, and comes equipped with the G-8 carb for easy set-up. The whole engine is designed with power and reliability in mind. It also comes with a new low price, making it ideal for modelers with a scale project on a low budget. This glow-type engine cranks out 1.55 HP @ 16,000 rpm, weighs 19.3 oz. w/o muffler, and has a .60 cu. in. displacement.

ALTECH MARKETING

The *Enya .60 XF TV* (No. JB-60X, No. JB-60W; Retail: See your dealer) is a Schnuerle-ported, hand-lapped engine with an aluminum liner that has been chrome plated. The piston is ringless and is machined from a high silicon content alloy casting. This engine features dual ball bearings and a compression ratio of 10.5 to 1, and a new metered carb for good response throughout the rpm range. This glow-type engine weighs 18.0 oz. w/o muffler, has a .60 cu. in. displacement, and delivers 1.65 HP @ 17,000 rpm.

ALTECH MARKETING

The *Enya .60 XL* (No. JB60E, Retail: See your dealer), a .60 Schnuerle rear exhaust engine, is probably one of the hottest pattern engines around. It was designed for use with the TM60BS70 tuned pipe system for top performance. The front mounted GM-9 carb offers the special mid-range mixture control so the engine never sags in lower rpm maneuvers, yet provides optimum top- and low-end control. The AAC construction of the lapped piston and cylinder provide a near-perfect thermal expansion ratio for gusty operation with 1.8 HP @ 17,000 rpm. You are in the winner's circle with this engine. This glow type engine weighs 20.0 oz. w/o muffler and has a .60 cu. in. displacement.

ALTECH MARKETING

Enya engines are noted for their high power output; but for the most demanding applications Enya has recognized your needs and developed the new 53-4C.

This engine looks compact yet is loaded with features and performance that advanced modelers have been requesting. The 53-4C produces 0.8 HP at 12,000 RPMs yet idles down smoothly to 2,500. The Enya GC 5.5mm carburetor is unbeatable for ease of operation; it comes with a spring loaded choke system for quick starting in bad weather. With a steel cylinder and a ringed aluminum alloy piston, you can be sure that the 53-4C will continue to churn out its power without a missed beat.

For ease of maintenance, a tool set consisting of wrenches, Allen wrench drivers, a screwdriver, and a feeler gauge is included.

ALTECH MARKETING

The *Enya .45 CX-TV* (No. JB45C for aircraft, No. JD45C for marine; Retail: See your dealer) is a Schnuerle-ported 45 featuring Enya's famous aluminum cylinder with chrome lining and aluminum piston for the best possible level of performance and light weight in one package. It comes with a muffler; but a special low-noise muffler SM402X is also available, as well as a tuned pipe set TM/40/49 and the bigger GM9 carb for more performance beyond its normal 1.3 HP at up to 17,000 rpm. This glow-type engine weighs 12.7 oz. without muffler and has a .456 cu. in. displacement. Also available in a marine version.

ALTECH MARKETING

The *Enya .60 B III BB TV-G8* (No. JA-60M; Retail: See your dealer) is an ideal engine for large-size airplanes. It features dual ball bearings and a compression ratio of 10:1. The famous G-8 carb provides smooth transition from idle to high speed, and it's one of the easiest to set up. It's a solid and reliable engine which will provide many hours of sheer enjoyment. The muffler comes with it. This glow-type engine delivers 1.45 HP @ 14,000 rpm, weighs 15.0 oz. w/o muffler, and has .606 cu. in. displacement.

FUTABA

The *YS.Futaba 45 F.S/45 F.R* ($179.95 retail) model aircraft engine is virtually hand-built and designed for maximum power output. This .45 size, glow type 2-cycle YS.Futaba engine features advanced CNC maching quality, ABC design, and Futaba's unique fuel injection system. Other features include Schneurle-porting, a special YS Butterfly-type throttle and convenient needle valve adjustments making this engine ideal for Sport and Competition flying. HP @ RPM: 2,000-18,000. The engine displaces 7.45cc with a 400g net weight. It comes available in both side and rear exhaust, with an optional muffler (FP-YS095).

HOBBY DYNAMICS DISTRIBUTORS

The *Webra Speed .50 Engine* ($185.99 - $199.99 retail) is a favorite among sport and helicopter modelers where the need for a powerful yet light engine is essential. This is a size .50, 2-cycle, glow-type engine.

HOBBY DYNAMICS DISTRIBUTORS

The *Silverline Engines with Mufflers* (No. WE1022RCS, .40, $99.99 retail; No. WE1020RCS, .61, $179.99 retail) have side exhaust, front intake, scavenged porting, ringed piston, ball-bearing-supported crankshaft, and TN barrel-type carburetor. They're available in .40 and .61 displacements.

O.S. ENGINES

O.S. FSR Classic Engines ($159.95 - $379.95 retail) are easy to start and exceptionally reliable. With standard features such as Schnuerle porting, ball-bearing supported crankshafts, specially-designed carburetors for maximum efficiency, mufflers, and parts that fit to precision tolerances, FSR Classics have been favored by flyers for years. Available are the .32 F ABC and the large 1.08 FSR. These engines weigh from 8.3 oz. to 26.5 oz.; have outputs ranging from 1.02 to 3.0 BHP @ 16,000 RPM; all are glow type.

O.S. ENGINES

The *O.S. SF Series Engines* ($134.95 - $349.95 retail) offer R/C pilots features and performance available nowhere else. Available in .25, .40, .46, and .61 sizes; both in ringed and ABC versions. The .61 long strokes offer more power in the 12,000 RPM range. The .46 and the .61 are available in pumped versions. All SF engines offer Schnuerle porting, double ball bearings, competition-type 4D carburetors, expansion mufflers and one-piece crankshafts, and are available with rings or ABC pistons. These engines weigh from 7.59 oz. to 20.44 oz. and all are 2-cycle glow type.

ROYAL PRODUCTS CORP.

The *Royal .45 RC Engine* ($124.95 retail) is Schnuerle-ported and has ABC to provide power when needed. It operates on low-nitro fuels, and is machined for quick break-in. Engine has twin ball bearings and full fuel metered carburetion.

SKYWARD R&D LABORATORY

The *60 FSR* (No. 60Fsr; Retail: See your dealer) is a 60 size, glow type, 2-cycle engine that is hand casted and machined for superior performance. It cranks 1.65 HP @ 14,500 RPM, is black anodized with Blue Head, ball bearing, and Schnuerle ported, with ABC construction. Muffler included. Net weight is 600 gr. and displacement is 9.82 cc.

SKYWARD R&D LABORATORY

The *Skyward 46Fsr Engine* (No. T46FSR) features RPM of 17,000, weighs 314g, has a 7.45cc cylinder, and puts out 1.40 HP.

UNITED MODEL DISTRIBUTORS

The *Saito FA-45S* ($241.99 retail) replaces the everpopular FA-45 MKII. This .45 size, glow-type 4-cycle FA-45S engine features a new carburetor, intake pipe, and the high lift cam gear design. Transition from idle to top end is smooth and strong. The engine features RPM range of 2,000-11,000, weighs 430 grams (15.1 oz.), has a 7.5cc displacement, and puts out 0.7 HP.

UNITED MODEL DISTRIBUTORS

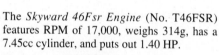

The *Saito FA-60T* (No. FA-60T, $694.99 retail) engine is the latest introduction from Saito. The FA-60T utilizes the same double throw crankshaft the large Saito twins do, for low vibration levels and efficiency. The FA-60T has an easy-to-adjust, single carburetor and comes complete with exhaust pipes. The FA-60T looks great in the Cub and other small planes where a small twin is needed.

Safety is Contagious...

UNITED MODEL DISTRIBUTORS

The *Saito FA-50* ($219.99 retail) engine features newly designed intake and outlet paths to boost charge of gases. This .50 size, glow-type 4-cycle FA-50 engine is precision machined and it can out-perform any .40 to .50 4-cycle engine. A real powerhouse that will fly most .40 two cycle aircraft. The engine features RPM range of 2,000-12,000, weighs 410 grams (14.4 oz.), has a 8.2cc displacement, and puts out 0.85 HP. Also available in the Golden Knight version finished in black and gold.

Engines

Aircraft .61 to .90

ALTECH MARKETING

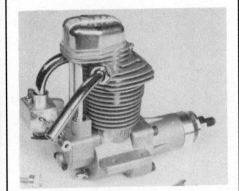

The *Enya .80-4C* (No. JC80X; Retail: See your dealer) is a .80 size 4-stroke engine that gives .60 scale fliers the power of an .80 in the package belonging to a .60, without so much extra weight. Practical rpms range 2,700 to 12,000—1.1 HP @ 11,500 rpm—for gutsy performance. A 7mm G-type carb takes care of the breathing chores, while the steel liner and ringed aluminum piston keep pumping away delivering power plus reliability. The manual choke valve helps you get going. This engine plus a big prop will get those large-scale birds going in a hurry. This glow-type engine weighs 1 lb. 4.5 oz. w/o muffler and has a .80 cu. in. displacement.

ALTECH MARKETING

The *Enya 80XF* (Retail: See your dealer) is one of Enya engineers' bigger, more reliable engines in a new compact form. The 80XF mounts in the same space as our 60XF yet will swing 14-inch propellers with authority. It is a ringed engine for fast break-ins and is equipped with a GM-10SB carburetor for optimum mixture control. This 2-cycle, glow-type engine delivers 2.0 HP at 16,200 rpm. It has a net weight of 18.69 oz. and a size/displ. of .80 cu. in.

ALTECH MARKETING

The *Enya .90-4C* (No. JC-90F; Retail: See your dealer) features an output of 1.3 HP at 11,500 rpm. Such a powerful, modern 4-stroke engine is hard to find. It comes with a muffler, choke, and tool set. A steel cylinder and ringed aluminum piston help insure maximum power output with top reliability. A SM-904C muffler, with 11-in. long flexible coupling, is an available option for certain applications. This glow-type engine weighs 28.4 oz. w/o muffler, and has a .90 cu. in. displacement.

FUTABA

The new *YS.Futaba 120FS* ($529.95 retail) is a four-stroke supercharged airplane engine. With YS.Futaba's unique fuel injection system, Schneurle-porting and increased power output throughout the rpm range (HP @ RPM: 2,000-12,500), 120FS produces superior performance during steep climbing or inverted flight and is not susceptible to 4-cycle detonation. YS.Futaba 120 FS was designed primarily for F3A Aerobatics, Scale Competition and the serious Sport Flyer. This glow type, 4-cycle engine has a 950g net weight and 19.96cc displacement.

FUTABA

The *YS.Futaba 61 F.S-H/61 F.R-H* ($239.95 retail) helicopter engine is virtually hand-built and designed for maximum power output. Features of this .61 size, glow-type 2-cycle engine include Schneurle-porting and Futaba's unique fuel-injection system. Coupled YS integrated carburetor design fuel flow is continuously and automatically regulated for superior throttle response when hovering. Performance is also unaffected by tank position or fuel level during rolls, loops, or inverted flight. In addition, the YS.Futaba 61 F-H incorporates a ringed piston for easy starting and cooler running in helicopter installations. HP @ RPM: 2,000-18,000. This engine weighs 565g net and has a 9.97cc displacement. Available in both side (61 F.S-H) and rear (61 F.R-H) exhaust.

FUTABA

The *YS.Futaba 61F.S Long Stroke* (Side exhaust/YS0080) and *61F.R Long Stroke* (Rear exhaust/YS0090) (Retail: See your dealer) are designed for pattern competition. The long stroke design of the 61F improves efficiency and increases power to allow use of a larger prop. The YS.Futaba VPS fuel injection system automatically adjusts the mixture to flying conditions and engine speed. The 61F is a direct replacement for the YS.Futaba 60F, and uses the same mounting bolt pattern. Bore: 23.0mm. Stroke: 24.0mm. This .61 size engine has a 9.97cc displacement and 565g net weight. HP @ RPM: 2,000-18,000.

HOBBY DYNAMICS DISTRIBUTORS

The *Webra Speed .61 Heli Engine* ($263.99 - $275.99 retail) has a track record that stands alone in the field of helicopter aerobatics. This is a size .61, 2-cycle, glow-type engine.

O.S. ENGINES

O.S. FSR Classic Engines ($159.95 - $379.95 retail) are easy to start and exceptionally reliable. With standard features such as Schnuerle porting, ball-bearing supported crankshafts, specially-designed carburetors for maximum efficiency, mufflers, and parts that fit to precision tolerances, FSR Classics have been favored by flyers for years. Available are the .32 F ABC, .50 FSR, .91 FSR, and the large 1.08 FSR. These engines weigh from 8.3 oz. to 26.5 oz.; have outputs ranging from 1.02 to 3.0 BHP @ 16,000 RPM; all are glow type.

SKYWARD R&D LABORATORY

O.S. ENGINES

The *O.S. SF Series Engines* ($134.95 - $349.95 retail) offer R/C pilots features and performance available nowhere else. Available in .25, .40, .46, and .61 sizes; both in ringed and ABC versions. The .61 long strokes offer more power in the 12,000 RPM range. The .46 and the .61 are available in pumped versions. All SF engines offer Schnuerle porting, double ball bearings, competition-type 4D carburetors, expansion mufflers and one-piece crankshafts, and are available with rings or ABC pistons. These engines weigh from 7.59 oz. to 20.44 oz. and all are 2-cycle glow type.

UNITED MODEL DISTRIBUTORS

The *Saito FA-90T* (No. 420190, $514.99 retail) engine utilizes a single-throw crankshaft as do all full-size radial engines. Because of this design, the engine is simple in construction, lightweight, and highly efficient. A patented vane-type air pump is used to maintain positive crankcase pressure and provides complete lubrication of all moving parts. This .90 size, glow-type 4-cycle FA-90T engine has been especially designed for light scale aircraft. The engine weighs 795 grams (1 lb. 9 oz.) net and has a 15cc displacement. 1.0 HP @ RPM: 2,500-9,000. Great for the Piper Cub, Cessna 150, and other similar size planes. A step up in displacement and performance, the FA-130T features RPM range of 2,000-10,000, weighs 1,300 grams, and puts out 1.9 HP.

The *Skyward 80Fsr Engine* (No. S80FSR) features RPM of 15,500, weighs 600g, has a 13.0cc cylinder, and puts out 2.20 HP.

O.S. ENGINES

The *O.S. 65 VR-DF ABC Ducted Fan Engine* (Retail: See your dealer) features a new drum valve induction system that improves performance, power, and reliability. It weighs only 20.30 oz. and has an rpm range from 2,500 to 25,000. This unit will fit most popular ducted fan units available.

UNITED MODEL DISTRIBUTORS

The *Saito FA-80* ($289.99 retail) engine is an incredible, lightweight, powerhouse. This .80 size, glow-type 4-cycle engine weighs 540 grams (1 lb. 2 oz.) and the output is 1.3 HP! Excellent for flying most all .60 two cycle engined models. Lighter in weight, the FA-80 has the same mounting holes as the FA-65. The engine features RPM range of 2,000-11,500 and has a 13.1cc displacement. Also available in the Golden Knight version finished in black and gold.

UNITED MODEL DISTRIBUTORS

Engines

Aircraft
Over .90

The *Saito FA-65* ($254.99 retail) engine is the most powerful 4-stroke engine in this displacement category. This .65 size, glow-type 4-cycle engine will fly most all 40 two-stroke models and some .60 two-stroke models. The FA-65 features an ABC piston/liner with a ring for high performance and long life. The engine features an RPM range of 2,000-11,500, weighs 550 grams (1 lb. 3 oz.), has a 10.6cc displacement, and puts out .95 HP. Also available in the Golden Knight version.

ALTECH MARKETING

The *Enya R1.20-4C* (No. JC99R; Retail: See your dealer) engine is intended for use by the demanding R/C flier who wants power, reliability, and versatility all in one package. An rpm range of 2,500 to 13,000—2.1 HP @ 12,500 rpm—bespeaks ultra-high power and torque. A special G-type 9mm carb uses a spring-loaded choke plus a reversible carb mount for more flexible throttle pushrod installation. A muffler, plus a good selection of tools, add plenty of value to an engine already loaded with engineering features for long life and low maintenance. This engine has more power and value than any other nationally advertised 4-cycle 120 engine. It is glow type, weighs 2 lbs. w/o muffler and has a 1.2 cu. in. displacement.

ALTECH MARKETING

The *Enya GP R120-4C* (Retail: See your dealer) adds a solid, reliable gear pump to an Enya R120-4C engine to make a good thing even better. The pump is easy to connect, comes factory preset, and delivers solid fuel feed despite Hi-G maneuvers. This glow-type, 4-cycle engine delivers 2.2 HP @ 12,500 rpm, weighs 33.09 oz. net, and has a 1.2 cu. in. size/displacement.

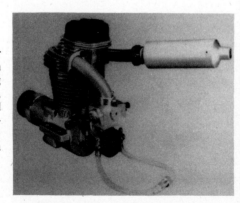

ALTECH MARKETING

The *VT 240 Four-Cycle Twin* (No. JC99Z; Retail: See your dealer) packs prettiness, power, and practicality in one package. This 4-cycle, glow-type engine uses alternate firing cylinders in an 80 degree Vee for less vibration, more power. It delivers 3.2 HP at 10,500 rpm, weighs 59.96 oz. net, and has a 2.4 cu. in. displacement. It comes with glow plugs, glow plug clips, fuel divider, engine mount, and other accessories.

ALTECH MARKETING

The *Enya 1.20-4C* (No. JC99F; Retail: See your dealer) is the power-plus reliability champ of the 4-cycles. With this 120-4C, you get two drive washers, each designed to meet your prop-mounting needs, plus tools, exhaust manifold, muffler, and the Enya G-8 carb with choke for easy starting and fine performance. You'll appreciate this glow-type engine's 1.6 HP at 11,000 rpm, which makes flying an exhilarating experience. The SM-904C muffler (with flexible tubing) is also available. The engine weighs 27.6 oz. w/o muffler, and has a 1.2 cu. in. displacement.

O.S. ENGINES

O.S. FSR Classic Engines ($159.95 - $379.95 retail) are easy to start and exceptionally reliable. With standard features such as Schnuerle porting, ball-bearing supported crankshafts, specially-designed carburetors for maximum efficiency, mufflers, and parts that fit to precision tolerances, FSR Classics have been favored by flyers for years. Available are the .32 F ABC, .50 FSR, .91 FSR, and the large 1.08 FSR. These engines weigh from 8.3 oz. to 26.5 oz.; have outputs ranging from 1.02 to 3.0 BHP @ 16,000 RPM; all are glow type.

O.S. ENGINES

The *O.S. BGX-3500* (No. OSMG0350, $499.95 retail) is a 2-cycle, glow-type engine designed specifically for giant-scale applications. The BGX-3500 features lower vibrations levels, higher output, and lighter weight. It weighs 20.07 oz. net, with a size/displ. of 2.135. Radial mount is included.

O.S. ENGINES

The *Surpass Series Engines* ($209.95 for the 26 Surpass to $799.95 for the Supercharged 120) are 4-cycle engines from O.S. These are the first name in 4-cycle power. They come in sizes such as 26, 40, 48, 70, and 91. The 120 Surpass comes in three versions, with and without pump and the incredible Supercharged 120 Surpass SP. The Surpass 4-strokes offer more power than ever before. These engines weigh from 9.45 oz. to 36.36 oz. and have outputs from .41 to 2.5 BHP @ 12,000 RPM. For power or realism, the Surpass 4-strokes from O.S. can't be beat.

O.S. ENGINES

The *FR5-3500* (No. OSMG1300, $1,999.95 retail) has excellent power-to-weight ratio, for 1/4-scale where realism and authenticity are important. It weighs 68.8 oz., and 1,800-9,000 rpm. 4.0/7,000BHP/rpm.

SUPERTIGRE

The *SuperTigre G-4500* (No. SUPG0270, $479.95 retail) is a powerful 45cc engine that will provide giant-scale modelers an engine big enough for the job at a low price. This 2-cycle, glow-type engine is 2.8 size with 45cc displacement, and delivers 4.5 HP at 8,600 rpm. Featuring a four-port Schnuerle induction, rear intake and 3 bearing design, the G-4500 is 50% bigger and more powerful than the S-3000.

QUADRA-AERROW INC.

The *Q35S* (No. 166501, $172.80 retail) and the *Q42P* (No. 167501, $198.60 retail) are direct descendants of the original Q35 of 1975 vintage. Equipped with mount and muffler, points ignition for easy propstarts. Reliable and trouble-free! For average plane weight of 18/22 lbs.; recommended prop, 18x10/18x12.

The *Q42CD* (No. 167503, $234.40 retail) is a deluxe model featuring 3 main bearings, mount muffler, CD Magneto ignition, and Q-Starter—3BHP. For average plane weight of 22 lbs.; recommended prop, 18x12.

More power in the trusted and familiar package, the *Q52S* (No. 303502, $314.10 retail) is much in demand! Swing 20x10 with ease and low vibration—4.5BHP. Interchangeable with Q35 and Q42. *Update kit* (No. 503523) will provide same power for older Q50s. For average plane weight of 28 lbs.

Proven RPV powerhouse since 1982 is the *Q100S* (No. 302903, $667.00 retail). For average plane weight of 45 lbs.; recommended prop, 24x12. This big brother with 8.5 BHP replaced the Q65 and the Q80.

The *Q35 Hobby Engine* (No.166506, $191.50 retail) and the *Q42H Hobby Engine* (No. 167506CCW, $216.50 retail) have served in R/C cars, boats, and helicopters for years. Water jacket not required. Power 2.4/2.9 BHP respectively. Weight is 5.5 lbs. including muffler. Tuned exhaust available.

The *Aerrow 2x50* (No. A2X50, $849.00 retail) is a Smooth Twin producing 8BHP. Weight is 6.6 lbs. Envelope 5.3"x11"x6.25". Fits inside most cowls. Swings 24x10 @ 6800. A TWIN IN THE QUADRA TRADITION!

SUPERTIGRE

SuperTigre's Giant-scale 2-cycle Engines (No. S-2000, $269.95 retail; No. S-3000, $369.95 retail) are perfect when you need the power. Equipped with Schnuerle porting, ball bearings, and lightweight pistons to reduce vibrations and weight. Large heat sinks and steel cylinder sleeves keep reliability high. These engines have displacements of 1.8 cubic inch; outputs of 3.0 BHP @ 9000 RPM; and are 2-cycle glow types. New from Supertigre, the S-2500.

U.S. QUADRA

If you're looking for a power plant for that next giant scale project, U.S. Quadra has the engine for you. U.S.Q. carries the full line of Quadra engines, parts, and accessories. Pictured is the *Q-42CD* ($205.00 retail). This engine develops 2.9 HP, weighs 4.0 lbs., and displaces 41.4c.c. (2.53 c.i.). It is 6.5 in. high, 6.4 in. long, and 5.4 in. wide. The Q-42 comes equipped with an aluminum die-cast mount, large volume muffler, and spring starter. The Q-42 is capable of turning a variety of propellers from 18-22 inches in diameter, with a pitch range of 6-12 inches.

UNITED MODEL DISTRIBUTORS

Since its introduction, the *Saito FA-120 AAC* (No. 420208, $409.99 retail) engine has become known for its reliability and easy handling. This 1.20 size, glow-type 4-cycle engine has pleased modelers with its performance in large sport and scale aircraft. Because of its massive power, it easily swings big efficient props. The 4-stroke engine features RPM range of 1,600-11,000, weighs 920 grams (2 lb. 2 oz.), has a 1.20 cu. in. displacement, puts out 1.8 HP, and also provides maximum economy. Also available is the FA-120S and FA-120S-DP engines that are higher performance versions of the FA-120. These two engines feature different carbs, intake pipes, combustion chamber shapes, and the FA-120S-DP also features dual glow plugs and a fuel pump system.

UNITED MODEL DISTRIBUTORS

The *Saito FA-270T-TDP* engine is a large alternate firing twin for 1/4-scale class models. This 2.7 size, glow-type 4-cycle engine's realistic sound and excellent performance have made the FA-270T-TDPs great reputation on the field and in the air. The engine features an RPM range of 1,500-8,100, weighs 1,750 grams (3 lb. 14 oz.), has a 45cc displacement, and puts out 3.6 HP. Also available is the new FA-300T for models that demand more power. The FA-300T weighs 300 grams less than FA-270T, has 1,000 more RPM and produces 4.7 HP. The FA-300T is also offered as the FA-300T-TDP, which like the FA-207T-TDP, features dual carbs, dual glow plugs per cylinder, and a fuel pump system.

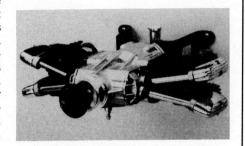

UNITED MODEL DISTRIBUTORS

The *Saito FA-325R-5D* ($2,129.99 retail) engine is a large alternate firing twin for large scale class models. This glow-type engine has realistic sound and excellent performance. The engine features an RPM range of 1,500-7,500, weighs 5 lbs. 4 oz. and has a 53cc displacement. Comes complete with silencers, operating instructions, parts list, exploded diagrams, glow plug, maintenance and tuning tools.

WILLIAMS BROS.

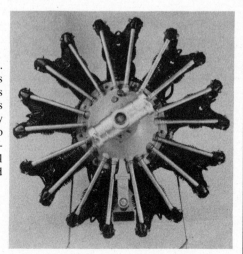

PRATT & WHITNEY "WASP" (Model 307). This record setting Golden Age engine is beautifully recreated in 1-1/2 inch scale. This highly detailed injection molded kit consists of more than 200 parts. Suitable for display or installation in a scale aircraft and also includes a display mount. It measures approximately 6-1/4 inches in. diameter. Individual cylinders available in 1, 1-1/2, 2, 2-1/2, and 3-inch scales.

WILLIAMS BROS.

Gnome Engine Cylinders (Model 725). The Gnome rotary engine was among the most famous power plants of the World War I era. You can now make 1/4-scale reproductions more easily with these detailed injection-molded cylinders.

PRICES AND SPECS ARE SUBJECT TO CHANGE

WILLIAMS BROS.

WILLIAMS BROS.

WRIGHT J-5 (Model 304). This highly detailed model kit represents more than a year of development. This precision injection-molded kit accurately recreates the J-5 which gained fame as the engine of the Spirit of St. Louis. In addition this engine was used in early military, mail planes, and Ford Tri-Motors. Individual cylinders available in 1, 1-1/2, 2, 2-1/2, and 3-inch scales.

WILLIAMS BROS.

R/C Radial Realism Engine/Cowl Kit (Model 325). Now have R/C engine realism the easy way. This kit comes complete with 5 highly detailed cylinders, streamlined cowling, dual ignition leads, as well as the intake tubes and exhaust stacks. It measures approximately 6-1/4 inches in diameter.

LeRhone Rotary (Model 301). A beautifully detailed display kit of this pioneer power plant. The kit consists of 9-cylinders, crankcase, and accessories such as movable gears and the throttle. Individual cylinders available in 1, 1-1/2 and 2-inch scales.

Engines

Boat

ALTECH MARKETING

The *Enya SS50 Ring Marine* (Retail: See your dealer) is a 2-cycle, glow-type engine that delivers 1.3 HP @ 16,000 rpm. Not-so-friendly water environments can make model boaters appreciate easy starts. The aluminum alloy ringed-piston Schnuerle porting, and a hardened steel cylinder on this solidly built marine engine deliver power. And the G-7 carburetor makes mixture adjustments a snap while the standard M402X muffler keeps the sound down. This .50 size engine weighs 325 grams net and has a .50 cu. in. displacement.

ALTECH MARKETING

The *Enya SS30 Ring Marine* (No. JB30M; Retail: See your dealer) packs some of the basic components of the famous SS30 helicopter engine into this marine product. Here's a Schnuerle-ported power plant with a low expansion aluminum alloy piston running in a steel cylinder. A G5.5 carburetor eases fuel adjustment, and two water line taps keep it cool. This 2-cycle, glow-type engine puts out 0.8 HP at 16,000 RPM, weighs 235 grams net, and has a .30 cu. in. size/displacement.

L.A.W. RACING PRODUCTS

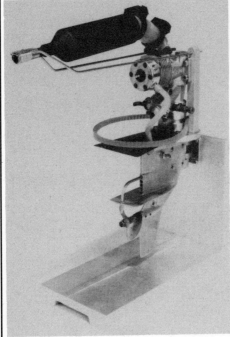

Boaters will now be able to utilize the OS EXM and very soon other similar engines. The *Outboard Engine Conversion Kit* ($82.95 retail) allows simple, lightweight mounting of the OS engine to existing or new K&B lower end outboard units. The mounting requires absolutely no modifications to the engine—it uses stock OS mounting hardware. Now there is an alternative—an alternative that will bring more competition to boat races across the nation.

L.A.W. RACING PRODUCTS

The *Exhaust Throttle* ($49.94 - $84.95 retail) immediately improves throttle response and reliability. The L.A.W. Throttle is the lightest, non-restricting, true round, race-proven throttle on the market today. We use hard clad aluminum barrels to reduce exhaust leakage, barrel wear and weight. Custom control arm, and water fittings are included. 12 and 20 degree mounting angles. Available for over 25 different marine engines.

L.A.W. RACING PRODUCTS

Available for over 25 different marine engines, the *L.A.W. Velocity Stack* ($29.95 - $49.95 retail) has been specifically designed for use with its exhaust throttle. The performance matched Velocity Stack and exhaust throttle eliminate engine acceleration lag, increases engine rpms, and greatly improves engine reliability.

L.A.W. RACING PRODUCTS

The *High Performance Head* ($24.95 - $34.95 retail)—sometimes known as the double bubble head—is computer machined to exceed manufacturers tolerances for fit and compression ratio. It increases compression and rpms with a cleaner, more efficient fuel burn at the head, yet increases fuel efficiency. Simple installation that does not require any configuration changes to your engine. Custom machined heads are also available.

IRVINE ENGINES

Irvine offers a quality line of *Marine Engines* ($85.95 - $209.95 retail) for various types of boats. Features are ABC construction, Schnuerle porting, fly wheel, and ball bearings. These engines range in sizes from .20 to .61 and are 2-cycle glow types. For performance at a value, Irvine Marine Engines are it.

O.S. ENGINES

O.S. Marine Engines come in all the major sizes (.10 to .81) for various applications. These engines weigh from 4.8 oz. to 29.6 oz.; have outputs ranging from .27 to 4.2 BHP; and are all 2-cycle glow types. For serious marine racers there is the VR-M Series, available in .40, .46, .61, .65, and .81. All VR-M feature rear exhaust, ABC construction, and double ball bearings. The .61, .65, and .81 utilize a drum induction system. The .10 and .20 FP-M offer excellent performance at a reasonable price. For the all-out power from a .20 size marine there is the .21 EX-M and the all new .21 RX-M putting out almost 2 horsepower.

Engines

Car

ALTECH MARKETING

The *Enya .09 TV Quick Buggy Engine* (No. JB09Q; Retail: See your dealer) is the ideal power plant for the new 1/10-scale R/C gas buggies hitting the market. You'll find the dual ball bearings on the crankshaft and special overall design leads to better power and easier starting. If you want to go off-road with your buggy in a hurry, this .09 TV Quicky by Enya is the way to go. The engine is glow type, delivers 0.18 HP @ 16,000 rpm, weighs 4.1 oz. w/o muffler, and has a .09 cu. in. displacement.

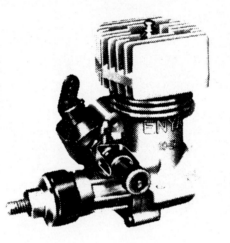

The *Enya .21 CX TV* (No. JB21R for cars, No. JB21W for boats; Retail: See your dealer) has a solid one-piece crankcase, two ball bearings on the crankshaft, and the ALL-chrome piston cylinder set-ups to put out 0.6 HP at 19,000 rpm. This glow-type engine weighs 8.4 oz. and has a .21 cu. in. displacement.

OFNA RACING DIVISION

OFNA Racing offers two types of .21 ABC rear exhaust engine used in all 1/8-scale off-road cars. The *Leo Pro Engine* (No. Leo-722-P EX-B type, $165.00 retail) is rated at 1.9ps at 32,000 RPM. This engine is highly finished with double brass bearing connecting rod, special piston, large port crank, polished case, and tall purple head. Also available is the *Leo Standard Engine* (No. Leo-722, RF-B type, $125.00 retail) and the *Leo Super Pro Engine* (No. Leo-722-PS, $249.00 retail).

ROYAL PRODUCTS CORP.

The *Royal .21 R/C Car Engine* ($109.95 retail) is a glow type, Schnuerle-ported ABC engine featuring oversize cooling fins, twin ball bearings, and massive one-piece crankshaft. It's designed to fit most gas buggies on the market in its size range. Displacement is .21 cu. in.

Engines

Helicopter

ALTECH MARKETING

ALTECH MARKETING

The *Enya 80XF-H Heli* (Retail: See your dealer) has the additional power needed for heavy-scale machines. Enya engines are being used in increasing numbers in helicopters everywhere. This 2-cycle, glow-type engine bolts into the same mount as the 60XF yet delivers more torque, and 2.0 HP @ 16,000 rpm. This ringed engine keeps its cool but uses its GM-10SB carburetor for solid throttle performance. It has a net weight of 19.75 oz. and a size/displ. of .80 cu. in.

The *Enya SS50 Heli GM* (No. JB39H, Retail: See your dealer) is the engine helicopter flyers have been waiting for. This Super Sport .50 cu. in., 2-cycle, glow-type engine comes with a heat sink head plus the famed Enya GM9SB carburetor with midrange mixture control for more power at all rpm ranges. The engine delivers 1.4 HP @ 16,000 rpm. The 1/4-28 crankshaft allows easy installation in many helicopter transmissions.

YOUR LOCAL HOBBY SHOP IS THERE TO HELP YOU SELECT THE BEST EQUIPMENT AND TO ANSWER YOUR QUESTIONS.

ALTECH MARKETING

The *Enya 80XF-H Heli* (Retail: See your dealer) has the additional power needed for heavy scale machines. Enya engines are being used in increasing numbers in helicopters everywhere. This 2-cycle, glow-type engine bolts into the same mount as the 60XF yet delivers more torque, and 2.0 HP @ 16,000 rpm. This ringed engine keeps its cool but uses its GM-10SB carburetor for solid throttle performance. It has a net weight of 19.75 oz. and a size/displ. of .80 cu. in.

ALTECH MARKETING

The *Enya SS35 Heli TN* (Retail: See your dealer) shows how Enya continues to pioneer new designs and develop new engines that can further advance the hobby of model helicopter flying. The 2-cycle, glow-type SS35 Heli TN will deliver plenty of "hover power" for all .30 size helicopters and then some. Its heat-sink head and ringed aluminum piston take the heat while the "new" twin needle 5.6mm carb allows for smooth mixture control at all rpms. The engine has a net weight of 8.46 oz., displaces .35 cu. in., and puts out 0.9 HP @ 16,000 rpm.

ALTECH MARKETING

The *GP 60XF-4* (No. JB60A for side exhaust version, No. JB60C for rear exhaust version, No. JB60B for side exhaust helicopter version; Retail: See your dealer) with gear pump is an excellent choice for severe aerobatic conditions. The GM-10GP carburetor delivers excellent throttle response at any rpm setting. The gear pump is preset at the factory. This 2-cycle, glow-type engine delivers 1.8 HP @ 17,000 rpm, weighs 19.36 oz. net, and has a size/displacement of .60 cu. in. No. JB60A is shown.

ROYAL PRODUCTS CORP.

The *Royal .28 R/C ABC Helicopter Engine* ($114.95 retail) is a glow type, Schnuerle-ported ABC engine that features twin ball bearings, massive one-piece crankshaft, and oversized heat-sink head. The unit accepts standard helicopter mufflers (not included). Displacement is .28 cu. in.

HOBBY DYNAMICS DISTRIBUTORS

Webra is known for reliability, lasting performance, and power. This engine is all that and more. The *Webra Speed .32 Heli engine with Muffler* (No. WE 1028RCH, $189.99 retail) is a favorite among helicopter modelers because it is extremely smooth running with excellent throttle characteristics and performance.

ROYAL PRODUCTS CORP.

The *Royal .46 Helicopter Engine* ($139.95 retail) is a 2 cycle glow type with .46 cu. in. displacement. It features fuel metered carburetion and twin ball bearings, this engine offers Schnuerle porting and ABC design. The unit comes with a heat sink head.

Engines

Miscellaneous

ALTECH MARKETING

Enya engines are noted for their high power output; but for the most demanding applications Enya has recognized your needs and developed the new *53-4C*.

This engine looks compact yet is loaded with features and performance that advanced modelers have been requesting. The 53-4C produces 0.8 HP at 12,000 RPMs yet idles down smoothly to 2,500. The Enya GC 5.5mm carburetor is unbeatable for ease of operation; it comes with a spring loaded choke system for quick starting in bad weather. With a steel cylinder and a ringed aluminum alloy piston, you can be sure that the 53-4C will continue to churn out its power without a missed beat.

For ease of maintenance, a tool set consisting of wrenches, Allen wrench drivers, a screwdriver, and a feeler gauge is included.

DU-BRO PRODUCTS, INC.

Du-Bro has hard to find 3.5 metric screws! Use the *Metric Socket Head Cap Screws* for replacement screws on engines, mufflers, helicopters, and R/C cars. Available in four sizes: 3.5 x 15mm (No. 521, $1.00 retail, 2/pkg.); 3.5 x 20mm (No. 522, $1.00 retail, 2/pkg.); 3.5 x 25mm (No. 523, $1.00 retail, 2/pkg.); and 3.5 x 30mm (No. 524, $1.00 retail, 2/pkg.). See your local dealer today!

L.A.W. RACING PRODUCTS

The *Exhaust Throttle* ($49.94 - $84.95 retail) immediately improves throttle response and reliability. The L.A.W. Throttle is the lightest, non-restricting, true round, race-proven throttle on the market today. We use hard clad aluminum barrels to reduce exhaust leakage, barrel wear, and weight. Custom control arm and water fittings are included. 12 and 20 degree mounting angles. Available for over 25 different marine engines.

L.A.W. RACING PRODUCTS

Available for over 25 different marine engines, the *L.A.W. Velocity Stack* ($29.95 - $49.95 retail) has been specifically designed for use with its exhaust throttle. The performance matched Velocity Stack and exhaust throttle eliminate engine acceleration lag, increases engine rpms, and greatly improves engine reliability.

L.A.W. RACING PRODUCTS

The *High Performance Head* ($24.95 - $34.95 retail)—sometimes known as the double bubble head—is computer machined to exceed manufacturers tolerances for fit and compression ratio. It increases compression and rpms with a cleaner, more efficient fuel burn at the head, yet increases fuel efficiency. Simple installation that does not require any configuration changes to your engine. Custom machined heads are also available.

L.A.W. RACING PRODUCTS

Boaters will now be able to utilize the OS EXM and very soon other similar engines. The *Outboard Engine Conversion Kit* ($82.95 retail) allows simple, lightweight mounting of the OS engine to existing or new K&B lower end outboard units. The mounting requires absolutely no modifications to the engine—it uses stock OS mounting hardware. Now there is an alternative—an alternative that will bring more competition to boat races across the nation.

Radio Control Accessories

By the Staff of Model Retailer

Have you ever met a good carpenter or a good auto mechanic who did not have a good selection of tools and accessories? If they're smart, they'll have the right tools for the job. Modeling is no different. If you don't select the accessories that will make you a better modeler, chances are you will never achieve the degree of enjoyment or satisfaction you should.

You don't have to buy the most expensive accessories on the market, but you should always shop for accessories that will give you trouble-free operation and provide maximum safety. Never compromise safety for a lower price.

Since we are covering the entire radio control hobby, we will review each category separately, although in some cases, one accessory applies to more than one category.

Cars and Monster Trucks

After you have decided which car or truck to buy, the first item you should give some serious consideration is a battery charger. The charger you select should be the AC/DC type, which means you can charge your batteries at home or off your car battery if you're out on a track. The charger should also have an automatic trickle charge feature, a pilot light to let you know when it's in a trickle mode, a charge/discharge switch, a large DC ampere meter, a volt meter jack, and a built-in universal output jack.

Some chargers come with large LED readout panels or meters. Normally, chargers with LED options are more expensive than dial-type chargers. There is no difference in performance between the two types, just a matter of personal preference.

After you have selected your charger, your next decision is what type, brand, and number of battery packs to buy. Depending on your budget, we recommend you start with at least two battery packs. Cars and trucks almost always require flat packs as compared to hump or saddle packs. Flat packs come in six-cell sets and are available in 7.2V and 8.4V packs. Battery packs also come in a wide range of miliamps (mAh) ranging from 1200 to 1700 mAh—even up to 1900 mAhs.

Prices will range from a low of $18.00 a pack to as much as $80.00 or higher if you get into the super-matched packs. Again, unless you plan on entering the competition-class racing, the lower-cost cells will perform well for you and last a long time—as long as you take care of them.

Some tips on how to prolong the life of your batteries are:
• Store fully charged when not in use.
• Avoid excessive heat or cold.
• Don't store them in the trunk of your car.
• Don't overcharge your batteries thinking that will give them longer running time.
• Inspect for leaks of electrolyte or bad connections. You can replace a bad cell without having to throw out the entire pack. Make repairs immediately.
• Discharge or cycle your batteries regularly to keep them at their peak.
• Give them a rest between races. This is the reason we recommend purchasing more than one pack.

Since battery packs come with one type of connector (Kyosho or Tamiya), we recommend you purchase or make your own connector harnesses. That way you don't have to rewire the connectors either on the charger or on the battery pack if they are not compatible. This harness also allows you to run the same pack with different cars/trucks, etc. Making your own connector harness is easy and very economical.

The next major purchasing decision is what type of radio to buy. Radios for cars and boats are called surface radios and normally come in a 2- or 3-channel configuration. These radios come in both stick or wheel formats. They both work the same so it's your own personal preference that should be the decisive factor. Normally, car/truck modelers prefer the wheel type because it resembles the steering wheel

of a car while boat modelers prefer the stick because of the throttle association with boats. Performance is the same.

Since a radio is one accessory that can be transferred from one model to another and because radios normally last a long time, think ahead when selecting a radio and buy the type of unit that will meet your needs in the months and years to come.

Another popular accessory, and well worth the money, is an electronic speed controller. Electronic speed controllers will significantly increase the performance of your model and decrease mechanical problems. (See the article on speed controllers in this Guide to find out the various types available).

You will save money and increase the life of your motors by replacing the motor brushes regularly. A minor replacement like this will keep you from having to buy new motors.

Finally, shop around for a good pit bag or car tote. These totes will help you protect your equipment while transporting or storing your car and accessories.

Boats

Many of the car accessories also apply to boats. Exceptions would be to have a supply of replacement props, cleaning supplies, "AA" batteries for both the radio inside the boat and for the radio, and a lubricant to keep the motor properly lubricated. Remember that heat is your model's worst enemy so keep your equipment well lubricated and well ventilated.

If you are running gas-powered boats, the list of accessories would include a supply of fuel recommended for that engine, a battery to supply power to the starter, an engine starter, glow plug igniters, and a fuel pump to fill and empty the tank. An extra fuel tank should also be a part of your parts kit.

Engine starters come with a variety of cones to fit the spinner of the engine. Make sure you have the correct size or you will damage the cone. A field box is again recommended to help you organize everything.

Airplanes

Airplanes traditionally require the most accessories and as stated earlier, safety should be the most important element when you are deciding what accessories to purchase.

The type and size of airplane you select will have a large effect on the type/size engine best suited for your model. The second largest expenditure will be the radio. Here again, think ahead when you are buying a radio. Do you anticipate staying with a 3- to 5-channel radio, which has very definite limitations as to the functions you can perform? Or do you want to buy a radio that has 5 to 7 channels which would give you flexibility and room to grow with your hobby without having to purchase a new radio? Brand is important and you should choose a brand that has a good reputation, with service readily available. Engines come in two and four stroke types.

Your field box, and we recommend you purchase a unit that will have enough room to hold all your accessories, should include glow plug igniters, an assortment of tools (pliers, screwdrivers, adhesives, rubber bands), an assortment of replacement props for your size aircraft, a battery charger to charge your glow plug igniter, extra glow plugs, extra fuel line, a fuel tank, several spare tires, an electric starter, a battery to power the starter, assorted nose cones for the starter, a fuel bulb, a fuel pump, and fuel.

When buying a field box, purchase a type that will take a power panel. A power panel will make engine starting much easier and safer. A good pair of sunglasses is highly recommended and always protect your hands when attempting to start your engine. A heavy pair of gloves may be just the thing to include in your field box. And don't forget a good CA (cyanoacrylate) and accelerator.

As you start flying at your local flying field, you will see new accessories used by others. Let that be your guide as far as which accessories you need to make flying more enjoyable. Happy flying!

AIRCRAFT ACCESSORIES: FLOATS

Aircraft Accessories

Floats

CARL GOLDBERG MODELS, INC.

Super Floats (No. 296, $59.99 retail) add a whole new dimension to flying. Super Floats are an accessory item for the popular Piper Cub kit that can be used with other 6-1/2- to 9-lb. airplanes as well. Constructed entirely of balsa and plywood, these easy-to-build floats weigh only 24 oz. and are 36 in. long. Because the floats come complete with all the necessary hardware for mounting and its own fully illustrated step-by-step instruction booklet, all the modeler needs is a bottle of Super Jet and a roll of Ultra-Cote to complete the kit.

GREAT PLANES MODEL MFG.

These *Sport Floats* (No. GPMQ1700, $44.95 retail) are 31-in. long. They are easy to build and are ideal for .60-size planes. This kit includes foam cores, all balsa and plywood sheeting, wire spreaders, and mounting blocks. Finished floats support up to 9 lbs.

HELIMAX

Helimax Heli Floats (No. HMXE2000, .30-.40 size, $19.95 retail; No. HMXE2005, .50-.60 size, $29.95 retail) are for your .30-.60 helicopters. They come in two sizes, one for .30-.40, and one for .50-.60. Heli Floats are made of heavy-duty vinyl and provide a safe landing on water or land.

SIG MANUFACTURING CO.

These *Giant Floats* (No. FK-001, $59.95 retail) are 46 in. long and are designed to fit the Sig 1/4 Scale Cub or any other large R/C airplane weighing 12 to 25 lbs. It has super-strong balsa and Lite-Ply construction; full-size plan and photo illustrated instruction book; complete water rudder assembly, including steering cables; pre-formed brace wires; and all mounting hardware.

PRICES AND SPECS ARE SUBJECT TO CHANGE

RADIO CONTROL BUYERS GUIDE 187

SURE FLITE ENTERPRISES

These *Floats* ($22.95 retail) are lightweight, strong, and can't fill with water. They can be used ''as is,'' painted, or fiberglassed. Good looking with a molded slot for the spruce spar included. For either wire or aluminum gear. These floats are constructed of shaped and molded closed cell foam and are 28 in. long. They have a capacity up to 5-1/2 lbs. and weigh 6 oz. per pair, including spars and attachment hardware.

U.S. AIRCORE

Explorer™ Floats (No. AC2060, Deluxe, $49.95 retail; No. AC2061, Standard, $39.95 retail) are quick-built, super tough floats made with AirCore's unique Fold & Fly™ Technology. Pre-decorated in AirCraft aluminum, they assemble in about three hours and fit most .40 to .60 sized planes weighing up to 7 lbs. The deluxe kit includes unique four-point landing gear which allows mounting to most high and low wing planes with minimum effort. Complete easy-to-follow instruction manual included. 100% Made in U.S.A.

R/C Flying is fun for the whole family!

Aircraft Accessories

— Landing Gear & Retracts

DAVE BROWN PRODUCTS

These *Southern Pro Retracts* (nosegear, $32.95 retail; 2-gear, $55.95 retail; 3-gear $85.95 retail) are designed by Ron Chidgey and feature down and up locks. These moving parts are supported by self-aligning bearings for low friction and feature one-servo actuation. Parts and service are available.

DU-BRO PRODUCTS

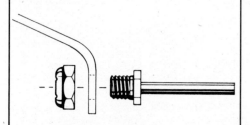

These *Spring Steel Axle Shafts* (No. 246 for 1-1/4-in. x 1/8-in., No. 247 for 1-1/4-in. x 5/32-in., No. 248 for 2-in. x 5/32-in., and No. 249 for 2-in. x 3/16-in.; $2.65/pack retail) are made of plated brass and bolt to any dural landing gear easily.

DU-BRO PRODUCTS

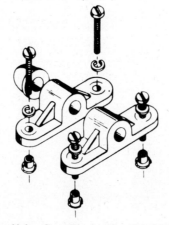

These *Nylon Gear Blocks* (No. 156, $1.70/set retail) are for use with a 5/32-in. wire. Each set includes two nylon blocks, four bolts, lock washers, nuts, and one nylon space.

DU-BRO PRODUCTS

These *Nylon Landing Gear Straps* (No. 238 for 1/8-in., No. 239 for 5/32-in.; $.80 retail) are made of strong nylon.

DU-BRO PRODUCTS

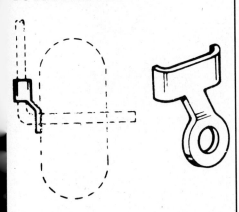

This *Right Angle Wheel Spacer* (No. 342, pack of three, $.75 retail) eliminates wheel lock-up. It positions the wheel a proper distance from the strut to keep wheel spinning freely. Use 5/32-in. wire.

DU-BRO PRODUCTS

7/32'' No. 243
1/4'' No. 244

These *Heavy-Duty Dura-Collars* (No. 243 for 7/32-in., and No. 244 for 1/4-in.; $1.35/two retail) are plated brass and made to fit 7/32-in. and 1/4-in. wire and can be reworked for other uses. Both have 1/2 OD and look like standard wheel collars.

DU-BRO PRODUCTS

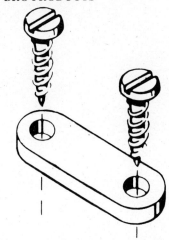

These *Steel Landing Gear Straps* (No. 158, $.75/pack retail) are light and strong. Packs include four straps and eight screws.

DU-BRO PRODUCTS

This *1/2A Steerable Nosegear* (No. 234, $3.00/set retail) is small, lightweight, and easy to install. It comes complete with mounting screws and a 3/32-in. wire.

DU-BRO PRODUCTS

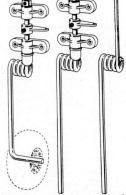

This quality *Steerable Nosegear* (No. 152 for bent, $3.75 retail; No. 153 for straight, $3.75 retail; No. 154 for Nosegear wire only with no blocks, $1.70 retail) is shock-absorbant and comes complete with nylon nosegear blocks, steering arm, and 5/32-in. heavy-duty wire.

DU-BRO PRODUCTS

These *Plated Brass Dura-Collars* (No. 137 for 1/16-in., No. 138 for 3/32-in., No. 139 for 1/8-in., No. 140 for 5/32-in., and No. 141 for 3/16-in.; Set of four, $1.10 retail) feature enough stock so threads don't strip plus they can be reworked for other uses. Each set includes an Allen wrench.

CARL GOLDBERG MODELS, INC.

Klett 5/32-in. Axle (No. 302, pack of two, $2.59 retail); *1/8-in. Axle* (No. 303, pack of two, $2.59 retail).

CARL GOLDBERG MODELS, INC.

Klett Landing Gear (No. 255 for .10/.20, $9.99 retail; No. 256 for .40/.60, $14.99 retail; No. 257 for 1/4 scale, $19.99 retail) are available in three sizes in high-tech glass-filled resin for superior strength and quality, yet they weigh less than aluminum. They won't "shed" paint like aluminum and best of all they absorb rough landings without bending out of shape. Cleanly machined, plated axles (not screws) are retained with special elastic stop nuts. Typical Klett attention to detail means the finest gear of its kind.

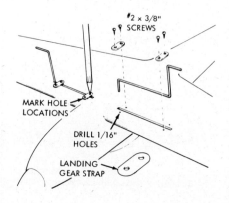

EDSON ENTERPRISES, INC.

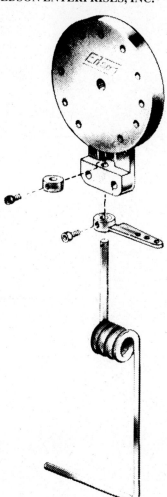

The *Edson Adjustable Nose Gear* (No. NG-55, $6.95 retail) is designed to receive the Edson M-50 Motor Mount. This combination allows a choice of 12 different positions to mount your engine without disturbing your nose gear. Complete instructions are supplied with the kit.

CARL GOLDBERG MODELS, INC.

Preassembled Tailwheel Steering Bracket (No. 232, $19.99 retail) includes one of the three optional tailwheel diameters: 1-1/2" (No. 238, $1.99 retail); 1-3/4" (No. 239, $1.99 retail); or 2" (No. 240, $1.99 retail). The scale appearance of this molded resin, glass-filled bracket is sure to attract your attention if quarter scale or larger is your pursuit. Weighing only 1.6 oz., this bracket is no lightweight when it comes to the rugged durability needed on the larger models and rough field conditions. The spring centering feature adds to the scale look and function, which is more effective on the larger models. However, should you damage this bracket, it will be replaced without charge.

CARL GOLDBERG MODELS, INC.

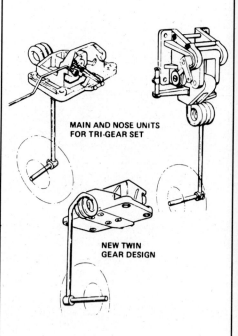

These *Retracts* (No. 250 for nosegear, $24.99 retail; No. 251 for twin-gear set, $29.99 retail; No. 252 for tri-gear set, $44.99 retail) are preferred by many experts for ruggedness and reliability. They feature long struts with adjustable axles, etc. Main gears are 1-in. high. Tri-gear set weighs 6 oz. Nylon moldings are broad-based, vibration absorbing, and have large bearing surfaces. One counterbalanced retract servo can actuate three units.

CARL GOLDBERG MODELS, INC.

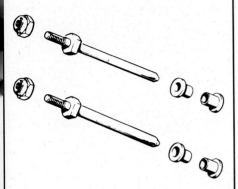

Klett 5/32-in. Axle with 3/16-in. Bushing (No. 304, Pack of two, $3.49 retail) is for use with wheels with 3/16-in. I.D. hub; *3/16-in. Axle with 1/4-in. Bushing* (No. 305, Pack of two, $3.49 retail) is for use with wheels with 1/4-in. I.D. hub.

CARL GOLDBERG MODELS, INC.

This *5/32 Steerable Nosegear with Adjustable Axle* (No. 267 for complete assembly, $5.99 retail; No. 272 for strut with axle only, $2.99 retail) is designed for use with large models. It comes complete with blind nuts, screws, 5/32-in. music wire strut, and adjustable axle.

CARL GOLDBERG MODELS, INC.

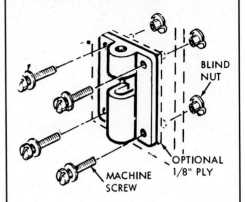

This *Nylon Nosegear Bearing* (No. 277 for 5/32-in., $1.99 each retail; No. 278 for 1/8-in., $1.99 each retail) is a one-piece design that mounts to the firewall. Included are blind nuts, screws, and washers.

CARL GOLDBERG MODELS, INC.

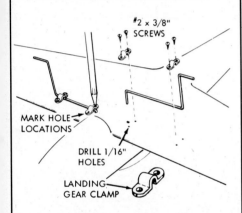

These *Landing Gear Clamps* (No. 287 for 5/32-in., $.99/pack retail; No. 286 for 1/8-in., $.99/pack retail) are molded of tough nylon. Each pack includes four clamps and eight screws.

CARL GOLDBERG MODELS, INC.

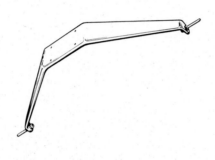

These tough nylon *Landing Gear Straps* (No. 290 for 3/8-in., $.99/set retail; No. 291 for 1/2-in., $.99/set retail) provide strong and electrically noiseless strut retention. Sets are of four straps and eight screws.

CARL GOLDBERG MODELS, INC.

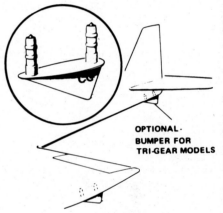

These nylon *Wing Skids* (No. 461, $1.29/three, retail) help prevent ugly scrapes. Even top fliers can't keep gusty winds from dropping a wing to the runway when landing.

CARL GOLDBERG MODELS, INC.

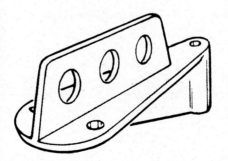

This *Nylon Tailwheel Bracket* (No. 460, $.99 retail) is a simple-to-install tailwheel mounting bracket. A slot in the rear bottom of the fuselage needs to be cut, then the glue fin epoxied, and the bracket slides into place.

CARL GOLDBERG MODELS, INC.

This *Steerable Nosegear* (Retail: $3.99 - $5.99 and $1.29 for arm only) is available in three sizes and comes with blind nuts, screws, etc. Order No. 260/SN332 for 3/32-in., No. 261/SN180 for 1/8-in., No. 262/ G16N for 5/32-in., No. 280/SA-180 for 1/8-in. steering arm only, and No. 281/SA-532 for 5/32-in.

CARL GOLDBERG MODELS, INC.

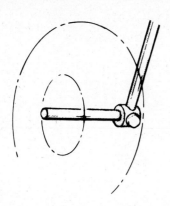

This *Adjustable Axle* (No. 300, $1.99 each retail) is for use with a 5/32-in. strut. The strut needs to be filed flat and the axle tightened into place. Axle and screw are made of hardened steel.

THE HALL COMPANY

This *Landing Gear* ($12.75 - $24.10 retail) is made of anodized, heat-treated aluminum for long life and strength. Stainless steel axle bolts are locked in place by a nylon insert. The nut is splined, press fitted, and clinched into the gear.

ROYAL PRODUCTS CORP.

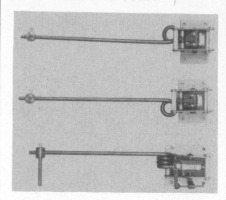

These *Retractable Landing Gear* (Trike set, $44.95 retail; Main retract set, $28.95 retail) are lightweight and economical. They are ideal for .60 size aircraft and feature adjustable axles, aluminum side plates, and fiberglass-filled nylon actuating parts.

L.A.W. RACING PRODUCTS

The *Snow Bird Skis* come in three sizes: .19-.40 size engines for planes to 6 lbs.; .40-.60 size for planes to 10 lbs.; and for planes up to 30 lbs. The Skis are machined from 6061 grade aircraft aluminum and come highly polished with attractive blue anodization. The Skis require no modification to the aircraft's existing landing gear and take just minutes to switch back and forth to wheels.

SIG MANUFACTURING CO.

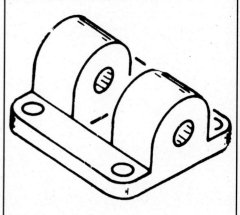

These *Nylon Nosegear Bearings* ($.85 retail) are molded from super-tough nylon. They're available alone or with blind nuts and bolts in 1/8-in. and 5/32-in. sizes.

SIG MANUFACTURING CO.

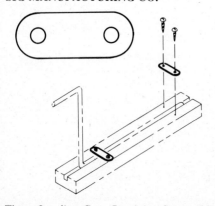

These *Landing Gear Retaining Straps* (No. SH-131, regular size, $.69 retail; No. SH-709, giant size, $.89 retail) are molded of tough nylon and come complete with mounting screws. It comes available in two sizes, four to a package.

SIG MANUFACTURING CO.

These *Nylon Steering Arms* ($.95/each retail) are extra heavy-duty. They have a brass bearing and are molded in Sig's manufacturing plant. Two sizes are available: 1/8-in. and 5/32-in.

SIG MANUFACTURING CO.

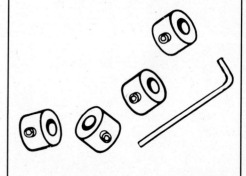

These *Wheel Collars* ($1.35/pack of four retail) are top quality, plated, and come four to a package, complete with set screws and allen wrench. Order No. SH-584 for 1/16-in., No. SH-585 for 3/32-in., No. SH-586 for 1/8-in., No. SH-587 for 5/32-in., and No. SH-588 for 3/16-in.

SIG MANUFACTURING CO.

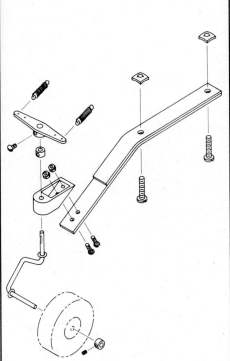

This *X-Large Leaf-Spring Tailwheel Assembly* (No. SH-730, $17.95 retail) is super strong for giant-size models weighing over 15 pounds. Scale-like design features hardened steel leaf-spring, pre-bent axle wire, molded super-tuff nylon control horns, and complete hardware. Fits up to 2 1/4-in. diameter wheels.

SPRING AIR PRODUCTS INT'L INC.

These *Retracts* (Retail: See your dealer) have a new 100% fail-safe design that is smaller and lighter than other retracts but with no sacrifice in strength. Completely self-contained. Can be operated with single mini-servo.

SPRING AIR PRODUCTS INT'L INC.

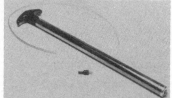

A *Hand Pump with Pressure Gauge* (No. 117; Retail: See your dealer)—no more guessing about the amount of air in the system. For all pneumatic systems. Hand Pump without Pressure Gauge (No. 118; Retail: See your dealer) is also available.

Aircraft Accessories
Pilot Figures

MGA ENTERPRISES

From the top of his helmet with the blazing red squadron eagle to the silver bars proudly gracing his shoulders, this MGA 1/8-scale *Jet Pilot Bust—Top Gun* (No. 008, $24.95 retail) says it all. MGA Quarter-scale state-of-the-art finished pilots in *WWI* (No. 100B), *WWII* (No. 200B), and *Civilian/ Sport* (No. 300B) retail for $19.95 each.

MGA ENTERPRISES

GERMAN LUFTWAFFE PILOT BUST

READY TO FLY
⅕ LUFTWAFFE
⅕ USAAF
⅑ JAPANESE

Achtung! *Luftwaffe Ace* (No. 700, $24.95 retail) is dressed in black jacket, red and silver emblems with yellow squadron scarf and has a poseable head. USAAF (No. 600, $24.95) and *Imperial Japanese Navy* (No. 009, $19.95 retail) are also available.

Aircraft Accessories

Propellors

DU-BRO PRODUCTS

The *Tru-Spin Prop Balancer* (No. 499, $26.95 retail) is completely adjustable for large and small props, helicopter blades, jet fans, car wheels and even motor gears. The lockable adjusting cone of the balancing shaft gives the Tru-Spin a sure-hold-grip to insure the precise balance you need.

DU-BRO PRODUCTS, INC.

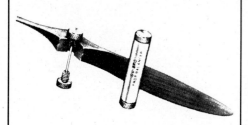

The *Prop Balancer* (No. 160, $4.25 retail) fits all prop sizes. It's bored for 1/4-in. shafts and shows balance on long and side axis. It's made of a knurled base cap, one cone piece, and precision-ground steel balance pin.

DYNATHRUST PROPS INC.

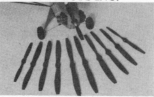

These *Glass-Filled Composite Molded Props* are precision injection-molded and feature true pitch and money saving durability. Now available with logo and tips painted.

Sizes	Price
11x7.75	$2.00
12x6, 8	$3.00
13x6, 8	$4.00
14x6, 8	$5.00
15x6, 8	$7.00
16x6, 8	$8.00
18x6, 8, 10	$10.00
20x6, 8, 10	$14.00
22x8, 10	$18.00

CARL GOLDBERG MODELS, INC.

The new *4-pin Snap-On Spinners* ($2.59-5.29 retail) from Carl Goldberg take larger props, shafts, and hubs without sacrificing performance or convenience. With 5 prop shaft adapters (included) and 2 new sizes (2-3/4-in. and 3-in.), the improved 4-pin design fits most props, eliminating reaming the back plate or trimming the spinner. The Goldberg spinner is pre-balanced, lighter than aluminum, and free of unsightly surface screw holes. It's perfect shape and polished finish make it the most popular spinner available.

CARL GOLDBERG MODELS, INC.

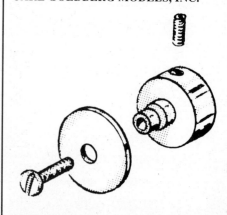

This *Propeller Mount* (No. 676/PMT, $2.99 retail) is precision-machined aluminum. It fits standard unthreaded 1/8-in. electric motor shafts. Especially designed for use with or without CG Snap-On Spinners.

THE MIDWAY MODEL COMPANY

Taipan Propellers are a high performance glass-filled nylon prop from Australia. Originally designed by Gordon Burford, world renowned designer of the Taipan Engines of the 1970s, the propellers were engineered competition performance. The high performance designs will allow you to get the best out of your sleeve or ball bearing engine as well as out of your electrics. The blade shape provides maximum thrust to the hub. The blades increase in cord to a center cuff to get the maximum performance out of the center area of the prop. This feature provides extra performance over most plastic and traditional wooden propellers. Give them a test and experience the performance advantage.

C.B. TATONE, INC.

C.B. Associates Aluminum Spinners (1-1/2-in., $11.50 retail; 1-3/4-in., $13.95 retail; 2-in., $14.95 retail; 2-1/4-in., $15.50 retail; 2-1/2-in. $17.25 retail) are precision machined and offer a modeler a low cost way to dress up his model. Aluminum spinners are available in five sizes: 1-1/2-in., 1-3/4-in., 2-in., 2-1/4-in., and 2-1/2-in.

C.B. TATONE, INC.

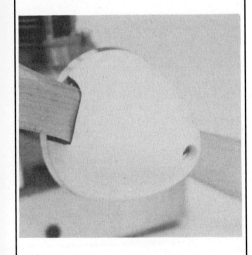

C.B. Associates Plastic Spinners "With Aluminum Back Plate" ($5.30 - $22.95 retail) come complete with spinner, spinner nut and bushing. Spinner cones are strong, and available in white, red, and black. Available from size 1-3/4-in. to 4-1/4-in. Send for complete catalog.

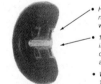

Aircraft Accessories ———— Wheels

DAVE BROWN PRODUCTS

Lite Flite Wheels ($3.25 - $16.95 retail) for aircraft are extremely light yet very durable. They are available from size 1-1/2-in. through 6-in. to fit every model. The wheels have a snap-together nylon hub for longer wear. No threads to jam axles. Now available: Lectra-Lite narrow light wheels.

DU-BRO PRODUCTS

These *Low Bounce Tread Wheels* ($3.75-$5.50/pair retail) are top quality, treaded, and hand inspected. They feature top quality workmanship, an authentic scale look, and realistic looking aluminum-finish wheel hubs. Order No. 175-T for 1-3/4-in., No. 200-T for 2-in., No. 225-T for 2-1/4-in., No. 250-T for 2-1/2-in., No. 275-T for 2-3/4-in., No. 300-T for 3-in., No. 325-T for 3-1/4-in., and No. 350-T for 3-1/2-in.

DU-BRO PRODUCTS

These *Smooth-Surface Wheels* ($3.75-$5.50/pair retail) are hand-inspected and picked to match tire pressure and softness. They're designed to hug the field when landing. Order No. 175-R for 1-3/4-in., No. 200-R for 2-in., No. 225-R for 2-1/4-in., No. 250-R for 2-1/2-in., No. 275-R for 2-3/4-in., No. 300-R for 3-in., No. 325-R for 3-1/4-in., and No. 350-R for 3-1/2-in.

DU-BRO PRODUCTS

This *Big Wheel Tire Inflator* (No. 333, $1.00 retail) can be used with Du-Bro's Big Wheel Tire Pump to inflate Du-Bro inflatable tires.

DU-BRO PRODUCTS

These *J-3 Cub Wheels–1/5, 1/4 and 1/3 Scale* ($20.95-$27.95 retail) are realistic looking 8.00-4 tires with bolt together hubs and authentically scaled ''Cub'' wheelcovers. The 1/4- and 1/3-scale wheels are easy to inflate with Du-Bro's positive seal air valves and inflate valve. The 1/5-scale wheels are low bounce and non-inflatable. Order No. 338TC for 1/5-scale, 3-3/8-in. dia. ($20.95); No. 425TC for 1/4-scale, 4-1/4-in. dia. ($25.95); and No. 558TC for 1/3-scale, 5-5/8-in. dia. ($27.95).

DU-BRO PRODUCTS

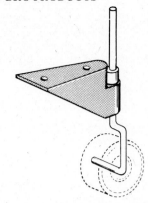

These *Tailwheel Brackets* (No. 375 for small–.40-size, $1.75 retail; No. 376 for medium–.60-size, $2.25 retail; No. 377 for large–1/4-scale, $2.75 retail) are made of lightweight durable nylon and are available in three sizes to fit most planes.

DU-BRO PRODUCTS

These *Large Scale Treaded Wheels* ($9.95-$14.95/each retail) are inflatable wheels which add realism and final detail to your plane. They feature a positive-seal air valve and inflator valve for ease of inflation. The large-diameter hub is made of high-impact nylon for strength and tire support. The standard axle diameter of 3/16-in. can be drilled out to 1/4-in. Order No. 375TV for 3-3/4-in. ($9.95); No. 400TV for 4-in. ($10.95); No. 450TV for 4-1/2-in. ($11.95); No. 500TV for 5-in. ($12.95); No. 550TV for 5-1/2-in. ($13.95); and No. 600TV for 6-in. ($14.95).

DU-BRO PRODUCTS

These realistic looking *Big Wheels* ($11.95-$20.95 retail) are smooth inflatable tires. They feature a positive-seal air valve, two-piece bolt-together hub and cap. They can be inflated and deflated through a tiny valve in the side of the tire. Order No. 400RV for 4-in. ($11.95), No. 450RV for 4-1/2-in. ($13.95), No. 500RV for 5-in. ($16.95), No. 550RV for 5-1/2-in. ($18.95), and No. 600RV for 6-in. ($20.95).

DU-BRO PRODUCTS

This *Nose Wheel Brake and Link Hook-Up* (No. 157, $3.50/set retail) is a complete 10-piece nose wheel brake and linkage hook-up.

DU-BRO PRODUCTS

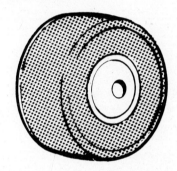

These low-bounce *Tailwheels* ($1.20-$1.95 retail) have a one-piece aluminum hub and are available in four sizes. Order No. 75TW for 3/4-in., 1/16-in.-axle .40-size planes ($1.20); No. 100TW for 1-in., 3/32-in.-axle .60-size ($1.45); No. 125TW for 1-1/4-in., 3/32-in.-axle .60-size ($1.70); and No. 150TW for 1-1/2-in., 1/8-in.-axle 1/4-scale ($1.95).

DU-BRO PRODUCTS

This *Big Wheel Tire Pump* (No. 332, $5.95 retail) can be used as a quick and easy way to inflate all Du-Bro's inflatable tires.

KDI

The *KDI Wheel Pant* ($24.95 retail) is the perfect way to dress up .40 to .60 size models. Pattern ships can save .5-1.0 lb. by using this gear instead of retracts. The durable vinyl material is lightweight and attractive. The slimline wheels help compliment the aerodynamic shape. Bright colors include white, red, and yellow. Comes assembled with 2-1/4" Slimline wheels including one left and one right.

C.B. TATONE, INC.

The *C.B. Tatone Big Wheels* ($22.95 - $29.95 retail) are lightweight foam low-bounce wheels with aluminum bearings in strong glass-filled nylon hubs which will support up to 100 lbs. Available in 3-1/2-in., 4-in., 4-1/2-in., 5-in., 5-1/2-in., 6-in., 6-1/2-in., and 7-in. A size for every modeler's need.

WILLIAMS BROS.

Smooth Contour Style Wheel. This type of wheel and tire was used from the late 1930s through early World War II. Wheel disc covers axle collar for a clean appearance. Wheel may be painted to match your aircraft, and like all Williams Bros. wheels, the larger sizes include foam core inserts installed. Available in the following sizes: 3/4, 1, 1-1/4, 1-1/2, 2-1/4, 2-3/4, 3-1/4, 3-3/4, 4-1/2, and 5-1/4 inch diameters.

WILLIAMS BROS.

Balloon Style Scale Wheels. These balloon wheels are ideal for aircraft from the 1930s to present. The larger sizes come with foam core inserts installed. Available in the following sizes: 2-1/2, 3-1/4, 3-3/4, 4-1/2, and 5-1/4 inch diameters.

WILLIAMS BROS.

Vintage Style Scale Wheel. This style of wheel is typical of the high-pressure type used during World War I and on to the mid-1930s. Highly detailed and easily paintable, the Vintage style wheel is available in the following sizes for your modeling pleasure: 1-1/2, 1-7/8, 2-1/2, 3-1/8, 3-3/4, 4-3/8, 5, and 5-1/4 inch diameters. For giant-scale, it is offered in 6-5/8 diameter.

WILLIAMS BROS.

Golden Age Scale Wheel. This disc type wheel was used extensively on aircraft from the late twenties to early thirties. Well detailed and very durable, these Golden Age wheels will make a beautiful addition to your scale aircraft. Available in the following sizes: 1-1/2, 1-7/8, 2-1/2, 3-1/8, 3-3/4, 4-3/8, and 5 inch diameters along with the giant-scale 6-1/2 in. diameter.

Aircraft Access.

—— Misc.

AEROTREND PRODUCTS

Parts Pots (No. 1213, $4.99 retail) are handy workbench helpers for holding small parts. They have a molded-in bump and ridge that allow the biggest hands to pick up the smallest parts. Come four to a package.

AEROTREND PRODUCTS

Skid Stops ($4.99 retail) are 3/4" long pieces of specially formulated silicone which protect the helicopter skids from excessive wear and damage and lessen the vibration—therefore helping to steady the helicopter before takeoff and landing—stopping the skid!! They come eight per package—all black, all white, or a combination of both and are approved by top helicopter fliers. Order Large—No. 1270 B/W Combo, No. 1271 White, No. 1272 Black; or Small—No. 1273 B/W Combo, No. 1274 White, No. 1275 Black.

C.J.T. ENTERPRISES INC.

Perfect for the den or office. These unique *clocks and thermometers* ($29.95 retail each) are double scale replicas of aviation instruments. Each instrument measures 6.5 inches square, is molded from high impact polystyrene and features a glass lens. All models are warranted for one year against manufacturers defects. The quartz clocks require one AA battery. Make a truly distinctive promotional gift by having the altimeter clock customized with your corporate logo.

DAVE BROWN PRODUCTS

The *RCHS R/C Helicopter Simulator and the RCFS R/C Flight Simulator* (Program, $53.95; Program and joystick TX, $152.95) are for IBM or compatible (special Tandy 1000 version available). This program, designed by John Kallend, successfully simulates R/C flight from take-off to landing (or crashing). The dual joystick transmitter takes the place of your computer's joystick. Also available for Commodore 64 and Apple II (Program, $49.95 retail; Program and joystick, $139.00 retail).

DU-BRO PRODUCTS

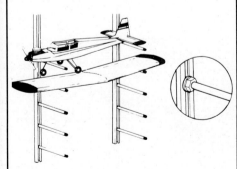

This *Wing-N-Fuselage Rack* (No. 350, $24.95 retail) is the easy and safe way to store airplanes free from damage. It's a must for every modeler's home. Features include a 3-ft.-long track system for easy adjustment. Five pairs of anodized aluminum rods are included.

DU-BRO PRODUCTS

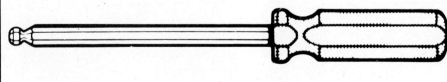

Standard and Metric Ball Wrenches ($2.25 retail) are the perfect tool for getting at those hard-to-reach places. Ball wrenches make it possible to turn socket head screws or bolts from any angle. Standard Ball Wrenches: No. 2151—5/64 (2-56 Skt. Hd.), No. 2152—3/32 (4-40 Skt. Hd.). Metric Ball Wrenches: No. 2153—1.5mm (2.0mm Skt. Hd.), No. 2154—2.0mm (2.5mm Skt. Hd.), No. 2155—2.5mm (3.0mm Skt. Hd.).

G&A PRODUCTS

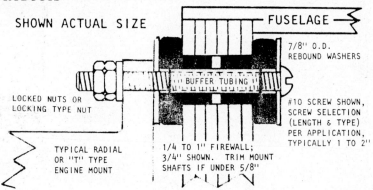

SHOWN ACTUAL SIZE

FUSELAGE

7/8" O.D.
REBOUND WASHERS

BUFFER TUBING

LOCKED NUTS OR
LOCKING TYPE NUT

#10 SCREW SHOWN,
SCREW SELECTION
(LENGTH & TYPE)
PER APPLICATION,
TYPICALLY 1 TO 2"

TYPICAL RADIAL
OR "T" TYPE
ENGINE MOUNT

1/4 TO 1" FIREWALL;
3/4" SHOWN. TRIM MOUNT
SHAFTS IF UNDER 5/8"

PATENT PENDING

G&A Products manufactures the *Vend Mount* (Standard Kit $12.00 mail order) system of soft engine mounts. Called the 'Vibration Killer,' the system offers the user a guaranteed vibration reduction of at least 70%. Plus no pull, shear, or tear modes; fuel proof rubber and fail-safe design. The standard four point kit covers engines to 1.20, firewalls from 1/4 to 1 in. thick and fits all engine mounts (radial, 'T' type, etc.). Kit includes 8 mounts to isolate 4 points, your choice of washers and buffer tubing for #6, #8, or #10 screws (SPECIFY), and instructions. Special 6 and 8 point kits are available for large engines (Quadras, etc.), (INQUIRE).

FIBERGLASS MASTER

Fiberglass Cowls and Wheelpants (Retail: See your dealer). All products are exact duplicates of the manufacturer's original. Made of fiberglass cloth and resin, these strong, flexible units do not require any assembly. The entire line of products is fuel-proof, reinforced at stress points and resistant to cracking from impact or vibration.

GRANITE STATE R/C PRODUCTS

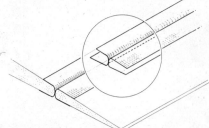

The *Iron-On Gapless Hinge* (No. 610, 45 in., $2.49 retail) is nothing new to some of the old-time control line fliers. They used cloth, sewed it together, and glued it in place. Using glue was a little messy, but well worth it, because the hinge outlasted the model. With all the new materials available to R/Cers, this is the easiest hinge to install today. It can be painted or Monokoted® —just line it up and heat it on with your iron. It seals the gap, stops aileron warping and flutter.

PECK-POLYMERS

3/8
1/8
1/4

1/2
7/16
1/4

PA-1 FOR 1/32 PROP SHAFT — PA-6 FOR 3/64 PROP SHAFT

These precision nylon thrust *Nose Bearings* (Nos. PA-1, PA-1B, and PA-6; 1.20/six, retail) are for rubber-powered models. Small is for 1/32-in. prop shaft; large is for 3/64-in. prop shaft.

K & S ENGINEERING

Pro-Lube Oil (No. 700, 4 oz. bottle, $2.95 retail) is a new premium-quality oil specially designed for 2-cycle and 4-cycle model engines. It penetrates quickly to neutralize acids from the combustion of glo-fuel, protects metal parts with an invisible barrier against corrosion, and provides a protective coating for internal parts of the engine while in storage.

PECK-POLYMERS

These beautiful *Spoked Wheels* (No. PW-100, $10.00 to $100.00 retail) are for antique rubber-powered models and R/C models. Small wheels are balsa construction over 1-1/2-in. stainless steel. Sizes include 1/2-in. dia. to 6-1/2-in. dia.

PECK-POLYMERS

These *Dummy Engine & Cylinders Kits* (Nos. WB 404 to WB 410, $2.29 to $2.60 retail) are only for scale detail: 5 cylinders 3/8 scale 1/2, 3/4—$1.49 retail; Engine kits 5 cylinders 3/8 scale 1/2, 3/4—$2.98 retail. Also 7, 9 cylinder kits.

ROYAL PRODUCTS CORP.

These *Scale Spun-Aluminum Spinners* ($8.95 - $10.95 retail) are designed to fit Royal and similar scale aircraft. The 2- and 3-blade styles are available in sizes for Royal Zero (Sr. and Jr.), FW-190, ME-109, Spitfire Sr., P-51 Jr., and Stuka.

ROYAL PRODUCTS CORP.

These *Scale Cockpit Kits* ($8.95 - $19.95 retail) are available in 10 sizes: P-51 1/2A-.60, Corsair 1/2A-.60, Spitfire, Bearcat, FW-190, P-38, Zero 1/2A-.60, B-25, B-17, and Cessnas.

ROYAL PRODUCTS CORP.

STANDARD

MILITARY

The *Royal Canopies* ($0.45-$2.75 retail) are available in military- or standard-style designs. They're molded from the fine butyrate and range in size from 4-in. to 16-in.

SERMOS R/C SNAP CONNECTORS, INC.

These *High-Amp Powerpole Snap Connectors* (Retail: Available from Sermos) are modular "silver-plated" connectors for your electric planes, cars, or boats. They're designed for a high-vibration environment. Cycled ten thousand times without electrical failure, they're designed for anything electrical requiring quick disconnects. Color coordinated and rated 30 amps at 600 DC, internal resistance is rated 250 micro ohms. Silver-plated contact accepts AWG sizes 12 to 16. For dealer information send to Sermos.

SERMOS R/C SNAP CONNECTORS, INC.

This *Insertion/Extraction Tool* (No. G-2 TOOL, $5.00 retail) is a quick and easy way to assemble and disassemble the Sermos R/C Snap Connectors.

SIG MANUFACTURING CO.

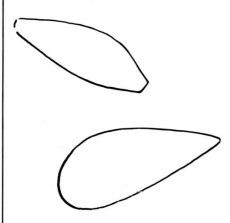

Canopies ($.85 - $4.65 retail)

	Width (Inches)	Height (Inches)	Length (Inches)	
WC-805	1-5/8	1-1/4	5	$1.05
WC-807	1-7/8	1-3/4	7	$1.30
WC-809	2-3/8	2-1/4	9	$1.75
WC-811	2-7/8	2-3/4	11	$2.10
WC-813	3-3/8	3-1/4	13	$3.65
WC-815	4-1/4	3-3/4	15	$4.65
CS-004	1-1/8	1	4	$ .85
CS-005	1-3/16	1	5	$ .89
CS-006	1-1/2	1-3/8	6	$1.05
CS-007	1-7/8	1-1/2	7	$1.15
CS-008	2	1-5/8	8	$1.65
CS-009	2	1-3/4	9	$1.75
CS-010	2-1/4	2	10	$1.85
CS-011	2-1/2	2	11	$2.10
CS-012	2-3/4	2-1/4	12	$2.75
CS-013	2-7/8	2-5/8	13	$3.45
CS-014	3-1/8	2-1/2	14	$3.85
CS-015	3-1/8	2-5/8	15	$4.15
CS-016	3-1/4	2-5/8	16	$4.50

SMC/LIGHTNING PRODUCTS

Designed specifically for airplanes, the *AirCraft Workstation* (No. ACW-1, $55.00 retail) foam padded carriages hold most fuselages up to and over planes with .90 engines. Hook/loop cinch straps allow just the right pressure to hold plane secure without damaging the fuselage. Clamp system tilts 180°, rotates 360°, and heavy-duty design holds work steady regardless of angle.

VORTAC MFG. CO., INC.

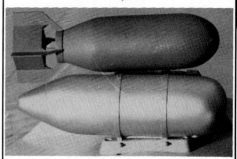

This *Reusable Exploding Bomb* ($4.98 each or $9.98 per two, retail) is a WW II-type bomb that scales out to 500-lb. size for Top Flite stand-off scale models, and 1000-lb. size for House of Balsa .40 powered P-51. It separates on impact to discharge a payload of chalk or flour. It's compatible with Vortac's Bomb Release Mechanism. It's available in bright orange and scale green.

VORTAC MFG. CO., INC.

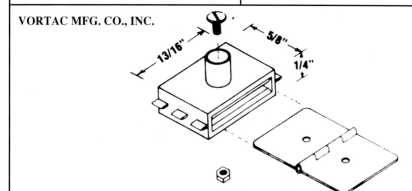

These *Hinge Holders* (12-piece set, $2.39 retail; 30-piece set, $4.98 retail) provide a revolutionary new way to install regular size pinned hinges. They automatically provide a 1/64-in. hinge gap. They secure your hinges with a steel bolt and clamping action and can be easily built into 1/4-in. sheet balsa and built-up surfaces. No more slotting and gluing hinges together. Control surfaces can be removed and worn hinges replaced simply by removing the bolts. All that shows are the recessed bolt heads in the underside of the control surfaces. All hardware, except hinges, is included. The 12-piece set mounts six hinges. The 30-piece set mounts 15 hinges.

VORTAC MFG., INC.

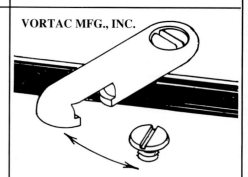

These *Gear Locks* (Pack of four, $1.98 retail) enable you to remove and reinstall wire landing gears and bipe wings in seconds for storage, repair, and transport without using tools. This lock mounts in the same space as a standard gear strap, but won't bend like metal straps and is stronger than nylon straps. It fits wire landing gears up to 5/32-in. Positive snap-action secures gear lock to bolt head.

C.B. TATONE, INC.

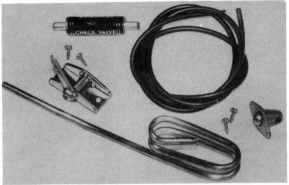

"Lotsa Smoke" Kits (No. 17016 for Tatone's 11314, 11334 and 11354, $22.95 retail; No. 17036 for 11754, 11913, 11933, 11434 and 11454, $22.95 retail; No. 17056 for all Tatone mufflers for Quadra, Kioritz, Magnum, Kawasaki, Max .90 and Webra .91 engines, $22.95 retail; and 17076 for Quadra-50 factory muffler, $26.95 retail) are smoke-making kits for mufflers. Each kit includes a pressure fitting, check valve, smoke shut-off valve, fuel line regulator, preheater coil, smoke fuel tubing and mounting screws, as well as complete instructions.

VORTAC MFG. CO., INC.

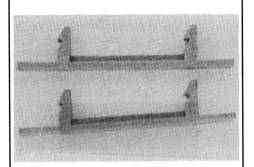

These *Release Clips* ($.98/two retail) are extras for Vortac's Release Mechanism. They can be epoxied or drilled and screwed to your bomb or drop tank. They're made of gray nylon and measure 2-in. x 1/4-in.

VORTAC MFG. CO., INC.

This *Bomb & Drop Tank Release Mechanism MK II* ($6.98 retail) is perfect for scale models and fun-fly bomb drops. It's small enough to be mounted anywhere on an aircraft or in a scale ordnance pylon. It can be linked to a servo by pushrod or pull cord. It can be connected to the rudder servo or throttle override. An extra servo is not needed. A spring-loaded positive-lock loads bombs instantly and the side-mounted release arm allows manual unloading independent of servo operation. It's compatible with Vortac's Release Clips and Exploding Bomb. Measures: 2-3/4-in. x 3/8-in.

XURON CORP.

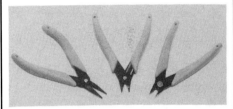

The *Shears* (No. 475 C, Combination Plier, $14.99 retail; No. 410 T, High Precision Shear, $9.99 retail; No. 450, Tweezernose Plier, $15.99 retail) that set the standard in civilian and military electronics and aerospace are now available to RC hobbyists. The shearing cut of XURON Micro-Shear® flushcutters is so clean and square that post-cutting clean up may not be required. Ask for XURON when you want the cuts that are so good their patented.

Heli Accessories

HOBBY DYNAMICS DISTRIBUTORS

Kalt's new Whisper Battery Pack (No. K40002, $61.99 retail) is here and ready to put the Whisper in flight. This new 9.6V, 1,100mAH, 8-cell SCR battery was specifically designed for the new Kalt Whisper electric helicopter. Its optimum weight-to-power ratio allows for maximum flight capabilities.

HELIMAX

The *Heli-Max Heliport* (No. HMXE1000, $99.95 retail) securely holds your model for easy maintenance at home or at the field. The handy tilt feature allows access to even the hardest to reach areas of your helicopter.

SMC/LIGHTNING PRODUCTS

Designed specifically for helicopters, the *RotorCraft Workstation* (No. RCW-1, $80.00 retail) special skid clamps hold most sizes. Clamping system tilts 180° and rotates 360°, providing infinite number of work angles. Heavy-duty design holds helis steady at steepest angle. Base tray holds tools, catches parts, and can be mounted on sturdy tripod to serve as portable field workstand.

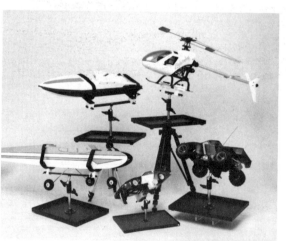

Boat Accessories

Electrical

HUGHEY BOATS, INC.

The *Geared Single 05 Power Unit* ($38.00 assembled without motor, $33.00 kit, $45.00 Twin Ball Bearing) with its completely NEW more versatile design is a lighter, smaller companion to the famous HUGHEY Dual/Single Power Unit. Both rigid and grommet mounting plates are supplied. The Unit is very strong with easy self-aligning assembly. Only one motor is used. Width: 2-1/4". Weight: 2 oz. less motor. Many gear ratios are available between 1.5 and 4.0 to 1. Measured speeds to 35 mph. Order no. E2300BB2, E2300, or E2310 for kit.

HUGHEY BOATS, INC.

New concept high current, four position *H4RS Racing Speed Control* ($42.00 retail) for 4-14 cell FAST ELECTRIC racing and sport. Fused output. Minimal voltage loss compares to electronic types. The unit gives proportional like speeds with less motor sparking than most electronic controls. Water does not affect operation. Circuit board is coated for long-term protection. Three sizes are available for mounting ease. Length: 2-7/16", 2-15/16", or 3-1/2". Width: 1-3/8". Order no. E1100, E1110, or E1120 for 8-14 cells; or E1105 or E1115 for 4-8 cells.

HUGHEY BOATS, INC.

The *Geared Dual/Single 05 Power Unit* ($40.00 assembled without motor, $35.00 kit, $50.00 Twin Ball Bearing; all without motors) is the dominant RECORD SETTING AND RACE WINNING 6-16 cell power package. Current IMPBA record is 51.2 mph. Powers larger boats than direct drive. Ideal for both SCALE and FAST ELECTRIC classes. Unit width: approximately 3". Weight: 14.5 oz. with 2 motors. Single motor can be either center or side mounted. Includes precision molded gears, metal hubs, and .187 stainless steel shaft with .125 output nut. Turns props to 47MM at 5-20,000 rpms depending on motor turns and battery voltage. Parts available separately. Order no. E1400 with 1.68, 1.81, or 1.95 ratio. Order no. E1500 with 2.09, 2.24, or 2.40 ratio.

HUGHEY BOATS, INC.

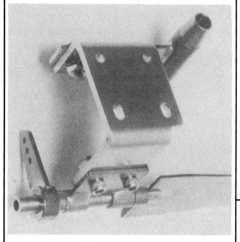

The *Electric Hardware Package* ($50.00 retail) comes with complete strut assembly with kickup rudder, flexible shaft with drive dog, rudder arm, teflon tubing, screws, etc. Clean, rugged, efficient record setting outdrive assembly. Fabricated stainless strut with bronze and lead teflon bearings. New lightweight aluminum U bracket for easy strut angle change. For highest electric speeds with Tunnels, Hydros, Riggers, and Deep-vees. Order no. E1360T or specify different strut depth or angle.

HUGHEY BOATS, INC.

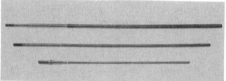

The *Flex Shaft System* ($4.00 - $32.00 retail) is the original inboard flex drive system featuring a large assortment of stainless shaft ends and complete flex shafts. Shafts are available for all model boats including mono, hydro, Deep-vee, gas, and electric. Sizes include .093, .125, .150, .187, and .250.

LINDBERG/CRAFT HOUSE CORP.

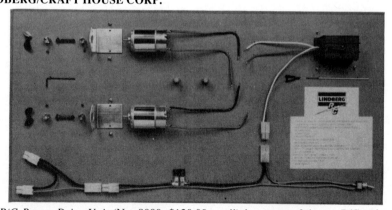

This *R/C Power Drive Unit* (No. 8000, $120.00 retail) is a state-of-the-art R/C twin engine power drive system for boats. It is a plug-in electric system designed for Lindberg R/C boats (PT Boat, Chris Craft Constellation, and Sport Fisherman) and other boats of similar size and includes two hi-performance 12-volt shielded and pre-wired "550" motors, 5-position speed control with control rod, brass turned universals with connectors and props, aluminum motor mounts, dual pack battery connector, plus a pre-wired harness with switch and safety fuse.

MRC

The *RB495 Delta Peak Quick Charger* (No. RB495; Retail: See your dealer), powered from 12 volts DC, uses race-car technology and can charge NiCads from 450-1800 mAH, in 4-7 cell configuration, with an adjustable current output from 1-9 amps. Standard features include a high-grade current/ voltage meter, and a unique melody-maker to notify you of the completed quick-charge.

VANTEC

This *Speed Controller* (No. HW-55, $109.95 retail) features proportional forward and proportional reverse. It replaces throttle servo and rheostat. With 416 amps MOSFET ratings for '05 motors, this 1.80 x 1.87 x .82-in. unit is optically isolated with Hi-Rate PWM for smooth low speed.

STAGE III

Super 13 Wire (2 ft. each of black and orange, $5.25 retail; Rolls available: 25 ft., $33.00 retail; 50 ft., $60.00 retail.) and *Super 13 B* (2 ft. each of black and orange, $3.00 retail; Rolls available: 25 ft., $33.00 retail; 50 ft., $60.00 retail.) were recently top-rated by R/C Car Action Magazine. They are high performance wires for all types of R/C. The wire is composed of 805 strands of 99.9% pure copper, tinned for easy soldering and corrosion resistance, and coated with super flexible silicone. Super 13 and 13 B are rated at a whopping 55 amps, and have 20% less resistance than typical 14 gauge wire.

STAGE III

Dragin' Wire (Packaged with 2 ft. of black and 2 ft. of orange silicone-coated 12 gauge wire, $7.50 retail) is extra-capacity, high-performance wire, designed for high current flow and high voltages typical in R/C power-boating, drag racing, and truck pulling. With 1,666 strands; this new 12 gauge wire has 33% more capacity than its state-of-the-art Super 13 wire which has all the same quality and features: 99.9% pure copper stranding, tinned for fast soldering and corrosion resistance, super flexibility, and burn-proof silicone insulation. Dragin' Wire was recently top-rated by R/C Car Action Magazine. When only the best will do, Stage III is the only way to go!

SERMOS R/C SNAP CONNECTORS, INC.

These *High-Amp Powerpole Snap Connectors* (Retail: Available from Sermos) are modular "silver-plated" connectors for your electric planes, cars, or boats. They're designed for a high-vibration environment. Cycled ten thousand times without electrical failure, they're designed for anything electrical requiring quick disconnects. Color coordinated and rated 30 amps at 600 DC, internal resistance is rated 250 micro ohms. Silver-plated contact accepts AWG sizes 12 to 16. For dealer information send to Sermos.

VANTEC

This *Speed Control* (No. RET-44, $79.95 retail) has fully-proportional reverse and forward for boats, tanks, and robots. It replaces the throttle servo and cumbersome rheostats. Optically isolated MOSFET design features Hi-Rate PWM for smoother control of motors up to 12 amps, 14 volts, and measures 1.80 x 1.87 x .82-in. It works with Futaba AM, FM, or PCM, Airtronics, Cirrus, ACOMS, Challenger, MRC, and most others. Higher power models are available to 70 continuous duty amps.

Boat Accessories

Non-Electrical

L.A.W. RACING PRODUCTS

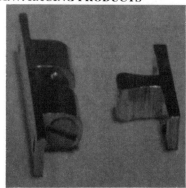

The *Hatch Latch* ($6.95 retail) is a two-piece brass, multi-purpose latch. It's operation can be a straight pull to 90 degrees to each other. The Latch has an adjustable spring tensioned controlled ball bearing detent mechanism. Dimensions are: Length—1-9/16", width—9/32", and weight—0.6 ozs.

L.A.W. RACING PRODUCTS

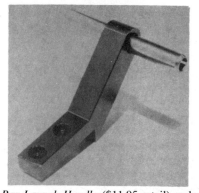

T-Bar Launch Handle ($11.95 retail) makes launching safer and more controlled. The handle is very functional, lightweight, and attractive. The unit is blue anodized aluminum with stainless steel bar. The universal mount comes with complete stainless steel hardware.

L.A.W. RACING PRODUCTS

The following *Water Fittings* ($1.50 - $3.95 retail) are available.
Aluminum 10-32, 90 degree right angle with brass jam nuts.
Brass 10-32 straight, with 3/8" long barbs.
Brass 10-32 straight, with 1/2" long barbs.
Brass bulkhead fittings, 7/16" long, 3.16" dia. barbs, with 5/16" jam nuts.

OCTURA MODELS, INC.

The *Twin-Drive Strudder* (Retail: See your dealer) has the same features as the Strudder but this is for twin-drive applications.

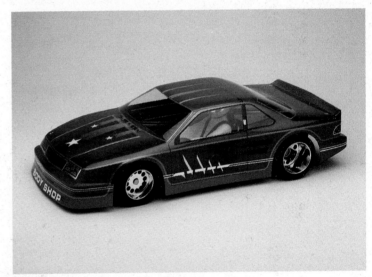

Clockwise from top left:
A radio controlled *America's Cup
sailboat* from A. G. Industries can also
be built as a static model. The *20 size
Royal Air Trainer* from Royal Products.
A beautifully *detailed body* painted
by Coverite Products.
The popular *Days of Thunder NASCAR
racer* from Parma International.

Clockwise from top left:
The Kyosho *Viper R/C Boat*
with driver figures. The *Focus
6 FM System* from hitec. The
original *Flying Saucer* from
the archives of the Vintage
R/C Society. The Kyosho
Concept 60 helicopter.
A *high-performance
transmission* for R/C cars
and trucks from Traxxas.

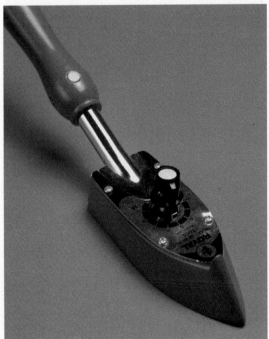

Clockwise from top:
The *1/16-scale ready-to-run truck* from Nikko.
The *JR-PRO off-road racer* from Team Losi.
A *WWII Japanese navy pilot Bust* from MGA
Enterprises. Royal's *Deluxe Heat Sealing Iron*
makes covering airplanes easy.

Clockwise from top left:
The *JR-X-347 PCM Helicopter System. Cyclone Motors* for R/C cars/trucks from Parma International. The *Baby Ace* built by Bob Burnstein of the WRAM club. The *MA-4 FM System* from JR Radio.

The AWARF advantage: More flying time with your friends.

Your friendship was like a secret club. Every day after school, you and your best buddies crammed into the back seat of the bus, throwing aside Mrs. Grundy's homework to plot some devilish scheme against sissy girls.

Today you're older and probably wiser, but free time still means the same thing: time together. Now there's less of it to go around, so finding the best way to spend that time is a must.

Introducing the **Hobbico AWARF** family. Quality all-wood ARFs that are as strong, beautiful, and exciting to fly as the hand-built models you discovered R/C flight together with years ago.

Hobbico AWARFs feature all-wood construction and pre-built parts already covered with tough, brilliantly colored polyester film. They require no painting, and include extensive hardware packages. Out of the box, they're already 80% assembled.

Which means you can unwind for a few evenings after work by putting the finishing touches to a top-notch kit...spend the rest of the week getting to know your kids...and still make the field Saturday morning. Just you and the guys.

At the flight line, all three Hobbico AWARFs shine. With its broad, 64" wing

AWARFs set a high standard for ARF quality. Construction is all-wood and parts are already handsomely pre-covered.

span and flat-bottom airfoil, the **Flightstar 40** is a dependable trainer with rock-solid stability.

Intermediate fliers can send the 60" span **Avistar 40** through aerobatic maneuvers courtesy of its semi-symmetrical airfoil.

A high-wing design, semi-symmetrical airfoil, huge wing area, and trainer-like wing loading make the 71" span **Hobbistar 60** an easy-flying step up to .60-sized dimensions.

The world's changed a lot since you and your friends first met. So have ARF airplanes. See the Hobbico AWARF family of high-quality models at your hobby dealer today. Mrs. Grundy would be so proud — you've all finally learned to straighten up and fly right.

DISTRIBUTED TO LEADING RETAILERS NATIONWIDE EXCLUSIVELY THROUGH

GREAT PLANES ™
MODEL DISTRIBUTORS COMPANY
P.O. BOX 4021, CHAMPAIGN, IL 61824-4021

HOBBICO®
AWARF SERIES ™
All Wood — Almost Ready To Fly

© 1990, Hobbico, Inc.

Hitec's Focus.
R/C Fun.

Hitec's NEW Focus series R/C systems join our popular master line of highest quality and performance R/C products.

Focus on Value, Focus on Performance!

Hitec's Focus comes standard with RCD's 1991 AMA-Listed "Bullet Proof" Receivers. This Hitec/RCD combination far surpasses AMA guidelines for 1991 narrow band performance at prices that make clear sense.

NEW!

FOUR FM MODELS

- *FOCUS 4 Basic System*
- *FOCUS 4E For Electrics*
- *FOCUS Heli 5 with all Mixing*
- *FOCUS 6 with Ch.6 Propo*

The Best Value & Quality R/C
Including These Standard Features:

- **AMA 1991-Listed RCD "BULLET PROOF" Receivers & Gold Sticker Transmitters!**
- **All-Channel Servo Reversing!**
- **Sanyo Flight-Pack Nicads!**
- **Ergonomically Designed Case for The Ultimate in Comfort!**

- **Superior Quality Servos!**
- **Channels 1-4 END-POINT Adjustments!**
- **Exclusive Master-Student Trainer System!**
- **Exclusive Nationwide Service!**
- **Full One Year Warranty!**
- **All Systems are FM!**

Hitec Focus Systems are available at leading hobby shops across the country. Call Hitec at (619) 449-1112 for the hobby shop location nearest you.

The R/Cer's Partner

Distributed in Canada
by Hobbycraft, Canada
(416) 738-6556 FAX (416) 738-6329

9419 Abraham Way • Santee, CA 92071
(619) 449-1112 FAX (619) 449-1002

© 1991 HITEC R/C USA, INC.

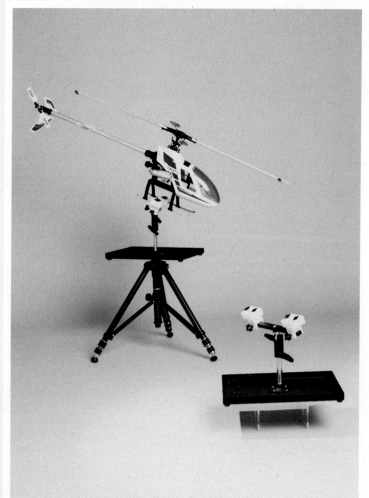

Clockwise from top:
Assorted *Decals* for R/C cars from Parma International add the finishing touch to any model. A *Chevrolet NASCAR body* shows off its sponsors' logos. A *"Rotorcraft" workstation* is ideal for holding your helicopter securely while making adjustments or building the model.

Clockwise from top left:
The *Hot Head glow-plug igniter* from Royal Products. Team Novak's *610-RV reversible Speed Control.* The Bob Violett *Aggessor Jet* built by Lou Scarlino of the WRAM club. The *Heavy Metal multi-terrain monster tank* from Kyosho.

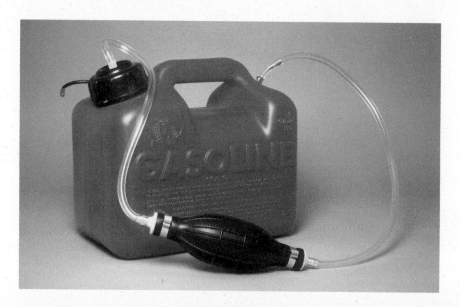

Left:
The *Squeez-Me E/Z Fill Fuel Pump* from Du-Bro Products can be used for fueling and defueling any gas-powered model and for priming engines.

Below:
The *Traxxas Hawk racing truck* in action.

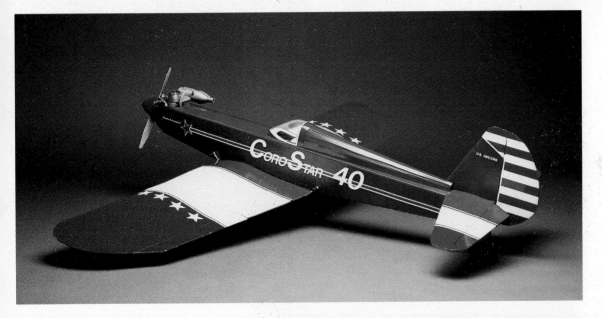

Top:
The Cox Hobbies *.049 GTP Nissan* gas-powered *Indy Racer*. Above: The *CoroStar 40 Sport Plane* from U.S. AirCore.

Right:
The Kyosho *Concept 60* provides power and versatility for this size of chopper.

Of all the speed secrets you can give a beginner, the best ones are under wraps

1 Exclusive Shotgun tube construction stiffens pack without gluing.

2 Cell insulators eliminate any chance of shorting.

3 Hand welded tabs for perfect reliability and lowest resistance.

4 Special Panasonic cells have great capacity, yet handle overcharge abuse.

5 Special endcap design reduces chaffing of 14 gauge Superflex wire.

When someone asks what battery to buy, do 'em a favor and recommend PTI's Sport Pack. It's produced with unique processes that result in a fast, reliable pack that will give long lasting performance.

Batteries made by the biggest name in consumer electronics.

In choosing the cell for our not-so-ordinary Sport Pack, we needed an extraordinary battery to match. We searched the world over, and finally settled on the biggest and best name in electronics: Panasonic. Their P130 cell has huge capacity and high voltage that puts it in a premium performance category for a sport cell. Specially designed to handle the overcharge

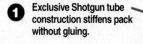

VOLTS

DISCHARGE TIME IN SECONDS AT 10 AMP RATE

High voltage means high speeds...with great capacity for extended runs.

abuse frequently encountered with timed chargers, the Panasonic cell has proven over a million times that it was the right choice for our most popular pack.

Hand assembled to be the best.

Automation may be good for some things, but pack production isn't one of them. By hand assembling, the tabbing is kept shorter than automated for overall lower resistance. Each contact is double welded and then given a quality control inspection that eliminates any chance of a bad weld. The result? A pack that handles the knocks and shocks of the toughest R/C action.

Automated systems require a "W" tab design that wastes energy. Our efficient "V" design not only reduces resistance, but even makes the pack shorter for a better fit in cars like the RC10.

Special assembly technique allows us to use the best welding tabs possible.

Exclusive tube makes a clear difference.

When all the cells' welds are complete, we start adding in the options. Superflex 14 gauge silicone wire is added for low voltage loss. The whole pack is then slipped into our very own clear plastic Shotgun tube. This not only stiffens the pack for great shock resistance, but does so without cumbersome gluing of cells which means cells can be easily replaced.

Do your friend or customer a favor. Recommend a PTi Sport Pack. And let 'em in on a speed secret that they'll appreciate for years!

PROGRESSIVE TECHNOLOGIES, INC.
P. O. Box 4648, Winston-Salem, NC 27115

Distributed through Horizon Hobby Distributors, Inc.

Clockwise from top left:
The *USA-1 Monster Truck* from Kyosho. *Ultra narrow band FM receiver* from RCD. A *T-Bird 1/10-scale body* from Associated Electrics. A *Royal Air Force Spitfire* photographed at the WRAM flying field. The *Lanier Laser* built by Frank DeVore of the WRAM club.

Right:
A *Lanier Fun Fly 40 trainer.*
Center: The internationally acclaimed *RC10L racer* from Associated Electrics. Below: Sig's *1/4-scale Cub* built by Lou Scarlino of the WRAM club.

SQUEEZE ME

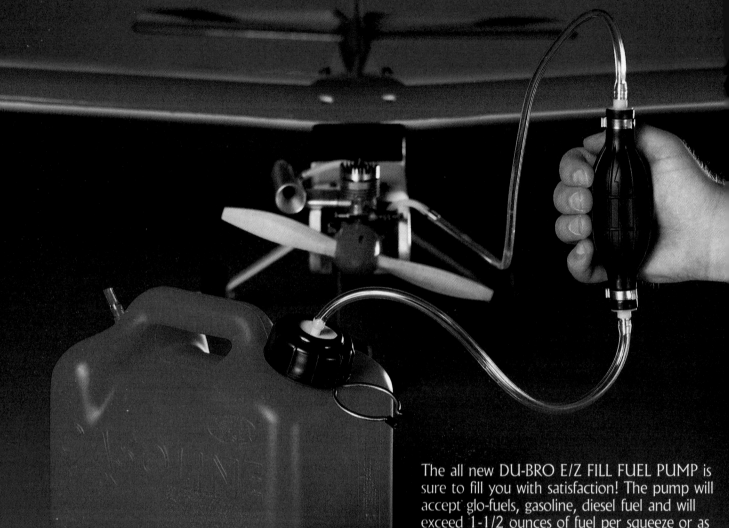

The all new DU-BRO E/Z FILL FUEL PUMP is sure to fill you with satisfaction! The pump will accept glo-fuels, gasoline, diesel fuel and will exceed 1-1/2 ounces of fuel per squeeze or as little as a drop or two for priming. Emptying your fuel tank is also made easy by simply turning the pump over 180° as shown in the picture below.

The new E/Z FILL FUEL PUMP is sold separately or comes complete with a sturdy one gallon no-tip fuel container, which will not tip over in your car.

See your local Hobby Dealer TODAY!

No. 519 E/Z Fill Fuel Pump
No. 520 E/Z Fill Fuel Pump & 1 gal. container

Easy to transport to the field.

Turn pump 180° for emptying your fuel tank.

DU-BRO PRODUCTS INC.   480 BONNER RD., WAUCONDA, IL 60084   (708) 526-2136

OCTURA MODELS, INC.

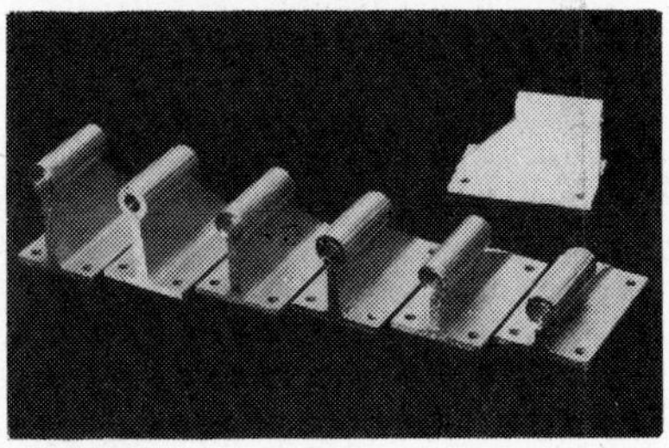

These *Struts* (Retail: See your dealer) are propeller mounting struts for R/C boats made of extruded aluminum. Depths range from 1/2-in. to 2-in. below bottom. Four T-nuts and screws are included.

OCTURA MODELS, INC.

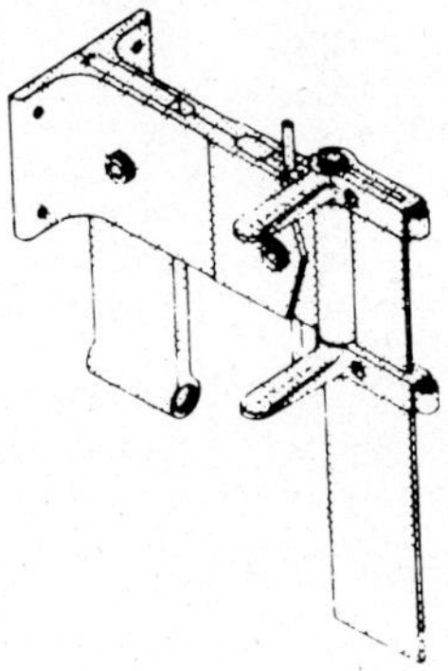

This *Strudder* (Retail: See your dealer) is available in four rudder versions: single strut/single wedge; single strut/single offset wedge; single strut/twin wedge; and twin strut/single offset. Strudders are also available with strut-blade profile machined and unmachined.

OCTURA MODELS, INC.

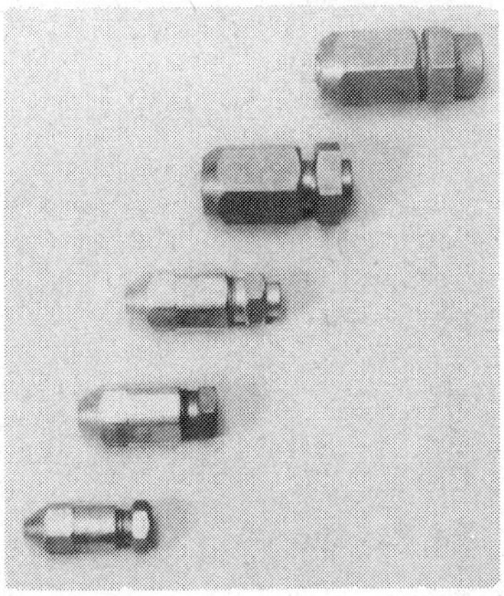

These *''Flex-Hex'' Couplings* (Retail: See your dealer) are for use with flexible shafts. They're available to fit 5/16-24, 1/4-28, 10-32, 8mm, 7mm, 6mm, and 5mm threads with .250, .187, .150 and .135 collets. Features include no fraying the shaft with set screws, and easy to clamp and release. Order by specifying thread and collet size.

OCTURA MODELS, INC.

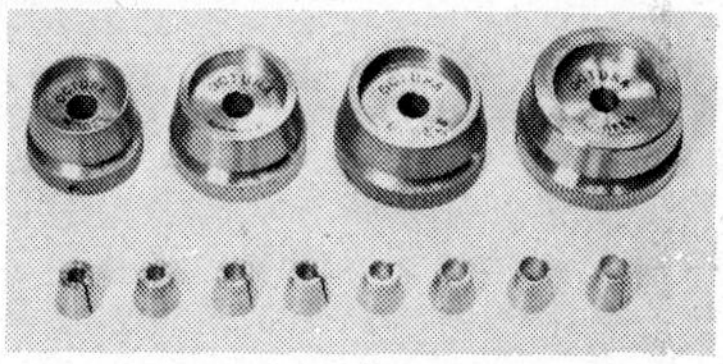

These *Flywheels* (Retail: See your dealer) are for running model plane engines in R/C model power boats. They're available in four sizes and two styles (plated-steel and color anodized aluminum). A brass conversion collet is included with each flywheel.

OCTURA MODELS, INC.

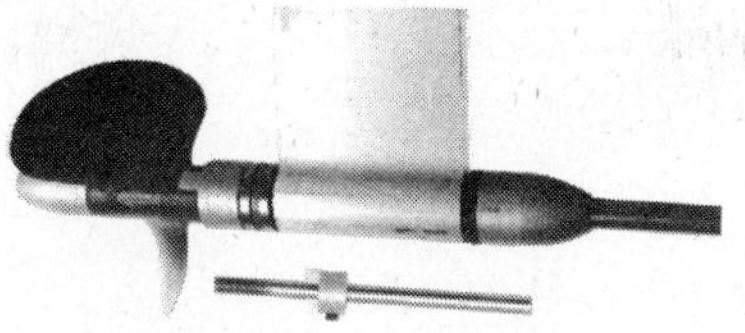

These *Underwater Fittings* (Retail: See your dealer) are for nearly any application including universal joints, flexible drive shafts, fins, bearings, screws, etc.

OCTURA MODELS, INC.

Octura offers a complete line of *Universal Joints* (Retail: See your dealer) for R/C model power boats made of hardened, plated steel, proven in competition-running for over 10 years. Sizes are available to fit all popular model engines. Underwater versions are also available.

SERMOS R/C SNAP CONNECTORS, INC.

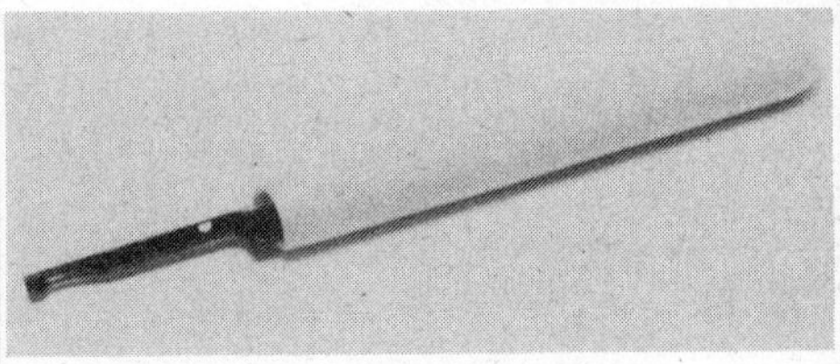

This *Insertion/Extraction Tool* (No. G-2 TOOL, $5.00 retail) is a quick and easy way to assemble and disassemble the Sermos R/C Snap Connectors.

SMC/LIGHTNING PRODUCTS

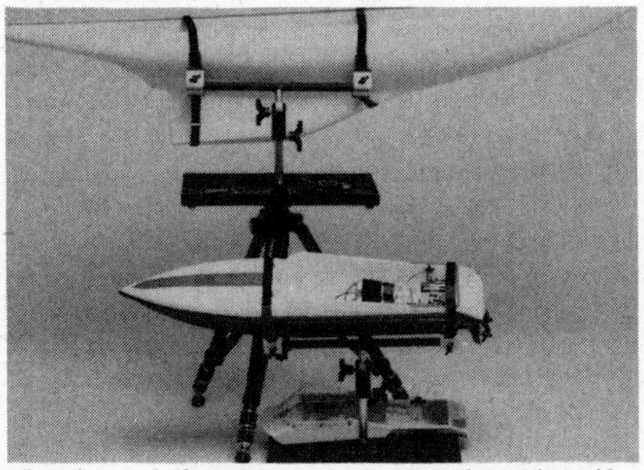

Designed for motor powered and sail, *MarineCraft Workstation* (No. MCW-1, $58.00 retail) foam padded cradles hold most mono-hulled boats and many twin- and tri-hulled boats. Cradles are offset and adjust to keels. Hook/loop straps allow just the right pressure to hold securely without damaging hull. System tilts 180°, rotates 360°, and is mounted to heavy-duty tray.

Boat Accessories

——————— Propellors

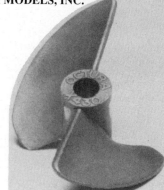

OCTURA MODELS, INC.

This *Boat Propeller* (No. X430-RH, $8.95 retail) is for electric-powered boats, using direct-drive with .125-diameter propeller shafts. Intended for .05 twin motors, this is a right-hand rotation propeller, cast in beryllium copper. Also available in silicon brass or aluminum.

OCTURA MODELS, INC.

This beryllium copper *Strut Blade* (No. OC4SBE, $9.95 retail) is a smaller version of the optional stainless steel strut blades used on Octura's famous Strudders. This is approximately 1/2 the size of the original strut blade with a .250 diameter shaft housing and a .187 diameter bore. The strut has a skeg and has a blade width of about .687. Lead teflon sleeve bearings are available to support a .125 diameter shaft. Shown with these accessories: *Lead Teflon Sleeve Bearings*—two required (No. OC4LTS, $1.15 retail), *Brass Nose Piece* (No. OC4NP, $1.45 retail), *Brass Prop Tail Nut* (No. OC4PN, $1.45 retail), *Brass Drive Dog* for 1/8-in.-dia. shaft (No. OC4D, $1.75), Stainless Steel Stub Shaft counter bored .098, 5/16 deep with the opposite end threaded 5-40 to fit the above tail nut (No. OC4PS, $2.50 retail), OC4SBE with two OC4LTS and an OC4NP installed (No. OC4SBEPA, $13.75 retail).

OCTURA MODELS, INC.

This *Boat Propeller* (No. 1630, $8.95 retail) is intended for cobalt 40 motors. Made of beryllium copper with left-hand rotation. For electric-powered boats, using direct-drive with .125-diameter propeller shafts.

OCTURA MODELS, INC.

This *3-blade Boat Propeller* (No. 0937/3, $12.00 retail) has left-hand rotation, and is intended for hi-torque motors. For electric-powered boats, using direct-drive with .125-diameter propeller shafts.

OCTURA MODELS, INC.

This beryllium copper *Boat Propeller* (No. 0930, $8.95 retail) with left-hand rotation is intended for 540 motors. For electric-powered boats, using direct-drive with .125-diameter propeller shafts.

OCTURA MODELS, INC.

This *Boat Propeller* (No. X430, $8.95 retail) is for electric-powered boats, using direct-drive with .125-diameter propeller shafts. Intended for .05 twin motors, this is a left-hand rotation propeller, cast in beryllium copper.

OCTURA MODELS, INC.

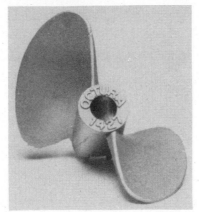

Boat Propeller (No. 1427, $8.95 retail) intended for 540 motors, cast in beryllium copper. Left-hand rotation. For electric-powered boats, using direct-drive with .125-diameter propeller shafts.

OCTURA MODELS, INC.

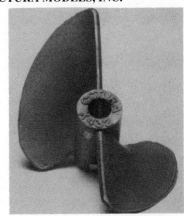

Boat Propeller (No. X432, $8.95 retail) intended for hot wind motors, cast in beryllium copper. Left-hand rotation. For electric-powered boats, using direct-drive with .125-diameter propeller shafts.

OCTURA MODELS, INC.

Boat Propeller (No. X427, $8.95 retail) intended for 540 motors. This is a left-hand rotation propeller cast in beryllium copper. For electric-powered boats, using direct-drive with .125-diameter propeller shafts.

OCTURA MODELS, INC.

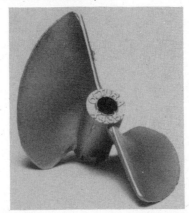

Boat Propeller (No. X435, $9.25 retail) intended for hi-torque motors, cast in beryllium copper. For electric-powered boats, using direct-drive with .125-diameter propeller shafts. Left-hand rotation.

OCTURA MODELS, INC.

These *Propellers* (Retail: See your dealer) are specially designed for R/C model power boats. They're available in plastic and metal to fit 3/16-in. shafts. They're left-hand rotation for .15 to 1.8 engines. Right-hand rotation is available for some sizes. Three-blade props are also available.

OCTURA MODELS, INC.

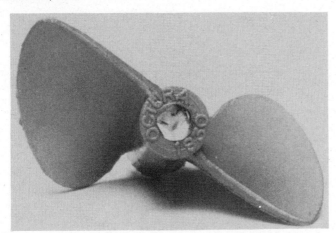

Boat Propeller (No. 1930, $8.95 retail) intended for cobalt 40 motors, cast in beryllium copper with left-hand rotation. For electric-powered boats, using direct-drive with .125-diameter propeller shafts.

PRATHER PRODUCTS INC.

Prather Hi Performance Boat Props ($11.95 - $19.95 retail) are precision made and performance tested. All are available in beryllium copper and our new stainless steel alloy for more strength and better performance. There are 14 sizes available.

Car Accessories

Bearings

AEROTREND PRODUCTS

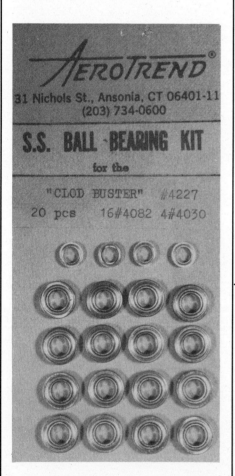

AEROTREND PRODUCTS

Stainless Steel Ball Bearing Kits (Send for catalog), as well as a long list of bearings for individual applications, are available from Aerotrend Products for all major R/C cars. This includes Teflon Sealed R/C 10 Rr. Support Bearings as well as a complete set for the Clodbuster. Installing bearings into your R/C vehicle is one of the most important moves that you can make to improve its performance.

AEROTREND PRODUCTS

Teflon Sealed Rear Support Bearings (No. 4358, Special $20.00! Sug. retail $21.99) are stainless steel bearings Teflon sealed on both sides to keep out dirt and sand that gets into regular rear support bearings. These are for the Assoc. R/C 10. 2/pkg.

The *Clodbuster Bearing Kit* (No. 4227, Special $45.00! Sug. retail $79.99) is a complete 20-piece stainless steel shielded bearing kit which includes the four small ones for the transmission. Because of its size and weight, the Clodbuster needs bearings for better performance.

BOCA BEARINGS

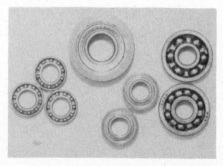

Boca Bearings are high quality bearings to fit all popular R/C cars including Associated, AYK, BoLink, Futaba, Kyosho, MRP, Marui, Tamiya, Team Losi, Traxxas, World, and others. Now available are helicopter bearings for GMP, Kalt, Miniature Aircraft, and Schulter.

BOCA BEARINGS

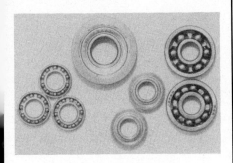

New *Boca Bearings Ultra Seals* are the frictionless sealed bearing that requires no maintenance or further lubrication. Ultra-Seals are available for the RC10, TQ10, RC10L, RC12L, Eliminator 10/12, Lynx, Predator, Hyper 10, JR-X2, JR-XT, Pro 10, and others.

HORIZON HOBBY DISTRIBUTORS, INC.

Horizon Hobby Distributors offers premium-quality *Dynamite Bearings* which give your car or truck higher speeds and lower maintenance. Dynamite Bearings give you a competitive edge at an affordable price. They come in chrome or stainless steel, in singles or sets, in U.S. standard metric sizes for the most popular cars and trucks. See your hobby shop for the entire line of Dynamite Bearings.

TEAM PIT STOP

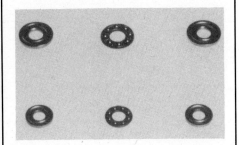

Team Pit Stop makes both a large and small *Super Thrust Bearing*. The *Large* (No. 9016, $29.99 retail) is for the JRX-2, Schumacher Cat and Couger, the old R/C-10 transmission, and the new Associated slipper. The *Small* (No. 9030-32, $18.99 retail) is for the TPS and R/C-10 Stealth, differentials, MIP, Ultima, Lazer, and Yokomo.

Car Accessories

1/10 Scale Bodies

ANDY'S R/C PRODUCTS

The 1/10 off-road buggy, *Pro Arrow* (No. 3019, $16.00 retail) fits the RC-10. Andy's *Chevy extended cab "off-road" race truck* (No. 3032, $18.95 retail) fits JRXT and long wheel base trucks. The *Chevy Lumina Super Speedway body* (No. 3172, $18.95 retail) fits narrow chassis cars. This is just one of four narrow NASCAR bodies. Other 1/10-scale bodies include: *91 Nissan NTP* (No. 3153, $18.95 retail), *Porsche 962 GTP long tail* (No. 3150, $18.95 retail), and the *Porsche 962 Group C short tail* (No. 3151, $18.95 retail).

ASSOCIATED ELECTRICS

The *RC10-Sidewinder* (No. 6161; Retail: See your dealer) is a new body that gives more downforce to the World Champion RC10 Car, giving it more steering and more rear traction.

DAHM'S RACING BODIES

DAHM'S *FX Wings* (No. D111, 5" FX Wing, $5.98 retail; No. D116, 6" FX Wing, $6.98 retail; and No. D131, 8" FX Wing, $8.98 retail) are formed from .030 GE Lexan. They are Bi-Level, adjustable, and come in three sizes—5", 6", and 8". FX Wings are assembled with nylon nuts and bolts (which are included) or you can use them as two separate wings!

The 6 in. FX Wing is shown with DAHM'S WARRIOR II racing body (No. D170) on the RC10 Graphite.

DAHM'S RACING BODIES

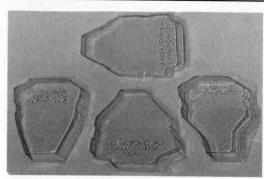

DAHM'S *RACING BODIES* makes Lexan Power Pans (Underbodies) for its outstanding dune buggy bodies, monster trucks, and NOW, DAHM'S makes aerodynamic underbodies for its high performance NASCAR bodies!!!

DAHM'S *Power Pans* ($10.98 retail) for monster and dune buggy: No. D126—Monster; No. D140—Warrior; No. D141—Terror; No. D143—Champion; No. D145—Ultra; No. D155—Razer; No. D165—Dirt Dancer; No. D175—Warrior II.

DAHM'S *Thunderbodies* ($16.98 retail) for NASCAR: No. D122—1991 Lumina (Standard); No. D123—1990 Pontiac (Std.); No. D124—1990 T-Bird (Std.); No. D127—1991 Lumina (Narrow); No. D128—1991 Pontiac (Nrw.); No. D129—1991 T-Bird (Nrw.).

DAHM'S RACING BODIES

DAHM'S *Devastator* (No. D180, Clear, $20.98 retail; and No. D180P, Painted, $34.98 retail) Lexan racing body is designed to fit most 10-scale dirt oval racing cars and conversions. The large hood scoop is designed to fit over the shock towers on RC10 and JRX conversions for a low fit without cutting clearance holes in the body!

Devastator features smooth aerodynamic styling, a large hood scoop with molded-in air cleaner detail, and an asymmetrical driver's compartment.

Devastator comes with finishing instructions, window templates, and a DAHM'S decal.

DAHM'S *Windjammer* (No. D185, $10.98 retail) side dam and spoiler kit is available for the Devastator.

DAHM'S RACING BODIES

DAHM'S exciting new *Jeep Cherokee* (No. D194, $19.98 retail) racing truck body is formed from .030 Lexan for lightweight and strength. The Cherokee is designed to fit most monster trucks, stadium race trucks, conversions, and narrow (RC10LSS size) on-road cars. Note: you may need long body mounts for some trucks. The Cherokee is shown on the Tamiya Toyota Hi Lux truck with DAHM'S Smoke Grey Instant-Tint (No. D814, Window Tinting Film, $5.98 retail).

The Jeep Cherokee features aerodynamic styling, realistic proportions and detailing, and wide wheel flares.

DAHM'S RACING BODIES

DAHM'S exciting new Lexan racing body, the *Warrior II* (No. D170, Clear, $17.98 retail; No. D170P, Painted, $29.98 retail; and No. D171, Clear body and underbody combo, $26.98 retail) is designed to fit the RC10, TQ10, and RC10 Graphite, and has molded-in trim lines for these cars. The Warrior II can also be easily trimmed to fit most other 2WD off-road cars.

Warrior II features smooth aerodynamic styling, cooling vents, and a very low profile! Warrior II is shown on the RC10 Graphite with DAHM'S Warrior II Power Pan (No. D175, Lexan Underbody, $10.98 retail) and DAHM'S 6" FX Wing (No. D116, Lexan Bi-Level Wing, $6.98 retail).

DAHM'S Warrior II comes with finishing instructions, window templates, and a DAHM'S decal.

DAHM'S RACING BODIES

This futuristic, aerodynamic Lexan racing body has molded-in trim lines for the JRX2 and the Optima Mid. The *Ultra* (No. D120, Clear, $17.98 retail; No. D120P, Painted, $29.98 retail; and No. D121, Clear body and underbody combo, $26.98 retail) can also be easily trimmed to fit the Ultima Pro, Ultima II, and many other 2WD and 4WD off-road cars.

The Ultra is shown on the JRX2 with DAHM'S *Ultra Power Pan* (No. D145, Lexan underbody, $10.98 retail) and DAHM'S 6" FX Wing (No. D116, Bi-Level Adjustable Lexan Wing, $6.98 retail).

The Ultra body comes with finishing instructions, window templates, a DAHM'S decal, and a FREE $3.98 Super Fin Wing!

DAHM'S RACING BODIES

DAHM'S new super-detailed, aerodynamic *Spice GTP* (No. D135, $20.98 retail) body is shown on the RC10L with DAHM'S 8" FX Wing (No. D131, Bi-Level Lexan Wing, $8.98 retail). The Spice GTP can easily be painted as a Firebird, Chevy, Buick, or Ferrari Spice GTP.

DAHM'S 10-scale Spice GTP includes finishing instructions, a DAHM'S decal, and a FREE $3.98 8" GTP Wing!

DAHM'S RACING BODIES

DAHM'S *Razer* (No. D150, Clear, $17.98 retail; No. D150P, Painted, $29.98 retail; and No. D151, Clear body and underbody combo, $26.98 retail) racing body is designed to fit the Yokomo YZ10, and has molded-in trim lines for this car. This strong, lightweight .030 Lexan racing body features aerodynamic styling, cooling intake vents, and a FREE $3.98, 6" Super Fin Wing!

Use DAHM'S *Razer Power Pan* (No. D155, Lexan Underbody, $10.98 retail) to keep the dirt out, protect your frame, and make your car more aerodynamic!

The Razer is shown on the YZ10 with the Razer Power Pan (No. D155) and DAHM'S 6" FX Wing (No. D116, Lexan Bi-Level Wing, $6.98 retail).

The Razer comes with finishing instructions, window templates, and a FREE $3.98, 6" Super Fin Wing.

DAHM'S RACING BODIES

DAHM'S *Dirt Dancer* (No. D160, Clear, $17.98 retail; No. D160P, Painted, $29.98 retail; and No. D161, Clear body and underbody combo, $26.98 retail) racing body is designed to fit the Ultima Pro and Ultima II. It has molded-in trim lines for the Ultima Pro. The Dirt Dancer is shown on the Ultima Pro with Pro Lines monster truck conversions, DAHM'S Dirt Dancer Power Pan (No. D165, Lexan underbody, $10.98 retail), and DAHM'S 5" FX Wing (No. D111, Lexan Bi-Level Adjustable Wing, $5.98 retail).

DAHM'S Dirt Dancer Lexan racing body comes with finishing instructions, window templates, a DAHM's decal, and a FREE $3.98, 6" Super Fin Wing!

DAHM'S RACING BODIES

The *Champion* (No. D109, Clear, $17.98 retail; No. D109P, Painted, $29.98 retail; and No. D112, Clear body and underbody combo, $26.98 retail) body features smooth aerodynamic styling, stability fins, a wrap-around windshield, escape hatch, and a cool air scoop that directs cool air right down onto your motor!

The new Lexan racing body has molded-in trim lines for the RC10, TQ10, and RC10 Graphite. It can easily be trimmed to fit most other 2WD off-road cars.

The Champion is shown on the RC10 with DAHM'S *Champion Power Pan* (No. D143, Lexan Underbody, $10.98 retail) and DAHM'S 6" Super Fin Wing (No. D117, Lexan Wing, $3.98 retail). The Champion comes with finishing instructions and a DAHM'S decal.

DAHM'S RACING BODIES

This hot Lexan racing body is designed for the RC10 (with aluminum tub frame). The Warrior's low, wide shape can easily be trimmed to fit most other 2WD off-road cars. The *Warrior* (No. D105, Clear, $17.98 retail; No. D105P, Painted, $29.98 retail; and No. D106, Clear body and underbody combo, $26.98 retail) is shown on the RC10 Graphite with DAHM'S *Warrior Power Pan* (No. D140, Lexan underbody, $10.98 retail) and DAHM'S 6" FX Wing (No. D116, Lexan Bi-Level Adjustable Wing, $6.98 retail). Warrior comes with finishing instructions, window templates, a DAHM'S decal, and a FREE $3.98, 6" Super Fin Wing!

DAHM'S RACING BODIES

DAHM'S exciting new *Ford Thunderbird NASCAR* (Body, $19.98 retail; Thunderbody, $16.98 retail) racing bodies come in both *Standard width* (No. D139 for RC10L size cars) and *Narrow width* (No. D103 for RC10LSS size cars). These strong, lightweight .030 Lexan racing bodies are the ultimate in performance, aerodynamic styling, and fine detailing. DAHM'S NASCAR racing bodies are the first and only NASCAR racing bodies with realistic bolt-on, adjustable rear spoilers! Plus—the New Thunderbird Thunderbody improves aerodynamics, strengthens the body, and protects the frame! (No. D129 Lexan Thunderbody for Narrow T-Bird, $16.98 retail; No. D124, Lexan Thunderbody for Standard T-Bird, $16.98). No. D103C—Narrow body and Thunderbody combo, No. D139C—Standard body and Thunderbody combo; $35.98 retail.

DAHM'S RACING BODIES

DAHM'S new 1932 Ford Panel Truck, the *Persuader* (No. D137, $19.98 retail), is designed to fit most 10-scale on-road cars. It can also be easily trimmed to fit many monster trucks. Persuader features include realistic proportions and styling, fine detailing, a custom-chopped top, sun roof, and an optional supercharger.

This crystal-clear Lexan body can also be painted to look like a 1932 Ford Sedan by leaving the rear/side window areas clear!

The Persuader comes with finishing instructions, a Lexan Supercharger, and a DAHM'S decal.

DAHM'S RACING BODIES

The *Super Sport 454* (No. D125, $20.98 retail) is designed to fit most 10th scale off-road racing cars and trucks. The SS454 is a low-riding street truck on the RC10L. It's a hot off-road stadium race truck on the JRXT, and the Super Sport 454 is a powerful monster truck on the Blackfoot, Clodbuster, or USA-1.

This strong, lightweight .030 racing truck features a swept-back front end, custom hood scoop with vents, chopped top, and a tailgate spoiler. The Super Sport 454 comes with finishing instructions, a Lexan Supercharger, and a DAHM'S decal.

DAHM'S RACING BODIES

This new, aerodynamic Lexan racing body fits the JRX Pro, Junior Two, and JRX2 (with 'H' arms). Trim lines for the JRX Pro are molded in! The *Terror's* (No. D107, Clear, $17.98 retail; No. D107P, Painted, $29.98 retail; and No. D108, Clear body and underbody combo, $26.98 retail) sculptured shape closely fits the JRX Pro frame.

The Terror features molded-in cooling vents which can be cut out to direct cool air to the batteries and speed control.

The Terror is shown on the JRX Pro with DAHM'S 6" FX Wing (No. D116, Adjustable, Bi-Level Lexan Wing, $6.98 retail). The Terror comes with finishing instructions, window templates, and a DAHM'S decal.

DAHM'S RACING BODIES

Thriller (No. D191, $19.98 retail)—DAHM'S custom Nissan Pathfinder is designed to fit most 10th scale monster trucks, conversions, stadium racing trucks, and narrow (RC10LSS size) on-road cars. Note: You may need long rear body mounts for some trucks. The Thriller body can be set up as a stadium race truck, monster truck, desert racer, mud bogger, puller, crew truck, or a low-riding on-road custom Pathfinder. The Thriller is shown on a RC10 truck conversion with DAHM's Smoke Grey Instant-Tint (No. D814, Window Tinting Film, $5.98).

Thriller features aerodynamic styling, realistic proportions and details, and wide wheel flares.

DAHM'S RACING BODIES

DAHM'S exciting new Dodge Dakota Lexan racing truck body—*Fever* (No. D193, $19.98 retail)—is designed to fit most 10th scale monster trucks, stadium race trucks, conversions and narrow (RC10LSS size) on-road cars. Fever can be set up as a monster truck, drag truck, puller, mud bogger, or a hot low-riding custom street truck.

Fever features a molded-in Supercharger, cab extension, wheel flares, aerodynamic style, and fine detailing. Fever is shown on Clodbuster with DAHM'S Smoke Grey Instant-Tint (No. D814, Window Tinting Film).

DAHM'S RACING BODIES

DAHM'S *Tuff-E-Nuff Ford Ranger* (No. D190, $19.98 retail) Lexan racing truck body is designed to fit most monster trucks, stadium racers, monster truck conversions, and narrow (RC10LSS size) on-road cars. The Tuff-E-Nuff can be set up as a monster truck, puller, mud bogger, drag truck, or a low-riding street tuff truck!

Tuff-E-Nuff features a molded-in Supercharger, wheel flares, molded-in cab extension, and fine detailing. Tuff-E-Nuff is shown on the Clodbuster with DAHM's Sky Blue Instant-Tint (No. D815, Window Tinting Film, $5.98).

DAHM'S RACING BODIES

DAHM'S exciting new *Chevrolet Lumina NASCAR* (Body, $19.98 retail; Thunderbody, $16.98 retail) racing bodies come in both *Standard width* (No. D133 for RC10L size cars) and *Narrow width* (No. D101 for RC10LSS size cars). These strong, lightweight .030 Lexan racing bodies are the ultimate in performance, aerodynamic styling, and fine detailing. DAHM'S NASCAR racing bodies are the first and only NASCAR racing bodies with realistic bolt-on, adjustable rear spoilers! Plus—the New Lumina Thunderbody improves aerodynamics, strengthens the body, and protects the frame! (No. D127 Lexan Thunderbody for DAHM'S Narrow Lumina, $16.98 retail; No. D122, Lexan Thunderbody for DAHM'S Standard Lumina, $16.98). No. D101C—Narrow body and Thunderbody combo, No. D133C—Standard body and Thunderbody combo; $35.98 retail.

DAHM'S RACING BODIES

Avenger 2000 (No. D195, $20.98 retail) is the van of the future! Avenger 2000 is designed to fit most 10th scale cars and trucks, from the Associated RC10 to the Tamiya Clodbuster. Note: Long body mounts may be needed for some cars. The Avenger 2000 can be set up as a monster van, drag van, street racing van, or a futuristic commercial delivery van. Avenger 2000 is shown on the Clodbuster. This strong, lightweight body is formed from .030 Lexan and comes with finishing instructions and a DAHM'S decal.

DAHM'S RACING BODIES

DAHM'S custom Ford Aerostar van, the *Starfighter* (No. D196, $19.98 retail), is formed from .030 Lexan for light weight and strength. Starfighter is designed to fit most monster trucks, conversions, and narrow (RC10LSS size) on-roads cars. Note: long rear body mounts may be needed on some cars.

The Starfighter features realistic proportions and details, wide wheel wells, sunroof, and a custom chopped top!

Starfighter is shown on the Kyosho USA-1 with DAHM'S Cherry Red Instant-Tint (No. D816, Window Tinting Film, $5.98).

Starfighter comes with finishing instructions and a DAHM'S decal.

DAHM'S RACING BODIES

DAHM'S exciting new *Pontiac Grand Prix NASCAR* (Body, $19.98 retail; Thunderbody, $16.98 retail) racing bodies come in both *Standard width* (No. D138 for RC10L size cars) and *Narrow width* (No. D102 for RC10LSS size cars). These strong, lightweight .030 Lexan racing bodies are the ultimate in performance, aerodynamic styling, and fine detailing. DAHM'S NASCAR racing bodies are the first and only NASCAR racing bodies with realistic bolt-on, adjustable rear spoilers! Plus—the New Pontiac Thunderbody improves aerodynamics, strengthens the body, and protects the frame! (No. D128 Lexan Thunderbody for DAHM'S Narrow Lumina, $16.98 retail; No. D123, Lexan Thunderbody for DAHM'S Standard Lumina, $16.98). No. D102C—Narrow body and Thunderbody combo, No. D138C—Standard body and Thunderbody combo; $35.98 retail.

DAHM'S RACING BODIES

DAHM'S exciting new *Camino 2000* (No. D199, $20.98 retail) is a futuristic El Camino style body, designed to fit most 10th scale cars from the Associated RC10L to the Tamiya Clodbuster. This outstanding crystal clear body features super aerodynamic styling, fine detailing, and is formed from .030 GE Lexan for light weight and strength.

Camino 2000 is shown on the Clodbuster with headlights and taillights made from DAHM'S Headlight & Taillight Kit (No. D210, $3.98 retail).

Camino 2000 comes back from the future to transform ordinary R/C cars and trucks into exciting new racing vehicles. Camino 2000 comes with finishing instructions and a DAHM'S decal.

DAHM'S RACING BODIES

DAHM's proudly presents a revolutionary new innovation for NASCAR and Pro Stock Drag racing! Aerodynamic "ground effects" underbodies for all of DAHM's NASCAR bodies—both the standard and new narrow widths! DAHM'S *Lexan Thunderbodies* ($16.98 retail) feature: aerodynamic ground effects design, progressive air channels, body mounting slots, and trim lines.

Order Nos. D122—Lumina Std., D127—Lumina Narrow, D123—Pontiac Std., D128—Pontiac Narrow, D124—T-Bird Std., and D129—T-Bird Narrow.

DAHM'S RACING BODIES

DAHM'S *Monster Power Pan* (No. D126, $10.98 retail) (Lexan Underbody) is designed to fit most monster trucks, stadium race trucks, and desert racers with flat bottom frames. The Monster Power Pan helps keep dirt out of your electronics, protects your frame, and makes your truck more aerodynamic.

The Monster Power Pan is formed from .030 GE Lexan for light weight and strength. It is shown on a RC10 truck conversion. The Monster Power Pan comes with mounting instructions, a clear Lexan Supercharger, and a DAHM'S decal.

DAHM'S RACING BODIES

DAHM'S exciting new super aerodynamic *Lumina NASCAR racing body and underbody* fit 10th scale Narrow on-road racing cars. The Lumina Body and Lumina Thunderbody are shown on the RC10LSS.

This lightweight .030 Lexan racing body features: an authentic, bolt-on, adjustable rear spoiler (including mounting bolts), realistic styling and detail.

The Thunderbody (Lexan Underbody) mounts to the bottom of the frame and to the Lumina body. The Thunderbody features aerodynamic "ground effects" design, progressive air channels, body mounting slots, and molded-in trim lines. The Thunderbody increases your top speed, improves handling, and protects the body and frame! The Lumina body and Lumina Thunderbody are available separately or together in a combo package with instructions and decals.

Order Nos: D101—1991 Chevrolet Lumina NASCAR (Narrow Width), $19.98; D127—1991 Lumina (Narrow) Thunderbody, $16.98; and D101C—1991 Lumina (Narrow) Body and Thunderbody Combo, $35.98.

DAHM'S RACING BODIES

DAHM'S exciting new Chevy S-10 Lexan racing truck body—*Ruff-E-Nuff* (No. D192, $19.98 retail)—is designed to fit most 10th scale stadium race trucks, monster trucks, conversions, and narrow (RC10LSS size) on-road cars. Ruff-E-Nuff can be set up as a stadium racer, monster truck, mud bogger, puller, drag truck, desert racer, or a low-riding street truck.

Ruff-E-Nuff is shown on the JRX-T with number plates and rear spoiler made from DAHM'S .030 sheet Lexan (No. D301) using full size templates included with the racing truck body. Ruff-E-Nuff is only 6" wide, so the body clears most stadium race truck tires completely! Ruff-E-Nuff comes with finishing instructions, a Lexan Supercharger, number plate, and rear spoiler templates, and a DAHM'S decal.

J.G. MANUFACTURING

The *J.G. Nissan King Cab Replacement Body* has awesome detail for precise realism. Body adapts to all trucks and conversions including all J.G. truck conversions, Jr-XT, Kyosho trucks, etc. Body is narrow, only 6-1/2 inches wide, so there is no need for excessive wheel well tire clearance.

MCALLISTER RACING

Venom—Single Seater (No. B-154, $15.95 retail)
Ultron—Single Seater (No. B-155, $15.95 retail)

Iron Man Toyota Pick-Up Desert Racer (No. B-153, $20.00 retail)
Toyota SR5 Racing Mini Pick Up (No. B-108, $18.00 retail)

Jeep Cherokee Narrow Race Truck (No. B-152, $20.00 retail)
Nissan Racing Mini Pick Up (No. B-128, $20.00 retail)

MCALLISTER RACING

'70 Barracuda (No. B-134, $20.00 retail)
1970 Boss 302 Mustang (No. B-136, $20.00 retail)

'48 Ford Panel Truck (No. B-145, $20.00 retail)
'73 El Camino (No. B-142, $20.00 retail)

'51 Mercury Pro Stocker (No. B-159, $19.95 retail)
Street Rod Coupe (No. B-129, $20.00 retail)

MCALLISTER RACING

T-Bird NASCAR Stocker (B-127, $20.00 retail)
Chevy Lumina NASCAR Stocker (B-130, $20.00 retail)

Nissan 300 Z (No..B-132, $20.00 retail)
Nissan GTP (No. B-116, $20.00 retail)

Firebird Pro Stock (No. B-140, $20.00 retail)
Baretta Pro Stock—Narrow (No. B-143, $20.00 retail)

J.G. MANUFACTURING

The *Chevy Long Wheel Base Stadium Truck Body* (No. P/N 4018) is made of clear Lexan. Also available painted (No. P/N 4018P). The Ford Long Wheel Base Stadium Truck Body (No. P/N 4019) is made of clear Lexan. Also available painted (No. P/N 4019P).

MRP

1/10-scale Nissan Stadium Truck Body (No. 31-1178, $29.99 retail) with Roger Mears/ Budweiser racing decals is made from .040 genuine GE Lexan®. This body will stand up to a punishing day in the dirt and still sparkle in the winner's circle.

MRP

From its first IMSA GTP race, the *1/10-scale Jaguar XJR-10* (No. 30-1167, $19.99 retail) has shown it superiority. Low, sleek, with the covered rear tires for exceptional aerodynamics, this body is a winner. Made from crystal clear .040 Lexan® including a detailed wing.

MRP

The *1/10-scale T-Bird Clear Stock Car body with Budweiser racing decals* (No. 31-1169, $29.99 retail) is a highly detailed body that is sure to be a crowd pleaser in the tradition of the Budweiser racing family. Crystal clear .040 Lexan® provides strong, fast surfaces.

PARMA INTERNATIONAL

This is the new *1/10-Scale 1956 Chevy Nomad Clear Body* (No. 10298, $19.00 retail). Also available is a 1/10-scale Hemi Kit (No. 10411, $12.00 retail) with chrome plate which will add realism to the car.

PARMA INTERNATIONAL

New for dirt oval fans. The *1990 Chevy Lumina Wedge body* (No. 10303, Clear, $19.00 retail). This 1/10 scale Lexan rocket has been wind tunnel tested for all the right angles for maximum downforce. The new Parma Lumina Wedge is designed to fit all off- and on-road cars. Great for 2 or 4 wheel drive action.

PARMA INTERNATIONAL

This *1/10-Scale '58 Corvette* (No. 10326, clear, $19.00 retail) lets you cruise your neighborhood in classic style. This 1/10-scale reproduction has detail you never thought possible in a Lexan body. Check it out at a fine hobby shop near you.

PARMA INTERNATIONAL

The *JRX-2* (No. 10299, $15.00 retail) is a direct replacement body for the two-wheel drive 1/10 off-road buggy. This body will fit stock body mounts.

PARMA INTERNATIONAL

Parma introduces the *1/10-scale '85 Dodge Van Body* (No. 10281, $19.00 retail) and *Lexan Car Trailer Kit* (No. 10294, trailer only, $21.95 retail; No. 10295, trailer w/dual wheel kit, $59.95 retail; No. 10279, '37 Ford sedan, $19.00 retail). This dynamic duo is shown here with the '37 Ford riding on back, complete with Parma "graphics" decals. All come in clear Lexan and all feature the quality of detail you expect from Parma bodies. Ask for them at your local Parma dealer.

PARMA INTERNATIONAL

Now the same aerodynamic qualities that you have found in our .040, 1/10 scale Mercedes and Toyota Group C bodies are compounded in these new lightweight pro versions. The *1/10 Mercedes Group C Lightweight* (No. 10305L, $19.00 retail) and the *1/10 Toyota Group C Lightweight* (No. 10309L, $19.00 retail) are vacuum-formed in .030 Lexan and have all the characteristic detail and clarity you would expect from any Parma body. Wind-tunnel tested and race proven, these Parma bodies are just two more clear winners.

PARMA INTERNATIONAL

The *1/10-Scale Porsche 911 Clear Body with Wing* (No. 10307, $19.00 retail) is molded in clear Lexan and comes completely detailed. The wing adds the final touch to this body.

PARMA INTERNATIONAL

This *Cobra Body* (No. 10254, $19.00 retail) is molded in clear Lexan with outstanding detail. This body can also be used as a convertible by removing the roof, side windows, and rear window.

PARMA INTERNATIONAL

The *Classic 1957 Chevrolet* (No. 10234, $22.00 retail) is Parma's latest 1/10-scale body. Available in clear Lexan, it sets the standard for detail and realism.

PARMA INTERNATIONAL

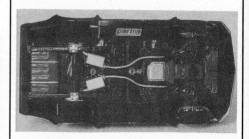

The *Parma 1/10-Scale Lexan Display Chassis* (No. 10327, clear chassis, $19.00 retail; No. 10328, clear chassis w/axle kit, $35.95 retail) comes in sturdy .050 thick Lexan with or without the axle kit. It's the final touch you've been seeking for your next Concourse entry. From top to bottom, Parma has all your concourse winning needs. Ask for it at your favorite Parma dealer today.

PARMA INTERNATIONAL

Lightweight Super Speedway Bodies, all ROAR Legal. Parma's wind tunnel-tested, lightweight Super Speedway series of 1/10-scale NASCAR racing bodies are more detailed than any others available today. All are .030 Lexan. 10319—Buick (shown)—$19.00; 10320—LeBarron—$19.00; 10321—Lumina—$19.00; 10322—Oldsmobile—$19.00; 10323—Pontiac—$19.00; 10324—T-Bird—$19.00; 10324CP—T-Bird, custom painted—$35.00. See our latest catalogue for complete listings.

PARMA INTERNATIONAL

Aerospace technology and wind tunnel testing combine to bring you Parma Pro-Series Racing Bodies. The very first entry, by the world's largest Lexan body manufacturer, is the *1/10 scale Sauber Mercedes* (No. 10305, $19.00 retail). Notice the sleek sweeping lines and low profile. Every surface has been designed to funnel airflow to the rear wing for maximum downforce and minimum drag. This land missile has been created to do one thing; win races. And now it's available in a *Lightweight* version (No. 10305L, $19.00 retail) also!

PARMA INTERNATIONAL

The European version of the Merkur Scorpio, the *1/10 Sapphire R/S for Off-Road with Wing* (No. 10330, Clear, $21.00 retail), is a sure-fire winner. It will easily mount on the most popular off-road chassis and comes complete with wing! If you are planning on racing Rally bodies, the RS 540 Sapphire is a must. This body is destined to be a popular stocking stuffer this Christmas. Order your RS 540 Sapphire today from your local hobby shop.

Car Access. —1/12 Scale Bodies

ANDY'S R/C PRODUCTS

The *Lotec GTP body* (No. 4152, $11.95 retail) is one of the most popular and best working body in a field of 20 other fine bodies we have for 1/12-scale cars.

PARMA INTERNATIONAL

1/12 Scale Stock car racing just got better. Parma introduces the *1/12 scale Chevy Lumina body* (No. 1967, $11.00 retail). With all the exceptional detail you would expect from Parma, this crystal clear Lexan stocker is available now. Visit your local hobby shop and insist on Parma bodies.

PARMA INTERNATIONAL

This *Midnight Pumpkin Truck Body* (No. 10272, $19.00 retail) is a direct replacement for the Tamiya car. Molded in clear Lexan, it features all the detail of the styrene body, but with the crash resistance and easy painting qualities of Lexan.

PARMA INTERNATIONAL

Parma's latest entry in 1/12 racing, the newly R.O.A.R. approved Nissan NPT (No. 1968, Clear, $11.00 retail). This new racing body balances on the fine line of downforce and drag for superior performance. Call today or fax your order.

PARMA INTERNATIONAL

This *1/12-Scale Dodge Van Body* (No. 10256; Retail: See your dealer) is a direct replacement for the Tamiya Lunch Box and also fits other off-road chassis with the use of No. 10483 Body Mounting Kit.

Car Accessories ——— Body/Chassis Parts

ANDY'S R/C PRODUCTS

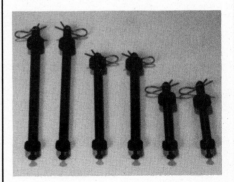

On-road Body Posts are available in 2, 3, and 4 inch lengths. (No. 3206, 2" high, $3.25 retail; No. 3207, 3" high, $3.50 retail; No. 3208, 4" high, $3.75 retail). Sold in pairs.

ANDY'S R/C PRODUCTS

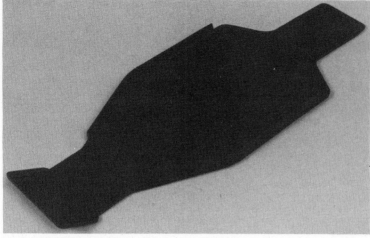

The *RC-10 Molded Graphite Chassis* (No. 3480, $59.95 retail) will add strength to your RC-10 while significantly reducing body weight.

ANDY'S R/C PRODUCTS

This *RC-10 Rear Oval Body Mount* (No. 3419, $5.95 retail) fits the RC-10 and comes in black.

ANDY'S R/C PRODUCTS

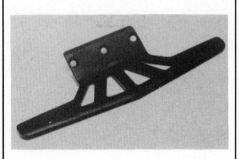

This *RC-10 Front Bumper Body Mount* oval (No. 3412, $6.95 retail) fits the RC-10 and comes in black.

ANDY'S R/C PRODUCTS

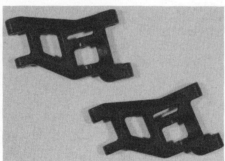

Wide Track Front Arms (No. 3400, $11.95 retail) and *Lightweight Rear Arms* (No. 3402, $11.95 retail) are for the RC-10. Finished in black.

BUD'S RACING PRODUCTS

Mini Pop Rivets (No. 7571, 2.95/18 pieces retail) from Bud's Racing Products are great for attaching spoilers, side dams, and reinforcing wings. Lightweight and easy to use!

CUSTOM CHROME PARTS

The *Lunch Box/Midnight Pumpkin Chrome Chassis* (No. CCP2500, $18.95 retail) will add a super shine to your monster truck. A real eye-catcher!!

CUSTOM CHROME PARTS

The *King Cab/Hi Lux Chassis* (No. CCP2700, $24.95 retail) has quality chromed parts that are specifically made for the King Cab. The entire chassis, suspension, and wheels are chrome-plated with a two-step process for maximum brightness and durability.

CUSTOM CHROME PARTS

The *Blackfoot/Beetle/Mudblaster Chassis Set* (No. CCP2600, $24.95 retail). CCP has taken the Tamiya stock chassis and chromed it with its unique 2-step chroming process that will make you the center of attraction.

CUSTOM CHROME PARTS

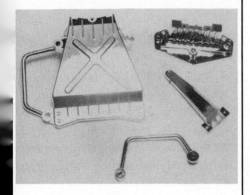

The *Midnight Pumpkin/Lunchbox Lower Chassis* (No. CCP2501, $15.95 retail) will dress up your monster truck with a lustrous, deep chrome finish.

DU-BRO PRODUCTS

These *Adjustable Body Mounting Posts* (No. 2167, 2/pkg, $2.75 retail) are the most universal body mounting system on the market. Constructed out of nylon, these 10-32 diameter body mounts allow you 3 in. adjustment. These body mounts were designed to fit almost any car/body combination on the market today.

Trim off excess

DU-BRO PRODUCTS

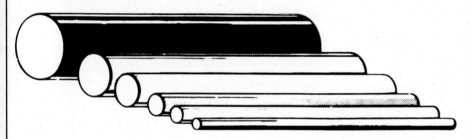

Heat Shrink Tubing (Nos. 2144-2149, $1.15 retail; No. 2150, $3.75 retail) is the ideal solution for many of your modeling needs. This tubing has been specially formulated to shrink up to one half its original diameter simply by using a heat gun, soldering iron, or cigarette lighter. Ideal for insulating electrical splices, and also covering electrical plugs and connectors. A must for every modeler's workshop and field box. Packaged in 3-in. lengths. Order No. 2144, 1/16" dia. Heat Shrink Tubing-Blu (4/pkg); No. 2145, 3/32-in. dia. Heat Shrink Tubing-Grn (4/pkg); No. 2146, 1/8-in. dia. Heat Shrink Tubing-Red (4/pkg); No. 2147, 3/16-in. dia. Heat Shrink Tubing Wht (3/pkg); No. 2148, 1/4-in. dia. Heat Shrink Tubing-Blk (3/pkg); No. 2150, Heat Shrink Tubing–(Asst. pack 2 ea/pkg).

DU-BRO PRODUCTS

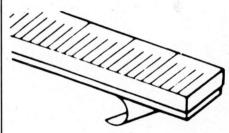

Kwik-Stik Lead Weights (No. 2142, 2/pkg, $2.90 retail) are perfect for adding extra weight to your R/C cars. Strong stick tape on back for easy installation. Two 3 oz. strips divided into 1/20- and 1/4-oz. increments.

DU-BRO PRODUCTS

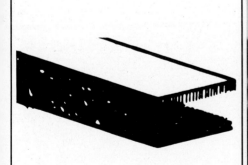

This *Hook & Loop Mounting Material* (No. 2143, 1/pkg, $3.00 retail) is super tough with a glue-like stick—good for mounting receivers, batteries—unlimited uses! Adhesive back on one side allows for easy mounting.

HOLESHOT RACING PRODUCTS

Our *Super Cooler 2001 Heatsink* (No. 2011, $30.95 retail) will fit our (12L) Associated Upper Plate. Our Plate is made of black G-10 material for lightness and strength. Kit contains one Upper Plate and one Super Cooler 2001.

MAXTRAX

The *Maxtrax Wedge* (No. MTXC1000, $299.95 retail) is a 1/10-scale, 2WD rolling chassis kit designed specifically for R/C pulling competition. This steel chassis includes steel black powder-coated finish, 1/4-in. rear axle with ball bearings, and adjustable wheelbase. Motor and speed control are not included.

OFNA RACING DIVISION

OFNA Racing distributes a *special style polycarbonate truck body* (No. PC-1T, $44.00 retail) for any 1/8-scale off-road chassis. The body is styled for full suspension travel under large fenders. Fits Pirate M1, Kyosho Burns, and Mungen.

PARMA INTERNATIONAL

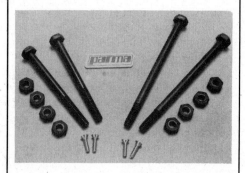

Super-Strong Nylon Body Posts. 18039—2 inch—$3.00 pr.; 8040—3 inch—$3.00 pr.; 8041—4 inch—$4.00 pr.; 8042—5 inch—$5.00 pr. See our latest catalogue for complete listings.

PARMA INTERNATIONAL

Bumper to Bumper parts. (Shown is No. 13221).
12801—4-40 rod ends—$1.20 ea., $7.20/6;
12815—4-40 threaded connecting rod— $1.00 ea., $ 6.00/6;
12825—Losi super heavy duty rod ends— $20.00;
12827—Frog & Grasshopper rod end kit— $6.50;
12828—R/C 10 rod ends & tie rods—$22.50;
12846—Lunch Box dual wheel adaptors— Pair. $10.00;
12848—Blacktoot steering blocks—$7 00;
12857—Losi steering brace, fits all Losi kits —$5.00;
13200—King Cab skid plate bumper—$6.00;
13203—R/C 10 skid plate bumper—$4.00;
13214—R/C 10 rear bumper—$3.00;
13217—Optima Mid skid plate bumper— $5.00;
13221—Universal front bumper, fits most on/off road cars & trucks—$8.00;
13223—Losi full width kydex front bumper, fits all Losi kits—$4.75.
See our latest catalogue for complete listings.

PARMA INTERNATIONAL

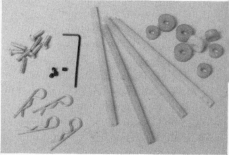

Universal Body Mount Kit (No. 10450, $6.50 retail). Parma makes a wide range of parts and accessories for many on- and off-road kits. The Parma Universal Body Mount Kit works on any R/C car or truck, in any scale. It perfectly mounts any brand of body with no-hassle! The kit includes a wrench and is fully adjustable. Other body mounts and accessories are:
8012—Adjustable lightweight body mounts —$5.50;
8037—Lightweight racing hood pins— $1.75/8;
8038—''Super Gripper'' hood pins—$1.75/6;
8039—''Quick Clip'' bent hood pins— $1.75/4;
8055—Servo tape, 1-in. x 3-ft.—$2.75;
10450—Universal adjustable body mounts fits all cars—$6.50;
10451—Adjustable body mounts for Frog, Blackfoot—$6.75;
10453—Tall body mount kit for sedan & truck bodies—$6.50;
10457—Velcro (hook & loop), 5/8-in. x 6-in. —$3.50;
18039—2" super strong nylon body posts— $3.00 pr.;
18040—3" super strong nylon body posts— $3.00 pr.;
18041—4" super strong nylon body posts— $4.00 pr.;
18042—5" super strong nylon body posts— $5.00 pr.

PARMA INTERNATIONAL

Tapes are out, discs are in. Don't waste your time with sticky and expensive teflon tapes while Parma offers *Solid Teflon Dampener Discs* (No. 18620, $2.50/2 retail). These discs give your ride the ultra-guide slide. So slip down to your favorite raceway or hobby shop and pick up yours. While you're there, check out our complete line of racing accessories.

UNITED MODEL DISTRIBUTORS

R/C Chrome Works ($4.99-$23.99 retail) is a line of the highest quality chrome parts for the Blackfoot, Clodbuster, and King Cab. These parts are genuine original equipment parts that are high-glossed-chrome and directly replace stock parts with classy-looking chrome. The R/C Chrome Works line of parts will really bring your vehicle to life.

On The Cover

Sticker Sheets - $1.35

#RRP 9302 - White
#RRP 9303 - Fluorescent Pink
#RRP 9304 - Black/Fluorescent Pink
#RRP 9305 - Black/Yellow
#RRP 9306 - Black

T-Shirts - $9.95

#RRP 9308 - All Sizes (Specify)

Sweat Shirts - $14.50

#RRP 9309 - All Sizes (Specify)

Pinion Gear Checker $9.95

#RRP 0250 - Gear Checker (32P, 48P & 64P Tooth Counter)

32 Pitch Pinion Gears

Standard Alloy Pinion Gears - $2.95

#RRP 0090 - 9T	#RRP 0170 - 17T
#RRP 0100 - 10T	#RRP 0180 - 18T
#RRP 0110 - 11T	#RRP 0190 - 19T
#RRP 0120 - 12T	#RRP 0200 - 20T
#RRP 0130 - 13T	#RRP 0210 - 21T
#RRP 0140 - 14T	#RRP 0220 - 22T
#RRP 0150 - 15T	
#RRP 0160 - 16T	

NEW! Super Light Pinion Gears.

48 Pitch Pinion Gears

Set Screws $1.00

#RRP 1000 - pkg. of 5

Standard Alloy Pinion Gears - $2.95

#RRP 1012 - 12T	#RRP 1019 - 19T	#RRP 1027 - 2?
#RRP 1013 - 13T	#RRP 1020 - 20T	#RRP 1028 - 28
#RRP 1014 - 14T	#RRP 1021 - 21T	#RRP 1029 - 29
#RRP 1015 - 15T	#RRP 1022 - 22T	#RRP 1030 - 30
#RRP 1016 - 16T	#RRP 1023 - 23T	#RRP 1031 - 3?
#RRP 1017 - 17T	#RRP 1024 - 24T	#RRP 1032 - 32
#RRP 1018 - 18T	#RRP 1025 - 25T	#RRP 1033 - 33
	#RRP 1026 - 26T	#RRP 1034 - 34
		#RRP 1035 - 35

NEW! Super Light Pinion Gears.

Metric Pinion Gears - $3.95

#RRP 1112 - 12T	#RRP 1116 - 16T
#RRP 1113 - 13T	#RRP 1117 - 17T
#RRP 1114 - 14T	#RRP 1118 - 18T
#RRP 1115 - 15T	#RRP 1119 - 19T
	#RRP 1120 - 20T
	#RRP 1121 - 21T
	#RRP 1122 - 22T
	#RRP 1123 - 23T
	#RRP 1124 - 24T

NEW! Super Light Pinion Gears.

"Titanium Gold" Pinion Gears - $4.95

#RRP 1212 - 12T	#RRP 1220 - 20T	#RRP 1228 - 28?
#RRP 1213 - 13T	#RRP 1221 - 21T	#RRP 1229 - 29?
#RRP 1214 - 14T	#RRP 1222 - 22T	#RRP 1230 - 30?
#RRP 1215 - 15T	#RRP 1223 - 23T	#RRP 1231 - 31?
#RRP 1216 - 16T	#RRP 1224 - 24T	#RRP 1232 - 32?
#RRP 1217 - 17T	#RRP 1225 - 25T	#RRP 1233 - 33?
#RRP 1218 - 18T	#RRP 1226 - 26T	#RRP 1234 - 34?
#RRP 1219 - 19T	#RRP 1227 - 27T	#RRP 1235 - 35?

NEW! Super Light Pinion Gears.

48 Pitch Super Spur Gears

48 Pitch Machined Super Spurs - $6.95

#RRP 1972 - 72T
#RRP 1975 - 75T
#RRP 1978 - 78T
#RRP 1981 - 81T
#RRP 1985 - 85T
#RRP 1987 - 87T
#RRP 1990 - 90T
#RRP 1993 - 93T
#RRP 1996 - 96T

RRP's New super thin Super Spur with RRP's Ultra-Precise White Machined Spur

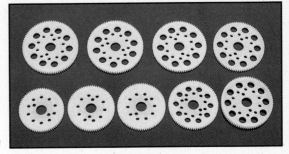

High Quality Machine Process

Titanium Ball Ends

Titanium Studded Ball Ends

$4.50   **$12.99**

#RRP 2014 - Pkg of 4   #RRP 2015 - Pkg of 12

18° King Pin/Castor Block/Axle Kits

RC10 - $22.50

#RRP 2020 - 20° Kit
#RRP 2030 - 30° Kit
#RRP 2040 - 40° Kit

$9.50/pair

#RRP 2001 - Aluminum Axles
#RRP 2010 - King Pins

$6.50/pair

#RRP 2002 - - Steering Arms
#RRP 2008 - 20° Castor Blocks
#RRP 2009 - 30° Castor Blocks

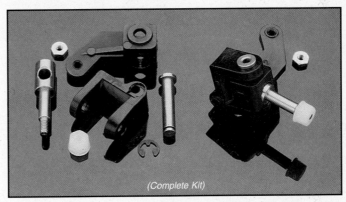

(Complete Kit)

Monster Truck Parts

48 Pitch Hardened Pinions
10-12T $6.95
13-15T $5.95

#RRP MT10 - 10T
#RRP MT11 - 11T
#RRP MT12 - 12T
#RRP MT13 - 13T
#RRP MT14 - 14T
#RRP MT15 - 15T

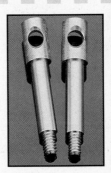

Front Axle Set
$9.50

#RRP 2000 - 18°
Stainless Steel

Adjustable & Fixed Rear Toe-In

RC10
$16.95

#RRP 2005 - Adjustable

RC10
$5.95

#RRP 2025 - 2.5° Fixed
#RRP 2003 - 3.0° Fixed
#RRP 2035 - 3.5° Fixed
#RRP 2004 - 4.0° Fixed

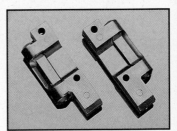

More For The RC10

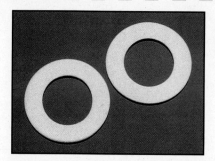

**"Titanium Gold"
Diff Rings
$4.50**

#RRP 2050

**Bearing Cover
$2.00**

#RRP 2007 - RC10

RC10 Race Package - $75.60

#RRP PKG-1 Includes:
1 - RC10 Adjustable Rear Toe-In Kit
3 - Black Teflon Molded Spur Gears In 81, 85 & 90T
15 - Alloy Steel Pinion Gears In 12 Through 26T

48 & 32 Pitch Spur Gears

**48 Pitch Machined
$6.95**

#RRP 2066 - 66T	*#RRP 2085 - 85T*
#RRP 2068 - 68T	*#RRP 2087 - 87T*
#RRP 2070 - 70T	*#RRP 2090 - 90T*
#RRP 2072 - 72T	*#RRP 2093 - 93T*
#RRP 2075 - 75T	*#RRP 2096 - 96T*
#RRP 2078 - 78T	
#RRP 2081 - 81T	

High Quality Machine Process

**48 Pitch Molded
$2.95**

#RRP 2181 - 81T	*#RRP 2190 - 90T*
#RRP 2185 - 85T	*#RRP 2193 - 93T*
#RRP 2187 - 87T	

Injection Molded Process

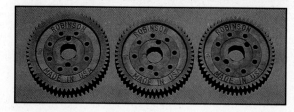

**32 Pitch Molded
$2.95**

#RRP 2254 - 54T
#RRP 2256 - 56T
#RRP 2260 - 60T

Injection Molded Process

For The Ultima Pro/Outlaw/Turbo & Optima Mid

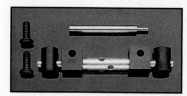

**Ultima Series
$17.95**

*#RRP 3005
Adjustable Rear
Toe-In*

**Optima Mid
$22.50**

*#RRP 3010
Adjustable Rear
Toe-In*

Ultima Series Race Package $146.05

#RRP PKG-2 Includes:
1 - Ultima Adjustable Rear Toe-In Kit
3 - Ultima Conversion Kits In 58, 62 & 66T
15 - Alloy Steel Pinion Gears In 12 Through 26T

Optima Mid Race Package $96.60

#RRP PKG-3 Includes:
1 - Optima Mid Adjustable Rear Toe-In Kit
3 - White Machined Spur Gears In 81, 85 & 90T
15 - Alloy Steel Pinion Gears In 12 Through 26T

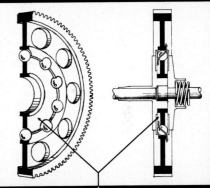

FACTS NOT FRICTION.

The current Off-Road World Champion top three 2WD drivers all ran Robinson Racing's 48 Pitch White Machined Spur Gears to victory. The world's best trusted Robinson Racing, shouldn't you?

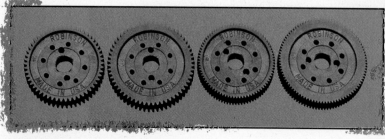

18° King Pin/Castor Block/Axle Kits

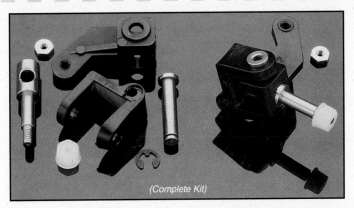

Ultima - $22.50
#RRP 3020 - 20° Kit
#RRP 3030 - 30° Kit

Ultima
$9.50/pair

#RRP 3001 - Axles
#RRP 3009 - King Pins

Ultima
$6.50/pair

#RRP 3004 Steering Arms
#RRP 3008 20° Castor Blocks
#RRP 3009 30° Castor Blocks

(Complete Kit)

48 Pitch Gear Kits

For The Ultima Pro/Outlaw/Turbo
$27.95

#RRP 3054 - 54T Conversion Kit
#RRP 3058 - 58T Conversion Kit
#RRP 3060 - 60T Conversion Kit
#RRP 3062 - 62T Conversion Kit
#RRP 3064 - 64T Conversion Kit
#RRP 3066 - 66T Conversion Kit

More For The Ultima Pro/Outlaw/Pro & Optima

48 Pitch Ultima Pro/Outlaw/Turbo
Cluster - $17.95

#RRP 3154 - 54T   #RRP 3162 - 62T
#RRP 3158 - 58T   #RRP 3164 - 64T
#RRP 3160 - 60T   #RRP 3166 - 66T

48 Pitch Ultima Pro/Outlaw/Turbo
Spur Gear - $8.95

#RRP 3254 - 54T   #RRP 3262 - 62T
#RRP 3258 - 58T   #RRP 3264 - 64T
#RRP 3260 - 60T   #RRP 3266 - 66T

48 Pitch Ball Differential
Conversion Kits - $17.95

#RRP 3300 - Ultima/Thorp (Car)
#RRP 3310 - Ultima/Thorp
                  (Monster Truck)
#RRP 3305 - Ultima/Kyosho (Car)
#RRP 3315 - Ultima/Kyosho
                  (Monster Truck)

48 Pitch
Ultima Pro/
Outlaw/Turbo
Outdrive Gear
$9.95

#RRP 3142
42T Machined

Ultima Pro/
Outlaw/Turbo
Gear & Collar
Set - $9.50

#RRP 3127
Stainless Steel

For The Traxxas Hawk/Sledgehammer

48 Pitch
Conversion
Kit - $29.50

#RRP 3600
(5x8 bearings
required)

Bearings
$9.95

#RRP 3604 - 5x8

32 Pitch
Conversion
Kit - $29.50

#RRP 3601
(5x8 bearings
required)

High Quality
Machine Process

48 Pitch Spurs
$6.95

#RRP 3554 - 54T
#RRP 3562 - 62T
#RRP 3566 - 66T
#RRP 3572 - 72T

Outdrive - $6.95

#RRP 3550 - 32P
#RRP 3551 - 48P
(ball diff recommended)

Gear Adaptor - $11.50

#RRP 3552 - 32P (5x8 bearings required)
#RRP 3553 - 48P (5x8 bearings required,
ball diff recommended)

Final Pinion
$8.95

#RRP 3602 - 32P
#RRP 3603 - 48P

48 Pitch Optima Mid Gears

High Quality Machine Process

Machined Idler $13.95

#RRP 3750 - Machined Idler

Machined Spurs $9.50

#RRP 3781 - 81T
#RRP 3785 - 85T
#RRP 3787 - 87T
#RRP 3790 - 90T
#RRP 3793 - 93T

48 Pitch Spur Gears For Lazer

Machined Spur Gears $13.50

#RRP 3796 - 96T
#RRP 3800 - 100T
#RRP 3808 - 108T
#RRP 3815 - 115T

High Quality Machine Process

64 Pitch Pinion Gears

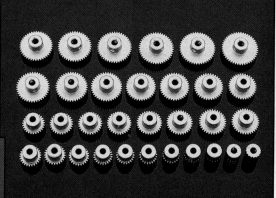

"Titanium Gold" Pinion Gears - $4.95

#RRP 4016 - 16T	#RRP 4029 - 29T	#RRP 4042 - 42T
#RRP 4017 - 17T	#RRP 4030 - 30T	#RRP 4043 - 43T
#RRP 4018 - 18T	#RRP 4031 - 31T	#RRP 4044 - 44T
#RRP 4019 - 19T	#RRP 4032 - 32T	#RRP 4045 - 45T
#RRP 4020 - 20T	#RRP 4033 - 33T	#RRP 4046 - 46T
#RRP 4021 - 21T	#RRP 4034 - 34T	#RRP 4047 - 47T
#RRP 4022 - 22T	#RRP 4035 - 35T	
#RRP 4023 - 23T	#RRP 4036 - 36T	
#RRP 4024 - 24T	#RRP 4037 - 37T	
#RRP 4025 - 25T	#RRP 4038 - 38T	
#RRP 4026 - 26T	#RRP 4039 - 39T	
#RRP 4027 - 27T	#RRP 4040 - 40T	
#RRP 4028 - 28T	#RRP 4041 - 41T	

NEW! Super Light Pinion Gears.

64 Pitch Machined Spur Gears

Machined Spurs $6.95

#RRP 4088 - 88T	#RRP 4108 - 108T
#RRP 4093 - 93T	#RRP 4115 - 115T
#RRP 4096 - 96T	#RRP 4120 - 120T
#RRP 4100 - 100T	#RRP 4125 - 125T
#RRP 4104 - 104T	

High Quality Machine Process

64 Pitch Super Spur Gears

Machined Super Spurs $6.95

#RRP 4196 - 96T
#RRP 4200 - 100T
#RRP 4204 - 104T
#RRP 4208 - 108T
#RRP 4215 - 115T
#RRP 4220 - 120T
#RRP 4225 - 125T

RRP's New super thin Super Spur with RRP's Ultra-Precise White Machined Spur

High Quality Machine Process

Blackfoot Diff/Universal/Axle Kits & Parts

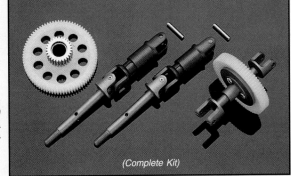

(Complete Kit)

Complete Kits
$89.50

#RRP 5000 - 32 Pitch
#RRP 5005 - 48 Pitch

Differential Gears
$8.50

#RRP 5002 - 32 Pitch
#RRP 5007 - 48 Pitch

Differentials
$40.00

#RRP 5001 - 32 Pitch
#RRP 5006 - 48 Pitch

Outdrives
$6.00

#RRP 5013 - Right
#RRP 5014 - Left

Universal/Axle Kit
$27.50

#RRP 5010 - Kit

Axles
$8.00

#RRP 5012 - Each

Universals
$8.50

#RRP 5011 - Pair

Gear Adaptors
$11.50

#RRP 5003 - 32 Pitch
#RRP 5008 - 48 Pitch

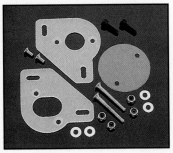

Differential Plates
$5.00

#RRP 5015 - Right
#RRP 5016 - Left

Bearings
$15.00

#RRP 5019 - 5x8mm

Thrust Retainer - $6.00

#RRP 5017

Springs
$2.00/pair

#RRP 5020

Diff Rebuild Kit - $6.00

#RRP 5018 - Balls & Thrust Kit

Clusters
$17.50

#RRP 5052 - 32 Pitch 52T
#RRP 5072 - 48 Pitch 72T
#RRP 5078 - 48 Pitch 78T
#RRP 5081 - 48 Pitch 81T

Spurs
$8.50

#RRP 5152 - 32 Pitch 52T
#RRP 5172 - 48 Pitch 72T
#RRP 5178 - 48 Pitch 78T
#RRP 5181 - 48 Pitch 81T

Adjustable Motor Mount Plate
$9.95

#RRP 5009

King Cab Adaptor & Gears

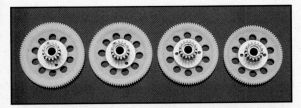

48 Pitch Cluster
$18.50

#RRP 5281 - 81T
#RRP 5285 - 85T
#RRP 5287 - 87T
#RRP 5290 - 90T

48 Pitch Spur Gear
$9.95

#RRP 5381 - 81T
#RRP 5385 - 85T
#RRP 5387 - 87T
#RRP 5390 - 90T

Gear Adaptor
$13.50

#RRP 5200 - Adaptor

JR-X2 & JR-XT Gears, Adaptors & Parts

JR-X2 Gear Adaptor $6.95

#RRP 8500

JR-X2 Side Bulkheads $6.95

#RRP 8501 - Pair

JR-X2 Toe-In $16.95

#RRP 8505 - Adjustable

JR-X2 64 Pitch Spurs $5.95

#RRP 7096 - 96T
#RRP 7100 - 100T
#RRP 7108 - 108T
#RRP 7115 - 115T
#RRP 7120 - 120T
#RRP 7125 - 125T

High Quality Machined Process

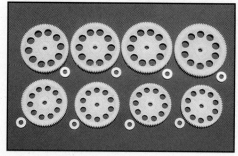

JR-X2 48 Pitch Spurs $5.95

#RRP 8572 - 72T
#RRP 8575 - 75T
#RRP 8578 - 78T
#RRP 8581 - 81T
#RRP 8585 - 85T
#RRP 8587 - 87T
#RRP 8590 - 90T
#RRP 8593 - 93T

JR-X2 18° King Pin/ Castor/Axle Kits $22.50

#RRP 8520 - 20° Kit
#RRP 8530 - 30° Kit

Castor Blocks $6.50/pair

#RRP 8508 - 20°
#RRP 8509 - 30°

JR-XT Rear A-Arms $17.00/pair

#RRP 8502 - Front
#RRP 8503 - Rear

Rear Castor Blocks $7.00/pair

#RRP 8504 - Rear

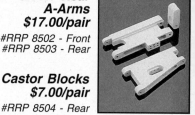

JR-X2 Race Package $84.95

#RRP PKG-4 Includes:

1 - JR-XT Adjustable Rear Toe-In Kit
3 - Black Teflon Molded Spur Gears In 81, 85 & 90T
19 - Alloy Steel Pinion Gears In 12 Through 30T
1 - JR-X2/ROBINSON Gear Adaptor

Cat & YZ10 Gears

YZ10 Pully Collar $9.50

#RRP 8115 - Stainless Steel

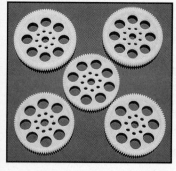

48 Pitch Cat Machined Spurs $9.95

#RRP 8081 - 81T
#RRP 8085 - 85T
#RRP 8087 - 87T
#RRP 8090 - 90T
#RRP 8093 - 93T

High Quality Machined Process

YZ10 Gear Adaptor $17.95

#RRP 8100 - One Way Bearing

48 Pitch YZ10 Clusters $24.95

#RRP 8181 - 81T
#RRP 8185 - 85T
#RRP 8187 - 87T

YZ10 Spurs $9.95

#RRP 8281 - 81T
#RRP 8285 - 85T
#RRP 8287 - 87T

Shock Oil

Shock Oil - 2oz. $3.00 Each

#RRP 9005 - 5wt.
#RRP 9010 - 10wt.
#RRP 9015 - 15wt.
#RRP 9020 - 20wt.

#RRP 9025 - 25wt.
#RRP 9030 - 30wt.
#RRP 9040 - 40wt.
#RRP 9050 - 50wt.
#RRP 9060 - 60wt.
#RRP 9070 - 70wt.
#RRP 9090 - 90wt.
#RRP 9120 - 120wt.
#RRP 9140 - 140wt.

Car Accessories

Suspension

AEROTREND PRODUCTS

The *Chassis Saver Kit* (No. 3410, Special $12.00! Sug. retail $16.99) is the result of extensive testing and development. The final production kit has been tested again and again, each time with positive results. This 15-piece kit consists of three aluminum plates that attach to the chassis, where the suspension pivot balls then attach to it. The holes in each plate are manufactured to close tolerances to insure proper fit. Kit includes ALL mounting hardware.

DU-BRO PRODUCTS

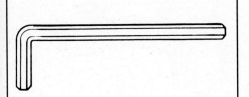

Metric Hex Wrench (No. 2128 for 2mm, No. 2129 for 2.5mm, No. 2130 for 3mm, and No. 2131 for 4mm; $.50 retail).

DU-BRO PRODUCTS

The *2-56 Threaded Ball* (No. 2163, $1.25, retail) is a replacement threaded ball for 2-56 threaded ball link (2/pkg).

DU-BRO PRODUCTS

Swivel Ball Link Shims (No. 2165, $.75, retail; No. 2166, $.85, retail) for Du-Bro swivel ball links. No. 2165 (No. 2) fits 2-56 and 2mm ball links; No. 2166 (No. 4) fits 4-40 ball links (4/pkg).

DU-BRO PRODUCTS

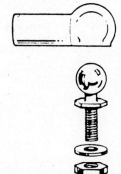

This *2-56 Threaded Ball Link* (No. 2162, $2.25 each, retail) is a 4-piece ball link set, excellent for off-set steering, throttle and servo hook-ups. Ball is threaded for 2-56 nut. Threaded coupler 3/4-in. with 3/8-in. 2-56 thread, for up to .072 wire. Self-threading nylon socket, washer, and 2-56 nut.

DU-BRO PRODUCTS

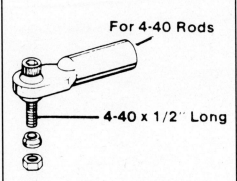

These high quality *4-40 Swivel Ball Links* (No. 2160, without hardware–2/pkg, $1.50 retail; No. 2161, with hardware–2/pkg, $2.50 retail) feature burnished brass swivel balls for smooth operation.

DU-BRO PRODUCTS

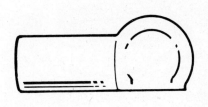

This *2-56 Ball Link Socket* (No. 2164, $1.10 each retail) is a replacement socket for 2-56 threaded ball link (4/pkg).

DU-BRO PRODUCTS

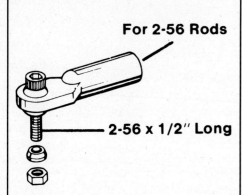

For 2-56 Rods

2-56 x 1/2" Long

These high quality *2-56 Swivel Ball Links* (No. 2134, without hardware–2/pkg, $1.50 retail; No. 2135, with hardware–2/pkg, $2.50 retail) feature burnished brass swivel balls for smooth operation.

DU-BRO PRODUCTS

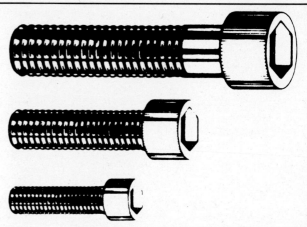

Socket Head Cap Screws (Pack of four, $1.25 retail). Order No. 2111 for 2mm x 4, No. 2112 for 2mm x 6, No. 2113 for 2mm x 10, No. 2114 for 2mm x 12, No. 2115 for 2.5mm x 4, No. 2116 for 2.5mm x 6, No. 2117 for 2.5mm x 8, No. 2118 for 2.5mm x 10, No. 2119 for 2.5mm x 15, No. 2120 for 3mm x 4, No. 2121 for 3mm x 6, No. 2122 for 3mm x 8, No. 2123 for 3mm x 10, No. 2124 for 3mm x 15, No. 2125 for 3mm x 18, No. 2126 for 3mm x 20, and No. 2127 for 3mm x 30.

DU-BRO PRODUCTS

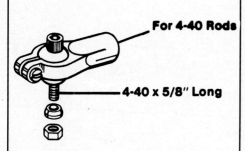

For 4-40 Rods

4-40 x 5/8" Long

This *4-40 E/Z Adjust Ball Link (Short)* (No. 2140, without hardware, $2.00 retail; No. 2141, with hardware, $3.00 retail) has adjustable ball tension, high-quality burnished brass swivel ball for smooth/friction-free operation.

DU-BRO PRODUCTS

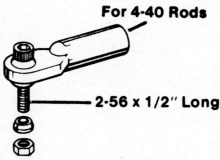

For 4-40 Rods

2-56 x 1/2" Long

These high-quality *2-56 Swivel Ball Links for 4-40 Rods* (No. 2138, without hardware –2/pkg, $1.50 retail; No. 2139, with hardware–2/pkg, $2.50 retail) feature burnished brass swivel balls for smooth operation.

DU-BRO PRODUCTS

Hex Nuts (No. 2103 for 2mm, No. 2104 for 2.5mm, No. 2105 for 3mm, and No. 2106 for 4mm; pack of four, $.50 retail).

DU-BRO PRODUCTS

Nylon Insert Lock Nuts (No. 2101 for 3mm, No. 2102 for 4mm; pack of four, $.75 retail).

DU-BRO PRODUCTS

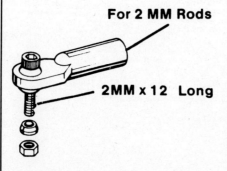

For 2 MM Rods

2MM x 12 Long

These high-quality *2mm Swivel Ball Links* (No. 2132, without hardware–2/pkg, $1.50 retail; No. 2133, with hardware–2/pkg, $2.50 retail) feature burnished brass swivel balls for smooth operation.

DU-BRO PRODUCTS

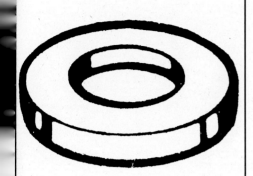

Flat Washers (No. 2107 for 2mm, No. 2108 for 2.5mm, No. 2109 for 3mm, and No. 2110 for 4mm; pack of eight, $.50 retail).

DU-BRO PRODUCTS

Swivel Ball Link Shims (No. 2165, $.75 each, retail; No. 2166, $.85 each, retail) for Du-Bro swivel ball links. No. 2165 (No. 2) fits 2-56 and 2mm ball links; No. 2166 (No. 4) fits 4-40 ball links (4/pkg).

DU-BRO PRODUCTS

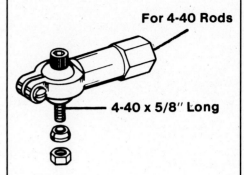

For 4-40 Rods

4-40 x 5/8" Long

This *4-40 E/Z Adjust Ball Link* (No. 2136, without hardware; pack of two, $2.00 retail; No. 2137, with hardware; Pack of two, $3.00 retail) has adjustable ball tension, high-quality burnished brass swivel ball for smooth/friction-free operation.

DURATRAX

Duratrax Competition Shocks (No. DTXC3500, 4-in., $24.95/pair retail; No. DTXC3501, 3-in. gold anodized, $24.95/ pair retail) let you hop up your car or truck at a low cost. Just add oil and they're ready to install.

KYOSHO

Option House Adjustable Pressure Shocks (No. KYOC5692 for short, $29.95 retail; No. KYOC5693 for long, $29.95 retail) are the best yet from Kyosho, already famous for shocks. Adjustable pressure shocks are available in both long and short versions, will fit most electric buggies, and are completely adjustable for any track condition.

MAXTRAX

New from Kyosho, *USA-1 Cantilever Suspension System* (No. MTXC1300, $79.95 retail) gives you stadium truck-like performance, a high-tech suspension patterned after the latest full-scale monster trucks. It improves handling and suspension travel, it is fully adjustable—fits both stock chassis and sassy chassis equipped trucks. It is made of heavy-duty aluminum bellcranks with bushings and shock mounts. The bellcranks can be upgraded with ball bearings for an even smoother operation. The 4-in. long shocks are not included.

PARMA INTERNATIONAL

Extremely smooth and durable, these revolutionary *Ceramic Diff Balls* (No. 17302, $18.00/12 retail) are formed to the highest tolerances possible and are perfect for R/C cars. Put the "smooth moves" on the competition. They'll wonder what happened.

PORTA-POWER INDUSTRIES

The *P.P.I. Tweak Board* (No. Tweak Board, $54.95 retail) is a precision instrument for calibrating the suspension on 1/10- or 1/12-scale R/C cars. Our Tweak Board is manufactured to exacting tolerances and utilizes two surface levels, ground and polished swivel shaft, three adjustment knobs for leveling and precision car alignment lines perfectly set from the center swivel point to achieve total accuracy. This item is a must for the serious racing enthusiast.

TEAM LOSI INC.

Pure Synthetic Shock Fluid (Retail: See your dealer) from Team Losi is an absolute must for winning performance. The exacting certified viscosity and hand-color coding make tuning simple for consistent performance. This non-heat sensitive fluid does not attack o-ring or plastic parts, which extends the shock life.

TEAM PIT STOP

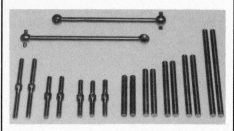

Team Pit Stop's *Lightweight Titanium Hinge Pins, Dog Bones, and Turnbuckles* (#4000 Series) are available for all popular cars. *Hinge Pins* come in both 1/8" and .117" diameter. *Turnbuckles* are available in both titanium and nickle plated steel in complete kits and also in pairs in the following lengths: 7/8". 1", 1-1/4", 1-1/2", 1-5/8", 1-7/8", 2-1/4", anbd 2-1/2". *Dog Bones* are available for TPS NOVA, R/C-10, and Ultima.

TEAM PIT STOP

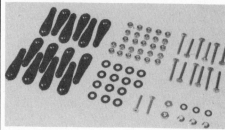

Using lightweight hardware and Heim ends, Team Pit Stop's complete *Steering and Suspension End Systems* (#4000, $29.99 retail) replace ball caps to improve performance and reliability, available for all popular on-road and off-road cars.

TEAM PIT STOP

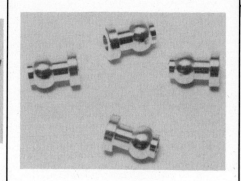

Team Pit Stop's *Lightweight Aluminum Bottom Shock Pivot Balls* (No. 4185, $4.99 retail) are available for Associated and Kyosho shocks. Reduce insprung weight by 1/10 ounce.

Car Accessories Tires

DURATRAX

Duratrax BBS Wheels and Tires (Retail: See your dealer) are ideal for 1/10-scale on-road racing. These tires are available in three compounds. BBS Tires are available as donuts or pre-mounted on rims.

AEROTREND PRODUCTS

Front and Rear Street Tires (No. 3967, Special $8.00! Sug. retail $9.99; No. 3968, Special $9.50! Sug. retail $12.99) give your car the extra mile!! Made of 100% rubber!! Extra wide—extra tread—extra versatile. Run on any hard surface.

YOUR LOCAL HOBBY SHOP IS THERE TO HELP YOU SELECT THE BEST EQUIPMENT AND TO ANSWER YOUR QUESTIONS.

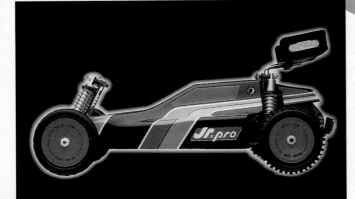

HOBBY PRODUCTS INT'L INC.

HPI offers high quality *Mounted Foam Tires* ($15.00 to $29.95/pr. retail) for various R/C car applications. The tires are incorporated with high-quality, high-impact nylon wheels, and high traction quality foam tires. The tires are available for various 1/10-scale Monster/Stadium Trucks, 1/10-scale Off-Road Cars, and 1/10-scale Direct Drive Cars. These tires are ideal for asphalt and carpet surface. The Super Star MTD Tires are available in Black and White. The Deep Dish are available in White, Black, Yellow, Pink, and Blue.

J.G. MANUFACTURING

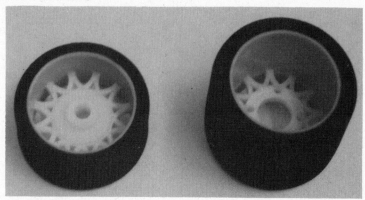

The *J.G. 1/10 On-Road Ultra Light Weight Nylon Rims-Foam Tires* are BBS style nylon rims which have less unsprung weight. We use the finest foam available, glued and trued to perfection. This combination is as light or lighter than any other rims and tire combination currently on the market. Rims fit Associated 10L cars, etc. Order Nos.: P/N 2158 front green-dot, P/N 2159 front blue-dot, P/N 2160 front orange-dot, P/N 2161 rear green-dot, P/N 2162 rear yellow-dot, P/N 2163 front black-dot, and P/N 2164 rear black-dot. Available now!

TEAM LOSI INC.

Team Losi "Naturals" Racing Tires ($10.00 - $16.00 retail) are the choice of champions worldwide. The 1/10 scale off-road "Naturals" line of natural rubber race tires has proven its superiority on race tracks around the country and around the world. The competition-developed carcass construction, tread design, and rubber compounds offer the right tire for every need.

TEAM LOSI INC.

Jammin Off-Road Racing Tires (No. J-701 and J-705, $11.00/pr.) offer track-tested design and race-proven Team Losi "H.T." rubber compound for maximum traction on most dirt surfaces. The No. 701 features a full radius carcass with the popular mini-pin tread pattern. The No. 705 utilizes a "cross hatch" lug pattern that can be trimmed to suit the most demanding track conditions.

J.G. MANUFACTURING

The new *Ultra Light Mini Pan Spike 2.2 Truck Tires* are 1/8" spike four per row staggered. Available in *Synthetic Rubber* (No. P/N 1422, $15.95 retail) or *Natural Rubber* (No. P/N 1423, $17.95 retail). Also pictured, *Ultra Light Soft Compound Mini-Mini Diamond Pin Spike 2.2 Truck Tires* (No. P/N 1424, $15.59 retail), 1/16" base with 1/8" high spikes.

OFNA RACING DIVISION

OFNA Racing has the widest selection of *high-grade, long-wear tires for the 1/8-scale gas racer* offered. Tires fit Pirate M1, Kyosho Burns, and Mungen cars. Selections include different compounds and patterns. Also available are foam inserts, for soft and medium tire compounds, and street foam tires (foam type) pre-mounted on Pirate M1 wheels. Wheel styles fit Pirate M1 and Mungen hubs.

TEAM PIT STOP

Team Pit Stop's *Pre-Trued 2.9" Diameter Front and Rear Foam Donuts* (#2400 Series) for dirt oval and off-road mount directly on 2" rear and 2.1" front single piece off-road rims. The 3/4" wide fronts ($11.99 retail) and 1-1/2" wide rear ($12.99 retail) are available in blue, green, and yellow compounds.

Car Accessories
——————— Wheels

ASSOCIATED ELECTRICS

Three-Piece Front Wheels (No. 6854, $4.00 retail) are specifically designed for mounting two 1/8-in. front tires without gluing them on. These wheels are designed to be used over and over.

ASSOCIATED ELECTRICS

Three-Piece Rear Wheels (No. 6804, $6.00 retail) are designed to mount 2 in. rear tires without having to glue them on. This reduces weight and allows the wheels to be used over and over.

CUSTOM CHROME PARTS

The *King Cab/Hi-Lux Front and Rear Wheels* (No. CCP2714, $21.95 retail) are the highest quality real chrome 2-step plating process that guarantees the brightest shine possible. These front and rear wheels come in a set of 4 or No. CCP2712 for Front, $12.95; or No. CCP2713 for Rear, $12.95.

CUSTOM CHROME PARTS

The *Clod/Bullhead Chrome Rims* (No. CCP1006-2, $26.95 retail/2 pair) are the original stock rims which are put through our unique 2-step chroming process for that CCP shine. Also available is one pair (No. CCP1006-1, $16.95 retail).

Safety is no accident

HOBBY PRODUCTS INT'L INC.

HPI Deep Dish Mounted Tires ($15.00 to $29.95/pr. retail) fit most American-made 1/10-scale direct-drive cars. The wheels are made of high-impact nylon, so they are rigid, durable, and lightweight. This 1.80-in. dia. wheels provide quick and crisp steering responses to your cars. The tires are available with various foam compounds and rubber caps. Also, the tires are available with White, Black, Yellow, Pink, and Blue wheels. HPI Mounted Tires are Modified and Stock '90 NORRCA National Champions.

T.M. R/C RACING COMPONENTS

T.M. introduces its new design of *BBS Style On-road Wheels* which will fit most of the popular 1/10 scale on-road cars available today. All wheels are manufactured in super tough nylon which resist breaking or cracking and are covered with one piece low profile sponge tires. Front wheels are 1-1/8" wide and rear are 2" wide.

Also available are replacement un-trued donuts for those who like the NASCAR look. T.M. introduces its new NASCAR Style Wheels and Tires. T.M.'s NASCAR wheels are manufactured in the same super tough nylon as its other wheels and covered with low profile one piece sponge tires. Front wheels are 1-1/8" wide and rear are 2" wide.

Order No. 5104, $14.95; No. 5110, $17.95; No. 5004, $15.00; and No. 5010, $18.00.

TECNACRAFT

1/4 Scale Wheels (Set of four, $249.95 retail) of modular aluminum are available from Tecnacraft with Indy, Grand National, or Sprint spoke patterns.

TECNACRAFT

Clod Buster Wheels (No. 18-04, Set of four, $149.95 retail) of modular aluminum are available from Tecnacraft with any of the various Tecnacraft spoke patterns and finishes for the Clod Buster.

TECNACRAFT

On-Road Wheels (No. 17-04, $99.95 retail) from Tecnacraft are available for BoLink, TRC, and most other 1/10 scale on-road cars. The spoke centers are available machined or gold anodized.

Car Accessories
Miscellaneous

AEROTREND PRODUCTS

Parts Pots (No. 1213, $4.99 retail) are handy workbench helpers for holding small parts. They have a molded-in bump and ridge that allow the biggest hands to pick up the smallest parts. Come four to a package.

A & D RACING PRODUCTS

The *A & D Racing Products Pro Pack* (price varies with match time) includes everything you need for a national-caliber battery pack. The pack includes: select cells, two 6 inch pieces of A & D Pro 13 wire in black and hot fluorescent pink, Dan's Gold Bars, shrink-wrap and two sheets of decals. Look for the Pro Pack now from A & D. A & D Pro Packs are available in 4-, 6-, and 7-cell packages of individual cells.

AEROTREND PRODUCTS

Motor Tubes (No. 3926, Special $2.00! Sug. retail $2.69 retail) are handy and convenient cases for protecting your motors and/or other small parts. 2 per package.

AEROTREND PRODUCTS

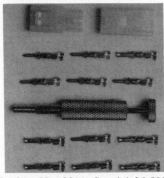

Pin Pusher (No. 3911, Special $6.50! Sug. retail $7.50) and *Pin Pusher Plus* (No. 3912, Special $12.00! Sug. retail $13.99) easily remove Tamiya and other types of connectors without damaging them. The Pin Pusher is constructed of brass. The Plus model comes with 6 each GOLD male and female pins plus connectors.

AEROTREND PRODUCTS

Series "Y" Harness (No. 3903, Special $5.00! Sug. retail $5.99) and *Parallel Wire Harness* (No. 3902, $5.99 retail) double the run time by allowing you to connect 2 SIMILAR battery packs to your speed controller.

AEROTREND PRODUCTS

End Caps (No. 3928, Special $.75! Sug. retail $.99) are made of high density nylon, perfect for the hobbyist who makes and repairs his own battery packs.

AEROTREND PRODUCTS

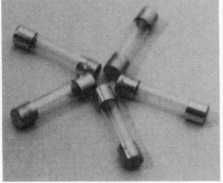

Replacement Fuses (Nos. 3941 - 3960, Special $1.75! Sug. retail $2.29) are available from Aerotrend in the .75- to 30-amp range. Ideal for battery chargers or any other circuit that requires fuse protection.

R/C Car Racing... Feel the Heat!

BUD'S RACING PRODUCTS

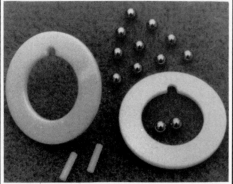

Bud's Racing Products brings this hi-tech, space-age material to the R/C racer. Super hard, precision *Ceramic Diff. Drive Ring Kit* (No. 2115, $24.95 retail) will give you the ultimate diff. Our proto set had over 200 4-min. runs and two 500-lap enduros on them. Used by many of the top R/C drivers.

C&M MFG.

Cobra Trackside Truer ($124.95 retail) the first easy and inexpensive way to true foam tires right at the track! By truing foam tires, you get much more accuracy and prolonged tire life. The TT is small, portable, and lightweight. Although easy to use, it is accurate within .002". It is powered by your 6-cell battery pack. The TT comes with arbors for 1/10 scale, but also available and sold separately are 1/12 scale, RC10, Dominator, and Corrally Arbors. Buy the regular TT or get the Deluxe model which comes with bearings and belt drive system ($159.95 retail).

CUSTOM CHROME PARTS

The *Clod/Bullhead Gearcase* (No. CCP1003, $24.95 retail) from CCP comes with 2 gearcases (1 front and 1 rear to a package). These gearcases will make your truck stand out in a crowd with an awesome shine you've come to expect from CCP.

CUSTOM CHROME PARTS

The *Pumpkin/Lunch Box Gearcases* (No. CCP2502, $14.95 retail) are plated with the best quality chrome and the unique two-step chrome process guarantees the best plating quality unmatched by any other manufacturer.

DURO ART IND., INC.

Graphics: complete packages of Vinyl Letters and Numbers ($2.49 and up retail). Manufactured in the following sizes: 1/4", 1/2", 3/4", 1", 2", and 3". Also 4" and 6" packages of Vinyl Letters and Numbers only. Available in 8 colors: black, white, red, blue, green, yellow, matte finish gold, and silver. (Fuel modelers should spray with poly varnish.)

HOBBY PRODUCTS INT'L INC.

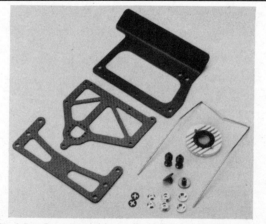

HPI offers various high quality machined *Pro Parts* (variable retail prices) for 1/10-scale cars. The graphite parts shown are Aero Lower Brace, Pro Upper Brace, and Pro Arm Brace. They are available for RC10L, RC12L, and RC10L Super Speedway cars. Quick Fit Wing Wire (adjustable width, pre bent, black), Motor Cooling Plate with dust protector, Aluminum Wing Buttons, Aluminum Wing Wire Mounts, Fr. Axle Stopper Washers, Cone Linkage Spacers, and Cone/Concave Washers are also shown.

Your local hobby shop is there to help you select the best equipment and to answer your questions

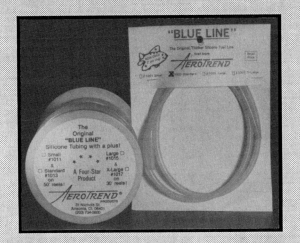

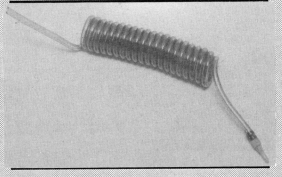
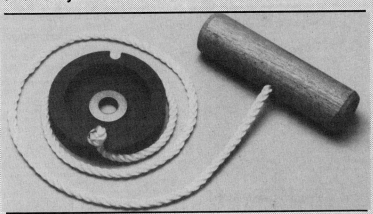

HOBBY PRODUCTS INT'L INC.

HPI offers various *Alum. Washers* ($3.50 to $4.00/6 pcs. retail) and spacers for R/C car applications. Alum. Cone Linkage Spacers are best used at the steering linkage system where smooth action is needed. Alum. Cone Washers are best used to secure cap screws. Alum. Concave Washers are best used to secure flat head screws. The washers and spacers are available for M2.0/2.6/3.0/4.0 and 2-56/3-48/4-40 screws. There are 6 washers per package.

HOLESHOT RACING PRODUCTS

The *Super Cooler 2000* (No. 2000, $23.50 retail) is the most efficient and effective heatsink on the market. Used by all the top drivers in the country, it's made of black anodized aluminum and weighs only a little over 1/2 oz. The Super Cooler 2000 will allow your motor to run 25°-30° cooler. Fits most 2WD off-road and on-road cars, trucks, and truck conversions. RC10 requires minor modifications.

HOLESHOT RACING PRODUCTS

The *Super Cooler 2001* (No. 2001, $21.50 retail) is designed to fit on-road cars with limited open space in the upper support plate such as the Associated 10L, Cheetah 10L Narrow Rear End, and Hyperdrive cars. It has 13-sq. in. of cooling surface, weighs only 1/2 oz., and can be used on off-road cars. It's made of black anodized aluminum.

KIMBROUGH PRODUCTS

KIMBROUGH PRODUCTS

NO TRICKS - NO MAGIC
NO GIMMICKS

JUST RELIABLE HIGH QUALITY R/C MODEL CAR ACCESSORYS AT REASONABLE PRICES.

Manufacturers of reliable, high quality *R/C model car accessories* at reasonable prices. Products include servo mounted, servo savers, servo arms, 32 and 48 pitch differential gears, 48 pitch pinion gears, gear adapters, diamond wing fasteners, transmitter wheel grips, and tire horns, for gluing foam tires.

J.G. MANUFACTURING

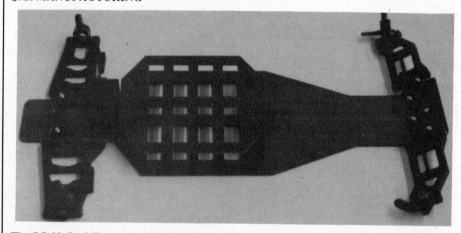

The *RC-10 Oval Conversion Kit* (No. P/N A-27, $45.95 retail) is one complete package for oval racing. Kit includes front oval bumper/body mount, rear oval body mount, front and rear lower shock towers, body post kit, foam body post spacers, nerf wing, and 3-D instructions. Also available with Graphite shock towers (No. A-27G, $56.95 retail). All parts are also sold separately.

KYOSHO

The *Kyosho Motor Checker DX* (No. KYOP1225, $129.95 retail) is a motor checker and break-in machine—all in one unit. Compact go-anywhere unit allows you to properly break in a motor and perform accurate motor checks between.

MAXTRAX

The *Maxtrax Heavy Duty Steel Gear Set* (No. MTXC0500, $79.95 retail) is a direct drop in replacement for all Kyosho trucks. Differential has been replaced to improve strength. Ball bearings are recommended. This unit is recommended for truck pulling.

MRC

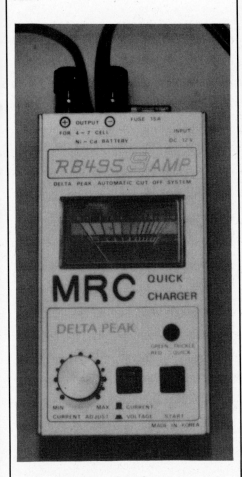

The *RB495 Delta Peak Quick Charger* (No. RB495; Retail: See your dealer), powered from 12 volts DC, uses race-car technology and can charge NiCads from 450-1800 mAH, in 4-7 cell configuration, with an adjustable current output from 1-9 amps. Standard features include a high-grade current/ voltage meter, and a unique melody-maker to notify you of the completed quick-charge.

MRC-TAMIYA

The *Dynatech 02H* (No. U53044; Retail: See your dealer) is cool running, and to win a race, you and your motor must keep cool. A lightweight miniature fan ventilates this car and rotor, and the case has cooling fins. To adjust brush tension, you merely move the end of the brush springs to one of three settings. Hop-up options are available.

RADIO CONTROL DEVELOPMENT, INC.

The *Shredder Micro 2-Channel AM* is the smallest, most affordable receiver available. As a result of its SMT construction (Surface Mount Technology), the Shredder is about 2/3 the size of any other and offers the best performance around. The Shredder is available on both 27 and 75mhz and is compatible with most existing two channel AM transmitters. No. RCD0010 for Futaba ''J'' 27mhz, No. RCD0020 for Airtronics 27mhz, No. RCD0030 for Hitec 27mhz, No. RCD0015 for Futaba ''J'' 75mhz, No. RCD0025 for Airtronics 75mhz, and No. RCD0045 for Hitec 75mhz.

SERMOS R/C SNAP CONNECTORS, INC.

These *High-Amp Powerpole Snap Connectors* (Retail: Available from Sermos) are modular ''silver-plated'' connectors for your electric planes, cars, or boats. They're designed for a high-vibration environment. Cycled ten thousand times without electrical failure, they're designed for anything electrical requiring quick disconnects. Color coordinated and rated 30 amps at 600 DC, internal resistance is rated 250 micro ohms. Silver-plated contact accepts AWG sizes 12 to 16. For dealer information send to Sermos.

SERMOS R/C SNAP CONNECTORS, INC.

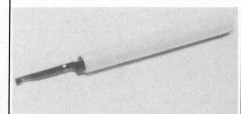

This *Insertion/Extraction Tool* (No. G-2 TOOL, $5.00 retail) is a quick and easy way to assemble and disassemble the Sermos R/C Snap Connectors.

RACING SILKS

Cartoon Plaques ($12.00 retail) for R/C Fanatics: Chuckle at the R/C Racer, the R/C Admiral, and Race Day—all depicting those all-too-familiar but laughable situations that R/C enthusiasts will recognize. These full-color 11x14 Plaques are mounted on wood and laminated to create a ready-to-hang decoration, or they can be framed for a custom look. They make great gifts for your favorite R/C nut!

SMC/LIGHTNING PRODUCTS

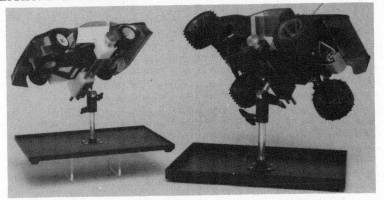

The *Steady Lift Jr.* (No. SLJ-1, $40.00 retail) and heavy-duty *Steady Lift Pro* (No. SLP-1, $65.00 retail) are designed for a wide range of R/C cars and trucks. Made of durable high-tech materials, they securely hold models up to 1/10 scale. Adjustable clamping device opens from 2-1/4 in. to 8-1/2 in. Clamp system rotates 360°, tilts 180°, and is mounted offset to provide maximum accessibility to chassis. Base tray holds tools and catches stray parts. Pedestal base can be attached directly to workbench or table.

STAGE III

TEAM PIT STOP

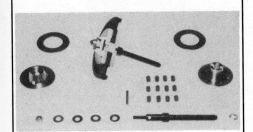

Team Pit Stop is the original developer for the *Slipper Clutch* (#9015 Series, $34.99 retail) and to date it is still the finest and best made. Available for the TPS chain drive, JRX-2, MIP, Schumacher, and Trackmaster transmissions.

TEAM PIT STOP

The Team Pit Stop's *Chain Drive Transmission* (Nos. 9030-S, 9031, 9032-S) with full ball bearing, 8 ball differential and slipper clutch is now available with up to six internal radios of 1.5, 1.6, 1.87, 2.0, 2.14, and 2.28 for TPS NOVA, R/C-10, and Ultima ($129.99 retail each); and JRX-2 ($134.99 retail). The fastest transmissions in the world.

Ultrabraid (2-ft. pkg., $4.50 retail; 50-ft. roll, $90.00 retail; 100-ft. roll, $160.00 retail) high-capacity, low resistance 12 ga. 99.9% pure copper braid for maximum current flow! Used as a shunt between cells in pack assembly. Ultrabraid has the lowest cost per connection, low resistance, and flexibility too!!

TEAM PIT STOP

Team Pit Stop's *Lightweight Universal Wing Mounts* (No. 8113, $4.99 retail) mount vertically or horizontally. They are aluminum with knurl and tapped holes length and across. Shipped with aluminum mounting screws.

TREATMENT PRODUCTS LTD.

The *Final Detail Model Wax* ($2.75 retail) from the Treatment allows for a good wax job of any model or R/C car. It's pure Carnauba formula will not scratch or leave a dusty residue like automotive waxes. Great for Lexan and all plastic surfaces. Removes fine scratches and smudges from finished surfaces. Protects surface from oils and natural acids. Recommended by top professionals!

WINNING EDGE PRODUCTS

Pro-Steer ($49.95) is a rack and pinion steering system designed to give true linear movement with double ball bearing smoothness. It has a Futaba size splined shaft and is currently available for the JR-X2, JR-XT, RC-10, RC-10 Graphite, and a universal model which can be used in trucks as well as other cars.

WINNING EDGE PRODUCTS

Turbo Motor Cooler's ($29.95 retail) unique design lets the motor breathe by allowing the air flow created by the spinning armature to be released through the slots allowing cool air to enter. The contact plate draws heat from the motor and dissipates through the heat sink.

XURON CORP.

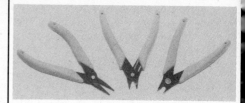

The *Shears* (No. 475 C, Combination Plier, $14.99 retail; No. 410 T, High Precision Shear, $9.99 retail; No. 450, Tweezernose Plier, $15.99 retail) that set the standard in civilian and military electronics and aerospace are now available to RC hobbyists. The shearing cut of XURON Micro-Shear® flushcutters is so clean and square that post-cutting clean up may not be required. Ask for XURON when you want the cuts that are so good their patented.

Truck Accessories

CUSTOM CHROME PARTS

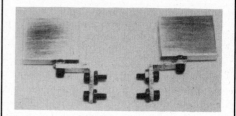

These *Universal Aluminum Side View Mirrors* (No. CCP10113, $34.95) fit all monster trucks and come two mirrors to a card. These mirrors are made of highly polished aluminum and are completely adjustable. Easy to install on plastic and Lexan bodies.

A & D RACING PRODUCTS

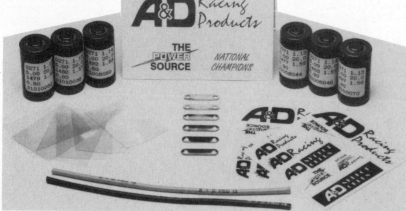

The *A & D Racing Products Pro Pack* (price varies with match time) includes everything you need for a national-caliber battery pack. The pack includes: select cells, two 6 inch pieces of A & D Pro 13 wire in black and hot fluorescent pink, Dan's Gold Bars, shrink-wrap and two sheets of decals. Look for the Pro Pack now from A & D. A & D Pro Packs are available in 4-, 6-, and 7-cell packages of individual cells.

CUSTOM CHROME PARTS

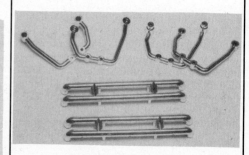

These *Front and Rear Clod/Bullhead Gearcase Bumpers* (No. CCP1002, $12.95 retail) are plated using CCP's 2-step chroming process for the lustrous, deep finish that replaces the red/yellow Tamiya original parts.

ADVANCE ENGINEERING & MFG. CO.

Advance Engineering & Mfg. offers this new
  Tuff Truck Stuff:
Scale Depth Box Kit—$4.95
Aluminum Box Liner—$7.95
Vinyl Tailgate Net—$4.95
Aluminum Front Bumper—$14.95
Aluminum Rear Bumper—$14.95
Aluminum Roll Bar—$19.95
Aluminum Blk Front Wheels—$35.95 per pair
Aluminum Clod B Wheels—$74.95 per pair
Adapters Inc. with purchase of aluminum wheels
Plastic Clod B Wheels—$6.95 per pair
Adapters for plastic wheels—$19.95 per set
Clod Buster Tires—$24.95 per pair
Advance Engineering Brochure—$2.00

CUSTOM CHROME PARTS

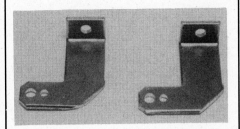

The *Clod/Bullhead Aluminum Gearcase Braces* (No. CCP10110, $15.95 retail/pair) which are direct replacements for the original plastic parts will beef up your gearcases and are guaranteed not to break. A must replacement for all Clod/Bullhead owners.

CUSTOM CHROME PARTS

The *Complete Chrome Package* is the ideal way to convert your monster truck from an ordinary looking truck to one that will outshine the competition! Custom Chrome uses only genuine Tamiya parts to ensure quality and fit. All parts that came with your original kit, but in a lustrous, deep chrome finish, so for a full chrome job order:
  No. CCP-1015—Clodbuster/Bullhead ($216.25); No. CCP-2512—Lunchbox/Pumpkin ($101.60); No. CCP-2611—Blackfoot/Mudblaster ($125.45); No. CCP-2715—King Cab/Hi-Lux ($163.35). Custom Chrome also sells individual packaged parts for the vehicles listed above.

CUSTOM CHROME PARTS

The *Clod/Bullhead Ladder Bars* (No. CCP1000, $21.95 retail/set of 4). Replace your original ladder bars with CCP's unique 2-step chrome finish which is unmatched by any other manufacturer.

CUSTOM CHROME PARTS

The *Clod/Bullhead Aluminum Steering Mechanism* (No. CCP10111, $39.95 retail/set) were designed for both front and rear steering on the Clod/Bullhead. This steering mechanism replaces the stock with aluminum parts for added durability and guaranteed not to break.

CUSTOM CHROME PARTS

The *EZ fit Clod Windshield Visor* (CCP10112, $16.95 retail) fits the Clodbuster and is made from .040 brushed aluminum and clear anodized for a CCP shine. It installs in less than 5 minutes with only a Phillips head screwdriver. All edges have been sanded and polished.
  Also available: No. CCP-10114—Bullhead ($16.95 retail) and No. CCP-10116—Blackfoot ($16.95 retail).

CUSTOM CHROME PARTS

The *Clod/Bullhead Axle Housing* (No. CCP1010, $13.95 retail) add these to Custom Chrome gearcases for a full shine drive train.

CUSTOM CHROME PARTS

These *Clod/Bullhead Steering Knuckles* (No. CCP1011, $16.95 retail) come packed in a set of 4 and will enhance the look of your monster truck. Used with CCP's chrome gearcases and axle tubes.

Outshine the Competition

CCP-6000

MONSTERIZE your Blackfoot with Custom Chrome unbreakable aluminum Clod wheel adapters. Also available for other MRC and Kyosho trucks.

NEW

Clodbuster Parts

CCP-10112	Clodbuster windshield visor	$16.95
CCP-10113	Clodbuster side view mirrors	(pair) 29.95
CCP-10110	Aluminum gear case braces (2)	15.95
CCP-10111	Aluminum Clodbuster steering (front & rear)	39.95
CCP-8002	Clodbuster steel gears new improved EMC	149.95
CCP-7000	Clod duel wheel adapters (steel)	59.95
CCP-7001	Clod duel wheel adapters (lightweight)	59.95
CCP-321	Clodbuster aluminum chassis w/lift	99.95
CCP-10114	Bullhead Windshield Visor	16.95
CCP-10116	Blackfoot Windshield Visor	16.95

Order now by phone or by mail. Or see your local hobby dealer.

Custom Chrome Parts for Clodbuster

CCP-1000	Ladder bars (4 pcs.)	$21.95
CCP-1001	Suspension braces	9.95
CCP-1002	Front & rear bumpers	12.95
CCP-1003	2 Gear cases	24.95
CCP-1004	Body mounts (4 pcs.)	5.95
CCP-1005	8 shock covers & mounts	13.95
CCP-1006	Clod rims (1 pr.)	16.95
CCP-1006-2	Chrome rims (2 prs.)	26.95
CCP-1007	Rod ends (16 pcs.)	5.95
CCP-1008	Clodbuster hubs (4)	5.95
CCP-1009	Chassis	25.95
CCP-1010	Axle housings (4 pcs.)	13.95
CCP-1011	Steering knuckles (4 pcs.)	16.95
CCP-1012	Battery covers	9.95
CCP-1013	Upper radio plate & chassis plate	12.95
CCP-1014	Body mount braces & servo mounts & horns	7.95
CCP-1015	**Complete Chrome Clodbuster Package**	216.95

Custom Chrome Parts for Midnight Pumpkin/Lunch Box

CCP-2500	Chassis	$18.95
CCP-2501	Lower chassis	15.95
CCP-2502	Gear cases	14.95
CCP-2503	Lower arms & rear trailing arms	11.95
CCP-2504	Shock ends	3.00
CCP-2505	Rear hubs	4.95
CCP-2506	Servo mounts & horns	5.95
CCP-2508	Bumper	6.95
CCP-2509	Front wheels (2)	10.95
CCP-2510	Rear wheels (2)	10.95
CCP-2511	Front & rear wheels (4 pcs.)	18.95
CCP-2512	**Complete Chrome Midnight Pumpkin/Lunch Box Package**	$101.60

Custom Chrome Parts for Blackfoot

CCP-2600	Chassis set	$24.95
CCP-2601	Front suspension (8 pcs.)	14.95
CCP-2602	Gear case, motor cover, spacers, rear trailing arms	15.95
CCP-2603	Front & rear shock mounts & top servo cover	13.95
CCP-2604	Body mounts (front & rear)	10.95
CCP-2605	Rear hubs	4.95
CCP-2606	Front & rear shocks	10.95
CCP-2607	Fog lights & roll bar	10.95
CCP-2608	Bumper (front guard)	6.95
CCP-2609	Steering uprights	5.95
CCP-2610	Servo horns	4.95
CCP-2611	**Complete Chrome Blackfoot Package**	$125.45

Custom Chrome Parts for Monster Beetle

CCP-2614	Fog lights & light bar	$10.95
CCP-2615	Gear case guard & antenna mount	9.95
CCP-2616	Front & rear body mounts	10.95

Custom Chrome Parts for Mudblaster

CCP-2617	Roll bar	$9.95
CCP-2618	Front brush guard	6.95
CCP-2619	Body mount set	10.95

Wheel Adapters to Mount Stock Clodbuster Tires & Wheels to these Trucks

CCP-5000	Big Brute, Big Boss, Double Dare & High Rider Corvette	$49.95
CCP-6000	Blackfoot, Mudblaster, Monster Beetle, Lunch Box & Midnight Pumpkin	59.95
CCP-6001	Adapter for **CCP-6000**. For use with Thorpe Blackfoot hubs/axles	15.95

...with Custom Chrome

from Custom Chrome Parts

CCP-10110   CCP-10111

New unbreakable gear case braces and steering mechanism assemblies for Clodbuster. They'll never need replacement again.

Real chrome. Real shine. Real pride. That's what the competition will see whenever you run your custom chromed machine. The winner's circle is nice. But, when you run the race in style, you'll always be the center of attention.

Custom Chrome Parts has been making it happen worldwide. Because Custom Chrome Parts is the only place on earth where you can get the real thing. We take genuine MRC parts and put them through a true two-step chroming process. We've got real chrome parts for Clodbuster, Midnight Pumpkin or Lunch Box, Blackfoot, Monster Beetle, Mudblaster and now King Cab.

And now we're introducing new unbreakable aluminum gear case braces and steering mechanism assemblies for Clodbuster, and Clod wheel adapters to monsterize your Blackfoot, and other MRC and Kyosho trucks.

So, be a winner. Get Custom Chrome Parts and outshine the competition.

CUSTOM CHROME PARTS

The *Blackfoot/Beetle/Mud Blaster Gearcase & Trailing Arm* package (No. CCP2602, $15.95 retail) is enhanced with Custom Chrome's 2-step plating process that will add a shine to the rear of the truck.

HOBBY PRODUCTS INT'L INC.

HPI offers *Super Star Wheels* ($5.00 to $9.50/pr. retail) for various 1/10-scale cars. Super Star MT Wheels have a 2.2-in.-dia. and are made for various monster/stadium trucks. The wheels are incorporated with ONE FITS ALL design, so the wheels can be mounted on various models with the adaptors included in the package. The Super Star Wheels are also available in 2.0-in. and 2.2-in.-dia. for regular off-road cars. The Wheels are available in White, Black, Yellow, Pink, Green, Chrome, and Gold.

CUSTOM CHROME PARTS

These *Truck Pull Weights* (No. CCP500, $10.95 retail and CCP501, $12.95 retail) are designed to add realism and weight to R/C monster truck pulling contestants. Model CCP500 contains 4-1/4 lb. weights and Model CCP501 contains 2-1/2 lb. weights.

J.G. MANUFACTURING

All *Complete Monster Truck Conversion Kits* ($83.95 retail) include front and rear nylon direct bolt on rims, front and rear truck body mounts, body post kit, foam body post spacers, front and rear monster truck tires, Lexan truck body, and 3-D instructions. Order Nos.: P/N A-22 for RC-10, P/N A-22CE for RC-10 Championship Edition, P/N 9021 for Ultima, P/N 1522 for Optima Mid, P/N 1811 for Jr-x2, P/N 1611 for Yokomo YZ-10, and P/N 2407 for Kyosho Lazer.

J.G. MANUFACTURING

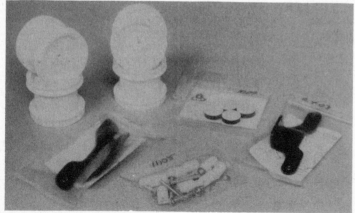

All *Basic Truck Conversion Kits* ($38.95 retail) include front and rear nylon direct bolt on rims, front and rear truck body mounts, body post kit, foam body post spacers, and 3-D instructions. Order Nos.: P/N A-17 for RC-10, P/N A-17CE for RC-10 Championship Edition, P/N 9016 for Ultima, P/N 1518 for Optima Mid, P/N 1809 for Jr-x2, P/N 1610 for Yokomo YZ-10, and P/N 2406 for Kyosho Lazer.

J.G. MANUFACTURING

The *J.G. Nissan King Cab Replacement Body* has awesome detail for precise realism. Body adapts to all trucks and conversions including all J.G. truck conversions, Jr-XT, Kyosho trucks, etc. Body is narrow, only 6-1/2 inches wide, so there is no need for excessive wheel well tire clearance.

J.G. MANUFACTURING

The *RC-10 J.G. Stadium Truck Wide Truck Arms* extend the front and rear width of trucks to maximum legal width of 13", for trucks only. Front and rear arms, used in conjunction with each other, increase the stability of truck over jumps and in cornering. Because of added width, we include longer tie rods in both front and rear arm kits. Rear arms need extended dog bones, which are also included in rear arm kits. Arms are available machined (Nos. P/N A-38 front and P/N A-39 rear) or injection molded (Nos. P/N A-40 front and P/N A-41 rear). Also, rear arms are available with Titanium dog bones (Nos. P/N A-39T rear machined and P/N A-41T rear injection molded). Extended ''long'' dog bones are also sold separately (Nos. P/N A-42 Steel and P/N A-43 Titanium).

J.G. MANUFACTURING

The *J.G. Direct Bolt on Rims* are nylon and ultra light weight for less unsprung weight. Both front and rear rims are ribbed across back of rim for super strength. Available for RC-10 (Nos. P/N 1453 and P/N 1454), Kyosho (Nos. P/N 1455 and P/N 1456), YZ-10 (No. P/N 1457), Jr-x2 (Nos. P/N 1458 and P/N 1459), Tamiya Nissan King Cab (Rear only, No. P/N 1460), and for RC-10 Championship Edition (No. P/N 1461). All rims are available in White dyable Nylon, Fluorescent Neon Orange or Yellow, and Chrome Plated or Simulated Gold Plated.

MAXTRAX

Maxtrax Aluminum Hubs (No. MTXC0100, $19.95/pair, retail) have strong machined aluminum construction. Package of two will fit the front or rear of all Kyosho Monster trucks.

J.G. MANUFACTURING

The *Chevy Long Wheel Base Stadium Truck Body* (No. P/N 4018) is made of clear Lexan. Also available painted (No. P/N 4018P). The Ford Long Wheel Base Stadium Truck Body (No. P/N 4019) is made of clear Lexan. Also available painted (No. P/N 4019P).

MAXTRAX

These *Maxtrax Shock Towers* (No. MTXC0200 & No. MTXC0300, $24.95/set, retail) have a gold anodized finish. They are available for the front and rear of a Monster truck. Optional mounting for shocks will lower truck 1/2 inch.

MAXTRAX

Four different *Maxtrax Truck Hitches* (Nos. MTXC0800, 0801, 0802, & 0803; $24.95 each, retail) are available for most Monster trucks, and are recommended for use in truck pulling competition.

PARMA INTERNATIONAL

Parma now offers the ideal *1/10 Stadium truck body* (No. 10329, Clear, $19.00 retail). It combines great looks and great design for superior performance. Be the first in your area to win with this new body. Rush down to your local hobby shop.

PARMA INTERNATIONAL

The *Parma Bigfoot® 4x4x4®* (No. 10293, Bigfoot body & decal, $25.00 retail; No. 10659, Bigfoot decal only, $5.00 retail) is the original Monster Truck®. This awesome '89 Ford truck body and decal have the style and detail Parma is famous for, recreated in perfect 1/10 scale. It is designed to be a direct replacement for the Clod Buster and fits many other trucks with the use of Parma body mount kits. See it at your local Parma dealer.

PARMA INTERNATIONAL

The *Clodbuster Replacement Body* (No. 10270, $19.00 retail) is molded in clear Lexan and features the ease of painting and impact-resistance of Lexan, while keeping all the detail of the ''kit'' styrene body.

PARMA INTERNATIONAL

This *Midnight Pumpkin Truck Body* (No. 10272, $19.00 retail) is a direct replacement for the Tamiya car. Molded in clear Lexan, it features all the detail of the styrene body, but with the crash resistance and easy painting qualities of Lexan.

PARMA INTERNATIONAL

This *1/12-Scale Dodge Van Body* (No. 10256; Retail: See your dealer) is a direct replacement for the Tamiya Lunch Box and also fits other off-road chassis with the use of No. 10483 Body Mounting Kit.

PARMA INTERNATIONAL

The very popular California Sport Truck Kit from Parma, now has an alter-ego. For all you Ford fans who demand equal rights, Parma offers this ''hot'' *1/10 scale Ford Sport Truck Body* (No. 10337, Clear, $23.50 retail) with ground effects and exclusive decal design. If you're looking for a new look for your sport truck, look no further! Parma has got it all.

PARMA INTERNATIONAL

Parma now has the most realistic 1/10 scale Lexan semi of any kind available. It's a *Kenworth Tractor* (No. 10332, Clear, $23.00 retail) with a double sleeper cab and fifth wheel/chassis area. This truck will fit almost any on-road chassis or monster truck. The detail is second to none and makes a great "rig" to get your race car to the track.

PARMA INTERNATIONAL

You asked for it, and here it is; Parma's *1/10 Ford Puller body* (No. 10336, Clear, $21.00 retail)! With all the clarity and detail you expect from Parma Lexan bodies, this new addition will be welcomed by all of you who have been wanting to drive a Ford lately. The rear end has no wheel well trim lines to give you flexibility in fitting it to your pulling truck.

PARMA INTERNATIONAL

The *1/10 scale '90 Ford Ranger body* (No. 10338, Clear, $19.00 retail) is just what you Ford fans have been waiting for. Sleek and detailed, this crystal clear body captures the realism you expect from all Parma bodies. Ride high using Parma's Ford Ranger truck body and Parma's tall body mounts.

PARMA INTERNATIONAL

Our new *'91 SS454 Chevy Truck body* (No. 10331, Clear, $19.00 retail) is now available with all the graphics decals needed to create the *1/10 scale "Equalizer"* (No. 10341, Clear, $25.00 retail). This is one of the hottest TNT Motorsports trucks in existence. A basic paint job and some decal work is all you need to finish off this "killer" combination.

PARMA INTERNATIONAL

Another blast from the past; the Parma *1/10 scale '56 Outlaw Ford Pickup* (No. 10258, Clear, $19.00 retail) is great for any off-road chassis including monster trucks.

PARMA INTERNATIONAL

The Parma VW *"Whaletale" body* (No. 10340, Clear, $19.00 retail) is a perfect replacement for the Tamiya Monster Beetle, or as a unique facelift for any Off-Road vehicle. Vacuum-formed from .040 Lexan, this 1/10 scale body will not disappoint you with it's detail and realism.

PARMA INTERNATIONAL

Parma International and TNT Motor Sports are proud to introduce Dennis Anderson's *"Grave Digger"* (No. 10310, Clear, $25.00 retail) in a crystal clear 1/10 scale Lexan body that comes with a "7" color decal. The *"Grave Digger"* is the ultimate monster truck body. With the highly detailed decal, the hobbyist can easily create a concours winner. Run, don't walk to your local hobby shop to get your Grave Digger monster truck body.

PARMA INTERNATIONAL

Keep on Truckin'! Now the Ultimate detail for any 1/10 scale R/C truck is available from Parma. This *interior* (No. 10342, Clear, $4.25 retail) is perfect for concours competition. It includes simulate upholstered seats, dash detail and separate steering wheel. It is vacuum-formed in .040 thick clear Lexan. Now you can cruise the streets of our neighborhood in style! The Parma 1/10 interior is a perfect compliment to the popular Hemi Motor and is great for sport trucks, stadium racers, monster trucks, the new Kenworth tractor and others!

TEAM LOSI INC.

Team Losi *"Tru-Pitch"* Precision Gears ($3.50 to $4.00 retail) offer unequaled design, quality, and performance. The 48 and 32 pitch pinions are precision tooled in nickel steel alloy utilizing a unique tooth contour producing unmatched repeatability and less than .002" T.I.R. Each pinion is size marked and AFL coated to further reduce friction. Spurs are color coded for easy identification.

AMERICAN POWER BOAT ASSOCIATION

17640 East Nine Mile Rd. • P.O. Box 377
East Detroit, MI 48021 • 313-773-9700

APBA Office Use:

APPLICATION FOR COMPETITION MEMBERSHIP for year ending Oct 31, 1991 **MODEL BOAT**

If under 18, a Minor Release
must be completed

NAME _____ DATE OF BIRTH _____

ADDRESS _____

CITY _____ STATE _____ ZIP _____

HOME PHONE ( ) _____ BUSINESS PHONE ( ) _____

OCCUPATION _____ SOCIAL SECURITY # _____

DISTRICT NUMBER _____ CLUB AFFILIATION _____

APBA NUMBER _____ APBA BOAT NUMBER _____

DO YOU HAVE OTHER MEDICAL INSURANCE? YES_____ NO_____

TO BE COMPLETED BY APBA	**APBA MODEL BOAT RACING MEMBERSHIP FEES:**
APBA NO. _____	FULL MEMBER FEE. $45.00
BOAT NO. _____	AFTER **1/3/91** (renewals only)...50.00
REGION _____	ADDITIONAL FAMILY MEMBER.................................30.00
	AMOUNT ENCLOSED ....$___.___

**IN ORDER TO BE VALID, THIS APPLICATION FOR APBA MODEL BOAT MEMBERSHIP
MUST BE SIGNED AND WITNESSED ON PAGE 2.**

The Agreement of release, on the reverse side hereof, must be signed before this application can be considered. Furthermore, said applicant and/or owner certifies to the truth of all statements made in this application and agrees to abide by all rules; and to accept as final all decisions of properly authorized race officials.

ROAR MEMBERSHIP FORM

PLEASE TYPE OR PRINT NEATLY

LAST NAME   FIRST NAME   M.I.

ADDRESS

CITY   STATE   ZIP CODE

R.O.A.R. # $ _____ PHONE ( ) _____

      AMOUNT ENCLOSED

☐ 1 8 SCALE ROAD   ☐ 1 8 SCALE OFF ROAD*   ☐ 1 8 SCALE SPRINT CARS*   ☐ DRAG CARS*   ☐ 1 10 SCALE OFF ROAD   ☐ 1 10 SCALE DIRT OVAL*   ☐ 1 12 SCALE ROAD

PLEASE CHECK APPROPRIATE BOXES

☐ NEW MEMBER   ☐ OPEN MEMBER   ☐ BULK RATE POST

☐ RENEWAL   ☐ FAMILY MEMBERSHIP   ☐ FIRST CLASS POSTAGE

SEE OTHER SIDE FOR DETAILS & DUES RATES   (include $ amt in pmt)

*INDICATES CLASS OF CARS RULES CAN BE DEVELOPED FOR IF INTEREST WARRANTS

RECD _____ CASH _____

MAILED _____ CHECK _____

FOR OFFICE USE ONLY

USE SECOND APPLICATION CARD IF MORE THAN 3 ADDITIONAL FAMILY MEMBERS.

R.O.A.R. #   LAST NAME   FIRST NAME   M.I.

R.O.A.R. #   LAST NAME   FIRST NAME   M.I.

R.O.A.R. #   LAST NAME   FIRST NAME   M.I.

TRAXXAS

WINNING EDGE PRODUCTS

WINNING EDGE PRODUCTS

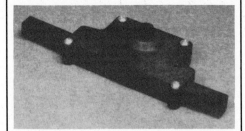

Traxxas' new *Pro-Series Transmission* (Model No. 1920, $90.00 retail) for off-roaders incorporates both a slipper clutch and a fully-adjustable ball differential. The low 2.72 final drive ratio is matched perfectly for use with truck wheels and tires. The 48-pitch gears are molded in a special material for quiet and efficient operation. Standard shaft size accepts all 3/8" i.d. spur gears. Ratios are adjustable from 6:1 to 20.04:1.

Pro-Steer ($49.95) is a rack and pinion steering system designed to give true linear movement with double ball bearing smoothness. It has a Futaba size splined shaft and is currently available for the JR-X2, JR-XT, RC-10, RC-10 Graphite, and a universal model which can be used in trucks as well as other cars.

Turbo Motor Cooler's ($29.95 retail) unique design lets the motor breathe by allowing the air flow created by the spinning armature to be released through the slots allowing cool air to enter. The contact plate draws heat from the motor and dissipates through the heat sink.

Speed Controls—What's Best for You

By Tyree Phillips

It's time to consider purchasing a speed control. You walk into your local hobby shop and you see a plethora of speed controls. There are low frequency speed controls, high frequency speed controls, speed controls with current limiting and torque control, speed controls with five transistors all the way up to 14 or more transistors. How do you decide which speed control to purchase?

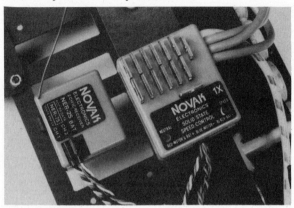

Low or High Frequency

First, let's separate speed controls into two categories; low frequency and high frequency speed controls. Up until 1990 low frequency speed controls were the standard for model vehicle use. These speed controls operate at 60 hertz. This means the speed control pulses current to the motor at a rate of 60 times a second.

Since 1990, many manufacturers have introduced high frequency speed controls. These speed controls operate at about 2500 hertz (depending on the manufacturer), and pulse current to the motor at a rate of 2500 times a second.

High frequency speed controls have two main advantages. The first is they provide a linear control range which makes them much easier to drive. The second advantage is high frequency speed controls are regenerative. This means they actually charge your batteries while you race—increasing your run time. This new technology does come at a price. High frequency speed controls tend to be more expensive than their low frequency counterparts.

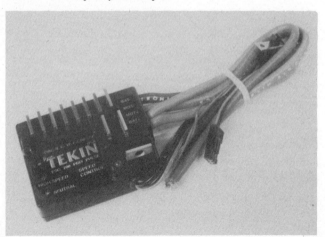

Racer or Recreationist

Now you have a little background on the basic differences between the two categories of speed controls. Let's discuss how to decide which speed control fits your particular needs. First determine how many cells the speed control needs to handle. The next step is tricky! You have to be honest with yourself. Are you going racing or are you a recreational enthusiast? The answer to this question will tell you which direction to go.

For this article, I'll limit the number of cells to the 4- to 10-cell range. If you're going to race, you'll want the most efficient speed control available. You will probably want to look for a high frequency speed control with current limiting and the lowest on-resistance. Novak Electronics' 410-M1c and 410-MXc speed controls are good examples. Both speed controls are high frequency and come with current limiting. Current limiting or torque control is a feature that allows the user to adjust the amount of current passed through the speed control. The M1c is a five-transistor speed control, and has an on-resistance of 0.003Ω. This means if your speed control is passing 10 amps, the voltage loss through the speed control is 0.03 volts. The MXc speed control has 12 drive transistors and has an on-resistance of 0.0015Ω. This means if you're passing 10 amps through an MXc speed control the voltage loss is 0.015 volts. Your pocketbook will decide which speed control to purchase.

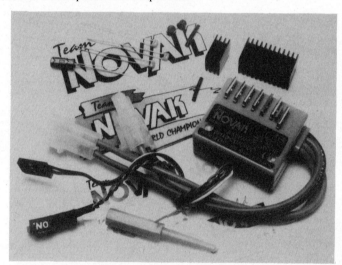

If you're a recreational enthusiast, you do not need to spend extra money on things like current limiting. For your needs, a reliable low frequency speed control would be sufficient, such as the Duratrax DTX-4. If you are into new and state-of-the-art products, there are speed controls that will give you all the advantages of high frequency without the extra cost of the current limiter. An example of this type of speed control is the 410-M5 by Novak Electronics. It features high-frequency operation and the same on-resistance as the M1c without current limiting, at two-thirds the cost.

Hopefully, you're a little less confused about speed controls. The pages in this *Guide* will show you what is available. Follow the information above and you should have no trouble deciding which speed control is best for your application.

Editor's Comment: Our thanks to Tyree Phillips of Novak Electronics for preparing this article.

Electrical Accessories

Failsafe Devices

MRC-TAMIYA

The *MRC-Tamiya Digital Multimeter* with case is one of the handiest tools around. This pocket size instrument measures up to 250 volts AC, 250 volts DC, and 20 meg-ohms of resistance. The built-in buzzer checks for continuity; use it also to check the condition of voltage-dropping diodes.

Safety is no accident!

VICTOR ENGINEERING

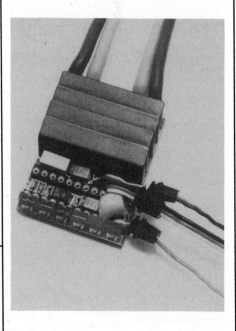

The *Computerized Deglitching/Fail-Safe Micro-Module* ($29.95 retail) for any channel works with any R/C system. Install in line with any servo or speed control. Custom computer chip. Negligible weight, size. Computer chip replaces faulty throttle signal by most probable substitution. Selectable fail-safe channel setting in case of loss of radio signal.

The *Computerized In-Race Remaining Battery Time* ($169.00 retail) is displayed in the windshield and works with any radio. Custom computer chip. Negligible weight, easy to install, and is used in electric-powered crafts.

Electrical Accessories
Speed Controllers

ARISTO CRAFT/POLK'S MODEL CRAFT HOBBIES INC.

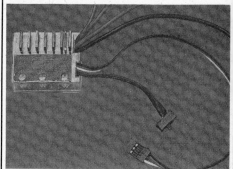

New also is a line of micro sized *"Equalizer" Speed Controls* that are as bullet proof as any on the market. They take second place to no one in quality, capacity, and endurance, yet are competitively priced. All of the speed controls are relayless, state-of-the-art, high frequency types, and are miniature in size.

ARISTO CRAFT/POLK'S MODEL CRAFT HOBBIES INC.

Speed Control Reverse Module adds reverse capability to your existing forward/brake only competition speed control. Complete with plugs to plug right in to an ARISTO-CRAFT or other speed control, easy to put in and take out. Great fun for sport drivers. Allows stunt driving. Handles 6-7 cells, stock motors, and modified motors down to 16 turns. Handles much more power than most reverse type speed controls. Small size and lightweight. Wide operating voltage.

DURATRAX

The *DTX-4 Electronic Speed Control* (Nos: DTXM1000, DTXM1005, DTXM1010, DTXM1015, $99.95 retail) utilizes tempfet technology to protect your investment by shutting down before damage occurs. It is fully proportional and designed for years of service. It is available with your choice of Connector, Futaba, Airtronics, Kyosho, or JR. The unit weighs 1.75 oz. and it is made in the USA.

FUTABA

MC112B (MC12B) MOS/FET Electronic Speed Control ($79.95 retail) has braking and one-speed reverse, and includes LED check circuits. Capacity: 7.2V-8.4V/100A, (400 amp surge).

FUTABA

MC 111B (MC-11B) MOS/FET Electronic Speed Control ($109.95 retail) has variable braking with reverse, LED check circuits, and motor connectors. Capacity: 7.2V-8.4V/130A, (500A surge). 1.81" x 1.59" x 0.78"/2.16 oz.

FUTABA

The *MC116 Competition Electronic Speed Control* (Retail: See your retailer) is designed for the serious R/C car racer. Six high power MOSFETs are used in the MC116 for low voltage drop and high efficiency necessary for competition. Using the built-in power curve adjuster, the MC116 can be tuned to suit individual driving styles or tracks. Its compact size and light weight make the MC116 perfect for on- or off-road racing, and power handling capabilities let you run 6 or 7 cell NiCad power supplies.

FUTABA

The *MC110T (MC10T) Electronic Speed Control* ($129.95 retail) features proportional forward and brake. Size: 1.27" x 1.46" x .55"; weight: .9 oz.; 6-9.6 volts 75 amp continuous with 300 amp surge (also available with "J" connector MC10T).

FUTABA

The *MC9T (MC109T) Competition Electronic Speed Control* ($159.95 retail) has proportional forward and brake and check circuits. Size is 1.17" x 1.59" x .61"; weight is 1 oz.; 6-9.6 volt 150 amp continuous with 450 amp surge (also available with "J" connector MC109T).

FUTABA

The *MCR-4A* ($159.95 retail) is a 4-channel integrated MOS/FET electronic throttle. 1.24" x 2.92" x 1.12"; 1.5 oz./72 MHz only. Capacity: 100A (continuous); 450A (surge). Motor: 280 to 540 size.

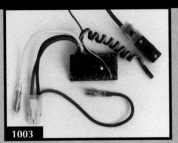
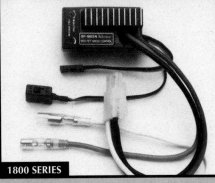
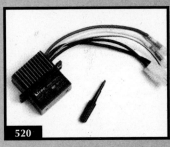
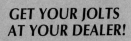
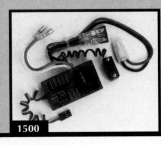

HITEC R/C USA, INC.

The *SP-1801* (No. HSP0050) speed control is ideally suited for small electric aircraft where size is a factor. Lightweight and compact, the 1801 will operate with 5-7 cell battery packs. Equipped with B.E.C. and auto cut-off, this speed control is the choice of sport fliers.

HITEC R/C USA, INC.

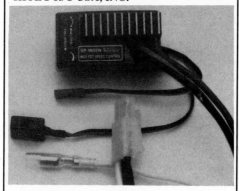

The *1802N* (No. HSP0065) and the 1802DL (No. HSP0070) speed controls are forward-only designed with the racer in mind. The 1802N was developed for the stock classes while the 1802DL can handle the massive power of the modifieds. Both are compact and lightweight.

HITEC R/C USA, INC.

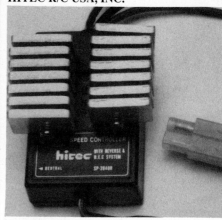

Great for cars and trucks as well as boats, the *SP-2040R* (No. HSP0030) forward and reverse speed control features fully proportional reverse, B.E.C., and will work with 5 to 7 cell battery packs.

HITEC R/C USA, INC.

The hitec *SP-1500* (No. HSP0040) is a heavy-duty forward and reverse speed control with brake. Great for monster trucks and boats, it handles 5 to 7 cell batteries with a maximum current rating of 400 amps.

HITEC R/C USA, INC.

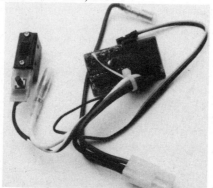

The hitec *SP-1003* (No. HSP0130) electronic on/off control unit is very popular with the electric sail plane pilots. Designed to work with 3 or 4 channel systems, it features a brake for folding propellers, and auto cut off. B.E.C. working voltage is 6 to 12 volts (5 to 10 cell packs).

HOLESHOT RACING PRODUCTS

Holeshot Racing Products now offers a more efficient heatsink for electronic speed controls. *Electronic Speed Control Heatsink* (No. 2020, $15.95 retail) was designed to allow better cooling without adding weight. It fits Novak 410MXC, 828HV, T-1X, and all other double row Mosfet speed controls. Three heatsinks are included—one large and two small. It's made of black anodized aluminum.

NOVAK ELECTRONICS, INC.

The *M1c* is a true digital, high-frequency speed control designed to give the racer the absolute advantage on the race track. The M1c features ruggedized MEGAFET transistors for a low 0.0030Ω ON-resistance, regenerative battery recharging for longer run times, increased motor commutator life, linear acceleration for ultra-smooth driving, an adjustable current limiter for maximum efficiency and performance, and Novak's exclusive user-repairable Solder Pop Fuse™ for protection against reverse voltage. Additional features include thermal shutdown protection, continuous current rating of 250 amps, 50 amps of braking power, 4 to 10 cell operation, compatibility with FET servos, and a dual color LED. The Novak Input Plug System™ makes the ESC compatible with Airtronics, Futaba J, KO, Kyosho, or JR systems. Includes heat sinks, pot adjustment screwdriver, mounting tape, Deans power plugs, motor capacitors, pot hole plugs, decal sheet, instruction manual, and a 90-day warranty. Made in the U.S.A. Size: 1.58" x 1.40" x 0.62". Weight: 1.84 oz.

Safety is Contagious...

NOVAK ELECTRONICS, INC.

The *MXc* incorporates the same features of the Novak 410-M1c, but has 12 MEGAFET transistors to allow for an incredible on-resistance of 0.0015 ohms—making it the most efficient speed control available in its class. Chosen by top oval and off-road pros, the MXc features regenerative battery charging for longer run times, linear acceleration for smooth driving, longer motor commutator life, adjustable current limiting, and a continuous current rating of 500 amps. Additional features include Novak's Solder Pop Fuse™ for protection against reverse voltage, thermal shutdown protection, 50 amps braking power, and a dual color LED. The MXc includes the Novak Input Plug System™, heat sinks, pot adjustment screwdriver, mounting tape, Deans power plugs, motor capacitors, pot hole plugs, a decal sheet, instruction manual, and a 90-day warranty. Made in U.S.A. Size: 1.58" x 1.78" x 0.62". Weight: 2.45 oz.

NOVAK ELECTRONICS, INC.

The *828-HV Hi-Voltage Megafet ESC* (No. 1520; $199.00 retail) was specially designed for high-voltage and high-current applications from 8 to 28 cells. The 828-HV incorporates Novak's latest high-frequency technology for more efficient recharging of batteries during partial throttle and braking, 0.0018 ohms ON-Resistance, dual color LED for easy adjustment of the neutral and high speed pots, input signal noise filter, linear throttle response, and a dirt- and moisture-resistant case. The 828-HV has a rated transistor current of up to 500 amps, with 50 amps of braking current. Includes motor and battery connectors, heat sinks, pot-adjusting screwdriver, pot hole plugs, motor capacitors, decal sheet, complete instructions, trouble-shooting guide, and a 90-day warranty. Also includes the Novak Input Plug System™ which allows the input harness to be compatible with the Airtronics, Futaba J, KO, Kyosho, or JR system. It weighs (w/plugs) 2.51 oz., and is 1.80" x 1.62" x 0.62".

NOVAK ELECTRONICS, INC.

Designed specifically for use with electronic speed controls, the *NER-2X* is compact and light (weighs in at only half an ounce!). The 2X operates at a low input voltage to prevent annoying glitches during heavy acceleration and to minimize adjacent channel interference. Features a user-friendly 18-inch antenna and has a long receiving range. This receiver is designed for surface models only and is available in both 27 and 75 MHz frequency bands with Airtronics, Futaba G, Futaba J, or KO plugs. Made in the U.S.A. Size: 1.10" x 1.28" x 0.53".

NOVAK ELECTRONICS, INC.

The *610-RV Hi-Frequency Megafet ESC with Reverse* (No. 1820, $165.00 retail) is a high-

frequency speed control that is proportional in both the forward and reverse directions. It features Team Novak's latest high-frequency technology, adjustable time delay (0 to 4 sec.), 0.0090 ohms ON-Resistance, operation from 6 to 10 cells, 100 amps of proportional braking, and a rated transistor current of up to 200 amps in the forward direction and 100 amps in the reverse direction. It includes motor and battery connectors, heat sinks, pot-adjusting screwdriver, pot hole plugs, motor capacitors, decal sheet, instruction book, trouble-shooting guide, and a 90-day warranty. Also includes the Novak Input Plug System™ which allows the input harness to be compatible with the Airtronics, Futaba J, KO, Kyosho, or JR system. It weighs (w/plugs) 2.21 oz. and is 1.58" x 1.78" x 0.62".

SCHUMACHER

TRACO TRAction COntrol Electronic Speed Control (No. G-913). The TRACO is our best Electronic Speed Control (E.S.C.) with many innovative features. All transmitter settings are easily programmed using a simple push button. The settings are permanently stored in memory. Also there is high frequency FET switching, ABS anti-lock brakes, and LED indicator for neutral, full power, and interface. In addition to the above, the TRACO offers a Traction Control system of programmable rates of acceleration and breaking providing the ultimate performance in power control.

TEKIN ELECTRONICS

The *Tekin TSC 410S Speed Control* is suitable for stock and modified racing and is the lowest-price speed controller available with torque control. This speed control contains all the desirable features found in the more expensive ESCs and comes with a fuse protection device.

TEKIN ELECTRONICS

The *Tekin TSC 411P Speed Control* is a perfect example of what can be accomplished with miniature electronics. The heart of the TSC 411P is a 28-pin, custom, surface-mount large-scale integrated chip. The controller makes extensive use of surface-mount components and the high tech construction provides all the performance demanded by today's serious R/C car racer. Coming soon National Champion "GOLDFET" version.

TEKIN ELECTRONICS

The *Tekin TSC 408S Speed Control* is the latest in state-of-the-art digital high-frequency speed controls and features high performance Mosfets that are rated to 250 amps and come with 15 gauge wire for more power and longer life. Special digital anti-glitch circuit stops glitches. The TSC 408S has a simple, easy plug-in installation with only two adjustments. Smooth proportional throttle control from slow-crawl to wide open with powerful adjustable built-in brakes. All at an economical price.

TEKIN ELECTRONICS

The *Tekin TSC 420F Speed Control* is Tekin's newest controller and is a direct replacement for the Tekin ESC 700. This makes it Tekin's top-of-the-line controller and features high frequency switching that results in a very smooth throttle response and allows motor commutators to last two to five times longer and also increases the length of motor runs.

TRAXXAS

The *XL-1 Electronic Speed Control* (Model No. 3006, $75.00 retail) is simply the best FWD/REV speed control available, featuring high current capability and digital proportional control in both directions. Heavy-duty design and extra large heat sinks make the XL-1 great for the big-wheeled monster trucks that are notorious for cooking ordinary speed controls. The neutral and proportional controls are easy to adjust with the built in L.E.D. Current handling is 150 amps peak and 75 amps nominal.

TRAXXAS

The *XL-3 Electronic Speed Control* (Model No. 3009) achieves an incredible 99.6% current efficiency with fewer transistors and less weight. The XL-3 weighs only 2.1 ounces with full length wires and heat sink —a full ounce less than some comparably fitted competitors in the same class. The XL-3 has no time delay or current squelching devices so it can instantly supply full power on demand. Peak current handling capacity is 1788 amps and both the forward and brake output sections are thermally protected against overload. No other speed control can give you more efficiency and current handling with less weight.

TRAXXAS

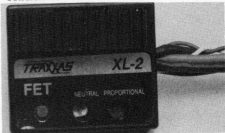

The *XL-2 Electronic Speed Control* (Model No. 3008, $85.00 retail) FWD/BRAKE E.S.C. is the best racing value on the market, combining efficient MOS-FET technology with incredible low price. Performance features include current handling rated at 300 amps peak, 4-8 cell operation, and proportional braking. The built-in L.E.D. allows easy adjustment of the neutral and proportional controls. The black anodized aluminum heat sink is included.

VANTEC

This *Dual Forward/Reverse Speed Control* (No. DFRM-2 through 26 EB, $199.95 retail) has a series of dual controllers with built-in steering mixing for tanks, twin screw boats, and robots or any vehicle powered by a right motor and a left motor. Call (805) 929-5055 for details.

VANTEC

This *Speed Controller* (No. HW-55, $109.95 retail) features proportional forward and proportional reverse. It replaces throttle servo and rheostat. With 416 amps MOSFET ratings for '05 motors, this 1.80 x 1.87 x .82-in. unit is optically isolated with Hi-Rate PWM for smooth low speed.

VICTOR ENGINEERING

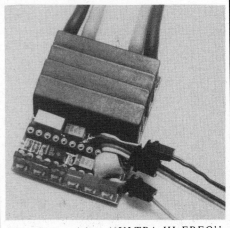

The *Competition "ULTRA-HI-FREQ"* computerized ESC is much more than any other ESC.
• Lowest on-resistance
• Victor custom computer chip
• ULTRA-HI-FREQUENCY, adjustable (!) from 2000-62000Hz (!)
• Computerized "fuel economy" plus torque control
• Calculated overload protection
• Track data recording
• Longest run times due to Victor exclusive "ULTRA-HI-FREQ FLY-BACK" battery recharging
• Computerized deglitching
• Reverse battery protection with no fuse (!)
• Auto-adjusting neutral plus HI points
• 7 adjustments from one solid state key or from TX- no pots
• 6 LEDs
• 2.5A, 5.7V regulator with auto-switch to external RX pack
• Fail-safe
• Power-down memory
• Ultra-compact
• Surface mount, multi-layer PCB
• HI-TEK plus HI-Q yet affordable
• Optional "SMART" reverse/brake module

VANTEC

This *Speed Control* (No. RET-44, $79.95 retail) has fully-proportional reverse and forward for boats, tanks, and robots. Replaces the throttle servo and cumbersome rheostats. Optically isolated MOSFET design features Hi-Rate PWM for smoother control of motors up to 12 amps, 14 volts and measures 1.80 x 1.87 x .82-in. It works with Futaba AM, FM, or PCM, Airtronics, Cirrus, ACOMS, Challenger, MRC, and most others. Higher power models are available to 70 continuous duty amps.

VANTEC

This *Speed Controller* (No. FB-55, $99.95 retail) has proportional forward and brake for competition. Replaces throttle servo and rheostat. It has 416 amps and .004 ohm conduction control for hot wind motors. The 1.80 x 1.87 x .82-in. unit features Hi-Rate PWM for precise control and calibrated braking. No relays, extra modules, heat sinks or awkward rate adjustments are needed. Optically isolated from your radio, it plugs into your receiver like a servo but draws no receiver power. It works with Futaba AM, FM, or PCM, Airtronics, Cirrus, ACOMS, Challenger, MRC, and most others.

Engine Accessories

Engine Mounts Aircraft

DAVE BROWN PRODUCTS

These *Glass-Filled Motor Mounts* ($1.95 - $5.50 retail) are lightweight and strong and available in 13 sizes to fit engines size .049 to 1.20. Now in 4 stroke sizes.

EDSON ENTERPRISES, INC.

This nylon *Thrust Ring* (No. TR-56, $2.50 retail) is mounted between the motor mount and firewall or between the motor mount and nose gear. It allows you to position your motor in the desired direction of thrust.

EDSON ENTERPRISES, INC.

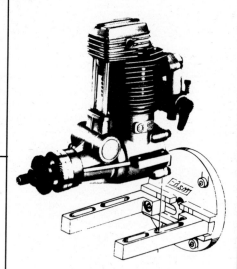

This *Adjustable Motor Mount 4-Cycle* (No. M-50-LP, $9.95 retail) fits Saito .40, .45; OS Max .20, .40, .61; Enya .46, .60; HP .20, .49; and others .20-.65.

EDSON ENTERPRISES, INC.

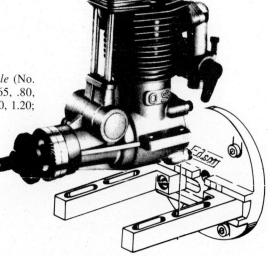

This *Adjustable Motor Mount 4-Cycle* (No. M-60-FC, $16.95 retail) fits Saito .65, .80, 1.20; OS Max .90, 1.20; Enya .80, .90, 1.20; Weber .80; and others .80, 1.20.

EDSON ENTERPRISES, INC.

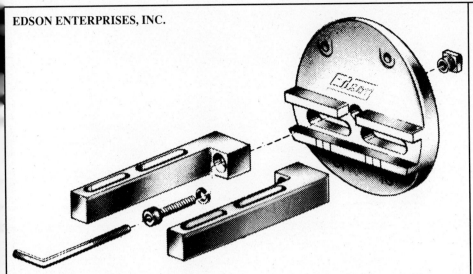

Motor Mount Assembly ($9.95 retail) is available for (No. M50-S) .15 to .35; (No. M50-L) .40 to .80; and (No. M50-Kit) .15 and .80.

EDSON ENTERPRISES, INC.

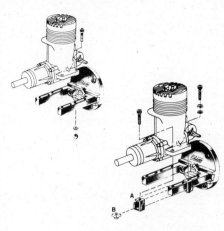

The *Socket Head/Hardened Bolt Set Spring Locknut Retainer* is now available (Retail: $1.19 HD-5/HD-6, $2.95 M51-5/M51-6).

HAYES PRODUCTS

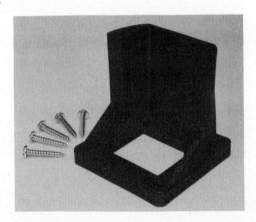

These *Glass-Filled Engine Mounts* (Retail: See your dealer) have a unique bottom support design that provides aluminum strength at half the weight. They're pre-drilled to accept nose gear mounting. They're available in 12 short and nine long sizes to fit all popular engines from .09 to .91.

J'TEC

Add-on *Engine Accessories* ($20.00 - $29.95 retail) for Max .91-1.08, Como-ST .61-.75-.90, anbd SuperTigre 2500-3000 engines include engine mount, five various incowl mufflers, and a Pitts-style muffler.

J'TEC

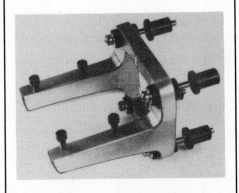

''Snuf-Vibe'' *Isolated Engine Mounts* ($14.95 to $27.95 retail) for any of our regular line of engine mounts. Just add 'SV' to existing catalog numbers plus $5.95 each.

SIG MANUFACTURING CO.

These *Aluminum Engine Mounts* (No. SH-477, Small, for .09-.25 engines, $2.10/pair retail; No. SH-478, Medium, for .19-.60 engines, $2.99/pair retail; No. SH-626, Large, for .60-.91 engines, $3.65/pair retail) are rugged, low-vibration mounts extruded from tough aluminum alloys.

C.B. TATONE, INC.

Giant Scale G-38/62 and Quadra 30/40/50/ 80 (No. 5330; Retail: See your dealer) come in 1/3 - 1/4 scale and have the same mounting pattern as TML MT. Deep enough to enclose spring starter.

C.B. TATONE, INC.

Four-Cycle Aluminum Engine Mounts ($8.00 - $19.95 retail) are made of cast aluminum. They're precision machined and bright polished. Hardened steel socket cap screws are included. The mounts are drilled and tapped for Enya 4-C- 35, 40, 46, 60, 80, 90, 120, R120, HP VT 21, 49, OS FS 20, 40, 61, 60, 90, 120, Max 1.08, Saito FA 30, 40, 45, 50, 65, 80, 120, Supertigre 2000 series, and Webra TR-40, 80.

Engine Accessories

A/C Soft Mounts

G&A PRODUCTS

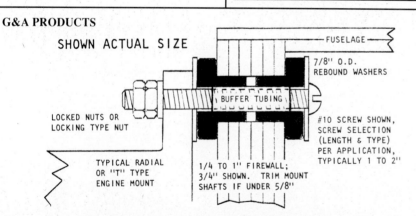

SHOWN ACTUAL SIZE

FUSELAGE

7/8" O.D. REBOUND WASHERS

BUFFER TUBING

LOCKED NUTS OR LOCKING TYPE NUT

#10 SCREW SHOWN, SCREW SELECTION (LENGTH & TYPE) PER APPLICATION, TYPICALLY 1 TO 2"

TYPICAL RADIAL OR "T" TYPE ENGINE MOUNT

1/4 TO 1" FIREWALL; 3/4" SHOWN. TRIM MOUNT SHAFTS IF UNDER 5/8"

PATENT PENDING

G&A Products manufactures the *Vend Mount* (Standard Kit $12.00 mail order) system of soft engine mounts. Called the 'Vibration Killer,' the system offers the user a guaranteed vibration reduction of at least 70%. Plus no pull, shear, or tear modes; fuel proof rubber and fail-safe design. The standard four point kit covers engines to 1.20, firewalls from 1/4 to 1 in. thick and fits all engine mounts (radial, 'T' type, etc.). Kit includes 8 mounts to isolate 4 points, your choice of washers and buffer tubing for #6, #8, or #10 screws (SPECIFY), and instructions. Special 6 and 8 point kits are available for large engines (Quadras, etc.), (INQUIRE).

Engine Accessories

—————— Engine Mounts Boat

OCTURA MODELS, INC.

This *4-50 Motor Mount* (Retail: See your dealer) is extruded from high-strength aluminum and anodized gold. It's interchangeable with the 4-40 mount and is of heavier construction. It's for use with Octura's Wing Ding 40.

OCTURA MODELS, INC.

OCTURA MODELS, INC.

This *5-55 Motor Mount* (Retail: See your dealer) is extruded from high-strength aluminum and anodized gold. It's designed to mount .40 (6.5cc) through .60 (10cc) engines in Deep-V hulls. Machined end pads fit between engine bearers space 5-in. apart on the crankshaft centerline. Engine mounting pads are machined but undrilled and untapped. Four 6-32 socket-head bolts are included.

OCTURA MODELS, INC.

This *.60 Multi Motor Mount* is for use with engines from .40 (6.5cc) to .60 (10cc). End pads are machined to fit engine bearers spaced 5 in. apart. End pad holes are 1-11/16 in. apart and 11/16 in. below engine mounting pads. Engine mounting pads are machined but undrilled and untapped. Four 6-32 socket-head bolts are included.

This *3-30 Motor Mount* (Retail: See your dealer) is designed for engines up to .21 (3.5cc). It's extruded from high-strength aluminum and anodized gold. End pads are machined to fit 3-in. engine bearer spacing. End pad holes are 1/4-in. apart on crankshaft centerline. Engine mounting pads are machined but undrilled and untapped. Four 4-40 socket head bolts are included for engine mounting.

OCTURA MODELS, INC.

The *4-40 Motor Mount* (Retail: See your dealer) is extruded from high-strength aluminum and anodized gold. It's designed for use with engines up to .40 (6.5cc). The end pads are machined to fit 4-in. bearer spacing. The end pad holes are 1-11/16-in. apart on the crankshaft centerline. The engine mounting pads are machined but undrilled and untapped. Four 6-32 socket-head bolts are included.

OCTURA MODELS, INC.

This *Swift Switch Motor Mount* (Retail: See your dealer) is 5 in. wide and interchanges with Octura's 5-50 and 5-60 Motor Mounts. It's designed to facilitate the quick change from a .60 to a .40 engine and vice versa. It does not require removing the entire mount from the hull (just the insert on which the engine itself is mounted). It's ideally suited for Deep-V hulls. Its one-piece base and insert are made of extruded aluminum. Engines are not included.

OCTURA MODELS, INC.

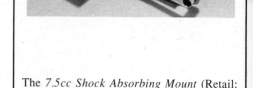

The *7.5cc Shock Absorbing Mount* (Retail: See your dealer) is for fiberglass Deep Vees and Tunnels. Interchangeable with the Swift Switch Mount. The .90 mount is 5 in. wide.

OCTURA MODELS, INC.

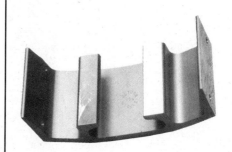

This *5-60 Motor Mount* (Retail: See your dealer) is interchangeable with the 5-55 and it's of heavier construction. It's extruded from high-strength aluminum and anodized gold. It's for use with Octura's Wing Ding 60 outrigger.

OCTURA MODELS, INC.

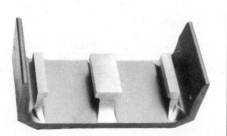

The *Twin .40* and *Twin .60 Motor Mounts* (Retail: See your dealer) have been designed by Octura. The Twin .40 is 5 in. wide and interchanges with Octura's 5-55 and 5-60. The Twin .60 is machined to take either two K&B 6.5s, two OPS 40s, two OPS 40Ss on 2-1/16-in. centers, two K&B 3.5s, or two OPS 3.5s. They're both extruded from high-strength aluminum and anodized in either black or gold.

OCTURA MODELS, INC.

This *Twin .20 Motor Mount* (Retail: See your dealer) is for mounting two 3.5 engines, side by side, in a 4-in. wide mount. It's interchageable with 4-40 and 4-50 mounts and permits installation in a Wing Ding 40. K&B's 3.5 aircraft engine is well suited for twin installation but the horizontal carb of the marine version might cause problems. Twin .20 engines can also be mounted on the Twin .40 Motor Mount which is 5 in. wide.

OCTURA MODELS, INC.

This *Omni Motor Mount* (Retail: See your dealer) is similar to Octura's Multi-Mount but doesn't have the end flanges. It's extruded from high-strength aluminum and anodized gold.

Engine Accessories
Glow Plug Igniters & Chargers

ALTECH MARKETING

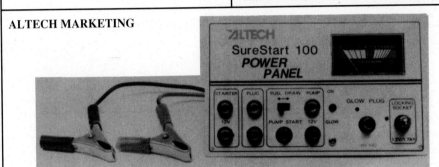

Altech Marketing, with its experience with Enya engines, has developed a 12-volt starter panel that sets a new standard for convenience, versatility, and utility. It's called the *Surestart 12 Volt Power Panel—Autodriver* (No. HV100); and it is packed with features that make starting model gas engines a "breeze."

The advanced electronics incorporate a 1.5 volt glow plug driver circuit named the Autodriver that matches any 1.5 volt glow plug. The next rewarding feature is our Locking Socket that can recharge your glow plug NiCad starters!

The panel provides 12 volt electric starter power, 12 volt pump power with fuel/drain and on/off switches, a meter that monitors current to the glow plug, a LED lamp to indicate proper contact, and an on/off switch for the glow plug Autodriver and Locking Socket circuit.

DU-BRO PRODUCTS

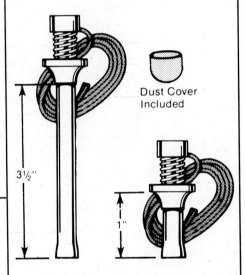

Dust Cover Included

3½"

1"

The *Kwik-Klip II "One Bite on Tite"* (No. 337, 1/pkg, $6.50 retail; No. 338, Extra Long, 1/pkg, $8.50 retail) is a locking glo-plug connector for standard and 4-cycle plugs. * Spring loaded...fits any size glo-plug with more contact area. * Large finger flange for easy non-slip grip. * Press to clip on—Press to release. * 30" wire leads. * Won't loosen, rotate, or fall off under heavy engine vibrations.

DU-BRO PRODUCTS

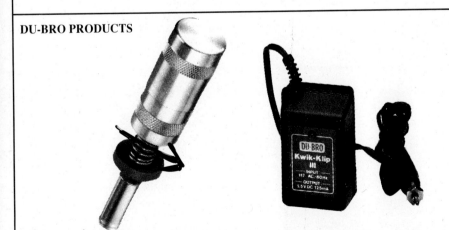

The *Kwik Klip III* ($12.95-$26.95 retail) uses a replaceable NiCad battery and fits all standard and 4-cycle glow plugs. The spring-loaded socket makes the Kwik Klip easy to use. The aluminum battery housing unscrews like a flashlight to hold a 1.2 volt, 1200mah rechargeable NiCad battery. The LED charger is rated at 125mA output. Order No. 396, Kwik Klip III with charger, $24.95; No. 397, Kwik Klip III without charger, $12.95; No. 398, Kwik Klip III XL with charger, $26.95; No. 399, Kwik Klip III XL without charger, $14.95.

PRICES AND SPECS ARE SUBJECT TO CHANGE

DU-BRO PRODUCTS

The *Glo-Plug Caddy* (No. 498, $2.25 retail) is a must for every modeler's field box. Made of tough fuel resistant rubber, it holds 12-cycle and 4-cycle glo plugs. Helps protect glo plug elements from dirt, moisture, and hard knocks.

DU-BRO PRODUCTS

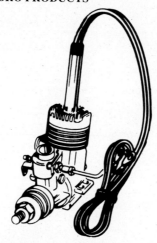

The *Kwik-Glo Glow Plug Connector* (No. 147, $3.50 retail) is for use with .10 and up engines. It's suitable for hard-to-get-at plugs.

ROYAL PRODUCTS CORP.

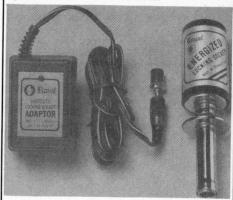

The *Energized Locking Socket* ($25.95 retail) is a feature of this engine starting system that locks onto any glow plug (including 4-cycle plugs) and doesn't let go until it's released. It's rechargeable hundreds of times. The injection-molded case is easily portable.

ROYAL PRODUCTS CORP.

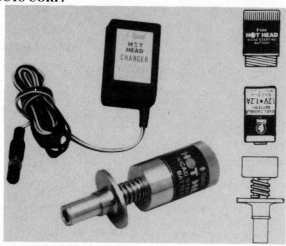

Royal's new *Hot Head NiCad Starting Battery* ($11.95 to $19.95 retail) features locking socket clip that holds until released and screw-apart case that allows battery replacement. It comes with or without charger and/or battery.

ROYAL PRODUCTS CORP.

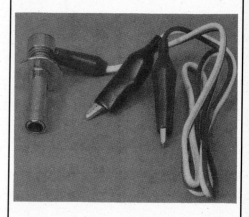

This *Locking Socket* ($6.95 retail) is a unique glow clip that locks on any glow plugs (even 4-cycle) and won't let go until it's released. Simple thumb pressure is all that's needed.

SIG MANUFACTURING CO.

Sig's *Glow Plugs* (No. GP-001, for 4-stroke, $2.95 retail; No. GP-002, for tuned pipe, $2.35 retail; No. GP-003, for R/C Long with idle bar, $2.35 retail) are high-quality platinum, designed for long life and come in three styles.

SKYWARD R&D LABORATORY

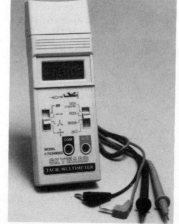

The *Skyward 1620 Tach Multimeter* is a tachometer for 2-, 3-, and 4-bladed props. Measures voltages DC 2V and DC 20V. Resistance to 2K ohms. LCD display.

Your local Hobby Shop is there to help you select the best equipment and to answer your questions.

~

Engine Accessories — Starters

HOBBICO

The *Hot Shots* (No. HCAP2505, $25.95 retail; No. HCAP2510, $39.95 retail) from Hobbico are portable and rechargeable glow-starters. They come in two sizes to fit 2- or 4-cycle glow engines. The Hot Shot is 1.2 volt, 1400 mAh rechargeable NiCad. The Super Hot Shot includes a long reach plug clip and a 4000 mAh NiCad battery, enough for an entire week's worth of starts, or one hour of continuous use. Both come with an overnight charger.

HOBBICO

Hobbico's *Torqmaster 90 and 180* are high powered starters. The Torqmaster 90 is for engine sizes up to .90 cu. in., and the Torqmaster 180 is for engines sizes up to 1.80 cu. in. The starters feature red endbells, molded-in stands to keep the switches clean, and includes a 5-ft. DC input cord that coils out of the way when not in use. It is perfect for airplanes, boats, helicopters, and cars.

HOBBY DYNAMICS DISTRIBUTORS

The new *HD Super Starter* (HDD104, $47.49 retail) is a high-powered starter with a 12V DC motor and will handle up to 120 size engines with no problems. It is perfect for use with 1/4-scale size engines. This is a top-quality starter with great features.

HOBBY DYNAMICS DISTRIBUTORS

The *Deluxe Super Starter 90* (1/4-scale) (No. HDD110, $55.99 retail) has a 12V DC motor that can handle up to 120-size engines and is perfect for use with 1/4-scale engines. Its features include an extra-long, heavy-duty cord; factory-installed battery clips; all-metal case; built-in rest stand; and non-mar rubber drive cone.

KDI

The *Power Handle and Cord* ($24.95 retail) is the perfect match for a gel cell battery and Sullivan-type starter motor. It's contoured non-slip handle and 6 foot cord offer the ultimate in runway restarts. Molded into the handle is a holster for the NiCad glow plug battery. Perfect portable starting system for experienced and new modelers.

MILLER R/C PRODUCTS

Big Grip (No. BG701, $29.95 retail) is engineered to start those "big" nose cones. The 3-in. cup is black anodized aluminum and comes with a hi-tech material insert to start big motors. Big Grip is machined to fit Sullivan and Royal starters or comes blank for individual applications.

MILLER R/C PRODUCTS

These inserts don't fly out, mar models, and are heat-resistant to fuels and igniters. *Polar Grip* (No. PG101, $6.49 retail) is for 3.5 and 7.5 outboards and ducted fans. *Polar Grip II* (No. PG101-2, $6.49 retail) is designed for the K&B 7.5 outboard that has the cut-down flywheel. *Sky Grip* (No. SG201, $6.49 retail) is for planes with nose cones. *Tuff Grip* (No. TG301, $6.99 retail) is for nut-washer, quads, 1/2-As, and rear start choppers.

MILLER R/C PRODUCTS

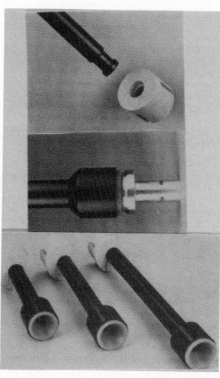

These *Helicopter Starting Extensions* (No. EX75 for 7-1/2 in., EX55 for 5-1/2 in. and EX40 for 4 in.; $18.99 - $19.99 retail) are configured with a large head to fit down further for a better grip. They're black anodized aluminum with Miller's rubber insert. They're made to fit Sullivan and Royal Starters. They are rubbed mounted.

ROYAL PRODUCTS CORP.

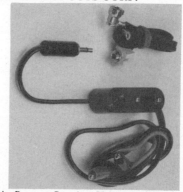

This *Remote Starting Harness* ($6.95 retail) is a handy accessory that's ideal for cowled-in engines. Special adapter stays in place on engine and all you do is plug in anywhere on exterior of fuselage to fire the glow plug. Unit has indicator light to note current flow and on-off switch.

MILLER R/C PRODUCTS

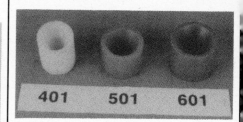

These *Heli-Grips Starting inserts* (No. 401 for Schluter, No. 501 for GMP, and No. 601 for Miller R/C; $4.99 retail) are designed to fit helicopter engine cones. They're constructed of high-tech materials.

MILLER R/C PRODUCTS

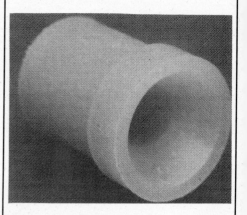

This new *Mini-Grip Starting Insert* (No. MG801, $4.99 retail) is engineered to fit the Astro Mini Starter as a replacement insert. It will NOT mar the nose cones.

ROYAL PRODUCTS CORP.

This *Jumbo Engine Starter* ($64.95 retail) is designed to handle 1/4-scale engines. It has an all-metal case, aluminum drive cone with belt groove, factory-attached battery clips, simple thumb-actuated switch, and is easy to grip/handle.

ROYAL PRODUCTS CORP.

The *Heavy-Duty Starter* ($48.95 retail) has the new power plus design offering the most power in its class size. Start engines easily up to 1.20 cubic inch displacement. It is made of a sturdy all metal case with a coil cord design and tapered silicone drive cone that will not mar your spinner.

Engine Accessories

Mufflers & Pipes

AEROTREND PRODUCTS

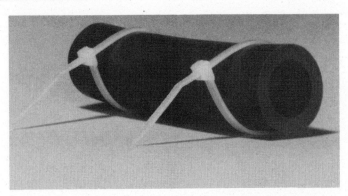

The *Ultra-Blue Tuned Pipe Connection Set-Up* ($2.39 - $3.69 retail) is a top quality tuned pipe coupler at a reasonable price. It features high performance heavy-gauge silicone that's specially formulated for tuned pipe connections. It's highly heat-resistant, strong, and does the job. The set-up includes a 4-in. piece of silicone and two nylon ties which is enough for two connections. Available in three sizes: No. 1033 for 1/2" ID; No. 1034 for 5/8" ID; and No. 1035 for 3/4" ID. Also available by the foot or more.

AEROTREND PRODUCTS

The *Cream Tuned Pipe Coupler* ($2.29 and up retail) has been specially developed for high-nitro (25-60%) applications. Extreme heat from high-nitro/closed canopy installations has no adverse effect on this coupler. Available in 3" or 12" lengths. For 3" lengths order No. 1051 for 1/2" ID, No. 1053 for 5/8" ID, No. 1055 for 3/4" ID, and No. 1057 for 7/8" ID. For 12" lengths order Nos. 1061, 1063, 1065, and 1067. Longer pieces are available.

AEROTREND PRODUCTS

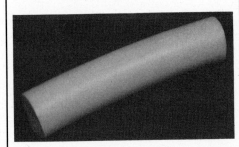

The *Ultra-Blue Tuned Pipe Coupler* ($6.69 - $10.39 retail) is a 12" straight piece of "Ultra-Blue" high performance heavy-gauge silicone. It's specially formulated for tuned pipe connections. Available in three sizes. Order No. 1037 for 1/2" ID, No. 1038 for 5/8" ID, and No. 1039 for 3/4" ID. Longer pieces are available for other applications.

AEROTREND PRODUCTS

These *Coupler Clamps* ($1.69 retail) offer the best method known for a tight hold on tubing, exhaust stacks, and tuned pipe couplers. They're made of nylon which doesn't conduct heat like metal clamps. They're designed to clamp on with ease and hold tight, yet a twist of the finger will release them. Available in 11 sizes. Order No. 1224 for 1/4" OD, No. 1225 for 11/32" OD, No. 1227 for 5/16" OD, No. 1228 for 5/8" OD, No. 1229 for 3/4" OD, No. 1230 for 13/16" OD, No. 1231 for 7/8" OD, No. 1233 for 1" OD, No. 1234 for 1 1/16" OD, No. 1235 for 1 3/16" OD, and No. 1237 for 1 1/4" OD.

AEROTREND PRODUCTS

"Blue Line" Exhaust Stacks ($2.89 - $4.09 retail) are silicone tubing formulated to keep excess residue from reaching your plane, boat, etc. Each pack contains 1 ft. of tubing. Order No. 1023 for 1/4" ID x 7/64" wall; No. 1024 for 3/8" ID x 1/8" wall; No. 1025 for 3/8" ID x 1/8" wall; No. 1026 for 5/8" ID x 1/8" wall; No. 1027 for 3/4" ID x 1/8" wall.

CONDOR R/C SPECIALTIES

Magic Mufflers ($24.95-$52.95 retail) are compact "folded" tuned pipes for extra power and silencing. Total of 22 different types to fit .12 to .90 two-stroke engines in sport and scale aircraft, ducted fans, pylon racers, helicopters, I/B and O/B powerboats, cars and buggies. Free applications chart on request. New 90/180 for larger engines now available.

DU-BRO PRODUCTS

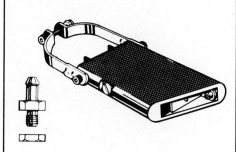

The *Universal Muff-L-Aire II* (No. 235, $11.50 retail) is for engines from .29-.80. A new and improved baffle in the exhaust exit further reduces the noise level of your engine. Back pressure and noise level are factory set but can be altered.

DU-BRO PRODUCTS

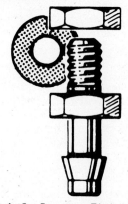

This *Bolt On Pressure Fitting* (No. 241, 1/pkg, $1.15 retail) includes brass pressure fitting, nut and fibre washer. Easily mounted anywhere on muffler by drilling a hole (No. 28 drill) and bolting it, or tap smaller hole for 6-32 threads.

DU-BRO PRODUCTS

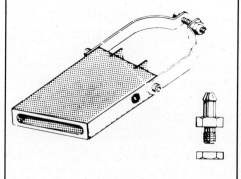

The *Universal Mini-Muff-L-Aire II* (No. 236, 1/pkg, $8.50 retail) is for engines .09-.25. Lightweight aluminum body with tapered end exits exhaust straight away from plane. Perfect for cowled-in engines. Includes pressure fitting.

DU-BRO PRODUCTS

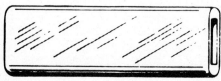

With this *6-in. Aluminum Exhaust Extension* (No. 213, $4.50 retail) you can custom make your own muffler extension. It fits most .29-.80 engines and most mufflers. This stock can be cut, drilled, tapped, and welded

FUTABA

The *YS/Futaba 45 Muffler* (FP-YS0495) ($24.50 retail) is designed specifically for the YS/Futaba 45 side exhaust engines. This new muffler is quieter without sacrificing performance. Precision cast in light alloy, this one-piece design is perfect for the Sport flyer seeking optimum efficiency from the unique YS/Futaba fuel injection system.

J'TEC

These *Giant Size Mufflers* ($29.95 retail) are designed to fit inside cowls with bolt-on mounting for upright, side, or inverted engines (Quadra, Zenoah, Super Tigre, Sachs-Dolmar, etc.).

J'TEC

These *In-Cowl 4-Cycle Mufflers* ($20.00 - $25.00 retail) are designed to fit inside cowls with bolt-on mounting for upright, side, or inverted engines. They're made to easily produce smoke. They're for use with Enya, OS Max, and Saito 4-cycle engines.

KDI

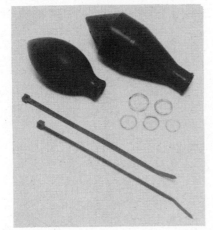

Rubber-After Mufflers (.20-.49 size, $19.95 retail; .50-.90 size, $29.95 retail) are made from a special high-temperature silicone that can withstand both the heat and exhaust residues of 2-stroke engines. 4-10 dB sound reduction is obtained with little if any RPM loss. They are extremely lightweight, .5 and .75 oz. respectively, and are aerodynamic in shape. They are easily installed, inexpensive, and are receiving reviewers' highest praises.

SLIMLINE MANUFACTURING

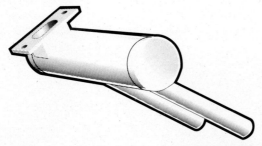

To meet the noise reduction demands of today's modelers, Slimline Mfg. has developed new *Large-Volume, Low-Noise Mufflers*. These mufflers, currently designed for side installations, will closely fit your engine becoming less visible and creating a larger volume for exhaust gases to be channeled through. This, coupled with our special baffling, noticeably decreases exhaust noise level and creates a lower, throatier exhaust note similar to 4-cycle sound.

Another unique feature of the Large-Volume, Low-Noise Muffler is the internal smoke coil (optional). The stainless steel coil is designed in such a way that it preheats the smoke oil, enabling it to quickly atomize and combine with exhaust gases, forming dense trails of cloud-white smoke.

Send for your complete catalog of all Slimline products today!

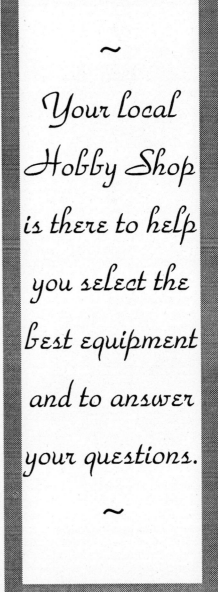

~

Your local Hobby Shop is there to help you select the best equipment and to answer your questions.

~

SLIMLINE MANUFACTURING

Slimline Mfg. has developed new *Giant Scale Mufflers* for Zenoah, Sachs-Dolmer, Super Tiger, Quadra, Webra, O.S. Max, A&M, and others. These mufflers, designed for inverted installations, wrap around the rear of your engine becoming less visible and creating a larger volume for exhaust gases to be channeled through. This, coupled with a special baffling system, noticeably decreases exhaust noise level and produces a smooth, pleasing sound without significant power loss.

Another unique feature of the Giant Scale Muffler is the internal smoke coil (optional). The stainless steel coil is designed in such a way that it preheats the smoke oil, enabling it to quickly atomize and combine with exhaust gases, forming dense trails of cloud-white smoke.

Send for your complete catalog of all Slimline products today!

C.B. TATONE, INC.

These *In Cowl Exhaust Manifolds* (No. 11012 for .09-.19, $12.80 retail; No. 11033 for .29-.40, $13.95 retail; No. 11054 for .45-.80, $15.25 retail) are made in three sizes to fit most engines. They're designed to fit into cramped quarters. Three tail-tubes suit various engine positions. Tailpipe extension and all mounting hardware is included.

C.B. TATONE, INC.

These *Exhaust Manifolds* (Bottom inverted exhaust: No. 11213 for .29-.40, $16.05 retail; and No. 11314 for .45-.80, $17.50 retail. Top upright exhaust: No. 11233 for .29-.40, $16.05 retail; and No. 11334 for .45-.80, $17.50 retail. Side exhaust: No. 11253 for .20-.40, $17.75 retail; and No. 11354 for .45-.80, $18.50 retail) are designed to fit inside most scale model cowlings. Rubber outlet tubes are included to exit the exhaust from the cowl. Three styles are available.

C.B. TATONE, INC.

This *.60 to 1.3 Universal Muffler-Manifold* (No. 13075 for inverted or upright engines, $19.95 retail; No. 13095 for side, inverted, or upright engines, $20.95 retail) is designed to fit inside cowls with limited space. It bolts onto most .60-1.3 side exhaust engines. Neoprene tail pipe extensions are included.

C.B. TATONE, INC.

These *Giant Mufflers* ($23.50 - $25.50 retail) fit most .90-1.5 engines. The narrow contour design fits most cowlings. They're quiet with little or no power loss on most engines. They either attach to the engine with stainless steel screw-style clamps or they bolt directly on with screws. Available in three versions.

C.B. TATONE, INC.

The *Zenoah G-38 Muffler* (No. 12915, $24.95 retail) bolts on and is quiet with little power loss.

C.B. TATONE, INC.

Pitts-Style Scale Mufflers (No. 11413, for .29-.40, $19.25; No. 11434, for .45-.80, $21.35; No. 11455, for. 90-.91, $25.75) are for use with scale aircraft such as Pitts and Cessna 150. They're designed and machined to fit most side-mounted engines and have two angled outlets at the bottom. An adjustable screw, strap clamp, neoprene exhaust tubing, and nylon tubing are supplied.

Field Accessories

Field Boxes

CUSTOM WOODCRAFT

This *Flight Box* ($139.95 retail) is manufactured from selected birch plywood and maple hardwood which have been sanded, stained, and finished with Pactra Formula ''U.'' The box features folding legs, adjustable folding/locking fuselage holders, folding wing holders, and two drawers. Also featured is a take-out power module that holds the starter and battery and has a built-in tool rack. Options include: Sonic-Tronics Power Panel ($48.95 retail, installed, and optional 4-Drawer Unit for left or right side ($14.95 retail).

CARL GOLDBERG MODELS, INC.

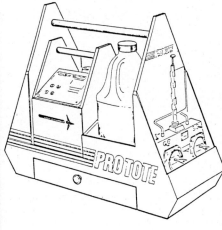

The style line design of the new Carl Goldberg *PRO-TOTE* (No. 100, $49.99 retail) field support box includes many features. Among these uniquely thought-out concepts is the hassle-free removable Satellite Power Module. With the Satellite, the modeler is able to quickly service an ''out of the pits'' aircraft with a new prop, glow plug and field restart, all without taking the whole field box to the model, or retrieving the model back to the pit area. The PRO-TOTE is designed with a narrow range carrying balance. This feature proves valuable when the fuel container gets close to empty or with the Satellite removed, the carrying point stays the same. The self-fixturing of the parts during construction, delivers an accurate and successful result. You won't be spending a lot of your time building a field box when you could be out flying. Let the PRO-TOTE be the last field support system you will ever build!

CARL GOLDBERG MODELS, INC.

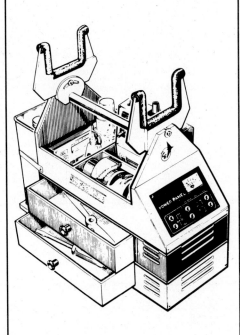

The *Super Tote Field Box* (No. 102-ST-1, $29.99 retail) is a compact field tote engineered to hold your 12V battery, power panel, and sufficient equipment required at field. Fuselage cradles are adjustable for width and slant. Step-by-step photo instruction booklet for easy assembly of precisely-cut wood components is included. It carries easily with its balanced loading and slim profile.

CARL GOLDBERG MODELS, INC.

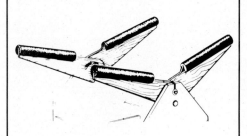

These *90-degree Adjustable Cradles* (No. 103, $6.99 retail) are designed for the Super Tote for use with boats, cars, and planes.

GREAT PLANES MODEL MFG.

The *Great Planes Master Caddy* (No. GPMP1000, $39.95 retail) with Auxiliary Power Station (APS) is crafted from plywood and comes ready to assemble. It can be finished to meet the modeler's desires. The APS will accommodate any power panel. Vents built into the side panels allow cooling air to circulate around the 12-volt battery. Two large drawers are also provided to store needed accessories.

HOBBICO

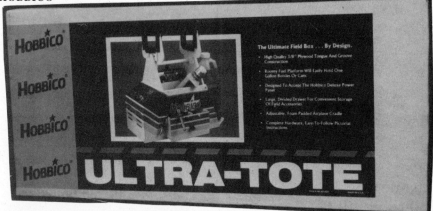

The *Hobbico Ultra Tote* (No. HCAP5020, $34.95 retail) features tongue and groove assembly with 3/8-in. mahogany wood for many years of service. It features a separate 12-volt battery compartment with a removable vented front panel. Also included is a foam-padded cradle that provides a secure and easy hold-down while working on the aircraft. All the upgrades and features desired by modelers can be found on this field box.

HOBBICO

Hobbico's *Tool Brute* (No. HCAR3030, $11.95 retail) is a handy tote molded of durable high-impact plastic. It keeps tools, small parts, and equipment organized and ready for use in the workshop or for taking to the field.

HOBBY DYNAMICS DISTRIBUTORS

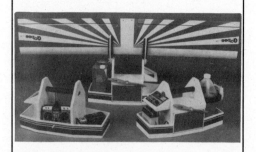

Hobby Dynamics Fieldboxes ($23.99, $34.99 and $40.99 retail) are attractive looking and nicely priced. The *Fieldmate, Flymate I, and II* are mahogany and poplar boxes. They have a pre-cut panel section and a sturdy foam covered handle. Each is cradle adaptable. (Cradles sold separately.)

ROYAL PRODUCTS CORP.

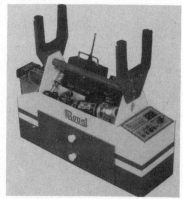

The *Royal Escort Field Box Kit* ($40.95 retail; Assembled version, $59.95 retail) features machine cut 1/4 mahogany plywood, two smooth tracking drawers, adjustable cradles, detailed pictorial instructions and space for fuel can/jug and power panel.

SIG MANUFACTURING CO.

This *Field Box* (No. BX-001, $1.75 retail) has lots of room for tools, batteries, and fuel. This inexpensive tote box made of heavy corrugated cardboard measures 7 in. x 11 in. x 8 in. high, with 4 in deep compartments. Handy for carrying only what you need, and no more, to the flight line.

SIG MANUFACTURING CO.

Field Accessories

Power Panels

Pure Magic Model Cleaner (Pint with sprayer, $2.95 retail; Pint refill, $1.75 retail; Qt. refill, $2.75 retail; 1/2 gal. refill, $3.95 retail) cuts through dirt and oil for a quick clean up. Spray on—wipe off! It removes messy exhaust residue without harming painted finishes or iron-on coverings. Non-hazardous, non-flammable, biodegradable, odor-free, and inexpensive to use and it keeps your models looking good!

ALTECH MARKETING

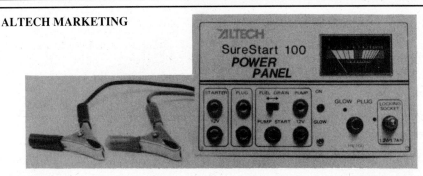

Altech Marketing, with its experience with Enya engines, has developed a 12-volt starter panel that sets a new standard for convenience, versatility, and utility. It's called the *Surestart 12 Volt Power Panel—Autodriver* (No. HV100); and it is packed with features that make starting model gas engines a "breeze."

The advanced electronics incorporate a 1.5 volt glow plug driver circuit named the Autodriver that matches any 1.5 volt glow plug. The next rewarding feature is our Locking Socket that can recharge your glow plug NiCad starters!

The panel provides 12 volt electric starter power, 12 volt pump power with fuel/drain and on/off switches, a meter that monitors current to the glow plug, a LED lamp to indicate proper contact, and an on/off switch for the glow plug Autodriver and Locking Socket circuit.

CARL GOLDBERG MODELS, INC.

The new *CGX 500 Power Panel* (No. 107, $79.99 retail) is so tough it comes with a lifetime warranty! The CGX manages your power for glow plug, starter, and electric fuel pump. It's overload-resistant with extra-rugged construction (enclosed back prevents shorts) and low current-consuming glow drive circuitry. All mounting and hookup hardware are included with an easy-to-follow instruction booklet.

HOBBICO

Hobbico's *Power Panel* (HCAP0300, $34.95 retail) allows you to power all of your field electric equipment from a single 12 volt battery. Not only can you hook up your starter and 6 volt or 12 volt fuel pump you can switch direction of the pump to fill or drain your model. The hook-up for the glow plug allows you to monitor and control the amount of current being supplied.

HOBBY DYNAMICS DISTRIBUTORS

Hobby Dynamics' *Deluxe Power Panel* (No. HDD106, $39.99 retail) can be used with any type of sealed or wet 12V battery. It will supply power for a 12V engine starter, 12V and 6V fuel pumps, and a 1.5V glow plug. An on/off switch allows you to start and stop the fuel pump at any time.

PORTA-POWER INDUSTRIES

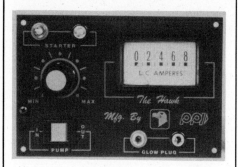

The *Deluxe 'Hawk' Power Panel* ($44.95 retail) features solid state circuitry, adjustable output current for glow plugs, a receptacle for engine starters, and 6- or 12-volt adjustable pump. Can also charge transmitter and receiver battery packs in the field.

ROYAL PRODUCTS CORP.

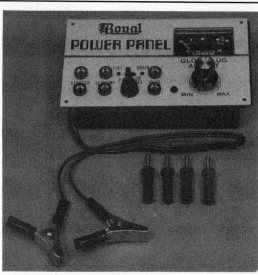

Royal's *Power Panel* ($29.95 retail) will fast charge your receiver battery, operate your fuel pump, starter and starting clip. It comes with back cover and six plug connectors.

SKYWARD R&D LABORATORY

The *Skyward Manual Power Panel* (No. 4059) is glow plug output, 12V starter output, 6V or 12V pump output, with power meter. Pump switch for in/out. Manual power adjustment for controlling plug voltage. Heavy metal construction. On/off switch.

Field Accessories

——— Miscellaneous

AEROTREND PRODUCTS

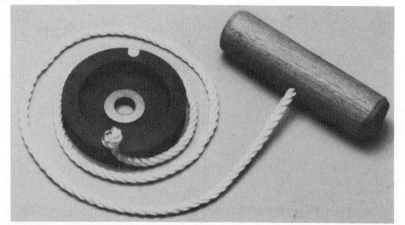

The *''Aerostart''* (No. 1218, $19.99 retail) is a handy, lightweight, inexpensive starter pulley for your large-size engines. It will start stubborn engines, is virtually maintenance free. It can be adapted to fit most large engines, plus you will NEVER have to carry a big bulky battery again. Gentleman, start your engines!

ALTECH MARKETING

Altech Marketing, with its experience with Enya engines, has developed a 12-volt starter panel that sets a new standard for convenience, versatility, and utility. It's called the *Surestart 12 Volt Power Panel—Autodriver* (No. HV100); and it is packed with features that make starting model gas engines a "breeze."

The advanced electronics incorporate a 1.5 volt glow plug driver circuit named the Autodriver that matches any 1.5 volt glow plug. The next rewarding feature is our Locking Socket that can recharge your glow plug NiCad starters!

The panel provides 12 volt electric starter power, 12 volt pump power with fuel/drain and on/off switches, a meter that monitors current to the glow plug, a LED lamp to indicate proper contact, and an on/off switch for the glow plug Autodriver and Locking Socket circuit.

COX HOBBIES, INC.

This *Deluxe Modeler's Kit* (No. 990; Retail: See your dealer) is a handsome, black leather-grained, plastic tool case that holds a half-pint of Super Power fuel, a filler hose, a 1-1/2 V starting battery, a glow head clip, multipurpose wrenches for .020 and .049 engines, a control handle, and Dacron control line.

COX HOBBIES, INC.

This *All-Purpose Starting Kit* (No. 400; Retail: See your dealer) includes everything needed to get a car, boat, or airplane engine started right (1/2-pint Super Power fuel, filler hose, 1-1/2 V starting battery, glow head clip, and multi-purpose .049 engine wrenches).

HITEC R/C USA, INC.

The *hitec Power-Mate* (No. HMS0100) is a dual range battery checker for testing 5 or 6 cell receiver packs. The Power-Mate has a range from 0 to 120% charge capacity (empty to full). After a couple of flights, plug the Power-Mate into the receiver pack to see if it is safe to fly again. The Power-Mate will also tell you if an old pack is up to snuff by giving you the capacity of a freshly charged battery pack.

HOBBY DYNAMICS DISTRIBUTORS

The *Wet Cell Battery* (No. HDDQ636, $18.99 retail) just can't be beat as an electric starter battery. The HD 5.5 amp 12 volt Wet Cell Battery is just the right size for slipping into most flight boxes and provides extra power over other wet cell batteries for operating electric motors and power panels.

HOBBY DYNAMICS DISTRIBUTORS

Hobby Dynamics' new *Mini-Tach* (No. HDD107, $58.99 retail) comes assembled and ready to use. The four watch/calculator batteries are already installed. The Mini-Tach allows you to test the effectiveness of fuel and the performance of your engine. The operating range of the Mini-Tach is 0-29,000 RPM.

HOBBY DYNAMICS DISTRIBUTORS

The *HD 6mAH Sealed Battery* (No. HDD102, $37.99 retail) is a rechargeable battery that will provide all the power that's necessary at the field without the mess of a wet cell.

HOBBY DYNAMICS DISTRIBUTORS

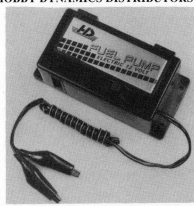

Hobby Dynamics' *12V Electric Fuel Pump* (No. HDD108, $19.99 retail) is designed for model glow and diesel fuel. This versatile pump will either fill or drain and can be mounted either to the side of the fuel can or to the side of your field box.

HOBBY DYNAMICS DISTRIBUTORS

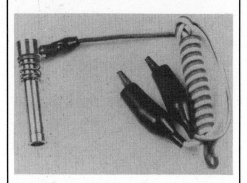

The Hobby Dynamics' *Glow Plug Adapter* (No. HDD120, $5.95 retail) fits right in with the other quality HD accessories. This chrome-plated glow-plug adapter has a positive locking mechanism and comes complete with alligator clips.

MILLER R/C PRODUCTS

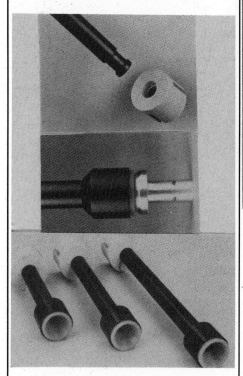

These *Helicopter Starting Extensions* (No. EX75 for 7-1/2 in., EX55 for 5-1/2 in. and EX40 for 4 in.; $18.99 - $19.99 retail) are configured with a large head to fit down further for a better grip. They're black anodized aluminum with Miller's rubber insert. They're made to fit Sullivan and Royal Starters. They are rubbed mounted.

MILLER R/C PRODUCTS

These inserts don't fly out, mar models, and are heat-resistant to fuels and igniters. *Polar Grip* (No. PG101, $6.49 retail) is for 3.5 and 7.5 outboards and ducted fans. *Polar Grip II* (No. PG101-2, $6.49 retail) is designed for the K&B 7.5 outboard that has the cut-down flywheel. *Sky Grip* (No. SG201, $6.49 retail) is for planes with nose cones. *Tuff Grip* (No. TG301, $6.99 retail) is for nut-washer, quads, 1/2-As, and rear start choppers.

MILLER R/C PRODUCTS

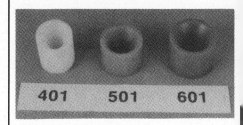

These *Heli-Grips Starting inserts* (No. 401 for Schluter, No. 501 for GMP, and No. 601 for Miller R/C; $4.99 retail) are designed to fit helicopter engine cones. They're constructed of high-tech materials.

MILLER R/C PRODUCTS

Big Grip (No. BG701, $29.95 retail) is engineered to start those ''big'' nose cones. The 3-in. cup is black anodized aluminum and comes with a hi-tech material insert to start big motors. Big Grip is machined to fit Sullivan and Royal starters or comes blank for individual applications.

MILLER R/C PRODUCTS

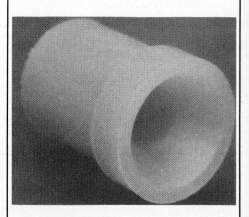

This new *Mini-Grip Starting Insert* (No. MG801, $4.99 retail) is engineered to fit the Astro Mini Starter as a replacement insert. It will NOT mar the nose cones.

MRC-TAMIYA

The *MRC-Tamiya Digital Multimeter* with case is one of the handiest tools around. This pocket size instrument measures up to 250 volts AC, 250 volts DC, and 20 meg-ohms of resistance. The built-in buzzer checks for continuity; use it also to check the condition of voltage-dropping diodes.

ROYAL PRODUCTS CORP.

This *Digital Tachometer* ($42.95 retail) is a handy field box-size unit featuring liquid crystal display and has an RPM range of 100-29,000. Photo cell pick-up allows modeler to keep a safe distance from engine. Will read 2 or 3 blade props.

ROYAL PRODUCTS CORP.

This handy *Analog Tachometer* ($42.95 retail) will read engine RPM from 0-32,000 on 2-, 3-, or 4-blade props. It features photocell pick-up, analog style meter, and 9-volt operation.

SWEEN I.D. PRODUCTS INC.

We guarantee you'll like *Fast Clean* (No. 7632, 8 oz., $4.95 retail; No. 7633, 64 oz., $7.95 retail) better than your home brew. It's made with a combination of non-alkaline soapless cleaners and wetting agents. It is safe for all painted or iron-on surfaces. It only takes a little Fast Clean and a clean towel to get your plane squeaky clean! It comes in an 8 oz. spray bottle or a one-half gallon (64 oz.) size with a free 4 oz. spray bottle for your flight box.

XURON CORP.

The *Shears* (No. 475 C, Combination Plier, $14.99 retail; No. 410 T, High Precision Shear, $9.99 retail; No. 450, Tweezernose Plier, $15.99 retail) that set the standard in civilian and military electronics and aerospace are now available to RC hobbyists. The shearing cut of XURON Micro-Shear® flushcutters is so clean and square that post-cutting clean up may not be required. Ask for XURON when you want the cuts that are so good their patented.

Safety is Contagious

Fuel & Fuel Accessories

Fuel

COX HOBBIES, INC.

Super Power Fuel and Racing Fuel (No. 550 for half-pint of Super Power, No. 551 for pint of Super Power; No. 510 for pint of Racing; Retail: See your dealer) offer their own distinctive blends. The Super Power Fuel is advanced, 15% nitromethane fuel which provides a powerful formula for maximum performance and ease of starting. The Racing Fuel is a special blend for all-out speed. It's 30% nitromethane and specially formulated for competition use and high-speed engines.

FHS SUPPLY INC.

Red Max Fuel (Retail: See your dealer) uses a new space-age lubricant that has ten times the film strength of castor oil to allow expensive engines to last longer. Available are the following nitro percentages: 0%, 5%, 10%, 12%, 15%, 25%, 40%, and 60%. Also available in 54-gallon drums.

LANIER R/C

Hot Stuff Fuel (Retail: $10.00 - $20.00) uses the finest and purest ingredients—AA castor oil only. It's available in 5%, 10%, 12%, 15% and 25%. It's also available for 4-cycle engines. Pints, quarts, gallons, and 55-gallon quantities are available.

SWEEN I.D. PRODUCTS INC.

End the frustration (and embarrassment) of hard-to-start 2- and 4-cycle glow model engines! *Fast Start* (No. 7621, cold weather, $4.95 retail; No. 7624, hot weather, $4.95 retail) helps to prevent drowning the glow plug by providing a high percentage of ignitable fuel and oxygen to the engine's combustion chamber. Works wonders on hot days, hot and flooded engines, quickly starts your engine on cold days when everyone else is having trouble. Just add a few drops to the carburetor prior to propping.

SIG MANUFACTURING CO.

SIG MANUFACTURING CO.

Champion RC Model Engine Fuel ($3.25-$25.95 retail) blends are cool-burning, clean, and deliver maximum power and a dependable idle. They're made with Klotz top-quality racing/castor oil mix to provide lubrication and long engine life. Price depends on nitro content (0% to 35% available) and size.

Sig 4-Stroke Fuel (No. FS-003 for 10%, $13.25/gallon retail; No. FS-007 for 15%, $15.25 retail) was two years in development. This special blend was designed for peak performance in all 4-strokers. Available with 10% or 15% nitro in gallon size.

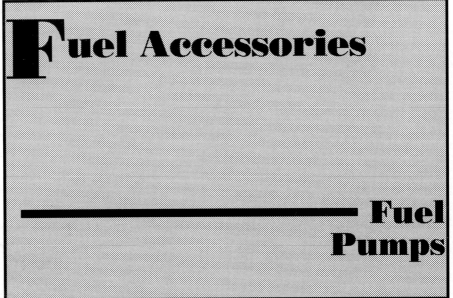

Fuel Accessories — Fuel Pumps

AEROTREND PRODUCTS

"Squeezme" Fuel Bulbs ($3.95 - $7.95 retail) are guaranteed for life. These fuel bulbs are specially formulated to eliminate internal flaking and deterioration. All-brass fittings are included and the regular version includes "Blue Line" Silicone fuel line and nylon nozzle. Order No. 1101 for 2-oz., No. 1103 for 4-oz., No. 1105 for 6-oz., No. 1107 for 8-oz., and No. 1109 for 10-oz. A fast-fill version is available for the 6-oz., 8-oz., and 10-oz. sizes ($1.00 extra).

DAVE BROWN PRODUCTS

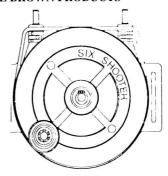

The *Six-Shooter* ($11.95 retail) is an industrial strength high-volume hand-operated pump designed specifically for model use. It features a silicone pumping element for fuel resistance and has no seals or valves to leak or wear out. It's virtually indestructible and guaranteed for a year. It's also available in a gas/diesel version (same price).

DAVE BROWN PRODUCTS

The *Pour N Pump system* ($21.95 retail) is a completely ready to use fueling station. It comes completely ready to use with six shooter pump, high quality silicone fuel tubing, and brass fittings already installed. Simply pour your fuel into it and pump it into your model. Can with fittings available separately for $9.95.

ROYAL PRODUCTS CORP.

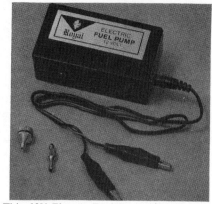

This *12V Electric Fuel Pump* ($22.95 retail) is a high-speed pump designed to handle model fuels of any nitro content and diesel fuel for smoker applications. The unit has a jack attachment, built-in fuel can hooks, and a fill and drain switch.

SWEEN I.D. PRODUCTS INC.

This is the original and very popular *Fuel Wizzard* (No. 7601, $9.95 retail) that mounts on your gallon plastic fuel bottles and comes with 1-1/2 feet of Lifetime Fuel Line. It pumps one full ounce of fuel per stroke and is all fuel safe.

SWEEN I.D. PRODUCTS INC.

The *Fuel Wizzard Model 2* (No. 7602, $21.50 retail) comes mounted on a heavy-duty metal gallon can to keep your fuel safe and fresh. It comes fully assembled, including four feet of Lifetime Fuel and is ready to use right out of the box. The Model 2 will fuel or defuel the largest tanks in just seconds at 1 full ounce per stroke and will do that with all types of fuels.

SWEEN I.D. PRODUCTS INC.

We have modified the original *Fuel Wizzard pump* (No. 7603, $10.95 retail) to fit on your gallon metal can. It still pumps all fuels at one ounce per stroke through the 1-1/2 feet of Lifetime Fuel Line furnished with pump.

DU-BRO PRODUCTS, INC.

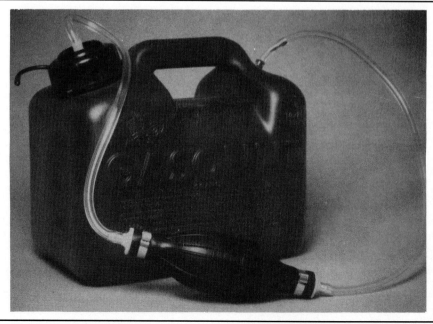

The all-new *Du-Bro E/Z Fill Fuel Pump* (No. 519, $12.95 retail) is sure to fill you with satisfaction! The pump will accept glo-fuels, gasoline, diesel fuel and will exceed 1-1/2 ounces of fuel per squeeze or as little as a drop or two for priming. Emptying your fuel tank is also made easy by simply turning the pump over 180° as shown in the picture. The new E/Z Fill Fuel Pump is sold separately or comes complete with a sturdy one gallon no-tip fuel container (No. 520, $19.95 retail), which will not tip over in your car. See your local hobby dealer today!

Fuel Accessories

Fuel Tanks

DU-BRO PRODUCTS

These *Fuel Tanks* (Nos. 402-424; ($2.45-$4.45 retail) include all tank hardware, soft brass tubing, and positive flow clunk fuel pick-up. Ten sizes are available, from 2-oz. to 24-oz.

DU-BRO PRODUCTS

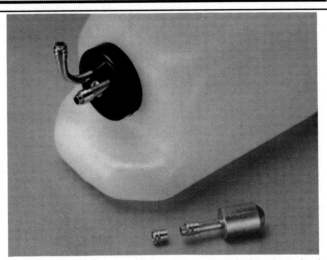

This *1/8″ Fuel Line Barb* (No. 512, 5/pkg., $1.75 retail) is a new product designed to take the fear out of fuel lines coming off your fuel tanks and clunks. As you can see, all the modeler has to do is solder a fuel barb on brass tubing or clunk and the fuel line will stay on securely. This is a very simple solution instead of fuel line clamps.

HAYES PRODUCTS

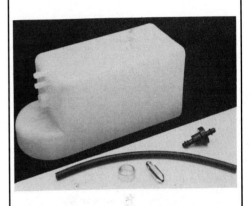

These *Polyethylene Fuel Tanks* (Retail: See your dealer) come in regular and slim-line models. The regular tanks are available in 4-, 6-, 11-, and 13-oz. The slim-line tanks are available in 4-, 8-, 12-, 16-, and 24-oz.

Fuel Accessories

Fuel Tubing & Valves

AEROTREND PRODUCTS

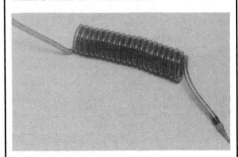

The *"Coiler"* (No. 1089, $5.49 retail) is a new filler set-up for those tired of stepping on their filler hoses. It consists of a 6 ft. long coil of heavy duty fuel-proof tubing plus "End-of-the-Line" nozzle. Specially made for filling the tanks on all glo-fuel and gas/diesel engines, "Coiler" uncurls for ease of filling and then curls back for storage. A must for the avid hobbyist.

AEROTREND PRODUCTS

"Blue Line" Silicone Tubing (3-ft. pack, $1.99 retail; 30- and 50-ft. reels, $.64/ft. retail) is thick, strong, highly heat resistant, and flexible. Four sizes, small through extra-large, are available for every application. Order Nos. 1001 to 1007 for packs, and Nos. 1011 to 1019 for reels.

AEROTREND PRODUCTS

"Aqua Blue" Gas/Diesel Fuel Line (3-ft. pack, $1.89 retail; reels, $.62/ft. retail) is for 1/4-scale, Quadra-type engines. This gas/diesel fuel line stays pliable, heat resistant, and is translucent. Order No. 1081 for small, No. 1083 for large, No. 1085 for small reel, and No. 1087 for large reel.

AEROTREND PRODUCTS

The *Super Blue Set-Up* (No. 1009, 5-ft. pack, $4.19 retail) is super-large fuel tubing (5/32" ID x 3/32" wall). Perfect for electric fuel pumps, water jackets, etc. It has super strength and it's flexible. Nozzle and ties are included. A 30-ft. reel is also available.

AEROTREND PRODUCTS

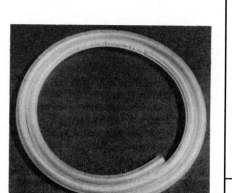

"EasyFlex" Gas/Diesel Fuel Tubing (No. 1073, 2-ft. pack, $1.99 retail; No. 1077, 30-ft. reel, $.99/ft. retail) is the alternative to neoprene for gas and diesel fuel line. It's for 1/4-scale engines (Quadra type). It's highly heat-resistant yet stays pliable at very low temperatures. It's translucent, flexible, yet maintains a thick wall for strength.

AEROTREND PRODUCTS

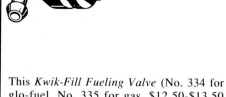

"End-Of-The-Line" fittings (Pack of 3, $1.29 retail) are designed to do what their name suggests: end the line. They can be used to join two similar fuel line pieces, simplify fuel tank installation, connect the pump line to the tank. There are two different colors for ease of identification.

DU-BRO PRODUCTS

This *Final Filter* (No. 162, $2.50 retail) is an in-line aluminum filter with twice as much fuel filtering capacity as most filters. It features an extremely fine, 130-micron polyester screen which filters out even the smallest particles.

DU-BRO PRODUCTS

This *Kwik-Fill Fueling Valve* (No. 334 for glo-fuel, No. 335 for gas, $12.50-$13.50 retail; and No. 339 for replacement fueling probe, $1.10 retail) mounts to fuselage with 3/8-in. hole to eliminate disconnecting fuel line from carburetor to fill fuel tank. It automatically shuts off when refueling.

DU-BRO PRODUCTS

These universal *Fuel-Can Cap Fittings* (No. 192, $2.60/set retail) sets are for quick-and-easy fuel pump hook-ups. They feature a nylon filter for any 1-1/4-in. and larger standard size. The set includes four 1/4-in. nuts, three top-quality brass fittings, and a fuel filter.

DU-BRO PRODUCTS

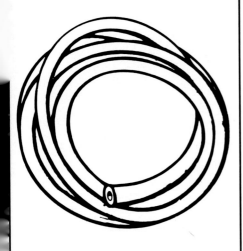

Fuel Tubing
Super Blue Silicone Fuel Tubing
For Glo-Fuel Only

No.	Size	Pkg.
196	Small	50 ft. spl.
221	Small	2 ft. length.
197	Medium	50 ft. spl.
222	Medium	2 ft. length.
204	Large	30 ft. spl.
223	Large	2 ft. length.

Neoprene Fuel Tubing
For Gas, Oil, Diesel or Glo-Fuel

No.	Size	Pkg.
199	Medium	50 ft. spl.
225	Medium	2 ft. length.

Tygon Fuel Tubing
For Gasoline and Diesel Fuel

No.	Size	Pkg.
505	Medium	50 ft. spl.
506	Large	30 ft. spl.

DU-BRO PRODUCTS

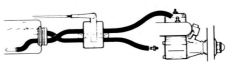

The *Super Smoker* (No. 255, $9.00 retail) features a positive, no-leak fuel and pressure shutoff valve. It's compact enough to mount anywhere. It requires one extra servo to operate. Included are 34-in. of Neoprene Fuel Tubing and hardware.

DU-BRO PRODUCTS

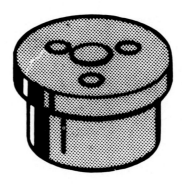

This *Gas Conversion Stopper* (No. 400, $1.10 retail) is a specially-formulated replacement stopper. It's all that's needed to convert any size Du-Bro Fuel Tank to gas. When converting to gas, Du-Bro's neoprene Fuel Tubing (No. 225 or equivalent) can be used.

DU-BRO PRODUCTS

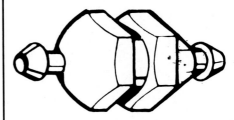

This *In-Line Fuel Filter* (No. 340, standard size, $2.25 retail; No. 341, large scale, $2.50 retail) is constructed of two threaded aluminum parts which separate for ease in cleaning. A 130-micron mesh screen is included to filter out the smallest particles and an O-ring properly seals against leakage.

DU-BRO PRODUCTS

This *Tank Filter* (No. 161, $1.65 retail) is a combination weight and filter made of sintered bronze. It's designed to fit all clunk tanks.

HAYES PRODUCTS

Fuel Filter (Retail: See your dealer).

SIG MANUFACTURING CO.

This *Heat-Proof Silicone Fuel Line* ($.99-$17.95 retail) is top quality tubing—completely heat-proof and impervious to alcohol, nitromethane, and oil. It will not harden or deteriorate in glow fuel and won't melt even if resting against the hottest part of the engine. Available in three diameters to fit any engine size, it comes packaged in 1 ft., 2 ft., and 25 ft. rolls.

SIG MANUFACTURING CO.

This *Surgical Tubing* ($.99-$12.95 retail) is pure latex—thin walled and very flexible. It's ideal for use with free flight timers and other special applications and is available in two diameters and packed in 1 ft., 2 ft., and 25 ft. rolls.

SWEEN I.D. PRODUCTS INC.

One fuel line for gas, glow, smoke, or diesel fuel! We've designed the *Lifetime Fuel Tubing* (No. 7650, $5.95 retail) with thick walls for strength and durability, yet flexible for easy installation. Each package contains 5 feet of 1/8" ID x 1/4" O.D. turbine so you'll have enough to convert several airplanes and your fuel pumping system. Free fuel line coupling included in each package.

C.B. TATONE, INC.

This *Carburetor Choke* (No. 52115, $10.25 retail) is for use with Tillotson and Walbro carbs. Most chain saw engines require lots of choking and a cowl. This simply bolts to the carb using the two existing screws. Choke can then be operated either manually or with a servo control.

C.B. TATONE, INC.

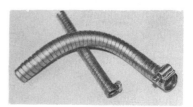

''Flex Off'' Metal Tubing (No. 15216 for 1/2-in. ID, $5.75 retail; No. 15236 for 5/8-in. ID, $6.00 retail; No. 15256 for 3/4-in. ID, and No. 15276 for 7/8-in. ID, $6.50 retail) is flexible metal tubing for use with most muffler tail pipes. Four 12-in. long sizes are available.

Building & Covering Materials

DAVE BROWN PRODUCTS

The revolutionary new *Skyloft Covering Material* (Pack, $3.25 retail) replaces silk and silkspan. It's a continuous filament spin-bonded nylon with extreme strength, is ultra lightweight, and features ease of manipulation and tremendous ''fillability'' (completely fill with three coats of dope). It's attractively priced and complete instructions are included. Each pack is of 3-sq.-yds.

DAVE BROWN PRODUCTS

Flex-All Plasticizer (4 oz., $2.95 retail) is for acrylic lacquer and primer and butyrate dope. In acrylic it completely eliminates cracking and spiderwebbing. It also aids in gloss retention. In dope, it helps reduce shrinking.

COMPOSITE STRUCTURES TECHNOLOGY

Rohacell is a light, rigid, high-quality, polymethacrylimide foam. Rohacell's high compression strength makes it ideal for use in solid core or sandwich composite structures. Pure white in color, Rohacell is compatible with most modeling adhesives and finishes including epoxy, CA, and dope. Three densities are available: 2 lb./ft.3, 3.2 lb./ft.3, and 4.7 lb./ft.3 in a wide range of sheet thicknesses and sizes. Rohacell is easily shaped with common woodworking tools or sandpaper.

COMPOSITE STRUCTURES TECHNOLOGY

CST offers a full line of *Composite Materials* for today's high tech modelers. Carbon is available in sheets, strips, fabrics, and tow in a wide variety of sizes. The unidirectional carbon fabric is pictured along with samples of their Kevlar fabrics. CST also offers seven weights of fiberglass cloth to meet every need.

COVERITE

Micafilm (Nos. 2500 - 2612; Small rolls, $7.50 - $9.95 retail; Large rolls, $20.75 - $27.50 retail) consists of a film bonded to thin mica fibres. It is 1/2 the weight of other films, yet 7 times the rip strength. Since it has no adhesive coating, it will never sag or become brittle. It is applied with Balsarite. Also, a remarkable Pre-Primed Micafilm has been developed. It comes in pearly white, transparent red, yellow, orange, blue, aluminum, opaque pearly white, metallic blue, ultralight 3/4-oz. clear and pre-primed for a paintable surface. Available in small and large 15-foot rolls.

COVERITE

Ironex (No. 3200, $4.50 retail) prevents adhesive buildup on tack irons. It also thins Balsarite and removes any excess. Ironex also cleans oil, grease, etc. from engines.

COVERITE

Balsarite (Nos. 6000 - 6001 for Fabric Formula, Nos. 6002 - 6003 for Film Formula; $4.95/ 1/2-pt., $8.75/pt. retail) is a crystal-clear liquid which is brushed on wood planes and boats. Its deep penetration seals and moisture proofs, strengthens, and makes all iron-on coverings stick better. It reduces sagging, fuel creep, and bubbling.

COVERITE

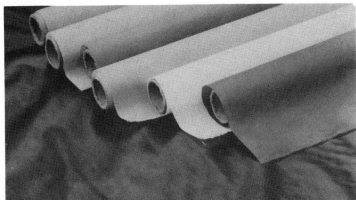

Unpainted Fabric Iron-On Coverings (Small rolls, $9.80 - $9.95; Large rolls, $32.50 - $47.15) are available from Coverite in two different types, made of 100% polyester, both with Coverite's unique soft iron-on adhesive coating. They are tough, lightweight, and easy to apply. Unpainted Super comes in red, white, blue, yellow, orange, and antique. Silkspun comes in white only. Both versions are available in small or large rolls.

COVERITE

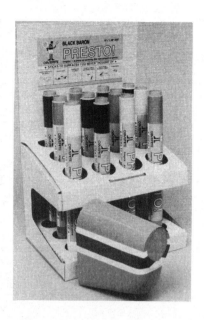

Black Baron "Presto" (Nos. 9310 - 9426; $7.95 retail for regular colors, $8.50 retail for metallics, 12-1/2 in. wide x 4 feet; $1.75 retail for Mini Presto , 6 in. x 12-1/2 in.) is a revolutionary covering for all solid surfaces: wood, plastic, fiberglass. Just peel and press on—no iron required. But, with heat, "Presto" stretches and shrinks. It's also the best trim material ever. 12 colors that match Black Baron Film are fire red, Fokker red, white, lite blue, flag blue, cub yellow, black, orange, cream, metalflake blue, metalflake red, and chrome.

COVERITE

Black Baron Film (Nos. 9110 - 9225; 6 ft., $12.99 - $13.99 retail; 15 ft., $32.48 - $34.98 retail) is the ultimate low heat iron-on film. It was judged best in all five tests: 1) puncturing, 2) contouring, 3) wrinkles and bubbles, 4) opacity, and 5) sticking to everything including directly onto foam. It requires no surface prep. Vivid colors are matched by Coverite's Black Baron Epoxy Paint. It's available in 27-in. x 72-in. sheets and 15-ft. rolls and in the colors fire red, cub yellow, flag blue, light blue, orange, black, white, cream, Fokker red, and real, honest-to-goodness metal flakes in red, blue, and silver, and transparent red, blue, and yellow.

COVERITE

21st Century Paint (No. 8100 - 8113, 13 oz. net wt., $6.95 retail) is fuelproof overnight and dries in 15 minutes. Insensitive to weather conditions. Twelve colors plus primer available. More colors and brush-on formula for spray equipment to come.

21st Century Film (No. 8200 - 8212, 27" x 72". $14.95 - $15.95 retail) is a mechanically-advanced polyester film with easy-to-use Multi-Temp Adhesive™. Totally fuelproof. Can be re-positioned without separation. Shines like a high-gloss paint job—not like plastic. Twelve colors including three metallics are available. More colors to come.

21st Century Fabric (No. 8300 - 8408, 27" x 72", Small Roll $17.95 retail; 27" x 15 ft., Large Roll $44.88 retail) is pre-painted fabric that looks like hand-rubbed lacquer. Lightweight, durable, and totally fuelproof. Exceptional adhesion, even to itself. Goes on easier than film. Eight colors are available.

COVERITE

Glaskote (No. 4500, $5.95 retail) is a clear liquid to brush or spray over any painted surface and produce a tough, lightweight outerskin. New quick-dry formula takes only 15 minutes! It's 94% clear, hi-gloss, and fuel proof. It's available in 1/2-pint cans.

DU-BRO PRODUCTS

Heat Shrink Tubing (Nos. 435-440, $1.15 retail; No. 441, $3.75 retail) is ideal for sleeving, plugs, or connectors. The tubing is easy to shrink, simply use a butane cigarette lighter, heat gun, or solder iron. The tubing shrinks up to half its original diameter. Color-coded for easy identification. Available in six sizes. Order No. 435 for 1/16-in. blue, No. 436 for 3/32-in. green, No. 437 for 1/8-in. red, No. 438 for 3/16-in. white, No. 439 for 1/4-in. yellow, No. 440 for 3/8-in. black, and No. 441 for assortment pack (two of each).

RADIO CONTROL BUYERS GUIDE

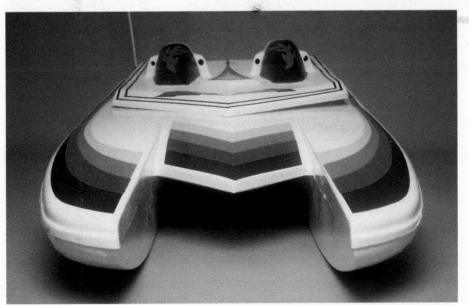

Clockwise from top left: A 2-channel surface radio. the *Alpina,* from JR for use with R/C boats and cars. Dramatic views of the *Concept* helicopter from Kyosho. A bow shot of the *Wildcat* twin-hull off-shore racer from Great Planes Mfg. The beautifully detailed William Bros. *Bee Gee* static model.

Clockwise from left:
The Advance Engineering *pickup bed* showing the fine detail of the roll bar, tail-gate net, and floor bed. The massive 4WD monster truck, the *Bullhead,* from MRC/Tamiya. The ever-popular *Clodbuster* monster truck from MRC/Tamiya shown in its natural environment.

Clockwise from top left:
MRC/Tamiya's off-road racer, the *Saint Dragon.* Parma's *Grave Digger* body mounted on a monster truck chassis. The *King Cab Nissan* from MRC/Tamiya, in action. The newest monster truck from Great Planes/Kyosho, the *Outlaw Rampage.* A beatifully detailed *monster truck body* from McAllister Racing.

Clockwise from left:
Futaba's state-of-the-art *PCM 1024H* radio system designed for helicopter application. Midwest Products *Boothbay* lobsterboat at anchor. A scale replica of a 44 ft. unsinkable *search and rescue cutter* from Dumas Products still in active service with the US Coast Guard.

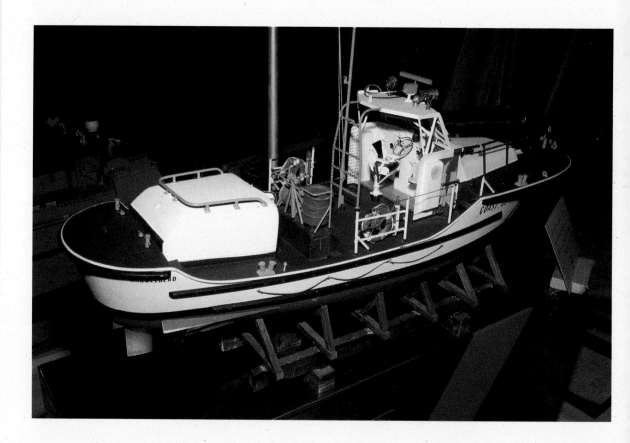

Superb engineering and hand crafted quality are a tradition at *SKYWARD R+D*. The fact that our Model *40* and Model *60* were voted ARF trainers of the year proves it.

And now, in the same tradition of excellence, we're proud to introduce the **SKYWARD 120**. A giant 1/4-scale version of the ultimate ARF trainer.

SKYWARD's reputation is founded on rugged design and leading edge technology. **Our ARF's are built to fly right and land light.** But at SKYWARD we know what trainers go through. So we build them tough to withstand punishment.

✳ All components pre-built, factory finished, ready to fly ✳ Quick assembly slotted joints for left and right wing segments ✳ Flat bottom airfoil [Model 25 and 40] and Horner type wingtips to ensure maximum control ✳ Slotted fuselage provides perfect dorsal and stabilizer alignment for optimum directional stability ✳ Zero-styrofoam, lightweight balsa construction allows easy repair ✳ Pre-molded see through windows ✳ Highest quality hardware and fittings throughout.

At *SKYWARD R+D* we think ahead. When you've mastered the art of flight with your SKYWARD 40, you can modify it using our high performance, semi-symmetrical Sport Wing (sold serparately).

Whatever your flying skill, *SKYWARD* is the way to go.

Sold only at better hobby shops the world over.

Skyward	25	40	60[1]	120[1]
2-cycle engine	20–25	35–45	45–61	108
4-cycle engine	20–26	48–61	60–91	120
Wing span	53"	63"	72"	108"
Length	37"	44.25"	56"	76"
R/C channels	3–4	3–4	4	4
Wing area*	449	730	909	2127

* (sq.in.)   [1] *SEMI-SYMMETRICAL AIRFOIL*

DEALER INQUIRIES ARE INVITED.
Skyward Research + Development Laboratory
4660 Decarie Blvd. Montreal,
Quebec H3X 2H5
Telephone: (514) 481-8107
Facsimile: (514) 487- 5383

TM

✕ SKYWARD
RESEARCH + DEVELOPMENT

TM

THE SKYWARD 40 FSR

Engine Size: 40
Displacement: 6.40 cc
Net Weight: 420 gr

Two Stroke/ Glow Plug
.97 HP @ 15,000 rpm

ABC Construction
Double Ball Bearing

Schnuerle Porting

Muffler included

Black Anodized*

The SKYWARD Line
of Engines includes:
Sizes 25*, 28, 40*, 46,
and 61*

Skyward engines are hand cast and machined for superior performance.

The Micropro 8000 Lets You
Get In Touch With The Future!

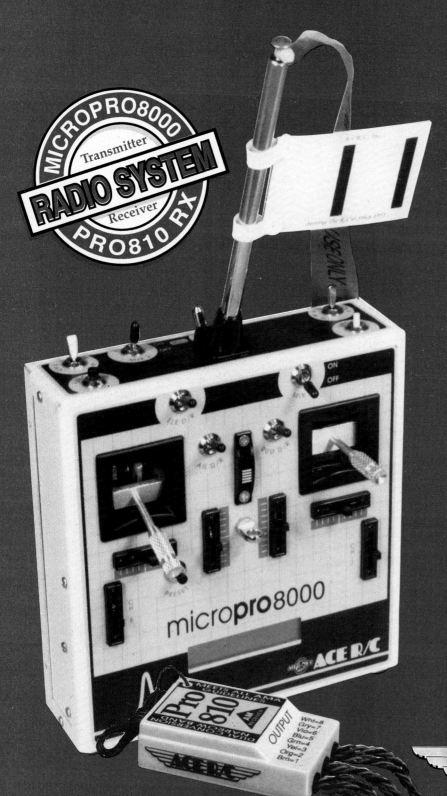

Ace R/C's Micropro 8000 goes well beyond what you normally expect of a computer radio. Not only does it provide the utmost in performance and dependability, it unleases the tremendous power of the computer and puts it to work for you with features not seen in any other radio.

With logical and understandable menu-driven software written by Americans, you will learn how to operate your Micropro quickly and not have to continually refer to the instruction manual. You will find that trim levers become obsolete as you use the Micropro's Autotrim feature. You will experience totally universal mixing capabilities, limited only by your imagination. You will also enjoy more of its features such as eight aircraft non-volatile memory, multi-task capabilities, over 5 hour battery capacity, expo rate, flight and battery timers, audio alarm, and digital voltmeter.

More importantly, you will be in touch with what the future will bring. As a registered Micropro user, you will be advised of software upgrades as they become available and can incorporate them in minutes at a nominal charge. That way, your Micropro will always be up-to-date. It is the radio for a lifetime.

If that isn't enough, you can incorporate the RS-232 option and link your Micropro with a IBM PC compatible or MacIntosh computer and really unleash its power. Set-ups can be transferred and manipulated on the computer, making it even easier! Thousands of aircraft configurations can be saved on disc; users can exchange data; transmitters can talk to one another; you can take your laptop to the field. It is even feasible to dream of, in the future, having a flight simulator that can test your manipulations before risking an airplane. And with the Micropro you **can** dream because you are in touch with the future.

Although the Micropro will operate any AM receiver on the same channel, a perfect companion to the Micropro transmitter is the Pro810 receiver. It is an eight channel, dual conversion, narrow-band receiver that exceeds the AMA guidelines for operating with all even and odd channels. It also works great as a replacement receiver for existing transmitters.

Call for FREE brochure...
1.816.584.7121

A Quality Radio System by...

ACE R/C

"Made in the U.S.A." since 1953!

Ace R/C Inc., 116 W. 19th St., P.O.Box 511 Dept#651, Higginsville MO 64037 816.584.7121

IF YOU'RE REALLY SERIOUS ABOUT RACING,

THINK BIG.

AT TEAM ASSOCIATED WE ALWAYS THINK BIG. AND WIN BIG.

Like *World Championships*. Team Associated cars and drivers have won an unparalleled six, including titles in 1:12, 1:10 and 1:8 scale competition. No other R/C car manufacturer's team has won more than two.

Associated cars win more than just the biggest races, too. Readers of *Radio Control Car Action* magazine voted the RC10 the 1988 R/C Car of the Year, and by a resounding margin of six to one over the second place car! Thank you very much, readers.

Radio Control CAR ACTION RC10 1988 R/C CAR OF THE YEAR

Radio Control Car Action also held a shootout between the RC10 and the next most popular car, and the RC10 came out a winner again!

And at the Reedy Race of Champions (called a re-run of the World Championships because all the drivers from *Europe, Japan,* and the *USA* who made the A Main at the World Championships were present), the RC10 finished first and second.

Racers, readers and dealers all agree. Performance, reliability and readily available spares make the RC10 a big Number One.

Whoops, gotta go now. I want to watch *World Champion Jammin' Jay Halsey* take a victory lap with his RC10.

Associated Electrics
3585 Cadillac Avenue/Costa Mesa, CA 92626

Actual, custom-detailed RC10, with custom wheels.

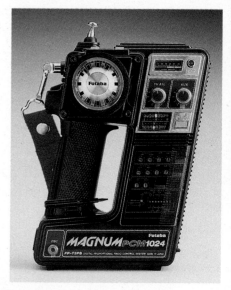

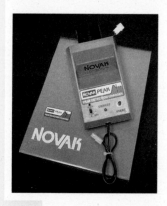

Clockwise from top:
The popular *Hemi Coupe* from Parma International painted in different color schemes. The Futaba *Magnum PCM 1024* radio system. U.S. AirCore's *40 size ARP* with optional pontoons. Novak's *Peak Detection charger.* The Traxxas *Villain IV* and MRP's *Fountain* racing boats.

Clockwise from top left: A beautifully detailed *trainer aircraft* ready for its maiden flight. An O.S. *FP-40 glo engine* with mounted muffler. The MRC/Tamiya *Ferrari F-189.* The *Big John,* built by Fred Coleman of the WRAM club. A *Chevy station wagon body* from yesteryear from Parma International.

Clockwise from top: The *Seamaster 40* from Ace R/C with its single engine mounted on top of the wing. Tekin's *Peak Detection charger.* MRC/Tamiya's *Vanquish* off-road racer. Various *work stations* from Lightning Products showing their numerous applications.

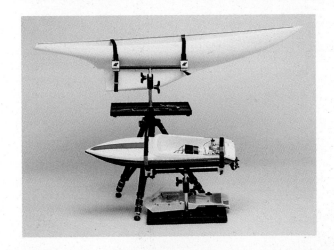

IT'S NOT MATH.
IT'S ELECTRONICS.

And the answer is M5—Team Novak's new High Frequency MEGAFET speed control.

The Novak T4 was a legend—the most rugged, reliable speed control ever, by Team Novak. Combine it with the revolutionary new Novak M1c (a World Champion in its very first year), and you get the new Novak M5.

Team Novak's high-frequency technology lets the M5 deliver smooth, linear acceleration for excellent control. It also has super-low on-resistance for instant response and a quick burst of power.

The M5 features ruggedized MEGAFET transistors and Novak's specially designed battery-regeneration circuitry for extra long run time. It comes pre-wired with the most popular battery and motor plugs for easy installation. The M5 even sports the industry's simplest reverse voltage protection system—with no extra fuses to buy or replace! So simple, it's not only better, it's more convenient and less expensive, too.

Math and electronics are easy if you know the answer. And for the Ultimate Sport Speed Control, the right answer is the new Novak M5. Pick one up today and get an A for the class.

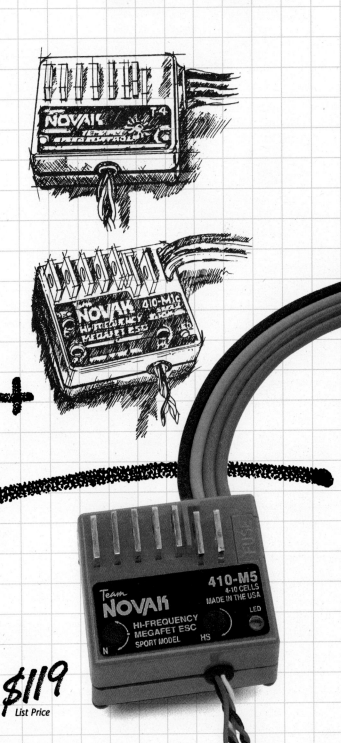

410-M5 (#1920)	
Voltage Input	4-10 cells
On-Resistance	0.0030 ohms
Rated Current	250 Amps

$119
List Price

**OFF COPIED,
NEVER DUPLICATED.**

For more information contact: NOVAK ELECTRONICS, INC. 128-C East Dyer Road, Santa Ana, CA 92707 • (714) 549-3741

©1991 Novak Electronics, Inc.

Clockwise from top right: The *Kenworth* truck from Parma International. The *Stocker .049* gas-powered racer from Cox Hobbies. The Futaba *Field Force 3 PCM 1024* radio system. Twister's *Premier* racing machine. The *Aggressor,* built by Lou Scarlino of the WRAM club. The *Stinger* trainer from Lanier R/C.

Clockwise:
Detailing at its finest can be seen on this Kyosho *Ferrari F-40* coming down the straightway. Dumas' *Hot Shot Sprint 3.5* gas-powered boat, is built for speed. The Associated Electric *RC10T* race truck showing the placement of its electronics and other components. Topflite's *SE-5*, built by Bob Foshay of the WRAM club.

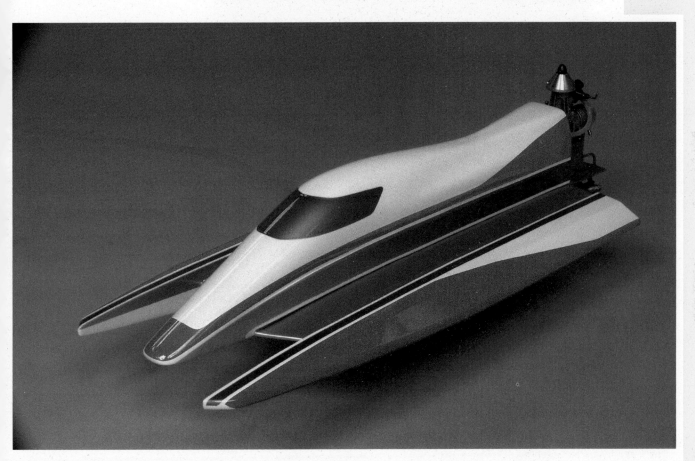

DU-BRO PRODUCTS

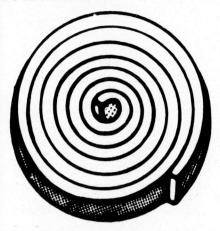

This quality *Foam Tape* (No. 163, 3-ft. roll, $1.40 retail) is super sticky on one side. It cuts down on vibration and it's ideal for wing saddles.

DU-BRO PRODUCTS

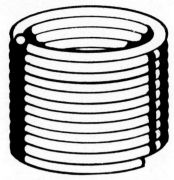

This *Rosin Core Solder* (No. 494, .025 dia./15 ft., $1.40 retail; No. 495, .031 dia./15 ft., $1.65 retail; No. 496, .050 dia./15 ft., $1.90 retail) is the highest quality available on the market. Made of 60% tin and 40% lead. Available in three different diameters for No-Flux soldering.

CARL GOLDBERG MODELS, INC.

This *Clean Scuff Guard/1-in. x 1-ft. Strip* (No. 480/SG1, $1.49 retail) provides protection for wing tips and other easily damaged areas. It's long lasting, fuelproof, and clear (with a ready contact adhesive that cures with age). Simply remove protective backing to apply to a curved or flat finished surface.

CARL GOLDBERG MODELS, INC.

This *Nylon Reinforcing Tape* (No. 450 for 3/4-in., No. 451 for 2 1/2-in., No. 452 for 4-in., and No. 453 for 6-in.,$.99 - $2.29 retail) is extremely tough when applied with epoxy or heavy coats of cement. All widths come in 5-ft. lengths.

CARL GOLDBERG MODELS, INC.

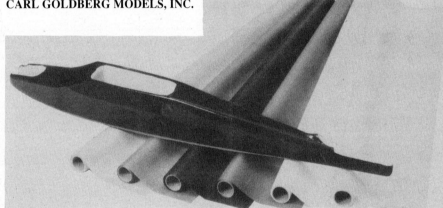

ColorTex (No. 860 for brilliant white, No. 861 for cub yellow, No. 862 for medium blue, No. 863 for red, No. 864 for orange, and No. 865 for antique, $15.99 retail) is a cover that can be applied at low-iron-heat directly onto foam. It goes around compound curves easily and won't bubble-up when applied over itself or sheeted areas. Two light coats of clear finish give a scale "aircraft fabric" appearance (fuselage pictured was covered with one piece of ColorTex). Illustrated instructions are included.

CARL GOLDBERG MODELS, INC.

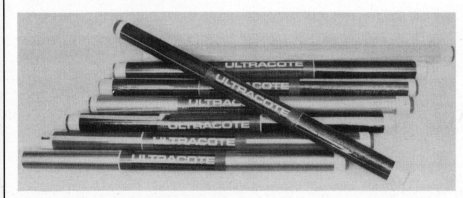

UltraCote (Retail: See your dealer) has a high-tech polymerized film-to-color bond and broad heat range that let you coax it around tough curves and reposition it without fear of layer-separation or "breakdown." UltraCote's streamlined 24 in. width and 81 in. length put more covering material where it belongs—on your plane, instead of on the floor. UltraCote's fade-free colors even have a richer, more realistic gloss that won't leave your plane looking like a shrink-wrapped plastic toy.

CARL GOLDBERG MODELS, INC.

Each roll of *Color-Stripe* (Retail, sold by width: 1/16-in. for $2.99, 3/32-in. for $3.69, 1/8-in. for $3.89, and 1/4-in. for $4.79) comes packed in its own convenient "dispensing blister." Top modelers are using Color-Stripe because it performs like no other tape. It's very thin and has a special expensive adhesive which allows it to bond permanently and adhere like paint. Sunlight gives it final fuelproof bonding. A beautiful model is assured with no problems from shrinking, lifting up, and getting dirty. It's marketed exclusively by Carl Goldberg Models and is available in many colors (red, white, black, gold, blue, yellow, light cream, dark cream, sky blue, deep red, orange, burgandy, silver, and smoke), and four widths (each 36-in. long).

CARL GOLDBERG MODELS, INC.

This *R/C Foam Rubber* (No. 481 for FR25 1/4-in. x 8-in. x 12-in., $2.99 retail; No. 482 for FR50 1/2-in. x 8-in. x 12-in., $3.99 retail) is latex material that helps protect R/C equipment from shock and vibration. It also protects and secures fuel tanks in place. It's the only material recommended by leading R/C manufacturers.

K & S ENGINEERING

This *Tube/Wire Center* (No. 4800, $385.00 retail) features 36-in. lengths of steel music wire in 15 sizes from .015-in. to 1/4-in. diameter. Also included are 11 sizes of round brass tubing, eight sizes of round aluminum tubing, and six sizes of streamline tubing. Also, four sizes of solid brass rod from 1/16-in. to 5/32-in. diameter is included.

GRANITE STATE R/C PRODUCTS

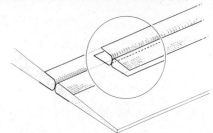

The *Iron-On Gapless Hinge* (No. 610, 45 in., $2.49 retail) is nothing new to some of the old-time control line fliers. They used cloth, sewed it together, and glued it in place. Using glue was a little messy, but well worth it, because the hinge outlasted the model. With all the new materials available to R/Cers, this is the easiest hinge to install today. It can be painted or Monokoted —just line it up and heat it on with your iron. It seals the gap, stops aileron warping and flutter.

K & S ENGINEERING

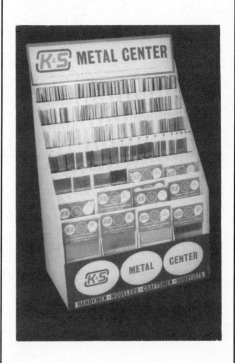

The *Metal Center* (No. 1005, $420.00 retail) has a complete assortment that includes a large variety of precision metal tubing and miscellaneous metal shapes. Available at your favorite dealer.

MIDWEST PRODUCTS CO.

Thin Plywood ($1.50-$19.25 retail) is a popular wood for all types of woodworking projects. Midwest's Thin Plywood takes paint and varnish well, and produces an outstanding finished piece. Available in the following types: Poplar, Beech, Meranti, and Aircraft Grade. Available only from your local hobby shop.

MIDWEST PRODUCTS CO.

Midwest's *Micro-Cut Quality Balsa* ($0.20-$20.50 retail) is available in a wide assortment of 36 in. strips, and 36 in. sheets in 1-in., 3-in, 4-in., and 6-in. widths, plus a wide assortment of blocks and 4 x 48-in. planks. Special shapes include triangles, tapered trailing edges, shaped leading edges, aileron stock in 36 in. lengths and cove-fillet in 24 in. lengths. Available only from your local hobby shop.

MIDWEST PRODUCTS CO.

Micro-Cut Quality Basswood ($0.16-$6.20 retail) is available in 24 inch lengths in a wide variety of strips, and 1 in., 3 in., and 4 in. sheets. Available only from your local hobby shop.

ROYAL PRODUCTS CORP.

The *Deluxe Heat Sealing Tool* ($20.95 retail) is the top of the line covering tool that has improved top end temperature and comes with a cotton anti-scratch bootie, heat stand and heat indicator light. The Teflon shoe has a unique tip that combines a trim tool and iron all in one.

ROYAL PRODUCTS CORP.

The *Economy Heat Sealing Tool* ($15.95 retail) is a good basic covering tool that features the same long life component as our deluxe iron and the same unique Teflon shoe design that combines trim tool and iron all in one. A heat stand is included with the model.

SIG MANUFACTURING CO.

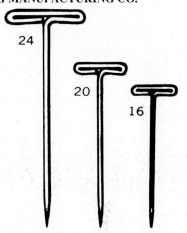

These *T-Pins* ($1.49 - $7.25 retail) are super sharp, chrome-plated, and easy to use. There are three sizes and three different quantity packages to choose from.

SIG MANUFACTURING CO.

Supercoat Covering ($10.95/roll retail) is an iron-on plastic covering that's easy to use, goes around curves without wrinkles, and is very affordable. Works with low heat so it can be put directly on foam parts without melting them. Available in 16 beautiful high-gloss colors, many of them color matched to Sig Supercoat Dope. Standard 27 in. x 6 ft. rolls.

SCC-410	Waco Red	
SCC-418	Cub Yellow	
SCC-411	Fokker Red	
SCC-419	Black	
SCC-412	White	
SCC-425	Midnight Blue	
SCC-413	Dark Blue	
SCC-421	Transparent Red	
SCC-414	Sky Blue	
SCC-422	Transparent Yellow	
SCC-415	Medium Blue	
SCC-423	Transparent Blue	
SCC-416	Dark Orange	
SCC-424	Transparent Orange	
SCC-420	Silver	
SCC-417	Antique	SCC-426 — Neon Red ($11.95) SCC-427 — Neon Yellow ($11.95) SCC-428 — Neon Green ($11.95)

BUILDING & COVERING MATERIALS

SIG MANUFACTURING CO.

SuperTrim ($6.49/roll retail) is the companion to Sig Supercoat Iron-on Plastic Covering. SuperTrim is the same thin, lightweight covering material with a self-stick adhesive on the back. It's perfect for adding stripes, sunbursts, checker-boards, lettering, and insignia to your model—simply cut out a design, peel off the back, and stick it on the model. It comes standard 13 in. x 36 in. rolls.

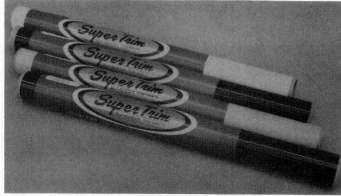

SCT-510	Waco Red
SCT-511	Fokker Red
SCT-512	White
SCT-513	Dark Blue
SCT-514	Sky Blue
SCT-515	Medium Blue
SCT-516	Dark Orange
SCT-520	Silver
SCT-518	Cub Yellow
SCT-519	Black
SCT-525	Midnight Blue
SCT-526	Metallic Blue
SCT-527	Metallic Red
SCT-528	Metallic Gold

SCT-529 — Neon Red   SCT-530 — Neon Yellow   SCT-531 — Neon Green (Neon colors $7.49/roll)

SIG MANUFACTURING CO.

Stix-It (No. SX-001, 8 oz., $4.65 retail; No. SX-002, Pint, $7.65 retail) features a heat-sensitive adhesive which lets you iron on Koverall or almost any other cover material. It works great with plastic films and other iron-ons. It helps eliminate bags, wrinkles, and pull-ups.

SIG MANUFACTURING CO.

Koverall (48-in. x 36-in., $3.95 retail; 48-in. x 72-in., $6.95 retail; 48-in. x 5-yd., $14.95 retail) is a lightweight polyester-based fabric that can be applied like silk and shrinks tight with an iron. It can be finished with dope, enamel, and epoxy. It has very high impact strength.

SIG MANUFACTURING CO.

Sig AAA Balsa (Retail: Write for free price list) is available in more than 300 stock sizes.

TOP FLITE MODELS, INC.

The *Super Monokote* (opaque and transparent, 13.99; metallic, 15.99; frosted, 16.99, retail.) is a revolutionary coverign with a built-in finish which eliminates the need for sanding, sealing, doping, and polishing. It simply irons on. It comes in four color groups, each 26-in. x 6-ft. (opaque: red, orange, yellow, white, aluminum, sky blue, insignia blue, black, olive drab, gray, chrome, paintable clear, cream, green, pink, maroon, tan, blue mist, dark red and salmon; metallic: blue, brown, green, purple, red, gold, charcoal, and platinum; transparent: red, green, orange, yellow, and blue; frosted: wine, blue, and aluminum).

SIG MANUFACTURING CO.

Super Stripe Color Trim Tape ($1.99-$4.25 retail) is the finishing touch for all models, whether covered with plastic film or painted. As thin as a coat of paint, Super Stripe Color Trim lays down flat and smooth going around tight curves with ease. Completely fuel proof. In tests with raw fuel, the tape simply would not budge, lift, or separate. It comes in economical 36-foot rolls and is available in 5 different widths (1/16-, 3/32-, 1/8-, 3/16-, and 1/4-in.) and 8 brilliant, glossy colors (red, white, medium blue, dark blue, yellow, orange, black, silver).

Decals & Decorating Materials

AUTOGRAPHICS

Quality *R/C Decal Graphics* (Retail: See your dealer) come in a wide assortment from Autographics of California. These decals are available at your local hobby shop.

COVERITE

Our *Graphics* (Nos. 7000 - 7514, $2.50 - $6.95 retail) are fuelproof, paintable, and can be repositioned during the first hour. Genuine cast-vinyl, razor-sharp, pressure sensitive, die-cut letters, numbers, stars, stripes, and trimsheets won't crack, chip, or peel. Graphics come in five colors.

COVERITE

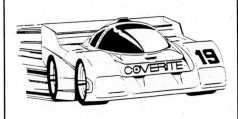

Presto Trimsheets for Lexan Bodies (Nos. 9410 - 9426, $1.75 per sheet, retail) are easy to use for logos, racing numbers, bumpers, or any other design. Unique ''inside/outside'' trim has color on both sides so you can leave them inside and paint over them. Nine colors including real metal flakes.

COVERITE

Bodyshop Pinstripes for Lexan Bodies (Nos. 200-207, $3.95 per sheet, retail) are press-on stripes that stay down even on 90 degree angles! Colored on both sides, there's a total of 50 feet for less than you would pay for one roll of 36 feet. Each sheet has 5 widths from 1/16'' to 1/4'' and are available in seven colors.

COVERITE

The *American Aircraft Art Decals* (No. 2300 - 2365, 4" size, $2.50 retail; 2-1/2" pairs, $2.95 retail) are a series of fuelproof vinyl decals that were inspired by cartoons that appeared on noses of WWII bombers. Silkscreened in up to 6 vivid colors, they look great on noses, wings, and tails of any models. Will stick to any surface including field boxes, helmets, skateboards, etc. 15 designs in 4" size; 5 designs in 2-1/2" pairs (left and right image).

DAHM'S RACING BODIES

DAHM'S Instant-Tint ($3.98 retail for Small, $5.98 retail for Large) self-adhesive, window tinting film comes in Smoke Grey (No. D810, Small; No. D814, Large), Sky Blue (No. D811, Small; No. D815, Large), and Cherry Red (No. D812, Small; No. D816, Large). This transparent, flexible film makes tinting of windows fast and easy. Using Instant-Tint is as simple as putting on stickers. Instant-Tint is great for finishing cars, boats, trains, and planes!

DOLANITE CUSTOM GRAPHICS, INC.

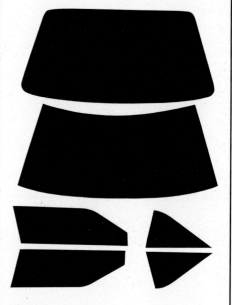

Miracle Mask Window Cuts ($4.99, retail) is a low track, high-performance vinyl mask material. After application, it can be repositioned and also may be reused. The material is then cut to fit the windows of your body style. Just peel, stick, and paint. Available for most of the popular bodies from Andy's, Associated, BoLink, Parma, Custom Works, BBR, and many more, including most of the new narrow styles. Write or call for current (free) price list.

DURO ART IND., INC.

Graphics: complete packages of *Vinyl Letters and Numbers* ($2.49 and up retail). Manufactured in the following sizes: 1/4", 1/2", 3/4", 1", 2", and 3". Also 4" and 6" packages of Vinyl Letters and Numbers only. Available in 8 colors: black, white, red, blue, green, yellow, matte finish gold, and silver. (Fuel modelers should spray with poly varnish.)

J'TEC

Authentic Scale Instruments ($7.50 - $8.50 retail) for planes, boats, and cars. 83 assorted instrument faces, 20 bezels with clear plastic faces. Scale sizes: 1/3, 1/4, 1/5, 1/6, 1/7, 1/8, 1/9, 1/10, and 1/12.

MCALLISTER RACING

Toyota GTP Decals (No. D-222, $3.75 retail)
Super Speedway Stock Car Decals (No. D-221, $3.75 retail)
Mini Logo Decals: Toyota (No. D-224), Nissan (No. D-223), Ford (No. 226), and Chevrolet (No. D225) are $2.00 retail.

MIDWEST PRODUCTS CO.

Midwest Easy Trim (No.1052-1061, standard colors-$18.95 or neon-$19.95 retail) can save 6 to 8 hours on your airplane and turn your single-color model into a multi-colored beauty. Easy Trim is a line of pressure-sensitive graphic sheets with pre-printed patterns that adhere to all covering materials and painted surfaces. Four pattern styles to choose from—Thunderbird, Starburst, Shooting Star, and Hot Stripes. Available only from your local hobby shop.

PARMA INTERNATIONAL

PARMA INTERNATIONAL

These *1/10-scale NASCAR Numbers and Detail Sheets* ($3.00 each retail) are new from Parma. They are available from 0-9. With the added detail items you can finish your Parma NASCAR body just like your favorite stock car driver's race car. This decal sheet makes it easy to finish an award winning body. No. 106600, NASCAR #0; No. 106601, NASCAR #1; No. 106602, NASCAR #2; No. 106603, NASCAR #3; No. 106604, NASCAR #4; No. 106605, NASCAR #5; No. 106606, NASCAR #6; No. 106607, NASCAR #7; No. 106608, NASCAR #8; No. 106609, NASCAR #9. Included are NASCAR # and detail sheet.

Decals (No. 766-oval racing, 3x4, $2.75; No. 758-flames, 3x4, $2.25; No. 763-hot rod, 3x4, $2.75; No. 750-MTV, 3x4, $2.50; No. 749-Halvoline, 3x4, $2.50; No. 755-Ratical rat, 3x4, $2.75) Parma makes decals for all scales and applications. Shown are a few of the 1/24-scale various style decals. All of Parma's decals are beautifully silk-screened on clear mylar and sealed in a protective clear bag to extend shelf-life. See our latest catalogue for complete listings.

PARMA INTERNATIONAL

PARMA INTERNATIONAL

PARMA INTERNATIONAL

Officially Licensed Decals (No. 10706, Gravedigger™ Monster Truck, 9x12, $7.50 retail; No. 10690, Miller® Genuine Draft, 9x12, $7.00 retail). Parma makes decals for all scales and applications. Shown are a few of the 1/10-scale sponsor style decals. All of Parma's decals are beautifully silk-screened on clear mylar and sealed in a protective clear bag to extend shelf-life. See our latest catalogue for complete listings.

Decals! Parma makes decals for all scales and applications. Shown are a few of the 1/8-scale sponsor and graphics style decals. All of Parma's decals are beautifully silk-screened on clear mylar and sealed in a protective clear bag to extend shelf life. 1351–Folgers 9x12–$6.00; 1352–Oval racing 9x12–$6.50; 1353–NASCAR 9x12–$6.50; 1354–WYNN's/K-Mart 9x12–$7.00; 1355–Havoline 9x12–$6.00; 1356–Valvoline 9x12–$6.00; 1361–Graphics #1/Checkers 9x12–$7.00; 1365–Graphics #6/3-D Ribbon 9x12–$7.00. See our latest catalogue for complete listings.

Parma makes decals for all scales and applications. Shown are a few of the graphics style decals. All of Parma's decals are beautifully silk-screened on clear mylar and sealed in a protective clear bag to extend shelf life. 10696–Domino's® Pizza 6X8–$4.00; 10692–Panel Graphics 6X8–$4.50; 10691–Splash Graphics 6X8–$4.50; 10698–Surfin' Noid® 6X8–$5.00; 10685–MTV 6X8–$3.75; 10704–Ratical Rat 6X8–$4.50. See our latest catalogue for complete listings.

PARMA INTERNATIONAL

Make your own big screen excitement with Parma's complete range of *Days of Thunder decals and body/decal sets* ($29.95 retail). Collect all five including, Mello Yello®, Hardee's®, City Chevrolet, Exxon®, and Superflo™. Two huge decal sheets provide all the graphics, details and painting instructions necessary to make a realistic reproduction of each full scale car! The body/decal sets include the same high quality, crystal clear, Chevrolet Lumina body the decals were designed to fit

PARMA INTERNATIONAL

By popular demand, Parma International now offers the entire *Days of Thunder™ series* decal/detail sheets (No. 10712, $12.50 retail) and *body/decal sets* (No. 10291E, $29.95 retail) separately. Each includes two 9"x12" multi-colored sheets to capture the big screen excitement of the movie. Even the most discerning concours judges would agree; when Parma makes a decal, they do it right.

PARMA INTERNATIONAL

Carolina Crusher, Awesome Kong, Clydesdale, Mad Dog, and Wild Hair are the most popular GM monster trucks on the TNT Racing Circuit. Now you can have their logos and graphics all on one sheet! The new *9"x12", seven color decal sheet* (No. 10731, $7.50 retail) is an inexpensive way to turn your next 5 truck bodies into real killers!

PARMA INTERNATIONAL

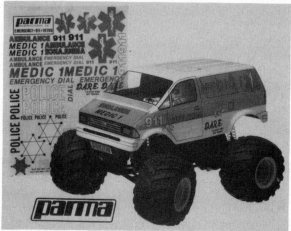

For years R/C hobbyists have been hand painting replicas of police, fire, and rescue vehicles. Now, Parma saves them countless hours of painstaking work with the *Emergency #911 Multicolor 9"x12" Decal Sheet* (No. 10700, $6.50 retail). Shop owners and hobbyists will be amazed by the versatility this decal sheet has. Turn any Lexan body into your own personal rescue vehicle.

PARMA INTERNATIONAL

Big screen oval thrills are now available in 1/24 scale! Parma releases their *Days of Thunder™* line ready-to-run cars and slot car starter sets. Collectors and dealers note: these are limited edition collectors cars and are selling out fast. Each Flexi-Kar® features a 16-D motor, custom painted body and complete decals. Each starter set includes a car, decals, Sebring controller, T.Q. Jr. oiler, extra body, braid clips, and pit box.

PARMA INTERNATIONAL

Now, everything you need to do a first class job of detailing your Lexan bodies is available in one package. Parma International, the world's leader in body shells, now offers their *Body Finishing Kit* (No. 10397, $13.50 retail). In this kit you get a bottle of liquid mask, speedwax, curved surgical scissors for those tricky angles, a body detailing pen with both broad and fine points, plus two Parma stickers. Get yours today at your favorite hobby shop.

PARMA INTERNATIONAL

By popular demand, Parma International now offers the entire *Days of Thunder*™ *series decal/detail sheets* (No. 10710, $12.50 retail) and *body/decal sets* (No. 10291C, $29.95 retail) separately. Each includes two 9"x12" multi-colored sheets to capture the big screen excitement of the movie. Even the most discerning concours judges would agree; when Parma makes a decal, they do it right.

PARMA INTERNATIONAL

Shown are Parma's new *Nissan/GTP* (No. 10717) and the ever-popular *Flames* (No. 10604/Red and No. 10604-B/Blue) decals. All Parma decals now are packaged in clear plastic sleeves to keep them clean and free of accidental scratching and dog-ears. You have trusted Parma to make the decals you want when you want them, but now you can be sure they will retain their original condition until you're ready to use them.

PARMA INTERNATIONAL

By popular demand, Parma International now offers the entire *Days of Thunder*™ *series decal/detail sheets* (No. 10708, $12.50 retail) and *body/decal sets* (No. 10291A, $29.95 retail) separately. Each includes two 9"x12" multi-colored sheets to capture the big screen excitement of the movie. Even the most discerning concours judges would agree; when Parma makes a decal, they do it right.

PARMA INTERNATIONAL

By popular demand, Parma International now offers the entire *Days of Thunder*™ *series decal/detail sheets* (No. 10709, $12.50 retail) and *body/decal sets* (No. 10291B, $29.95 retail) separately. Each includes two 9"x12" multi-colored sheets to capture the big screen excitement of the movie. Even the most discerning concours judges would agree; when Parma makes a decal, they do it right.

PARMA INTERNATIONAL

Now, the added touch of realism you've been looking for to detail up that Parma Hemi Motor Kit. With the new Parma *V-8 Hemi Motor Wiring Kit* (No. 10411A, $5.00 retail) and your paints, you can turn the basic *V-8 Hemi Motor Kit* (No. 10411, $12.95 retail) into a ground pounding monster. Stiff yellow wires are perfect for spark plug wires and the braided wire is a great way to represent fuel lines.

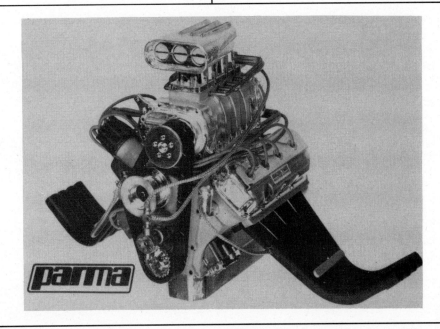

PARMA INTERNATIONAL

Parma makes decals for all scales and applications. Shown are a few of the 1/10-scale sponsor style decals. All of Parma's decals are beautifully silk-screened on clear mylar and sealed in a protective clear bag to extend shelf life. 10601–*Off Road* 6X8–$4.00; 10602–*Oval Racing 6X8*–$4.00; 10687– *Winston Fender 6X8*–$4.50; 10701–*Coat of Arms (auto mfg.) 6X8*–$4.50; 10661–*Mr. Goodwrench 6X8*–$3.75; 10707–*Snickers 6X8*–$3.50. See our latest catalogue for complete listings.

ROYAL PRODUCTS CORP.

These super-detail *Water Transfer Decals* ($3.95 - $16.95 retail) come complete with stencil markings for Corsair Sr., Jr., P-38, Curtiss Hawk, Bearcat, Zero Sr., Jr., P-51, C-47, B-17, and Staggerwing Beech. Most sets include markings for two paint schemes.

SIG MANUFACTURING CO.

These *aircraft Decals* (Retail: See your dealer) are pressure-sensitive and come in many shapes and sizes from 1- to 4-in. Replacement Sig kit decals, U.S. Air Force decals, German crosses, etc., are available.

R/C Boating is a Family Sport!
Join in some family fun!

Paint & Paint Accessories

BADGER AIR BRUSH COMPANY

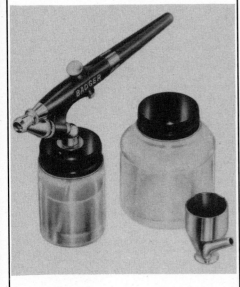

The *Model 350 Bottom Feed, Single-Action, External Mix Air-brush* (No. 350, $38.00 retail) is easy to operate and maintain. Its "external mix" refers to the manner in which the air and paint came together outside the tip of the air-brush. This method causes the spray to have a larger dot pattern than the internal mix air brushes. This makes the Model 350 excellent for stippling and spraying larger areas. The 350 is the perfect choice for beginning students, hobbyists, ceramists, van and motorcycle painters, and crafts persons or anyone who wishes to spray materials of a high viscosity. The 350 will spray ceramic glazes and stains, hobby enamels, properly reduced acrylics, inks, dyes, watercolors, acrylic lacquers, and enamels.

BADGER AIR BRUSH COMPANY

Cyclone I Model 180-1 (No. 180-1, $169.00 retail) portable oilless diaphragm-type compressor has internal bleed allowing use with any make air-brush. Develops .80 CFM at 25 PSI. Compact, lightweight and quiet, it can be carried from room to room. This compressor never needs lubrication and has a 6 ft. electric cord with 3 prong plug.

BADGER AIR-BRUSH CO.

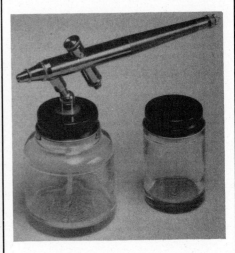

The *Model 200 Air-Brush* (No. 200, $55.00 retail) is simpler to operate than any other Badger air-brush, whether you are just beginning or are a R/C modeling pro of many years. The Model 200 will spray modeling paints, acrylic enamels and lacquers, properly reduced acrylics, and Air-Opaque air-brush colors. The 200 offers a choice of three reservoirs: 3/4 and 2 oz. paint jars, plus 1/4 oz. color cup. This air-brush can adapt to three different heads: fine, medium, and heavy, making it possible to spray any type material.

BADGER AIR-BRUSH CO.

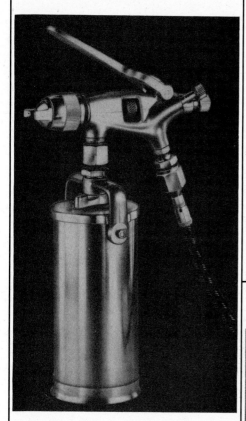

The *Badger Model 400 Detail/Touch-Up Gun* (No. 400, $110.00 retail) is the perfect tool to use for finishing the larger R/C models. It is compact, lightweight, and bridges the gap between the small-precision air-brush and the larger guns with bigger spray patterns. It may be adjusted for round or fan-spray patterns. Available with fine, medium, or heavy spray tips, it can be operated with air compressor, CO2 tank, or pressure tank. Most use an air compressor that develops 2.0 CFM at 30 psi.

BINKS MFG. CO.

The *Chameleon Color Changer with Carrier Outfit* (No. 59-355) includes compressor, regulator-filter, and Chameleon with Raven II Airbrush in an easy-to-carry base. With a twist of the dial, the Chameleon puts up to nine colors at your finger tips.

BINKS MFG. CO.

Three Wren Airbrush models are available. *Model A:* for precise airbrush work. A small-size nozzle opening can spray fine lines, detailed stenciling, and shading with inks, stains, dyes, and other light materials.

Model B: A medium-size nozzle opening atomizes thinned lacquers, enamels, and similar coatings for beautiful finishes on models and other projects.

Model C: for maximum airbrush capacity. A large-size nozzle opening applies ceramic under-glazing, thinned overglazing, and heavier materials. All models are available in sets including hose, connections, and choice of bottle sizes. This is the original hobby airbrush. It's made by the people who make precision spray painting equipment for automobiles, appliances, and furniture.

BINKS MFG. CO.

The *Model 115 touch-up gun* sprays a wide range of pigmented and clear coatings including enamels, lacquers, and shellacs. One-finger trigger allows precise control. Fully-adjustable spray pattern and fluid adjustments are featured. It atomizes evenly and thoroughly and cleans quickly. It's made of sturdy but lightweight forged aluminum. The siphon cup holds 8 oz. It's ideal for shading, stenciling, and touch-up work.

BINKS MFG. CO.

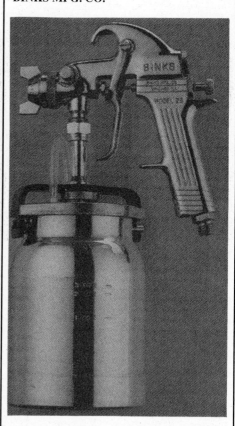

This professional *Model 26 spray gun* is lightweight and ideal for the serious craftsman. It has a rugged aluminum body with brass fluid passages for long service life. The spray pattern is fully adjustable. It's available with nozzle combinations for spraying fluids ranging from dyes to house paints (siphon or pressure feed, with or without cup). The needle valve adjusts to compensate for wear. A full range of accessories is available including hose with connections, compressors, etc. Binks specialty is spray paint application.

BINKS MFG. CO.

Wren Airbrush Kit (No. 59-10015) are fine-tuned to your unique hobby/household needs, including all needed accessories (from hairline detailing to hundreds of household touch-ups). Atomizing air and fluid controls allow a wide range of spray adjustments. A compact air compressor is included in the price. Combinations of bottle sizes of 1/4, 1/2, and 2-1/2 fl. oz. are included. Three nozzle sizes are available as well as a 6-ft. plastic or heavy duty braided hose with connections. It's packaged in an attractive, durable styrene case.

BINKS MFG. CO.

The new *Raven II* (No. 59-220) is a superior double-action airbrush for spray painting very fine lines and it features a plated brass handle with needle adjustment assembly. Control is achieved with an adjustable air cap, needle, and trigger assembly, to produce spray patterns from 1/2-in. to a pencil-thin line.

CHEVERON

Perfect Paint (4 oz., $5.50 retail; 8 oz., $6.99 retail; 11 oz., $7.20 retail) features an actual paint chip on each can's label to aid in color selection. The 15 Monokote Matching Colors are computer color matches to Monokote's wing covering. The 16 Camouflage Colors are computer matched to the Federal standards for authentic color reproduction of military aircraft. These colors use non-toxic pigment, are virtually odorless, will not affect styrofoam and feature excellent flow and adhesion. Balsa fillers, primers, display racks, engine cleaners and thinners.

COVERITE

Black Baron Epoxy Paint, Aerosol or Brush-On (Nos. 9000 - 9099, $5.95 retail) features all the advantages of two-part epoxies without the fuss and short pot-life. It's fuelproof, lightweight, super tough, leaves a high gloss shine in one or two coats, and is very flexible. It's for use on fabric, wood, metal, and many plastics. A total of 14 colors, 2 flats, and a clear and sandable primer are available. Many colors match Coverite's Black Baron Film, its Permagloss Fabric, and other coverings.

COVERITE

Primex Nitrate Dope (No. 3101, 1/2-pt. thinner, $4.75 retail; No. 3100, 1/2-pt. primer, $5.50 retail) is the recommended primer for Coverite fabric coverings. Primex provides great adhesion so when you remove masking tape the paint job stays down. It's ultra light, smooth, and quick-drying. It's also easy to apply and easy to sand. You can put any paint on top. It's the only primer to use on Coverite Super, Silkspun, and Permagloss. It's also great on wood, tissue, silk, dacron, and nylon.

COVERITE

Bodyshop WindowMask for Lexan Bodies (No. 275, $2.25 per sheet, retail) comes in a handy 6-in. x 12-1/2-in. sheet—enough for all the windows on the average car. Instead of cutting individual strips from a roll, with WindowMask you can cut the whole window out in one piece. Instructions are easy, and when properly applied, paint won't leak underneath, producing razor sharp edges.

COVERITE

Bodyshop Lexan Car Paint (Nos. 100 - 112, $3.75 per can) comes in a man-sized 6-oz. can and features a patented nozzle that puts out a misty pattern like a spraygun. "Sticks to Lexan like bugs on flypaper!" Works wonders with BodyShop WindowMask, Pinstripes, Presto Trim, and other Coverite Graphics that stick to inside or outside of Lexan.

DU-BRO PRODUCTS

Mix-It Stix (No. 346, pack of 25, $.75 retail) are handy to have when mixing paint or epoxy—inexpensive, too.

DURO ART IND., INC.

Our *Duro Gold* (Golden Taklon) Brushes (No. 6015, $565.50 retail) has the snap, spring, and shape retention of red sable, and the resilience, ease of cleaning, and durability of synthetic hair. Duro Gold Brushes are manufactured with the finest seamless nickel plated ferrules and thick hardwood handles.

DURO ART IND., INC.

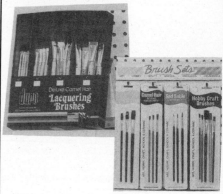

Fast selling all purpose *Brushes* (No. 5640. $163.20 retail; No. 5620, $114.00 retail) for detail, broad coverage, and doping. Quality products and very low retail sill add to your sales. We also have a complete line of artists materials available. Call or write for catalog.

KARODEN HOBBY PRODUCTS

Flex-Mask (No. 101 for 1/4-in., $3.50 retail; No. 102 for 1/8-in., $3.25 retail) is ultra-flexible masking tape that lays flat around 1/2-in. radius curves. It's extremely thin, low tack, and one roll does many ships. It was used by the best-finish winner at Toledo and WRAMS shows.

SIG MANUFACTURING CO.

Plastinamel (4 oz., $3.49 retail; 8 oz., $5.79 retail) is high-gloss fuel-proof paint for molded foam. It requires no filler so it can be painted directly onto foam. Eight brilliant colors are available.

SIG MANUFACTURING CO.

Sig Supercoat Dope ($2.59 - $32.99 retail) is the traditional painted finish for models and full-scale aircraft. It provides a durable fuel-proof finish when used in conjunction with a plain cloth or paper covering material. Sig Supercoat Butyrate Dope comes in 30 brilliant high-gloss colors, regular clear, Lite-Coat low-shrink clear, and Flat-Coat non-glossy clear. All Supercoat Dopes can be brushed or sprayed with excellent results. Available in 4-oz., 8-oz., pint, quart, and gallon sizes.

SUPPORT YOUR LOCAL HOBBY SHOP.

SIG MANUFACTURING CO.

Skybrite ($4.65 - $15.45 retail) paint system features two perfectly matched products: super-easy-sanding white primer and seven brilliant high-gloss color paints. Convenient, one-part formulas are developed especially for model use. Additional features include beautiful finish, fuel-proof, fast-drying, tack-free in 20-30 minutes, high-gloss deep brilliant colors, excellent coverage with fewer coats and less weight, brushes beautifully, simple to make invisible repairs, and an exceptional dollar value.

Brushes

DU-BRO PRODUCTS

These *Epoxy Brushes* (No. 345, pack of six, $1.20 retail) are a must for spreading epoxy and resin glue evenly. They're also ideal for engine cleaning.

DURO ART IND., INC.

Our *Duro Gold (Golden Taklon) Brushes* (No. 6015, $565.50 retail) has the snap, spring, and shape retention of red sable, and the resilience, ease of cleaning, and durability of synthetic hair. Duro Gold Brushes are manufactured with the finest seamless nickel plated ferrules and thick hardwood handles.

DURO ART IND., INC.

Fast selling all purpose *Brushes* (No. 5640. $163.20 retail; No. 5620, $114.00 retail) for detail, broad coverage, and doping. Quality products and very low retail sill add to your sales. We also have a complete line of artists materials available. Call or write for catalog.

Glues

Adhesives

DAVE BROWN PRODUCTS

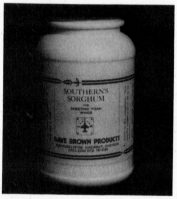

Sorghum Contact Adhesive (7 oz., $3.25 retail) is for sheeting foam wings and tail surfaces. It's extremely lightweight, has tremendous adhesion, ease of manipulation, and a very noncritical ''open'' time of 30 minutes to 3-4 hours.

DU-BRO PRODUCTS

Duco Cement (No. 6244, 1 3/4 oz. net wt., $2.00 retail) is the world-famous household cement for china, glass, wood, metal, leather, and paper. Dries fast, clear, and tough.

DU-BRO PRODUCTS

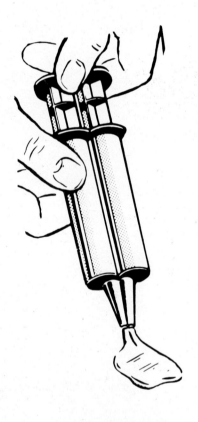

Dev-Tube (No. S-208, $3.39 retail) is 5-minute epoxy in the revolutionary two-in-one dispenser. Just snip off end of double nozzle and push out equal parts of epoxy and hardener, automatically, then mix and apply. When finished, close nozzles for future use with special cap. This epoxy is famous for super-fast repairs even in thin films and at low temperatures.

DU-BRO PRODUCTS

This *Clear Silicone Rubber* (No. S-250, $4.03 retail) is a clear, waterproof silicone adhesive/sealant. It won't crack or dry out. Flexible from -75° to 500° F.

DU-BRO PRODUCTS

Devcon (No. S-209 for 5-minute, No. S-33 for 30-minute, $11.94 each, retail), the 5-minute and 30-minute epoxy, comes in big 4 1/2-oz. non-breakable squeeze bottles. This is the ideal modeler's cement. It bonds all metals, wood, fiberglass, and most plastics. It's clear and fuel proof with a 9-oz. combined weight.

DU-BRO PRODUCTS

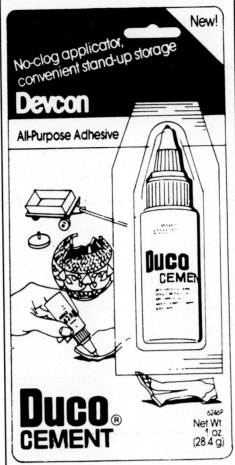

World-famous *Duco® Cement* (No. 6246P, 1 oz. net wt., $2.03 retail) in a new no-clog applicator bottle, is easy-open, easy-close with convenient stand-up storage. Dries clear.

DU-BRO PRODUCTS

Duco Model Cement (No. 9022, 3/4 oz. net wt., $1.61 retail) is ideal for polystyrene plastic models and toys. For the hobbyist it's fast! It's easy! Dries clear.

Support Your Model Boating National Organizations. Join *AMYA*, *IMPBR* or *NAMBA* Today!

DU-BRO PRODUCTS, INC.

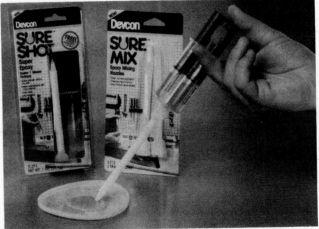

The *Devcon Sure Shot 1 Minute Epoxy* (No. S-211, $4.99 retail) and the *Sure Mix Epoxy Mixing Nozzles* (No. S-212, $2.39 retail) give the modeler the epoxy strength without the wait. The package comes complete with a syringe type applicator with free automatic mixing nozzle.

DU-BRO PRODUCTS

The *Plastic Welder* (No. S-720, 1 oz. net wt., $4.28 retail) is a truly unique plastic bonding system for most R/C car parts. Makes an extremely tough bond between plastic to plastic, plastic to metal, and metal to metal. Creates a permanent bond is 15 to 30 minutes.

DU-BRO PRODUCTS

Super-Lock (No. S-360, $2.19 retail) keeps nuts and bolts from getting loose but lets you remove them when you need to. Cures in the absence of air (an anaerobic).

DU-BRO PRODUCTS

Contact Cement (No. S-180, 1 oz., $1.94 retail) is a super adhesive for making a permanent bond without pressure or clamps. It dries to a thin film in 30 seconds and to a heavy coat in 10 minutes. It bonds to wood, rubber, metal, plastics, and paper.

CARL GOLDBERG MODELS, INC.

Model Magic Filler (No. 795, 8 fl. oz., $5.99 retail) is a stronger, lightweight, non-shrinking filler to use with all modeling woods, foam, and fiberglass. When it's dry, it's carvable, sandable, and paintable.

CARL GOLDBERG MODELS, INC.

The new *Jet-Tips* (No. 788, $1.49 retail) provide the modeler with pinpoint precision gluing, in addition to a more controlled flow of JET glue, and extended reach. The clear, clog-resistant tip, snugly clings to the existing applicator using a matched taper fit-up. This permits hassle-free removal when you wish to return to the original tip. The Jet-Tips fit all JET bottle sizes. The tip also fits the DISSOLVE bottle for uncompromising application of glue joints no longer required. The Jet-Tips are available 6 per package.

HOBBY DYNAMICS DISTRIBUTORS

This industrial-quality *6-Minute Epoxy* (No. HDDR1000, $9.95 retail) has proven itself to be a very good seller as well as an exceptional value. With its six minute cure time and superior bonding strength this glue has hundreds of uses. (2 part, 2-4.5 oz. bottles.)

SIG MANUFACTURING CO.

Sig-Ment (2 oz., $1.79 retail; 4 oz., $2.59 retail; 8 oz., $4.99 retail; pint, $6.99 retail) is fuel-proof/waterproof model airplane cement, specially formulated to combine extra strength with fast drying. Provides deep penetration, permanent bond, and good adhesion to ABS plastic.

SIG MANUFACTURING CO.

Sig Bond Adhesive (No. SB-001, 2 oz., $1.79 retail; No. SB-002, 4 oz., $2.99 retail; No. SB-003, 8 oz., $4.49 retail; No. SB-004, 16 oz., $6.49 retail) is especially recommended for structural assembly. Completely dope-proof and lacquer-proof. Sands clean, provides extra-strong joints, and is rapid drying.

SIG MANUFACTURING CO.

Core-Bond (No. CB-001, $8.50 retail) is a completely different type adhesive for bonding balsa, ply, and plastic skins to foams. It's exceptionally light and has good bonding characteristics. It doesn't attack foam in any way.

Glues

——— Cyanoacrylates

ART GROSS ENTERPRISES

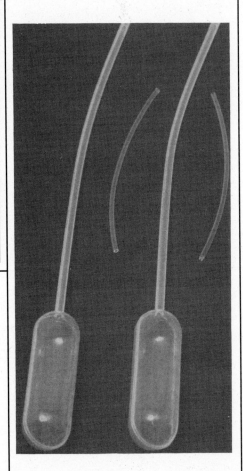

You'll be a-mazed!! At the savings in C/A glue! Art Gross' *Drop-Et* "A Non-Pluggable C/A Glue Dispenser" lays on a tiny line of CA without runs, drips, fuss, or muss. Your building projects will look like a MILLION, and no plugging.

CARL GOLDBERG MODELS, INC.

Slo-Jet (No. 772, 1/2 oz., $3.49 retail; No. 773, 1 oz., $5.29 retail; No. 776, 2 oz., $9.99 retail) is a high-quality extra-thick cyanoacrylate adhesive. It allows extra time to insure components are positioned properly before it bonds permanently. Once satisfied with proper positioning, bonding time can be accelerated rapidly with a fine spray application from CG Jet Set.

CARL GOLDBERG MODELS, INC.

Jet Instant Glue (No. 761, 1/4 oz., $2.79 retail; No. 762, 1/2 oz., $3.49 retail; No. 763, 1 oz., $5.29 retail; No. 764, 2 oz., $9.99 retail) is the best buy in high-quality cyanoacrylate adhesives. It provides high strength, bonds in seconds, and lots of modelers say the new bottle design doesn't clog as often.

CARL GOLDBERG MODELS, INC.

Jet Set (No. 776, $4.99 retail) is a 3-oz. aerosol spray accelerant for all brands of cyanoacrylate adhesives.

CARL GOLDBERG MODELS, INC.

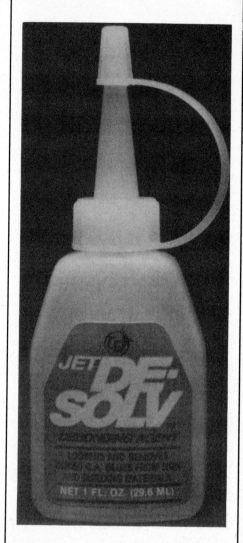

Jet De-Solv (No. 781, $3.29 retail) is for loosening and removing cyanoacrylate glues from skin and building materials. It comes in a 1-oz. size.

CARL GOLDBERG MODELS, INC.

Super Jet Instant Glue (No. 766, 1/4 oz., $2.79 retail; No. 767, 1/2 oz., $3.49 retail; No. 768, 1 oz., $5.29 retail; No. 769, 2 oz., $9.99 retail; No. 770, 4 oz., $17.99 retail) is a revolutionary instant glue—it has body like regular model cement. What a difference body makes! Now your joints don't have to be perfect—Super Jet fills in slight errors. Try it—and see for yourself why good modelers are excited about Super Jet—it makes a difference!

CARL GOLDBERG MODELS, INC.

Jet Pack (No. 789, $3.99/pack retail) includes accessory tips, spare cap, five extra-fine tips and 12 in. of medium-bore capillary tubing.

HOBBICO

Hobbico's *Bullet CA+* (No. HCAR3550, 1 oz., $4.59 retail; No. HCAR3650, 2 oz., $8.49 retail) is a thicker CA glue that can be used to fill small gaps.

HOBBICO

Bullet CA- (No. HCAR3570, 1 oz., $4.59 retail; No. HCAR3670, 2 oz., $8.59 retail) is a thick CA glue that has a slower curing time. This gives you a little more time to position the items you want to bond.

SIG MANUFACTURING CO.

Sig CA (Retail: See below) is a complete CA adhesive system developed especially for model use. Has all the features modelers want—high strength, low odor, fast bonding, and a long shelf life. Special tip design virtually eliminates tip clogging. The Sig line includes three different adhesives: CA Thin for fast penetrating action, CA Plus for general purpose construction, and CA Slow for gap filling and maximum working time. Also Kwik-Shot CA Accelerator for instant curing of all three Sig CA glues, and Debonder for removing cured CA glue from hands, clothing, and models.

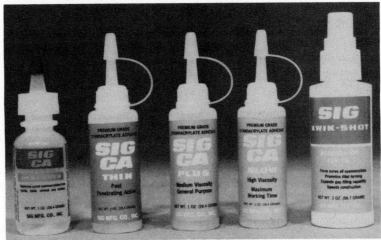

Sig CA Thin Formula
  No. CA-001 1/2 oz. $3.25 retail
  No. CA-002 1 oz. $4.95 retail
  No. CA-003 2 oz. $9.49 retail
Sig CA Plus—Medium Viscosity
  No. CA-010 1/2 oz. $3.25 retail
  No. CA-011 1 oz. $4.95 retail
  No. CA-012 2 oz. $9.49 retail
Sig CA Slow Formula
  No. CA-020 1 oz. $5.15 retail
  No. CA-021 2 oz. $9.99 retail
Sig Kwik-Shot CA Accelerator
  No. CA-030 2 oz. w/sprayer $3.95 retail
  No. CA-031 8 oz. Refill $6.95 retail
Sig CA Debonder
  No. CA-040 1 oz. $2.95 retail

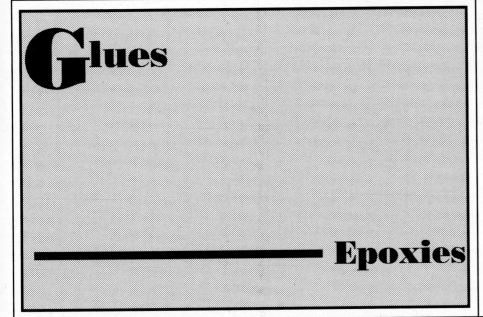

Glues

Epoxies

CARL GOLDBERG MODELS, INC.

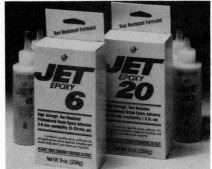

Formulated to withstand the high-vibration punishment of today's R/C environment, these state-of-the-art *Jet Epoxies* (No. 9106) even apply easier than ordinary brands. Besides producing stronger bonds with a wider variety of materials, Jet Epoxies are formulated to retain the perfect degree of elasticity to prevent vibration-caused failures.

DU-BRO PRODUCTS

Devcon 5-Minute Epoxy (No. S-205, 1 oz., $2.89 retail; No. S-206, 2 1/2 oz., $5.25 retail) is for super-fast repairs. It's been tried and true for modelers everywhere. It's the ideal model builder's cement. It features great strength, fast setting, and it's fuel-proof.

CARL GOLDBERG MODELS, INC.

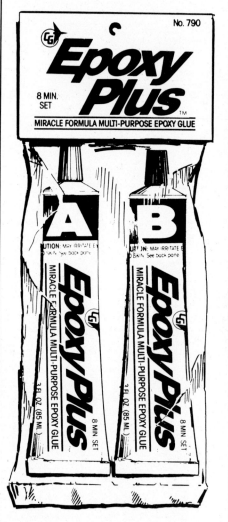

Epoxy Plus (No. 790, 6 fl. oz., $9.99 retail) is a lightweight, penetrating, and gap-filling, 8-min. epoxy glue which provides a high-strength bond for your favorite project (6 oz. is equivalent to 8 oz. of competitive products).

HOBBICO

Hobbico's *Bullet Epoxy* (No. HCAR3800, $6.95 retail; No. HCAR3900, $9.95 retail; No. HCAR3950, $9.95 retail) offers high-quality, excellent strength at a great value. Ideal for bonding high stress areas and fuel proofing, it can be used to bond dissimilar materials such as wood, plastic, metal, and ceramics and glass.

SIG MANUFACTURING CO.

This *Glass Cloth* ($5.00 - $11.95 retail) is top quality for all your modeling needs. Two sizes and four weights are available. 38-in. x 36-in.

No. GF-007 *Ultra-Light Weight* (.56 oz.) $5.95 retail

No. GF-003 *Light Weight* (.75 oz.) $5.50 retail

No. GF-001 *Regular Weight* (1.5 oz.) $5.25 retail

No. GF-002 *Heavy Weight* (6 oz.) $5.00 retail 38-in. x 72-in.

No. GF-008 *Ultra-Light Weight* (.56 oz.) $11.95 retail

No. GF-004 *Light Weight* (.75 oz.) $10.75 retail

No. GF-005 *Regular Weight* (1.5 oz.) $9.50 retail

No. GF-006 *Heavy Weight* (6 oz.) $9.25 retail

SIG MANUFACTURING CO.

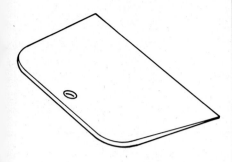

Epoxy Spreader (No. SH-678, $.75 retail) is handy and flexible—just what you need when working with fiberglass resin, epoxy glue, and fillers. Lay on a thin, smooth coat right where you want it!

SIG MANUFACTURING CO.

Glass Resin (No. GR-001, 8 oz., $4.95 retail; No. GR-002, pint, $7.25 retail; No. GR-003, quart, $11.75 retail) is a general purpose polyester resin to use with fiberglass cloth for molding your own cowlings, wheel pants, fuselage shells, boat hulls, etc.

SIG MANUFACTURING CO.

Finishing Resin (No. FR-001, pint, $6.95 retail; No. FR-002, quart, $11.50 retail) is a thinner version of Sig polyester Glass Resin designed for creating a glass-smooth base for an epoxy or enamel painted finish.

SIG MANUFACTURING CO.

These *Mixing Sticks* (No. SH-528, Pack of two, $.79 retail) are 6-in. long round wood sticks, handy for stirring paint and mixing epoxy or other two-part finishing products.

SIG MANUFACTURING CO.

These *Epoxy Brushes* (No. SH-534, Pack of six, $.99 retail) are 3/8 in.-wide nylon bristle brushes with metal handles that are handy for spreading epoxy glue, fiberglass resin, and any other liquid. They're also ideal for cleaning engines, and are economical enough to throw away. Metal handles.

SIG MANUFACTURING CO.

This *Epoxy Glue* (No. EG-001, 1 1/2 oz., $3.25 retail; No. EG-002, 3 oz., $4.25 retail; No. EG-003, 12 oz., $10.49 retail) has been the top choice of modelers for many years in areas where high strength is critical. The strongest bond available in a modeling adhesive, it bonds balsa, hardwood, metal, fiberglass, and plastic. It's fuel proof when dry and sets up in 2 hours.

SIG MANUFACTURING CO.

Sig Epoxolite Epoxy Putty (No. EP-001, 5 oz., $7.99 retail; No. EP-002, 8.75 oz., $12.99 retail) is light but strong, used for making wing fillets and repairs, and it doesn't shrink.

SIG MANUFACTURING CO.

Kwik-Set Epoxy (No. KS-001, 2 oz., $3.99 retail; No. KS-002, 4 oz., $6.39 retail; No. KS-003, 8 oz., $9.99 retail) is an exclusive formula developed especially for model building. Tough yet flexible when dry. Bonds balsa, hardwood, metal fiberglass, and plastic. Completely fuel proof. Sets up in 5 minutes, it's good for field repairs.

Hardware

Aircraft

AEROTREND PRODUCTS

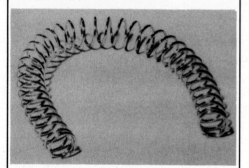

Each *"Ezeebend" Spring* (Pack of 6, $1.99 and up retail) is made of a 3" piece of chromated high-tensile closed-coil steel with the primary purpose of eliminating collapse of tubing in extreme bend situations. Order No. 1261 for 1/8" ID, No. 1262 for 1/4" ID, No. 1263 for 3/8" ID, No. 1264 for 1/2" ID, No. 1265 for 5/8" ID, and No. 1266 for 3/4" ID.

AEROTREND PRODUCTS

Ti-M-Ups (No. 1201 for small—12/pack, No. 1203 for large—8/pack; $1.29 retail) are reusable nylon ties for securing pressure lines, fuel lines, radio wires, etc. They have no sharp edges, are self-locking, and may be unlocked.

AEROTREND PRODUCTS

Stainless Steel Aircraft Nuts (Pack of 4, $.99 retail) are 18-8 insert nuts. They come in six sizes, four per pack. Order No. 2302 for 2-56, No. 2303 for 3-48, No. 2304 for 4-40, No. 2306 for 6-32, No. 2308 for 8-32, and No. 2310 for 10-32.

DU-BRO PRODUCTS

This *Nylon Wing Mounting Kit* (No. 159 for 10-32, pack of two sets, $1.75 retail) is for use in fastening wings to fuselage. Each 11-piece set includes nylon bolts and nylon threaded blocks.

DU-BRO PRODUCTS

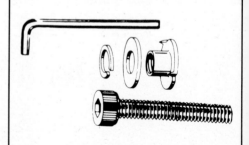

This *Socket-Head Bolt/Blind Nut Set* (No. 129 for 4-40, No. 130 for 6-32; $1.50/set retail) consists of 17 pieces made of high strength steel and includes four each of bolts, flat washers, lock washers, blind nuts, plus an Allen wrench.

DU-BRO PRODUCTS

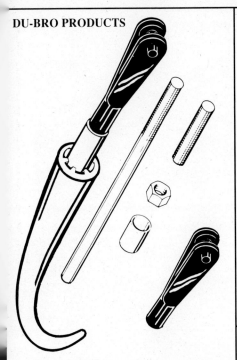

These *Lazer Rods* (No. 500, $4.00 retail; No. 501, $4.50 retail) are the result of a highly controlled process through which Du-Bro stabilized the push rod material so heat and cold have very little effect on trim settings. In fact, in our tests we found 75% less growth or shrinkage than any push rod on the market. Again, Du-Bro's technology has made a good product even better. Just look at these features! * The red outer housing has 6-contact points giving the inner push rod a smooth positive control. * Inner push rod is translucent in color to better match your color scheme and give your model a more realistic look. * 4-in. threaded rod slides inside inner push rod to give a stiffer exit to control horn. * Two push rods per package—available in 36-in. and 48-in. lengths. * All hardware included. * Just the right flexibility and strength for the perfect installation.

DU-BRO PRODUCTS

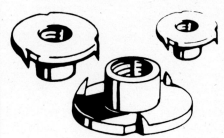

These *Blind Nuts* (Nos. 133, 134, 135 and 136: set of four, $.60 retail; No. 347, $.79 retail) can be used on 1/8-in. or thicker plywood without sticking through. Order No. 133 for 2-56, No. 134 for 3-48, No. 135 for 4-40, No. 136 for 6-32, and No. 347 for 8-32.

DU-BRO PRODUCTS

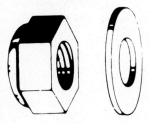

These *Bolt Sets with Lock Nuts* ($.80-$.90 retail) are aircraft quality and made of high strength steel. Included are four each (total of 12) of bolts, flat washers, and lock nuts. Order No. 174 for 1/2-in. 2-56, No. 175 for 3/4-in., No. 176 for 1-1/4-in. 4-40, and No. 177 for 1-1/4-in. 6-32.

DU-BRO PRODUCTS

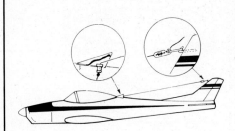

This *Antenna Cowling, Hook, and Keeper* (No. 349, $1.15 retail) is the perfect cowling for antenna exit because it carefully exits the antenna through a radiused bushing giving your airplane that finished look. A completely adjustable wire keeper and hook lets you fasten any length antenna on any size airplane.

DU-BRO PRODUCTS

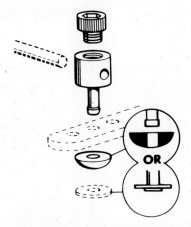

Heavy Duty E/Z Connector (Steel) (No. 489, $1.25 retail; No. 490, $1.50 retail) for those tough connections. Made of steel for a lock-tight grip. Two nylon snap-ons included, or if you prefer, just peen on washer for a permanent installation. Hex head screw for more torque. Order No. 489 for Heavy Duty E/Z Con-nector (Steel) (2/pkg), No. 490 for Heavy Duty 4-40 E/Z Connector (Steel) (2/pkg).

DU-BRO PRODUCTS

This *Threaded Stud Driver* (No. 504, $2.95 retail) has a unique design that takes the hassle out of threading studs and threading threaded rods into plastic push rods (such as Du-Bro Lazer Rods and other push rods on the market). To use, simply thread your stud or rod into either the 4-40 or 2-56 end of the driver until it bottoms out, then thread rod/stud into plastic push rod until desired length is reached and finally, back off driver. It's fast and easy! No more damaging threads with pliers.

DU-BRO PRODUCTS

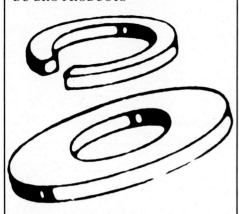

Flat/Split Washers (Pack of 8, $.50 retail). Flat Washers: Order No. 321 for -2, No. 323 for -4, No. 325 for -6, No. 327 for -8. Split Washers: Order No. 322 for -2, No. 324 for -4, No. 326 for -6, and No. 328 for -8.

DU-BRO PRODUCTS

Socket-Head Cap Screw (All 4/pack; Retail: Nos. 309, 310, 311, and 312, $.69; No. 313, $.79; No. 314, $.89; No. 315, $.69; No. 316, $.79; No. 317, $.89; No. 318, $.69; No. 319, $.79; and No. 320, $1.10). Order No. 309 for 2-56x1/4 (10/pack); No. 310 for 2-56x1/2 (8/pack); No. 311 for 2-56x3/4 (6/pack); 1-in. sizes: No. 312 for 4-40 (10/pack), No. 315 for 6-32 (10/pack), and No. 318 for 8-32 (8/pack); 1-1/4-in. sizes: No. 313 for 4-40 (8/pack), No. 316 for 6-32 (8/pack), and No. 319 for 8-32 (4/pack); 1-1/2-in. sizes: No. 314 for 4-40 (6/pack), No. 317 for 6-32 (6/pack), and No. 320 for 8-32 (4/pack).

DU-BRO PRODUCTS

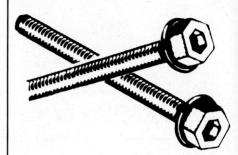

These *Nylon Wing Bolts* (No. 142 for 2-in. 1/4-20, and No. 164 for 2-in. 10-32; pack of four, $1.10/pack retail) are fitted on the outside hex head by a glow plug/prop nut wrench and on the inside socket by a 3/16-in. Allen wrench. Both provide safe, non-slip ways to secure or loosen wing bolts.

DU-BRO PRODUCTS

These *Nylon Insert Lock Nuts* (Nos. 168, 169, 170, 171 and 329: $.65 retail) are aircraft quality. Packs are 12 pieces. Order No. 168 for 2-56, No. 169 for 3-48, No. 170 for 4-40, No. 171 for 6-32, and No. 329 for 8-32.

DU-BRO PRODUCTS

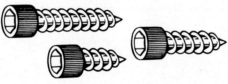

These *Socket Head Sheet Metal Screws* (Nos. 380-390, $1.25 each (8/pkg.), retail) are fully threaded and have more applications than wood screws. The non-slip socket head makes hard-to-get-at places easy! Perfect for mounting servos, landing gear straps, motor mounts, etc. Available in 11 sizes. Order No. 380 for No. 2 x 3/8-in., No. 381 for No. 2 x 1/2-in., No. 382 for No. 4 x 1/2-in., No. 383 for No. 4 x 3/4-in., No. 384 for No. 4 x 1-in., No. 385 for No. 6 x 1/2-in., No. 386 for No. 6 x 3/4-in., No. 387 for No. 6 x 1-in., No. 388 for No. 8 x 1/2-in., No. 389 for No. 8 x 3/4-in., and No. 390 for No. 8 x 1-in.

DU-BRO PRODUCTS

This *Socket-Head Bolts with Lock Nuts Set* (No. 178 for 4-40, and No. 179 for 6-32; $1.50/set retail) is aircraft quality. Sets include four each of nuts, bolts, flat washers, and lock nuts. They're 1-in. long and made of high strength steel.

DU-BRO PRODUCTS

These *1/4 Scale Turnbuckles* (No. 300, $7.25/pair retail) are nickel plated. They not only look good, they're fully functional. When attached to your guy wires (flying wires), they add a working touch of class.

DU-BRO PRODUCTS

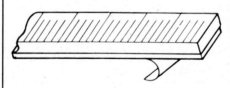

These *Kwik Stik Lead Weights* (No. 351, Pack of two, $2.90 retail) are perfect for adding extra weight to planes, trains, boats, pine wood derby cars, etc. Strong stick tape is on back for easy installation. There are 1/20-oz. and 1/4-oz. increments.

DU-BRO PRODUCTS

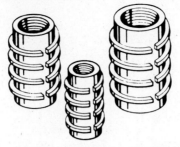

This *Hook & Loop Mounting Material* (No. 348, $3.00 retail) is a super tough material that sticks like glue. Adhesive back on one side is for easy mounting. It's good for mounting receivers, batteries, and other unlimited uses.

DU-BRO PRODUCTS

These brass *Threaded Inserts* (Nos. 391, 392 and 393, $1.25 retail; No. 394, $1.75 retail; No. 395, $2.25 retail) are the perfect way to put threads into wood and mount engines to wood mounting rails. Threaded Inserts make a simple and effective way to make wing hold downs. Can be used where blind nuts are hard to fit. Available in five sizes. Order No. 391 for 4-40, No. 392 for 6-32, No. 393 for 8-32, No. 394 for 10-32, and No. 395 for 1/4-20.

DU-BRO PRODUCTS

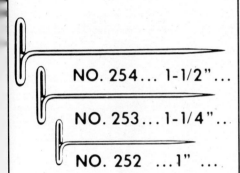

NO. 254... 1-1/2"...

NO. 253... 1-1/4"...

NO. 252 ...1" ...

These *Plated-Steel T-Pins* (Packs of 100, $2.25-$3.60 retail) are strong, smooth, and sharp. Order No. 252 for 1-in., No. 253 for 1-1/4-in., and No. 254 for 1-1/2-in.

DU-BRO PRODUCTS

This *Mounting Bolt/Blind Nut Set* (Nos. 125 and 126, $1.00 retail; Nos. 127 and 128 $1.10 retail) is for mounting engines. Included are four each of bolts, flat washers, and blind nuts. Order No. 125 for 1/2 2-56, No. 126 for 3/4 3-48, No. 127 for 1-1/4 4-40, and No. 128 for 1-1/4 6-32.

DU-BRO PRODUCTS

The *.050 Right Angle Ball Wrench* (No. 508, 1/pkg., $.60 retail) is 3-in. long and fits 4-40 socket set screws. Ideal for some of our wheel collars and other hardware set screws.

DU-BRO PRODUCTS

The *.050 Ball Wrench* (No. 507, 1/pkg., $2.00 retail) is the perfect wrench to fit our wheel collars and other hardware set screws.

DU-BRO PRODUCTS, INC.

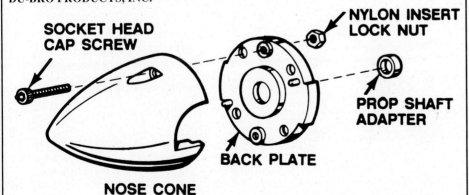

SOCKET HEAD CAP SCREW

NYLON INSERT LOCK NUT

PROP SHAFT ADAPTER

BACK PLATE

NOSE CONE

Spinners (No. 260 - 299, $2.79 - $6.00 retail) feature a nose cone that has 4 alignment pins which glide smoothly into a back plate. The nose cone is then held securely with 2 socket head screws that thread into 2 nylon insert lock nuts which are press fitted into the back plate. It's easy...simple...and safe. Available in 7 sizes: 1-1/2", 1-3/4", 2", 2-1/4", 2-1/2", 2-3/4", and 3". Four mirror finish colors—black, white, red, and yellow. Each spinner comes with 4 shaft adapters: 6mm, 1/4", 7mm, and 5/16" shafts.

CARL GOLDBERG MODELS, INC.

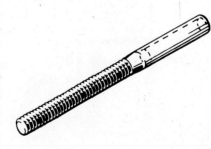

This *1/16" Threaded Coupler* (No. 359, TC116, pack of 2, $.89 retail) is made by a different manufacturing method from other couplers, creating a stronger unit where the thread ends, reducing potential breakage where the thread adjoins the body. Two per package, for joining 1/16-in. wire to clevis.

CARL GOLDBERG MODELS, INC.

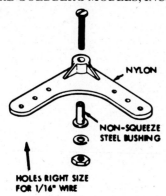

This *Aileron Bellcrank* (No. 420, $.99 retail) has steel bushing of proper size, so crank can be screwed firmly in place without binding. No electrical noise—all metal parts are screwed tightly together. Two cranks, etc., per pkg.

CARL GOLDBERG MODELS, INC.

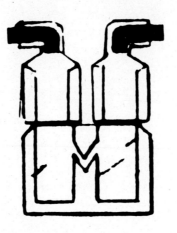

This *20-Amp Fuse* (No. 677/FF, $1.99/two, retail) is for use with Turbo 500 motor assembly and other comparable connectors.

HAYES PRODUCTS

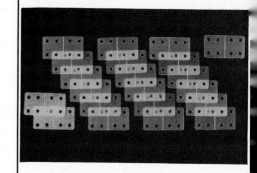

Hinges (Retail: See your dealer).

SIG MANUFACTURING CO.

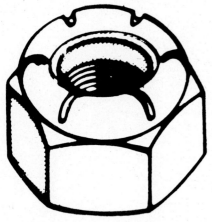

These steel *Aircraft Lock Nuts* ($.85/eight, retail) come with a special nylon insert to help prevent loosening from vibration. Sizes available are 4-40, 6-32, 8-32, and 10-32.

SIG MANUFACTURING CO.

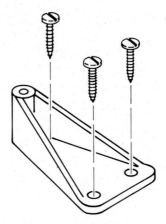

This *Nylon Tailwheel Bracket* (No. SH-132, $.75 retail) provides a convenient method of attaching a steerable tailwheel. It comes complete with mounting screws.

SIG MANUFACTURING CO.

These *Sheet Metal Screws* (Pack of 10, $.69-$.85 retail) are for mounting engines to wood engine mounts. Order No. 1 x 3/8, No. 2 x 3/8, No. 2 x 1/2, No. 2 x 3/4, No. 4 x 3/8, No. 4 x 1/2, and No. 6 x 3/4.

SIG MANUFACTURING CO.

These *Blind Mount Nuts* (Sizes 4-40, 6-32, Pack of four, $.69 retail; Size 10-32 and 8-32, Pack of four, $.79 retail) are available in four-piece packs in size 4-40, 6-32, 8-32, and 10-32.

SIG MANUFACTURING CO.

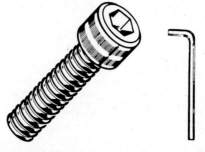

Socket Head Bolts (Pack of four w/ wrench, $.85 - $1.10 retail).
   No. SH-103 4-40 x 3/8 in. $.85 retail
   No. SH-104 4-40 x 3/4 in. $.85 retail
   No. SH-670 4-40 x 1 in. $.85 retail
   No. SH-582 6-32 x 3/4 in. $.85 retail
   No. SH-105 6-32 x 1 in. $.85 retail
   No. SH-106 8-32 x 1-1/2 in. $1.10 retail
   No. SH-684 10-32 x + $1.10 retail

SIG MANUFACTURING CO.

Nylon Wing Bolts (Pack of four, $.65-.85 retail) are available in a variety of sizes:
   No. SH-171 4-40 x 1/2 in. $.65 retail
   No. SH-172 4-40 x 1 in. $.65 retail
   No. SH-173 8-32 x 1 in. $.65 retail
   No. SH-530 10-32 x 1 in. $.65 retail
   No. SH-526 1/4-20 x 5/8 in. $.65 retail
   No. SH-174 1/4-20 x 1 in. $.85 retail
   No. SH-175 1/4-20 x 1 1/2 in. $.85 retail
   No. SH-520 1/4-20 x 2 in. $.85 retail
   No. SH-687 10-32 x 1 1/4-in. $.65 retail

SIG MANUFACTURING CO.

This *Heavy Duty Rudder Control Horn* (No. SH-716, $1.49 retail) is designed for cable control systems in giant-size models. Molded of super-tough nylon. It's ideal for attaching tailwheel steering springs to rudder.

SIG MANUFACTURING CO.

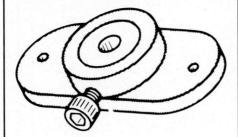

Wheel Pant Mounts ($2.95 - $3.95 per pair, retail) are available if four sizes:
No. SH-726 for 1/8 in. Axles, $2.95 per pair, retail;
No. SH-727 for 5/32 in. Axles, $2.95 per pair, retail;
No. SH-720 for 3/16 in. Axles, $3.95 per pair, retail; and
No. SH-721 for 1/4 in. Axles, $3.95 per pair, retail.

SIG MANUFACTURING CO.

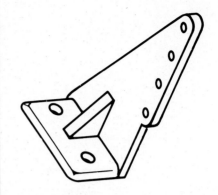

These *Heavy Duty Nylon Control Horns* (No. SH-694, Pack of two, $.99 retail) were designed for Giant models. They are extra thick for strength but still allow 4-40 clevises to latch on completely.

SIG MANUFACTURING CO.

Wing Cushions (No. SH-545 for 1/8-in. x 3/8-in., $1.35 retail; No. SH-546 for 1/4-in. x 1/4-in., $1.45 retail) are made from this white fuel-proof self-adhesive foam tape. When applied to fuselage wing cut-outs it creates a cushion for the wing which saves the finish and seals the fuselage interior.

SIG MANUFACTURING CO.

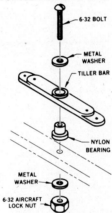

This *Heavy Duty Tiller Bar* (No. SH-715, $1.49 retail) is designed for cable control systems in giant-size models. Molded of durable nylon, it is the perfect companion to the Sig Rudder Control Horn.

VORTAC MFG. CO., INC.

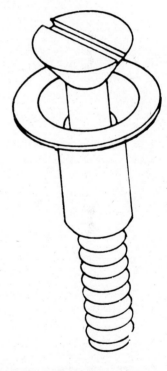

These *Flush Head Captive Wing Bolts* ($2.98/set retail; Replacement bolts, 4-pc pack, $1.98 retail) are aircraft-type, flush 2 1/4-in.-20 head bolts that stay in the wing after it's removed from the fuselage. They're easily removable, if desired. With these, there are no more unsightly bolt heads sticking out of the wing. They're easily installed in the aircraft you're now flying. Made of nylon, these bolts can be easily cut to any length. A large contact area eliminates crushing. The thread length is controlled to provide 3/8-in. free vertical travel. This aids in aligning the bolts and eliminates jacking tendencies. A complete 6-piece wing mounting set includes two bolts, two sleeves, and two 2 1/4-in.-20 blind nuts. Replacement bolts are also available.

C.B. TATONE, INC.

The *Engine Test Stand* (No. 51616, $16.65 retail) is made of cast aluminum for strength and heat dissipation. The test stand is fully adjustable to test engines up to size .80 and includes steel restraining pins and bench mounting screws.

C.B. TATONE, INC.

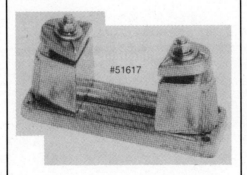

The *Giant Size Engine Test Stand* (No. 51617, $27.50 retail) will accommodate engines up to size 1.3. It is made of cast aluminum for strength and heat dissipation. It has a large engine base and mounting supports with all required hardware.

Hardware

—— Pushrods, Clevises Hinges & Linkages

DU-BRO PRODUCTS

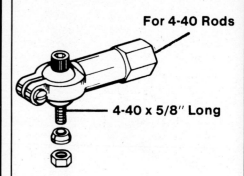

For 4-40 Rods

4-40 x 5/8" Long

This *Heavy-Duty 4-40 Ball Link* (No. 259, $1.60 retail) is perfect for any 1/4-scale application. Each five-piece kit includes one ball with 4-40 thread, one self-threading 4-40 nylon socket, one 4-40 stud, one 3/32 ID brass coupler, and one 4-40 lock nut.

DU-BRO PRODUCTS

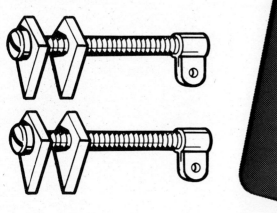

Our new *Adjustable Control Horn* (No. 493, $1.75 retail) mounts between two molded nylon pads for a strong solid mount. A 1-1/2-in. 5-40 bolt allows you the full range of height adjustment. Two to a package.

DU-BRO PRODUCTS

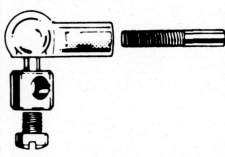

These *Aileron Horn Wire Ball Links* (No. 189, $2.25 retail) enable you to change old strip aileron connectors to ball link control. They're useful as dual take-off connectors, too. Each eight-piece set includes two horn wire ball links for 3/32-in.-dia. wire, two self-threading nylon sockets, two threaded couplers 3/4-in. long 1/16-in. ID with 3/8-in. 2-56 threads, and two 4-40 screws.

DU-BRO PRODUCTS

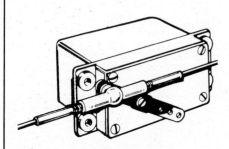

This *Aileron Connector Ball Link* (No. 183, $1.35 retail) is a five-piece set. It includes one two-way/self-threading nylon socket, two threaded couplers 3/4-in. long with 3/8-in. 2-56 threads for up to .072 wire, one 1/16-in.-dia. ball threaded for 0-80, and one 0-80 nut.

DU-BRO PRODUCTS

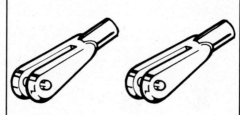

These sure-lock *Nylon Kwik-Links* (No. 122, Pack of two, $.45 retail) are the same size as Du-Bro's steel kwik-links. They're self-threading nylon for use with 2-56 rods or threaded couplers.

DU-BRO PRODUCTS

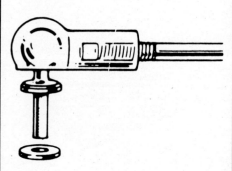

This *Rivit Ball Link* (No. 182, $1.25 retail) is ideal for throttle hook-ups. Each four-piece set includes one steel ball with pin and washer for peening on, one self-threading nylon socket, one threaded coupler 3/4-in. long with 3/8-in. 2-56 threads for up to .072 wire.

DU-BRO PRODUCTS

These *Nylon Bearings* (No. 124, $1.10/four retail) are ideal for aileron and elevator linkage. They can also be used for tail-wheel mounting bracket with .093 3/32-in. wire.

DU-BRO PRODUCTS

These *Rigging Couplers* (No. 201, $1.65/ four retail) thread into Du-Bro steel Kwik-Links and are perfect for cable controls, flying wires, and other linkage requirements. They're strong enough for 1/4-scale applications. Specs: 7/8-in.-long, 2-56 thread, 1/32-in. eye.

DU-BRO PRODUCTS

These *Nylon Kwik Links with Rod* (No. 123, available 12/tube, $.45 each retail; No. 184, 5 pieces per skin-packed card, $2.05 retail) are on a 12-in./.072-dia. rod with 2/4-in. 2-56 threads.

DU-BRO PRODUCTS

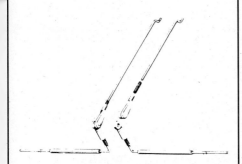

This *1/2A Aileron Linkage* (No. 231, $1.90/ set retail) is easy to install. It's lightweight and compact and made especially for 1/2A planes. Each set features Mini Kwik Links, spring thread couplers, nylon rod ends, brass tubes, and 1/16-in. wire.

DU-BRO PRODUCTS

These *Waterproof Pushrod Fittings* (No. 214, pack of 3, $1.50 retail) are nylon and are perfect for pushrod exits and seaplanes.

DU-BRO PRODUCTS

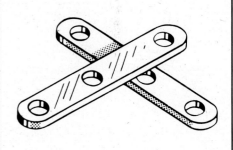

These *Nickel-Plated Steel Straps* (No. 302, pack of 2, $2.95 retail) are pre-drilled for 4-40 screws and bolts. They fit Du-Bro's No. 302 and No. 303 Rod Ends (1/16-in.). They can be bent and reworked to specific applications.

DU-BRO PRODUCTS

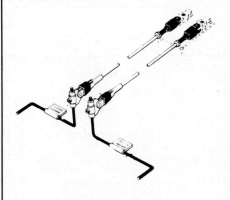

This *Strip Aileron Linkage* (No. 101, $3.90 retail) can be used on any high-, mid-, and low-wing plane. Each complete, fully adjustable 22-piece set includes all hardware for 2-56 thread spring steel Kwik Link and link guard for safety under heavy stress (3/32 horn wire).

DU-BRO PRODUCTS

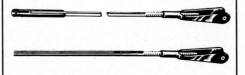

These *Kwik-Link with Rod* ($.65-$3.20 retail) assemblies are for any control linkage. They allow easy removal for on-field adjustments. Order No. 106 for 4-in./.072 3/4-in./ 2-56 split coupling sleeves (.$90, one per pack), No. 108 for 12-in./.072 3/4-in./2-56 sold individually ($.65, 12 per tube), No. 185 for 12-in./.072 3/4-in./2-56 skin-packed ($3.20, 5 per card), No. 306 for 12-in./.093 3/4-in./4-40 sold individually ($.95, 12 per tube).

DU-BRO PRODUCTS

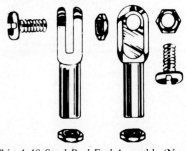

This *4-40 Steel Rod End Assembly* (No. 205, pack of 2, $7.50) is perfect for many 1/4-scale applications including strut attachments, flying wires, tail-fin stab bracing, and biplane aileron connectors. Each assembly includes two No. 303 Solder Rod Ends, two No. 302 Threaded Rod Ends, four No. 202 Steel Straps, two 12-in. .093-in. rods with 3/4-in. 4-40 thread, four 1/4-in. x 4-40 screws, and four 4-40 nuts.

DU-BRO PRODUCTS

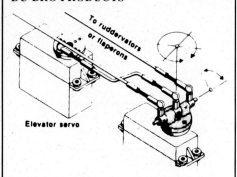

This *V-Tail Mixer* (No. 215, $6.25/set retail) is for V-tails, flying wings, and for rudder-vators and flaperon control. It utilizes ball links throughout for absolute no-play linkage. It's light, compact, and fully adjustable. Included are 3-32 collars and ball links with 4-40 threads, 2-56 threaded pushrod, and nylon self-threading sockets.

DU-BRO PRODUCTS

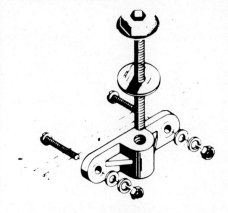

This *1/4-20 Wing-Bolt Set* (No. 256, $1.95/pack retail) provides an up-to-date way to fasten wings to fuselage. One 11-piece set includes nylon bolts and nylon threaded blocks. Each pack is two sets.

DU-BRO PRODUCTS

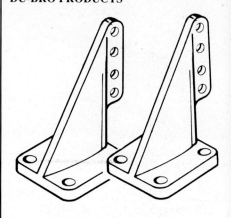

These *Large Scale T-Style Control Horns* (No. 366, pack of two, $1.55 retail) were aerodynamically designed with large-scale airplanes in mind. 1-3/8-in. long with four adjustment positions and four mounting holes.

DU-BRO PRODUCTS

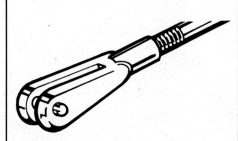

The *Mini Nylon Kwik-Link with Rod* ($.45-$2.05 retail) is Du-Bro's No. 228 nylon Mini Kwik-Link on a 12-in./.072 rod with 3/4/2-56 threads. Order No. 229 ($.45 individually or 18/tube), and No. 230 for skin packed ($2.05, 5 per card).

DU-BRO PRODUCTS

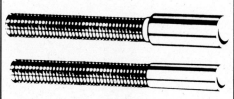

These *Threaded Couplers* ($.75-$1.90 per pack, retail) are designed for use with Du-Bro Kwik-Links and Mini Kwik-Links. Both styles are 3/4-in./2-56 threaded. Overall length is 1 1/4-in. Order No. 111 for 1/16-in. wire ($.75, two/pack), and No. 212 for .072 wire ($1.90, five/pack).

DU-BRO PRODUCTS

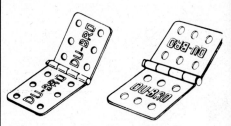

These *Nylon Hinges* ($1.29-$2.90 per pack, retail) are precision-molded, inspected, and assembled with locked-in hinge pin. They're flash-free and simple to install. Hinges have six holes on each side for maximum loading power. Order No. 116 for Standard–6/pack ($1.45), No. 117 for Standard–15/pack ($2.90), No. 118 for Mini–6/pack ($1.29), and No. 119 for Mini–15/pack ($2.35).

DU-BRO PRODUCTS

This *Engine Control Flex-Cable* (No. 165 for 20-in., $1.90 retail; No. 343 for 36-in., $2.50 retail; No. 344 for 48-in., $3.00 retail) provides the ultimate in control cable assembly. It's highly flexible, free-running, and adjustable at control horn. Comes in 20-in., 36-in., and 48-in. lengths. Each assembly includes one each of No. 228 Mini-Kwik-Link, No. 112 Solder Link, 2-56 Tthreaded Coupler, Flex-Cable, and Nylon Sleeve.

DU-BRO PRODUCTS

Each set of these *Strip Aileron Horn Wires with Bearings* (No. 104, $1.40/set retail) includes two .093 (3/32-in.) horn wires with nylon bearings attached. They're for use with hi-, mid-, and low-wing planes.

YOUR LOCAL HOBBY SHOP IS THERE TO HELP YOU SELECT THE BEST EQUIPMENT AND TO ANSWER YOUR QUESTIONS.

DU-BRO PRODUCTS

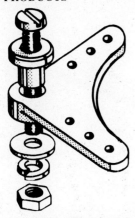

Each *90 Degree Nylon Bellcrank Assembly* (No. 167, two sets, $.90 retail) set includes a 90 degree nylon bellcrank with a brass bushing, a 4-40 x 3/4-in. screw, washer, lock washer, and 4-40 nut.

DU-BRO PRODUCTS

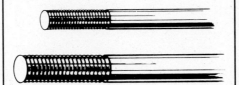

These *Threaded Rods* ($.30-$.65 retail) can be used with nylon or steel Kwik-Links or with ball links where extra-long pushrods are needed. They're bendable and strong. Rods are available with 3/4-in. thread on one end, .072 rods with 2-56 threads, .093 rods with 4-40 threads. Order No. 172 for 12-in./.072/2-56 ($.30, 36/tube), No. 173 for 30-in./.072 ($.50, 36/tube), No. 144 for 12-in./.093/4-40 ($.35, 24/tube), and No. 145 for 30-in./.093/4-40 ($.65, 24/tube).

DU-BRO PRODUCTS

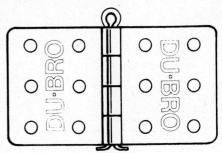

This *Heavy-Duty Nylon Hinge* (No. 257, 15 per pack, $4.25 retail) is built to take heavy loads and it's ideal for 1/4-scale. It's 3/4-in. wide and 1-3/8-in. long and .040 thick. A removable 3/64-in. Cotter Pin (No. 307, Replacement Cotter Pins, 10 per pack, $.65 retail) is included for maximum convenience and strength.

DU-BRO PRODUCTS

Socket Set Screw (Nos. 2168-2171, $1.00 each, retail). No. 2168, 3mm x 3 Socket Set Screw (4/pkg.); No. 2169, 3mm x 5 Socket Set Screw (4/pkg.); No. 2170, 4mm x 4 Socket Set Screw (4/pkg.); No. 2171, 4mm x 6 Socket Set Screw (4/pkg.).

DU-BRO PRODUCTS

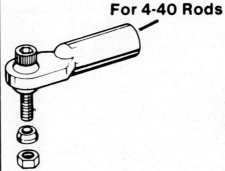

For 4-40 Rods

These high-quality *Swivel Ball Links for 4-40 Rods* (No. 369 for 2-56 THD, No. 497 for 4-40 THD; $1.25 retail) feature burnished brass swivel balls for smooth operation.

DU-BRO PRODUCTS

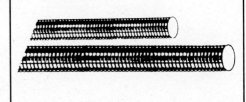

These *12-in. Fully Threaded Rods* (No. 378, 2-56, $.70 retail; No. 379, 4-40, $.85 retail) are stainless steel. They're perfect for making custom lengths to the size you need.

DU-BRO PRODUCTS

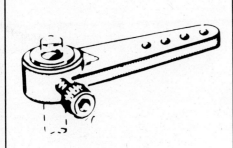

This *Nylon Steering Arm* (No. 166, $1.10/set retail) set is 1-1/4-in. A 5/32-in. nose gear wire attaches to the arm. A hardened socket-head screw passes through a heavy brass bushing.

DU-BRO PRODUCTS

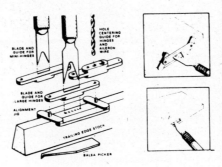

This *Kwik-Hinge Slotter* (No. 216, $2.25 retail) centers and guides to provide perfectly aligned slots for any hinge. Three blades fit No. 2 X-Acto handle. Three snap-on jig guides are included.

DU-BRO PRODUCTS

These *2-56 and 2mm Swivel Ball Links* (No. 367 for 2-56, No. 368 for 2mm; $1.25/set retail) are high quality ball links featuring burnished brass swivel balls for smooth operation.

PRICES AND SPECS ARE SUBJECT TO CHANGE

DU-BRO PRODUCTS

These *Ball Link Sockets* (No. 188, pack of four, $1.10 retail) are self-threading nylon. They're for use when switching radio to another plane. You can keep the same trim setting for future flights by leaving the nylon links on the pushrods. They're for use with up to .072 wire.

DU-BRO PRODUCTS

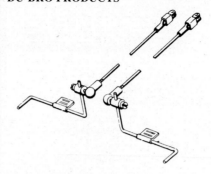

This *Strip Aileron* (No. 186, $4.00 retail) is a fully adjustable 16-piece aileron hook-up set featuring no play, no binding, and super precision. It eliminates differential throw and can be used on hi-, mid-, or low-wing planes utilizing strip ailerons. Includes all hardware for 2-56 thread and link guards for safety under heavy stress. Horn wire 3/32-in. dia.

DU-BRO PRODUCTS

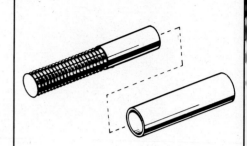

These *4-40 Threaded Couplers* (No. 336, set of two, $1.25 retail) are .093 dia. and designed for use with Du-Bro's No. 304 4-40 Spring Steel Kwik-Links. Thread length is 5/8-in., and overall length is 1-3/8-in. They're pre-tinned for easy soldering.

DU-BRO PRODUCTS

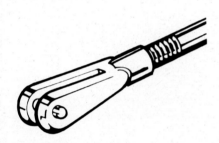

This *Ny-Steel Kwik-Rod Assembly* (No. 102, pack of one, $1.85 retail) is no-shrink, no-stretch, free-running, and fully adjustable at control horn. Each 31-in. assembly includes a No. 112 Solder Link, a No. 109 Kwik-Link, a flexible nylon sleeve, a 30-in. .072-in. rod with 3/4-in. 2-56 thread, and two link guards.

DU-BRO PRODUCTS

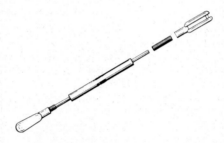

This *Mini Ny-Steel Pushrod Assembly* (No. 113, $2.00 retail) is perfect for 1/2A planes. It's no-shrink, no-stretch, free running, lightweight, flexible, and strong. Each 20-in. assembly includes four No. 228 Mini Kwik-Links, four No. 232 Spring Threaded Couplers, two 20-in. .047-in. wires, and two nylon sleeves.

DU-BRO PRODUCTS

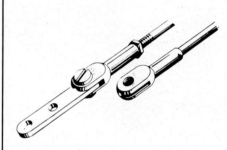

4-40 Steel Solder Rod Ends (No. 303, pack of two, $2.95 retail).

DU-BRO PRODUCTS

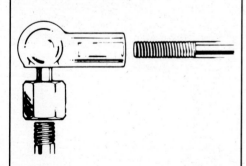

This *Bolt-On Ball Link* (No. 180, $1.25 retail) is a three-piece set. It readily adapts for many linkage hook-ups. Ball joint action eliminates binging. The ball is threaded for use with a 4-40 rod or bolt. The threaded coupler is 3/4-in. long with 3/8-in. 2-56 threads for up to .072 wire. Self-threading nylon sockets included.

DU-BRO PRODUCTS

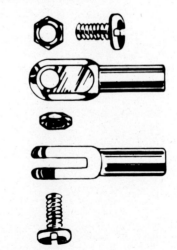

4-40 Threaded Rod Ends (No. 302, pack of two, $2.95 retail).

Safety is Contagious...

DU-BRO PRODUCTS

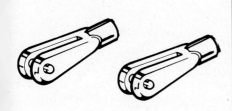

These sure-lock *Mini Nylon Kwik-Links* (No. 228, pack of two, $.45 retail) are perfect for 1/2A airplanes or any throttle hook-up. They're self-threading nylon for use with 2-56 rods or threaded couplers.

DU-BRO PRODUCTS

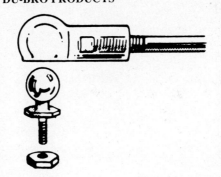

This *2-56 Threaded Ball Link* (No. 181, $1.25 retail) is a five-piece set. It is excellent for off-set steering, throttle, and servo hook-ups. Included: a 2-56 threaded ball, 3/4-in. coupler that's 3/8-in. 2-56 threaded for up to .072 wire, self-threading nylon socket, washer, and 2-56 nuts.

DU-BRO PRODUCTS

The *Spring Steel Kwik-Links Clevis* (No. 109 for 2-56/.072 with link guards, pack of two, $.90 retail; No. 304 for 4-40/.093 with spring keepers, pack of two, $1.20 retail) is a top-quality tried-and-true spring steel kwik-link. It's ideal for any controllinkage and hook-ups. It can be used with threaded rods or threaded couplers.

DU-BRO PRODUCTS

These *Solder Kwik-Links* (No. 112 for 2-56/.072 with link guards, pack of two, $.90 retail; No. 305 for 4-40/.093 with spring keepers, pack of two, $1.20 retail) make a strong, attractive, and easy-to-solder connector for servo or horn.

DU-BRO PRODUCTS

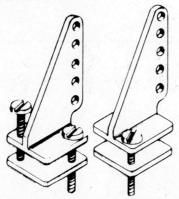

These *T-Style Nylon Control Horns* (No. 237, $.65/set retail) are 1-1/8-in. long and have five adjustment positions. Each set includes two control horns that are centered on base, two self-threading nut plates, and four 2-56 x 5/8-in. screws.

DU-BRO PRODUCTS

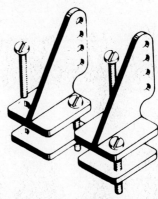

These *1/2A T-Style Nylon Control Horns* (No. 107, $.65/set retail) are 3/8-in.-long with four adjustment positions. Each set includes two control horns centered on base, two self-threading nut plates, and four 2-56 x 3/8-in. screws.

DU-BRO PRODUCTS

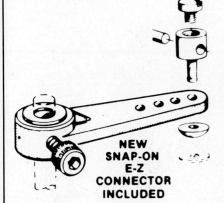

NEW SNAP-ON E-Z CONNECTOR INCLUDED

This *Steering Arm Assembly* (No. 155, $1.70/set retail) is 1-1/4-in. The nylon steering arm and brass bushing/set-screw fit a 5/32-in. nose gear wire. A snap-on E-Z connector is included.

DU-BRO PRODUCTS

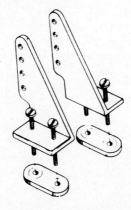

These *Nylon Control Horns* (No. 105, pack of two, $.65 retail) are 1-1/8-in. long with four adjustment positions. Included are one right and one left control horn, two self-threading nut plates, and four 2-56 x 5/8-in. screws.

DU-BRO PRODUCTS

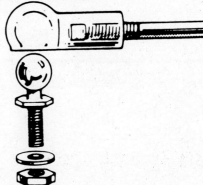

This *1/16 Threaded Ball Link* (No. 190, $1.25 retail) is a four-piece set. It fits perfectly in servo arm hole, bellcranks, nylon horns, and throttle arms. Included: one ball threaded for 0-80 (1/16-in.-dia. thread), one self-threading nylon socket, one 3/4-in.-long/1/16 ID threaded coupler with 3/8-in. 2-56 thread.

DU-BRO PRODUCTS

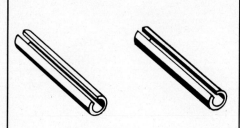

These *Split Coupling Sleeves* (No. 110, $.55/four retail) are .062-.078-dia. sleeves. They are pre-tinned for easy soldering. They're designed for use with Du-Bro Kwik-Links.

DU-BRO PRODUCTS

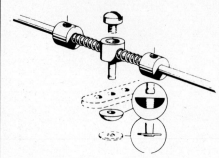

This *Control Over-Ride Servo Saver* (No. 120, $1.40 retail) is an adjustable, spring-action assembly. It protects the servo from shock and stalling. It's excellent for throttle or rudder nosewheel hook-ups. Lightweight and heavy-duty springs are included for .072-dia. control rods.

DU-BRO PRODUCTS

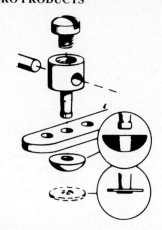

These *E-Z Connectors* (No. 121, $1.10 retail) include two of Du-Bro's nylon snap-ons in every pack. *Nylon Replacement Washers* (No. 308, 12/pack, $.60 retail) are also available.

DU-BRO PRODUCTS, INC.

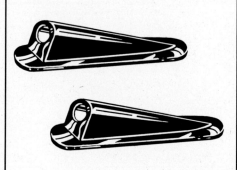

Try our new *Lazer Rod Push Rod Exits* (No. 502, 2/pkg., $1.95 retail) when outfitting your airplane with Lazer Rods. Our push rod exits give your model a nice clean look. Comes with two push rod exits per package.

DU-BRO PRODUCTS, INC.

Our new *Pull-Pull Systems* are available in two sizes, *2-56* (No. 517, $4.95, 1/pkg.) and *4-40* (No. 518, $5.95, 1/pkg.). They come complete with nylon coated cable and all mounting hardware. Ideal for pull-pull installations on rudder, elevator, tail wheels, etc.

DU-BRO PRODUCTS

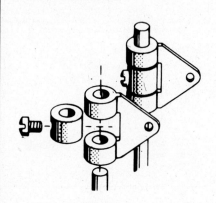

These *Strip Aileron Horn Connectors* (No. 103, $1.25/two retail) are for use with .093 wire. They simplify servo link hook-ups. Each pack includes 3-32 Dura-collars, two nylon horn connectors, and two slot-head screws.

CARL GOLDBERG MODELS, INC.

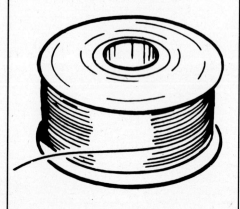

The *1/2-A Flying Line* (No. 431, $1.49/ spool, retail) on this 56-ft. spool is strong, minimum-stretch, Dacron thread. It's good for binding pushrods, sewing hinges, etc.

CARL GOLDBERG MODELS, INC.

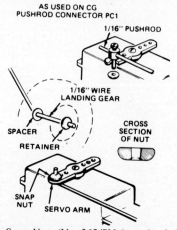

These *Snap-Nuts* (No. 362/SN-1, pack of six, $.79 retail) are used with 1/16-in. wire as a retainer or spacer. They're replacement for CG's Pushrod Connector (No. PC-1).

CARL GOLDBERG MODELS, INC.

Snap-Link and Mini Snap-Link (No. 340 for Snap-Link with rod—$.59 each; No. 341 for Mini Snap-Link with rod, $.59 each; No. 310 for Snap-Link without rod, $.59/two; No. 311 for Mini Snap-Link without rod, $.59/two; No. 350 for link rods, $1.49/six; No. 320-1 for valve pack of six links w/rod, $1.49) are truly safe links. Features include a tiny, 45 degree shoulder which snaps through the arm preventing accidental opening, a one-piece design so no separate pieces come apart.

CARL GOLDBERG MODELS, INC.

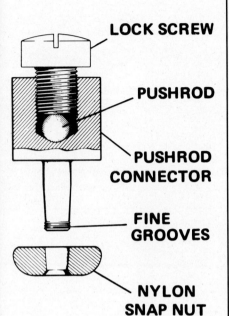

LOCK SCREW

PUSHROD

PUSHROD
CONNECTOR

FINE
GROOVES

NYLON
SNAP NUT

These new *Pushrod Connectors* (No. 360, two sets, $1.49 retail) require no soldering or preening. The tough nylon snap-nut snaps easily over fine grooves, yet requires a knife blade to pry off. They can be reused over and over. Once again, a CG accessory turns a tough, irritating job into a breeze.

CARL GOLDBERG MODELS, INC.

The design of *Klett Flex-Point Hinges* (No. 204 for large, No. 203 for small, package of 18, $1.40 retail) has a number of advantages: the web area, combined with the barbed shank, absorbs vibration and flutter permitting the hinge to flex only at the hinge line; the web allows visual axis alignment; it's easy to get the ailerons very close to the wing for maximum effect; simplest possible installation (drill holes, then apply any aliphatic resin glue or epoxy); and they're made from virgin poly-propylene.

CARL GOLDBERG MODELS, INC.

This *Aileron Coupler* (No. 363/AC1, $1.19 retail) is a simple way, at last, to couple conventional aileron pushrods to your servo output arm. The diagram shows how it's done. The coupler can be used for steerable nosegear linkage and throttle linkage. It features 1/16-in. I.D. brass tube, nylon coupler, lock screw, adjusting screw, and mini-snap.

CARL GOLDBERG MODELS, INC.

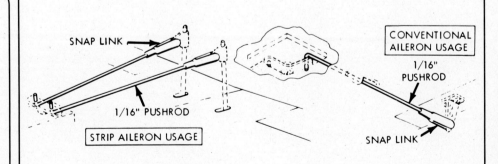

SNAP LINK

1/16" PUSHROD

STRIP AILERON USAGE

CONVENTIONAL
AILERON USAGE

1/16"
PUSHROD

SNAP LINK

These are *True 1/16-in. Pushrods* (No. 351/AP-1, $1.99/pair retail). Now you can stop drilling out your aileron servo output arms. These aileron Pushrods are made of 1/16-in. wire and feature two of Carl Goldberg Models' patented Snap-Links and two 7-in. rods. Modelers say this product has really been needed a long time.

CARL GOLDBERG MODELS, INC.

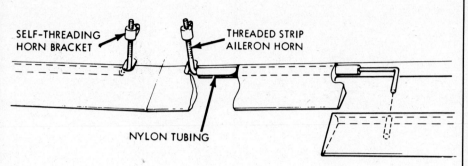

This simple *Strip Aileron Horn Set* (No. 402 for 3/32-in. Medium, $1.59/pair retail; No. 403 for 1/8-in. Large, $2.99/pair retail) provides easy adjustment of throw and long-reach torque rods. It can be used with Carl Goldberg's aileron Pushrods.

CARL GOLDBERG MODELS, INC.

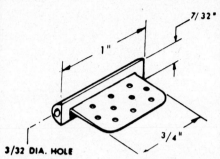

This nylon *Klett Aileron Horn Bearing* (No. 421, $.99/pair retail) is for 3/32-in. wire ailerons, horns, and elevator joiners. The thin, tapered web makes for easy entry into the slot, and the holes insure a good glue joint.

CARL GOLDBERG MODELS, INC.

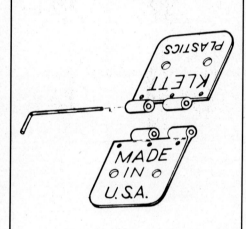

These *Klett Nylon Hinges* (No. 205 for RK2s, pack of 7, $1.29 retail; No. 206 for RK2s, pack of 15, $2.29 retail; No. 207 for RK3s, pack of 7, $1.45 retail: No. 208 for RK3s, pack of 15, $2.75 retail) are the slickest work you've ever seen. For years, expert modelers have carefully cleaned out the tiny "flash" preventing smooth operation in most hinges. Now Roy Klett, originator of the world-famous RK Hinges, has designed and manufactured two sizes of hinges that put an end to annoying click and play. The RK2s are strong and small (7/16-in. by 1/2-in.), and are so thin that all you need is a knife slit. The RK3s are regular size (1/2-in. by 5/8-in.). Both sizes have the fine lines and holes needed for security in gluing. The music wire pin is removable when desired. Ask to see the world's best—Klett hinges, exclusive with Carl Goldberg Models.

CARL GOLDBERG MODELS, INC.

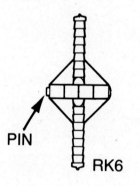

These *Klett Pin-Point Hinges* (No. 200 for 7-piece set, $1.35 retail; No. 201 for 15-piece set, $2.50 retail) allow the simplest installation possible: just drill two holes and apply Super Jet or epoxy glue. Unlike other barbed hinges, this broad gusset web allows visual alignment. The web braces the hinges stiffly against flight loads. Close-fitting pin minimizes flutter and vibration. A total of 16 barbs provide a solid anchor for glue. Silk-smooth in operation, Klett hinges are, traditionally, the world's highest quality. They're used by top fliers and are recommended by many leading designers.

CARL GOLDBERG MODELS, INC.

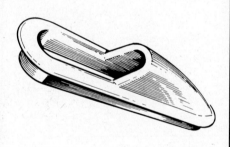

These *Klett Hooded Pushrod Exit Guides* (No. 373 for 1/16-in., No. 372 for 5/64-in.; $.69/pair retail) are decorative and help keep dust and dirt out of your ship.

CARL GOLDBERG MODELS, INC.

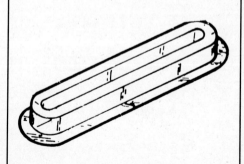

These *Klett Pushrod Exit Guides* (No. 370 for 5/64-in., No. 371 for 1/16-in.; pack of two, $.69 retail) protect your fuselage and insure smooth operation of pushrods. Precision-made of tough nylon, they're easy to install.

CARL GOLDBERG MODELS, INC.

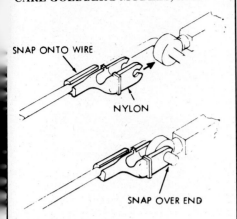

The *Nylon Snap'r Keeper* (No. 361/SK-1, $.99/four, retail) is the quickest, handiest way to secure pushrod wire ends to servos, horns, etc. It works on 3/64-in. wire and holds firmly.

CARL GOLDBERG MODELS, INC.

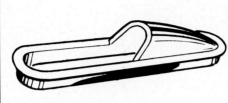

Klett Aileron Pushrod Exits (No. 374, $.69/pair retail) are beautiful fairings to be used where the aileron pushrod exits your wing. Roy Klett again has used his special quality touch to produce the finest item of its kind.

CARL GOLDBERG MODELS, INC.

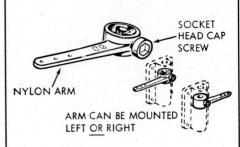

This *Nylon Steering Arm* (No. 281 for 5/32-in. wire, No. 280 for 1/8-in. wire; $1.29/set retail), with hardened-steel collar and screw, is stiff enough for good control yet can flex under shock to protect servo.

SIG MANUFACTURING CO.

These *Rod Couplers* (No. SH-127 for 2-56 1/16 I.D., pack of four, $.55 retail; No. SH-551 for 4-40 7/64 I.D. pack of 4, $.95 retail) are pre-tinned for easy soldering.

SIG MANUFACTURING CO.

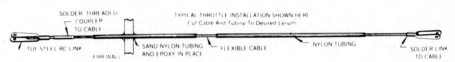

This *Aero-Shaft Pushrod* ($4.95 retail) is the ultimate rigid pushrod. It's made from super-strong, lightweight graphite (a modern high-tech material). It works with any size model including 1/4 scale. Complete hardware is included.

SIG MANUFACTURING CO.

These *Nylon Tubing Pushrods* (30-in., $2.45 retail; 48-in., $2.85 retail) feature two super-slipper telescoping nylon tubes in a free-running, flexible pushrod assembly. Complete hardware is included.

SIG MANUFACTURING CO.

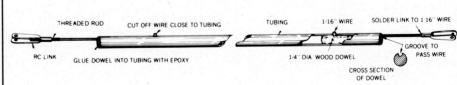

This *Flexible Cable Pushrod* (20-in., $2.15 retail; 36-in., $2.55 retail) is great for throttle and steerable nosegear hookups. It features a stainless steel cable that runs inside a nylon outer tube for flexible, free-running installation. Complete hardware is included.

PUSHRODS, CLEVISES, HINGES, & LINKAGES

SIG MANUFACTURING CO.

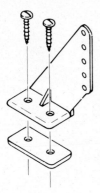

These *Nylon Control Horns* (Pack of two, $.65 retail; Pack of four, $.99 retail) are precision-molded and available in three lengths, in packages of two or four. Complete with retainer plates and screws. Order Nos. SH-220, -221, -222, -547, -549, and -550.

SIG MANUFACTURING CO.

Tuf-Steel R/C Links are available in two sizes: *Standard* (2-56 thread R/C links with 10-in. steel rods, $1.10/two, retail; Links only, $.85/two, retail) and *Heavy Duty* (4-40 thread links with 8-in. steel rods, $1.65/two, retail; Links only, $1.15/two, retail).

SIG MANUFACTURING CO.

Easy Hinges (No. SH-710, Pack of 24, $2.95 retail) are the unique new hinges that are revolutionizing the way people hinge model airplane control surfaces. They are super thin, super strong, and super fast! Simply slot the wood, insert the hinges, and glue in place with thin CA glue. Suitable for all size models. Once you try them, you'll never use another hinge!

SIG MANUFACTURING CO.

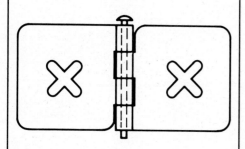

Brand-X Hinges (No. SH-216, pack of six, $1.20 retail; No. SH-217, pack of 15, $2.65 retail) are two-piece pinned. They're molded from tempered nylon for easy installation and alignment, and smooth operation.

SIG MANUFACTURING CO.

These *Solder Clevises* (No. SH-527/2-56 for .0625 wire or cable, $.85 retail; No. SH-700/4-40 for .093 wire or cable, $1.15 retail) are a strong spring steel that can be soldered directly to wire or scale. They're specially plated for easy soldering.

SIG MANUFACTURING CO.

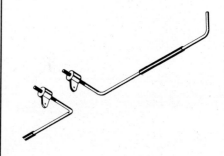

These *Strip Aileron Sets* (No. SH-628 for Mini, $1.59 retail; No. SH-594 for Large, $1.69 retail) feature two self-threaded aileron connectors molded in super-tough nylon. On the Mini set, two strong formed steel horns and brass bearings have 2-56 threads. On the Large set, 4-40 threads.

SIG MANUFACTURING CO.

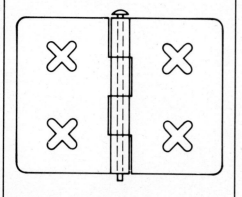

The *Brand-XX Giant Scale Hinge* (No. SH-701, Pack of 15, $3.95 retail) was designed especially for giant-scale modelers. These molded nylon pinned hinges can really handle heavy loads. They come unassembled.

SIG MANUFACTURING CO.

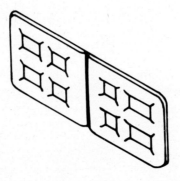

These *Molded Poly Hinges* (No. SH-543, pack of 20, $.99 retail) are a one-piece unpinned design molded from polypropylene for strength and flexibility, plus easy installation.

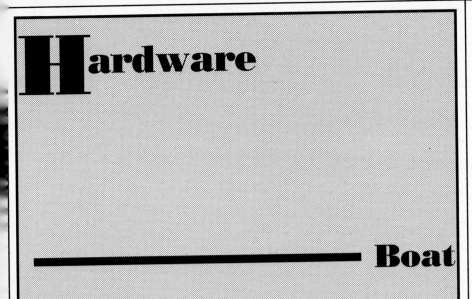

Hardware

Boat

AEROTREND PRODUCTS

These *18-8 Stainless Steel Cotter Pins* (Pack, $.79 retail) come in six sizes. Order No. 2402 for 1/16" x 1/2", No. 2404 for 3/32" x 3/4", No. 2406 for 3/32" x 1 1/2", and No. 2408 for 1/8" x 1".

AEROTREND PRODUCTS

These *18-8 Stainless Steel Star Washers* (Pack of 12, $.69 retail) come in six sizes. Order No. 2242 for No. 2s, No. 2243 for No. 3s, No. 2244 for No. 4s, No. 2246 for No. 6s, No. 2248 for No. 8s, and No. 2250 for No. 10s.

AEROTREND PRODUCTS

These *18-8 Stainless Steel Socket-Head Cap Screws* (Pack of 4, $.99 retail, except 1-1/2" sizes, which are $1.99 retail) come four per pack in nine sizes. Two 3/4" sizes: No. 2172 for 2-56, and No. 2175 for 4-40. Three 1" sizes: No. 2178 for 6-32, No. 2181 for 8-32, and No. 2184 for 10-32. One 1 1/4" size: No. 2177 for 4-40. Three 1-1/2" sizes: No. 2179 for 6-32, No. 2182 for 8-32, and No. 2185 for 10-32.

AEROTREND PRODUCTS

These *18-8 Stainless Steel Hex Nuts* (Pack, $.79 retail) come in six sizes. No. 2342 for 2-56, No. 2343 for 3-48, No. 2344 for 4-40, No. 2346 for 6-32, No. 2348 for 8-32, and No. 2350 for 10-32.

AEROTREND PRODUCTS

These *18-8 Stainless Steel Machine Screws* (Pack, $.89 retail, except for 1 1/2" size, which are $1.99 retail) come in four lengths. Four 1/4" sizes: No. 2102 for 2-56, No. 2108 for 3-48, No. 2114 for 4-40, and No. 2120 for 6-32. Four 1/2" sizes: No. 2104 for 2-56, No. 2110 for 2-48, No. 2116 for 4-40, and No. 2122 for 6-32. Four 1" sizes: No. 2106 for 2-56, No. 2112 for 3-48, No. 2118 for 4-40, and No. 2124 for 6-32. Six 1-1/2" sizes: No. 2107 for 2-56, No. 2113 for 3-48, No. 2119 for 4-40, No. 2125 for 6-32, No. 2131 for 8-32, and No. 2137 for 10-32.

AEROTREND PRODUCTS

Super Blue Set-Up (No. 1009, 5-ft. pack, $4.19 retail) fuel tubing is super-large (5/32" ID x 3/32" wall). Perfect for electric fuel pumps, water jackets, etc. It has super strength and it's flexible. Nozzle and ties are included. A 30-ft. reel is also available.

AEROTREND PRODUCTS

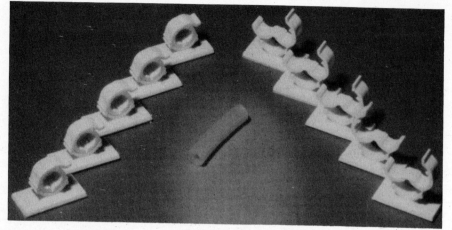

The *"Hold 'Em Tite"* Clamp (No. 1251 for 2 pack, No. 1253 for 10 pack, $1.19 retail) is a reusable nylon clip that will last for years. It's for multi-purpose use and won't rust. It has a 1/4" OD and comes with a bushing. It's backed with a super-strong self-adhering tape.

AEROTREND PRODUCTS

This *Stainless Steel Machine Screw Combination* (Pack of 4 sets, $2.29) consists of 18-8 1 1/2" screws, nuts, and washers. Order No. 2502 for 2-56, No. 2503 for 3-48, No. 2504 for 4-40, No. 2506 for 6-32, No. 2508 for 8-32, and No. 2510 for 10-32.

AEROTREND PRODUCTS

These *18-8 Stainless Steel Lock Washers* (Pack of 12, $.39 retail) come in six sizes. Order No. 2202 for No. 2s, No. 2203 for No. 3s, No. 2204 for No. 4s, No. 2206 for No. 6s, No. 2208 for No. 8s, and No. 2210 for No. 10s.

AEROTREND PRODUCTS

These *18-8 Stainless Steel Flat Washers* (Pack of 12, $.59 retail) come in six sizes. Order No. 2222 for No. 2s, No. 2223 for No. 3s, No. 2224 for No. 4s, No. 2226 for No. 6s, No. 2228 for No. 8s, and No. 2230 for No. 10s.

AEROTREND PRODUCTS

Stainless Steel Socket Head/Cap Screw Combinations (Pack of 4 sets, $2.39 retail) consist of 18-8 1 1/2" screws, nuts, and washers. Order No. 2602 for 2-56, No. 2604 for 4-40, No. 2606 for 6-32, No. 2608 for 8-32, and 2610 for 10-32.

AEROTREND PRODUCTS

Ti-M-Ups (No. 1201 for small—12/pack, No. 1203 for large—8/pack, $1.29 retail) are reusable nylon ties for securing pressure lines, fuel lines, radio wires, etc. They have no sharp edges, are self-locking, and may be unlocked.

AEROTREND PRODUCTS

These *18-8 Stainless Steel Sheet-Metal Screws* (Pack, $.79 retail) are panhead screws and come in eight sizes. Order No. 2142 for 2 x 3/8", No. 2144 for 2 x 1/2", No. 2146 for 4 x 3/8", No. 2148 for 4 x 1/2", No. 2150 for 6 x 1/2", No. 2152 for 6 x 3/4", No. 2154 for 8 x 3/4", and No. 2156 for 8 x 1".

CARL GOLDBERG MODELS, INC.

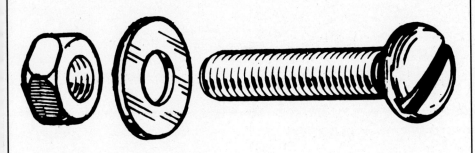

These *2-56 Plated Panhead Machine Screws* come with all necessary washers and nuts. Order No. 542 for 1/4-in., $.99/eight; No. 544 for 1/2-in., $.99/eight; No. 545 for 3/4-in., $.99/eight; No. 546 for 1-in., $.99/eight. All prices retail.

CARL GOLDBERG MODELS, INC.

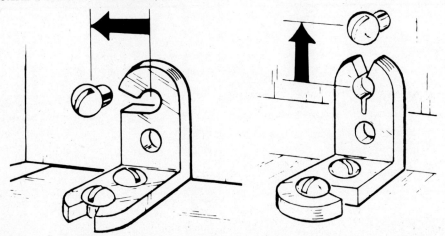

These *Two-Way Angle Hold-Down Brackets* (No. 464/AH1, $1.29/four, retail) are made from nylon for easy snap-on/snap-off attachment of hatches, cowls, doors, servo trays, and unlimited applications. Side-action makes them virtually foolproof. Screws and instructions are included.

CARL GOLDBERG MODELS, INC.

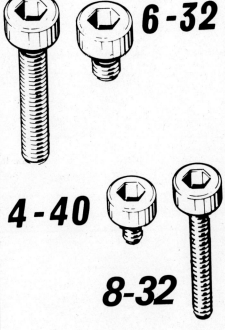

*Socket Head Screws—4-40, 6-32, 8-32—*1/8-in. to 1 1/2-in. (Nos. 501-8 for 4-40, Nos. 511-18 for 6-32, and Nos. 524-28 for 8-32; retail: $.99 -$1.29/set) have long been favored by expert modelers. They're made of higher alloy steel and can be torqued down precisely. These short and long lengths come in three popular thread sizes. Each set comes with four each of screws and washers.

CARL GOLDBERG MODELS, INC.

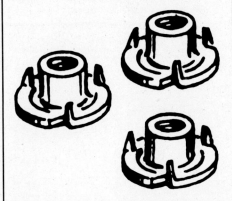

The *4-40, 6-32, and 8-32 Blind Mounting Nuts* (No. 571/BN4 for 4-40, No. 572/BN6 for 6-32, No. 573/BN8 for 8-32; $.99/four, retail) are, by far, the most popular sizes. They're made of high quality steel and plated to prevent corrosion.

CARL GOLDBERG MODELS, INC.

These *Sheet-Metal Screws* (Nos. 563-4, 7-8; $.99/pack retail) are like wood screws but better. They're sharp, clean, hard, and strong with full-depth threads. They're excellent for mounting servos, etc. Washers are included. The 2 x 3/8-in. and 2 x 1/2-in. sizes come 10 per pack; and 4 x 3/8-in. and 4 x 1/2-in. come 8 per pack.

CARL GOLDBERG MODELS, INC.

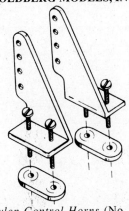

These *Nylon Control Horns* (No. 440 for long, No. 441 for short; $.79/pair retail) have the upright part rising from the center of the base for maximum stability. The nut-plate, with 1/16-in. holes, is for easy mounting. Screws are included.

CARL GOLDBERG MODELS, INC.

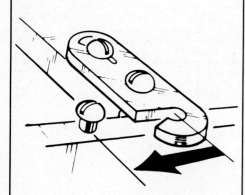

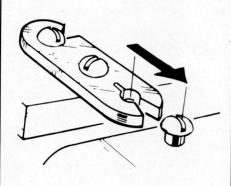

These *Two-Way Flat Hold-Downs* (No. 463/FH1, $1.29/four, retail) are made from nylon for easy snap-on/snap-off attachment of glider canopies, hatches, doors, and servo trays. They can also be used as an antenna fin clip or for other unlimited applications. Instructions and screws are included.

CARL GOLDBERG MODELS, INC.

These *90 degree Mounting Brackets* (No. 462. $.99/four, retail) are molded of nylon and have dozens of uses. They can be used to mount cowls, canopies, internal pushrod guides, etc. Screws are included.

VORTAC MFG. CO., INC.

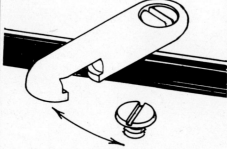

These *Gear Locks* (Pack of four, $1.98 retail) enable you to remove and reinstall wire landing gears and bipe wings in seconds for storage, repair, and transport without using tools. This lock mounts in the same space as a standard gear strap, but won't bend like metal straps and is stronger than nylon straps. It fits wire landing gears up to 5/32-in. Positive snap-action secures gear lock to bolt head.

CARL GOLDBERG MODELS, INC.

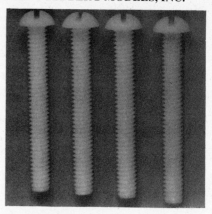

These *Nylon Wing Bolts* (No. 575/WB2 for 2-in., No. 586/WB3 for 3-in.; $1.29/pair retail) won't rust, bind, or seize. Excellent as wing hold-downs and for mounting landing gears. Available in two lengths of 1/4-20 threading

VORTAC MFG. CO., INC.

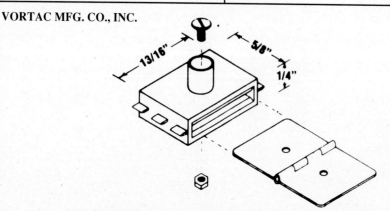

These *Hinge Holders* (12-piece set, $2.39 retail; 30-piece set, $4.98 retail) provide a revolutionary new way to install regular size pinned hinges. They automatically provide a 1/64-in. hinge gap. They secure your hinges with a steel bolt and clamping action and can be easily built into 1/4-in. sheet balsa and built-up surfaces. No more slotting and gluing hinges together. Control surfaces can be removed and worn hinges replaced simply by removing the bolts. All that shows are the recessed bolt heads in the underside of the control surfaces. All hardware, except hinges, is included. The 12-piece set mounts six hinges. The 30-piece set mounts 15 hinges.

Hardware — Car

The *"Hold 'Em Tite"* Clamp (No. 1251 for 2/pack, No. 1253 for 10/pack, $1.19 retail) is a reusable nylon clip that will last for years. It's for multi-purpose use and won't rust. It has a 1/4" OD and comes with a bushing. It's backed with a super-strong self-adhering tape.

DU-BRO PRODUCTS

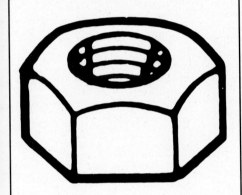

Metric Hex Nuts (No. 2103 for 2mm, No. 2104 for 2.5mm, No. 2105 for 3mm, and No. 2106 for 4mm; Pack of four, $.50 retail).

DU-BRO PRODUCTS

Metric Flat Washers (No. 2107 for 2mm, No. 2108 for 2.5mm, No. 2109 for 3mm, and No. 2110 for 4mm; Pack of eight, $.50 retail).

DU-BRO PRODUCTS

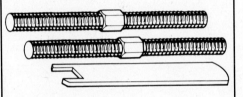

4-40 Turnbuckles enable you to get the ultimate in handling performance by replacing your stock linkage. Precise toe-in, toe-out and camber adjustments can be made with ease. Order No. 2156, 4-40 Turnbuckles with wrench, 2/pkg., $2.95 retail; No. 2157, 4-40 Turnbuckles, 2/pkg., $2.35 retail; No. 2158, 2-56 Turnbuckles with wrench, 2/pkg., $2.95 retail; No. 2159, 2-56 Turnbuckles, 2/pkg., $2.35 retail.

DU-BRO PRODUCTS

This 2-56 Threaded Ball Link (No. 2162, $2.25 each, retail) is a 4-piece set, excellent for off-set steering, throttle, and servo hook-ups. Ball is threaded for 2-56 nut. Threaded coupler 3/4-in. with 3/8-in. 2-56 thread, for up to .072 wire. Self-threading nylon socket, washer, and 2-56 nut.

DU-BRO PRODUCTS

This 2-56 Threaded Ball (No. 2163, $1.25 each, retail) is a replacement threaded ball for 2-56 threaded ball link (2/pkg).

DU-BRO PRODUCTS

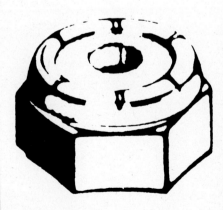

Metric Nylon Insert Lock Nuts (No. 2101 for 3mm, No. 2102 for 4mm; Pack of four, $.75 retail).

DU-BRO PRODUCTS

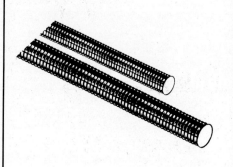

These *12-in. Fully Threaded Rods* (No. 378 for 2-56, $.70 retail; No. 379 for 4-40, $.85 retail) are stainless steel. They are perfect for making custom lengths to the size you need.

DU-BRO PRODUCTS

These *Metric Socket Head Cap Screws* (Pack of four, $1.25 retail) are replacement screws for R/C cars. They're great for easy installation and removal. Order No. 2111 for 2mm x 4, No. 2112 for 2mm x 6, No. 2113 for 2mm x 10, No. 2114 for 2mm x 12, No. 2115 for 2.5mm x 4, No. 2116 for 2.5mm x 6, No. 2117 for 2.5mm x 8, No. 2118 for 2.5mm x 10, No. 2119 for 2.5mm x 15, No. 2120 for 3mm x 4, No. 2121 for 3mm x 6, No. 2122 for 3mm x 8, No. 2123 for 3mm x 10, No. 2124 for 3mm x 15, No. 2125 for 3mm x 18, No. 2126 for 3mm x 20, and No. 2127 for 3mm x 30.

HOBBICO

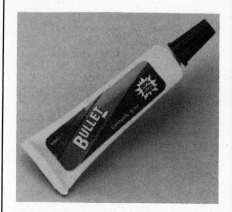

Hobbico's *Bullet Threadlock* (Retail: See your dealer) is 6 oz. of a blue medium viscosity semi-permanent compound that is used to lock screws and nuts. Protect valuable equipment from damage due to vibration.

HOLESHOT RACING PRODUCTS

Splined Set Screws and Wrenches (Nos. 4030, 4031, 5030, 5031; $3.50 and $4.50 retail) are designed to allow maximum torque while tightening pinion gears without rounding off set screw or splined wrench, thus eliminating the need for gear pullers due to stripped set screws. Available in 4-40 and 5-40 (Losi pinion) sizes. Packaged 10 set screws per bag and one splined wrench. Also available are splined wrenchs, two to a bag.

HYPERDRIVE RACING SYSTEMS

Seven times 1991 R.O.A.R. National Champion Hyperdrive's new *Platinum Series "Super Gears"* offers you the widest selection of ratios available on the market: 64 Pitch gears available in 14 through 44 tooth and 48 Pitch in 10 through 40 tooth. Comes in both super hard coated aluminum with a slip coat and stealthcoat steel with nearly 80 C Rockwell hardness. Four out of five invitational races at the Race of Champions at Lake Whippoorwill and every single "A" Main in both 10th and 12th scale at the 1991 ROAR Nationals were won with the new Platinum Series Gears. Each gear is machine hollowed to average 40% less weight with the lowest rotating mass in the industry. HYPERDRIVE: The Ultimate in Racing.

TEAM PIT STOP

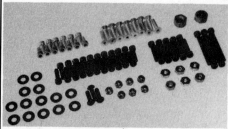

Team Pit Stop's *Aluminum Lightening Systems for R/C Cars* (#5000 Series, $32.99 retail) replace the steel screws, nuts, and washers with lightweight hardened aluminum ones to reduce weight up to 3 ounces per car. Available for all popular cars and trucks.

R/C Racing is a family sport.

Tools and Building Tips

By Douglas R. Pratt

If you're buying your first model, there are some things you'll need beyond what came in the kit box.

It doesn't take much to set up a model workshop, but there are some basic requirements. The first is a smooth, straight, flat surface to build on. Any warps in your work table will show up as warps in the structures you build!

I like to build on a surface that I can push pins into. This is very useful for holding balsa parts precisely in position. A sheet of smooth-surfaced ceiling tile is ideal. Tape the plans down onto this, and tape a sheet of waxed paper or cellophane over the plans to keep the glue from sticking to them.

You'll need a sharp knife. Traditional hobby knives with the standard pointed #11 blade are the most useful.

Other useful tools include lightweight needle nose pliers; a sharp pair of scissors; small screwdrivers, both slotted and Phillips head; a drill; sandpaper; a covering iron; and consider a heat gun.

Adhesives

We used to build model airplanes with cellulose cement, white glue, and aliphatic resins. Cyanoacrylate super glues revolutionized modeling. Now these glues are used in most aspects of model building. They're available in different grades for different purposes. When you see a reference to "CyA" or "CA" glues, they're talking about the cyanoacrylates.

What sets these glues apart is their chemistry. Common glues harden by letting their solvents evaporate. CyA glues polymerize, forming long chains molecules that bind the surfaces together. CyA glues are available in three common grades.

The thinnest CyA (Jet, Zap, Hot Stuff, Sig Red Label, etc.) is best for when the glue joint is perfect—the parts must match exactly, and the glue is dripped onto the seam rather than being applied to one surface. Thin CyA sets the fastest.

The medium grade (Super Jet, Hot Stuff Super T, Zap-A-Gap, Sig Blue Label, etc.) is the most all-around useful grade. It is applied the way you expect glue to go on: put it on one surface and press the two surfaces together. It will fill small gaps and uneven surfaces, and is useful for bonding dissimilar materials, like wood to plastic or metal.

Thick CyA (Slow Jet, Slow Zap, etc.) is useful for many applications where you would ordinarily use epoxy. Because it takes several minutes to set, it is usually used with an accelerator.

One of the best things about building with CyA glues is the fact that you can use accelerators. An accelerator is a chemical that causes the glue to polymerize almost instantly. It usually comes in a spray bottle. Spray it on the glue joint, and pow—the glue is hard. Pretty amazing to have a glue that sets when you push a button! If you have a joint that is particularly difficult to work with, spray accelerator on one surface and put medium or thick CyA on the other surface. When you press them together, you get an instant bond. Some accelerators will fog clear plastic, so be wary of using them on windows or canopies.

You can also buy debonders for CyA glue. These are chemicals that dissolve the polymerized CyA, freeing the glue joint. They will work on wood, if you're careful and patient. Debonders are most useful for the times when you accidentally glue your fingers to your airplane. Don't laugh, it happens to all of us.

Epoxy

You'll need at least one kind of epoxy on your workbench. Epoxy should be used where you need a very strong bond, or to reinforce a weak area It is also useful for fuelproofmg the engine and fuel tank compartments. For this use, you can take advantage of the fact that epoxy flows more easily when it's warm. Spreading epoxy is much easier if you use a heat gun to warm it up; another reason for owning a heat gun!

The two useful epoxy grades are five-minute and thirty-minute. This refers to the amount of time it takes for the epoxy to harden. Five-minute epoxy is great for making repairs, or in small batches for parts that have to be clamped or held together. Thirty-minute epoxy has

better penetration and will make a stronger joint, besides giving you enough time to get everything straight before it hardens.

Traditional Cements

Many people still build models with the cellulose-based cements (Sig-Ment, Ambroid, Testors, etc.). It takes no longer to set than CyA glues, and it smells funny. But, it's much easier to sand the dried glue. If, for example, you need to lay balsa sheeting across the top of your wing, and you need to edge-glue two thin sheets together, consider using cellulose cement. You can put on plenty of it, then sand the ridge of dried glue right down smooth.

Covering a model

You need a sealing iron to do a good job covering your model. Go ahead and buy one now. A small travel iron might work, but why cause yourself unnecessary trouble by having less than the best to work with?

Ask your dealer for advice when selecting a covering. There are several brands of plastic film available, suitable for different purposes. You should look for a strong film for your first model, since it can be expected to endure some bumps and scratches.

Another essential tool is a thermometer to measure the temperature of your iron. Believe me, it's very important to have the iron in the temperature range that the covering needs. I remember struggling with one new brand of film for almost an hour, before I gave up and read the instructions. When I (sheepishly) set my iron to the right temperature, the covering went on like butter on toast.

You'll be covering two types of structures: solid, like the side of the fuselage; and open framework, like the wings. Naturally, you use two different methods to cover them.

When you're covering a fuselage side or other solid structure, start by cutting a piece of covering that's about 1/2 inch larger than the structure all the way around. Cover one panel at a time; don't try to run the covering up one side, across the top, and down the other. Lay the film on the structure, check your iron temperature, and apply the iron to a spot in the center of the surface. Work slowly outward, holding the film tight as you go. Be careful not to trap air bubbles under the film. If some get in anyway, poke them with your knife and iron them down. When you're out to the edge, work your way around the curves in the sides, holding the film smooth. It's good practice to cover the top and bottom of a fuselage, then the sides...this helps hide the seams.

Covering an open framework like a wing panel isn't quite as simple but it isn't hard. Start by cutting a piece of film that's about 1/2 inch oversize. Lay it on the panel, making sure that it's centered. It's good policy to cover the bottom of the wing, then the top. This lets you overlap the seams onto the bottom, where they're less noticeable. Now tack down one corner of the covering. Move diagonally to the opposite corner, pull the covering tight, and tack it down. Tack down the other two corners. If you have to remove one corner to keep the covering smooth, it's easy at this point.

Finally, when you have all four corners down and the covering smooth, tack down a spot in the center of the leading edge, holding the covering tight all the time. Move across the leading edge, tacking down spots that are separated by the width of the iron, until you can smooth down the entire leading edge with no wrinkles. When the leading edge is secure, move to the trailing edge and attach it the same way. The leading edge will give you a solid foundation to pull against as you keep the covering taut.

When the leading and trailing edges are down, do the sides the same way. Use heat and pressure to pull and stretch the covering around curved wingtips. If you get wrinkles, heat it up and try it again. A heat gun is very useful at this point.

Finally, when the covering is down along all four sides, use the heat gun to shrink the center section of the covering. This will not only give you a good smooth surface, but the heat will attach the covering cleanly to the ribs underneath.

If you run into any problems building your model, remember to call your hobby dealer. He's your best source of information and inspiration.

Tools

APPLIED DESIGN CORP.

Our *Mini Sander* (No. 111, $285.00 retail) makes for handy sanding with "the littlest miracle of the workshop." The ever-taut sanding belt has a patented locking mechanism that snaps into place with a finger pull. It fits into small and large concave recesses and over small and large beads. Knife-edge sides sand as close to right angle fittings as possible.

APPLIED DESIGN CORP.

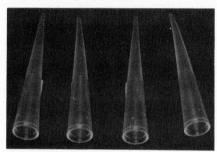

These *Mini Glue Tips* (No. 121, $1.05/6 retail) give you exact placement of the correct amount of glue. It lets you keep models neat and light and preserves expensive glue. Precision molded of durable polypropylene, the long reach gets into hard places and seals with a pin. Makes any glue tube an "instant glue gun."

APPLIED DESIGN CORP.

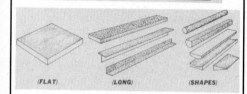

Customize Your Sanding Like The "PROS"

(FLAT) (LONG) (SHAPES)

With *Ruff Stuff* (No. 131, $1.25/pk. retail) you can customize your sanding like the pros when you use this self-adhesive sheet sandpaper that adheres to metal, plastic, glass, rubber, or wood. Make your own special sanding shapes. It's easy—just cut to shape, peel, and stick for instant use for sanding. Packed 36 sheets to a pack.

APPLIED DESIGN CORP.

The *Mini Tee Bar* (No. 140, $3.15 retail) offers precision sanding and shaping with this 4-1/2" custom aluminum extrusion sanding block that features true 90 degree corners for hard to reach spots. Especially designed for small, precision sanding jobs, the mini won't wear out, even when you use it again and again. It's straight and flat for level finishing and comes complete with 3 sheets peel and stick sandpaper.

APPLIED DESIGN CORP.

Mini-T-Stuff (No. 140RS, $2.00/6 retail) is the precision die-cut replacement PSA sandpaper and comes in medium (No. 100), fine (No. 180), and super fine (No. 280) grit. It's easy to apply, just peel and stick for complete coverage of all sanding surfaces.

APPLIED DESIGN CORP.

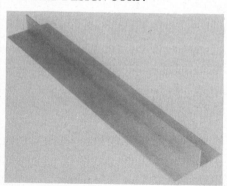

Large Tee Bars offer two sizes—11" (No. 141, $3.10 retail) or 22" (No. 142, $4.65 retail)—to choose from in this handy aluminum extrusion sanding block for use with Rite-Stuff self adhesive sandpaper. The large, true surface won't wear out. These are handy to use.

APPLIED DESIGN CORP.

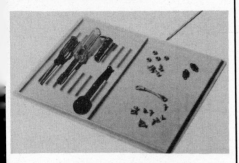

The *Stay-Tray* (No. 151, $2.10 retail) lets you keep everything in place neatly with this organizer for your hobby materials. End lost parts and frustration by keeping tools and instruments where you need them. It's handy to use because small parts are easy to see and they don't get lost. Made of unbreakable, low-density polyethylene that is not damaged by chemicals. Washable finish.

APPLIED DESIGN CORP.

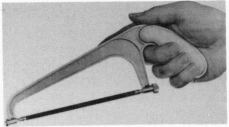

This compact *10" Mini Saw* (No. 161, $9.00 retail) saws anything, anywhere. The rugged, die-cast frame has a comfortable, chip-proof plastic inset handle. The receding nose and adjustable 6" blade gives good work access. Cuts wood, plastic, metal, and hardened music wire. Blade can be quickly and easily turned to six positive positions.

APPLIED DESIGN CORP.

Fine tooth replacement *Mini Sawblades* (No. 162, $2.10/3 retail) for the 10" mini saw. These 6" blades are tempered to cut wood, plastic, metal, and hardened music wire. Blades do not twist or buckle. Fine teeth leave minimum burr on tubing.

BLUE RIDGE MACHINERY & TOOLS INC.

The new *Emco Maier Unimat PC* (No. 170.00A, Base Machine Package $950.00 retail) allows the R/C enthusiast maximum precision in machining, convenient operation, versatility, and up-to-date technology. Base machine includes: electronic variable speed control, power feed, gear quadrant for thread cutting, live center, 3 jaw lathe chuck. *IBM or IBM-compatible with at least 640 kB RAM memory.

COVERITE

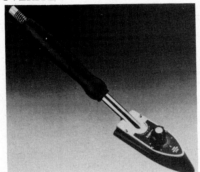

The *Black Baron Iron* (No. 6201, $22.95 retail) has exclusive "roll bars" that fit into fillets and undercambers. Coating is 100% Blackstone—a big improvement over less expensive coatings. Slides like butter, even over tacky surfaces. Reduces temperature drift to only 5 degrees while ordinary irons vary up to 40 degrees.

COVERITE

This *Pocket Thermometer* (No. 6200, $7.50 retail) is a precision tool that tells you the exact temperature of your iron so you can install any covering correctly. It also reads engine temperatures to avoid damage due to overheating.

COMPOSITE STRUCTURES TECHNOLOGY

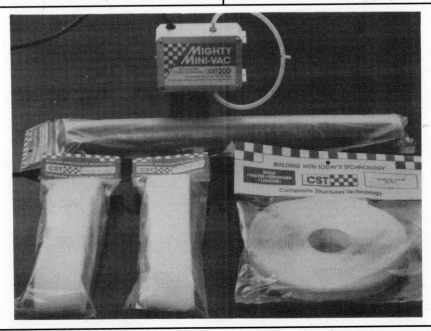

CST's *MIGHTY MINI-VAC* ($74.95 retail; $199.95 retail for the Professional System) electric vacuum bagging system for foam core wings is very quiet. The continuous operation electric Mini-Vac pump pressure is preset to be safe for skinning 1 to 1.5 lb./ft.3 styrene foam cores without distorting or crushing. The system includes 3 yards of nylon bagging tube, vacuum bag sealant, breather strip, tubing, and T-fitting. The system is complete for vacuum bagging wood skins over foam cores. Optional mylar is recommended for vacuum bagging fabric skins over foam cores where a slick finish is desired. CST offers a variety of vacuum bagging systems for advanced vacuum bagging techniques. A complete line of vacuum bagging supplies is also available.

CUSTOM MODEL PRODUCTS INC.

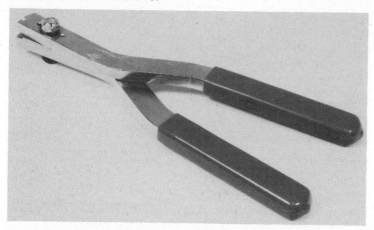

The addition of *Z-pliers* (No. 0616, $24.95 retail) to your workshop tools will speed installation of pushrods, eliminate solder joints (a potential point of failure), and kwik-links. Z-pliers also ease the chore of cutting music wire. Available in chrome for bending 1/16" (.062") music wire or gold for bending threaded rod .078".

DREMEL

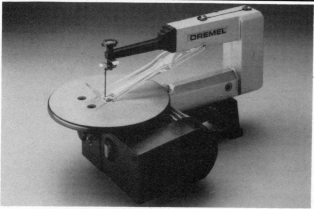

The *Model 1371 Dremel 13" Scroll Saw* (Retail: See your dealer) is designed for detailed craft, hobby, and beginning woodworking projects. It features a die-cast aluminum frame and heavy cast-iron base. It's powered by a 0.9 amp direct-drive induction motor to produce 1720 strokes per minute. The saw uses a 5-inch pin and plain end blades. Also included are a clear plastic guard, front-mounted blade tension control, and an adjustable 10-inch diameter steel table which pivots from 0 degrees to 45 degrees and locks in position for accurate bevel cuts. Built-in storage tray.

DREMEL

The *Model 1731 Disc-Belt Sander* (No. 1731; Retail: See your dealer) is the perfect addition to those home workshops that require the diversity of a disc/belt sander. It has a 1 in. wide by 30 in. long belt and a 5-in. diameter disc, which will sharpen, sand, deburr and polish metal, wood, plastic, and even ceramic material. Both tables pivot and the disc table includes a miter gauge for compound angle work. Long running, maintenance-free induction motor provides dependable trouble-free operation. Outlet for standard vacuum hose provided.

DREMEL

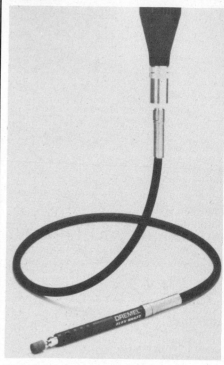

The *Model 225 Flex-Shaft Attachment* (No. 225; Retail: Available from Dremel or see your dealer) has been introduced for use with Dremel's new Moto-Tool line. The 36-in. cable and pencil-thin handpiece attaches to the Moto-Tool to provide lightweight, fingertip control. The cable attaches easily to Dremel Moto-Tool Models 395, 285, and 275. The handpiece uses a collet to hold a variety of Moto-Tool cutting, carving, and engraving bits. When using the Flex-Shaft, the Moto-Tool can be hung in a stationary upright position, freeing the work area of added clutter. It also reduces the operating weight of the Moto-Tool for intricate applications. The 1/2-in. dia. ballbearing handpiece is cool running and handles all Dremel accessory bits.

DREMEL

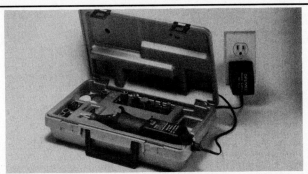

The *Freewheeler*™ *Cordless Moto-Tool* (No. 850, No. 8508; Retail: See your dealer) is currently available in two models. The Model 850 includes the Freewheeler and charging unit, plus a keyless chuck for quickly changing bits. The deluxe 8508 includes the Freewheeler, charger unit, carrying case, keyless chuck, and a 30-piece accessory set. With speeds of 15,000 and 20,000 RPM, the Dremel Freewheeler can cut, grind, sand, saw, drill, and polish its way through all kinds of materials: wood, metal, plastic, and even ceramic tile. It's a top performing tool in other ways, too. The Dremel Freewheeler is made of the highest quality materials and molded into a sleek, comfortable shape. It is engineered to hold a charge through the toughest workouts and recharge quickly in just three hours. What's more, the Freewheeler is compatible with all Dremel attachments, accessories, and bits, making its versatility virtually endless.

DREMEL

The *Model 1671 Two-Speed Scroll Saw* (Retail: See your dealer) has all the features you want in your home workshop. This 16-in. saw has a two-speed direct drive motor—1,790 SPM at high speed, 890 SPM at slow speed. 12-in. round cast aluminum table makes cutting easier. Cast iron frame gives strength and stability. Sawdust blower keeps cutting surface clear. Accepts pin and plain end blades so you can select the best blade for the application. It comes with a built-in blade storage case.

DREMEL

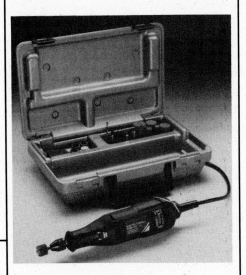

The *Moto-Tool*® (Retail: See your dealer) has been redesigned to be compact and lightweight with increased speed up to 30,000 RPM. Improvements include addition of keyless chuck capability for use with bits up to 1/8-in. and a tapered housing shape for comfortable finger-tip control. The Moto-Tool is double insulated, eliminating the need for grounding. The custom-designed shatter-resistant housing fits comfortably in your hand to provide precise finger-tip control. A new thrust bearing provides greater drilling capability. Three models are available as variable speed, two speed, and single speed kits with various accessory/bit assortments.

DREMEL

The *Model 230 Router Attachment* (Retail: See your dealer) can be used with Moto-Tool Nos. 245, 250, 270, 275, 280, 285, 370, 380, 395, and 850. Ideal for edging, shaping, grooving, recessing and freehand routing. Cat. No. 650 1/8-in. straight bit is included. Bushings are included to hold all the above Moto-Tools.

PRICES AND SPECS ARE SUBJECT TO CHANGE

DREMEL

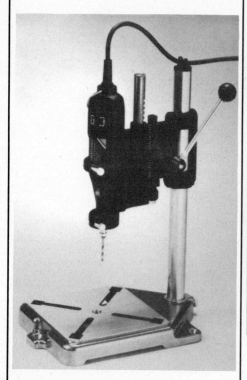

DREMEL

DU-BRO PRODUCTS

This *Ball Link Tool* (No. 187, $1.00 retail) serves two purposes: 1) safely separates ball links with its curved end, and 2) fits the 1/16-in. threaded ball link nut.

DU-BRO PRODUCTS

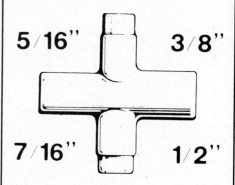

This *4-Way Socket Wrench* (No. 251, $4.25 retail) is perfect for glo-plugs, prop nuts, and nylon bolts. Sockets for 5/16-in., 3/8-in., 7/16-in., and 1/2-in., as well as 8mm to 13mm metric sizes.

The *Model 212 Drill Press Stand* (No. 212; Retail: Available from Dremel or see your dealer) accepts the new Dremel Moto-Tool Models 395, 285, and 275, and is designed for precision drilling, routing, and grooving. The Model 212 features a 36-sq.-in. worksurface and a 3-in. throat depth. The table is slotted for both guides and hold downs, and the tool carriage is adjustable from 0 to 3 in.

The *Dremel MiniMite Model 750 Compact Cordless Rotary Tool* ($48.00 retail) is designed for precision projects. Use it anywhere precision drilling, sanding, shaping, or grinding is required. The Model 750 can be used with all 1/8-in. and smaller shank Dremel tool bits. It comes equipped with a rechargeable, removable battery pack and its own unique plug-in battery charger. Additional battery packs are available so you are never without the convenience of the MiniMite.

DU-BRO PRODUCTS

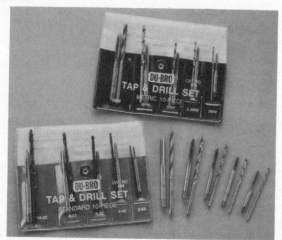

Standard Tap & Drill Set (No. 509, contains 2-56, 4-40, 6-32, 8-32, 10-32 drill & taps, $19.95/set retail). Metric Tap & Drill Set (No. 510, contains 2mm, 2.5mm, 3mm, 4mm & 5mm metric drill & tap sets, $24.95/ set retail).

DU-BRO PRODUCTS

The *No. 499 Tru-Spin Prop Balancer* ($26.95 retail) is completely adjustable for large and small props, helicopter blades, jet fans, car wheels, and even motor gears. The lockable adjusting cone of the balancing shaft gives the Tru-Spin a sure-hold-grip to insure the precise balance you need.

DU-BRO PRODUCTS

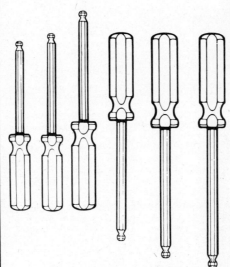

Standard & Metric Ball Wrenches (Retail: $2.25-$3.25 each, $10.95-$11.95 per set) are the perfect tool for getting at those hard-to-reach places. Ball wrenches make it possible to turn socket head screws or bolts from any angle. Now available in five sizes for both standard and metric socket head screws or bolts. Standard Ball Wrenches: No. 442, 5/64 (2-56 Skt. Hd.), $2.25; No. 443, 3/32 (4-40 Skt. Hd.), $2.25; No. 444, 7/64 (6-32 Skt. Hd.), $2.25; No. 445, 9/64 (8-32 Skt. Hd.), $2.75; No. 446, 5/32 (10-32 Skt. Hd.), $3.25; No. 447, 5 pc. Standard Set, $11.95. Metric Ball Wrenches: No. 448, 1.5mm (2mm Skt. Hd.), $2.25; No. 449, 2.0mm (2.5mm Skt. Hd.), $2.25; No. 450, 2.5mm (3.0mm Skt. Hd.), $2.25; No. 451, 3.0mm (4.0mm Skt. Hd.), $2.25; No. 452, 4.0mm(5.0mm Skt. Hd.), $2.25; No. 453, 5 pc. Metric Set, $10.95.

DU-BRO PRODUCTS

These *1-1/4-in. Cut-Off Wheels* (No. 352, pack of two, $2.95 retail) are perfect for cutting through most woods, plastics, and metals. They're designed with fiberglass reinforcement to prevent brittleness.

DU-BRO PRODUCTS

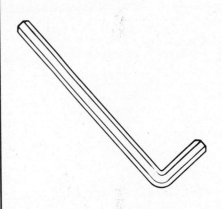

Metric Hex Wrench (No. 2128 for 2mm, No. 2129 for 2.5mm, No. 2130 for 3mm, and No. 2131 for 4mm; $.50 each, retail).

DU-BRO PRODUCTS

This *Cut-Off Wheel with Mandril* (No. 353, $2.95/set retail) is 1-1/4-in. It's great for cutting most woods, plastics, and metals.

DU-BRO PRODUCTS, INC.

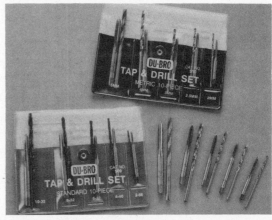

For the modeler who would like to have a complete set of taps and drills at a 13% savings over purchasing individual sets. The five piece set assortment comes complete in vinyl pouch.

10 Piece Standard Tap and Drill Set (No. 509, 1/pkg., $19.95 retail) comes complete with 2056, 4-40, 6-32, 8-32, and 10-32 tap and drill sets.

10 Piece Metric Tap and Drill Set (No. 510, 1/pkg., $24.95 retail) comes complete with 2mm, 2.5mm, 3.0mm, 4.0mm, and 5.0mm tap and drill sets.

PRICES AND SPECS ARE SUBJECT TO CHANGE

DU-BRO PRODUCTS

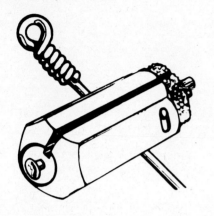

The *Kwik Twist* (No. 301, $8.95 retail) is a tool that ties perfect barrel wraps to each end of piano wire (up to .032 dia.) to make beautiful guy wires.

DU-BRO PRODUCTS

These *6-In. Allen Wrenches* (No. 131, pack of two, $1.75 retail) fit 4-40 and 6-32 socket head bolts.

DU-BRO PRODUCTS, INC.

These *Tap and Drill Sets* ($4.00 - $5.95 retail) are made of high-quality steel and are available in the following sizes: No. 359 for 10-32, No. 360 for 2-56, No. 361 for 4-40, No. 362 for 6-32, No. 363 for 8-32, No. 364 for 1/4-20, No. 370 for 2mm, No. 371 for 2.5mm, No. 372 for 3mm, No. 373 for 4mm, and No. 374 for 5mm.

EXCEL HOBBY BLADES CORP.

The *Grip-On Art Knife Non-Roll* (No. K18, $2.99 retail) comes in five assorted colors: blue, black, red, pink, and green. It also has a four chuck jaw with a soft rubber touch and is supplied with free safety cap.

EXCEL HOBBY BLADES CORP.

The *Deluxe Railroad Set* (No. 44289) includes #1, 5 knives snap knife, plier, mitre box, pinvise, 6-in. ruler, B490 saw blade, sanding stick, Swiss hammer, 2 screwdrivers (Phillips and regular), 2 files (flat and round), 3 assorted D drills, and 3 assorted D blades.

FOREDOM ELECTRIC CO.

Foredom 2272 General Applications Kit (Retail: See your dealer) contains Foredom's most popular 1/8 HP motor, chuck-style handpiece, new FCT-1 foot control, and 35 assorted accessories. This kit is the best general purpose, professional quality, flexible-shaft power tool kit available. The 2272 now comes in exciting display packaging.

CARL GOLDBERG MODELS, INC.

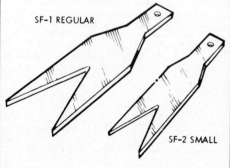

These *Slotting Fork Blades* (No. 601 for Klett RK-5 regular, No. 602 for Klett RK-4 small; $.99 retail) are designed to fit the CG hinge slotting kit handle.

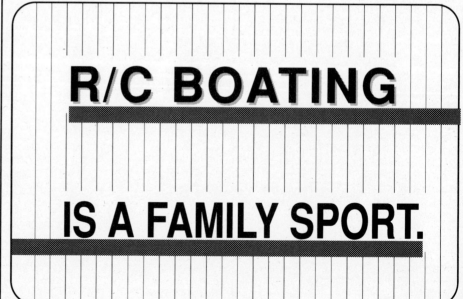

CARL GOLDBERG MODELS, INC.

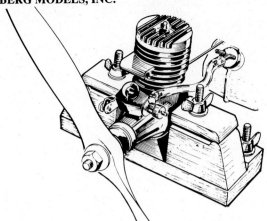

This *Engine Test Stand* (No. 620/ETS-1, $19.99 retail) is made of rock hard Canadian Maple. It's husky enough to handle a big .61 and adjustable down to a T.D. .049. It's finished in a clear lacquer, fully assembled, and includes all mounting bolts, restraining lug pins, and guide pins to help break in engines.

ART GROSS ENTERPRISES

CARL GOLDBERG MODELS, INC.

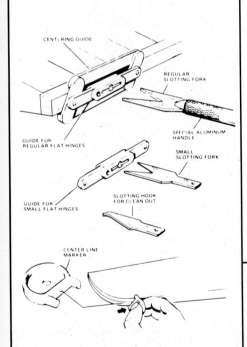

This *New Hinge Slotting Kit* (No. 600 for HSK-2 Complete Kit, $4.99 retail) is the deluxe version of CG's famous hinge slotting kit. It serves every common hinging need including "point" hinges. Included are the centering guide, special aluminum handle, center line marker, regular and small slotting fork blades, and a hook blade. (Individual components: No. 606 for CG-1 centering guide, $1.49; No. 601 for SF-1 regular slotting fork blade, $.99; No. 602 for SF-2 small slotting fork blade, $.99; No. 603 for SH-1 slotting hook blade, $.99; and No. 607 for HM-1 center line marker, $.69. All prices retail).

GRANLUND ENGINEERING

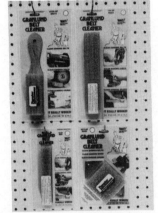

Sanding Belt/Disc Cleaner ($2.95-12.95 retail) Granlund's complete line of tools which clean the grit on clogged sanding belts, discs, drums, and sheets to restore "like new" cutting action.

GYROS PRODUCTS

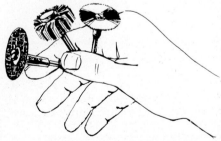

Gyros offers a complete line of *Mini-Tools* (Retail: See your dealer) for today's modeler, including: 1) fiber-cutting discs for hard and soft metals as well as ceramics (sizes 1-in. through 2 1/2-in.); 2) flap wheels in 80, 180 and 360 grits 1/2-in. through 1 1/2-in. diameter; and 3) coarse and fine circular saws 1/2-in. through 2-in. and NEW 7/8-in. x .005-in. fine and 7/8-in. x .021-in. coarse, with teeth set for wood.

This is the only sanding block that wears a belt. The *Hand Belt Sander* by wedg-lock will give you the smoothest, best finish (on any material) with less work, at a lower cost and in less time than any other hand sanding block sold today.

H & N ELECTRONICS

Supersafe Solder Flux (Liquid, $2.85 retail; Gel, $3.70 retail) contains no resins, zinc-ammonium chloride, or other strong corrosives. When heated, it becomes chemically neutral, non-corrosive, non hygroscopic, and electrically non-conductive. It is water-soluble and cleans up with water.

HOBBY DYNAMICS DISTRIBUTORS

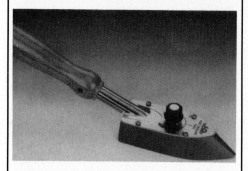

Hobby Dynamics' *Sealing Iron* (No. HDD101, $20.99 retail) is controlled by a thermostat and has a non-stick, coated surface. This light, versatile tool has a sturdy one-piece, formed-steel handle and a shoejoining plate that won't separate. Special features include tapered sides for perfect bonding and rounded edges to prevent scratching.

HOBBY DYNAMICS DISTRIBUTORS

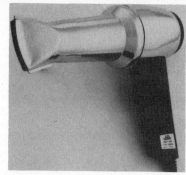

Hobby Dynamics' *Heat Gun 110V* (No. HDD100, $25.99 retail) is perfectly suited for any brand of heat-shrinkable fabric or film used for covering model airplane framework. The nozzle can be removed to concentrate heat where needed. This light-weight gun has a low-noise design and a three-position control switch (hot/cool/off).

HOBBY DYNAMICS DISTRIBUTORS

Hobby Dynamics announces its new *Lexan Curved Scissors* (No. HDD115, $12.99 retail). These curved tip scissors cut easily through Lexan and other light, vacuum formed types of plastics. The curved tip design, and dual large loop handle design allows easy cutting around inside and outside corners as well as comfortable left or right hand operation.

HORIZON HOBBY DISTRIBUTORS, INC.

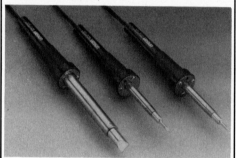

Ungar's EconoIrons are available in a wide range of sizes, all with interchangeable tips. Every 700-degree F 25W (No. UNG3125, $13.95 retail) and 900-degree F 40W (No. UNG3140, $19.95 retail) chisel-tip model includes an iron holder. The 1000-degree F 80W Iron (No. UNG3180, $31.95 retail) has a wide chisel tip.

HORIZON HOBBY DISTRIBUTORS, INC.

Ungar's top-quality pistol *Soldering Guns* (No. UNG2075, 5-piece, $29.95 retail; No. UNG2100, 8-piece, $43.95 retail) heat up very quickly. A 75W version, designed for general work, has a solid copper tip. A dual-heat 100/140W output gun includes a trigger-activated light for work illumination. Also included are two solder tools and three tips.

HORIZON HOBBY DISTRIBUTORS, INC.

The modular construction of the top-quality, blue-handled *Ungar SL series Soldering Irons* allows you to interchange both tip styles and heaters for a life-time of use. The special "cool handle" design ensures that heat goes into the project, not into your hand. The Irons are available in 25-watt output (No. UNGSL325, $36.95 retail), 35-watt (No. UNGSL335, $37.95 retail), and 45-watt (No. UNGSL345, $39.95 retail) outputs. An SL model, when combined with one of Ungar's stands, makes an outstanding bench unit at an affordable price.

HORIZON HOBBY DISTRIBUTORS, INC.

Ungar's Race Station (No. UNG200R, $124.95 retail) and Super Race Station (No. UNG300S, $134.95 retail) have exclusive Thermal Thrust Tips, an adjustable temperature range (from a mild 400 degrees F for fine work to a blistering 800 degrees F for heavy-duty battery-pack assembly), and electronic temperature control. Other features include handy base units with an iron holder to keep the iron safely off the bench and a sponge to keep the tip clean. The Race Station has a micro-handle and is perfect for small jobs that require great control. General work is best accomplished with the slightly larger Super Race Station.

HORIZON HOBBY DISTRIBUTORS, INC.

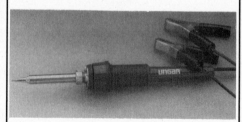

Announcing *Ungar's RaceIron* (No. UNG3012, $54.95 retail), a 12V portable soldering iron with enough power for all your soldering needs. The RaceIron features: 12-foot cord, low current draw, 1-minute heat-up time, insulated handle, 30W output, and modular tip design for great flexibility. And don't worry: the RaceIron won't false-trip your peak detector chargers. (Stand not included.)

HORIZON HOBBY DISTRIBUTORS, INC.

Overpower the competition with Ungar's *SL500 Super Iron* (UNGSL500, $44.95 retail). Ungar introduces a new 50 watt modular iron. The AC powered SL500 comes stock with a 50 watt heater, long tapered chisel tip and a red handle that looks good and stays cool. Because of its modular design, the SL500 can be modified to adjust to your soldering needs by changing 1 of the 6 available tips or 1 of the 4 available heaters.

HORIZON HOBBY DISTRIBUTORS, INC.

For safety, an *Iron Holder* is recommended, Ungar offers three holders from left to right: Economy (No. UNG8000, $14.50 retail); Micro (No. UNG9800, $19.95 retail); and Deluxe (No. UNG8800, $29.50 retail).

K & S ENGINEERING

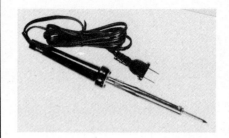

This heavy-duty *Soldering Iron* (No. 910, $7.95 retail) has a 110V/60 watt capacity.

K & S ENGINEERING

Kwik-Change Tool Sets (No. 425, $7.95 retail) are screwdriver sets that include five different tools. They're the right size for the hobbyist and perfect for the R/C flight box.

K & S ENGINEERING

This *Tubing Bender Kit* (No. 321, $1.75 retail) solves tube bending problems for 1/16, 3/32, 1/8, 5/32, and 3/16 tubing.

K & S ENGINEERING

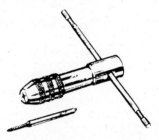

Threading Dies and Taps (All dies $4.95 retail; All taps $2.95 retail; Die handle $9.95 retail; Tap handle $4.95 retail). Order No. 415 for #0-80 die, No. 416 for #1-72 die, No. 417 for #2-56 die, No. 418 for #3-48 die, No. 419 for #4-40 die, and No. 420 for die handle. Order No. 435 for #0-80 tap, No. 436 for #1-72 tap, No. 437 for #2-56 tap, No. 438 for #3-48 tap, No. 439 for #4-40 tap, and No. 434 for tap handle.

K & S ENGINEERING

These *Standard Tool Sets* (No. 422 for nut drivers (5), No. 423 for open end wrenches (5), No. 424 for Phillips/Allen (5), and No. 426 for screwdrivers (6); $9.95 retail) are top quality and have individual swivel handles. They're ideal for home, workshop, and field use.

K & S ENGINEERING

This fine *Sandpaper* (No. 475, $.59/pack, retail) is available in an assortment of all popular grits.

K & S ENGINEERING

This *Soldering Gun* (No. 1210, $15.95 retail) provides 100 watts capacity and heats instantly for those tough soldering jobs.

K & S ENGINEERING

This *Tubing Cutter* (No. 296, $3.95 retail) cuts brass, copper, and aluminum tubing from 3/32-in. to 5/8-in. It's made of nylon and, by reducing friction, makes cutting easy.

K & S ENGINEERING

Flex-I-Grit ($1.09/pack, retail) is a tough sanding film. It won't crack, peel, clog, or break down, and can be used wet or dry. It outlasts ordinary sandpaper and is available in assorted grits of garnet, aluminum oxide, and silicon carbide. Sheet size: 4-in. x 5-1/2-in.

K & S ENGINEERING

These jeweler's *Needle Files* (No. 430, $8.95 retail) are for use in all hobbies and crafts. There are 10 files per set which feature round handled files of tough tempered steel and a handy pouch for easy storage.

K & S ENGINEERING

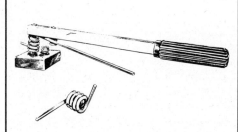

With this *Coil Winder* (No. 324, $19.95 retail) you can produce coils in 5/32-in. and 3/16-in. music wire. Just clamp the base in a vise and wind coils. Using this tool, you can customize landing gears, steering arms, springs, or any wire project you may be doing.

K & S ENGINEERING

These *Mini and Mighty Wire Benders* (No. 323 for Mini, 1/8 wire and smaller, $7.95 retail; No. 322 for Mighty, 1/8 to 1/4 wire, $19.95 retail) are simple, precision made tools with a protective oxidized finish and a vinyl grip. They bend square and rectangular-shaped metal and will handle most bending problems.

KYOSHO

This *Kyosho Lexan Body Scissors and Sander Set* (No. KYOR1010, $12.95 retail) features scissors with curved stainless steel blades to make cutting and trimming 1/10- and 1/12-scale Lexan bodies much easier. The included sander has an ABS handle with flat and curved surfaces for sanding down rough spots and "frosting" plastic bodies.

MRC-TAMIYA

The *MRC-Tamiya Digital Multimeter* with case is one of the handiest tools around. This pocket size instrument measures up to 250 volts AC, 250 volts DC, and 20 meg-ohms of resistance. The built-in buzzer checks for continuity; use it also to check the condition of voltage-dropping diodes.

PANAVISE PRODUCTS INC.

The *375 R/C Car Chassis Vise* (No. 375, $79.95 retail) has specially grooved jaws to gently hold a 10- or 12-scale R/C car chassis. Single knob permits tilt, turn, and rotate. Tray base has 6 finger trays for small parts and tools. Includes accessory jaws with neoprene pads for work on other items. Accepts all standard PanaVise interchangeable heads.

PORTA-POWER INDUSTRIES

The *Shop Mate Lathe and Machining Center* ($1,495.00 retail) is a heavy duty production machine manufactured to exacting tolerances, .001" and less. The lathe has metal gears, a 36 speed power feed with 6 spindle speeds and comes complete with the following accessories: 3-jaw chuck with inside and outside jaws, drill chuck with key, 4-way tool post, lathe centers, wrenches, and drift. At last there is an affordable lathe and machining center for the hobby industry, car and motorcycle repair shop, or small manufacturer. In comparison, the Shop Mate makes the competition look like a child's toy.

ROYAL PRODUCTS CORP.

This *Heat Gun* ($23.95 retail) features improved airflow and top-end temperature range, asbestos-free, and chrome metal housing with plastic handle.

ROYAL PRODUCTS CORP.

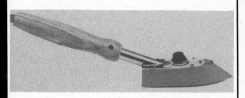

The *Deluxe Heat Sealing Tool* ($20.95 retail) is the top of the line covering tool that has improved top end temperature and comes with a cotton anti-scratch bootie, heat stand and head indicator light. The Teflon shoe has a unique tip that combines a trim tool and iron all in one.

ROYAL PRODUCTS CORP.

The *Economy Heat Sealing Tool* ($15.95 retail) is a good basic covering tool that features the same long life component as our deluxe iron and the same unique Teflon shoe design that combines trim tool and iron all in one. A heat stand is included with the model.

SHERLINE PRODUCTS, INC.

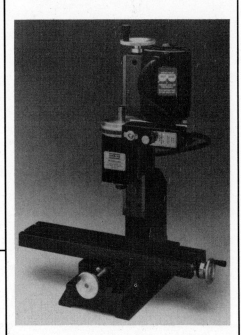

The *Vertical Mill* (No. 5000, $430.00 retail) is the ultimate tool for the miniature machinist. The overall size of this model is 12x14-1/2x17-in. The work table measures 13x1-3/4-in. Travel on the "X" axis is 9 inches. Travel on the "Y" axis is 3 inches. Travel on the "Z" axis is 6-1/2 inches. Standard features include a precision spindle, adjustable pre-load bearings, anti-backlash feed screws, fully dove-tailed machine slides, adjustable gibs, 1/4 HP variable speed motor, and more.

SHERLINE PRODUCTS, INC.

This *3.5 Inch Precision Lathe* (No. 4000A, $420.00 retail) is capable of great versatility and accuracy. It boasts a long list of standard features which are normally found only on much larger and more expensive machines. Standard features include adjustable pre-load bearings, anti-backlash feed screws, fully dove-tailed machine slides, adjustable gibs, 1/4 HP variable speed motor, and much more. Complete line of accessories available for the Model 4000 and 5000.

SMC/LIGHTNING PRODUCTS

SMC/Lighting Products manufactures a line of *Workstands* specifically designed for each R/C hobby. The *Steady Lift Jr.* and heavy-duty *Steady Lift Pro* for cars and trucks, the *AirCraft Workstation* for planes, the *RotorCraft Workstation* for helicopters and the *MarineCraft Workstation* for both motor powered and sail boats. The clamping system of each workstand is designed to hold the greatest variety and widest range of models for each specific hobby. Each system tilts 180° and rotates 360°, allowing an infinite number of work angles. All units have base trays for holding tools and catching parts, and can be mounted directly to a workbench or adapted for mounting on any sturdy tripod. See individual workstand for suggested retail price.

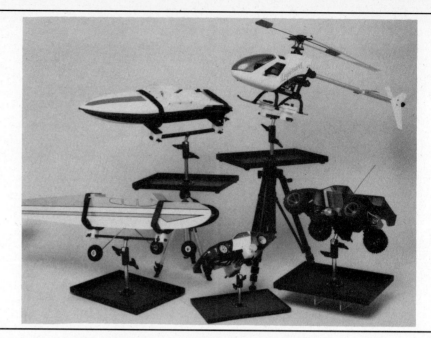

SIG MANUFACTURING CO.

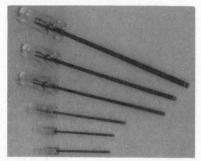

Sig Ball Drivers ($2.25 - $3.50 retail; Sets, $9.95 - $14.50 retail) come in the following standard and metric sizes: Standard Sizes
No. SH-688 5/32-in. Fits 10-32 Socket Head Screws (Shaft Length—7-7/16 in.) $3.50 retail
No. SH-689 9/64-in. Fits 8-32 Socket Head Bolts (Shaft Length—7 in.) $2.95 retail
No. SH-690 7/64-in. Fits 6-32 Socket Head Bolts (Shaft Length—6 in.) $2.95 retail
No. SH-723 5/64-in. Fits 2-56 Socket Head Bolts (Shaft Length—5-1/2 in.) $2.95 retail
No. SH-691 3/32-in. Fits 4-40 Socket Head Bolts (Shaft Length—5-1/2 in.) $2.95 retail
No. SH-692 1/16-in. Fits most large wheel collar sizes Shaft Length—3-5/16 in.) $2.25 retail
No. SH-693 .050-in. Fits most small wheel collar sizes (Shaft Length—3-3/16 in.) $2.25 retail
No. SH-707 Set of 6 Std. Balldrivers (1 of each size) $14.50 retail
Metric Sizes
No. SH-702 1.5mm (89 shaft length) $2.25 retail
No. SH-703 2.0mm (120mm shaft length) $2.95 retail
No. SH-704 2.5mm (140mm shaft length) $2.95 retail
No. SH-705 3.0mm (160mm shaft length) $2.95 retail
No. SH-706 Set of 4 Metric Balldrivers (1 of each size) $9.95 retail.

TWISTER MOTORS

Twister's *Mini Comm Lathe* (Retail: See your dealer) is completely portable and runs on a 4-cell pack or 5-volt power supply. At 4" x 4" x 3" it is the world's smallest and most accurate comm truer and is supplied with instructions and carrying case. Now you can keep you motors running perfectly anytime or anyplace.

XURON CORP.

The *Shears* (No. 475 C, Combination Plier, $14.99 retail; No. 410 T, High Precision Shear, $9.99 retail; No. 450, Tweezernose Plier, $15.99 retail) that set the standard in civilian and military electronics and aerospace are now available to RC hobbyists. The shearing cut of XURON Micro-Shear® flushcutters is so clean and square that post-cutting clean up may not be required. Ask for XURON when you want the cuts that are so good their patented.

Lubricants

WOODLAND SCENICS

Hob-E-Lube ($14.98 for 7-Pak or 2.98 each retail) is paint and plastic compatible. Whether you need lube that will make your servo more responsive or one that can cling to a vibrating prop shaft, you'll have it in the 7-Pak with clear instructions specifying your best selection.

Dry Graphite with molybdenum; Dry White Teflon Lube; Ultra-Lite Oil; Lite Oil; Gear Lube; Moly(bdenum) Grease and White Teflon Grease are all you will ever need for high friction, close tolerance requirements. They come with 4 in. extension tip applicators. The 7-Pak is a MUST for your tool box or workbench!

Publications

HELI IMAGES LTD.

HELISCENE ($6.00 per copy, $36.00 annual subscription) is an 84-page, high-quality, full-color magazine covering all aspects of radio controlled helicopters and associated equipment with full-size information. With stunning photography, unbiased facts, and kit reviews, worldwide and indepth U.S.A. coverage you will not want to be without the finest magazine of its kind.

PUBLICATIONS

CARSTENS PUBLICATIONS INC.

Flying Models magazine was established in 1928. Designed for model builders of all kinds; radio control, control line, free flight, gas, electric, or rubber power. Each monthly issue is packed with how-to features, new product news and reviews, plans, techniques, and troubleshooting. Also included is a monthly R/C boat column.

COMPETITION PLUS

Competition Plus ($3.25 retail) is the oldest monthly devoted exclusively to radio control cars. Each month, its readers are informed on the latest products and racing from around the country. The magazine's policy has always been no mail order ads, so you can stock Competition Plus with confidence knowing that you will not lose your valued customers to some discount house. Competition Plus is distributed by Kalmbach Publishing.

EDSON ENTERPRISES, INC.

The book, *Applying Heat Shrink Plastic Covering to Model Airplanes* ($6.75 retail), was written to help modelers achieve a beautiful finish with heat-shrink plastic covering. For many years, model aircraft builders were limited to finishing materials that required advanced skills in brushing and spraying. Since all materials were liquid, all were subject to a variety of problems. About 12 years ago, this new concept in model aircraft finishing was developed. With its ease of application, limitless finish life, simple repair qualities, and gorgeous coloring, this new material has become the standard in finishing methods for Sport and Competition modelers. The techniques shown were developed over many years and show the modeler how to use the covering to its very best advantage. The book includes 32 pages, full-color photos, and step-by-step instructions.

HARRY B. HIGLEY & SONS, INC.

Harry's Handbook (No. BOK001, $11.95 retail) is an easy-to-read complete treatment of engines. Starting with basic theory and including hop-up, it's acclaimed as the finest book of its type by experts. It includes 90 pages and 200 illustrations.

KALMBACH PUBLISHING CO.

Basics of Radio Control Modeling (No. 12025, $8.95 retail) by Fred M. Marks and William Winter, is an easy-to-read, all-purpose R/C guide with information on tools, materials, cars, engines, radio equipment, boats, and aircraft. Information for simple models as well as competition level models. Softcover, 8-1/4 in. x 11-1/4 in., 220 photos, 84 pages.

KALMBACH PUBLISHING CO.

KALMBACH PUBLISHING CO.

KALMBACH PUBLISHING CO.

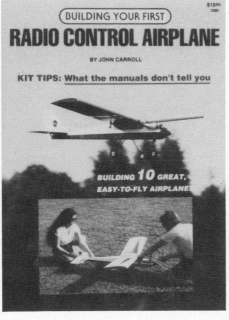

Basics of Radio Control Power Boat (No. 12054, $9.95 retail) by David Thomas, provides useful, how-to-do-it tips for building and operating radio control model boats. Includes descriptions of hull designs, construction methods, radio control systems, internal combustion engines, electric motors, and batteries. Also covers installation of R/C equipment and safe operating techniques. Softcover, 8-1/4 in. x 11-1/4 in., 180 photos, 80 pages.

Building Your First Radio Control Airplane (No. 12087, $10.95 retail) by John Carroll, is a helpful guide that goes one step further than kit instructions, filling in the gaps and holes prevalent in most manufacturers' instruction manuals. Explains how to cover models, align the tail, keep the landing gear from vibrating and support the receiver antenna. Also provides extensive tables listing all the tools and materials needed to build an airplane. Softcover, 8-1/4 in. x 11-1/4 in., 68 pages.

How to Build and Fly Radio Control Gliders (No. 12044, $4.95 retail) by Jack E. Schroder, explains how to choose and build a glider, basic flying techniques, performing challenging aerobatic maneuvers, and glider care and repair. Written in clear, simple language. Chapters cover ground school, clubs, contests, and opportunities. Softcover, 8-1/4 in. x 11-1/4 in., 32 pages.

KALMBACH PUBLISHING CO.

Learning to Fly Radio Control Model Airplanes (No. 12073, $9.95 retail) by John Carroll, tells how to choose a trainer airplane, engine and radio equipment, and describes the qualities to look for in an instructor. The book then covers taxing tests and basic, intermediate, and advanced flight maneuvers. Teaches the skills and reflexes that make a proficient radio control pilot. Softcover, 8-1/4 in. x 11-1/4 in., 184 photos, 84 pages.

KALMBACH PUBLISHING CO.

Building and Flying Electric-Powered Model Aircraft (No. 12069, $9.95 retail) by Mitch Poling, is a complete guide to building and flying electric-powered model airplanes. Teaches how to choose an electric plane, charge and care for batteries, troubleshoot motors, and fly many types of electric-powered models. Also suggests advanced projects to tackle. Softcover, 8-1/4 in. x 11-1/4 in., 76 pages.

KALMBACH PUBLISHING CO.

Building and Racing Electric RC Cars & Trucks (No. 12096, $8.95 retail) by John Carroll, tells beginners how to build a race-winning car, and how to win all the time. Chapters cover what to buy, assembling the vehicle, race tuning, racing strategies, and step-by-step building. Softcover, 160 black-and-white photos, 10 color photos, 15 illustrations, 8-1/4 in. x 10-3/4 in., 64 pages.

KALMBACH PUBLISHING CO.

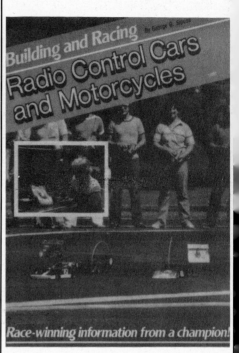

Building and Racing Radio Control Cars and Motorcycles (No. 12052, $7.50 retail) by George G. Siposs, offers race-winning information on choosing gas versus electric power and 1/12 scale versus 1/8 scale. Covers all aspects of the hobby, including how radio control works, chassis, gearing, brake, axles and suspension, wheels and tires, engines, batteries, bodywork, assembly, tools, learning to drive, off-road racing, and troubleshooting. Softcover, 8-1/4 in. x 11-1/4 in., 160 photos, 80 pages.

KALMBACH PUBLISHING CO.

Basics of Model Rocketry (No. 12051, $7.95 retail) by Douglas R. Pratt, is a clear and informative guide that gets new modelers started in the hobby. Chapters explain where to get a first model rocket and basic flying techniques. Further chapters cover some advanced building and flying techniques. Softcover, 8-1/4 in. x 11-1/4 in., 48 pages.

KALMBACH PUBLISHING CO.

If you are into Auto Racing... Become a Member of ROAR.

KALMBACH PUBLISHING CO.

Second Stage: Advanced Model Rocketry (No. 12074, $8.50 retail) by Michael Banks, will challenge and thrill experienced modelers with fun advanced projects. Chapters on high-power model rockets, aerial photography, contest-winning scale models, and home computer programs incorporate the diverse interests of the hobby. Softcover, 8-1/4 in. x 11-1/4 in., 64 pages.

RCM PUBLICATIONS

Now available is the new, full-size *R.C.M. Plans Catalog* ($4.00 retail), providing the scratch-builder with a complete listing of all plans available from R/C Modeler. Plans are listed in chronological order; each includes a photo of the completed model and lists its general specifications. This pictorial listing will greatly ease the modeler's chore of locating plans for that "Special Model" for which he has been looking.

PARMA INTERNATIONAL

Parma 1991 Catalog and *How to Open a Raceway Booklet*. No hobbyist should be without this beautiful, back-to-back full color catalogue. It is packed full of helpful information and handy partsfinder charts covering Parma's entire line of R/C and slot products. ''Slot?'' you say. That's right, those tiny little racers from the 60s are back! If you want to know how you can open your own commercial slot raceway, be sure to contact Parma and ask for the info-pak called: ''Just The Facts.'' It includes the booklet shown.

RCMB, INC.

Model Builder ($4.00 retail; one-year U.S. subscription, 12 issues, with full-size plans available, $25.00) is a comprehensive model magazine, specializing in radio control. This monthly magazine is highly valued by genuine, here-to-stay hobbyists who enjoy building their own models just as much as flying them. Also covers C/L and F/F.

RCMB, INC.

U.S. Boat & Ship Modeler ($4.50 retail; one-year subscription, 4 issues, $13.95) is a quarterly how-to magazine devoted to all types of model boats and ships: R/C, steam, electric, sail, racing, sport, static, and operational scale. Also construction articles on all types, with full-size plans and patterns available, complete with reprint of building instructions.

RCMB, INC.

Radio Control Model Cars ($4.00 retail; one-year U.S. subscription, 12 issues, $25.00) is a monthly magazine devoted entirely to radio control gas- and electric-powered model cars and trucks in all scale sizes. Features product reviews, competition news, how-to articles, and much more.

RCM PUBLICATIONS

Now in its 28th year, *Radio Control Modeler Magazine* ($2.95 cover price, $24.00 one-year subscription) continues to be the world's leading publication for the radio control enthusiast. Devoted entirely to radio control modeling, R.C.M. provides its readers with the highest quality columns, articles, and product reviews. Its columns, construction articles, and plans continue to set the standard for the R/C industry and give readers the most information possible. RCM is by, and for, R/C modelers!

RCM PUBLICATIONS

A Complete Guide to O.S. Model 4-Strokes ($7.95 retail) was developed for the modelers as a guide to O.S. 4-stroke engine service and repair. This 5-3/8" x 8-3/8", 59 page book covers all O.S. single and twin cylinder 4-stroke engines. The text is written in a simple, easy-to-follow "how-to" style and each section is loaded with illustrations and exploded views to take the mystery out of servicing these popular engines.

ZENITH BOOKS

The *Zenith Books Catalog* ($2.00 retail) is packed with R/C modeling books, plus a tremendous selection of aviation books with incredible detail for the modeler, cutaways, three-view drawings, crisp color photos, complete specs, and more on every type of aircraft. Zenith Books, PO Box 1, Osceola, WI 54020. Call (1-800) 826-6600.

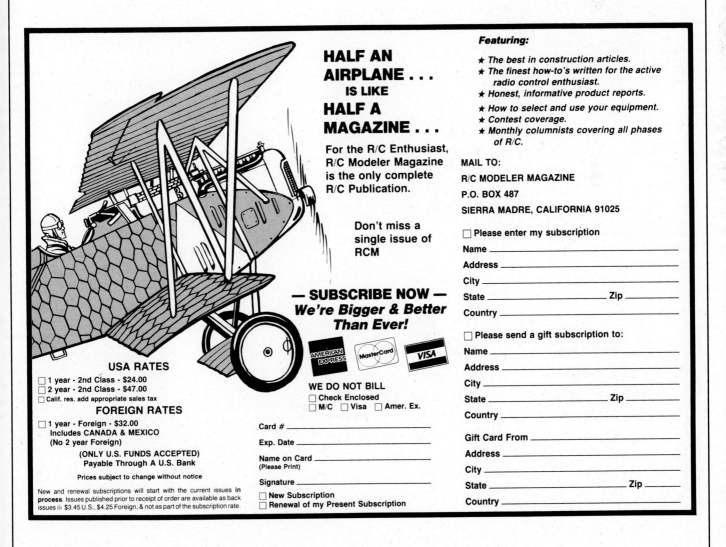

SQUADRON/SIGNAL PUBLICATIONS

Video Tapes

9991A $1.00

squadron/signal publications

1991 FALL CATALOG OF BOOKS

Squadron/Signal publishes books dealing with military aircraft, vehicles, and combat troops. These *softcover books* provide the modeler, historian, and buff with an in-depth, comprehensive study of each subject.

ASSOCIATED ELECTRICS

The *R/C Off-Road Video* (No. 6972, $14.95 retail) depicts the excitement and competition that takes place at off-road races around the world. This tape is designed for the serious modeler who is interested in picking up racing tips from the experts.

COX HOBBIES, INC.

In 1990, Cox Hobbies introduced a new concept of building and flight instructions for its airplane kits. This new concept consists of a brief video with each kit entitled *Video-Copilot*™ (Retail: Free with each kit). Their purpose is to enhance the written assembly and flight instructions that come with each kit.

CARL GOLDBERG MODELS, INC.

It's the *"Wring It Out"* (No. 9105, $24.99 retail) aerobatic instruction series featuring Dave Patrick. Even if you've been flying for some time, work through all three tapes for a complete refresher that'll leave you flying with the kind of refinement you've always admired in the pros. Their real-time split-screen imaging and ideal blend of voice-over and live sound gives "Wring It Out" a real edge over less-professional products, and your progress will be the proof.

RC VIDEO MAGAZINE

The *Top Gun Tournament "Special"* ($24.95 retail) is an exciting example of how video can bring you the ultimate in radio control today. This program was produced with the finest in broadcast equipment and captured in a way to bring you the inside story. Scale radio-control aircraft have reached a new level of sophistication, not only in detail but flight presentation as well. If you enjoy seeing fine scale models flown with skill in a professionally produced program you'll want to OWN THIS TAPE!

SIG MANUFACTURING CO.

The *Sig Video Tour* ($25.00 retail) takes you on a fascinating tour of the Sig plant, shows the models and Hazel Sig's full-scale Clipped-Wing Cub in flight. Professionally done in VHS or Beta.

Rockets

COX HOBBIES INC.

The *Saturn 1B Rocket* is 2.15 in. tall and is made of injection-molded material, fully assembled, decaled, and painted. The Saturn 1B rocket comes with the required parachute, wadding, and engine retainer. Standard solid fuel model rocket engines are required and all Cox rockets can be launched with standard launching systems.

COX HOBBIES, INC.

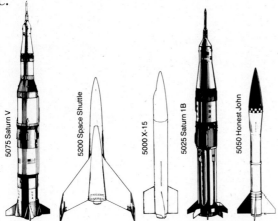

All Cox model *Rockets* (No. 5200 for Space Shuttle, No. 5075 for Saturn V, No. 5000 for X-15, No. 5025 for Saturn 1B, and No. 5050 for Honest John; Retail: See your dealer) are packed with chutes, wadding, and engine retainers. Striking realism shows in the precise scale and factory paint of these ready-to-fly models. Injection-molded construction withstands severe impacts.

COX HOBBIES INC.

The *Honest John Rocket* is 13 in. tall and the *Saturn V* rocket is 34 in. tall. Both rockets are made of injection-molded material, come fully assembled, decaled, and painted. Both rockets come with parachute, wadding, and engine retainer. Standard solid fuel model rocket engines are required.

MRC

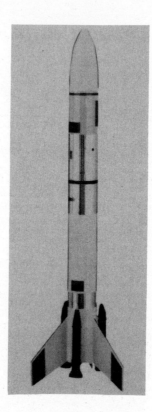

The *Iron Man* (No. LS-100; Retail: See your dealer) is a new super-hero in the rocket world. It has three molded recruit, textured body wraps, three pre-cut fins and a Kevlar Shock cord. There are three FX engine mounts, and each molded recruit can also hold an FX engine. The Iron Man is 24 in. long and 2.0 in. in diameter. It weighs 4.0 oz. and an 18-in. fabric parachute recovery system is included. This is a skill level three (advanced) rocket; recommended engines are C6-3, D12-5 FX (use with C6-3 or D12-5).

MRC

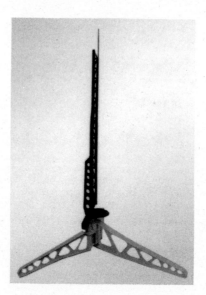

This *Sounding Rocket Launcher* (No. LS-201; Retail: See your dealer) is styled after real sounding rocket launchers used by NASA and even works like the real ones. With 30-degree tilting capability and built-in "C-Rail" guide, this kit also has a molded matching launch lug. Some assembly.

MRC

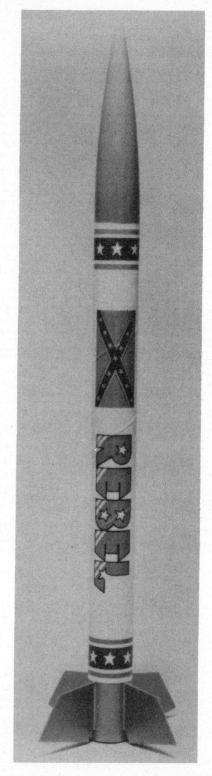

The *TR202 Rebel* (Retail: See your dealer) is one of many types of rockets available from MRC. It features quick, simple assembly; can attain altitudes of 1,200 feet or more; has a computer-aided design (CAD) for stable, high altitude flights, and requires no painting. The Rebel is 15.8 in. long, and weighs 1.17 oz. A 12-in. diameter parachute recovery system is included. Recommended engine sizes are 1/2A6-2, A8-3 (for the first flight), B4-4, B6-4, C6-5 or C6-7.

MRC

The *Trailblazer* (No. LS-104; Retail: See your dealer) sounding rocket in 1/17th scale is for master modelers (skill level four). With a 34.3 in. length and 1.75 in. diameter, it weighs 4 oz. and has 4 molded fins, molded transition and payload, molded recruit motors, and Kevlar shock cord. Also featured are 3 FX engine mounts and ejection baffle. Recovery is made with an 18-in. fabric parachute. Recommended engines are C6-3 and D12-7 FX (use with C6-3 or D12-7).

MRC

This *Dual Electric Launch Control Panel* (No. LS-205; Retail: See your dealer) comes in a sturdy molded case that contains a printed circuit board and all-soldered connections. There's an adapter plug for sources such as an R/C car 7.2V rechargeable pack. Two independent launching circuits allow separate ignition of engines.

MRC

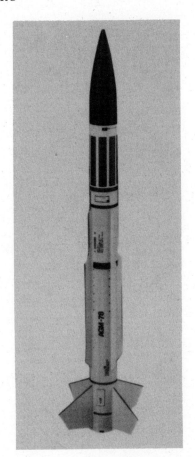

The *Standard Arm* (No. LS-101; Retail: See your dealer) will be welcomed by skill level two (intermediate) rocketeers. This new MRC product is a 25-in. model with pre-marked body tube ejection baffle, four molded fins, and molded nose cone. It's a 1/14-scale sport model. Diameter is 1.75 in., weight is 3.2 oz., and recovery is made with an 18-in. fabric parachute. Recommended engines are C6-3, D12-7 FX (use with C6-3 or D12-7).

MRC

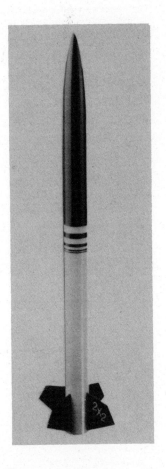

The *2X2* (No. LS-102; Retail: See your dealer) is a skill level one beginner rocket with a 27-in. length full of get-up-and-go. Color-coded parts, ejection baffle, three FX engine mounts, a Kevlar shock cord, four molded fins, and a molded nose cone are featured. The diameter is 1.75 in. It weighs 3.1 oz. and recovery is made with an 18-in. fabric parachute. Recommended engines are C6-3 and D12-7 FX (use with C6-3 or D12-7).

Apparel

RACING SILKS

PARMA INTERNATIONAL

Get the "new" Parma *Ferrari F-40 T-shirt* before they are gone. It boasts 10 vivid colors on the front and back. The F-40 symbolizes the high quality of Parma products. Add one of the new Parma fluorescent hats and win in style. Ask for it at your favorite Parma clothier (hobby shop) or raceway.

TEKIN ELECTRONICS

A complete line of *Tekin Team Apparel* is available in assorted sizes. *Hats and Visors* come in red, blue, and black. *T-shirts* come in small, medium, large, and extra large. *Sweatshirts* also come in small, medium, large, and extra large. Stickers which are suitable for attaching to cars, field boxes, etc., as well as Banners for use in race tracks are available at nominal prices.

VICTOR ENGINEERING

The *Team Victor T-Shirt* ($11.95 retail) is 2 sided, top quality four fluorescent color. The *Team Victor Sweat Shirt* ($19.95 retail) has the same colors as the T-shirt. The *Victor Engineering Hat* ($5.95 retail) has red and white logo. The *"I Have a HI-IQ" Hat* ($5.95 retail) comes in three colors.

Racing Silks' *Tee Shirts* ($12.00 retail) and *Sweatshirts* ($21.00 retail) are the latest in our original line of racing apparel. This realistic but humorous artwork will appeal to all ages of R/C enthusiasts, and to the hard-core racer as well as the Saturday afternoon hobbyist. The Tee Shirts and Sweatshirts are of the highest USA-made quality and the bright screen printed designs will withstand may washings and still retain their vibrant colors. Sizes are S-XL adult. Designs available: Racing Boats, YZ10, Dominator, JRX2, Lunchbox, Clodbuster, Big Brute, and 4 Wheel Fever.

RADIO CONTROL HOBBY SHOPS

116 S. Main St.
Enterprise, AL 36330
(205)393-3355

Radio Control
Airplanes & Helicopters
Plastic Models • Model Rockets
Building Supplies
MON-FRI 10:30-6 • SAT 10-4:30

ALABAMA

Red Baron R/C Hobbies, 116 S. Main St., Enterprise, AL 36330. (205) 393-3355. Mon.-Fri., 10:30-6; Sat., 10-4:30; Sun., closed. R/C airplanes and helicopters; plastic models, model rockets, and building supplies.

Wilson's Hobby Shop, 117 Governors Dr. SE, Huntsville, AL 35801. (205) 539-2259. Mon.-Fri., 9-6; Sat. 9-5; Sun., 12-5. North Alabama's model airplane headquarters. Complete line of R/C airplanes, freeflight, control-line; HO and N scale trains, model rockets, plastic models, and detailing accessories.

ARIZONA

HobbyTown USA, Smitty's Township Plaza, 1915 East Baseline Road, Gilbert, AZ 85234. (602) 892-0405. Mon.-Fri., 10-7; Sat., 10-6; Sun., 12-5. R/C cars, planes, boats, helicopters; models, adventure games, trains, sports cards, and so much more!

HobbyTown USA, Bell Canyon Pavilions, 2814 W. Bell Rd. #1485, Phoenix, AZ 85023. (602) 993-0122. Mon.-Fri., 10-8; Sat., 10-6; Sun., 1-5. R/C cars, planes, boats, helicopters; models, adventure games, trains, sports cards, and so much more!

HobbyTown USA, Scottsdale Pavilions, 9180 East Indian Bend Road, Scottsdale, AZ 85250. (602) 948-3946. Mon.-Fri., 10-8; Sat., 10-6; Sun., 12-5. R/C cars, planes, boats, helicopters; models, adventure games, trains, sports cards, and so much more!

CALIFORNIA

Eagle Hobbies Inc., 1270 Washington Ave., Colton, CA 92324. (714) 825-9706. Mon.-Fri., 10-8; Sat.-Sun., 10-6. Specializing in R/C cars and planes. Support accessories, rockets, plastic models, gaming, family craft, and building supplies. Always ready to help with your hobby projects.

Wilson's **HOBBY SHOP**
117 Governors Drive SE, Huntsville, AL 35801
**North Alabama's
Model Airplane Headquarters**
Complete line of radio control airplanes, freeflight, control-line, HO & N scale trains, model rockets, plastic model and detailing accessories
205-539-2259
Mon-Fri 9-6 • Sat 9-5 • Sun 12-5

HobbyTown USA
A NATIONAL FRANCHISE
*Imagine it...
then find it here!*
•R/C Cars, Planes, Boats, Helicopters
•Models, Adventure Games, Trains
•Sports Cards, and So Much More!!
(602) 892-0405
Smitty's Township Plaza
1915 East Baseline Road
Gilbert, AZ 85234
M-F 10-7 • Sat 10-6 • Sun 12-5

HobbyTown USA
A NATIONAL FRANCHISE
*Imagine it...
then find it here!*
•R/C Cars, Planes, Boats, Helicopters
•Models, Adventure Games, Trains
•Sports Cards, and So Much More!!
(602) 948-3946
Scottsdale Pavilions
9180 East Indian Bend Road
Scottsdale, AZ 85250
M-F 10-8 • Sat 10-6 • Sun 12-5

HobbyTown USA
A NATIONAL FRANCHISE
*Imagine it...
then find it here!*
•R/C Cars, Planes, Boats, Helicopters
•Models, Adventure Games, Trains
•Sports Cards, and So Much More!!
(602) 993-0122
Bell Canyon Pavilions
2814 W. Bell Rd. #1485
Phoenix, AZ 85023
M-F 10-8 • Sat 10-6 • Sun 1-5

EAGLE HOBBIES
1270 Washington Ave. • Colton, CA 92324
• **PLASTIC MODELS • GAMES
TRAINS • CLOCKWORKS
ROCKETS & ACCESSORIES
RADIO CONTROL**
We can special order
BEGINNERS OR EXPERTS
(714) 825-9706
Open 7 days ~ Mon-Fri 10-8 • Sat & Sun 10-6

Flying Machine Model Center, The, 24208 Crenshaw Blvd., Torrance, CA 90505. (213) 325-6194. Mon.-Fri., 10-7; Sat., 10-6; Sun., 11-5. Knowledgeable help and a wide selection of hardware, fine woods, boats, cars, trains, rockets, planes, and helicopters. M/C, Visa, Amex, and Discover.

Ground to Air Hobbies, 18212 Imperial Hwy., Yorba Linda, CA 92686. (714) 579-7488. Mon.-Fri., 11-8; Sat., 11-6; Sun., 11-5. Stock car parts—Kyosho, MRC, Traxxas, BoLink, ASC, JRX, and accessories.

Hobbie Corner, 1287-D N. Main St., Salinas, CA 93906. (408) 449-5824. Mon.-Thurs., 11-7; Fri.-Sat., 10-8; Sun., closed. R/C cars, boats, planes, and helicopters. Plastic models, Nintendo rentals, tools, baseball cards, and trains. Will ship anywhere. Fast, friendly service is our specialty!

HobbyTown USA, 1356 West Valley Rd., Escondido, CA 92025. (619) 739-0672. Mon.-Fri., 10-8; Sat., 10-6; Sun., 11-5. R/C cars, planes, boats, helicopters; models, adventure games, trains, sports cards, and so much more!

HobbyTown USA, 4160 Oceanside Blvd., Oceanside, CA 92056. (619) 758-8125. Mon.-Fri., 10-8; Sat., 10-6; Sun., 11-5. R/C cars, planes, boats, helicopters; models, adventure games, trains, sports cards, and so much more!

HobbyTown USA, 2061 North Oxnard Blvd., Oxnard, CA 93033. (805) 988-4838. Mon.-Fri., 10-8; Sat., 10-6; Sun., 11-4. R/C cars, planes, boats, helicopters; models, adventure games, trains, sports cards, and so much more!

HobbyTown USA, The Brickyard, 4006 Foothills Blvd., Roseville, CA 95678. (916) 773-5061. Mon.-Sat., 12-7; Sun., 12-5. R/C cars, planes, boats, helicopters; models, adventure games, trains, sports cards, and so much more!

HobbyTown USA, The Crossroads, 3850 Barranca Pkwy., Irvine, CA 92714. (714) 733-1126. Mon.-Fri., 10-8; Sat., 10-6; Sun., 12-5. R/C cars, planes, boats, helicopters; models, adventure games, trains, sports cards, and so much more!

HobbyTown USA, 445 Encinitas Blvd., Encinitas, CA 92024. (619) 942-2014. Mon.-Fri., 10-8; Sat., 10-6; Sun., 11-5. R/C cars, planes, boats, helicopters; models, adventure games, trains, sports cards, and so much more!

J.B. Hobbies, 3490 Palmer Dr., Ste. #3K, Cameron Park, CA 95682. (916) 676-8697. Mon.-Fri., 9-6; Sat., 10-5; Sun., closed. We specialize in radio control planes, cars, boats, and helicopters. We carry all major brands of products. Special orders no problem. Mail order available.

Jack's Hobbies & Crafts, 1032 Sixth St., Los Banos, CA 93635. (209) 826-3595. Mon.-Fri., 9-6; Sat., 10-4; Sun., closed. Full service dealer specializing in radio control planes, cars, trucks, boats, and accessories. Plus plastics, rockets, trains, and building supplies. M/C and Visa accepted.

RC Sports, 1009 Alamo Dr., Vacaville, CA 95688. (707) 446-5555. Mon.,-Fri., 10-7; Sat., 10-6; Sun., closed except on race weekends. Largest selection of R/C cars and parts in northern CA. 1/10 and 1/12 scale on road races held twice monthly all year. Trophies every event. The place to race!

Ultimate Hobbies, 2143 N. Tustin, Orange, CA 92665. (714) 921-0424. Mon.-Fri., 11-7; Sat., 10-6; Sun., 11-5. Radio control cars, planes, and boats. Rockets, plastic models, trains, and complete selection of baseball cards.

COLORADO

HobbyTown USA, 839 N. Academy Blvd., Colorado Springs, CO 80909. (719) 637-0404. Mon.-Fri., 10-8; Sat., 10-6; Sun., 12:30-5. R/C cars, planes, boats, helicopters; models, adventure games, trains, sports cards, and so much more!

HobbyTown USA, 1728 Dublin Blvd., Colorado Springs, CO 80918. (719) 531-0404. Mon.-Fri., 10-8; Sat., 10-6; Sun., 12:30-5. R/C cars, planes, boats, helicopters; models, adventure games, trains, sports cards, and so much more!

HobbyTown USA, Drake Crossing, 2100 Drake Rd., Fort Collins, CO 80526. (303) 224-5445. Mon.-Fri., 10-8; Sat., 9-6; Sun. 12-5. R/C cars, planes, boats, helicopters; models, adventure games, trains, sports cards, and so much more!

HobbyTown USA, 6975 W. 88th Ave., Westminster, CO 80020. (303) 431-0482. Mon.-Fri., 10-8; Sat., 10-6; Sun., 11-5. R/C cars, planes, boats, helicopters; models, adventure games, trains, sports cards, and so much more!

CONNECTICUT

Danbury Hobby Center, 366 Main St., Danbury, CT 06810. (203) 743-9052. Tue.-Fri., 9-6; Sat., 9-5; Sun., 9-3. R/C boats, cars, planes, and heli. Adventure games, trains (HO), plastic models, wooden ships, and rockets. All your building needs.

Davis Hobbies Inc., 45A Welles St., Fox Run Mall, Glastonbury, CT 06033. (203) 633-3056. Tue., 10-6; Wed., 10-9; Fri., 10-9; Sat., 10-5. Closed Sun. and Mon. Specializing in radio control planes, cars, boats, helicopters and accessories; plastics, rockets, trains and building supplies.

HobbyTown USA, Fairway Shops, 70 East Main St., Avon, CT 06001. Mon.-Fri., 10-8; Sat., 10-6; Sun., 12-5. R/C cars, planes, boats, helicopters; models, adventure games, trains, sports cards, and so much more!

HobbyTown USA, Groton Square, 220 Route 12, Groton, CT 06340. Mon.-Sat., 10-9; Sun., 12-6. R/C cars, planes, boats, helicopters; models, adventure games, trains, sports cards, and so much more!

HobbyTown USA, Clock Tower Square, 477 Main St., Monroe, CT 06468. Mon.-Fri., 10-7; Sat., 10-5; Sun., 11-5. R/C cars, planes, boats, helicopters; models, adventure games, trains, sports cards, and so much more!

Radio-Active Hobbies, 374 New Haven Ave., Milford, CT 06460. (203) 877-8200. Tue.-Fri., 12-8; Sat., 10-4. Closed Sun. and Mon. "Our name says it all." Radio control only. Planes and helicopter specialists. Free Flying Lessons. Compare our prices!

FLORIDA

Ace Hobbies, 2127 So. Ridgewood Ave., So. Daytona, FL 32119. (904) 761-9780. Mon.-Fri., 12-8; Sat., 10-4; Sun., 12-5. Specializing in R/C airplanes, cars, boats, helicopters; HO and N scale trains, plastic kits, and supplies.

Bob's Hobby Center, Inc., 7333 Lake Underhill Rd., Orlando, FL 32822. (407) 277-1248. Mon.-Thurs., 10-6; Fri., 10-8; Sat., 10-6; Sun., closed. Specializing in R/C airplanes, helicopters, boats, and cars; rockets, trains, plastic models, and tools.

Bob Fiorenze Hobby Center, 420 W. S.R. 434, Winter Springs, FL 32708. (407) 327-6353. Mon.-Fri., 11-7; Sat., 10-6. Jets, airplanes, cars, boats, rockets, plastics, and tools. Complete line of hobby accessories. 35 minutes from Disney, visit our showroom.

Han's Hobby Shop, 1202 W. Waters Ave., Tampa, FL 33604. (1-800) 326-4131. Mon.-Fri., 10-8; Sat., 10-6; Sun., 12-5. We carry a complete line of R/C cars, boats, and planes; plastic models, games, trains, tools, and paints. We welcome mail order.

Orange Blossom Hobbies, 1975 N.W. 36th St., Miami, FL 33142. (305) 633-2522. Mon.-Fri., 9:30-6; Sat., 9-6; Sun., closed. R/C planes, R/C boats, R/C cars, R/C helicopters. Trains, plastic models, tools. Full service dealer.

R.C. Hobbies Inc., 6800 N. University Dr., Ft. Lauderdale, FL 33321. (305) 721-5720. Mon., Tue., Thurs., Fri., 9-8; Sat., 10-5; Sun., 10-3; Wed., closed. Fort Lauderdale's largest discount hobby shop—boats, cars, planes, plastics, helis, trains, rockets, live steam, and kites.

Scott's Gun & Hobbies—Branford R/C Speedway, Rt. 3, Box 240, Branford, FL 32008. (904) 935-0758. Mon.-Sat., 10-6; Sun., every other on race day and all races. R/C cars, planes, and boats; plastic car kits, trains (HO, N, G). Concrete tri-oval, clay tri-oval, and off-road combination. Full service, R/C car specialty. CB radios and accessories, and rockets.

Town & Country Hobbies, 7209 N.W. 4th Blvd., Gainesville, FL 32607. (904) 332-6624. Mon.-Fri., 10-8; Sat., 10-6; Sun., 12-5. R/C helicopter specialists featuring X-Cell and Concept 30/60. Free set up and flight instructions. Full line of R/C cars and planes; plastics, N gauge, dollhouses, and accessories.

Universal Hobbies, 141 S. State Rd. 7, Plantation, FL 33317 (305) 581-9390. Mon.-Fri., 9:30-8; Sat., 9:30-6; Sun., 11-4. Everything in R/C. Trains, planes, and automobiles. Kites, rockets, and tools.

HobbyTown USA, Regency Park, 9120 Metcalf, Overland Park, KS 66212. Mon.-Fri., 10-8; Sat., 10-6; Sun., 12-5. R/C cars, planes, boats, helicopters; models, adventure games, trains, sports cards, and so much more!

T.Q. Pro Shop & R/C Superdome, 14 East Ave "A", Hutchinson, KS 67501. Tue., Thurs., Fri., 4-9; Wed., practice race; Sat., 12 till races end (oval); Sun., 11 till races end (offroad). Specializing in R/C cars and trucks. Indoor track of 40'x90'. Dirt oval and offroad track. Complete service and friendship with a smile!

KENTUCKY

Perry's R/C Hobbies, 214 Globe St., Radcliff, KY 40160. (502) 351-RACE. Mon.-Fri., 11-7 (late on race nights). Specializing in R/C cars, boats, planes; and trains. Oval racing inside and outside twice weekly. Sales and service on all R/C products.

MARYLAND

HobbyTown USA, Burtonsville Crossing, 15751 Columbia Pike, Burtonsville, MD 20866. (301) 421-1819. Mon.-Sat., 10-9; Sun., 11-5. R/C cars, planes, boats, helicopters; models, adventure games, trains, sports cards, and so much more!

MASSACHUSETTS

Hobby USA, Westford Valley Marketplace II, 174 Littleton Road, Westford, MA 01886. (508) 392-9522. Mon.-Fri., 10-8; Sat., 10-6; Sun., 12-5. R/C cars, planes, boats, helicopters; models, adventure games, trains, sports cards, and so much more!

Hobby USA, Shaw's Town Line Plaza, 301 Pond Road, Ashland, MA 01886. (508) 881-1082. Mon.-Fri., 10-9; Sat., 10-6; Sun., 1-5. R/C cars, planes, boats, helicopters; models, adventure games, trains, sports cards, and so much more!

MICHIGAN

HobbyTown USA, K-Mart Plaza, 3514 Henry St., Muskegon, MI. (616) 733-9892. Mon.-Sat., 10-8; Sun., 12-5. R/C cars, planes, boats, helicopters; models, adventure games, trains, sports cards, and so much more!

Joe's Hobby Centers, 7845 Wyoming, Dearborn, MI 48126; (313) 933-6567. 17900 E. 10 Mile, East Detroit, MI 48021; (313) 773-8294. 35203 Grand River, Farmington, MI 48335; (313) 477-6266. 105 S. Livernois, Rochester, MI 48307; (313) 651-8842. Mon.-Fri., 11-8; Sat., 10-6. All stores are full-function hobby shops; well stocked all surround the Detroit Metro area. Use your own ides for layout if you want.

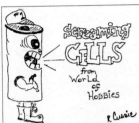

Trains Center Hobbies, 4508 N. Woodward Ave., Royal Oak, MI 48072. (313) 549-6500. Mon.-Fri., 10-8; Sat., 9-6; Sun., 10-5. Your headquarters for the latest in radio control products. Specializing in Schumacher, Associated, Losi, and Tamiya. We repair what we sell.

MISSISSIPPI

Jay's Craft & Hobbies, Maywood Shopping Center, I 55 N. at Northside Dr., Jackson, MS 39211. (601) 981-JAYS. Mon.-Fri., 9:30-6; Sat., 9:30-5. Complete line of foreign and domestic kits. Paints, tools, airbrushes, diorama supplies, and books. Also model railroading and R/C aircraft.

World of Hobbies, 4909 West Gate Hills Dr., Meridian, MS 39305. (601) 693-8368. Mon.-Fri., 12-8; Sat., 10-7. R/C car specialist, including Screamin Cell line of racing packs and accessories. Contact us for the latest racing products. Dealer inquiries welcome. Call/write today.

MISSOURI

Schaefer's Hobby Shop, Inc., 4206 Virginia Ave., St. Louis, MO 63111. (314) 352-3750. Mon.-Fri., 9-6; Sat., 9-5; Sun. closed. Established in 1946. Serving St. Louis and surrounding area with great selection of R/C planes, cars, and boats. Complete line of accessories.

NEBRASKA

HobbyTown USA, Conestoga Mall, 3404 W. 13th, Grand Island, NE 68803. (308) 382-3451. Mon.-Sun., 10-9. R/C cars, planes, boats, helicopters; models, adventure games, trains, sports cards, and so much more!

HobbyTown USA, Rockbrook Village, 11019 Elm St., Omaha, NE 68144. (402) 391-5669. Mon.-Fri., 10-8; Sat., 10-6; Sun., 12-5. R/C cars, planes, boats, helicopters; models, adventure games, trains, sports cards, and so much more!

HobbyTown USA, American Plaza, 701 Galvin Rd. S., Bellevue, NE 68005. (402) 291-0542. Mon.-Fri., 10-8; Sat., 10-6; Sun., 12-5. R/C cars, planes, boats, helicopters; models, adventure games, trains, sports cards, and so much more!

HobbyTown USA, Westgate Square, 1306 Norfolk Ave., Norfolk, NE 68701. (402) 371-2240. Mon.-Fri., 10-8; Sat., 10-5; Sun., 12-5. R/C cars, planes, boats, helicopters; models, adventure games, trains, sports cards, and so much more!

HobbyTown USA, Sutter Place Mall, 5221 S. 48th St., Lincoln, NE 68516. (402) 483-7427. Mon.-Fri., 10-8; Sat., 10-5; Sun., 12-5. R/C cars, planes, boats, helicopters; models, adventure games, trains, sports cards, and so much more!

HobbyTown USA, Galleria Plaza, 14465 West Center Rd., Omaha, NE 68144. (402) 697-9514. Mon.-Fri., 10-8; Sat., 10-6; Sun., 12-5. R/C cars, planes, boats, helicopters; models, adventure games, trains, sports cards, and so much more!

HobbyTown USA, East Park Plaza, 220 N. 66th St., Lincoln, NE 68505. (402) 464-2858. Mon.-Fri., 10-9; Sat., 10-6; Sun., 12-5. R/C cars, planes, boats, helicopters; models, adventure games, trains, sports cards, and so much more!

NEW JERSEY

HiFly Hobbies Inc., Marlton Sq. Shopping Ctr., 729 West Route 70, Marlton, NJ 08053. (609) 983-8060. Mon.-Fri., 10-8; Sat., 10-5; Sun., closed. We are specialists in R/C and we are all modelers. We can help anyone with any kind of problem.

Hobbymasters, 62 White St., Red Bank, NJ 07701. (908) 842-6020. Mon.-Wed., 10-6; Thurs., Fri., 10-8; Sat., 10-5; Sun., 12-4. One of New Jersey's most complete hobby centers. Largest model department on the East Coast. Will mail order anywhere in U.S.

HobbyTown USA, Berlin Circle Plaza, 116 Walker Ave., Berlin, NJ 08091. (609) 768-7550. Mon.-Fri., 10-8; Sat., 10-6; Sun., 12-5. R/C cars, planes, boats, helicopters; models, adventure games, trains, sports cards, and so much more!

HobbyTown USA, Turnersville Square, No. 2 Shoppers Lane, Turnersville, NJ 08012. (609) 227-3222. Mon.-Fri., 10-8; Sat., 10-6; Sun., 12-5. R/C cars, planes, boats, helicopters; models, adventure games, trains, sports cards, and so much more!

Kim's R/C Pit Stop, 357 A Union Blvd., Totowa, NJ 07512. (201) 942-5955. Mon.-Thurs., 11-9:30; Fri., 11-10:30; Sat.-Sun., 11-6. Specializing in R/C cars, planes, helicopters, boats, and much more! All repairs done on premises while you wait. Full stock on all parts!

Motor Bike Imports, Inc., 6005 S. Rt. 130, Pennsauken, NJ 08105. (609) 662-6110. Mon., Tue., 10-7; Thurs., Fri., 10-8; Sat., 10-5; Wed. and Sun., closed. R/C race car specialist. Hottest motors and batteries available. All the latest in trick parts: TRC, RC10, 10L, 12L, Losi, Kyosho, Corally, Novak, Tekin, Lavco, Futaba, Tamiya, and more!

Ricky G's R/C Hobby Center, 2208A Hamilton Blvd., So. Springfield, NJ 07080. (908) 753-1518. Mon.-Fri., 12-9; Sat., 10-10; Sun., 10-5. We specialize in radio control boats, cars, planes, and helicopters. We have an asphalt oval outdoor R/C track on premises.

Ridgefield Hobby, 508 Broad Ave., Ridgefield, NJ 07657. (201) 943-2636. Mon.-Fri., 9-7; Sat., 9:-6; Sun., 9:-1. North Jersey's complete hobby shop. R/C cars, airplanes, helicopters, and boats. Trains, plastics, balsa wood, miniature tools, and science projects. We service what we sell.

Sports America & Hobby Centre, Rt. 130 So., PO Box 255, Florence, NJ 08518. (609) 499-2992. Mon., 10-6; Tue., closed; Wed., 8-6; Thurs.-Fri., 8-8; Sat., 8-5; Sun., 8-4. We build and repair all types of R/C equipment. Area's largest off-road R/C track. HO train repair service available. Mail and phone orders welcome.

TECH-TOYS, 370 Rt. 46 W., Parsippany, NJ 07054. (201) 227-7012, Fax (201) 227-5032. Mon.-Fri., 12-9; Sat., 10-6; Sun., 12-5. Speed Shop for R/C Motor Sports. R/C cars, boats helicopters, and planes. Models and modeling supplies. Service department. Largest selection in N.J. 1/4 and 1/6 scale on display. We ship everywhere.

Zeppelin Hobbies & Raceway, 92 Route 23 North, Riverdale, NJ 07457. (201) 831-7717. Mon.-Wed., 10-9; Thurs.-Sat., 10-11; Sun., 10-6. R/C airplanes, cars, boats, helicopters, slot cars, and accessories. Slot and R/C raceways on site. Racing every night.

NEW YORK

A&D's FasTracks, 1000 N. Main St., Brewster, NY 10509. (914) 279-2065. Mon.-Fri., 2:30-9; Sat., 12-9; Sun., call. R/C hobby shop and indoor clay oval track. Weekly races/ AMB-Auto Score counting. Visa/MC accepted. Mail orders welcome.

Brockport International Speedway, 6000 Sweden Walker Rd., Brockport, NY 14420. (716) 637-6224. Mon.-Thurs., 4-9; Fri., 4-11; Sat., 12-11; Sun., 1-6. R/C cars and trucks. Repairs. Used equipment sales. Two tracks —indoor asphalt, outdoor dirt (seasonal).

HobbyTown USA, Plank Road Plaza, 629 Plank Rd., Clifton Park, NY 12065. (518) 383-1215. Mon.-Fri., 10-8; Sat., 10-6; Sun., 12-5. R/C cars, planes, boats, helicopters; models, adventure games, trains, sports cards, and so much more!

HO/RC Hobbies, 982 Monroe Ave., Rochester, NY 14610. (716) 244-8321. Mon.-Sat., 10-9; Sun., 12-5. Radio controlled cars, boats, and planes. HO slot cars. Skateboards, video games and systems, splatball guns, kites, and snowboards.

Ralph's Hobbies, 60-13 Northern Blvd., Woodside, NY 11377. (718) 728-7744. Mon., Tue., Fri., 10-6; Wed., Thurs., 10-8; Sat., 10-3; Sun., closed. Supporting all forms of R/C. Complete inventory of parts and accessories for all popular helicopters. If you can't find it, we've got it.

NORTH CAROLINA

Hobby USA, Fayetteville, NC. COMING SOON!

HobbyTown USA, Charlotte, NC. COMING SOON!

King R/C, Inc., PO Box 897, Five Forks Village, King, NC 27021. (919) 983-3969. Mon.-Fri., 10-8; Sat., 10-7; Sun., gone flying. We gratify the R/C hobbyist with their needs for racing, flying, sailing, or hovering, with kits, parts, and accessories.

OHIO

Aero Tech Hobbies, 902 N. Main St., North Canton, OH 44720. (216) 499-1300. Mon.-Fri., 10-8; Sat., 10-5; Sun., 12-4. (Nov.-May). We specialize in R/C cars, airplanes, helicopters, and boats. Summer outdoor dirt oval car track. Airplane flying classes and flying field all year around.

HobbyTown USA, Carriage Place, 2544 Bethel Rd., Columbus, OH 43220. (614) 457-1144. Mon.-Sat., 10-9; Sun., 12-5. R/C cars, planes, boats, helicopters; models, adventure games, trains, sports cards, and so much more!

Jinx Model Supply, 721 Rockwell Ave., Findlay, OH 45840. (419) 422-5589. Mon., Wed., Fri., 10-9; Tue., Thurs., 1-9; Sat., 10-5; Sun., open if we are here. We specialize in radio control airplanes, cars, and boats. Kits, accessories, tools, fuel, paint, and covering materials. All the little goodies to complete the kit.

Modeler's Haven, 4255 Portage N.W., Portage Square, North Canton, OH 44720. (216) 499-6000. Mon.-Fri., 11-8; Sat., 10-6; Sun., 12-5. Specialists in radio control airplanes, cars, boats, and helicopters. Many hard-to-find and after-market parts. High-performance matched batteries. Clay oval racing. Special orders welcomed—we'll ship to you.

The Racer's Choice, 1298 U.S. Rt. 42, Mason, OH 45040. (513) 398-5539. Mon.-Fri., 11:30-8:30; Sat., 11-7; Sun., 12-6. Specializing in R/C race cars. Also R/C boats and planes, slots, HO trains, accessories, hop-ups, and service. Outdoor off-road racing. Only minutes from Cincinnati and Kings Island.

Right Choice Hobbies & Raceway, 7760 Harrison Ave., Cincinnati, OH 45247. (513) 353-3343. Mon.-Sat., 12-10; Sun., 12-6. A complete line of radio controlled gas and electric-powered cars and airplanes. Indoor carpet track, outdoor dirt oval track. On-site AMA sanctioned flying field.

Trojan Hobby Center, 200 S. Wilson Rd., Troy, OH 45373. (513) 335-1272. Mon., Tue., Wed., Fri., 2-9; Sat., 10-2; Thurs. and Sun., closed. Specializing in R/C aircraft and supplies. Sig, Ace, Goldberg, Midwest, Model Tech, Futaba, Airtronics, ASP, Fox, K&B engines, Du-Bro, Sullivan, Pacer, Safety Plus glasses.

OREGON

Coin Corner & Hobbies, 215 7th St., Oregon City, OR 97045. (503) 656-1835. Mon.-Sat., 9:30-5:30; Sun., closed. We carry R/C cars, planes, and boats. Also N-gauge, HO, and Lionel trains. We have plastic kits, wood kits, baseball cards, coins, hobby tools, and HO slot cars.

HobbyTown USA, Clackamas Promenade, 8974 S.E. Sunnyside Rd., Portland, OR. (503) 652-5899. Mon.-Fri., 10-8; Sat., 10-6; Sun., closed. R/C cars, planes, boats, helicopters; models, adventure games, trains, sports cards, and so much more!

R/C Plus, 2029 & 2031 25th St. SE, Salem, OR 97302-1130. (503) 364-9188. Mon.-Sat., 11-7; Sun., racing. Salem, Oregon's radio control race car headquarters. Indoor and outdoor dirt radio control race tracks. Full line of parts and accessories for novice to pro.

Sky Sport, 4564 Commercial St. SE, Salem, OR 97302. (503) 363-4345. Mon.-Sat., 10-6; Sun., 1-5. Radio controlled aircraft, cars, and boats. Trains: HO, N, 027, and G. Plastic, Peanut scale, science kits, and more. All accessories and instruction.

PENNSYLVANIA

Cranberry Hobby Depot, 20327 Perry Hwy., Rt. 19N, Cranberry Gardens Plaza, Evans City, PA 16033. (412) 776-3640. Mon.-Fri.: 11:30-8; Sat., 10-5; Sun. 12-5. R/C planes, cars, and boats, plus parts department. Trains: LGB, Lionel, Playmobile; HO, N, & Z Gauge; art dept., rockets.

Marshall's Hilltop Hobbies, RR 4, Box 640, Honesdale, PA 18431. (717) 729-7458. Mon.-Fri., 2-9; Sat. 10-5; Sun., by appointment. We specialize in R/C cars, planes, and boats. We have both an indoor R/C car carpet oval plus an outdoor lighted dirt oval. Also a flying field.

R & D Hobbies, 11-13 So. Hanover St., Hummelstown, PA 17036. (717) 566-5655; Fax (717) 566-5644. Mon., Wed., Fri., 11-9; Tue., Thurs., 11-5; Sat., 12-5; Sun., closed. We offer performance R/C cars and parts. Racer services. Home of the Terminator dirt oval conversion kit. Large selection of NASCAR and performance scale models.

Z & Z Hobbies & Crafts, 229 Plaza Blvd. #22, Morrisville, PA 19067. (215) 736-3351. Tue.-Fri., 11-9; Sat., 11-6; Sun., 12-4; Mon., closed. We sell and service all types of R/C cars, planes, boats, and helicopters. We have all types of trains and collectibles (Lionel). We buy old trains!

SOUTH CAROLINA

HobbyTown USA, Belvedere Plaza, 3122 N. Main St., Anderson, SC 29621. (803) 261-8479. Mon.-Sat., 10-8; Sun., 1:30-6. R/C cars, planes, boats, helicopters; models, adventure games, trains, sports cards, and so much more!

TENNESSEE

HobbyTown USA, Knoxville, TN. COMING SOON!

TEXAS

HobbyTown USA, The Commons at Willowbrook, 7516 FM 1960 West, Houston, TX 77070. (713) 955-7097. Mon.-Fri., 10-8; Sat., 10-6; Sun., 1-5. R/C cars, planes, boats, helicopters; models, adventure games, trains, sports cards, and so much more!

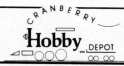

HobbyTown USA, 4107 Capital of Texas Highway, Austin, TX 78704. (512) 440-7877. Mon.-Sat., 10-8; Sun., 12-5. R/C cars, planes, boats, helicopters; models, adventure games, trains, sports cards, and so much more!

I & I Hobby Center, 6707 Chimney Rock, Bellaire, TX 77401. (713) 661-2270. Mon., 10:30-4; Tue.-Sat., 10-8; Sun., 11-6. Cars, planes, boats, helicopters, all kinds of model trains, tools and accessories. Repair, race tracks, boat pond.

R C Pro Shop, 3303 N. Midkiff, Midland, TX 79705. (915) 697-2723. Mon.-Fri., 10-6:30; Sat., 10-5; Sun., closed. R/C cars and parts. Indoor oval R/C track. Races: Tuesday and Friday 7:30 p.m.

Roy's Hobby Shop, 1309 N. Norwood Dr., Hurst, TX 76053. (817) 268-0210. Mon.-Fri., 11-7; Sat., 10-6; Sun., closed. R/C airplanes, cars, helicopters, and electric boats at discount prices.

Wild Bill's Hobby Shop, 535 E. Shady Grove, Irving, TX 75060. (214) 438-9224. Mon.-Thurs., 10-7; Fri., 10-9; Sat., 10-6; Sun., closed. We offer a terrific selection of R/C planes, cars, boats, helicopters, parts and accessories. Also, REA, LGB, Lionel, HO, and N gauge trains, plastic models.

World Wide Hobbies, 6850 Hwy. 6 South (Randall's Shopping Center), Houston, TX 77083. (713) 568-2898. Mon.-Sat., 10-7. R/C cars, planes, helicopters, and boats. Repair service. Collectors plastic kits, HO and N gauge, and rockets. Mail orders accepted. All major credit cards.

UTAH

Douglas Models, 2065 East 3300 South, Salt Lake City, UT 84109. (801) 487-7752. Mon.-Fri., 10-7 (School days, 12-7); Sat., 10-6; Closed Sun. and holidays. Since 1934, 13 different model railroad operations; all gauges. Your one stop model hobby shop.

VERMONT

Mammoth Hobbies, Rte. 131, Cavendish, VT 05142. (802) 226-7100. Mon.-Fri., 11-6; Sat., 9-6; Sun., 11-4. A full line hobby store specializing in radio control, trains, and 1/35 military models.

mike's hobbies & RACEWAY — Open 7 days

Vermont's Largest Full Service Hobby Shop

11,000 sq. ft. including N.E. finest high bank carpeted R/C raceway, family arcade & snackbar.

(802) 775-0059

Located in Central Vermont 1 mile north of junction at Routes 4 & 7.

OLDEST ESTABLISHED HOBBY SHOP IN WASHINGTON, D.C. METRO AREA (SINCE 1948)

Open
Sun 12-5
Mon, Thu, Fri 10-9
Tue, Wed, Sat 10-6

ARLINGTON HOBBY CRAFTERS
Willston Center, 6176 Arlington Blvd. (Rt. 50)
Falls Church, VA 22044 • (703) 532-2224

Hobby USA — A NATIONAL FRANCHISE

Imagine it... then find it here!
• R/C Cars, Planes, Boats, Helicopters
• Models, Adventure Games, Trains
• Sports Cards, and So Much More!!

COMING SOON!
Virginia Beach, VA

HobbyTown USA — A NATIONAL FRANCHISE

Imagine it... then find it here!
• R/C Cars, Planes, Boats, Helicopters
• Models, Adventure Games, Trains
• Sports Cards, and So Much More!!

(703) 330-1990
11696 Sudley Manor Drive
Manassas, VA 22110

M-F 10-8 • Sat 10-6 • Sun 12-5

Mike's Hobbies & Raceway, 162 North Main St., Rutland, VT 05701. (802) 775-0059. Open 7 days. Vermont's largest full service hobby shop. 11,000 sq. ft. including N.E. finest high bank carpeted R/C raceway, family arcade, and snackbar. Located in Central Vermont 1 mile north of junctions of Routes 4 and 7.

VIRGINIA

A-K-Z Hobbies, 940 Radford Road, Christiansburg, VA 24073. (703) 382-9811 or 1173. Mon.-Thurs., 9-5; Fri., 9-4; Sat., 9-7; Sun., 2-4. Remote control cars, supplies, airplanes, trains, models, and hobby items.

Arlington Hobby Crafters, Willston Center, 6176 Arlington Blvd. (Rt. 50), Falls Church, VA 22044. (703) 532-2224. Mon., Thurs., Fri., 10-9; Tue., Wed., Sat., 10-6; Sun., 12-5. Oldest established hobby shop in Washington, D.C. metropolitan area (since 1948). Model cars, boats, airplanes, hobby and model tools, model building supplies, model railroad, rockets and tanks, paint by numbers, radio control cars, boats, and airplanes.

Crossroads Hobbies & Crafts of Salem, 1104 W. Main St., Salem, VA 24153. (703) 387-3414. Mon.-Fri., 10-9; Sat., 10-6; Sun., 1-6. Roanoke Valley's most complete hobby and craft center. R/C cars and planes, plastic and wood models, ships, trains, tools, crafts, and art materials. Indoor carpet R/C car track. Just one mile from exit 40 off I-81 in Salem.

Hobby USA, Virginia Beach, VA. COMING SOON!

Hobby USA, Roanoke, VA. COMING SOON!

HobbyTown USA, 11696 Sudley Manor Dr., Manassas, VA 22110. (703) 330-1990. Mon.-Fri., 10-8; Sat., 10-6; Sun., 12-5. R/C cars, planes, boats, helicopters; models, adventure games, trains, sports cards, and so much more!

WASHINGTON

B&B Hobbies, 317-B S. Washington Ave., Kent, WA 98032; (206) 859-1585. E 907 Francis, Spokane, WA 99207; (509) 487-2122. 14506 NE 20th, Bellview, WA 98007; (206) 641-9722. 15752 Redmond Way, Redmond, WA 98052; (206) 861-4486. You name it we got it. We match Towers 91-92 catalog prices.

A-K-Z HOBBIES
Remote Control Cars, Supplies, Airplanes, Trains, Models & Hobby Items

Asphalt (250 ft.) oval track | Race 1:30 Sat & 1:00 Sun | Dirt (420 ft.) off road

M-Th 9-5, Fri 9-4, Sat 9-7, Sun 2-4
940 Radford Rd., Christiansburg VA 24073
(703) 382-9811

Crossroads Hobbies & Crafts of Salem

Roanoke Valley's most complete hobby & craft center. R/C Cars & Planes, Plastic & Wood Models, Ships, Trains, Tools, Crafts & Art Materials AND Indoor Carpet R/C Car Track. Just one mile from exit 40 off I-81 in Salem.

1104 W. Main Street Salem, VA 24153
703-387-3414
Mon-Fri: 10-9 • Sat: 10-6 • Sun: 1-6

Hobby USA — A NATIONAL FRANCHISE

Imagine it... then find it here!
• R/C Cars, Planes, Boats, Helicopters
• Models, Adventure Games, Trains
• Sports Cards, and So Much More!!

COMING SOON!
Roanoke, VA

B&B — You Name It We Got It

317-B S. Washington Ave. Kent, WA 98032 **206-859-1585**
E 907 Francis Spokane, WA 99207 **509-487-2122**
14506 NE 20th Bellview, WA 98007 **206-641-9722**
15752 Redmond Way Redmond, WA 98052 **206-861-4486**

We match Towers 91-92 catalog prices

WEST VIRGINIA

D.W. Reeds Hobby Shop Inc., 142 West Main St., Bridgeport, WV 26330. (304) 842-2742. Mon.-Fri., 11-7:30; Sat., 11-9; Sun., closed. We are a full line hobby shop. R/C planes, cars, and boats. Dollhouse supplies, trains Z-G, plastic models, diecast, collectables, paints, and tools.

WISCONSIN

ABC R/C Inc., 1441B East Main St., Waukesha, WI 53186. (414) 542-1245. Tue.-Fri., 12-9; Sat., 10-6; Sun., 10-4; Mon., closed. R/C airplanes, boats, cars, and helicopters. Complete kits and accessories. Outdoor dirt track. Racing Saturday afternoons. Truck pulls Tuesday evenings. We build and repair cars.

HobbyTown USA, Aviation Plaza, 2061 South Koeller, Oshkosh, WI. (414) 426-1840. Mon.-Fri., 10-8; Sat., 10-6; Sun., 12-5. R/C cars, planes, boats, helicopters; models, adventure games, trains, sports cards, and so much more!

Hobby USA, Madison, WI. COMING SOON!

AUSTRALIA

Hobbyco, 417 George St., Sydney, Australia 2000. +61 2 299-7461. Mon., Tue., Wed., Fri., 9-5:30; Thurs., 9-9; Sat., 9-4:30; Sun. 10-5. For people who take their fun seriously. Australia's largest general hobby shop with over 200 brands of plastic kits. Railroad— Australia, USA, Europe. Radio control cars, boats, and planes. Books, videos, wooden ships, and kites.

CANADA

Racer's Choice, 39 Ontario St., Bowmanville, Ontario L1C 2S4. (416) 623-8074. Tue.-Fri., 6-9; Sat., 9-5. Remote control cars and trucks. Most parts in stock: Traxxas, Tamiya, Associated, BoLink, Parma, Astro Flight. Plastic models. Custom built trucks. Repair and service available.

Silverwing Hobbies, 2838 E. Hastings, Vancouver, B.C. V5K 5C5 Canada. (604) 255-2838, Fax (604) 255-7088. Mon.-Sat., 10-7; Sun., closed. We specialize in both electric and gas R/C planes, helicopters, jets, boats, and cars. Large selection of Dremel tools, airbrushes, rockets, and plastic models. A one stop R/C super store.

Why Should You Belong to An Association?

Want to become a better modeler faster and enjoy your hobby to the fullest? You can do just that when you join a club or association.

But the benefits don't stop there. As a member, you'll be more apt to expand into other segments of the hobby which can add significantly to your enjoyment.

Also, many associations offer liability insurance to protect you in the event you hurt someone or even yourself and against loss of personal property.

And, of course you'll be helping to promote the growth of the hobby through your active participation and through your financial support.

What types of associations are there?

The Academy of Model Aeronautics (AMA)—If you are a model airplane or helicopter modeler, this is the association you should join. The AMA is located at 1810 Samuel Morse Drive, Reston, VA 22090. Its phone number is (703) 435-0750.

The AMA performs many functions to promote the model aviation hobby. Here are some of its most important contributions:

The AMA works closely with the Federal Aviation Administration (FAA) and the Federal Communications Commission (FCC) to ensure that a sufficient number of radio channels, or frequencies, are available to modelers to safely operate their planes, helicopters, boats, and cars, without infringing on other frequencies used by police, ambulances, etc.

Without this effort, the number of channels available would be seriously reduced because of increased pressure from other industries or municipalities to use the limited number of frequencies available.

Another important function of the AMA is to locate suitable sites that can be developed into safe radio-control flying fields and provide guidance in this connection.

The AMA also sanctions more than 1,900 flying events each year and charters more than 2,100 clubs nationwide and works towards the expansion of the aeromodeling hobby.

The AMA operates a state-of-the-art museum at its headquarters in Reston, Va., which contains an astonishing number of rare airplane models, engines, etc., as well as the latest designs.

When you become a member, you receive a license that allows you to fly in AMA contests and club fields.

Besides the liability coverage, you will have fire, theft, and vandalism coverage which will help you recover the cost of your equipment if it is stolen, damaged by vandals, or damaged by fire. This coverage applies if the loss occurs in your home, car, or at the flying field.

You'll receive the AMA official magazine *Model Aviation*. This monthly publication contains some 200 pages and is loaded with plans, new product information, pictures, and club news from around the country. The magazine is free with your full AMA membership.

Finally, you will be a part of an association that is 160,000-plus strong and growing. And, you'll have the satisfaction of knowing that you are a part of a national association that helps model aviation grow.

For more information on how to become a member of the AMA, see the full page ad in this *Guide*.

R/C Car and Truck Associations

NORRCA
NATIONAL ORGANIZATION FOR RACING RADIO CONTROL AUTOS

If you are a radio-control car or monster truck enthusiast, you'll get more enjoyment from your hobby if you become a member of one or more of these associations. When you become a member, you may attend regular meetings and take part in friendly competition races to win trophies and other prizes.

There are two radio-control car associations. The largest and oldest organization is **ROAR** or **Radio Operated Auto Racing Inc.,** located at 288 E. Maple, Suite 266, Burlington, MI 48009, telephone (313) 644-0669 and **The National Organization for Racing Radio Control Autos (NORRCA)** is located at 331 Mariposa Ct., Upland, CA 91786. Its phone number is (714) 981-9641.

NORRCA is more than 6,500 members strong and strives to bring more novice and informal racers to the hobby and the tracks.

As a NORRCA member, you receive year-round insurance coverage against injury. In addition, NORRCA provides qualified staff members to help tracks/clubs conduct sanctioned races.

ROAR has a much broader scope. In addition to performing the same functions as NORRCA in conducting sanctioned races, ROAR also sets the standards for parts and accessories, i.e. motors, bodies, tires, etc., that can be used on a car in sanctioned races.

ROAR also publishes a quarterly magazine which is full of race news and a slate of upcoming races.

For more information on these associations, see the membership application forms in this *Guide*.

R/C Boating Associations

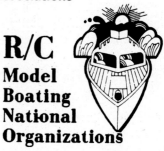

Boat modelers also have a number of organizations to choose from, depending on the type of model boating that interests them. The **American Model Yacht Association (AMYA)** would appeal to sail boat enthusiasts. They are located at 104 West Lake Dr., Sebring, FL 33870.

The **American Power Boat Association (APBA)** is the organization for gas and electric radio-control boats. The phone number for APBA is (313) 773-9700.

The **International Model Power Boat Association (IMPBA)** is involved with boat modelers residing in the Midwest and Florida and is located at RR2, Box 100F, Fountaintown, IN 46130.

The **North American Model Boat Association (NAMBA)** is for those modelers residing in the East and in some parts of the West. This association can be reached at (619) 424-6380.

Your annual dues provide conditional insurance protection and you will receive a monthly newsletter, etc. These associations help to establish racing rules and conduct and supervise races all over the country.

In summary, the few dollars you spend on annual membership dues will go a long way to increase the enjoyment of whatever segment of the hobby you participate in. What sounds better? Running a car or boat by yourself or participating in a friendly competition race with other modelers like you?

Join your favorite association and discover what a difference it can make!

DIRECT RESPONSE COUPON

SPECIAL OFFER:

25% OFF ON ANY HOLESHOT RACING PRODUCT.

SHIPPING IS FREE IF YOU ORDER OVER $25.00.

YOUR NAME:_____

ADDRESS:_____

CITY:_____ STATE:_____ ZIP:_____

PHONE: ( )_____

I've been modeling for _____ years. My primary interest is:

❑ Planes ❑ Boats ❑ Cars ❑ Helicopters

✂

DIRECT RESPONSE COUPON

SPECIAL OFFER:

I WOULD LIKE TO RECEIVE "HELISCENE" FOR $30.00, A SAVINGS OF $6.00 ON THE NORMAL ANNUAL SUBSCRIPTION OF $36.00. I WILL BE BILLED WITH THE FIRST ISSUE I RECEIVE.

YOUR NAME:_____

ADDRESS:_____

CITY:_____ STATE:_____ ZIP:_____

PHONE: ( )_____

I've been modeling for _____ years. My primary interest is:

❑ Planes ❑ Boats ❑ Cars ❑ Helicopters

✂

DIRECT RESPONSE COUPON

SPECIAL OFFER:

RECEIVE A 15% DISCOUNT ON YOUR NEXT ORDER. LIMIT 1 PER CUSTOMER. CANNOT BE APPLIED TOWARD TAX OR SHIPPING OR USED IN CONJUNCTION WITH OTHER DISCOUNTS OR PROMOTIONS. EXPIRES DEC. 31, 1991.

IF A MEMBER OF AMA, PLEASE PROVIDE NUMBER_____

YOUR NAME:_____

ADDRESS:_____

CITY:_____ STATE:_____ ZIP:_____

PHONE: ( )_____

I've been modeling for _____ years. My primary interest is:

❑ Planes ❑ Boats ❑ Cars ❑ Helicopters

To: HOLESHOT RACING PRODUCTS
      P.O. BOX 630
      CANTON, MA 02021

      Attn: TONY BERARDI

To: HELI IMAGES LTD.
      #2107 FLAMINGO PLAZA
      7601 E. TREASURE DRIVE
      NORTH BAY VILLAGE, FL 33141

      Attn: SUBSCRIPTIONS DEPT.

To: COMPOSITE STRUCTURES
      TECHNOLOGY
      P.O. BOX 4615
      LANCASTER, CA 93539

      Attn: DEPT. G

SPECIAL OFFER:

COMPLETE AND RETURN TO *LIGHTNING PRODUCTS*, AND RECEIVE 10% OFF SUGGESTED RETAIL PRICE ON ANY OF THE LIGHTNING PRODUCTS LISTED IN THE RADIO CONTROL BUYERS GUIDE. NO COPIES OR DUPLICATES.

YOUR NAME:_____

ADDRESS:_____

CITY:_____STATE:_____ZIP:_____

PHONE: (   )_____

I've been modeling for _____ years. My primary interest is:

❑ Planes   ❑ Boats   ❑ Cars   ❑ Helicopters

✂

SPECIAL OFFER:

CONSUMER OR HOBBY RETAILER: THIS COUPON ENTITLES BEARER TO 1 BLACK W/ FLUORESCENT GET BIT BY THE SNAKE TEAM COBRA T-SHIRT, 1 TEAM COBRA STICKER PACK, AND 1 FULL COLOR CATALOG FOR ONLY $7.95. REGULAR RETAIL VALUE ON THESE ITEMS IS $16.00. AND FOR ONLY $13.95 TOTAL, WE WILL THROW IN A BLACK W/ FLUORESCENT GET BIT BY THE SNAKE RACE BANNER. THIS IS REGULARLY A $46.00 RETAIL VALUE! ORDER YOURS TODAY!!! TO AVOID C.O.D. CHARGES, SEND MONEY ORDER/CASHIERS CHECK.

YOUR NAME:_____

ADDRESS:_____

CITY:_____STATE:_____ZIP:_____

PHONE: (   )_____

I've been modeling for _____ years. My primary interest is:

❑ Planes   ❑ Boats   ❑ Cars   ❑ Helicopters

✂

SPECIAL OFFER:

**FREE CATALOG OFFER!
SEND FOR YOUR FREE COPY OF THE FULL COLOR CARL GOLDBERG MODELS CATALOG. LOADED WITH EXCITING COLOR PHOTOGRAPHS.**

YOUR NAME:_____

ADDRESS:_____

CITY:_____STATE:_____ZIP:_____

PHONE: (   )_____

I've been modeling for _____ years. My primary interest is:

❑ Planes   ❑ Boats   ❑ Cars   ❑ Helicopters

To: LIGHTNING PRODUCTS
      P.O. BOX 1607
      TOMBALL, TX 77377-1607

      Attn: CHRIS ADAMS

DIRECT REPSONSE COUPON

To: C & M MFG. TEAM COBRA
      P.O. BOX 701-353
      W. VALLEY CITY, UT 84170

      Attn: CHRIS FARRELL

DIRECT REPSONSE COUPON

To: CARL GOLDBERG MODELS INC.
      4734 W. CHICAGO AVE.
      CHICAGO, IL 60651

      Attn: ORDER DEPT.

DIRECT REPSONSE COUPON

To: DAVE BROWN PRODUCTS
     4560 LAYHIGH ROAD
     HAMILTON, OH 45013

     Attn: ORDER DEPT.

DIRECT RESPONSE COUPON

To: COX HOBBIES, INC.
     350 WEST RINCON STREET
     CORONA, CA 91720

     Attn: CATALOG DEPT.

DIRECT RESPONSE COUPON

To: COX HOBBIES, INC.
     350 WEST RINCON STREET
     CORONA, CA 91720

     Attn: CUSTOMER SERVICE

DIRECT RESPONSE COUPON

DIRECT RESPONSE COUPON

SPECIAL OFFER:

SEND S.A.S.E. FOR A *FREE COPY* OF THE ALL NEW TEKIN PRODUCT CATALOG.

YOUR NAME:_____

ADDRESS:_____

CITY:_____ STATE:_____ ZIP:_____

PHONE: (   ) _____

I've been modeling for _____ years. My primary interest is:

❏ Planes   ❏ Boats   ❏ Cars   ❏ Helicopters

DIRECT RESPONSE COUPON

SPECIAL OFFER:

SEND $4.95 TO RECEIVE A DU-BRO HAT, PATCH, TWO DECALS AND UP-TO-DATE CATALOG. PLUS NEW PRODUCT INFO.

YOUR NAME:_____

ADDRESS:_____

CITY:_____ STATE:_____ ZIP:_____

PHONE: (   ) _____

I've been modeling for _____ years. My primary interest is:

❏ Planes   ❏ Boats   ❏ Cars   ❏ Helicopters

DIRECT RESPONSE COUPON

SPECIAL OFFER:

$5.00 OFF SELECT JR RADIOS, KALT HELICOPTERS OR HD BOATS! SEND FOR COUPON!

YOUR NAME:_____

ADDRESS:_____

CITY:_____ STATE:_____ ZIP:_____

PHONE: (   ) _____

I've been modeling for _____ years. My primary interest is:

❏ Planes   ❏ Boats   ❏ Cars   ❏ Helicopters

To: TEKIN ELECTRONICS, INC.
     970 CALLE NEGOCIO
     SAN CLEMENTE, CA 92672

     Attn: ORDER DEPT.

To: DU-BRO PRODUCTS INC.
     480 BONNER ROAD
     PO BOX 815
     WAUCONDA, IL 60084

     Attn: ORDER DEPT.

To: HOBBY DYNAMICS DISTRIBUTORS
     P.O. BOX 3726
     CHAMPAIGN, IL 61826-3726

     Attn: PROMOTIONS DEPT.

To: TEAM LOSI
       13848 MAGNOLIA
       CHINO, CA 91719

       Attn: ORDER DEPT.

DIRECT RESPONSE COUPON

To: MODEL RECTIFIER CORP.
       200 CARTER DRIVE
       EDISON, NJ 08817

       Attn: ORDER DEPT.

DIRECT RESPONSE COUPON

To: ROBART
       P.O. BOX 1247
       ST. CHARLES, IL. 60174

DIRECT RESPONSE COUPON

To: HOBBY LOBBY
5614 FRANKLIN PIKE CIRCLE
BRENTWOOD, TN 37027

Attn: TRENT DEVAULT

DIRECT RESPONSE COUPON

To: COMPETITION ELECTRONICS
3469 PRECISION DRIVE
ROCKFORD, IL 61109

Attn: ORDER DEPT.

DIRECT RESPONSE COUPON

To: AEROTREND PRODUCTS
31 NICHOLS STREET
ANSONIA, CT 06401

Attn: ORDER DEPARTMENT

DIRECT RESPONSE COUPON

ATTN: Product Manager
Kalmbach Publishing Co.
P.O. Box 1612
Waukesha, WI 53187-1612

DIRECT RESPONSE COUPON

$2.00 Rebate on Building and Racing Electric RC Cars and Trucks.

To receive your refund, mail completed coupon along with an original cash register receipt. Store must be identified, as well as date of purchase (on or before March 31,1992). Circle the price of **Building and Racing Electric RC Cars and Trucks** circled. Photocopy of cash register receipt is not acceptable.

We'll refund you $2.00 on **Building and Racing Electric RC Cars and Trucks** when you send this completed certificate along with the cash register receipt to:
ATTN: Product Manager
Kalmbach Publishing Co.
P.O. Box 1612
Waukesha, WI 53187-1612

Name_____

Address_____

City,State _____

Zip_____

Store Name_____

LIMIT: One refund per household. Refund requests must be made on this official certificate; reproduction of this official certificate is unacceptable and transfer is prohibited. Void where prohibited, licensed, restricted or taxed. Allow 6 to 8 weeks for refund. Refund requests must be postmarked no later than March 31,1992. Requests postmarked after this date will not be honored. Resellers not eligible for rebate.

90022

DIRECT RESPONSE COUPON

To: **TEAM LOSI INC.**
13848 MAGNOLIA AVE.
CHINO, CA 91710

Attn: DEPT. J

DIRECT RESPONSE COUPON

To: R/C MODELER MAGAZINE
       P.O. BOX 487
       SIERRA MADRE, CA 91025

       Attn: LOUISE STARK

DIRECT RESPONSE COUPON

To: ACE R/C INC.
       P.O. BOX 511
       HIGGINSVILLE, MO 64037

       Attn: CATALOG DEPT.

DIRECT RESPONSE COUPON

To: FUTABA CORP. OF AMERICA
       3 STUDEBAKER
       IRVINE, CA 92718

       Attn: CATALOG DEPT.

DIRECT RESPONSE COUPON

To: PROGRESSIVE TECHNOLOGIES, INC.
       HOBBY DIVISION, P.O. BOX 4648
       WINSTON-SALEM, NC 27115-4648

       Attn: RANDY SMITH

To: SKYWARD
       4660 DECARIE BLVD.
       MONTREAL QUEBEC
       CANADA, H3X 2H5

       Attn: ORDER DEPT.

To: SKYWARD
       4660 DECARIE BLVD.
       MONTREAL QUEBEC
       CANADA, H3X 2H5

       Attn: ORDER DEPT.

To: ASSOCIATED ELECTRICS INC.
3585 CADILLAC AVENUE
COSTA MESA, CA 92626

Attn: CATALOG DEPT.

To: TATONE PRODUCTS CORP.
21658 CLOUD WAY
HAYWARD, CA 94545

Attn: ORDER DEPT.

To: CUSTOM CHROME PARTS MFG.
34518 WARREN ROAD
SUITE 273
WESTLAND, MI 48185

Attn: ORDER DEPT.

To: ROBINSON RACING PRODUCTS
        165 N. MALENA
        ORANGE, CA 92669

Attn: ORDER DEPT.

PLACE
APPROPRIATE
POSTAGE
HERE

Great Planes Model Distributors Company
P.O. Box 4021
Champaign, Illinois 61824-4021

To:

Attn:

Manufacturers Index

— A —

A & D RACING PRODUCTS
12 Plaza 94, Suite 218
St. Peters, MO 63376
(1-800) 397-3488   Fax (314) 447-5662
Sales: Dealers, Distributors, and Direct
Catalog: Yes
Products: Matched battery packs and related
accessories. p. 142, 259, 266

AG INDUSTRIES, INC.
3832 148th Avenue, NE
Redmond, WA 98052
(206) 885-4599   Fax (206) 885-4672
Sales: Dealers
Catalog: Yes
Products: These are the only official models of The
America's Cup Challenge '87. They are considered
best in their class and are regarded as the fastest
models of their kind. p. 26, 70

AKS GONZO/WIMPY
418 Roberts Road
Chesterton, IN 46304
(219) 926-7925   Fax (219) 926-3462
Sales: Dealers
Catalog: Yes
Products: A variety of battery packs and motors for
the R/C car market. Matched Sanyo cells and built
battery packs. Modified, Stock, and Custom wind
motors. p. 143, 163

ACE RADIO CONTROL, INC.
PO Box 511, 116 W. 19th Street
Higginsville, MO 64037
(816) 584-7121   Fax (816) 584-7766
Orders: (800) 322-7121
Technical Support: (816) 584-6303
Sales: Dealers and Direct
Catalog: Yes
Products: Offer a complete line of R/C systems both
for air and boat use. Extensive line of electronic
support equipment. Tools, hardware, and
accessories. Manufacture over 28 different airplane
kits from sailplanes to seaplanes. p. 13, 24, 25, 41,
122, 128, 147

ADVANCE ENG. & MFG. CO.
PO Box 766
Woodland Park, CO 80866
(719) 687-2626   Fax (719) 687-1013
Sales: Dealers and Distributors
Catalog: Yes
Products: Monster truck parts and accessories and
high-performance on road cars and replacement
parts. p. 267

AEROTREND PRODUCTS
31 Nichols Street
Ansonia, CT 06401-1106
(203) 734-0600   Fax (203) 732-5668

Sales: Dealers, Distributors, and Direct
Catalog: $2.00
Products: Many Radio Control accessories for cars,
boats, planes, helicopters, including "BlueLine"
tubing, many size battery packs, bearing kits for
many R/C cars. p. 142, 147, 198, 199, 228, 251, 254,
258, 259, 293, 294, 300, 305, 307, 308, 352, 369,
370, 373

ALTECH MARKETING
PO Box 391
Edison, NJ 08818-0391
(908) 248-8738
Sales: Dealers
Catalog: $3.00
Products: Distributors of Enya engines, Acoms R/C
car radio systems and chargers, free-flight airplanes,
electric motors, Hirobo helicopters and parts, and
almost ready to cover wood airplane kits. p. 8, 14, 17,
21, 29, 30, 35, 41, 49, 130, 158, 159, 164, 165, 166,
169, 170, 171, 173, 174, 176, 177, 180, 181, 182,
183, 184, 185, 289, 299, 301

ANDY'S R/C PRODUCTS INC.
466 W. Arrow Highway, Unit M
San Dimas, CA 91773
(714) 592-4737   Fax (714) 592-0505
Sales: Distributors
Catalog: Yes
Products: After market radio controlled car parts
(Lexan bodies, injection molded suspension parts,
conversion kits). p. 229, 237, 238

APPLIED DESIGN CORP.
PO Box 3384
Torrance, CA 90510
(213) 375-4120
Sales: Dealers and Distributors
Catalog: $.75
Products: We manufacture small hand tools for
model and crafts. p. 376, 377

ASSOCIATED ELECTRICS INC.
3585 Cadillac Avenue
Costa Mesa, CA 92626
(714) 850-9342   Fax (714) 850-1744
Sales: Distributors
Catalog: Yes
Products: Manufacture R/C car kits in 1/12, 1/10, and
1/8 scales which have won 9 IFMAR World
Championships. There is none better. p. 76, 77, 86,
87, 158, 229, 257, 396

AUTOGRAPHICS OF CALIFORNIA
7401-1 White Lane
Bakersfield, CA 93309
(805) 836-2886   Fax (805) 836-0938
Sales: Distributors
Catalog: Yes
Products: Quality R/C decal graphics. p. 333

— B —

BADGER AIR BRUSH COMPANY
9128 West Belmont Avenue
Franklin Park, IL 60131
(708) 678-3104   Fax (708) 671-4352
Sales: Dealers and Distributors
Catalog: Yes
Products: Largest manufacturer of air brushes in the
United States. We manufacture a complete line of air
brushes and accessories including compressors,
paints, frisket film, stencils, books, and videos. p.
339, 340

BINKS MANUFACTURING CO.
9201 W. Belmont Avenue
Franklin Park, IL 60131
(708) 671-3000   Fax (708) 671-6489
Sales: Dealers, Distributors, and Direct
Catalog: Yes
Products: Manufacturer of air brushes, accessories,
and all spray equipment. p. 340, 341

BLUE RIDGE MACHINERY & TOOLS, INC.
PO Box 536-RCBG
Hurricane, WV 25526
(1-800) 872-6500   Fax (304) 562-5311
Sales: Direct
Catalog: $1.00
Products: Distribute lathes, milling machines, and
machine shop supplies to the hobby builders. We
stock Emco Maier, Myford, South Bend, Jet,
Sherline, Atlas parts and accessories. R/C books and
woodworking machinery available. p. 377

BOCA BEARING CO.
7040 W. Palmetto Park Road, Suite 2304
Boca Raton, FL 33433
(407) 998-0004   Fax (407) 998-0119
Sales: Dealers and Distributors
Catalog: $3.00
Products: Complete range of miniature bearings for
R/C cars, boats, helicopters, planes, engines, motors,
and small tools. p. 228, 229

DAVE BROWN PRODUCTS
4560 Layhigh Road
Hamilton, OH 45013
(513) 738-1576   Fax (513) 738-0152
Sales: Distributors
Catalog: Yes
Products: Manufacture model aircraft accessories,
wheels, motor mounts, pushrods, fuel pumps,
retracts, cordless starter pack, epoxy, contact
adhesive, CyA instant glues, etc. Also a computer
flight simulator for training purposes. p. 188, 196,
199, 284, 305, 306, 310, 344

BUD'S RACING PRODUCTS INC.
1575 Lowell St.
Elyria, OH 44035
(216) 284-0270   Fax (216) 284-0271

Sales: Distributors
Catalog: $2.00; include business size, 52¢
  stamped envelope, dealers N/C
Products: One of the leading manufacturers of hop
up racing accessories, wings, motors, bodies,
ceramic diff. rings and diff. parts, and fasteners. 1991
ROAR 1/12 National Champions! p. 143, 159, 238,
260

— C —

C.J.T. ENTERPRISES INC.
9965 Miramar Parkway, Suite 137
Miramar, FL 33025
(305) 436-2821   Fax (305) 436-1042
Sales: Dealers
Catalog: Free color product brochure
Products: C.J.T. Enterprises Inc. is a Florida-based
distributor of high-quality Trintec brand aviation and
marine novelty products. Trintec quartz clocks and
thermometers have a one year manufacturer's
warranty. C.J.T. also distributes Trintec desk top
alarm clocks, coasters, and keychains. p. 199

C & M Mfg.
PO Box 701-353
West Valley City, UT 84170
(801) 250-9747   Fax (801) 250-9792
Sales: Distributors
Catalog: $2.00 with sticker; pack-free to trade
Products: C & M Team Cobra is fast becoming the
one to beat in R/C! In business since 1987, we're a
company comprised of serious R/C racers. As a
result, we know what racers need and want in order
to win. We manufacture the Cobra line of 1/10, 1/12,
and 1/8 electric road race cars, the Trackside Truer—
portable tire truer, and the VR3000 and 3000T 0-30
AMP variable discharger and timer. We also make
selectrics—a full line of stock on road and off road
motors and handwound modifieds. We have a full
line of racing accessories such as battery equalizers,
body posts, and track grip tire compound; a line of
conversion items such as narrowed Yokomo chassis,
long front axles for JRX2/T, and much, much more!
p. 86, 88, 89, 156, 159, 260

CARSTENS PUBLICATIONS INC.
PO Box 700
Newton, NJ 07860-0700
(201) 383-3355   Fax (201) 383-4064
Sales: Dealers write for information
Catalog: Illustrated $2.00
  Canada and foreign $4.00.
Products: Publishers of *Flying Models* magazine, est.
1928, for the model builder; radio control, control line,
free flight. Gas, electric, and rubber power. Each
monthly issue packed with how-to features, new
product news and reviews, plans, techniques,
troubleshooting. Monthly R/C boat column.
Subscription: 1 year, $23.00; Canada add $6.00;
Foreign $9.00 US funds. Readers: Send No. 10 SAE
for brochure. p. 390

CHEVERON HOBBY PRODUCTS
PO Box 2480
Sandusky, OH 44870
(419) 797-2208
Sales: Dealers and Distributors
Catalog: Yes
Products: Monokote Matching Colors, Federal
Standard Matching Camouflage Colors, Non-Toxic
Pigment virtually odorless will not affect styrofoam,
excellent flow and adhesion. Balsa fillers, primers,
display racks, engine cleaners, and thinners. p. 341

CLASS RECREATIONAL PRODUCTS
Rd. #1 Box 187A
Utica, NY 13502
(315) 724-8052   Fax (315) 732-2034
Sales: Dealers, Distributors, and
  Direct with restrictions
Catalog: Free
Products: Class has earned a reputation for high
quality R/C car products. Our Model 188 Peak
Detector rewrote the standards for AC chargers. All

our products are race proven before being released.
Look for new high performance car and motor
accessories from Team Class. p. 154, 162

COMPETITION ELECTRONICS
3469 Precision Dr.
Rockford, IL 61109
(815) 874-8001   Fax (815) 874-8181
Sales: Distributors
Catalog: Yes
Products: Manufacturers of battery chargers and
matchers. Known for quality, reliability, and customer
service. Products manufactured in U.S.A. p. 147, 156

COMPETITION PLUS
16582 Gotharo St. Unit Q
Huntington Beach, CA 92647
(714) 842-3881   Fax (714) 848-2969
Sales: Dealers and Direct
Products: Radio controlled magazine dedicated
exclusively to cars with race coverage, technical
articles, product reviews, and interviews. No mail
order ads. p. 390

COMPOSITE STRUCTURES TECHNOLOGY
PO Box 4615
Lancaster, CA 93539
(805) 723-3783   Fax (805) 723-3783
Order Desk: (1-800) 338-1278
Sales: Dealers and Direct
Catalog: Yes
Products: CST specializes in high tech modeling
supplies including electric vacuum bagging systems,
equipment, and supplies as well as a full line of
composite materials including carbon, fiberglass,
Kevlar, Rohacell, and epoxies. p. 310, 311, 377

CONDOR R/C SPECIALTIES
1733 Monrovia Avenue #G
Costa Mesa, CA 92627
(714) 642-8020   Fax (714) 642-8021
Sales: Dealers and Direct
Catalog: Free
Products: Specialty R/C equipment and accessories
bridging the gap between normal recreational R/C
and industrial RPV, UAV, robotics applications. p. 133,
136, 137, 148, 294

COVERITE
420 Babylon Road
Horsham, PA 19044
(215) 672-6720   Fax (215) 672-9801
Sales: Distributors
Catalog: Yes
Products: Finishing materials for planes, cars, and
boats. Seven different airplane coverings (films and
fabrics). Epoxy paints for planes and boats. Lexan
paints for cars. Fuelproof die-cut press-ons. Sealing
irons, thermometers. Stripes, WindowMask, Presto
trim for cars and planes. p. 311, 312, 333, 334, 341,
377

COX HOBBIES, INC.
350 W. Rincon Street
Corona, CA 91720
(714) 278-1282   Fax (714) 278-2981
Sales: Distributors
Catalog: Yes
Products: R/C systems for aircraft, cars, and boats;
R/C aircraft, fuel, and electric-powered with
instructional videos; R/C fuel-powered cars, control
line, and free-flying fuel-powered models; .010 to .09
model engines; fuel; starting kits; and rockets. p. 6, 7,
8, 29, 86, 122, 129, 133, 166, 167, 301, 304, 396,
397, 398

CUSTOM CHROME PARTS MFG. INC.
24518 Warren Rd. Suite 273
Westland, MI 48185
(313) 591-0060   Fax (313) 591-5549
Sales: Dealers, Distributors, and Direct
Products: Custom Chrome Parts Mfg. is the
worldwide leader in R/C chrome-plated Tamiya parts
and also manufactures a line of aftermarket
replacement aluminum parts and truck pulling
accessories. Started in 1989, Custom Chrome's
unique 2-step chroming process is unmatched by any

other manufacturer in the R/C industry. p. 148, 238,
239, 257, 260, 266, 267, 270

CUSTOM MODEL PRODUCTS, INC.
1 Bert Dr. Unit 12
W. Bridgewater, MA 02379
(508) 580-1622   Fax (508) 586-0036
Sales: Dealers, Distributors, and Direct
Products: Model products for modelers by modelers.
p. 378

CUSTOM WOODCRAFT
#4 Pine Shadows Road
McArthur, CA 96056
(916) 336-6378
Sales: Dealers and Direct
Catalog: Flyer
Products: Manufacture field support systems for the
R/C model industry. This is the original Flight Box
since 1968! Made in America by Americans. p. 297

— D —

DAHM'S RACING BODIES
PO Box 360
Cotati, CA 94931-0360
(1-800) 232-4679 or (707) 792-1316
Fax (707) 792-0137
Sales: Dealers, Distributors, and Direct
Catalog: $2.00; free to trade
Products: DAHM'S RACING BODIES produces world
class Lexan racing bodies, wings, and underbodies
with exceptional styling, fine detailing, performance,
and quality! NEW! DAHM'S introduces aerodynamic
"ground effects" underbodies for NASCAR racing. p.
230, 231, 232, 233, 234, 334

DOLANITE CUSTOM GRAPHICS INC.
PO Box 206
Smyrna, DE 19977
(302) 653-2121
Sales: Dealers, Distributors, and Direct
Catalog: Free
Products: Dolanite is THE GRAPHICS OPTION FOR
THE HOBBY INDUSTRY. Our products include
Miracle Mask Window Cuts and DCG Window
Netting. We provide vinyl graphics services such as
banners, sponsor stickers, logos, and custom painted
bodies. p. 334

DREMEL
Div. Emerson Electric Co.
4915 21st Street
Racine, WI 53406
(414) 554-1390   Fax (414) 554-7654
Sales: Dealers, Distributors, and Direct
Catalog: Yes
Products: Corded and cordless Moto Tool high speed
rotary tools and kits, attachments and accessories,
scroll saw, disc/belt sander, Moto Flex Tool,
engraver. p. 378, 379, 380

DU-BRO PRODUCTS
PO Box 815
Wauconda, IL 60084
(708) 526-2136   Fax (708) 526-1604
Sales: Distributors
Catalog: $1.00
Products: A full line of R/C accessories and hardware
for the modeler. p. 137, 185, 188, 189, 190, 194, 196,
197, 199, 239, 251, 252, 253, 289, 290, 294, 306,
307, 308, 309, 312, 329, 342, 343, 344, 345, 346,
350, 352, 353, 354, 355, 358, 359, 360, 361, 362,
363, 364, 373, 374, 380, 381, 382

DUMAS PRODUCTS, INC.
909 E. 17th Street
Tucson, AZ 85719
(602) 623-3742   Fax (602) 620-1329
Sales: Distributors
Catalog: $2.00
Products: Dumas Products, Inc. has been a
manufacturer of radio controlled model boat kits and
related marine hardware since 1964. Dumas
Products has built its reputation on offering a wide

442   **PRICES AND SPECS ARE SUBJECT TO CHANGE**   **RADIO CONTROL BUYERS GUIDE**

selection, prompt efficient service, and high quality products. p. 59, 66, 67, 68, 70, 71, 72, 73

DURO ART IND., INC.
1832 Juneway Terrace
Chicago, IL 60626
(312) 743-3430   Fax (312) 743-3882
Sales: Dealers and Distributors
Catalog: Yes
Products: We manufacture and sell a service complete lettering and art supply departments. We offer top-quality products at a very low retail! You can be competitive with Duro. p. 260, 334, 342, 343

DURACRAFT
1007 Orchard Grove Dr.
Royal Oak, MI 48067
(313) 547-5082
Sales: Dealers and Distributors
Catalog: Yes
Products: Ready-to-fly airplanes. p. 50

DURATRAX
(See Great Planes Model Dist.)
p. 143, 253, 254, 278

DYNAMIC MODELS
Drawer "C"
Port Jefferson Station, NY 11776
(516) 928-8200
Sales: Dealers, Distributors, and Direct
Catalog: $5.00
Products: Dynamic has been a major manufacturer and distributor of high-quality model products for more than 30 years. Dynamic currently specializes in scale R/C model boats and accessories. p. 71, 157

DYNATHRUST PROPS, INC.
Box 91
Georgetown, TN 37336
(615) 476-2330
Sales: Dealers and Direct
Products: Precision-molded fiberglass reinforced propellers. p. 194

— E —

EDSON ENTERPRISES INC.
17 Speer Place
Nutley, NJ 07110
(201) 661-2310
Sales: Dealers, Distributors, and Direct
Catalog: Free
Products: Manufacture the only Adj. Mount in the world that fits over 90 engines. Plus nose gear, trust ring, spare parts, publish book on covering models with plastic and all hardware to mount airplane engines. p. 190, 284, 285, 390

EXCEL HOBBY BLADES, CORP.
399 Liberty St.
Little Ferry, NJ 07643
(201) 807-1772   Fax (201) 807-0395
Sales: Dealers and Distributors
Catalog: Yes
Products: Wide assortment of hobby knives, replacement blades, and hobby tool sets. p. 382

— F —

FHS SUPPLY INC.
PO Box 9, 239 Bethel Church Road
Clover, SC 29710
(803) 222-7488   Fax (803) 222-7285
Sales: Dealers and Direct
Products: Featuring nitro fuels for racing and model engines. p. 304

FIBERGLASS MASTER
Route 1, Box 530
Goodview, VA 24095
(703) 890-6017
Sales: Dealers and Direct

Catalog: $1.00
Products: We have cowls, wheelpants, and floats. All molded in fiberglass. p. 200

FOREDOM ELECTRIC CO.
Route 6
Bethel, CT 06801
(203) 792-8622   Fax (203) 790-9832
Sales: Dealers, Distributors, and Direct
Catalog: Yes
Products: Manufacturers of quality rotary power flexible shaft machines. Various models available from 1/4 horsepower to 1/15 horsepower with 1,000 different accessory items. p. 382

FUN-LINE MODELS
PO Box 2392
Shawnee Mission, KS 66201
(913) 262-1399
Sales: Dealers and Direct
Catalog: Free
Products: Manufacture the Ole Reliable Flying Machine Kit. p. 50

FUTABA CORPORATION OF AMERICA
4 Studebaker
Irvine, CA 92718
(714) 455-9888   Fax (714) 455-9899
Sales: Distributors
Catalog: Yes
Products: A complete line of radio control systems and accessories for aircraft, helicopter, sailplane, car, and boat models. Included are the only PCM 1024 systems, electronic speed controls, gyros and the largest selection of servos. Futaba also imports YS Futaba engines, Hatori mufflers, Hirobo planes, the FX10 car and Candy boat. p. 9, 30, 41, 50, 51, 77, 123, 124, 125, 126, 127, 128, 129, 130, 131, 133, 134, 138, 148, 171, 174, 278, 279, 295

— G —

G&A PRODUCTS
PO Box 36025
Sarasota, FL 34233
(813) 377-4252
Sales: Dealers, Distributors, and Direct
   Domestic, mail order, and hobby shops.
   Foreign via distributors. Inquires welcome.
Catalog: Info sheet; S.A.S.E.
Products: G&A specializes in the soft-mounting of model airplane engines. Known for the "VEND MOUNT" system; it is the only "soft-mount" ever remotely endorsed by John Preston, Model Aviation, Safety Comes First, August 1989. p. 200, 286

G.P.M.
(See Great Planes Model Dist.)
p. 62

CARL GOLDBERG MODELS INC.
4734 West Chicago Avenue
Chicago, IL 60651
Sales: Distributors
Catalog: $2.00
Products: Produces a full line of R/C airplanes and accessories for the novice and sports modelers. The line includes jet CyA glues, Model Magic filler and epoxies, Ultracote covering and Colorstripe detailing tape. p. 14, 15, 16, 17, 18, 26, 42, 51, 52, 157, 187, 190, 191, 192, 194, 297, 298, 299, 329, 330, 346, 347, 348, 349, 350, 355, 356, 364, 365, 366, 367, 371, 372, 382, 383, 396

GRANITE STATE R/C PRODUCTS
65 North Lowell St.
Methuen, MA 01844-2354
(508) 794-4442   Fax (508) 794-4442
Sales: Dealers and Distributors
Products: Granite State R/C Products developed and began selling Iron-On Gapless Hinges some 15 years ago. The Hinge features easy installation, no gaps, long lasting, stops aileron warping and flutter. It can be painted or covered with iron on coverings. p. 200, 330

GRANLUND ENGINEERING CO. INC.
Parker Street, PO Box 7
Ware, MA 01082
(1-800) 221-2940   Fax (413) 967-3265
Sales: Dealers and Distributors
Catalog: Yes
Products: Sanding belt, disc, and drum cleaners. p. 383

GREAT PLANES MODEL DIST.
PO Box 4021
Champaign, IL 61820
(217) 398-3630   Fax (217) 398-0008
Sales: Dealers
Catalog: Yes
Products: Distribute most of the hobby product lines including our proprietary lines-KYOSHO, O.S., SUPERTIGRE, IRVINE, HOBBICO, DURATRAX, and GREAT PLANES. Practically any product in the hobby industry can be found through Great Planes Model Distributors. p. 14, 18, 27, 42, 43, 44, 51, 52, 53, 159, 187, 298

ART GROSS ENTERPRISES
12516 Maplewood Ave.
Edmonds, WA 98026
(206) 743-9332   Fax (206) 743-9332
Sales: Distributors
Catalog: Yes
Products: Hand belt sanding blocks and replacement belts in assorted grits and CyA glue dispensers. p. 347, 383

GYROS PRODUCTS CO. INC.
PO Box 344
Monsey, NY 10952
Sales: Dealers and Distributors
Products: A wide assortment of modelmakers' tools, and artists' brushes. p. 383

— H —

H & N ELECTRONICS
10937 Rome Beauty Drive
California City, CA 93505-2338
(619) 373-8033
Sales: Dealers, Distributors, and Direct
Catalog: Flyers
Products: We offer the SAFE solder flux—SUPERSAFE. Also solid wire solders, electronic and silver. Solder products through dealers and direct. Also we have a fine line of electronic products (Tachometers, Voltmeters, and others) direct only. p. 384

THE HALL COMPANY
420 East Water Street
Urbana, OH 43078
(513) 652-1376   Fax (513) 653-7447
Sales: Dealers and Distributors
Catalog: Yes
Products: Anodized/heat treated aluminum alloy landing gear (black or clear) complete with stainless steel axles and locking nuts. Anodized surface-corrosion resistant, with improved adhesion to apply lacquer, enamel, or dope. p. 192

HAYES PRODUCTS
14325 Commerce Drive
Garden Grove, CA 92643
(714) 554-0531   Fax (714) 554-0173
Sales: Distributors
Catalog: Yes
Products: R/C accessories, fuel tanks, engine mounts, tires, antennas, etc. p. 285, 307, 309

HELI IMAGES LTD.
#2107 Flamingo Plaza
7601 E. Treasure Drive
North Bay Village, FL 33141
(305) 864-3740   Fax (305) 864-0107
Sales: Dealers and Direct
Products: *Heliscene* is a 84-page, full-color magazine covering all aspects of radio controlled helicopters and associated equipment and recognized as the finest magazine of its type. p. 31, 389

HELIMAX
(See Great Planes Model Dist.)
p. 187, 204

HARRY B. HIGLEY & SONS, INC.
433 Aquilla Drive
Glenwood, IL 60425
Sales: Dealers
Products: R/C tools and accessories. p. 390

HITEC R/C USA INC.
9419 Abraham Way
Santee, CA 92071
(1-800) 669-4672   Fax (619) 449-1002
Sales: Dealers
Products: Hitec is one of the largest manufacturers of R/C equipment and accessories. p. 9, 60, 125, 127, 131, 138, 148, 149, 280, 301

HOBBICO
(See Great Planes Model Dist.)
p. 9, 44, 53, 54, 138, 291, 298, 299, 349, 350, 374

HOBBY DYNAMICS DISTRIBUTORS
4105 Fieldstone Road
Champaign, IL 61821
(217) 355-0022   Fax (217) 355-0058
Sales: Dealers
Catalog: Free to dealers
Products: A full service distributor of radio control hobby products carrying more than 170 lines. Hobby Dynamics is the exclusive distributor of JR Radios and accessories, Kalt helicopters, Webra engines, Yoshioka planes, K & S of Japan, and HD brand products. p. 9, 27, 31, 44, 45, 54, 60, 123, 124, 125, 127, 129, 131, 134, 135, 149, 167, 171, 174, 184, 203, 291, 298, 299, 301, 302, 346, 384

HOBBY PRODUCTS INT'L, INC.
22600-C Lambert St., Suite 904
El Toro, CA 92630
(714) 837-3250   Fax (714) 837-3251
Sales: Dealers and Distributors
Catalog: $2.00
Products: HPI offers various types of motors, wheels, tires, and machined parts for 1/10 cars. The items such as Super Star Wheels, Uno Motors, and Pro parts shows our policy or marketing high-quality items at competitive prices. p. 160, 256, 257, 260, 262, 270

HOLESHOT RACING PRODUCTS
PO Box 630
Canton, MA 02021
(508) 587-0663   (508) 746-7243
Sales: Dealers, Distributors, and Direct
Catalog: Yes
Products: Holeshot Racing Products is best known for its Super Cooler 2000 and 2001 Snap on Heatsinks. Also for its splined set screws/ wrench and 24KT Gold braided wire battery kit. Holeshot Racing Products has new products that will be available in the near future. p. 143, 239, 262, 280, 374

HORIZON HOBBY DISTRIBUTORS
3102 Clark Road
Champaign, IL 61821
(217) 352-1913   Fax (217) 352-0355
Sales: Dealers
Catalog: Yes
Products: R/C cars, boats, planes, helicopters, and accessories; plastics; rockets; and tools. Exclusive distributor for Dynamite batteries and bearings, Ungar tools and accessories, and Sees wheels. Computer ordering—fast service. p. 143, 144, 229, 384, 385

HUGHEY BOATS INC.
6251 Coffman Road, PO Box 68328
Indianapolis, IN 46268
(317) 299-3303
Sales: Dealers, Distributors, and Direct
Products: R/C racing boats and accessories. p. 205, 206

HYPERDRIVE RACING SYSTEMS
3210 Howard Nickele Road
Fayetteville, AR 72703
(501) 444-8200   Fax (501) 444-8402
Sales: Dealers and Distributors
Catalog: $3.00
Products: Hyperdrive strives to provide the ultimate in racing systems with a complete line of high-quality cars and accessories. Revolutionized the industry with belt drive system. New products include: H10SC, H10SE, and the platinum series "Super Gears." p. 89, 374

—I—

IRVINE ENGINES
(See Great Planes Model Dist.)
p. 181

—J—

J. G. MANUFACTURING
PO Box 6014
Whittier, CA 90609-6014
(213) 947-1206   Fax (213) 693-2577
Sales: Dealers and Distributors
Catalog: $3.00
Products: Manufacturers of race-proven J.G. Stadium Race Trucks, also parts and accessories for top-of-the-line 1/10 scale R/C cars. The innovators of the monster truck conversions, on road, off road, oval, monster truck, tires, rims, bodies, and much more! p. 98, 234, 235, 256, 262, 270, 271

J & M PRODUCTS CO.
PO Box 214
Allen Park, MI 48101
(313) 381-5589   Fax (313) 381-3144
Sales: Dealers and Distributors
Catalog: Yes
Products: J&M kits have been known for their high quality, custom semi-built models since 1973. The kits offer superior strength, light weight, and outstanding performance with either gas or electric power. Models to 48 inches and all unsinkable. p. 62, 68

J'TEC
164 School Street
Daly City, CA 94014
(415) 756-3400
Sales: Dealers, Distributors, and Direct
Catalog: Yes
Products: Major manufacturer of two and four cycle engine mounts, two and four cycle mufflers, scale instrument kits, engine test stands, electric motor mounts, electric motor test stands, isolation mounts, and kits. p. 285, 295, 334

—K—

KDI
10426 SE 206 Pl.
Kent, WA 98031
(206) 854-8053
Sales: Dealers, Distributors, and Direct
Catalog: Information sheets
Products: Manufacturers of quality products such as transmitter trays, wheel pants, portable starting systems, and rubber after mufflers. p. 139, 198, 291, 295

K & S ENGINEERING
6917 West 59th Street
Chicago, IL 60638
(312) 586-8503   Fax (312) 586-8556
Sales: Dealers and Distributors
Catalog: $.50
Products: Brass tubing, squares, rods, angles, channels, strips, sheets, rectangles, and hexagons. Aluminum tubing and sheets. Copper tubing and sheets. Music wire. Tools and accessories for the hobbyist. p. 200, 330, 385, 386

KALMBACH PUBLISHING CO.
21027 Crossroads Circle, PO Box 1612
Waukesha, WI 53187
(1-800) 446-5489   Fax (414) 796-0126
Sales: Dealers, Distributors, and Direct
Catalog: Yes
Products: Publisher of quality radio control and modeling books. p. 390, 391, 392, 393

KARODEN HOBBY PRODUCTS
PO Box 601
Bergenfield, NJ 07621
Sales: Dealers, Distributors, and Direct
Products: Ultra-flexible masking tape solves masking problems on planes, cars, and boats. p. 342

KIMBROUGH PRODUCTS
1420 East St. Andrews Place, Unit F
Santa Ana, CA 92705
(714) 557-4530   Fax (714) 557-4609
Sales: Distributors and Manufactures only
Catalog: Yes
Products: Servo mounted, Servo Savers, Servo arms, heavy-duty 32 pitch dif. gears, 48 pitch dif. gears, 48 pitch pinion gears, Gear adapters, Diamond Wing Fasteners, Transmitter Wheel Grips, Tire Horns for gluing foam tires. p. 262

KYOSHO
(See Great Planes Model Dist.)
p. 10, 18, 27, 31, 32, 34, 60, 62, 63, 68, 71, 78, 79, 85, 89, 90, 91, 94, 98, 99, 126, 128, 131, 144, 150, 160, 253, 263, 386

—L—

L.A.W. RACING PRODUCTS
1229 Capitol Drive
Addison, IL 60101
(708) 543-2030   Fax (708) 543-6871
Sales: Dealers, Distributors, and Direct
Catalog: Free
Products: L.A.W. Racing Products are best known for their extensive line of computer-machined, "add-on" high performance marine engine accessories. Other products for the aviator include a unique radio transmitter tray and snow skis. p. 139, 181, 185, 192, 208

LANIER RC
PO Box 458
Oakwood, GA 30566
(404) 532-6401   Fax (404) 532-2163
Sales: Dealers and Distributors
Catalog: Yes
Products: Lanier RC manufactures 20 ARF kits and 1 giant scale balsa kit. Replacement parts available. Inquiries invited. Information and questions answered daily 9:00-5:30 EST. p. 7, 10, 11, 45, 54, 304

LINDBERG/CRAFT HOUSE CORP.
328 N. Westwood
Toledo, OH 43607
(419) 536-8351   Fax (419) 536-4159
Sales: Distributors
Catalog: $1.00
Products: Plastic model kits of cars, boats, planes, anatomical, armor, and R/C compatible model boats. p. 61, 63, 64, 69, 206

—M—

MGA ENTERPRISES
PO Box 5631
Fresno, CA 93755
(209) 224-4170   Fax (209) 224-2789
Sales: Dealers, Distributors, and Direct
Catalog: Yes
Products: Produces top-quality state-of-the-art factory finished pilots in scales from 1/9 through 1/4. These

ready-to-fly pilots are available in styles beginning with the early aviator to the present day jetpilot. p. 193

MAXTRAX
(See Great Planes Model Dist.)
p. 100, 239, 253, 263, 271, 272

MCALLISTER RACING INC.
2245 First Street #105
Simi Valley, CA 93065
(805) 583-4473   Fax (805) 582-0940
Sales: Distributors
Catalog: $2.00
Products: McAllister Racing leads the way in scale racing trends with a full line of top-quality bodies, decals, and accessories. Also featuring five complete car kits including the "00" oval only 1/10 car kit and the Fly'n "M" 18 wheeler kit. p. 91, 99, 234, 334

MIDWAY MODEL COMPANY, THE
PO Box 9
Midway City, CA 92655
(714) 895-6569   Fax (714) 895-6629
Sales: Dealers, Distributors,
and Direct (Last resort)
Catalog: Yes
Products: Manufacturer of old-timer sailplane and electric power airplane kits. US agent for Taipan propellers. We are noted for our quality kits that feature machine cut and sanded parts. p. 19, 20, 27, 32, 45, 195

MIDWEST PRODUCTS CO., INC.
400 S. Indiana St., PO Box 564
Hobart, IN 46342
(219) 942-1134   Fax (219) 947-2347
Sales: Distributors
Catalog: $1.00
Products: Manufacturer of Micro-Cut Quality®, Balsa, Basswood and Hardwoods, and Success Series® R/C airplane kits and Wooden Boat Model kits for display or radio control. p. 45, 46, 55, 64, 331, 334

MILLER R/C PRODUCTS
PO Box 425
Kenwood, CA 95452
(707) 833-5905   Fax (707) 539-0507
Sales: Dealers and Distributors
Products: Miller R/C Products is a major manufacturer of rubber starting inserts that fit all the different starters (different part numbers for different starters). Helicopter starting extension, and Big Grip starter cup for starting the big nose cones. p. 291, 292, 302

MODEL ENGINEERING OF NORWALK
54 Chestnut Hill Road
Norwalk, CT 06851
(203) 846-9090
Sales: Dealers, Distributors, and Direct
Catalog: Yes
Products: Manufacture the M.E.N. Trainer C-50/4 Auto Charger, Buzzard Bombshell, The Gabbler, HiStart Supplys, and other kits. p. 14, 28, 55, 150

MODEL RACING PRODUCTS, INC. (MRP)
18676 142nd Ave. NE
Woodinville, WA 98072
(206) 485-4100   Fax (206) 485-1229
Sales: Distributors
Catalog: $3.00
Products: MRP was the first to manufacture performance electric boats and still leads the way in speed and realism. The car bodies of 1/8, 1/10, and 1/12 scale have long been recognized as the most realistic and true-to-scale available. p. 65, 66, 235

MODEL RECTIFIER CORPORATION
200 Carter Drive
Edison, NJ 08817
(908) 248-0730   Fax (908) 248-0970
Sales: Distributors
Catalog: $6.30 each—MRC-Tamiya Encyclopedia, MRC-Tamiya Radio Control Guide Book
Free—Model Train Controls, Model Rocketry
Products: Manufacture and import items such as Tamiya R/C cars and accessories; R/C gas airplanes,

R/C electric boats, R/C systems, quick chargers, and batteries. p. 55, 61, 64, 65, 75, 76, 79, 80, 81, 82, 86, 87, 91, 92, 93, 94, 95, 96, 99, 100, 101, 102, 132, 144, 145, 150, 151, 158, 160, 207, 263, 264, 277, 303, 386, 398, 399

MOODY AUTOMOTIVE, INC.
755 Ash Street
Flossmoor, IL 60422
(708) 799-5597
Sales: Dealers and Direct
Catalog: $1.00
Products: One-eighth scale gas-powered radio control model sprint car for racing on clay or asphalt oval tracks. All-metal structural components, in-line drive, rear axle disc brake, heavy-duty clutch, aluminum chassis, ABS body, nickel-plated roll cage, and nerf bars. p. 95

MORLEY HELICOPTERS,
R/C MODELS USA
PO Box 6026
San Pedro, CA 90734
(213) 833-4700
Sales: Dealers and Direct
Catalog: Yes
Products: Scale model helicopters at a reasonable price. p. 32, 33

— N —

NIKKO AMERICA
2801 Summit Avenue
Plano, TX 75079
(214) 437-6677   Fax (214) 437-6704
Sales: Dealers and Distributors
Catalog: Free to Dealers
Products: Largest selection of R/C vehicles. Also carry R/C boats, hovercraft, airplanes, and race sets. All prices, all sizes. Quality engineered to last. p. 76

NOVAK ELECTRONICS, INC.
128-C East Dyer Road
Santa Ana, CA 92707
(714) 549-3741   Fax (714) 549-2740
Sales: Distributors
Catalog: Yes
Products: Leading manufacturer of electronic speed controls, 2 and 3 channel AM and FM receivers, peak chargers, servos, and accessories. p. 73, 102, 135, 139, 280, 281, 295

— O —

OFNA RACING DIVISION
771 West 19th Street, Ste. J
Costa Mesa, CA 92627
(714) 722-9388   Fax (714) 722-1480
Sales: Hobby Shops only
Products: OFNA Racing has been supplying the Priate M1 to the hobby industry for 2 years. OFNA Racing has the widest selection of 1/8 scale racing upgrade offered to the U.S. 1/8 scale racing marketing. p. 85, 182, 240, 256

OWI INC.
1160 Mahalo Place
Compton, CA 90220
(213) 638-4732   Fax (213) 638-8347
Sales: Dealers and Distributors
Catalog: Yes
Products: OWI is the manufacturer of MOVIT educational electronic robot kits and OWIKITS. The principles demonstrated by the MOVITs emulated those used in robots of all sizes, including large industrial models. The kits are intended for both the educational and adult hobby markets. p. 97

OCTURA MODELS, INC.
7351 N. Hamlin Avenue
Skokie, IL 60076
(708) 674-7351   Fax (708) 674-7351
Sales: Dealers

Products: Pioneer producer of quality model marine supplies. Largest selection of original design propellers in both plastic and metal for R/C model power boats. Price list and literature available at present. p. 208, 225, 226, 227, 287, 288, 289

O.S. ENGINES
(See Great Planes Model Dist.)
p. 11, 167, 168, 171, 172, 174, 175, 177, 181

— P —

PANAVISE PRODUCTS, INC.
1485 Southern Way
Sparks, NV 89431
(702) 353-2900   Fax (1-800) 395-8002
Sales: Distributors
Catalog: Yes
Products: Work-holding and positioning systems, with modular design for interchangeable heads and bases. p. 387

PARMA INTERNATIONAL INC.
13927 Progress Parkway
North Royalton, OH 44133
(216) 237-8650   Fax (216) 237-6333
Sales: Distributors only
Catalog: $4.00, full-color-free to trade
Products: Parma has been a major manufacturer of slot racing products since 1968, and of R/C replacement parts and kits since the 1970s. Parma is best known for its wide selection of crystal clear Lexan bodies for most scales; colorful mylar decals; Cyclone II motors; and 1/10 on-road kits like Days of Thunder™, California Sport Truck, and the Hemi Coupe. p. 92, 93, 94, 95, 145, 146, 159, 161, 162, 235, 236, 237, 240, 253, 272, 273, 335, 336, 337, 338, 394, 400

PECK-POLYMERS
PO Box 710399
Santee, CA 92072
(619) 448-1818   Fax (619) 448-1833
Sales: Dealers, Distributors, and Direct
Catalog: $2.00
Products: Fly Model Aircraft. Contest-quality rubber and R/C, including support accessories. R/C blimp also. p. 20, 21, 22, 28, 46, 56, 200

POLK'S MODEL CRAFT HOBBIES INC./
ARISTOCRAFT
346 Bergen Ave.
Jersey City, NJ 07304
(201) 332-8100   Fax (201) 332-0521
Sales: Distributors and Direct
Catalog: $3.00
Products: R/C systems, chargers, speed controls, and R/C cars. p. 122, 133, 136, 147, 278

PORTA-POWER INDUSTRIES
PO Box 34026
Chicago, IL 60634
(312) 637-5523   Fax (312) 637-6120
Sales: Dealers, Distributors, and Direct
Catalog: Yes
Products: Manufactures NiCad battery chargers, power panels, fuel pumps, voltmeters, tweak boards, battery charging caddies. p. 66, 151, 152, 253, 300, 387

PRATHER PRODUCTS, INC.
1660 Ravenna Avenue
Wilmington, CA 90744
(213) 835-4764
Sales: Distributors
Catalog: $2.00
Products: Manufacturers of epoxy-fiberglass model boat kits. A complete line of model boating accessories are available including boat props, running hardware, radio boxes, motor mounts, and much more. p. 68, 69, 227

PROCELL
PO Box 691831
Houston, TX 77269
(1-800) 966-1616   Fax (713) 537-2211
Sales: Dealers and Direct

Distributors, retail
Catalog: $3.00
Products: Procell complete battery service, matching and rematching. Matched packs—1200, 1400, 1700 SCRs, 1700 SCRs Motor Dyno stock and modifieds motors. All custom winds. p. 145, 160

PROTEC
3455 W. 6th Street
Los Angeles, CA 90020-9910
(213) 462-2437
Sales: Distributors
Catalog: Yes
Products: Quality battery chargers for the modeling industry. Eight available models to meet everyone's requirements. Sixty day warranty. p. 152

—Q—

QUADRA AERROW INC.
PO Box 183
Perth, Ontario, Canada K7H 3E3
(613) 264-0010   Fax (613) 264-8441
Sales: Distributors
Catalog: Product Sheet
Products: Our Quadra engine entered the aircraft model market in 1975. It became the nucleus around which the large model movement (1/4 and 1/3 scale) evolved. Its tradition remains GOOD PERFORMANCE AND EXCELLENT VALUE FOR ENGINES AND PARTS. No planned obsolescence! p. 178

—R—

RC VIDEO MAGAZINE
PO Box 319
Easton, MD 21601
(301) 820-6154
Sales: Dealers, Distributors, and Direct
Catalog: Yes
Products: RC Video Magazine has been creating high-quality programs since 1984. This year's programs will be better than ever. Utilizing the latest in state-of-the-art broadcast equipment combined with the talents of some of the best R/C modelers in the world with nearly thirty titles now available covering many areas of R/C hobby. p. 397

RCM PUBLICATIONS
PO Box 487
Sierra Madre, CA 91025
(818) 355-1476   Fax (818) 355-6415
Sales: Dealers, Distributors, and Direct
Products: Publishers of a monthly consumer radio control magazine covering all aspects of the R/C hobby. p. 393, 394, 395

RCMB, INC.
898 West 16th Street
Newport Beach, CA 92663
(714) 645-8830 (CA)   (1-800) 243-9593
Sales: Dealers, Distributors, and Direct
Catalog: Yes, samples
Products: The best up-to-date information in radio control. p. 394

RADIO CONTROL DEVELOPMENT, INC.
9419 Abraham Way
Santee, CA 92071
(1-800) 669-4672   Fax (619) 449-1002
Sales: Dealers and Direct
Catalog: Yes
Products: RCD is the manufacturer of the popular "bullet proof" receivers and high-quality servo packs. p. 135, 140, 264

RACING SILKS
PO Box 193
Pine Brook, NJ 07058
(201) 227-7434
Sales: Dealers, Distributors, and Direct
Catalog: Yes

Products: Wid assortment of silk screened T-shirts, hats, and other outerwear, with emphasis on radio control themes. p. 264, 400

ROYAL PRODUCTS CORP.
790 W. Tennessee Avenue
Denver, CO 80223
(303) 778-7711   Fax (303) 778-7721
Sales: Dealers and Distributors
Catalog: $5.00; free to dealers
Products: Radio control accessories, scale aircraft, engines, ready-to-fly aircraft, motorcycles, and R/C trucks. p. 7, 11, 14, 15, 20, 24, 33, 34, 35, 36, 37, 38, 39, 56, 96, 97, 102, 135, 153, 168, 172, 182, 184, 192, 201, 290, 292, 293, 298, 300, 303, 306, 331, 338, 387

—S—

SMC/LIGHTNING PRODUCTS DIVISION
12519 Wanda Lane
Houston, TX 77355
(713) 356-2584   Fax (713) 259-7801
Sales: Dealers, Distributors, and Direct
Catalog: Yes
Products: SMC/Lightning is the leading manufacturer of workstands for specific R/C hobbies; including R/C cars, trucks, airplanes, helicopters, and boats. Applications include the building, repairing, testing, tuning-up, transporting, and displaying of a wide range of model sizes and types. p. 202, 204, 225, 265, 388

SCHUMACHER INC.
6302 Benjamin Rd. Suite #404
Tampa, FL 33634
(813) 889-9691   Fax (813) 889-9593
Sales: Dealers and Distributors
Catalog: $3.00
Products: Schumacher Inc. is dedicated to giving quality service and excellent parts availability on all Schumacher products including Procat, Cougar, Shotgun Truck, and the exciting new NITRO 10 range of 1/10 scale gas car. p. 82, 83, 84, 153, 281

SERMOS R/C SNAP CONNECTORS, INC.
Cedar Corners Station, PO Box 16787
Stamford, CT 06905
(203) 322-6294
Sales: Dealers, Distributors, and Direct
Catalog: Yes
Products: Manufacture the #1 power pack connector rated at 600 volts AC or DC; contact resistance 250 microhms; special silver-plated contacts are salt water rated; modular Lexan color coded housing, #300 stainless steel retention springs assure positive contact in heavy vibration conditions. Cycled over 10,000 times without any failure or loss of power. The only franchised distributor and representative to the R/C industry for Anderson Power Products. p. 153, 158, 161, 202, 208, 225, 264

SHERLINE PRODUCTS, INC.
170 Navajo Street
San Marcos, CA 92069
(619) 744-3674   Fax (619) 744-1574
Sales: Dealers, Distributors, and Direct
Catalog: Yes
Products: Manufacture the Sherline 3.5 Inch Precision Lathe Vertical Mill and accessories for it. p. 387

SIG MANUFACTURING CO., INC.
401 S. Front Street
Montezuma, IA 50171
(515) 623-5154   Fax (515) 623-3922
Sales: Dealers
Catalog: $3.00
Products: Over 2,000 Sig-brand products for the model airplane enthusiast. Also a distributor for most other major brands of model airplane supplies. p. 15, 16, 17, 22, 24, 25, 28, 39, 40, 46, 47, 48, 56, 57, 187, 192, 193, 202, 285, 290, 298, 299, 305, 309, 331, 332, 333, 338, 342, 343, 347, 349, 350, 351, 356, 357, 367, 368, 388, 397

SKYWARD RESEARCH & DEVELOPMENT LABORATORY
4668 Decarie Boulevard
Montreal, Quebec H3X 2H5
(514) 482-6660   Fax (514) 487-5383
Sales: Dealers and Distributors
Catalog: Yes
Products: Radio control products for flying, car racing, boating. Manufacture quality products for the discerning modeler. p. 102, 103, 168, 169, 172, 175, 290, 300

SLIMLINE MANUFACTURING
PO Box 3295
Scottsdale, AZ 85257
(602) 967-5053   Fax (602) 967-5053
Sales: Dealers, Distributors, and Direct
Catalog: $1.00
Products: Slimline offers the most complete line of in-cowl mufflers, smoke mufflers, and exhaust systems. Designed to bolt on to each specific engine, these mufflers are machined out of high-quality aluminum bar and tubing. p. 295, 296

GLEN SPICKLER RADIOMODELS
1709 Benton Street
Bakersfield, CA 93304
(805) 831-6639
Sales: Dealers, Distributors, and Direct
Products: Products are American-made R/C sport and racing airplane kits. All kits are machine cut from balsa, ply, and spruce. p. 48, 49

SPRING AIR PRODUCTS
PO Box 201
Custer, WA 98240
(206) 366-5621   Fax (206) 366-5985
Sales: Dealers and Distributors
Products: Pneumatic retractable landing gear and related products. p.193

SQUADRON/SIGNAL PUBLICATIONS
1115 Crowley Dr.
Carrollton, TX 75011-5010
(214) 242-1485   Fax (214) 242-3775
Sales: Distributors
Catalog: $1.00
Products: Squadron/Signal publishes books dealing with military aircraft, vehicles, and combat troops. These softcover books provide the modeler, historian, and buff with an in-depth, comprehensive study of each subject. p. 396

STAGE III, INC.
"The Ultimate Cell Test"
1189 Chicago Road
Troy, MI 48083
(313) 585-1150   Fax (313) 978-9085
Sales: Dealers, Distributors, and Direct
Catalog: Yes
Products: An independent NiCad cell testing lab servicing distributors, dealers, and racers by matching new and used cells. Manufacture high-performance silicone wire and braid for R/C applications. p. 145, 146, 162, 163, 207, 265

SUPERTIGRE
(See Great Planes Model Dist.)
p. 177, 178

SURE FLITE ENTERPRISES INC.
571 Crane St. Bldg. H
Lake Elsinore, CA 92330
(714) 245-6343
Sales: Dealers and Distributors
Catalog: Brochure
Products: For almost twenty years Sure Flite has been manufacturing scale-type radio-control airplanes. Our aircraft are primarily constructed of fully shaped, injection-molded styrofoam. Replacement parts are available at reasonable prices. p. 40, 49, 56, 57, 188

SWEEN I.D. PRODUCTS, INC.
1940 Commerce Drive, PO Box 8300
No. Mankato, MN 56003
(507) 345-6200   Fax (507) 345-3291

Sales: Dealers and Direct
Products: High-performance fuel pumps and related accessories for the radio control model airplane hobby. p. 303, 304, 306, 310

—T—

C. B. TATONE, INC.
21658 Cloud Way
Hayward, CA 94545
Sales: Dealers and Direct
Products: R/C aircraft accessories, tires, mufflers, test stands, spinners, etc. p. 195, 198, 203, 286, 296, 310, 357

T.M. R/C RACING COMPONENTS
49679 Leona
Mt. Clemens, MI 48044
(313) 949-3506   Fax (313) 949-3506
Sales: Dealers and Distributors
Catalog: $2.00
Products: T.M. R/C Racing components has been a manufacturer of R/C wheels and sponge tires since 1986 for both 1/10 and 1/12 scale cars and also dragsters. All wheels are direct bolt on. p. 258

TEAM LOSI INC.
13848 Magnolia Ave.
Chino, CA 91710
(714) 465-9400   Fax (714) 590-1496
Sales: Dealers and Distributors
Catalog: $1.00
Products: Team Losi manufactures national champion R/C buggies and monster truck kits in both entrance and pro levels. Highest quality stock and modified motors, batteries, precision gears, shock fluid, and similar racing accessories. p. 84, 104, 163, 253, 256, 273

TEAM PIT STOP
12353 S.W. 132 Ct.
Miami, FL 33186
(305) 255-2887   Fax (305) 255-2970
Sales: Dealers and Distributors
Catalog: Yes
Products: Radio control cars, conversion kits, and related accessories. p. 84, 163, 229, 254, 256, 265, 374

TECNACRAFT
1335 B Dayton Street
Salinas, CA 93901
(408) 422-7466   Fax (408) 422-6703
Sales: Dealers, Distributors, and Direct
Catalog: $2.00
Products: Manufacture a high-end line of aluminum wheels for most popular cars and trucks, and titanium ti-rods for most all cars and trucks and aftermarket parts made of space-age alloys for the RC-10 and JRX-2. p. 258

TEKIN ELECTRONICS CORP.
970 Calle Negocio
San Clemente, CA 92672
(714) 498-9518   Fax (714) 498-6339
Sales: Distributors
Catalog: Yes
Products: Electronic speed controls, battery cyclers, receivers, and chargers for the competition-minded racer. Also additional R/C products geared to the R/C racer. p. 140, 154, 156, 282, 400

TOP FLITE MODELS, INC.
(See Great Planes Model Dist.)
p. 40, 332

TRAXXAS CORPORATION
12150 Shiloh Road
Dallas, TX 75228
(214) 613-3300   Fax (214) 613-3599
Sales: Distributors
Catalog: Yes
Products: Manufacturer of hobby class radio controlled cars, trucks, and boat kits ranging from the national championship winning Blue Eagle to the popular Hawk truck. Also manufacture speed

controls, radios, chargers, and accessories. Almost all models are also available fully assembled. p. 59, 76, 104, 154, 275, 282, 283

TREATMENT PRODUCTS LTD.
3057 N. Rockwell
Chicago, IL 60618
(312) 588-7777   Fax (312) 588-4414
Sales: Dealers and Distributors
Catalog: Yes
Products: Manufactures a model wax which protects body and finish from scuffs and scrapes. p. 265

TWISTER MOTORS
657 E. Arrow Highway #H
Glendora, CA 91740
(818) 914-6177   Fax (818) 335-1659
Sales: Dealers, Distributors, and Direct
Catalog: Yes
Products: Manufacture several lines of motors for cars, boats, and planes; a 1/10 scale road car; the famous Twister mini cathe. Well-known for on-time shipping, customer "hotline," and great service. p. 94, 163, 388

—U—

U.S. AIRCORE
4576 Claire Chennault, Hangar #7
Dallas, TX 75248
(214) 250-1914   Fax (214) 250-6532
Sales: Dealers and Distributors
Catalog: $3.00; free to trade
Products: U.S. AirCore manufactures a complete line of "Fold & Fly™' Aircraft and accessories, including pontoons. Using Aircore™ material, the company's products are three to four times more durable than balsa products, and build in a few evenings. All AirCore aircraft are compatible with the company's Power Cartridge™ or PC, which is a tray containing the customer's engine, radio, tank, and servos. The PC slides into the nose of the aircraft on a set of rails and can be moved from plane to plane in a few minutes at the field. p.12, 188

US Quadra
1032 East Manitowoc
Oak Creek, WI 53154
(414) 762-7155
Sales: Dealers, Distributors, and Direct
Products: Large-scale engines for model airplanes. Also provide repair services. p. 178

UNITED MODEL DISTRIBUTORS INC.
301 Holbrook Drive, PO Box "O"
Wheeling, IL 60090
(1-800) 323-1050   Fax (312) 459-4834
Sales: Dealers
Catalog: N/C
Products: A full line distributor for R/C cars, boats, planes, and related accessories plus trains and other hobby products. p. 12, 13, 146, 172, 173, 175, 176, 179, 240

—V—

VANTEC
460 Casa Real Place
Nipomo, CA 93444
(1-800) 8-VANTEC
Sales: Dealers, Distributors, and Direct
Catalog: $2.00
Products: Unique source for unusual electronic control system components for boats, cars, and R/C robots. We also manufacture custom R/C systems for professional and industrial applications. p. 129, 132, 154, 207, 208, 283

VICTOR ENGINEERING
380 Camino de Estrella Ste. 170
San Clemente, CA 92672
(714) 496-9701   Fax (714) 496-0608
Sales: Distributors

Catalog: Yes
Products: High-performance Hi-IQ battery chargers that also perform grading, cycling, and matching batteries and also conditions motors. p. 155, 277, 283, 400

VORTAC MFG. CO., INC.
PO Box 469
Oak Lawn, IL 60453
(708) 425-5885
Sales: Distributors
Catalog: $1.00
Products: Manufacturers of hinge and landing gear accessories, bombs, and bomb releases, and flush head wing bolts for all types of model airplanes. p. 202, 203, 357, 372

—W—

WILLIAMS BROS. INC.
181 Pawnee St.
San Marcos, CA 92069
(619) 744-3082   Fax (619) 744-1899
Sales: Dealers and Distributors
Catalog: $3.00 (color); free to trade
Products: Williams Bros. Inc., now in its 31st year, continues to produce one of the most sought after lines of model airplane kits and R/C aircraft accessories. Accuracy and attention to detail have made Williams Bros. kits and accessories traditionally the finest. p. 23, 179, 180, 198

WINNING EDGE PRODUCTS
1 Bert Dr., Unit A-11
W. Bridgewater, MA 02379
(508) 580-1622 or 559-6686   Fax (508) 586-0036
Sales: Dealers, Distributors, and Direct
Products: Winning Edge's products are competitive, common sense products for the car enthusiasts. p. 266, 275

WOODLAND SCENICS
PO Box 98, 101 E. Valley Drive
Linn Creek, MO 65052
(314) 346-5555   Fax (314) 346-3768
Sales: Distributors
Catalog: $1.25
Products: Highest grade lubricants; paint and plastic compatible. Detailed instructions to take the confusion out of which to use when. 7-PAK with extension-tip applicators is a tool box must. Available individually for 7-PAK replacements or spares. p. 389

—X—

XURON CORP.
60 Industrial Park Rd.
Saco, ME 04072
(207) 283-1401   Fax (207) 283-0594
Sales: Distributors
Catalog: Yes
Products: XURON is the inventor and patent holder of the Micro-Shear® flushcutter. These products set the standard in civilian and military electronics and aerospace. XURON is now making a selection of their shears and pliers available to R/C hobbyists. p. 203, 266, 303, 388

—Z—

ZENITH BOOKS
PO Box 1 / RCBG91
Osceola, WI 54020
(715) 294-3345   Fax (715) 294-4448
Sales: Dealers, Distributors, and Direct
Catalog: $3.95
Products: Zenith offers a complete selection of aviation and radio control books; featuring classic warbirds, modern military, and much more. Fantastic details for most aircraft. p. 395 ∎

Product Index

— B —

— C —

Advertisers
— Index —